CORPORATE RISK MANAGEMENT

CORPORATE RISK MANAGEMENT

Edited by Donald H. Chew

Columbia University Press

NEW YORK

Columbia University Press
Publishers Since 1893
New York   Chichester, West Sussex
Copyright © 2008 Morgan Stanley

Library of Congress Cataloging-in-Publication Data

Corporate risk management / edited by Donald H. Chew.
    p. cm.
  A collection of articles previously published in the Journal of applied corporate finance.
  Includes bibliographical references and index.
  ISBN 978-0-231-14362-2 (cloth : alk. paper)—ISBN
978-0-231-14363-9 (pbk. : alk. paper)—ISBN 978-0-231-51300-5 (ebook)
  1. Risk management.   2. Corporations—Finance—Management.   3. Business
enterprises—Finance—Management.   I. Chew, Donald H.   II. Title.
  HD61.C67 2008
  658.15'5—dc22   2007035844

Columbia University Press books are printed on permanent and durable acid-free paper.

This book is printed on paper with recycled content.

Printed in the United States of America

c 10 9 8 7 6 5 4 3 2 1
p 10 9 8 7 6 5 4 3 2 1

References to Internet Web sites (URLs) were accurate at the time of writing. Neither the author nor Columbia University Press is responsible for URLs that may have expired or changed since the manuscript was prepared.

Contents

Introduction

THE THEORY OF CORPORATE RISK MANAGEMENT has changed a lot in the past 25 years. And so has corporate practice, mainly in ways predicted by the theory.

In the 1980s and well into the 1990s, most large companies had a "risk manager" whose main job was to oversee the firm's insurance purchases. At the same time, financially savvy corporate treasurers, with little or no input from risk managers, began using newfangled securities called "derivatives" to hedge the firm's interest rate and currency exposures. In many of these companies, especially those where the treasury was encouraged to view itself as a profit center, the treasurers followed a practice known as "selective hedging." In practice, selective hedging meant leaving exposures unhedged (or, in some cases, maybe even enlarging them) when so directed by the treasurer's "view" of future prices. The main purpose of such hedging was to pad or smooth the corporate profit and loss statement, with the idea that shareholders place a premium on earnings stability, no matter how achieved.

But in the last 10 years, the scope and mission of corporate risk management have expanded well beyond insurance and opportunistic hedging to include all kinds of corporate operating and strategic risks. And, as oversight and control of these once compartmentalized activities has become more centralized, the corporate risk manager has given way to the "chief risk officer," a senior management function increasingly overseen by the board of directors. In many companies the mission of corporate risk management, once concerned mainly with smoothing out bumps in the earnings trajectory, has become protection of the firm's "franchise value"—that is, protection of all the firm's major sources of future earnings power. As Bob Anderson, executive director of the Committee of Chief Risk Officers, notes in the roundtable discussion that ends this book, corporate risk management is no longer "just a series of isolated transactions; it's a strategic activity . . . [that] encompasses everything from operating changes to financial hedging to the buying and selling of plants or new businesses—anything that affects the level and variability of cash flows going forward. When viewed in this light, risk management is clearly a senior management responsibility, one that requires input from and coordination of the company at all operating levels."

Chief among the factors driving this transformation of corporate risk management are increases in the scale and variety of uncertainties facing today's companies, everything from fluctuating commodity prices to threats of re-regulation and terrorist attacks. But, in addition to the increase in uncertainty and risk, another force for change in corporate practice has been developments in finance theory that came along earlier.

For decades after publication of the Modigliani–Miller Theorem (M&M) "irrelevance propositions" in the late 1950s and early 1960s, finance professors taught their students that neither a company's capital structure nor its dividend policy should affect its value. Both were viewed as nothing more than different ways of "repackaging" the firm's future earnings stream for investors (and it was this expected stream of operating earnings, together with the investments necessary to sustain it, that was seen as the main engine of value). Much the same was held to be true of corporate efforts to manage major risks. A company's stockholders, just by holding diversified portfolios, were said to "diversify away" any effects of currency, interest rate, or commodity price risks on the firm's cost of capital and value.

But starting in the late 1970s, finance scholars began to come up with explanations for how risk management—and changes in the right-hand side of the balance sheet in general—can increase corporate values. Although the tax benefits of substituting debt for equity, and stock repurchases for dividend payments, were well understood by corporate practitioners as well as theorists, the smoothing effect of corporate hedging on taxable earnings was shown to offer another means of lowering the firm's expected tax liability. But, as academics like Cliff Smith, David Mayers, and René Stulz argued in papers in the early 1980s, a potentially more important source of value is the use of risk management to help ensure a company's ability and willingness to fund its investment opportunities and carry out its strategic plan. In theory, value-maximizing managers are supposed to undertake all projects expected to earn more than the cost of capital. But in practice, a sharp downturn in earnings or cash flow, and the high cost of arranging new funding in such circumstances, could cause managers to cut back on promising investments. By limiting the probability of such a downturn, a risk management strategy can "protect" management from making short-sighted cutbacks in investment to avoid financial distress or meet a near-term earnings target.

Besides encouraging managers to carry out a company's strategic investments, risk management can also play a role in persuading outsiders to provide financing for such investments on advantageous terms. What's more, as Cliff Smith argues (in another roundtable in this book), "it's not only the firm's bondholders and creditors who appreciate risk management; reducing the probability of financial trouble also helps reassure the firm's other corporate 'stakeholders'—groups such as employees, suppliers, and regulators, who are generally willing to provide the firm with better terms (or more slack) when the possibility of Chapter 11 seems remote."

And there's another important stakeholder group—namely, management itself—that is likely to benefit significantly from enterprise risk management (ERM). In theory at least, the more predictable corporate earnings and cash flow stream that results from ERM should make managers more confident about their own future employment income; and with the reduction of uncertainty, they should be willing to work for less. What's more, *good* managers should be encouraged by the fact that their performance bonuses can now be tied to measures that, because they are now insulated from random fluctuations in commodity or currency prices, do a better job of reflecting managerial skill and effort. But, as Smith also suggests, the resulting reduction of uncertainty may be a mixed blessing for less competent managers:

> In the good old days before derivatives, whenever things turned out badly, the people in the hot seat could blame poor performance on things that weren't their fault. They could say that a jump in interest rates reduced the profitability of their book of loans, or that a plunge in oil prices was responsible for their drop in revenue. But thanks to the development of derivatives, we now have a set of markets that allow us to isolate those things that are outside the executive's control and take them off the table. As a result, we're left with a clearer picture of the true operating performance of a particular enterprise. So, in one sense, it makes the manager more comfortable by not being held responsible for events that he or she can't control. But from the corporate board's perspective, if things turn out badly, there are fewer places for managers to hide.

To sum up, then, enterprise-wide or strategic risk management has significant potential to add value by strengthening managers' incentives to invest for the long term and by reducing uncertainty for key corporate stakeholders, including creditors, managers, and employees. But having determined *when* and *why* to manage risks, companies then face the question of which risks to shed and which to keep?

The answer provided in these pages is fairly simple—one that draws on a very old principle of economics. At least since Adam Smith's demonstration of the gains from "division of labour" in the first chapter of *The Wealth of*

Nations, economists have been professing allegiance to the concepts of specialization and comparative advantage. As applied to corporate risk management, the basic idea is that companies should retain only those risks they have a comparative advantage in bearing and attempt to transfer all "non-core" risks to other firms (or investors) in a better position to bear them. For example, if interest rate risk poses a significant threat to a company's future ability to carry out its strategic plan, *and* if that risk can be shifted to a third party (presumably, a financial institution) at a relatively low cost, then that risk should be transferred. By contrast, although auto companies might like to hedge against declining gross domestic product and economy-wide car sales, and oil companies might wish to limit their exploration risk, they are unlikely to find takers at a reasonable price. And, as discussed in a case study called "Corporate Insurance Strategy: The Case of British Petroleum," though a company like BP might consider laying off their largest property-and-casualty and product-liability risks on insurers or re-insurers, the company's size and expertise makes it the natural bearer (and hence the self-insurer) of those risks.

This book consists of 18 chapters previously published as articles in the *Journal of Applied Corporate Finance,* which discuss the development and use of risk management products. Divided into three parts, the text offer an introduction to risk management tools along with considerable discussion of the theory of value at risk (VaR) value management and practical applications of the theory. Case studies of Merck, British Petroleum, and Nationwide Insurance focus on currency risk management, the uses of corporate insurance, and the implementation of enterprise risk management. The book ends with two roundtable discussions in which small groups of academics and practitioners explore the motives, aims, and methods of corporate risk management programs.

The dominant theme in these discussions—and the main focus of this book—is the use of risk management to support business strategies and increase corporate values. This is not, of course, to deny that the principal tools of risk management—derivatives such as forwards, futures, swaps, and options—have been and will continue to be used in ways that end up destroying value. The aim of this book is to give corporate practitioners a clear sense of when and how the use of such instruments is likely to be value-adding—that is, functioning as an enabler rather than a subverter of a company's primary business activities.

PART I

The Products

WALL-STREET BASHING IS a time-honored practice, even among economists. In the chapter that begins this book, "Financial Innovation: Achievements and Prospects," Merton Miller, Nobel laureate and widely regarded as "the father of modern finance," traces the popular skepticism about Wall Street and financial innovation to an 18th-century economic doctrine known as "Physiocracy." According to this theory, the ultimate source of national wealth lies in the production of physical commodities. All other forms of commercial activity are considered nonproductive, if not parasitic. "Modern-day Physiocrats," as Miller wrote, "automatically and enthusiastically consign to that nonproductive class all the many thousands on Wall Street and LaSalle Street now using the new instruments."

The subject of Miller's chapter is "the new instruments"—that is, the proliferation since the early 1970s of all variety of futures, swaps, and options. It is Miller's contention—and one of the major recurring themes of this book—that the social benefits of financial innovation far outweigh the costs.

What are these benefits? Perhaps the principal source of gain from the many securities innovations over the past 20 years has been an improvement in the allocation of risk within the financial system—which in turn has enabled the capital markets to do a better job of performing their basic task of channeling investor savings into productive corporate investment of all kinds. The foreign exchange futures market that started in 1972, together with the host of "derivative" products that have risen up since then, have dramatically reduced the cost of transferring risks to those market participants with a comparative advantage in bearing them. "Efficient risk-sharing," as Miller put it, "is what much of the futures and options revolution has been all about." By functioning much like "a gigantic insurance company," the options, futures, and other derivative markets also effectively raise the price investors pay for corporate securities, thus adding to corporate investment and general economic growth.

Consider, for example, the development of a national mortgage market that was made possible by investment bankers' pooling and repackaging of individual mortgages into securities. Such asset securitization, which in turn was made possible by the development of financial futures necessary to hedge the investment bankers' interest rate and prepayment exposures, has accomplished a massive transfer of interest rate risk away from financial institutions to well-diversified institutional investors. Besides lowering interest rates for homeowners (by as much as 100 basis points, according to some estimates), such risk-shifting has also helped prevent a repeat of the savings and loan debacle of the 1980s.

Futures, options, and the practice of risk management with derivatives in general continue, of course, to have a public relations problem—one that stems mainly from the fact that derivatives are used by "speculators" as well as "hedgers." But economists know that speculators serve a purpose: Besides keeping markets "efficient" by channeling information rapidly into prices, they also help supply the liquidity essential to these markets. And, as Miller argues further, the widespread charges that index futures and options were the cause of growing stock price volatility in the 1980s (including the "crash of 1987") have been contradicted by a growing weight of academic evidence. In short, popular indictments of the "new instruments" confound the messenger with the message. When price volatility shows up within the system, it is largely the reflection of fundamental events. Index futures, options, and other derivatives are simply methods that allow companies and investors to cope with the volatility.

In "The Evolution of Risk Management Products" (chapter 2), Waite Rawls and Charles Smithson point to sharp increases in uncertainty about oil prices and inflation that began in the early 1970s as the main catalyst for the wave of derivatives innovation that followed during the next two decades. In the face of this unprecedented price volatility, capital markets responded by creating new instruments to help investors and corporations in managing their exposures. The 1970s and 1980s saw the introduction of the following:

- futures contracts on foreign exchange contracts, interest rates, metals, and petroleum;

- currency, interest rate, and commodity swaps;

- options on futures and options; and

- hybrid securities combining standard debt issues with option- or forward-like features.

Most of these products, as the authors point out, were not entirely new when they appeared but, rather, were variations of basic instruments, some of which had been around for centuries. What was new, however, was the formation of active market exchanges that dramatically reduced the costs to individuals and corporations of using such risk management tools.

In "The Revolution in Corporate Risk Management: A Decade of Innovations in Process and Products" (chapter 3), Christopher Culp begins by describing the explosion of corporate risk management programs in the early 1990s as a hasty and ill-conceived reaction by U.S. corporations to the great "derivatives disasters" of that period. Anxious to avoid the fate of Barings and Procter & Gamble, most top executives were more concerned about crisis management than risk management. Many companies quickly installed expensive value-at-risk systems without paying much attention to how such systems fit their specific business requirements. Focused myopically on loss avoidance and technical risk measurement issues, the corporate risk management revolution of the 1990s thus got under way in a disorganized, ad hoc fashion, producing a curious amalgam of policies and procedures with no clear link to the corporate mission of maximizing value.

But as the risk management revolution unfolded over the last decade, the result has been the "convergence" of different risk management perspectives, processes, and products—and along with these developments, a coming together of insurance and capital markets. Culp begins by observing, "Before the 1990s, the worlds of insurance and capital markets were about as far apart as Mozart's Vienna and the Nashville of the Dixie Chicks." Insurance companies focused mainly on insuring their corporate clients against property and casualty losses, product liability suits, and other "insurable" events. And with the exception of private placements, the financing of corporate America was the near-exclusive province of commercial and investment banks. Moreover, this divide between insurance and capital markets was mirrored by a corporate structure that included a corporate risk manager who acted pretty much independently of the corporate treasury.

But starting around 2002, insurers like Swiss Re and American International Group (AIG) went into the business of providing their corporate clients with "contingent capital"—sub debt and equity lines of credit, if you will—while capital market investors began offering what amounts to hurricane and earthquake insurance in the form of catastrophe-linked (or "CAT") bonds. At around the same time, industrial companies began joining banks and other financial institutions in embracing "enterprise-wide risk management," which requires not only integration of risk management with the corporate treasury but far greater coordination between the finance function and the business operations of the firm. And, as the case of United Grain Growers illustrates (see the case study in Part III of the book), insurance companies have even come up with new "integrated risk management" products that combine protection against financial (e.g., currency and interest rate) risks and conventional insurance risks.

But underlying—and to a large extent driving—these outward forms of convergence is a more fundamental kind of convergence: the integration of *risk management* with corporate finance. As first corporate finance theorists and now practitioners have come to realize, decisions about a company's optimal capital structure, as well as the design of the securities it issues, cannot be made without first taking account of the firm's risks and its opportunities for managing them. Indeed, Culp argues in his chapter that a comprehensive approach to corporate finance must begin with a risk management strategy that incorporates the full range of available risk management products, including new risk finance products as well as well-established risk transfer instruments like interest rate and currency derivatives. The challenge confronting today's chief financial officer is to maximize firm value by choosing the mixture of securities and risk management products and solutions that give the company access to capital at the lowest possible cost.

In short, the function of risk management has now become an integral part of corporate strategic and financial planning. And as if to confirm Culp's argument, Lisa Meulbroek provides, in "A Senior Manager's Guide to Integrated Risk Management" (chapter 4), an enterprise-wide framework that aims to integrate risk management with corporate strategy. As Meulbroek points out at the outset, companies have three basic ways of managing risk: changing operations; adjusting capital structure; and using derivatives to manage any firm-wide net exposures that remain (after the optimal operational and debt structure have been decided on). The word "integration" refers here both to the combination of these three risk management techniques and the aggregation of all risks faced by the firm. In illustrating this functional analysis of integrated risk management, the chapter uses a wide-ranging set of illustrative situations to show how the risk management process influences, and is influenced by, a company's overall strategy and business activities.

CHAPTER 1

Financial Innovation: Achievements and Prospects

MERTON H. MILLER

THE WONDERMENT OF RIP VAN WINKLE, awakening after his sleep of 20 years to a changed world, would pale in comparison to that felt by one of his descendants in the banking or financial services industry falling asleep (presumably at his desk) in 1970 and waking two decades later. So rapid has been the pace of innovation in financial instruments and institutions over the last 20 years that nothing could have prepared him to understand such now commonplace notions as swaps and swaptions, index futures, program trading, butterfly spreads, puttable bonds, Eurobonds, collateralized mortgage bonds, zero-coupon bonds, portfolio insurance, or synthetic cash—to name just a few of the more exotic ones. No 20-year period has witnessed such a burst of innovative activity.

What could have produced this explosive growth? Has all this innovation really been worthwhile from society's point of view? Have we seen the end of the wave of innovations, or must we brace for more to come? These are the issues I now address.

Why the Great Burst of Financial Innovations Over the Last Twenty Years?

Several explanations have been offered for the sudden burst of financial innovations starting some 20 years ago.[1]

This chapter was previously published as an article in *Journal of Applied Corporate Finance* Vol. 4, No. 4 (Winter 1992): 4–11. The original article was reprinted in *Japan and the World Economy* Vol. 4, No. 2 (June 1992).

1. See, for example, Merton H. Miller, "Financial Innovation: The Last Twenty Years and the Next," *Journal of Financial and Quantitative Analysis* Vol. 21 (December 1986): 459–71; and James C. Van Horne, "Of Financial Innovations and Excesses," *Journal of Finance* Vol. 40 (July 1985): 621–36.

The Move to Floating Exchange Rates

A popular one locates the initiating impulse in the collapse of the Bretton Woods, fixed-exchange rate regime. In the early 1970s, the U.S. government, with strong prodding from academic economists, notably Milton Friedman, finally abandoned the tie of gold to the dollar. The wide fluctuations in exchange rates following soon after added major new uncertainty to all international transactions. One response to that uncertainty was the development of exchange-traded foreign-exchange futures contracts by the Chicago Mercantile Exchange (CME)—an innovation that spawned in turn a host of subsequent products as the turbulence spread from exchange rates to interest rates.

But cutting the tie to gold cannot be the whole story because financial futures, influential as they proved to be, were not the only major breakthrough of the early 1970s. Another product introduced only a few months later, and almost equally important to subsequent developments, was not so directly traceable to the monetary events of that period. The reference, of course, is to the exchange-traded options on common stock of the CME's cross-town rival, the Chicago Board of Trade (CBOT). That the CBOT's options did not precede the CME's financial futures was mainly luck of the bureaucratic draw. Both exchanges started the process of development at about the same time, impelled to diversify by the same stagnation in their traditional agricultural markets. Both needed the cooperation, or at least the toleration, of the appropriate regulators to break out in such novel directions.

The CME was the more fortunate in having to contend only with the U.S. Treasury and the Federal Reserve System—at a time, moreover, when both those agencies were strongly committed to the Nixon administration's push for floating exchange rates.[2] The CBOT, alas, faced the U.S. Securities and Exchange Commission (SEC), a New Deal reform agency always hypersensitive to anything smacking of speculative activity.[3] By the time the SEC had finished its detailed review of option trading, the CME had already won the race.

Computers and Information Technology

Another explanation for the sudden burst of financial innovation after 1970 finds the key in the information revolution and, especially, in the electronic

2. The then Secretary of the Treasury was George P. Shultz, a former colleague and long-time friend of Milton Friedman. The chairman of the Federal Reserve Board was Arthur Burns, another old friend. With Milton Friedman's blessing, both gave a cordial audience to Leo Melamed of the CME and at least a *nihil obstat* to his proposal for an International Monetary Exchange. See Leo Melamed, "The International Monetary Market," in *The Merits of Flexible Exchange Rates*, ed. Leo Melamed (Fairfax, VA: George Mason University Press, 1988), 417–29.

3. Under the SEC's original dispensation, only calls could be traded because puts were regarded as potentially destabilizing. Word of the put-call parity theorem had apparently not yet reached the SEC staff.

computer. Computers in one form or another had been available since the 1950s. But only in the late 1960s, with the perfection of transistorized circuitry, did computers become cheap and reliable enough to design new products and strategies such as stock index arbitrage and collateralized mortgage obligations. And certainly the immense volume of transactions we now see regularly could not have been handled without the data-processing capacities of the computer.

But the basic and most influential innovations, financial futures and exchange-traded options, did not require computers to make them commercially feasible. Options on commodities in fact had been traded regularly on the CBOT until the U.S. Congress, in one of its periodic bouts of post-crash, antispeculative zeal, ended the practice in 1934. That this long prior history of options trading is not better known may trace to the arcane CBOT terminology under which options were known as "privileges." But traded instruments designated with the modern terms puts and calls go back much further than that, to the Amsterdam Stock Exchange of the late 17th century.[4] Routine exchange trading of futures contracts has a history almost as long.

Innovation and World Economic Growth

Still another possibility, and the one I find most persuasive,[5] is that the seeming burst of innovation in the 1970s was merely a delayed return to the long-run growth path of financial improvement. The burst seems striking only in contrast to the dearth of major innovations during the long period of economic stagnation that began in the early 1930s and that for most of the world continued well into the 1950s.

The shrinkage in the world economy after 1929 was on a scale that few not actually experiencing it can readily imagine. The prolonged depression undermined any demand pull for developing new financial instruments and markets, and the increased regulatory role of the state throttled any impulses to innovate from the supply side. Much of this new regulation, particularly in the United States, was in fact a reaction to the supposed evils—notably the Crash of 1929—flowing from the development of exchange-traded, and hence relatively liquid, common stock as a major investment and financing vehicle in the 1920s. Prior to the 1920s, U.S. companies had relied almost exclusively on bonds and preferred stock for raising outside capital.

Even in the depressed 1930s, of course, financial innovation, though muted relative to the 1920s, did not come to a halt. But the major novelties tended to be government sponsored, rather than market induced. Examples are the special housing-related instruments such as the amortizing mortgage and the Federal

4. Joseph de la Vega, *Confusion de Confusiones* (Amsterdam, 1688, translated by Hermann Kellenbenz, 1957, reprinted by Baker Library, Harvard Business School, 1988).
5. See Miller, "Financial Innovation."

Home Administration loan guarantees. Another government initiative of the 1930s was the support direct and indirect of what later came to be called, rather unprophetically we now know, "thrift institutions." New U.S. Treasury instruments were developed, or at least used on a vastly expanded scale, notably Series E savings bonds for small savers and, at the other extreme, U.S. Treasury bills. Indeed, T-bills quickly became the leading short-term liquid asset for banks and corporate treasurers, displacing the commercial paper and call money instruments that had previously served that function.

Financial innovation by the private sector might perhaps have revived by the 1940s had not the war intervened. The war not only drained manpower and energy from normal market-oriented activity, but led to new regulatory restrictions on financial transactions, particularly international transactions.

Regulation and Deregulation as Stimuli to Financial Innovation

By a curious irony, the vast structure of financial regulation erected throughout the world during the 1930s and 1940s, though intended to and usually successful in throttling some kinds of financial innovation, actually served to stimulate the process along other dimensions. Substantial rewards were offered, in effect, to those successfully inventing around the government-erected obstacles. Many of these dodges, or "fiddles" as the British call them, turned out to have market potential far beyond anything dreamed of by their inventors; and the innovations thrived even after the regulation that gave rise to them was modified or abandoned.

The most striking example of such a regulation-propelled innovation may well be the swap in which one corporation exchanges its fixed-rate borrowing obligation for another's floating-rate obligation, or exchanges its yen-denominated obligations for another's mark-denominated obligations, and so on in an almost unimaginable number of permutations and combinations. Some swaps are arranged by brokers who bring the two counterparties directly together, others by banks who take the counterparty side to a customer order and then either hedge the position with forwards and futures or with an offsetting position with another customer.

The notional amount of such swaps, interest and currency, currently outstanding is in the trillions of dollars and rising rapidly. Yet, according to legend at least,[6] the arrangement arose modestly enough as vacation-home swapping by British overseas travelers, who were long severely limited in the amount of

6. The first currency swap appears to have been arranged by Continental Illinois' London merchant bank in 1976. The precise dates and places remain problematic because the originators sought secrecy in a vain attempt to maintain their competitive advantage. See Henry T.C. Hu, "Swaps, the Modern Process of Financial Innovation and the Vulnerability of a Regulatory Paradigm," *University of Pennsylvania Law Review* Vol. 128 (December 1989): 333–435, especially 363, note 73.

currency they could take abroad. Two weeks free occupancy of a London flat could compensate a French tourist for a corresponding stay in a Paris apartment or compensate an American for the use of a condominium at Aspen. If the ingenious British innovator happened to work for one of the merchant banks in the city, as is likely, the extension of the notion to corporate currency swaps was a natural one. The rest, as they say, is history.

> The burst of innovations in the past 20 years seems striking only in contrast to the dearth of major innovations during the long period of economic stagnation that began in the early 1930s and that for most of the world continued well into the 1950s.

The list of similar, regulation-induced or tax-induced innovations is long, and includes the Eurodollar market, the Eurobond market, and zero-coupon bonds, to name just some of the more far-reaching loopholes opened in the restrictive regulatory structure of the 1930s and 1940s.[7] Whether the private sector processes that produced the seemingly great wave of innovations after 1970 will continue to produce innovations if left unchecked is a topic to be taken up later. First let's consider some of the arguments currently being advanced for not leaving them unchecked.

Has the Wave of Financial Innovations Made Us Better or Worse Off?

Free market economists have a simple standard for judging whether a new product has increased social welfare: Are people willing to pay their hard-earned money for it? By this standard, of course, the new products of the 1970s and 1980s have proved their worth many times over. But why have they been so successful? Whence comes their real "value added"? The answer, in large part, is that they have substantially lowered the cost of carrying out many kinds of financial transactions.

Consider, for example, a pension fund or an insurance company with, say, $200 million currently in a well-diversified portfolio of common stocks. Suppose that, for some good reason, the sponsors of the fund believe that the interests of their beneficiaries would be better served at the moment by shifting funds from common stocks to Treasury bills. The direct way would be first to sell the stock portfolio company by company, incurring commissions, fees,

---

7. For a fuller account of tax- and regulation-induced innovations, see Miller, "Financial Innovations."

and "market impact" on each transaction. The cash proceeds, when collected, could then be put in Treasury bills, again incurring transaction costs. A second and much cheaper alternative, however, is simply to sell about 1,000 (at present price levels) Standard and Poor's (S&P) 500 index futures contracts. Thanks to the way the futures contracts must be priced to maintain intermarket equilibrium, that one transaction has the same consequences as the two transactions along the direct route. And at a fifth or even less of the cost in fees, commissions, and market impact!

Or, to take other kinds of financial costs, consider a bank maintaining an inventory of government bonds for resale. The availability of that inventory, like the goods on the shelf in a supermarket, means better and faster service for the bank's customers when they come to shop. But it also means considerable risk for the bank. Bond prices can fall, sometimes very substantially, even in the course of a single day.

To protect against such losses, the bank can hedge its inventory by selling Treasury bond futures. Should the price of the bonds fall during the life of the futures contract, the gain on that contract will offset the loss on the underlying inventory. Without this opportunity to shift the risk via futures, the bank must seek other and more costly ways of controlling its inventory exposure. Some banks might find no better solution than to shrink their inventory and, hence, the quality and immediacy of the services they offer. Others might well abandon the activity altogether.

Insurance and Risk Management

A bank's use of futures to hedge its own inventory does not, of course, eliminate the price risk of the underlying bonds. It merely transfers that risk to someone else who *does* want to bear the risk, either because he or she has stronger nerves, or more likely, because another firm or investor somewhere wants to hedge against a *rise* in bond prices. The futures and options exchanges have greatly reduced the time (and hence cost) that each risk-shifter might otherwise have spent searching for a counterparty with the opposite risk exposure.

The combined set of futures and options contracts and the markets, formal and informal, in which they are transferred has thus been likened to a gigantic insurance company—and rightly so. Efficient risk-sharing is what much of the futures and options revolution has been all about. And that is why the term "risk management" has come increasingly to be applied to the whole panoply of instruments and institutions that have followed in the wake of the introduction of foreign exchange futures in CME's International Money Market in 1972. Honesty requires one to acknowledge, however, that this essentially benign view of the recent great innovative wave is not universally shared by the general public or even by academic economists.

The Case Against the Innovations

Some of the complaints about the harmful social consequences of the financial innovations appear to be little more than updated versions of a once-popular 18th-century economic doctrine known as Physiocracy, which located the ultimate source of national wealth in the production of physical commodities, especially agricultural commodities. Occupations other than commodity production were nonproductive. Modern-day Physiocrats, disdaining consumer sovereignty, automatically and enthusiastically consign to that nonproductive class all the many thousands on Wall Street and LaSalle Street now using the new instruments.

A related complaint is that the new instruments, by lowering transactions costs, have led to too much short-term trading—trading that not only wastes resources, but which has unduly shortened the planning horizons of both firms and investors. That the volume of trading has in fact skyrocketed in recent years there can be no doubt. But the key stimulus to the surge in trading in the underlying stocks appears to have been less the introduction of index futures and options than the ending of the regime of high fixed commissions in 1974. For Treasury bonds, the spur was the huge expansion of federal government debt beginning in 1981.

But the critics are surely right in believing that lower trading costs will induce more trading. More trading, however, need not mean more waste from society's point of view. Trading is part of the process by which economic information, scattered as it necessarily is in isolated bits and pieces throughout the whole economy, is brought together, aggregated, and ultimately revealed to all. The prospect of trading profits is the bribe, so to speak, that society uses to motivate the collection, and ultimately the revelation, of the dispersed information about supply and demand.

Index Futures and Stock Market Volatility. Although many of the complaints against the new financial investments are merely standard visceral reactions against middlemen and speculators, some are specific enough to be tested against the available data. Notable here is the widespread view, expressed almost daily in the financial press, that stock market volatility has been rising in recent years and that stock index futures and options are responsible. The evidence, however, fails to support this widespread public perception of surging volatility.

Volatility, measured as the standard deviation of rates of return (whether computed over monthly, weekly, or even daily intervals), is only modestly higher now than during the more placid 1950s and 1960s, and is substantially below levels reached in the 1930s and 1940s.[8] Even the 1950s and 1960s had brief,

8. See G. William Schwert, "Why Does Stock Market Volatility Change over Time?" *Journal of Finance* Vol. 44 (December 1989): 1115–53.

transitory bursts of unusually high volatility, with a somewhat longer-lasting major burst occurring in the mid-1970s. The number of large, one-day moves (that is, moves of 3% or more in either direction) has indeed been higher in the 1980s than in any decade since the 1930s, but almost entirely due to the several days of violent movements in the market during and immediately following the crash of October 1987. Such increased volatility seems to accompany every major crash (as the Japanese stock market showed through much of 1990).

In fact, the tendency of volatility to rise after crashes and fall during booms is one of the few, well-documented facts researchers have been able to establish about the time-series properties of the volatility series. These bursts of post-crash volatility typically die out within a few months, and that has been basically the case as well for the crash of 1987. Indeed, what makes the 1930s so different from more recent experience is that the high levels of post–1929 crash volatility persisted so long into the next decade.

Index Products and the Crash of 1987. The failure to find a rising trend in volatility in the statistical record suggests that the public may be using the word volatility in a different and less technical sense. They may simply be taking the fact of the crash of 1987 itself (and the later so-called mini-crash of October 13, 1989) as their definition of market volatility. And without doubt, the 20% decline during the crash of 1987 was the largest one-day shock ever recorded. (The mini-crash of October 13, 1989, at about 6%, was high, but far from record breaking.) If the crash of 1987 is the source of the public perception of increased volatility, the task of checking for connections between the innovative instruments and volatility becomes the relatively straightforward one of establishing whether index futures and options really were responsible either for the occurrence or the size of the crash. On this score, signs of a consensus are emerging, at least within academia, with respect to the role of two of the most frequently criticized strategies involving futures and options, portfolio insurance and index arbitrage.

> The combined set of futures and options contracts and the markets, formal and informal, in which they are transferred has been likened to a gigantic insurance company—and rightly so. Efficient risk-sharing is what much of the futures and options revolution has been all about.

For portfolio insurance, the academic verdict is essentially "not guilty of causing the crash," but possibly guilty of the lesser charge of "contributing to the delinquency of the market." Portfolio insurance, after all, was strictly a U.S. phenomenon in 1987, and the crash seems to have gotten under way in the

Far East, well before trading opened in New York or Chicago. The extent of the fall in the various markets around the world, moreover, bore no relation to whether a country had index futures and options exchanges.[9] Even in the United States, nonportfolio insurance sales on the 19th, including sales by mutual funds induced by the cash redemptions of retail investors, were four to five times those of the portfolio insurers.

Still, portfolio insurance using futures, like some older, positive-feedback strategies such as stop-loss orders or margin pyramiding, can be shown, as a matter of theory, to be potentially destabilizing.[10] The qualification "using futures" is important here, however, because the potentially destabilizing impact of portfolio insurance is much reduced when carried out with index options (that is, essentially, by buying traded puts rather than attempting to replicate the puts synthetically with futures via craftily timed hedges). With exchange-traded puts, the bearishness in portfolio insurance would make its presence known immediately in the market prices and implicit volatility of the puts. With futures, by contrast, or with unhedged, over-the-counter puts, the bearishness may be lurking in the weeds, only to spring out on a less-than-perfectly forewarned public.[11]

Index Arbitrage: The New Villain. Whatever may or may not have been its role in the crash of 1987, portfolio insurance using futures rather than options has almost entirely vanished. Certainly it played no role in the mini-crash of October 13, 1989. Its place in the rogues' gallery of the financial press has been taken over by computerized "program trading" in general and by index arbitrage program trading in particular.

Why index arbitrage should have acquired such an unsavory public reputation is far from clear, however. Unlike portfolio insurance, which can be destabilizing when its presence as an information-less trade in the market is not fully understood, intermarket index arbitrage is essentially neutral in its market impact. The downward pressure of the selling leg in one market is always balanced by the equal and opposite buying pressure in the other. Only in rather special circumstances could these offsetting transactions affect either the level or the volatility of the combined market as a whole.

9. See Richard Roll, "The International Crash of October 1987," *Financial Analysts Journal* Vol. 22 (September 1988):19–35.
10. See Michael J. Brennan and Eduardo S. Schwartz, "Portfolio Insurance and Financial Market Equilibrium," *Journal of Business* Vol. 62 (October 1989): 455–72. Particularly interesting in their demonstration, however, is how small the destabilization potential really is, provided the rest of the investing public understands what is going on.
11. See Sanford J. Grossman, "An Analysis of the Implications for Stock and Futures Price Volatility of Program Trading and Dynamic Hedging Strategies," *Journal of Business* Vol. 61 (July 1988): 275–98.

Index arbitrage might, possibly, increase market volatility if an initial breakout of the arbitrage bounds somehow triggered sales in the less-liquid cash market so massive that the computed index fell by more than needed to bring the two markets back into line. A new wave of arbitrage selling might then be set off in the other direction.

Despite the concerns about such "whipsawing" often expressed by the SEC, however, no documented cases of it have yet been found.[12] Careful studies find the market's behavior after program trades entirely consistent with the view that prices are being driven by "news," not mere speculative "noise" coming from the futures markets as the critics of index futures have so often charged.

Nor should these findings be considered in any way remarkable. The low cost of trading index futures makes the futures market the natural entry port for new information about the macro economy. The news, if important enough to push prices through the arbitrage bounds, is then carried from the futures market to the cash market by the program trades of the arbitragers. Thanks to the electronic order routing systems of the New York Stock Exchange (NYSE), the delivery is fast. But arbitrage is still merely the medium, not the message.

That so much recent criticism has been directed against the messenger rather than the message may reflect only the inevitably slow reaction by the public to the vast changes that have transformed our capital markets and financial services institutions over the last 20 years. Index futures, after all, came of age less than 10 years ago. The shift from a predominantly retail stock market to one dominated by institutional investors began, in a big way, less than 15 years ago. In time, with more experience, the public's understanding of the new environment will catch up. Unless, of course, new waves of innovation are about to sweep in and leave the public's perceptions even further behind.

Financial Innovations: Another Wave on the Way?

Will the next 20 years see a continuation, or perhaps even an acceleration, in the flow of innovations that have so vastly altered the financial landscape over the last 20 years? I think not. Changes will still take place, of course. The new instruments and institutions will spread to every country in the developed world (and possibly even to the newly liberalized economies of Eastern Europe). Futures and options contracts will be written on an ever-widening set of underlying commodities and securities. But the process will be normal, slow,

---

12. See, for example, the very thorough searches described in Gregory Duffie, Paul Kupiec, and Patricia White, "A Primer on Program Trading and Stock Price Volatility: A Survey of the Issues and Evidence" (Unpublished working paper, Board of Governors, Federal Reserve System, Washington, DC, 1990).

evolutionary change, rather than the "punctuated equilibrium" of the recent past.[13]

Long-range predictions of this kind are rightly greeted with derision. Who can forget the U.S. Patent Office commissioner who recommended in the early 1900s that his agency be closed down because all patentable discoveries had by then been made? We know also that regulation and taxes, those two long-standing spurs to innovation, are still very much with us despite the substantial progress, at least until recently, in deregulation and in tax rate reduction. But something important has changed. In the *avant garde* academic literature of economics and finance today, few signs can be seen of new ideas and concepts like those that bubbled up in the 1960s and 1970s and came to fruition later in specific innovations.

The extent to which academic thinking and criticism prefigured the great wave of financial innovations of the 1970s and 1980s is still too little appreciated. Calls for the creation of a foreign exchange futures market and analysis of the economic benefits that would flow from such an institution were common in the 1950s and 1960s, as noted earlier, in the writings of the academic supporters of floating exchange rates, especially Milton Friedman. On the common stock front, major academic breakthroughs in the 1950s and 1960s were the Mean-Variance Portfolio selection model of Harry Markowitz and, building on it, the so-called Capital Asset Pricing Model of William Sharpe and John Lintner in which the concept of the "market portfolio" played a central role.

The notion of the market portfolio ultimately became a reality by the early 1970s when the first, passively managed index funds were brought on line. That the world would move from there to the trading of broad market portfolios, either as baskets or as index futures and options, was widely anticipated. The fundamental Black-Scholes and Robert Merton papers on rational option pricing were published in the early 1970s, though manuscript versions of them had been circulating informally among academics well before then. These and other exciting prospects abounded in the academic literature 20 years ago. At the moment, however, that cupboard seems bare of new concepts and ideas waiting for the day of practical implementation.

Such hints of future developments as the current literature does relate more to the structure of the exchanges themselves than to the products they trade. For academics, accustomed to spending their workdays staring at the screens of their personal computers (PCs), the near-term transition of the markets from floor trading to electronic trading is taken for granted. Frequent references can be found in the many articles on the crash of 1987 to the

---

13. Evolution also involves "extinctions." Some of the recent innovations will inevitably fail in the competitive struggle. Others may be killed by heavy-handed regulation.

presumed failings of the current exchange trading systems during that hectic period. Those systems are typically characterized pejoratively as "archaic" and "obsolete," in contrast to the screen-based trading systems in such non-exchange markets as government bonds or inter-bank foreign exchange.

That screen-based trading will someday supplant floor trading seems more than likely, but whether that transition will occur even by the end of this century is far from clear. The case of the steamship is instructive. The new steam technology was clearly superior to sail power in its ability to go upriver and against winds and tides. Steam quickly took over inland river traffic but not, at first, ocean traffic. There steam was better, but vastly more expensive. Steam thus found its niche in military applications and in the high-unit-value fast passenger trade. Only as fuel costs dropped did steam take over more and more of the low-unit-value bulk trade in ocean freight. For some bulk commodities such as lumber, in fact, sail was often the lower-cost alternative up until the start of World War I, more than 100 years after the first practical steamboat.

> The extent to which academic thinking and criticism prefigured the great wave of financial innovations of the 1970s and 1980s is still too little appreciated.

The same laws of comparative advantage apply to electronic trading systems. The open-outcry trading pits of the major futures exchanges may seem hopelessly chaotic and old-fashioned; but they are, for all that, a remarkably cheap way of handling transactions in large volume at great speed and frequency in a setting of high price volatility. Until recently, at least, electronic trading could not have come close to being cost-competitive in this arena. Screen trading found its niche elsewhere. And electronic computer systems found their niche in futures in tasks such as order routing, data processing, and some kinds of surveillance rather than on the trading floor.

But screen-trading technology, like that of computing technology generally, continues to advance and a possibly crucial watershed for the trading systems in futures may soon be crossed. By mid-1992 the Chicago exchanges hope finally to bring on line the long-delayed Globex electronic network for after-hours trading of futures contracts. Unlike some past experiments with screen trading of futures, the test this time will be a valid one. The contracts to be traded, Eurodollars and foreign exchange rates, have long proven viable; the underlying spot markets are themselves screen traded; and substantial potential trading demand for the contracts might well exist outside the United States and after U.S. trading hours.

Even a successful Globex, however, need not doom the exchanges to disappear as functioning business entities. The transactions facilities the exchanges provide through their trading floors are currently the major and certainly the most glamorous, but by no means the only, services they offer. The exchanges also provide such humdrum but critical functions as clearing and settlement, guarantees of contract performance, record-keeping and audit trails, and the collection and dissemination of price information. The market for these services in supporting financial transactions not currently carried out via exchanges is potentially huge. The futures exchanges, by virtue of their expertise and their substantial existing capital investments, are well positioned to enter and to capture a significant share of these new markets, just as they were 20 years ago when the shrinkage in their agricultural business propelled them into financial futures and options.

■ MERTON H. MILLER was the Robert R. McCormick Distinguished Service Professor at the University of Chicago's Graduate School of Business. In recognition of his contributions to financial economics, Professor Miller was awarded the Nobel Prize in Economics in 1990.

CHAPTER 2

The Evolution of Risk
Management Products

S. WAITE RAWLS III AND CHARLES W. SMITHSON

T ODAY, FINANCIAL PRICE RISK not only can affect quarterly profits but
may determine a firm's very survival. Unpredictable movements in exchange rates, interest rates, and commodity prices present risks that cannot be
ignored. It's no longer enough to be the firm with the most advanced production technology, the cheapest labor supply, or the best marketing team—because price volatility can put even well-run firms out of business.

Changes in exchange rates can create stiff competition where none previously existed. Similarly, commodity price fluctuations result in changes in input prices which can make substitute products—products made from different
inputs—more affordable to end-consumers. Changes in interest rates can put
pressure on the firm's costs; and, for those firms whose sales are hurt by higher
interest rates, rising interest rates can lead directly to financial distress as sales
dry up just when borrowing costs skyrocket.

Not surprisingly, the financial markets have responded to this increased
price volatility. The past 15 years have witnessed the evolution of a range of financial instruments and strategies that can be used to manage the resulting
exposures to financial price risk.

At one level, financial instruments now exist that permit the direct transfer of financial price risk to a third party more willing to accept that risk. For
example, with the development of foreign exchange futures contracts, a U.S.
exporter can transfer its foreign exchange risk to a firm with the opposite exposure or to a firm in the business of managing foreign exchange risk, leaving
the exporter free to focus on its core business.

This chapter was previously published as an article in *Journal of Applied Corporate Finance* Vol. 1,
No. 4 (Winter 1989): 18–26 and based on chapter 1 of *Managing Financial Risk* by Clifford W. Smith
Jr., Charles W. Smithson, and D. Sykes Wilford, Institutional Investor Series (New York: Ballinger,
1990).

At another level, the financial markets have evolved to the point that financial instruments can be combined with debt issuance so as to unbundle financial price risk from the other risks inherent in the process of raising capital. For example, by coupling their bond issues with swaps, issuing firms are able to separate interest rate risk from traditional credit risk.[1]

The World Became a More Risky Place . . .

There is general agreement that the financial environment is more risky today than it was in the past. Figure 2.1 provides some dramatic evidence of the change. Here we present what must be regarded as a long price series—namely the retail price index for England from 1666 to the mid-1980s. What jumps out at you from figure 2.1 is that, from the 17th century until the late 20th century, the price level in England was essentially stable. Prices did go up during wartime—the data series reflects conflicts like the one the British had with "that French person" in the early 19th century—but then fell to pre-war levels once the conflict ended.

In marked contrast, the price history for the last half of the 20th century indicates that the financial environment changed. For the first time, prices have gone up—and stayed up. And this is not only a U.K. phenomenon; a similar pattern of price level behavior exists for the United States (albeit, as British colleagues point out, with fewer data points). In fact, during this period of general uncertainty, the developed economies generally began to experience unexpected price changes (primarily increases).

In short, the financial markets were confronted with increased price uncertainty. And this increased uncertainty about inflation was soon followed by uncertainty about foreign exchange rates, interest rates, and commodity prices.

Foreign Exchange Rates Became More Risky . . .

Panel A of figure 2.2 shows monthly percentage changes in the U.S. dollar/ Japanese yen exchange rate since 1957. This figure provides a very clear indication that the foreign exchange market has become more risky. And the reason for the increased volatility of foreign exchange rates in the early 1970s is evident: the breakdown of the Bretton Woods system of fixed exchange rates.[2]

---

1. This decoupling of interest rate risk and credit risk is stressed in Marcelle Arak, Arturo Estrella, Laurie Goodman, and Andrew Silver, "Interest Rate Swaps: An Alternative Explanation," *Financial Management* Vol. 17, No. 2 (Summer 1988): 12–18.
2. A description of the Bretton Woods system and its effect on prices is contained in Bluford Putman and D. Sykes Wilford, eds., *The Monetary Approach to International Adjustment* (New York: Praeger, 1986).

FIGURE 2.1

Retail Price Index for England

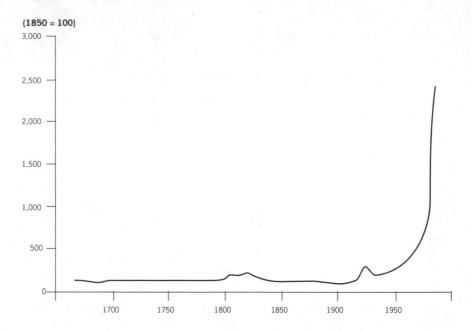

(1850 = 100)

Under the fixed exchange rate system of Bretton Woods, importers knew what they would pay for goods in their domestic currency and exporters knew how much they would receive in their local currency. If the importer could sell at a profit to the consumer, and the exporter's costs were below the export price, then gains from trade were had by all.

With the breakdown of Bretton Woods, the rules changed. Both sides to the transaction now faced exchange rate risk. Each party wanted to transact in his own currency to prevent being "whipsawed" by the market. The importer's profit margin could, and often did, evaporate if his currency weakened sharply and the imported goods were priced in the exporter's currency.

Exchange rate volatility also affects domestic producers. Exchange rate risk occurs whenever the value of future cash flows may change because of foreign exchange rate movements. With more volatile exchange rates, all market participants face greater exchange rate risk. The volatility of exchange rates also greatly affects the real return on domestic versus foreign financial assets. Adverse exchange rate movements can overshadow the interest payments or other income stream received on a foreign currency–denominated asset. Consequently, exchange rate volatility influences the currency distributions of

FIGURE 2.2

Exchange Rates

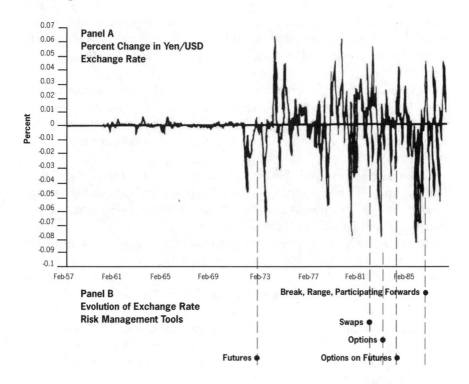

Panel A
Percent Change in Yen/USD
Exchange Rate

Panel B
Evolution of Exchange Rate
Risk Management Tools

Break, Range, Participating Forwards ●

Swaps ●

Options ●

Futures ●   Options on Futures ●

global portfolios, as both borrowers and lenders try to diversify their foreign exchange risk by holding assets or liabilities in different currencies.

Foreign exchange forward contracts had been available for decades. But, not surprisingly, it was only in the early 1970s that this market took on its own existence. But because a forward contract involves the extension of credit, the forward foreign exchange market had become primarily an interbank market.[3] For this reason, many firms confronted with foreign exchange risk were unable to take advantage of the forward market.

As illustrated in Panel B of figure 2.2, the financial market responded to this need by creating a range of risk management instruments. The first to appear was futures contracts on foreign exchange. In May 1972, the International Monetary Market of the Chicago Mercantile Exchange (CME) began trading

---

3. For a description of the credit risk aspects of a forward contract, see Smith et al., *Managing Financial Risk*, chapters 3 and 4.

futures contracts on the British pound, Canadian dollar, deutsche mark, japanese yen, and Swiss franc.[4]

Currency swaps were next to appear. While precursors to swaps such as back-to-back and parallel loans had been used since the onset of volatility in foreign exchange rates,[5] the public introduction of currency swaps is normally marked by the World Bank–International Business Machines (IBM) swap of August 1981.

Option contracts on foreign exchange followed closely on the heels of swaps. In December 1982 the Philadelphia Stock Exchange introduced an options contract on the British pound, which was followed by options on the Canadian dollar, deutsche mark, Japanese yen, and Swiss franc in January–February 1983.[6]

The Chicago Mercantile Exchange followed with the introduction of options on foreign exchange futures in the following currencies: deutsche mark, January 1984; British pound and Swiss franc, February 1985; Japanese yen, March 1986; and Canadian dollar, June 1986.[7]

Commercial banks responded by offering their clients over-the-counter foreign exchange options. They also created forward foreign exchange contracts with option-like characteristics. "Break forwards," "range forwards," and "participating forwards" had all entered the market lexicon by 1987.[8]

In addition to the financial instruments themselves, the rise in foreign exchange rate volatility spawned a number of "hybrid securities."[9] For example, dual currency loans—loans where the bank can convert the debt to another currency at a future date at a specified exchange rate—were introduced by Privatbanken in 1985.[10]

---

4. CME futures contracts on other currencies followed: French franc, September 1974; European currency unit (ECU), January 1986; and Australian dollar, January 1987.

5. For a description of the evolution of the currency swap from parallel loans, see Clifford W. Smith, Charles W. Smithson, and Lee Macdonald Wakeman, "The Evolving Market for Swaps," *Midland Corporate Finance Journal* Vol. 3, No. 4 (Winter 1986).

6. Option contracts on the French franc began trading in 1984, followed by the ECU in 1986 and Australian dollar in 1987.

7. Options on futures are not traded on the CME for French francs, the ECU, or Australian dollars.

8. In "Second-Generation Forwards: A Comparative Analysis," *Business International Money Report* (September 21, 1987), Sam Srivivasulu noted that "break forward" is the name used by Midland Bank. The same construction is known as Boston option (Bank of Boston), forward with optional exit (FOX) (Hambros Bank), and cancellable forward (Goldman Sachs). Likewise, "range forward" is the name used by Salomon Brothers. The same construction is known as collar (Midland Montagu), flexible forward (Manufacturers Hanover), cylinder option (Citicorp), option fence (Bank of America), and mini-max (Goldman Sachs).

9. In general, a hybrid security is one that is made up of a combination of a credit extension instrument and one or more of the financial instruments.

10. A dual currency loan is drawn in one currency, but the bank has the right to convert it to another currency at the spot rate on origination at a pre-arranged time, usually one year after drawing.

Interest Rates Became More Risky . . .

Surprisingly, the increased volatility evident in the foreign exchange market did not spill over into the U.S. domestic money market at first. Indeed, compared to interest rates in the late 1960s and early 1970s, rates actually became more stable in 1977 through 1979. As shown in Panel A of Figure 2.3, interest rate volatility declined during this period,[11] even though interest rates were rising in response to the inflation rate.[12]

As illustrated in Panel A of figure 2.3, however, uncertainty hit U.S. interest rates with a vengeance in 1979. On October 6, 1979, the newly appointed chairman of the Federal Reserve Board, Paul Volcker, abandoned the Fed practice of targeting interest rates and began to target money supply growth instead. As a consequence, interest rates became extremely volatile. For example, in the two years following October 1979, the volatility of 90-day Treasury bill interest rates was five times greater than that of the prior two years.

Perhaps the most widely cited example of the impact of the increased volatility of interest rates is the experience of the U.S. savings and loan (S&L) industry. In the 1970s, S&Ls looked like money machines. With an upward-sloping and *stable* yield curve, S&Ls profited by taking in short-term passbook deposits and making long-term, fixed-rate mortgage loans. In the 1980s, S&Ls changed from money machines to money pits. Those same long-term, low-rate loans to homeowners were now being financed with high-rate—and volatile— short-term funds. The increased interest rate risk changed the way the capital markets functioned. With the increased uncertainty about interest rates, financial institutions became less willing to make long-term rate commitments. They reacted by turning to floating-rate loans. Floating-rate loans first appeared following the increase in rates and volatility in 1973 and 1974; by the 1980s, this structure was being used in earnest.

Floating-rate loans did help banks and S&Ls to manage their exposure to interest rate movements. But it did so only by passing the interest rate risk to the borrower;[13] thus better tools for managing interest rate risk were required. And, as indicated in Panel B of Figure 2.3, they were not long in coming.

Consequently, the dual currency loan is made up of a standard loan and a foreign exchange option. See *International Financial Review* Vol. 742 (September 17, 1988): 2989. As noted in chapter 19 of Smith et al.'s *Managing Financial Risk*, a dual currency bond can be viewed as a combination of a standard bond and a long-dated foreign exchange forward contract.

11. For exposition, Figure 2.3 provides the monthly first difference in the rate rather than percentage change or some other measure more closely related to volatility.

12. Critics have argued that the then chairman of the Federal Reserve Board, Bill Miller, paid for these stable domestic interest rates with higher inflation and a weaker dollar.

13. While floating-rate loans did deal with the immediate problem of interest rate risk, they did not turn out to be the panacea some expected. By passing the market risk to the borrower, floating-rate loans increased the default risk of the borrower.

FIGURE 2.3

Interest Rates

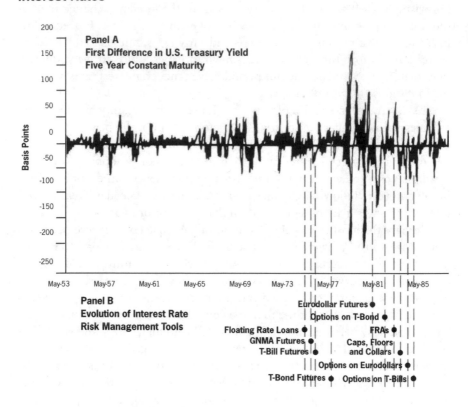

In contrast to the foreign exchange market, there was no historical forward market for interest rates. Consequently, financial futures were the first financial instrument designed to help firms manage their interest rate risk. The progression of futures contracts on U.S. dollar interest rates introduced on the Chicago Board of Trade (CBOT) and the Chicago Mercantile Exchange (CME) is presented below:

First Day Trading	Underlying Asset	Exchange
October 1975	Ginnie Mae	CBOT
January 1976	U.S. T-bills	CME
August 1977	U.S. T-bonds	CBOT
December 1981	Eurodollar	CME
May 1982	T-notes	CBOT

Although the futures exchanges had established a large lead on interest rate management products, banks finally responded to the demand for these products. Banks first reacted by providing interest rate swaps in 1982. Then, in early 1983, they provided the missing forward market for interest rates with the introduction of forward rate agreements (FRAs).

As was the case with foreign exchange, the options contracts followed closely. Option contracts on the underlying asset itself appeared on the Chicago Board Options Exchange (CBOE); options on futures on the underlying asset were introduced on the CBOT and the CME.

First Day Trading	Underlying Asset	Exchange
October 1982	T-bond futures	CBOT
October 1982	T-bond	CBOE
March 1985	Eurodollar futures	CME
May 1985	T-note futures	CBOT
July 1985	T-note	CBOE
April 1986	T-bill futures	CME

And, as in the case of foreign exchange, the banks responded to the exchanges by introducing over-the-counter options: caps, floors, and collars. These products first began to appear in late 1983.

Commodity Prices Became More Risky . . .

Volatility also increased in the commodity markets. The first commodity that comes to mind is oil. As Panel A-1 of figure 2.4 indicates, the price of petroleum products became more volatile in the 1970s. But so did the prices of most basic commodities. Panel A-2 of figure 2.4, for example, presents data on monthly volatility for metal prices.

Figure 2.5 provides another way of looking at commodity prices by displaying data on the relative prices of commodities. Much of the increase in basic commodity prices in the 1970s was driven by inflation. The declining purchasing power of dollars increased the demand for commodities as assets, with the result that the prices of real goods were bid up relative to financial assets.

In the 1970s, commodity-exporting countries experienced a windfall. Wealth was transferred from the industrialized West to commodity producers, especially those producers of oil in the Middle East. Consequently, a commodity-exporting country could become wealthy by recycling "petrodollars"—that is, by borrowing dollars, then subsequently repaying with dollars that had depreciated relative to its export prices. This simple process

FIGURE 2.4

Commodity Prices

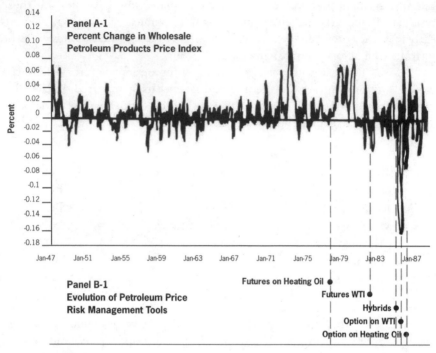

Panel A-1
Percent Change in Wholesale
Petroleum Products Price Index

Panel B-1
Evolution of Petroleum Price
Risk Management Tools

Futures on Heating Oil ●
Futures WTI ●
Hybrids ●
Option on WTI ●
Option on Heating Oil ●

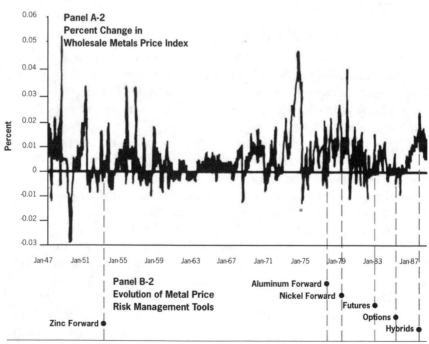

Panel A-2
Percent Change in
Wholesale Metals Price Index

Panel B-2
Evolution of Metal Price
Risk Management Tools

Aluminum Forward ●
Nickel Forward ●
Futures ●
Options ●
Zinc Forward ●
Hybrids ●

FIGURE 2.5

Relative Price of Commodities

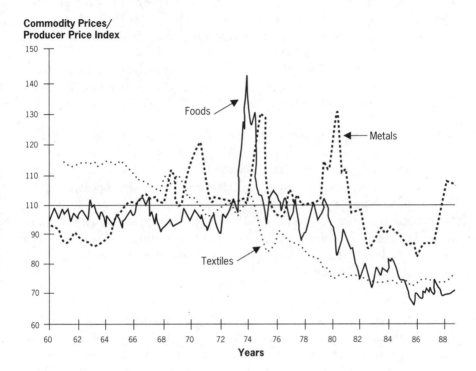

Commodity Prices/
Producer Price Index

Years

worked as long as the relative price of commodities was kept high by unantici-pated inflation.

But when real interest rates rose sharply after the October 1979 shift in U.S. monetary policy, the opportunity cost of holding inventories of com-modities also rose. So, the real value of commodities fell. Wealth was once again shifted, this time from the commodity producers to those holding floating-rate liens against those commodity assets. As figure 2.5 indicates, the relative prices of commodities have fallen dramatically from their peaks in 1974 and 1979.

As with foreign exchange and interest rates, the financial markets re-sponded to the increased commodity price risk with new instruments. The evolution of financial instruments to manage commodity price risk is traced in Panels B-1 and B-2 of figure 2.4.

Metals. The behavior of the price of metals differs from that of foreign exchange, interest rates, and oil prices in that metals experienced a period of increased price volatility in the 1950s as well as the 1970s. Given what we have seen so far, then, it should come as no surprise that a forward contract on zinc was introduced on the London Metal Exchange (LME) in 1953. (Forward contracts on copper had been traded on the LME since 1883.) With the increase in volatility in the 1970s, forward contracts began trading on the LME on aluminum in 1978 and nickel in 1979.

Futures contracts appeared later on the Commodity Exchange (CO-MEX)—on copper in July 1983 and on aluminum in December 1983. An option on copper futures began trading on the COMEX in April 1986.

Petroleum. Because of the preponderance of long-term contracting in the oil industry, forward contracts have never been a significant feature of the petroleum market. But with the increased volatility of oil prices, futures contracts were not long in appearing. Heating oil futures appeared on the New York Mercantile Exchange (NYME) in November 1978, and futures on West Texas Intermediate (WTI) crude oil appeared in March 1983. And, as with all of the other instruments we have watched, options followed. Options on WTI crude oil futures were introduced in November 1986 and options on heating oil futures in June 1987.

Hybrids. Hybrid securities involving commodities have also appeared. With its June 1986 issue of oil interest-indexed notes, Standard Oil made the first inroad into oil warrants. At maturity, the holder of the note will receive not only the principal amount, but an additional payment tied to the value of crude oil. Specifically, holders of the 1990 notes will receive the excess of the crude price over $25 multiplied by 170.[14] In effect, investors in the 1990 notes have an embedded four-year option on 170 barrels of crude oil.

Hybrids have also begun to appear that modify the timing of the options embedded in the bond. Magma Copper Company's copper interest-indexed senior subordinated notes of November 1988 represent a case in point. This 10-year issue pays a quarterly interest payment that varies with the prevailing price of copper as follows:[15]

Average Copper Price	Indexed Interest Rate	Average Copper Price	Indexed Interest Rate
$2.00 or above	21%	$1.20	16%
1.80	20	1.10	15
1.60	19	1.00	14

14. For more details, see the prospectus supplement of June 19, 1986. The holder of the 1992 note had the same payoff, but for 200 barrels instead of 170.
15. From the November 23, 1988, prospectus, page 5.

1.40	18	0.90	13
1.30	17	0.80 or below	12

Hence, at each coupon date, the holder of the debenture has an option position on copper prices.[16] In effect, this 10-year debenture has embedded in it 40 option positions on the price of copper: one with maturity 3 months, one with maturity 6 months, . . . , and one with maturity 10 years.

Commercial Bank Activities. In marked contrast to the markets for foreign exchange and interest rates, banks have not yet become active in providing risk management instruments for commodity prices. The Commodity Futures Trading Commission (CFTC) December 1987 release on hybrid instruments[17] has had, in the words of the Securities and Exchange Commission (SEC), a "chilling effect on new product development."[18] To date the activities of commercial banks in this area have been limited to a relatively small number of banks arranging commodity swaps offshore.

But How Much Is Really "New"?

In the preceding pages, we have traced evolution in the 1970s and 1980s of financial structures that have come to be called "innovations" in the capital markets: Forward rate agreements; futures contracts on foreign exchange rates, interest rates, metals, and petroleum; currency, interest rate, and commodity swaps; options on foreign exchange rates, interest rates, and petroleum; and hybrid securities—all these represent innovations in the sense that they provide firms with the ability to deal with today's more risky financial environment.

But, it is misleading to think of these financial instruments as recent "discoveries." If anything, these risk management instruments were "rediscovered" in the 1970s and 1980s.

For example, while we in Chicago point with pride to the fact that futures contracts have been traded since 1865 on the Chicago Board of Trade, futures contracts are actually much older.[19] Historians suggest that futures contracts first appeared in Japan in the 17th century. The feudal lords of

16. In effect the owner of the note is long a call option with an exercise price of $0.80 and is short a call with an exercise price of $2.00.

17. Commodity Futures Trading Commission, 17 CFR Part 34, Regulation of Hybrid and Related Instruments, Advance Notice of Proposed Rulemaking, December 11, 1987.

18. Response of the SEC to the CFTC, August 19, 1988, page 6.

19. The Board of Trade opened in 1842; but, in the early years of the board, it was forward rather than futures contracts which were traded. *Futures* (Chicago Board of Trade, 1988).

FIGURE 2.6

Cotton Bond

Japan used a market they called cho-ai-mai—"rice trade on book"—to manage the volatility in rice prices caused by weather, warfare, and other sources.[20] In Europe, formal futures markets also appeared in the Netherlands during the 17th century. Among the most notable of these early futures contracts were the tulip futures that developed during the height of the Dutch "tulipmania" in 1636.[21]

The forward contract is even older. Historians suggest that forward contracts were first used by Flemish traders who gathered for trade fairs on land held by the Counts of Champagne. At these medieval trade fairs, a document called a letter de faire—a forward contract specifying delivery at a later date—made its appearance in the 12th century.[22]

Of the financial instruments, options were the last to appear and therefore seem to be the most innovative. But options are not new. As early as the 17th century, options on a number of commodities were being traded in Amsterdam.[23]

And, even the hybrid securities are not new. In other periods of uncertainty, similar securities have appeared. As both of us are Southerners, we would conclude by reminding you of the "cotton bonds" issued by the Confederate States of America (fig. 2.6).

In 1863, the Confederacy issued a 20-year bond denominated not in Confederate dollars but in French francs and pounds sterling. The most interesting feature of this bond, however, is its convertibility (at the option of the bondholder) into cotton.[24] In the parlance of today's investment banker, the Confederate States of America issued a dual-currency, cotton-indexed bond.

---

20. Richard J. Teweles and Frank J. Jones, *The Futures Game*, 2nd ed. (McGraw-Hill, 1987).
21. Peter M. Garber, "The Tulipmania Legend" (Center for the Study of Futures Markets Working Paper #CSFM-139, August 1986).
22. Teweles and Jones, *Futures Game*.
23. *Futures & Options Trading in Commodity Markets* (Paris: International Chamber of Commerce, 1986).
24. The set rate was sixpence sterling per pound of cotton.

Concluding Remarks

From the perspective of financial markets, the changes in the financial environment in the 1970s are important because they stimulated demand for new financial instruments. The financial environment is the key determinant of the kinds of instruments that will be successful in the marketplace. In short, financial innovation is a demand-driven phenomenon.

If the financial environment is stable, the market will use simple instruments. In the late 19th century, for example, the financial instrument of choice was the consol: a bond with a fixed interest rate but no maturity—it lasted forever. Investors were quite happy to hold infinite-lived British government bonds because British sovereign credit was good and expected inflation was nil. Confidence in price level stability led to a stable interest rate environment and therefore to long-lived bonds.

But when the financial environment is filled with uncertainty, then we can expect to see the proliferation of new risk management instruments and hybrid securities. Thus, such uncertainty, though causing many economic problems and disruptions, has also provided the impetus for much valuable financial innovation. Through this process of innovation, financial intermediaries can expand their activities by offering their customers products to manage risk, or even the ability to turn such risk to their own advantage. Through innovation, moreover, financial institutions can better evaluate and manage their own portfolios. Because price uncertainty cannot be eliminated, the clear trend now is to manage risk actively rather than to try to predict price movements.

■ S. WAITE RAWLS is Vice Chairman, in charge of Global Trading and Risk Management, of the Continental Bank. He came to Continental in early 1988 after 12 years at Chemical Bank, where he was Managing Director, Global Securities and Foreign Exchange. Rawls is the current chairman of the Risk Management Center Committee in Chicago.

■ CHARLES W. SMITHSON is Vice President of the Risk Management Products division of Continental Bank. His past research, which focused on a wide range of microeconomic issues, has dealt with questions of regulation, production, discrimination in labor markets, natural resources, and issues in the delivery of health care. His current research concerns financial instruments and risk management.

CHAPTER 3

The Revolution in Corporate Risk Management

A Decade of Innovations in Process and Products

CHRISTOPHER L. CULP

WORLD WAR I, most historians agree, could easily have been prevented. It was the calamitous by-product of overreaction, miscommunication, and plain bad luck. But once the spark was thrown into the powder keg at Sarajevo, the chain of events that became the "Great War" was set in motion.

When economic historians get around to telling the story of the corporate risk management revolution of the 1990s, they will reach a similar conclusion. The explosion in popularity of "enterprise-wide" risk management in the early 1990s need not have happened—or at least not the way it did. The spark in this case was provided by sensational press accounts of the "great derivatives disasters," which in turn prompted hasty, ill-advised reactions by companies anxious to avoid the fate of Barings and Procter & Gamble. Thus, rather than evolving gradually and methodically, the corporate risk management revolution of the 1990s got under way in a disorganized, ad hoc fashion, producing a curious amalgam of policies and procedures with no clear link to the corporate mission of maximizing value. Focused myopically on loss avoidance and technical risk measurement issues, the resulting risk management programs often bore little resemblance to the predictions (or certainly the prescriptions) of finance theorists.

But as the risk management revolution has unfolded over the last decade, the result has been "convergence"—convergence of various perspectives on risk management once divided by extreme differences in vocabulary, concepts, and methods; convergence of organizational processes for managing an extraordinary variety of risks; convergence of risk management products offered

This chapter was previously published as an article in *Journal of Applied Corporate Finance* Vol. 14, No. 4 (Winter 2002): 8–26. The author is grateful to Don Chew, J.B. Heaton, Philippe Planchat, Angelika Schöchlin, Astrid Schornick, and Tom Skarek for their comments on earlier drafts. The usual disclaimer applies, and all remaining errors are the author's alone. In particular, the views expressed here do not necessarily represent those of CP Risk Management or any of its clients.

by hitherto completely separate industries like insurance and capital markets; and, finally, convergence of risk management with the quest for the corporate holy grail of optimal capital structure.

At the center of this convergence maelstrom is a fairly recent development called *alternative risk transfer* (ART). In my new book on the subject,[1] I define ART as the large and growing collection of "contracts, structures, and solutions" provided by insurance and/or reinsurance companies (a group henceforth referred to as "insurance companies" or "insurers") that enable companies to transfer or finance some of their risks in non-traditional ways. So defined, ART forms represent the foray of the insurance industry into the corporate financing and capital formation processes that were once the near-exclusive domain of commercial and investment banks.

To discuss risk management in a corporate finance context is still considered odd by some. Yet, as I argue in my new book—and as a handful of finance academics have suggested for well over a decade[2]—to discuss optimal corporate financing and capital structure without taking account of risk management opportunities is quite likely to lead to serious inefficiencies in how a firm manages risk or raises funds—if not both.

As I also argue in this article, a comprehensive approach to corporate finance must begin with a risk management process and strategy that aims explicitly at maximizing the value of the firm. Then, in executing that strategy, management must consider the full range of available risk management products, including new risk finance products such as "contingent capital" and "finite risk" contracts along with well-established risk transfer instruments like interest rate and currency derivatives. And because that range today encompasses both new and established products provided by insurance companies as well as commercial and investment banks, a comprehensive approach to corporate finance thus means taking account, and full advantage, of the convergence accomplished in the last decade. To some observers, particularly finance academics, such convergence has seemed slow in coming. But now that it has arrived, companies like Michelin and United Grain Growers that have adopted such a comprehensive approach will attest that there is no going back.

This article attempts to survey the last decade of innovations in risk management, from risk management as a process to risk management products, with emphasis throughout on the confluence of risk management and corporate finance. I begin with a discussion of where things stood *before* the series

1. C.L. Culp, *The ART of Risk Management: Alternative Risk Transfer, Capital Structure, and the Convergence of Insurance and Capital Markets* (New York: Wiley, 2002). Parts of this article draw heavily on this book.
2. See, for example, D. Mayers and C.W. Smith Jr., "On the Corporate Demand for Insurance," *Journal of Business* Vol. 55 (1982), and C.W. Smith Jr., and R.M. Stulz, "The Determinants of Firms' Hedging Policies," *Journal of Financial and Quantitative Analysis* Vol. 20, No. 4 (1985).

of financial scandals and disasters in the early 1990s. Specifically, I review different perspectives on risk management that, until the 1990s, happily co-existed in the almost eerily independent spheres of theory and practice. Next I discuss the forces of convergence that have worked together to unify these disparate risk management perspectives and practices in the last 10 years. The remainder of the article then describes some of the most important innovations, first in risk management as a process and then in risk management products.

Risk Management Before 1990—In the Eye of the Beholder

Until the early 1990s, most people seemed to have adopted the same approach to defining risk management that Justice Potter Stewart took when faced with the task of defining pornography: "I don't know how to define it, but I'll know it when I see it." To an environmental scientist, risk management means reducing sulfur dioxide emissions or preventing hazardous chemicals from making their way into the food chain. To a health care professional, risk management means analyzing the tradeoff between deaths caused when drugs like thalidomide come on the market too soon and deaths that result when drugs like penicillin are kept off the market by conservatism, delays, and overregulation. To a financial executive, risk management implies a range of concerns, from making the correct risk adjustment to the discount rate in a capital budgeting problem to protecting the principal invested in a pension plan. The lack of clear understanding about what risk management entails led to a seemingly chaotic variety of perspectives on risk management prior to the revolution of the 1990s.

"Non-Financial" versus "Financial Risk"

Until the 1990s, the idea that people would discuss "financial" and "non-financial" risks at the same time was nothing less than heretical. A financial risk is the possibility that certain events can unexpectedly and adversely affect a firm's financial performance, whether by reducing its net asset value or cash flows, or by lowering its reported earnings. The best-known and most widely managed forms of financial risk are market, credit, and liquidity risk. But there are clearly other risks of a more "physical" nature that can also have a financial impact. And this tendency of risk categories to overflow their bounds has forced the financial and non-financial risk worlds to bump up against one another in often uncomfortable ways.

Consider, for example, the Exxon *Valdez* disaster in 1989. When the captain ran the ship aground in Prince William Sound, causing the largest oil spill in history, the damage to Exxon included not only the costs of environmental cleanup and civil and administrative liability, but also the potential impact of the oil loss on the company's existing oil hedges—without the oil itself, any hedge suddenly became an outright position and thus a major source of risk. Needless to say, the effect of the *Valdez* incident on Exxon's hedge ratios was hardly a matter of concern for environmentalists intent on saving waterfowl; but it also meant little or nothing to the company's legal and insurance staff. The two disciplines—finance and insurance—had almost no common ground.

As the above example is meant to suggest, a financial risk can be defined as any event that can reduce a company's value, cash flow, or earnings. Now let's compare that definition to the three other categories of risk most familiar to insurance theorists and practitioners:[3]

Peril: a natural, man-made, or economic situation that may cause a personal or property loss;

Accident: an unexpected loss of resources arising from a peril; and

Hazard: something that increases the probability of a loss arising from a peril.

In the parlance of insurance, when a bad outcome occurs, it is no longer a type of risk—at that point, it becomes a loss. In the case of the *Valdez* disaster, the risk of an oil spill was thus both a peril and a financial risk. The disaster itself was an accident, the hazard in question was the captain's apparent penchant for alcohol—and in every way the risks translated into a loss.

For a long time, the world of perils, accidents, and hazards was an actuarial and physical world, whereas the world of financial risk was the province of accounting and finance. Expertise in one world implied a near total lack of expertise in the other. And this division of risks into "insurance" and "financial" was reflected not only in major differences in the training, expertise, and conceptual approach of individuals, but in the near-total separation of two entire industry groups—industries that, as people eventually recognized, were performing a similar economic function.

"Capital Markets" versus "Insurance" Perspectives on Risk Management

Until the 1990s, the worlds of capital markets and insurance were about as far apart as Mozart's Vienna and the Nashville of the Dixie Chicks. Even the basic vocabularies used by participants in these areas seemed like two distinct languages. Classical insurance deals with perils, hazards, and accidents and is populated by people who use terms like "retrocessionaires" and "funded retentions" and "attachment points." Financial risk has been the domain of

3. See, for example, J.F. Outreville, *Theory and Practice of Insurance* (Boston: Kluwer, 1998).

FIGURE 3.1

Fire Insurance as a Vertical Spread

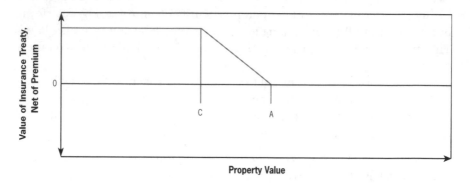

treasurers and traders familiar with concepts like "duration," "convexity," "delta," and "gamma." And to this day, most college and graduate insurance texts pay at most cursory attention to financial instruments while best-selling finance texts regularly fail even to mention insurance.

But on closer inspection, the actual *products* offered by the two industries are not that different. Consider the simple example of a firm that purchases fire insurance for its headquarters building. Suppose the building is initially worth $A and the firm buys insurance with a policy limit up to $C. The solid line in figure 3.1 depicts the value of this insurance contract to the company, net of the premium paid for the policy. An options user would immediately recognize that the payoff indicated by the solid line is exactly the same as the terminal payoff of a short "vertical option spread" written on the value of the firm's property—that is, a long put struck at $A and a short put struck at $C.

Traditional insurance contracts are characterized by several important features, one of which is that the purchaser of insurance must have an "insurable interest"—that is, the purchaser must sustain some economic loss in order to receive compensation under the contract.[4] The firm in figure 3.1 has an insurable interest in its headquarters office building because it sustains direct and material damage from a fire. But there is a potential "moral hazard" problem

4. This requirement originally was intended to distinguish insurance contracts from gambling. Especially with the proliferation of financial instruments excluded from anti-gambling laws through provisions other than insurable interest requirements, the insurable interest issue has become progressively less important over time. See, for example, C.A. Williams, M.L. Smith, and P.C. Young, *Risk Management and Insurance*, 7th ed. (New York: McGraw-Hill, 1995); R. Phifer, *Reinsurance Fundamentals: Treaty and Facultative* (New York: Wiley, 1996); and Outreville, *Theory and Practice.*

FIGURE 3.2

Fire Insurance with a Deductible and Co-insurance

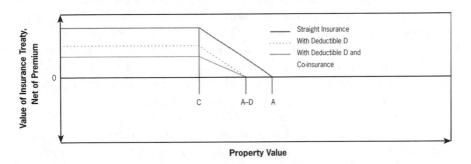

that stems from the fact that the payout on insurance is based on actual damages sustained, and that actions taken by the insured party are not perfectly observable by the insurer. Once insured, the firm may take fewer or less costly precautionary measures to reduce fire hazards, invest too little in fire risk management, or, in the extreme, burn down its own building.

To mitigate moral hazard, insurers include terms like co-payment or co-insurance provisions and deductibles. Figure 3.2 shows how these features alter the payoff structure (and hence the incentives) of the insured from the straight insurance policy shown in figure 3.1. If the building is worth $A and the insurance has a deductible of $D, the insurance is akin to an out-of-the-money vertical spread. And if the insured party must pay a certain percentage (call it α%) of all damages above $(A–D) and up to limit $C (that is, an α% co-insurance provision), then the insurance is equivalent to a short vertical option spread comprising a long puts struck at $(A–D) and α puts sold at $C.

The insurance and option spreads are truly identical, however, only if the options are also written specifically on the value of *this firm's property*.[5] Most derivatives transactions are not written this way and instead involve an *optionable interest* rather than an insurable interest. This means that the risks transferred in a derivatives contract need not be risks to which the derivatives counterparties are naturally exposed. In a typical pay fixed/receive London interbank offered rate (LIBOR) on an interest rate swap, for example, the fixed-rate payer need not have a natural exposure to rising LIBOR as a pre-condition for doing the swap. If LIBOR rises relative to the fixed swap rate, the fixed-rate payer is entitled to a net payment from the swap counterparty *regardless* of whether the fixed-rate payer has sustained any economic damage from the

---

5. Note that property ownership is not the key driver here, but rather the direct connection of the loss the property owner takes with the indemnity offered through the insurance contract.

interest rate increase. This would be impossible in a traditional insurance contract.

Because the payments on derivatives are optionable and generally *not* based on specific economic losses sustained by specific firms, derivatives counterparties need not worry about moral hazard. But the benefit of vanquishing moral hazard is attained at the cost of introducing *basis risk*. Because most derivatives and traditional capital market solutions have payments based on market indexes, the payment on the derivatives contract may not be perfectly correlated with the exact risk its user is trying to hedge.

The distinction between an insurable and an optionable interest is a critical one that separates traditional insurance and the risk management *products* offered in the capital markets. But the risk management *process* a firm undertakes to decide which solution makes sense should be the same regardless of which products are ultimately chosen to manage the exposure. Only vocabulary and culture continue to separate two industries whose outward differences have long obscured their common function. But, as we shall see below, all that is changing.

Risk Management "Process" versus "Products"

In addition to the gaps in corporate risk management stemming from differences in the type of risk and the industries supplying the risk products, still another chasm made it hard to reconcile different perspectives on risk management: the rift between risk management *as a process* and risk management *as products*. The extent of this separation could be seen most clearly in the distance between the worlds of corporate strategy and financial trading. Risk strategists were forever trying to define risk management in terms of business processes like corporate governance, information production and communication, product development, and management of customer relations. To traders, however, risk management was mainly just a code word for market timing and hedge ratio calculations.

For companies developing a risk management program, neither a process nor a product orientation is likely to prove disastrous. But, as I will argue below, a company's product choices should follow logically from its process. Unfortunately, companies prior to 1990 that failed to grasp this logic also generally lacked a common and consistent framework for answering questions like the following:

- How do I choose from among several similar risk management products?

- Should my reason for managing risk affect the products I use?

- Are substitutes for external risk management products available either on my balance sheet or in the context of my broader corporate financing decisions?

A "process," according to the *American Heritage Dictionary*, is a "series of actions, changes, or functions that bring about a result." In the case of risk management, the desired result is that the risks to which a company is *actually* exposed are the same as the risks to which the firm's security holders *want and expect the firm to be* exposed.[6] Like most business processes, this is an active and dynamic exercise that is never "complete" in any meaningful sense. Changes in the firm's assets and liabilities or changes in prevailing market conditions can easily cause a firm's actual risk profile to deviate from its "risk tolerance," making the risk management process an essentially continuous one. But even so, a company's risk management process can be viewed as having several distinct stages:[7]

- Identification of all material "natural" risk exposures—that is, those financial and non-financial risks to which the firm's primary businesses naturally expose the company;

- Risk retention decision by the firm's security holders (or, more precisely, representatives, top managers, and directors);

- Measurement or quantification of the firm's actual risk exposures for comparison to risk tolerances;

- Monitoring and reporting deviations between actual risk exposures and risk tolerances;

- Actions, processes, and systems required to control deviations between the firm's actual risk exposures and its tolerances; and

- Oversight, audit, tuning, and re-alignment of risk management as a continuous process—that is, regularly ensuring that the process accomplishes what it is supposed to *and* ensuring that the objectives of the process remain consistent with security holders' objectives.

The Retention Decision. One aspect of this process merits a bit more attention—namely, deciding which exposures to transfer and which to retain. A key part

---

6. Throughout this article, a firm's optimal investment and financing policies are presumed to have the goal of maximizing the market value of the firm, which is the same as maximizing the combined wealth of the firm's security holders. This is *not* the same as maximizing shareholder or stakeholder value—either of which can be shown to be suboptimal and unstable in a long-run equilibrium. See E.F. Fama, "The Effects of a Firm's Investment and Financing Decisions on the Welfare of its Security Holders," *American Economic Review* Vol. 68, No. 3 (1976), and M.C. Jensen, "Value Maximization, Stakeholder Theory, and the Corporate Objective Function," *Journal of Applied Corporate Finance* Vol. 14, No. 3 (Fall 2001).

7. For a much more detailed discussion of the different parts of this process, see C.L. Culp, *The Risk Management Process: Business Strategy and Tactics* (New York: Wiley, 2001).

of this process requires companies to separate their risks into "core" and "non-core" risks. The former are those risks that the firm is "in business to take," whereas the latter are risks the firm has no clear perceived comparative advantage in bearing. For each company, this classification may be different, thus underscoring the importance of a *formal determination* by a firm's board of what those core risks are.

Consider, for example, a trucking company whose financial risks include both rising gasoline prices that reduce operating margins and rising metal prices that increase the cost of replacement parts. The firm is naturally exposed to both fuel and metal price risks, but its management and board (again, as representatives of its security holders) may conclude that good management of the fleet—which *is* part of the core business—can keep the demand for metal parts under control. Accordingly, the firm's risk management strategy might dictate a focus on fuel price risk while leaving metal price risk to operating managers. As this example is meant to suggest, most of the risks that are explicitly addressed in the firm's risk management process are likely to be non-core risks. But in some cases management will decide to manage core risks as well, especially when such risks expose the firm to the possibility of financial distress.

For those risks the firm chooses not to bear, there are two alternatives. First, the firm can *transfer* the risk to another participant in the market, either by selling or securitizing assets or liabilities, or by using derivatives and other hedging instruments. Alternatively, the firm can *neutralize* the risk using techniques such as balance sheet or operational hedging, structured notes (including commodity- and currency-linked debt), and risk controls.[8]

Another critical component of a firm's retention definition concerns whether or not to secure *advance funding* for any losses resulting from risks the firm retains. To draw on insurance terminology again, an *unfunded retention* is a retained risk for which any losses are financed as they are incurred, whereas a *funded retention* involves the allocation of specific funds to specific expected losses. If funds are allocated to losses based on a price negotiated before the loss occurs, the funds are called *pre-loss financing*. Funds can also be obtained to finance losses from a specific risk but on *variable* price terms, in which case the firm has arranged *post-loss financing*.[9]

---

8. As an example, if British Airways expects a larger amount of dollar/sterling risk to arise on its expected U.S. ticket sales than its security holders want to bear, the company can (and does) issue dollar-denominated debt to help neutralize that exposure. See C.L. Culp, D. Furbush, and B.T. Kavanagh, "Structured Debt and Corporate Risk Management," *Journal of Applied Corporate Finance* Vol. 7, No. 3 (Fall 1994).
9. For a discussion of when pre-loss financing makes sense and when it does not, see chapters 9–13 of N.A. Doherty, *Integrated Risk Management* (New York: McGraw-Hill, 2000).

The Convergence Decade

In the wake of the derivatives disasters in the early 1990s, suggestions and formal proposals for reforming corporate risk management policies and procedures came quickly from all quarters. Some were constructive, but most were not. On the positive side, industry groups like the International Swaps and Derivatives Association and the Group of Thirty published recommended best practices in risk management that gave some badly needed uniformity to an extremely disparate field. Less helpful, a large number of regulators, legislators, and media commentators were lying in wait for the next finance scandal to replace the Milken/Boesky witch hunt that was at long last subsiding. The "evils of derivatives" and the need for draconian risk management became the new populist rallying cry.

As a consequence, the first part of the 1990s was more crisis management than risk management. Many companies jumped headlong onto the risk management bandwagon, more out of fear—both of losses and crusading politicians—than because the risk management process actually *made sense* as part of an overall corporate strategy to increase firm value. Many corporations hastily installed (often outrageously priced) value-at-risk (VaR) systems, for example, without paying much attention to how such systems fit their specific business requirements. For example, quite a number of non-financial clients that purchased VaR software ended up putting it back on the shelf. They learned the hard way that although VaR could be quite useful in helping dealers price exotic options and measure daily trading risk, it was of limited use (and in some cases positively misleading) for non-financial corporates attempting to manage exposures in less liquid markets over longer time horizons.

Complicating matters was the sudden huge demand for risk management professionals and technicians generated by political and regulatory pressure. What was needed at the beginning of the 1990s was greater integration between classical insurance and capital markets risk management, but what emerged was yet a third category of risk manager often better trained in physics than economics. Fueled by the need many boards felt to "be doing something," the risk management focus went straight to issues that were purely technical in nature—what distributional assumptions to make, how to model time-varying correlation matrices, and the like. Although useful in many risk management applications—especially at financial institutions with rapidly changing exposures in traded financial instruments—little thought and effort were devoted to harmonizing corporate risk management practice with the corporate objective of value maximization.

But this would begin to change over the next five years. The sheer amount of money being poured into risk management—reports of "chief risk officers" being hired for more than a million dollars a year were not unusual—ensured that corporations and academics alike would begin the struggle to plant risk management on a more solid foundation of corporate finance and business strategy. With the technology of risk measurement now firmly in their grasp, the question then became how to *use* such risk measurement in a manner consistent with the firm's business and risk management strategy—the question that should have come first.

Convergence in Risk Management as an Organizational Process

One direct outgrowth of publications like the Group of Thirty report was the widespread establishment by active derivatives dealers of independent risk management units that were segregated from "front office" risk-taking activities. But even within the realm of financial risk, these early risk management units were responsible mainly for *market* risk management—for example, administering a set of trading limits based on some analytical measure of market risk. This was the primary function of the so-called "middle office."

Slowly but surely, many financial institutions began to recognize that analytical risk measurement requirements alone created considerable economies of scope from merging market and credit risk management. The obvious next step was to measure and coordinate the management of *all* of a company's major risks in a manner consistent with the fundamental business objectives of the firm.

Enterprise-wide risk management (ERM), aims to *consolidate* and *integrate* both the process by which a firm manages its risks *and* the risks that are targeted in that process. Arthur Andersen usefully defines ERM as

> a structured and disciplined approach [that] aligns strategy, processes, people, technology and knowledge with the purpose of evaluating and managing the uncertainties the enterprise faces as it creates value. . . . It is a truly holistic, integrated, forward-looking and process-oriented approach managing all key business risks and opportunities—not just financial ones—with the intent of maximizing shareholder value for the enterprise as a whole.[10]

There are four basic differences between ERM and other less formal, more *ad hoc* approaches. First, ERM seeks to consolidate exposure types not just across financial risks but also across non-financial perils and hazards. In so doing, ERM seeks to differentiate between core risks and non-core risks—and, as part of that process, between those risks in which the firm has some perceived comparative informational advantage and those where it views itself as no better informed than other market participants.

10. J.W. DeLoach, *Enterprise-Wide Risk Management* (London: Financial Times-Prentice Hall, 2000), p. 5.

A second distinguishing feature of ERM is that it involves viewing all risks facing a company through some form of common lens, such as that provided by risk measurement frameworks like VaR and risk-adjusted return on capital (RAROC), which is discussed in more detail below. But at a more general level, ERM implies the ability of management to transform the chaotic variety of financial instruments into an orderly array of related—and in some respects interchangeable—tools for accomplishing the firm's overarching risk management goals. From this vantage point, what matters is *not* whether a risk is best managed through "swaps," "insurance," or "trading limits," but whether the company's resulting enterprise-wide risk exposure conforms to the risk tolerances of its security holders *and*, in the process, enables the firm to minimize its cost of capital.

A third characteristic of ERM is its attempt to consolidate the risk management process organizationally across systems, processes, and people. In other words, the "enterprise-wide" in ERM refers not just to a company's view of the risks it is facing, but also the degree of coordination and consolidation with which the firm manages those risks.

Finally, enterprise-wide risk managers are constantly looking for more integrated risk management products and solutions. Capital and insurance markets have been converging over the last decade on both the demand and supply sides. On the supply side, an investment banker might solicit a once-unheard-of meeting with the head of a corporation's captive insurance company instead of its chief financial officer (CFO). At the same time, several reinsurance companies now boast of relationships with corporate CFOs that are deeper than those most CFOs now have with their derivatives dealers. On the demand side, corporations with a growing ERM focus are increasingly seeking one-stop shopping for their risk management solutions, prompting insurance and reinsurance companies like American International Group (AIG) and Swiss Re to offer earnings per share insurance, and derivatives participants like Goldman Sachs and Lehman to set up licensed reinsurance subsidiaries.

Convergence on a Common Theme—Capital Structure Optimization

The recent trend toward convergence in risk management processes and products across different lines is much more fundamental than just growing similarities among institutions or the progressive integration of once separate markets like swaps and Eurodollar futures strips. The *real* convergence—the one that underlies and to a great extent is driving the others just discussed—is the integration of *corporate finance* and *risk management*. As I suggested at the outset of this article (and as Prakash Shimpi demonstrates) a company intent on finding its value-maximizing capital structure cannot do so without first assessing its major risks and determining, at least to a first approximation, its plan to transfer or retain (and perhaps pre-fund) them.[11] By the same token, a company's risk management policy, particularly its product choices, will generally have to be coordinated with its financing decisions, including the design of its securities.

At the most basic level, the company's capital structure decision is where corporate risk management converges with the theory and practice of corporate finance. After all, instead of transferring a given risk, a company can simply issue more equity to absorb the larger expected losses. And instead of using a risk financing product, a firm can borrow the old-fashioned way by issuing new debt or arranging a line of credit. In a very real sense, most risk transfer products are thus *synthetic equity*—and risk financing can be viewed as *synthetic debt*.

The challenge confronting today's CFO is thus to maximize firm value by choosing the mixture of securities and risk management products and solutions that gives the company access to capital at the lowest possible weighted cost. Corporations and suppliers of capital and risk management products increasingly recognize that the quest for optimal capital structure and the design of a risk management program are often driven by the same underlying economic considerations. And as will be shown later, the rising demand for products that allow firms to manage their risks and their capital *at the same time* is in large part responsible for the development of the rapidly evolving ART market.

Advances in Risk Management as a Process

Let's now turn to some of the major advances in risk management as an enterprise-wide process over the past decade. Although there have been countless incremental improvements in many aspects of the process, the focus here will be on major innovations that have strengthened *the entire process*.

Risk Management Should Aim to Increase Value

The most fundamental change in the process of corporate risk management has been the growing recognition that risk management must contribute to the overarching corporate goal of value maximization. But this begs the question: how does risk management increase value? In the M&M world of perfect capital markets that many of us were introduced to in business school, corporate risk management was largely a matter of indifference to the company's stockholders. Because such investors could diversify away the risks associated with fluctuations in interest rates or commodity prices simply by holding well-diversified portfolios, they would not pay a higher price/earnings (P/E) multi-

---

11. See Prakash A. Shimpi, *Integrating Corporate Risk Management* (New York: Texere, 2001); and Prakash Shimpi, "Integrating Risk Management and Capital Management," *Journal of Applied Corporate Finance* Vol. 14, No. 4 (Winter 2002): 27–40, which draws heavily on chapter 3 of Shimpi's *Integrating*.

ple (or, what amounts to the same thing, lower the cost of capital) for companies that chose to hedge such risk. So if hedging was unlikely to affect a firm's cost of capital and value, then why do it?

Two decades of theoretical and empirical work on the issue of "why firms hedge" have produced a number of plausible explanations for how risk management can increase firm value—that is, how it can increase the firm's expected cash flows even after taking account of the costs of setting up and administering the risk management program.[12] Summarized briefly, such research suggests that risk management can help companies increase (or protect) their expected net cash flows mainly in the following ways:[13]

- By reducing expected tax liabilities when the firm faces tax rates that rise with different levels of taxable income.

- By reducing the expected costs of financial distress caused by a downturn in cash flow or earnings, or a short-fall in the value of assets below liabilities. Although such costs include the out-of-pocket expenses associated with any formal (or informal) reorganization, more important considerations are the diversion of management time and focus, loss of valuable investment opportunities, and potential alienation of other important corporate stakeholders (customers, suppliers, and employees) that can stem from financial trouble.

- By reducing potential conflicts between a company's creditors and stockholders, including the possibility that "debt overhang" results in the sacrifice of valuable strategic investments.

- By overcoming the managerial risk aversion that (in the absence of hedging) could lead managers to invest in excessively conservative projects to protect their annual income and, ultimately, their job security.

- By reducing the possibility of corporate underinvestment that arises from unexpected depletions of internal cash when the firm faces costs of external finance that are high enough to outweigh the benefits of undertaking the new investment.

As this list suggests, value-increasing risk management has little to do with dampening swings in reported earnings (or even, as many academics have suggested, minimizing the "variance" of cash flows). For most companies, the main contribution of risk management is likely to be its role in minimizing the

12. In principle, risk management can also reduce the firm's cost of capital. For example, managing risk can lower the capital cost for a partnership whose shareholders have most of their own wealth tied up in the firm.
13. For a reasonably thorough summary of the different major theories, including some not explicitly mentioned here, see part I of Culp, *Risk Management Process*.

probability of *costly*[14] financial distress. In this sense, the optimal risk management policy may be one that provides a kind of insurance against "worst-case" scenarios or, to use an actual insurance term, "catastrophic" outcomes. And even when the company has relatively little debt, management may choose to purchase such catastrophic insurance to protect the company's ability to carry out the major investments that are part of its strategic plan. In the process of insuring against catastrophic outcomes and preserving a minimal level of cash flow, companies will generally discover that they can operate with less capital (or at least less equity capital) than if they left their exposures unmanaged. And to the extent that hedging proves to be a cheap substitute for capital, risk management is a value-adding proposition.[15]

Besides economizing on a firm's use of capital while protecting its strategic plan, there is another potentially value-increasing application of risk management—one that has largely escaped the attention of finance theorists. Increasingly, companies are also recognizing that the expertise required to reduce their own catastrophic risks can sometimes be leveraged into opportunities to increase expected revenues. Such revenues come *not* from taking open positions in financial markets, but from the risk management unit's ability to provide (and even sell) other valuable products and services without changing the net risk exposure of the firm.

The Risk Management Unit as a "Service Bureau." Having incurred the costs of setting up a risk management process and infrastructure, companies whose risk management units rely on diverse valuation and risk measurement models may discover that those units can function as an internal "service bureau" that provides financial modeling capability throughout the firm.[16] As one example of the kind of analysis that some risk units now can and do provide, many companies evaluate business opportunities with value-based management (VBM) concepts like economic value added (EVA) and shareholder value added (SVA). The systems required to measure EVA and SVA are essentially just large cash flow forecasting and risk-adjusted discounting systems, which are almost certainly *already housed* in a comprehensive ERM risk measurement system. Also found in many ERM

---

14. As the italics are meant to suggest, the possibility of financial distress is not necessarily value-reducing for all firms; in fact, for mature companies with large and stable operating cash flow and limited investment opportunities, high leverage, which of course raises the probability of financial distress, is likely to be a value-increasing strategy by reducing managers' natural tendency to spend (and thereby waste) excess cash flow.

15. For an example of how insurance has the potential to reduce a company's cost of capital, see Shimpi, "Integrating."

16. See C.L. Culp and P. Planchat, "New Risk Culture: An Opportunity for Business Growth and Innovation," *Derivatives Quarterly* Vol. 6, No. 4 (Summer 2000).

systems are tools for capital budgeting, risk-adjusted capital allocation, capital structure optimization, and scenario analysis that the firm's risk management unit could make accessible to other parts of the firm.

The Risk Management Unit as an Internal "Bank." Some companies have also discovered that significant efficiency gains can be achieved—both within and outside the internal risk management process—by allowing the risk management unit to function as a type of internal treasury department, or "internal bank," for the business units of the firm. In such arrangements, treasury is still responsible for *external* finance, but risk management increasingly takes care of the analytical service and financial product demands of business units for *internal* financial transactions.

Such risk management–cum–internal banking units also typically offer their analytical services to other business units, including risk management products and solutions. Mirroring risk control transactions, for example, are often executed between the risk unit and individual business units before being executed by and between the risk unit and an external counterparty like a swap dealer. This enables all risks to be transferred from the business units to the internal bank, which in turn gives the internal bank the comprehensive view of and control over the firm's total risks that are necessary to achieve enterprise-wide exposure management and portfolio-based risk measurement and control.

The trend in this area seems to be confined mainly to non-financial corporates, including companies like Novartis, ABB, Michelin, and Siemens. In the case of ABB (and several other firms whose names I'm not at liberty to disclose), risk units that serve as internal banks have also begun to offer *external* banking services. Both capital structure and banking products like letters of credit and risk management products like derivatives are routinely supplied to outside customers of the firm. In some cases, these external banking divisions also provide advisory services to customers in the area of risk and treasury management.

Why a Firm Manages Risk Should Affect How

From a practical standpoint, risk management can add to firm value when the risk management process is aimed at protecting value, cash flows, or earnings— *but not usually all three at once*. Hedging to reduce expected taxes is an earnings-based strategy, for example, while hedging to prevent a shortfall of assets below liabilities is value based. And hedging to reduce underinvestment stemming from prohibitive costs of external finance is designed to ensure minimal levels of internal funds.

Finance theorists, to be sure, have long maintained that the value of the firm is linked directly to its cash flows. And a firm's earnings are basically just its operating cash flow with the appropriate accounting rules overlaid. But despite the close relations of these three measures, they can be quite different when viewed through a risk manager's eyes. The difference between value on the one hand and either earnings or cash flows on the other, for example, is at bottom the difference between a *stock* and a *flow*. The value of the firm is its value *at any specific point in time*; the cash flows or earnings of a firm occur over some *interval* of time. As some firms have learned the hard way, controlling one of these variables does not always mean controlling the other.

Increased corporate awareness of the linkages between *why* risk is managed and *how* it should be managed has been one of the major advances in the risk management process over the last decade. A company's underlying rationale for risk management—that is, its understanding of how risk management is expected to add value—should in turn influence key aspects of the firm's risk management approach, including how it distinguishes between core and non-core risks and what measure of financial condition serves as the basic building block for the rest of the risk management process. As one example, a multinational corporation intent on maintaining sufficient cash flow to carry out its strategic investments is unlikely to hedge with futures, which are marked to market at least daily and thus can actually increase cash flow volatility even while locking in net asset value and earnings.

Consistency in Risk Measurement Methods

As discussed earlier, one major reason for the rapid growth in risk management "as a discipline unto itself" was the explosion of research on risk measurement and the use of summary risk measures as the basis for reporting, monitoring, and control systems. Progress over the past decade in the technology of risk measurement and reporting has been impressive, both for specific risk types as well as across different exposures.

Market Risk. A major by-product of the early years of the risk management revolution was the widespread adoption of forward-looking measures of market risk that express potential losses in terms of their probabilities. Such measures have been used to supplement, if not replace, less reliable risk measures such as static risk sensitivities like duration or the net interest income gap. Easily the most popular forward-looking market risk measure is value at risk (VaR) or its flow equivalent, cash flow at risk (CFaR). Apart from the adoption of VaR and related risk measures, most advances in market risk measurement have been methodological improvements. Notable among such advances are better parameter estimation methods for volatility and correlation used in the parametric normal VaR implementation, better "primitives" for use as proxies of actual positions, the use of "extreme value theory" (to take account of the possibility of low-probabilility, catastrophic events) for summary risk measurement,[17] and the use of non-parametric methods for loss measurement.[18]

Credit Risk. Significant advances have also been made within the area of credit risk measurement. In commercial banking applications, the core of any credit risk measurement model has always been *expected loss*.[19] Traditional transactional models define expected loss for any asset as the product of three terms: the expected default rate (DR) of an obligor, the expected loss (net of recoveries) in the event of default, and the potential credit exposure (PCE). Numerous improvements have been made in the past decade in the measurement of each of these terms. Two examples of such improvements are reasonably advanced credit scoring models and analytical models for DR estimation (including models that allow the DR to "migrate" across rating changes rather than remain constant)[20] and option-theoretic approaches for modeling the PCE of derivatives.[21] The last decade has also seen the development of *portfolio* measures of credit risk that capture interactions between the components of expected loss that were traditionally treated as independent.[22]

Operational Risk. The International Swaps and Derivatives Association, British Bankers' Association, and the Risk Management Association all define operational risk as "the risk of loss resulting from inadequate or failed internal processes, people, and systems or from external events."[23] Interest in "op risk" measurement has grown significantly since the promulgation in 1999 of a major revision in the Basel Capital Accord for banks. Among other things, the proposed revision creates a "whole capital charge" that reflects *all* the major risks facing banks, including op risk. On the one hand, the attempt to measure op risk seems to indicate greater integration between financial risk

17. See, for example, F.M. Longin, "From Value at Risk to Stress Testing: The Extreme Value Approach," *Journal of Banking and Finance* Vol. 24 (2000).
18. See, for example, Y. Aït-Sahalia and A.W. Lo, "Nonparametric Risk Management and Implied Risk Aversion," *Journal of Econometrics* Vol. 94 (2000).
19. See C. Matten, *Managing Bank Capital* (New York: Wiley, 2000).
20. See M. Crouhy, D. Galai, and R. Mark, "A Comparative Analysis of Current Credit Risk Models," *Journal of Banking & Finance* Vol. 24 (2000).
21. See, for example, C.W. Smithson, *Managing Financial Risk* (New York: McGraw-Hill, 1998).
22. For surveys of the major advances in credit risk measurement, see J.B. Caouette, E.I. Altman, and P. Narayanan, *Managing Credit Risk* (New York: Wiley, 1998); M. Ong, *Internal Credit Risk Models* (London: Risk Books, 1999); A. Saunders, *Credit Risk Measurement: New Approaches to Value at Risk and Other Paradigms* (New York: Wiley, 1999); D. Shimko, *Credit Risk: Models and Management* (London: Risk Books, 1999); and M. Crouhy, D. Galai, and R. Mark, *Risk Management* (New York: McGraw-Hill, 2001).
23. International Swaps and Derivatives Association, British Bankers' Association, and Risk Management Association, *Operational Risk: The Next Frontier* (December 1999).

and classic insurance perils and hazards. On the other hand, the current preoccupation with *measuring* op risk has led some to contend that more attention is paid to modeling op risk for its own sake than to *managing* op risk, which is arguably all that matters.

Integration Across Risks. In addition to advances in measuring and summarizing specific risk types, the last few years have also seen significant attention paid to *consolidated* measures of risk across types. Much of the interest in integrated risk measures can be attributed to the growth in corporate adoptions of ERM. Enterprise-wide risk *measurement*, after all, is a virtual necessity for enterprise-wide risk *management*. In addition, the desire by some firms to use risk measurement as the primary basis for explicitly tying internal capital allocation to capital structure has been a further impetus for integration in measures of different risk types.

Several portfolio-based measures of credit risk, for example, attempt to express credit exposure in a VaR-like fashion. And in some cases, risks have been explicitly integrated into a VaR framework, such as liquidity risk-adjusted VaR (L-VaR), a risk measure that reflects both market risk and the risk of widening spreads associated with selling an asset during illiquid market conditions.[24]

But far and away the most popular of the risk-based capital allocation systems are those that come under the name of RAROC (risk-adjusted return on capital).[25] RAROC is the expected net economic profit of a business line or activity divided by its economic capital at risk. Net economic profit is generally defined as the expected revenues of a business unit less expected costs and expected losses arising from that business line. Capital at risk is a measure of the capital necessary to support *all* risks that are associated with that business line's expected economic profit.

In order for RAROC to prove useful, capital at risk must be an integrated risk measure. Although some companies use measures like VaR as a measure of capital at risk, this does not work particularly well in allocating capital to, say, a lending business, where the major risk is credit risk. A much more comprehensive risk measure is required. As interest in integrated risk measures like capital at risk continues to rise, methodological improvements will doubtless continue to follow, as happened in the 1990s first with market risk and then with credit risk.

---

24. For a discussion of this and other related risk measurement extensions, see P. Jorion, *Value at Risk* (New York, McGraw-Hill, 2000); and Crouhy et al., *Risk Management*.
25. Alternatively, some focus on return on risk-adjusted capital. For a good discussion of alternative capital measures, see Matten, *Managing Bank Capital*.

Risk Control without Financial Instruments

A sound and comprehensive system of internal controls based on the risk exposures associated with the firm's assets and liabilities can go a long way toward keeping firms within their risk tolerances. Before the 1990s, firms often misconstrued this prescription as a call for internal controls on *specific* financial instruments, such as pre-trade authorization requirements. And the derivatives policies set up in response to the derivatives disasters of the 1990s actually compounded the problem. More aptly called "anti-derivatives policies," such policies had the effect of depriving risk managers of the hedging benefits of derivatives without actually helping to control the risks associated with derivatives use. As the shareholders of companies like Procter & Gamble learned to their dismay, financial institutions are capable of creating virtually any kind of synthetic derivative to circumvent product-specific trading limits.[26] And thus, as ERM momentum gradually replaced derivatives paranoia, companies began to realize that their internal controls should focus on controlling *exposures* rather than products whose names change and whose effects on firm value, cash flows, and earnings are impossible to infer from terminology alone.

The risk-adjusted capital allocation that is perhaps the most important output of a RAROC system can also be used to help companies keep their risks within the established tolerances. But if the number of non-financial corporate users of RAROC as a risk control tool has grown significantly in recent years, financial institutions continue to be by far the largest user group—one that includes Bank of America,[27] BankAustria, HypoVereins Bank, First Union, and Canadian Imperial Bank of Commerce.

Advances in Risk Management Products

Now let's turn to new risk management *products*. Rather than attempt to cite every new instrument developed in the last 10 years, the focus here is on several major *themes* in the product innovations of the 1990s.

"Equitized" Risk Transfer Products

When a company is seeking to reduce the expected costs of financial distress or reduce the underinvestment costs of debt overhang,[28] it can issue new equity.

---

26. Even in the case of actual derivatives like notional interest rate swaps, embedded options often make such instruments much riskier than the name "swaps" would suggest. See chapters 13, 14, and 22 of Culp, *Risk Management Process*.
27. See E.J. Zaik, G. Walter, G. Kelling, and C. James, "RAROC at Bank of America: From Theory to Practice," *Journal of Applied Corporate Finance* Vol. 9, No. 2 (Summer 1996).
28. Underinvestment in this context is a result of the agency costs of debt. See S.C. Myers, "The Determinants of Corporate Borrowing," *Journal of Financial Economics* Vol. 5 (1977).

But given the costs associated with equity offerings, the firm may instead choose to use derivatives to manage certain major financial exposures—an action that, as seen earlier, can reduce the firm's need for equity capital. But if these two approaches are similar in effect, they are not exact equivalents. Equity will absorb losses arising from *any* risk, whereas risk transfer products are usually aimed at one or two risks, such as commodity price or interest rate fluctuations. Issuing equity, moreover, results in an immediate inflow of paid-in capital, whereas risk transfer products effectively provide what amount to *options* on paid-in capital—that is, the firm receives the funds only in specific circumstances, such as the decline of LIBOR below the fixed rate in a pay floating/receive fixed swap.

One of the most important risk management product trends of the last decade has been the increasing popularity of "equitized" risk transfer products—products that have some of the distinctive features of an equity issue that are not generally found in conventional risk products. Examples can be found in the worlds of both derivatives and insurance.

Total Return Swaps. In the first half of the decade, the market for credit derivatives—over-the-counter transactions that effectively allow companies or investors to transfer credit risks—went from virtually nothing to a notional amount outstanding of around $40 billion.[29] By the end of June 2001, notional amounts of credit derivatives outstanding had exploded to almost $700 billion.[30]

One of the most popular types of credit derivatives is called a total return swap (TRS). In a TRS, a firm pays a fixed financing spread over LIBOR in exchange for receiving LIBOR plus all the income *and* the change in value on some underlying asset(s) or portfolio. The cash flows can be based on a representative index (like the Citibank loan index) or, provided the two parties to the swap can agree on an objective, a clearly specified measurement method for the change in value of the asset(s), on actual income and values.[31]

Intended to help firms manage the risk of either an actual default or a downgrade on the reference asset (or assets), the "total return" nature of a TRS makes the transaction economically equivalent to a sale of the asset. That is, the TRS removes *all* the risk and *all* the return of an asset in exchange for a fixed payment based on the *expected* income on the asset. And in the sense that

29. A.S. Kramer, *Financial Products: Taxation, Regulation, and Design* (New York: Aspen Publishers, Inc., 2001).
30. Bank for International Settlements, *Press Release: The Global OTC Derivatives Market at End-June 2001* (20 December 2001).
31. A TRS thus represents one of the very few derivatives whose payment may be based on actual economic values of one of the firm's assets, hence resembling an insurable interest.

it effectively provides funding in the case of a credit loss, a TRS can be viewed as providing a synthetic new equity issue.[32]

Multi-line Integrated Risk Management Policies and Earnings per Share Insurance. Integrated risk management (IRM) products are a type of alternative risk transfer product designed by insurance (and reinsurance) providers in a specific effort to target corporate customers pursuing ERM. They provide combined coverage for *all* the risks an institution may wish to bundle together under the same aggregate limits and deductible—risks like interest rate and professional indemnity that normally would be insured or hedged separately. In an IRM policy, losses arising from *any* of the individual risks can be used to satisfy the deductible and make a claim against the aggregate policy limit.[33]

The idea behind IRM programs is that a company that measures and manages risks on an enterprise-wide basis may find it economical to manage its net exposures with an enterprise-wide risk management *product*. The basic reason is this: Because losses on different risks (for example, casualty and interest rate) will be imperfectly correlated over time, the total amount of capital required to support all the risks in one program will typically be less than the capital required to support each risk in a separate policy.

Sometimes replacing a series of individual policies with a single IRM program results in less coverage in the catastrophic layers for certain risks. For example, if a company has six risks insured up to $300 million each and a seventh risk insured up to $1 billion, the IRM policy likely will have an aggregate limit of less than $1 billion. Although these numbers appear to suggest that the firm now has a "gap" in its coverage, the aggregate deductible and limits will be set to cover the firm's desired retention *on a portfolio basis* and thus reflect the recognition that all risks will not result in losses *at the same time*.[34] Thus, in a well-structured IRM, apparent gaps in coverage are not gaps at all, but rather efficiency enhancements that prevent capital from being parked idly in one risk silo when it could be covering a loss in another (or returned to shareholders).

Although multi-line programs can cover as few as two risks,[35] they can also be comprehensive enough to provide *earnings per share* (EPS) *insurance*. Ex-

32. For a numerical example, see C.L. Culp, "Contingent Capital: Integrating Corporate Financing and Risk Management Decisions," *Journal of Applied Corporate Finance* Vol. 15, No. 1 (Spring 2002): 46–56.

33. The discussion of the IRM of United Grain Growers provides an illustration of this point. See Scott Harrington, Greg Niehaus, and Kenneth Risko, "Enterprise Risk Management: The Case of United Grain Growers," *Journal of Applied Corporate Finance* Vol. 14, No. 4 (Winter 2002): 71–81.

34. The purveyors of IRM products—such as Swiss Re's multi-line aggregated and combined risk optimization (MACRO)—emphasize that a key to their success is careful analysis of clients' actual loss experiences and risks, which in turn leads to "optimal" limits and deductibles.

35. For a discussion of a range of different multi-line policies, see Culp, *ART of Risk Management*; and Shimpi.

amples are the COIN^{SM} and STORM^{SM} programs provided by AIG risk finance (which helped AIG win *Risk* magazine's 1999 Alternative Risk Management House of the Year award) and the structured finance EPS management program of Swiss Re. By including essentially all the major risk exposures that a firm faces, EPS insurance functions as a very close substitute for an infusion of equity. Any time EPS falls below a trigger (set relative to some deductible), the firm essentially obtains capital to cover that shortfall on pre-loss terms.

But despite the theoretical appeal of IRM programs, their track record has been marked by several notable failures. When Honeywell merged with Allied Signal, for example, an assessment of Honeywell's IRM program (covering its insurance and foreign exchange risks) revealed that Honeywell would have paid less overall if it had instead purchased separate insurance policies and engaged in conventional hedging solutions to address its exchange rate risk. The program was thus dismantled, as was Mobil Oil's IRM program in 1999—and for the same reasons. Utah-based petrochemical company Huntsman claims it opted not to buy an IRM product because its silo-by-silo coverage with 30 different insurers was simply cheaper.

But if IRM programs successfully bundle risks and involve set attachment points that reflect the correlation across those risk types, why are they more expensive? Part of the explanation, of course, is that insurers generally set premium as an "actuarial price" plus a "load." The former is the "true price" of the cash flow bundle; the latter reflects the insurer's cost of hedging or reinsurance. So, although IRM programs may involve actuarial prices that are lower than the sum of the component policies' actuarial premiums, the problem is likely to come in the hedging costs built into the load. Especially when an IRM program includes financial risks, the insurer will rarely retain 100% of the loss exposure across all risks. But if the insurer cannot hedge its underwriting risks on the same portfolio basis it offers to customers, the cost to the insurer of hedging will be the sum of the premiums of the risk transfer solutions *for each risk managed separately*—thus wiping out the actuarial cost savings. In other words, many IRM products merely push the unbundled pricing problem back one level.

Despite such setbacks, however, some multi-line policies have proven successful as of this date. Union Carbide recently renewed a major multi-line IRM product, and both Mead Corp. and Sun Microsystems claim to have saved more than 20% by consolidating their numerous risk transfer policies into a single structure.[36] This suggests that the providers of these policies either retained a big chunk of the risk, thus avoiding the hedging costs that render

36. Gerling Global Financial Products, Inc., *Modern ART Practice* (London: Euromoney Institutional Investor, 2000).

such programs uneconomic, or had much lower hedging costs than their customers.

Other multi-line success stories can be attributed to situations where the primary benefit of an integrated policy is optimized coverage rather than reduced costs. For example, Winnipeg-based United Grain Growers (UGG) was concerned that weather-related risks could adversely affect its grain volume and hence its revenues. Working with the insurance broker Willis, UGG entered into a 3 year deal with Swiss Re that effectively provides coverage of credit, counterparty, weather, environmental, inventory, property/casualty, and grain price risk. The key provision in UGG's policy is one that effectively guarantees payments from Swiss Re whenever UGG's grain shipments—and hence its expected earnings and cash flow—fall below a level deemed necessary to protect the company's ability to make strategic investments. As the UGG case illustrates, IRM products can be appealing because they allow companies to tailor their capital planning to their own risk profile.

The Appeal of Risk Finance

The 1990s also saw significant growth in risk management products aimed at helping companies finance their retained risks *on pre-loss terms* rather than transferring those risks.[37] Pre-loss risk finance makes particular sense for firms seeking to avoid underinvestment problems that can arise when a shortage of internal funds is accompanied by high external financing costs.[38] Under these circumstances,[39] rather than engaging in a risk transfer or an expensive new equity issue, the firm could issue new debt or arrange committed letters of credit *before* a loss occurs—or it could choose risk financing products.[40]

---

37. Doherty, derives the conditions under which pre-loss financing is of any real benefit.
38. More precisely, underinvestment occurs when external financing costs rise at a faster rate than internal funding rates. See K.A. Froot, D.S. Scharfstein, and J.C. Stein, "Risk Management: Coordinating Investment and Financing Policies," *Journal of Finance* Vol. 48, No. 5 (1993), and K.A. Froot, D.S. Scharfstein, and J.C. Stein, "A Framework for Risk Management," *Harvard Business Review* (November–December 1994).
39. Note that this is a different kind of underinvestment problem than in the previous section, where it was shown that if a company has too much debt for equity holders to benefit from new investments, the firm must engage in risk transfer or issue new equity to increase its debt capacity. Otherwise, the firm's stockholders are likely to reject positive net present value (NPV) projects because most of the benefits of such projects go to retiring the firm's debt. Here a different underinvestment problem, one involving a firm's *flow of funds* rather than the stock of its debt, is considered.
40. If the costs of external finance include adverse selection costs that give rise to a pecking order, risk finance instruments will be preferred to issuing new debt even during periods of strong earnings See S.C. Myers, "The Capital Structure Puzzle," *Journal of Finance* Vol. 39, No. 3 (1984); and S.C. Myers and N.S. Majluf, "Corporate Financing and Investment Decisions When Firms Have Information That Investors Do Not Have," *Journal of Financial Economics* Vol. 13 (1984).

Risk finance can be secured either through derivatives or ART forms. Income swaps, for example, can be used to exchange one stream of cash flows for another stream that is approximately equal in present value terms but with different timing. An income swap can convert a pool of assets paying interest semiannually into a quarterly cash flow stream—or it may be used to convert a pool paying interest on an actual/365 bond-equivalent basis to an actual/360 money market basis. Credit and market risk on the assets are not borne by the swap counterparty; the transaction affects only the timing of cash flows on the reference asset(s), and the swap dealer's only risk is that timing risk.

Before the 1990s, the principal way for companies to pre-fund losses was through the use of internal reserves, earmarked funds, self-insurance, or wholly owned insurance affiliates known as "captive" insurance companies. Captives deserve special mention since several of their features—including limited risk transfer, shared participation in any premium investment income, and premium rebate in the event of a favorable loss experience—are also found in most of the alternative risk transfer (ART) products created in the 1990s. What's more, the captive itself has evolved into more flexible forms of risk finance, including vehicles like rent-a-captives and protected cell companies.[41]

More recently, the insurance industry has developed specific products known as "finite risk" products and structures designed to help companies finance losses from retained risks.[42] For example, loss portfolio transfers (LPTs) are used by companies like Johns Manville and Hanson/Beazer to manage the timing risk of a known liability for which reserves have already been set aside. Even if the reserves are equal to the expected liability *in present value terms*, the firm still bears the risk that losses arrive faster than the reserves grow in value. To address that risk, the firm cedes both its reserves and its liability up to the amount of its reserves. If losses exceed total reserves, the firm is still on the hook, but it is now protected from the risk of an unexpectedly rapid loss development period.[43] In sum, loss portfolio transfers are the insurance analogues of income swaps.

Consider the following application of an LPT product. In a typical merger, the seller places money in escrow to cover its representations and warranties (R&Ws), and violations of those R&Ws can result in claims against the escrow account. Companies concerned that an R&W claim may scuttle an otherwise bene-

41. See P. Wöhrmann, "Swiss Developments in Alternative Risk Financing Models," *The European America Business Journal* (Spring 1998).

42. See R.G. Monti and A. Barile, *A Practical Guide to Finite Risk Insurance and Reinsurance* (New York: Wiley, 1995); and R. Carter, L. Lucas, and N. Ralph, *Reinsurance*, 4th ed. (London: Reactions Publishing Group in association with Guy Carpenter & Company, 2000).

43. Under several jurisdictions around the world, finite risk policies must involve some amount of underwriting risk as well, in order to receive tax, accounting, and regulatory treatment as insurance.

ficial transaction can insure their reps and warranties directly.[44] Alternatively, the firms might wish to retain that risk but instead improve the terms on which it is financed. Escrow funds are usually given to a collateral trustee and left to earn little more than the money market rate during the merger and acquisitions (M&A) negotiations. But by means of an LPT, the escrow could instead be ceded to a insurer that, besides providing explicit R&W insurance with a policy limit equal to the size of the escrow, would invest the funds in its broader, higher-yielding technical reserve portfolio. As in the case of most ART products, the benefits in the form of a higher yield would be split between the insured firm and the insurer. There would no real transfer of R&W risk, moreover, because the insurer can apply the escrow to claims up to the escrow amount and is protected from R&W claims above that amount by the policy limit. Thus, the insurer bears only the investment risk, but nothing else.

Two Distinctive Features of ART Forms

Having already discussed multi-line IRMs and finite risk products, let's now consider some of the features that often distinguish such ART products from more conventional insurance products and solutions. One distinguishing feature is the underwriting of financial risks together with non-financial perils—hence the classification of IRM programs as an ART form. Two other notable differences between ART and traditional insurance products are the former's extensive use of "double triggers" and "experience participation."

Double Triggers. A contract is considered an ART form if it contains two triggers, one of which is the occurrence of an economic loss by the insured; the second is in many cases tied to an index variable independent of the insured's performance and beyond its control or influence. The second trigger serves to reduce the cost of insurance in two main ways: (1) by limiting the moral hazard problem, and (2) by limiting the range of circumstances in which the policy pays off, in many cases just to situations when the firm is expected to have a significant need for funds. Although the second trigger does not affect the amount of the payment to the insured party, it guarantees that the insured cannot *access* those funds unless something occurs that is beyond its control. The insured firm is thus making a tradeoff: in exchange for a reduction in moral hazard (and the associated savings in its insurance premium), the firm is exposing itself to "basis risk" from the second trigger—namely, the possibility that the specific risk the firm is attempting to insure against turns out to have a

---

44. "Transactional insurance products" for M&As are discussed in T. Boundas and T.L. Ferro, "The Convergence of Insurance and Investment Banking: Representations & Warranties Insurance and Other Insurance Products Designed to Facilitate Corporate Transactions," in Culp, *ART of Risk Management.*

low correlation with the second trigger. The risk here is that although the risk and the firm's expected losses materialize, the second trigger fails to activate and the firm ends up "self-insuring."

The more equity-like a risk transfer product, the greater the potential for moral hazard problems and thus the greater the need for a second trigger. In the case of EPS insurance, for example, the moral hazard problem looms so large as to rule out the possibility of coverage for most companies. In the case of United Grain Growers discussed earlier, what allayed the insurer's concerns about moral hazard was the existence of an index of Canadian wheat shipments that, while highly correlated with the company's earnings, was clearly beyond the control of the insured.

In some cases, the second trigger on an ART form is used not so much to manage moral hazard as to help isolate and target the specific mixture of risks being managed. In such cases, the second trigger helps effectively provide customers with expanded risk coverage, which generally leads to an increase in the premiums. But in other cases, the second trigger is designed in large part to lower the overall cost of risk management to the customer. A good example of the latter is provided by Swiss Re's business interruption (BI) protection program, which is aimed specifically at telecommunication firms attempting to protect against underinvestment.[45] The policy pays out only when two conditions are met: (1) the purchaser sustains a loss in revenue (above the deductible) attributable directly to a business interruption, and (2) the purchaser's earnings before interest, taxes, depreciation, and amortization (EBITDA) growth rate falls more than a certain percentage below the growth rate of an index based on other telecom firms' EBITDAs. *If* the policy pays out, it reimburses the purchaser for actual damages from the business interruption; but the policy pays out only when such damages contribute to cash flow underperformance by the insured. The second trigger appears designed to limit Swiss Re's exposure to the telecom sector because it ensures that the policy is not activated by industry-wide cash flow problems, but only by the insured's failure to stay even with its competitors.

Experience Participation. Unlike traditional insurance and reinsurance, ART forms often involve some profit-sharing provision that allows the insured and insurer to share in the risks and returns of the transactions. The mechanics by which profit and loss sharing is accomplished in a particular ART form depend on the nature of the transaction. In the case of the finite risk products mentioned earlier, sharing is accomplished through the use of an *experience account* that tracks the paper profits and losses on the actual underlying deal. Premiums

---

45. See D. Imfeld, "Keeping an Eye on Interruption Risk," *Alternative Risk Strategies: Special Supplement to* Risk *Magazine* (December 2000).

paid by the insured to the insurer are credited to the account, as is interest on invested premium reserves. Losses and various charges incurred by the insurer are debited from the account. At the end of the term, the insurer and insured split the balance in the experience account. In some programs, the present value of expected future investment income may also be credited against the initial premium owed, which further reduces the total cost of the program.

Contingent Capital as a Risk Management Product

No innovation of the last decade serves to illustrate the convergence of risk management and corporate finance more clearly than contingent capital. Such capital is "contingent" in the sense that, like committed bank lines of credit, it effectively gives companies the *option* to raise capital (in some cases equity, in others debt) when they expect to need it most—for example, after the occurrence of an insurable loss *and* a depletion of internal funds. In this sense, contingent capital represents the new class of insurance products that enables firms to engage in financing and risk management decisions at the same time.

Such products come in several different forms, most of which function like "knock-in" put options on debt or equity. The "barrier" in question is the second trigger (with the first represented by the fact that the cost of raising capital through the option must be lower than that available in the open market for the insured to want to exercise it). Unlike double-trigger insurance, however, the second trigger on most contingent capital products is *not* an index, but rather a risk or loss specific to the purchaser of the facility. And, as suggested above, the value of such products consists mainly in the option it gives companies to raise capital in difficult circumstances, generally (though not always) on "pre-loss" terms.[46]

The best way to illustrate the design of contingent capital, as well as its advantages over old-fashioned lines of credit, is to focus on a specific product: the Committed Long-term Capital Solutions (CLOCS™) developed by Swiss Re New Markets in 1999. One recent CLOCS was placed by Swiss Re working together with Société Générale (SocGen) for Switzerland's Compagnie Financière Michelin, the financial and holding company for the well-known French tire manufacturer.

The Michelin deal is actually part bank debt and part CLOCS. SocGen has granted Michelin the right for 5 years to draw on a deeply subordinated long-term bank credit facility. Swiss Re has given Michelin an option over the same 5-year period to issue subordinated debt, at a pre-negotiated fixed spread, that matures in 2012. The bank line is a classic risk finance banking product with

---

46. As explored in more detail in Culp, contingent capital seems to be a highly innovative response to adverse selection problems that give rise to a "pecking order" in the sense of Myers, "Capital Structure Puzzle," and Myers and Majluf, "Corporate Financing."

no second trigger. The CLOCS option, by contrast, can be exercised only when the combined average growth rate of gross domestic product (GDP) across the European and U.S. markets (Michelin's main markets) falls below 1.5% during the period 2001–2003 or below 2% during 2004–2005.

The linking of the deal to low GDP growth was done for several reasons. The first is that Michelin's earnings are highly correlated with GDP growth in these markets; and because GDP growth is outside Michelin's control, the trigger avoids moral hazard while providing a fairly reliable proxy for low earnings.[47] Second, the firm is more likely to restructure in a low-earnings environment, and an infusion of fresh capital would facilitate any such restructuring. Third, the contingent capital will give Michelin access to adequate funds to exploit potential acquisition opportunities even following a transitory adverse earnings shock—that is, it enables the company to avoid underinvestment problems.

Viewed as a synthetic debt facility, the Michelin CLOCS structure can be regarded as a pre-loss risk financing solution for Michelin. If both facilities remain undrawn, Michelin pays a commitment fee of 35 basis points per annum and 30 basis points for the bank and sub-debt facilities, respectively. The lower arrangement fee for the sub-debt option is the direct result of the inclusion of a triggering mechanism.[48]

Advances in Structured Finance

As reported in a recent *New York Times* article, Citibank, a major lender to Enron, apparently protected itself from a significant portion of Enron's credit risk by passing it on to investors in credit-linked bonds. What the article did not mention, however, was that Citibank accomplished this risk transfer not through credit derivatives or insurance, but through an innovative transaction that *combines* credit derivatives and insurance with traditional securitization.[49] Similar in spirit to the 1997–98 J.P. Morgan "Bistro" transactions, these "synthetic securitizations" are representative of a major new trend in structured finance—namely, the increasing use of securitization to manage risk rather than to sell assets or raise funds.

---

47. As noted, however, most contingent capital structures do not rely on the second trigger to mitigate moral hazard.
48. For a more complete discussion of the economics of contingent capital and the other structures these products may take, see C.L. Culp, "Contingent Capital: Integrating Corporate Financing and Risk Management Decisions," *Journal of Applied Corporate Finance* Vol. 15, No. 1 (Spring 2002): 46–56.
49. A special purpose vehicle (SPV) set up and owned by Citibank issued credit-linked bonds to the public market that guaranteed payment of interest and principal as long as Enron made payments on its publicly traded bonds. But with Enron's declaration of bankruptcy, Citibank's SPV stopped payments to investors and substituted ownership of Enron bonds.

In the last several years alone, corporations and financial institutions alike have relied on securitization structures to manage a wide range or risks, in most cases "synthetically"—that is, without the actual sale of an asset that most of us associate with the securitization process. Risks managed in this manner have included the residual value risk on auto leases originated by Toyota and Lexus, mortgage default risk, trade credit default risk, and catastrophic risk.[50]

Beyond Plain Vanilla

A final theme of the risk management product revolution of the 1990s has been the development of risk transfer and risk financing solutions for exotic risks. As the sources of financial losses became more diverse in the 1990s, so too did insurance solutions. Following the rogue trader-related losses at Barings, Sumitomo, and other firms, Lloyd's syndicate SVB Financial Group began offering "rogue trader" insurance that reimburses a firm for damages sustained from unauthorized trading that has been concealed from management. The first reported buyer of such insurance was Chase Manhattan, which bought $300 million in rogue trader cover for an annual premium of $2 million.[51]

Op risk is also ripe for bundling into the multi-line IRM programs discussed earlier. Swiss Re New Markets offers several bundled op risk protection programs. One such program typically indemnifies only losses above a deductible of $50 to $100 million, but covers all losses arising from virtually any known risk, including unauthorized trading, professional indemnity, electronic computer crime, and employment liability. Contingent capital can also be used to help firms manage operational risk. For example, there is now an "op risk loss equity put" that enables buyers to fund any losses by issuing new securities at a pre-loss price.[52]

Other risks that insurance, derivatives, and ART products can now be used to manage include weather risk (i.e., arising from fluctuations in temperature and precipitation),[53] bandwidth price risk in emerging telecommunications markets, water price risk in emerging water markets, and unusual insurance risks such as aborted M&A bids and natural catastrophe property. The number and types of risks on which risk management products can be based seem virtually limitless.

---

50. For a discussion of catastrophic bonds and their role in managing catastrophic risk, see Angelika Schöchlin, "Where's the CAT Going? Some Observations on Catastrophe Bonds," *Journal of Applied Corporate Finance* Vol. 14, No. 4 (Winter 2002): 100–107.
51. L. Cooper, "Help Is at Hand," *Operational Risk Supplement to* Risk *Magazine* (July 1999).
52. A. Webb, "Controlling Operational Risk," *Derivatives Strategy* (January 1999).
53. See A.S. Kramer, "Weather Derivatives or Insurance? Considerations for Energy Companies," in Culp, *ART of Risk Management*; Gerling Global Financial Products, *Modern ART Practice*; and Shimpi.

Conclusion

Despite starting in a most accidental fashion, the risk management revolution of the 1990s now appears on an inevitable course of convergence with the modern theory of corporate finance. Companies today can focus selectively on risk finance or risk transfer, use features like triggers to control the cost of capital acquired through risk management products, integrate their financing and risk management decisions through the use of enterprise-wide products, and replace expensive paid-in capital with cheaper sources of contingent capital that provide an infusion of funds only when truly necessary. Such expanded products are likely to be beneficial, however, only if a company has the right risk management *process* in place—one in which corporate financial and risk management decisions are no longer made separately, but in a fully integrated way that is clearly informed by the goal of increasing firm value.

▪ CHRISTOPHER L. CULP is Managing Director of CP Risk Management LLC and Adjunct Associate Professor of Finance at the University of Chicago's Graduate School of Business.

CHAPTER 4

A Senior Manager's Guide to Integrated Risk Management

LISA K. MEULBROEK

M ANAGERS HAVE ALWAYS ATTEMPTED to measure and control the risks within their companies. The enormous growth and development in financial and electronic technologies, however, have enriched the palette of risk management techniques available to managers, offering important new opportunities for increasing shareholder value. "Integrated risk management" involves the identification and assessment of the collective risks that affect firm value and the implementation of a firm-wide strategy to manage those risks. For some managers, risk management immediately evokes thoughts of derivatives and strategies that magnify rather than reduce risk. But derivatives, when used as a risk management tool, are only a small part of the integrated risk management process. Moreover, a proper risk management strategy does not involve speculation or betting on future commodity prices or interest rates and, indeed, is the antithesis of such speculation. Instead, the goal of integrated risk management is to maximize value by shaping the firm's risk profile, shedding some risks while retaining others.

Companies have three fundamental ways of implementing risk management objectives: modifying the firm's operations, adjusting its capital structure, and employing targeted financial instruments (including derivatives). "Integration" refers both to the combination of these three risk management techniques and to the aggregation of all the risks faced by the firm. While managers have always practiced some form of risk management, implicit or explicit, in the past, risk management has not traditionally occurred in a systematic and integrated fashion across the firm. Integrated risk management has only recently become a practical possibility, both because of the enormous improvements in computer

This chapter was previously published as an article in the *Journal of Applied Corporate Finance* Vol. 14, No. 4 (Winter 2002): 56–70. The author gratefully acknowledges the financial support of Harvard Business School's Division of Research. Email: Lmeulbroek@hbs.edu.

and other communications technologies and because of the wide-ranging set of financial instruments and markets that have evolved over the past decade. A sophisticated and globally tested legal and accounting infrastructure is also now in place to support the use of such instruments on a large scale and at low cost. Of equal importance to this evolution in capital markets is the cumulative experience and success in applying modern finance theory to the practice of risk management. Today, managers can analyze and control various risks as part of a unified, or integrated, risk management policy.

Integrated risk management is by its nature "strategic" rather than "tactical." Tactical risk management, currently more common, has a narrower and more limited focus. It usually involves the hedging of contracts or other explicit future commitments of the firm such as interest rate exposures on its debt issues. Consider a U.S. dollar-based firm that buys steel from a Japanese firm for delivery in 3 months. The U.S. firm may decide to "tactically" hedge the dollar price of its steel purchase. By using forward currency contracts, the firm locks in the dollar cost of its steel purchase, offsetting the effect of dollar-yen exchange rate movements that may occur before delivery and payment. The treasurer's office of the firm typically executes such tactical currency hedging without consideration of other hedging or insuring activities carried out in the firm, even when the risks across units are significantly correlated. In contrast, strategic currency hedging addresses the broader question of how exchange rate fluctuations affect the value of the entire firm as well as the firm's competitive environment, including the pricing of its products, the quantity sold, the costs of its inputs, and the response of other firms in the same industry.

Exchange rate risk is, of course, only one potential risk a firm faces. Managers using an integrated risk management approach must depart from the standard practice of viewing each risk in isolation and instead devise a strategy to respond to the full range of risks, taking into account that a risk management policy designed solely to respond to exchange rate risk may have unintended consequences for the firm's other business operations. This chapter presents a managerial overview of integrated risk management, using a series of examples to illustrate the range of applicable management decisions and the benefits for the firm from its implementation.

By applying integrated risk management, managers will benefit from new insights about the interplay among different types of risk and traditional financial decision areas, connections easily missed without a comprehensive framework. Because the three ways to manage risk are functionally equivalent in their effect on risk, their use connects seemingly unrelated managerial decisions. For instance, because capital structure is one component of a firm's risk management strategy, effective capital structure decisions cannot be made in isolation from the firm's other risk management decisions. This chapter's discussion of the integrated risk management framework emphasizes the connection between the three mechanisms to alter the firm's risk profile, and offers guidance on their practical application.

There are those who question whether firm-wide risk management can add value to the firm. In the hypothetical Modigliani-Miller world of corporate finance, neither capital structure choices nor corporate risk management affects the value of the firm. Indeed, the direct expenses and distraction of management's attention would make risk management a negative net-present-value proposition for the firm. Thus, the next section describes the various ways that risk management can enhance the value of the firm in the imperfect environment of the real world. With this value proposition established, I offer a functional analysis of integrated risk management using a wide-ranging set of illustrative situations to show how the risk management process influences, and is influenced by, the overall business activities and strategy of the firm. Finally, I present an overall managerial framework for formulating and designing an enterprise-wide risk management system, and conclude by providing a perspective on the future evolution of risk management.

How Risk Management Adds Value

Managers seeking to implement a risk management program must consider a number of basic questions: Is the goal of the program to reduce earnings fluctuations, or to reduce fluctuations in firm value? Should the firm fully hedge its risk exposures, or only part of them? Should it hedge only the downside risk, while retaining the upside (as with an option or more traditional insurance contract)? Or should it hedge both the downside and the upside (as a forward contract would permit)? None of these questions can be answered in the abstract, because the answers will vary from firm to firm. Still, the fundamental goal of risk management is unambiguous: to maximize shareholder value. The *ability* to reduce risks does not automatically imply that the firm *should* reduce its risk. Because the benefits (and costs) of risk management vary by firm, a risk management strategy must be tailored to the individual company. For some firms, targeting a particular level of earnings or cash flow fluctuations will increase the value of the firm. For other firms, the value-maximizing strategy is to target a particular range of fluctuation in market value of the firm or shareholder equity.[1] To determine the optimal risk management policy, the manager must begin by understanding how the degree of uncertainty about

---

1. René Stulz offers another take on how risk management maximizes firm value; he argues that risk management should eliminate "costly lower-tail outcomes," that is, limiting the downside while preserving as much of the upside as possible. See R. Stulz, "Rethinking Risk Management," *Journal of Applied Corporate Finance* Vol. 9, No. 3 (Fall 1996).

future earnings and firm value affects the current market value of the firm. That is, to assess whether and to what extent the firm should target its risk, the manager must first understand the channels through which risk management can potentially affect firm value. This understanding forms the critical underpinning of any risk management strategy; without it, attempts to evaluate the costs and benefits of risk management within the context of a particular firm will prove fruitless.

Corporate Risk Management Can Facilitate Risk Management by the Firm's Stockholders

Financial theory distinguishes between systematic (market or beta) risk and total risk. Investors can reduce the amount of total risk they bear by diversifying their holdings. Systematic risk is the risk that remains after such diversification is fully implemented. If diversification opportunities are widely available to investors, systematic risk is the only risk for which they must be compensated. By definition, diversification by either the firm or its investors cannot reduce systematic risk. But investors can control their own exposures to systematic risk by adjusting their holdings of risky assets and cash or by using futures, forwards, or swap contracts. By holding a larger fraction of cash or by hedging with futures, forwards, and swaps, investors can limit their systematic risk exposures, but at the cost of reducing their expected returns. The availability of these targeted financial instruments greatly enhances the efficiency of investors in managing systematic risk exposures for themselves—provided, of course, they have a clear understanding of the firm's exposures.

The apparent ability of outside investors to adjust their own systematic risk exposures may seem to leave no role for firm-based risk management. Indeed, some observers conclude that attempts by managers of the firm to manage risk are at best redundant and at worst wasteful, because investors can easily increase or decrease their own risk exposures. But estimating the firm's risk can be difficult for investors, especially if it changes continually over time. Outside investors can estimate the systematic risk of the firm by using the volatility of past equity returns, but they typically do not have other information that would enable them to improve on that estimate. Managers, on the other hand, have proprietary information about the current and future activities of the firm, both in scale and scope, which bears directly on the firm's systematic risk. It may not be feasible or prudent from a competitive standpoint for managers to simply reveal this private information, but they can use it to manage the firm's risk in a way that shareholders cannot—again, because the shareholders do not fully understand the exposures. For this reason alone, the classic Modigliani-Miller argument for invariance of firm value to risk management does not always apply. That is, in cases where investors cannot hedge for themselves easily or cheaply, companies can use risk management to lower their cost of capital.

More precisely, investors may accept a smaller risk premium on the firm's equity in return for greater certainty about their own exposure to systematic risks from holding that equity.

To assist investors in managing risk and thereby lower the company's cost of capital, managers of the firm can target specific levels of systematic and total risk. Using risk management techniques, they can amplify or dampen the risk of the firm's operations to stabilize it at a targeted level. If the firm's risk level is held constant, investors can more easily adjust their own risk exposures, even if the firm's operations are otherwise opaque to them. Moreover, to the extent there are economies of scale in managing risk, corporate-level risk management is likely to be less expensive than risk management by investors. Thinking about the firm's risk profile in these terms may be new to many managers. However, such targeting has a clear analogue in the more familiar territory of debt policy: companies routinely use target debt ratios to maximize shareholder value, even though investors could certainly duplicate that level of debt in their own portfolios. By the same logic, corporate-level risk targets can increase shareholder wealth by facilitating investor-based risk management, even when investors assume much of the responsibility for managing risk. For example, a multinational with significant currency risk may increase its value by communicating to shareholders the extent of the exchange rate exposure remaining after it undertakes its risk management program.

But, as we now consider, corporate-level risk management can also create value in ways that investors cannot accomplish on their own. Specifically, as discussed below, corporate risk management can increase shareholder wealth by reducing the costs associated with financial distress, moderating the risk faced by important non-diversified investors and stakeholders, decreasing taxes, reducing monitoring costs, and lowering the firm's funding costs.

Risk Management Can Reduce Financial Distress Costs

By reducing the firm's total risk, risk management makes financial distress less likely. Even highly successful businesses are vulnerable to financial distress. Microsoft, for example, competes in a rapidly changing and volatile industry. If a bad turn of events were to create uncertainty about the company's future dominance, then customers, suppliers, or employees might alter their behavior, worsening the impact of the initial negative shock. Customers may defect, questioning Microsoft's ability to provide future service and upgrades; other software developers may be less likely to tailor their products to Microsoft's operating platform; and key employees may leave for a more stable environment. In short, financial distress has the ability to destroy substantial value.

Consider the fate of Thinking Machines Corp., a pioneer in massively parallel supercomputers. Despite its reputation for superior technology, Thinking

Machines encountered financial difficulties when the government cut its su-
percomputer funding, difficulties that hobbled its ability to compete. Intel and
International Business Machines (IBM) entered the market, luring customers
away from smaller and less stable companies like Thinking Machines. As the
president of Thinking Machines explained, "The issue of our viability kept arising. No one wants to spend $4 million on a machine from a company that may
not be around." Financial distress impaired the firm's ability to compete
against more stable companies, causing further erosion in firm value and ultimately bankruptcy.[2]

The potential destructiveness of financial distress is not limited to technology firms. Retailers, for example, rely heavily upon their suppliers for financing. These suppliers in turn regulate their own risk exposures through
their selection of customers, and tend to respond rapidly to changes in customer
creditworthiness. In 1999, Hechinger Co., a U.S.-based retailer of do-it-yourself
home products, defaulted on an interest payment. Anxious suppliers cut back
on credit, intensifying the company's cash crunch. During the critical warm
months when do-it-yourself sales typically peak, potential Hechinger customers were greeted by nearly empty stores, leading to further deterioration of the
firm's condition as customers left to shop elsewhere. Hechinger was soon forced
to liquidate its operations.

Even the mere prospect of financial distress can cast a costly shadow over
the firm. Hence, managers must estimate the probability of encountering distress. Again, this estimate will vary from firm to firm. The value of a company
in a cyclical industry may be more volatile and its probability of distress higher.
Before embarking upon a campaign to manage risk, such a firm also needs to
evaluate its costs once in distress. If some level of financial distress would not be
too disruptive to the business, a firm may choose to accept a relatively high
probability of distress. Leveraged buyouts (LBOs), for example, typically occur
in industries where the cost of financial distress is not high.

At the other end of the distress-cost spectrum are financial firms like insurance companies and commercial banks. In large part because their customers are also major liability holders, the costs of financial distress in such
credit-sensitive businesses are enormous. A consumer purchasing a retirement
life annuity, for example, is unlikely to buy the annuity from an insurance
company that is perceived as vulnerable to financial distress. No matter what
the initial "savings" and how favorable the terms, few customers would will-
ingly risk default on their retirement annuities. In sum, a proper analysis of the
costs of financial distress must consider both the probability of reaching distress and the expected costs once in distress. Risk management techniques can
be used to reduce either or both.

2. Aaron Zitner, "Fishman: Wariness from the Gut," *The Boston Globe*, August 16, 1994.

Risk Management Can Reduce the Risk Faced by Key Undiversified Investors

Another way that risk management can add value is by lowering the risk faced by managers who have most of their wealth invested in their company's stock. The dramatic increase in stock- and option-based compensation and the long-running bull market have created tremendous "paper" wealth for managers. Without the ability to diversify their holdings, however, managers find that the value of their personal wealth fluctuates in tandem with their company's equity. Such fluctuations can be substantial, especially in highly volatile technology stocks, where stock and option compensation reigns supreme. Risk management techniques can lower the risk faced by such managers.

But extreme volatility in the value of personal wealth is not a problem limited to managers in technology firms. In the first few months of 2000, the stock price of blue-chip Procter & Gamble (P&G) dropped by more than 50% from a high of $115 in January to $54 in March. Ninety percent of the value of the employees' retirement plans had been invested in P&G stock. In less than one calendar quarter, this unanticipated stock price drop halved the accumulated value of employees' retirement funds. Again, risk management can help prevent such severe fluctuations.

Of course, financial theory has long made the case for equity-based compensation plans as an effective means to align managers' incentives with those of shareholders. But if managers own significant stakes in the firm, they will, by necessity, have poorly diversified portfolios. In essence, the exposure to firm-specific risk that is essential for generating the right managerial incentives also imposes a cost on managers by compelling them to hold inadequately diversified investment portfolios.

Risk-averse managers will thus require higher compensation for bearing this "non-systematic" or diversifiable risk that ordinary investors do not face. With a higher required return for holding the firm's stock, managers will apply a larger discount rate to the expected future earnings of the firm in privately valuing their holdings. That is, they will typically place a lower private value on their holdings of the firm than the market value of the shares. And in such circumstances, to induce managers to have concentrated holdings of company stock, the firm must pay a higher total value in shares than would be required for straight cash compensation.

This "deadweight wedge" in value between equity compensation and cash compensation represents the cost to the firm of this compensation policy.[3] The

3. For a method of estimating this deadweight loss, see L. K. Meulbroek, "The Efficiency of Equity-Linked Compensation: Understanding the Full Cost of Awarding Executive Stock Options," *Financial Management* (Summer 2001): 5–30. Use of this method suggests that, in volatile firms, the

firm's deadweight loss is greatest for high-volatility firms whose managers have most of their personal wealth tied up in the firm. Note that the same type of costs apply to all forms of performance-based compensation, including options, phantom stock, and earnings-based bonuses. Therefore, a company with a large proportion of pay-for-performance compensation may be able to reduce the deadweight cost of that compensation by reducing the total risk of the firm without reducing the net present value of its projects.

Risk Management Can Reduce Taxes

Risk management also creates value by reducing a company's tax burden. A progressive tax structure gives firms an incentive to smooth earnings to minimize taxes, and risk management enables such smoothing. Progressive tax rates mean that a firm will do better by trying to stay consistently in the lower tax-rate region rather than have negative earnings one year and earnings that result in a higher tax rate the following year. Suppose that the tax rate for $10 million or less in earnings is 20%, and that above $10 million, the marginal tax rate is 30%. If a firm earns $10 million in each of two consecutive years, its total tax will be $4 million over the two-year period. But if first-year earnings are $0 and second-year earnings are $20 million, the total tax bill will now be $5 million, or $1 million higher than when earnings are evenly distributed over the two-year period.

As a practical matter, the "penalty" for volatility in taxable earnings is even greater whenever the ability of a company to carry its losses forward or backward is limited. For instance, if a firm has negative earnings for an extended period of time, it may never have enough positive earnings to offset its losses and use its tax credits. Using risk management, a firm can smooth its earnings and reduce its tax bill.

Risk management can also decrease the firm's taxes by increasing its debt capacity and the tax shield provided by interest payments. Debtholders care about total firm volatility, because it is the total risk—and not just the systematic-risk component of that risk—that determines the probability that the firm will default. If risk management can reduce a company's total risk without reducing the net present value of its operations, then the firm can support a greater debt-to-equity ratio and shelter more of its income from taxes.

The value of the incremental tax shield created by increased debt capacity will vary by firm. Many start-up firms, for example, have negative profits during their early years; at the margin these firms cannot capture the tax benefits of debt until they have used their net operating losses. But new risk manage-

private value an undiversified manager places on her stock options can be as little as half their market value.

ment techniques and instruments could present an opportunity for established, cash-generating companies to rethink their capital structures and raise their target debt levels.[4,5]

Risk Management Can Reduce Monitoring Costs by Improving Performance Evaluation

Risk targeting can lower the costs of evaluating and monitoring corporate performance for investors, creditors, customers, and corporate boards of directors. Performance evaluation requires a measure of the firm's risk in order to construct an appropriate benchmark for gauging performance.[6] If the firm's risk exposures are changing or if the firm's operations are opaque to outsiders, constructing such a benchmark is difficult. To the extent outside investors or creditors find monitoring and evaluation difficult and costly, they will require an additional expected return premium—and customers may even pay a lower price for the firm's products—to offset this higher monitoring cost. Although some companies may be able to avoid paying this premium by providing full disclosure about their operations and associated risk, such disclosure may not always be practical—again, perhaps for competitive reasons. By setting a "benchmark" level of either systematic or total risk, managers can facilitate investor monitoring without disclosing proprietary information about the firm's operations.

Another way that risk management can contribute to better performance evaluation is by making corporate disclosures more informative, not only to outside investors, but to corporate boards as well. For example, to the extent that the effect of oil price fluctuations are removed by hedging from an oil and gas company's reported earnings and cash flows, those measures can provide

4. Some firms appear to have begun this process. David Haushalter's study shows that oil and gas companies with higher leverage hedge more of their oil price risks. See G.D. Haushalter, "Financing Policy, Basis Risk, and Corporate Hedging: Evidence from Oil and Gas Producers," *Journal of Finance* Vol. 55, No. 1 (2000): 107–52. Walt Dolde also finds the same positive correlation between hedging and leverage (after controlling for primitive risk exposure). See W. Dolde, "Hedging, Leverage, and Primitive Risk," *Journal of Financial Engineering* Vol. 4, No. 2 (1995): 187–216.
5. Another way risk management—particularly, the communication of and adherence to a firm-wide risk target—can contribute to a firm's debt capacity is by reducing potential bondholder-stockholder conflicts that arise when higher debt ratios cause managers to increase asset volatility in the hopes of a higher equity payoff. By committing themselves to targeting a total risk level, management decreases the opportunity for risk shifting at the expense of debtholders.
6. Risk measurement is an integral part of performance evaluation. High-risk ventures may be accompanied by high returns, but investors cannot evaluate whether the firm has earned excess returns without an estimate of how much risk the firm took to achieve those returns. The Standard and Poor's (S&P) 500 index, for instance, is neither an appropriate benchmark if the firm invests in low-risk, market-neutral, or counter-cyclical projects, nor is it an appropriate benchmark if the firm invests in well-above average risk, pro-cyclical projects.

outside investors with a more accurate reflection of managerial ability and performance. And besides providing more useful information to outsiders, such risk-adjusted performance measures may also provide corporate boards with a more effective basis for management compensation, one that helps insulate managers from risks beyond their control.[7]

In addition to energy and mining companies, the financial services industry is another one in which risk exposure targeting can be particularly valuable. The asset and liability portfolios of banks, securities firms, and insurance companies are typically quite opaque to outsiders. Furthermore, relative to most non-financial firms, these companies have the ability to change the composition of their assets and liabilities rapidly without public detection, suggesting that an efficient way for investors to manage their risk is for the firm to target a specific risk level. Of course, the high leverage typical in this industry can mean that firm performance is very sensitive to its underlying risk exposures, providing another reason why financial firms may want to manage risk. It is therefore not surprising that financial institutions have been the pioneers in implementing sophisticated, integrated risk management. Industries that are rapidly evolving and changing, and that have few tangible assets (and therefore less transparency), might also be good candidates for risk exposure targeting.

Risk Management Can Provide Internal Funds for Investment

If a company needs funding for a potentially profitable project, and issuing debt or equity is either impossible or too costly, management must fund the project internally or forgo it. Internal funding requires that the firm either stockpile cash or have steady cash flows from other projects. By smoothing out cash flow volatility, risk management can help to ensure that the firm will be able to fund profitable projects internally.[8]

Internal funding, however, is a double-edged sword. Companies with too much cash on hand avoid the discipline of outside review that accompanies external capital raising and can prevent managers from proceeding with bad projects.[9] Thus, the benefit of internal funding will vary from firm to firm, but will tend to be greater for companies with more growth opportunities and a

---

7. For an extended discussion of this role of risk management in strengthening management incentives in the energy industry, see the roundtable discussion of "Derivatives and Corporate Risk Management: The Transformation of the U.S. Energy Industry," *Journal of Applied Corporate Finance Journal* Vol. 13, No. 4 (Winter 2001).

8. For more complete descriptions of how risk management enhances the firm's ability to internally-fund valuable new investments, see Kenneth Froot, David Scharfstein, and Jeremy Stein, "A Framework for Risk Management," *Harvard Business Review* Vol. 72, No. 6 (1994).

9. For an argument suggesting that the absence of capital market scrutiny for new investments leads to the acceptance of sub-optimal projects, see Peter Tufano, "Agency Costs of Corporate Risk Management," *Financial Management* Vol. 27, No. 1 (1998).

larger information gap between managers and investors. Larger firms, besides being less capital constrained, are less likely to suffer from such an information gap between managers and investors due to their greater analyst coverage. Consequently, the role of risk management as a means of ensuring internal funding should be more important for smaller, more specialized firms.

A Functional Approach to Integrated Risk Management

Integrated risk management extends across functional boundaries within the firm, and a risk management perspective yields insights into seemingly unrelated managerial decisions. Consider, for example, Microsoft's heavy reliance on temporary employees. Microsoft's personnel officer, Doug McKenna, explains that "we count on them [temps] to do a lot of important work for us. We use them to provide us with flexibility and to deal with uncertainty."[10] And the company's director of contingent staffing, Sharon Decker, adds that "we want to be very flexible as a company, to be able to react to competitive challenges and react quickly."[11] By reducing operating leverage (here the fixed costs of a more permanent workforce), Microsoft has greater flexibility to respond to unexpected shocks in demand, technology, or regulation.

Without such flexibility, a bad turn of events could create uncertainty about the company's competitive position and its ability to continue setting industry standards. Customers may begin to defect, as they question Microsoft's ability to provide future service and upgrades. With further deterioration, software developers may be less likely to tailor their products to Microsoft's operating platform. Key permanent employees may leave for a more stable environment. Microsoft's policy of using temporary workers allows the company to respond more rapidly to such shocks, thereby improving its chances of remaining a lead player in its industry.

And Microsoft's operational policies, at least in the sphere of risk management, are complemented by its financial policies. The company has no outstanding debt and, indeed, holds about $18 billion in cash. Besides providing financial flexibility that can help the company in responding to demand or other shocks, Microsoft's no-leverage (or negative leverage) policy may also reflect an attempt to reduce the risk borne by some of its senior executives, who together own a substantial fraction of the outstanding shares.

In sum, Microsoft's operational policy of using temporary employees and its no-leverage financial policy both serve to reduce its overall level of fixed costs, increase flexibility, and thereby reduce the firm's total risk. Both types of policies, although quite different in their application, are functionally equivalent

10. *Los Angeles Times*, December 7, 1997, p. D1.
11. *The News Tribune* (Tacoma, WA), February 21, 1999, p. G1.

and thus can be viewed as substitutes for one another.[12] An integrated risk management approach recognizes that a firm has many ways to manage its risk, and that both the optimal amount of risk retained and the tools used to achieve that level of risk will differ from firm to firm. What integrated risk management provides is a systematic way of thinking about risk and identifying its multidimensional effects on the firm, coupled with a framework for deciding upon the best strategy for implementation.

"Integration," then, means both integration of risks and integration of ways to manage risk. Integrated risk management evaluates the firm's total risk exposure, instead of evaluating each risk in isolation, because it is the total risk of the firm that typically "matters" to the assessment of the firm's value and its ability to fulfill its contractual obligations in the future. Furthermore, individual risks within the firm will partly or completely offset each other (thereby reducing the total expense of hedging or otherwise managing those risks). Thus, in implementing hedging and insurance transactions to manage the risk of the firm, one need only address the *net* exposures instead of covering each risk separately. This netting can significantly reduce transaction costs.

Moreover, such an analysis is essential in charting an effective risk management strategy because, by focusing narrowly on one specific risk, managers may create or exacerbate other types of risk for the company. Interactions between risks are not always obvious, especially when they occur among unrelated businesses within the firm. A nice example of this comes from the late 1980s, when Salomon Brothers, the investment bank, attempted to move into the merchant banking business on a large scale by leading an investment group in an unsuccessful effort to acquire control of RJR Nabisco in a leveraged buyout. Although it did not succeed, the attempt signaled bond rating agencies and other stakeholders that Salomon was prepared to increase the total risk it faced. This change in Salomon's risk profile hurt its existing customer-based derivatives business, which had been a significant source of profits.

---

12. Each policy, of course, has its particular costs and benefits. Without debt, Microsoft loses out on the debt tax shield. And temporary workers may not be as motivated as permanent employees in the words of one Microsoft permanent employee (a former temp): "Temps are temps—they come and go. They are probably not working as hard. They aren't invested in the company, so it's not in their interest to work 70-hour weeks." *Los Angeles Times*, December 7, 1997, p. D1. Microsoft seems fully aware of the incentive problem, and tries to compensate: "what they lack in status and benefits, temps often make up in salary; typically, their paychecks are 30 percent higher than a comparable Microsoft employee. And many non-traditional workers enjoy the flexibility of the arrangement." *Seattle Times*, December 16, 1997, p. A1. Sometimes the short-term nature of Microsoft's commitment to its temporary employees can engender dissatisfaction and resentment. "As a part-timer, you are like a tool," said Philip Hirschi, a Web designer who recent left a temporary job at Microsoft to take a full-time position elsewhere. "If you are a Phillips screwdriver, and they need a flat head, they just get rid of you, they won't retool you." *Los Angeles Times*, December 7, 1997, p. D1. This perception suggests that at least some temporary employees may be less willing to invest in firm-specific human capital.

Salomon's prospective merchant banking business would seem to have little connection to its existing customer-based derivatives business: the employees were different, the technology was different, the customers were different, even the buildings housing the businesses were different. But because Salomon owned both businesses, its shift into a riskier business affected the overall risk and creditworthiness of the company. The value of derivative contracts is acutely sensitive to the credit ratings of derivatives providers. Just by contemplating a move into the merchant banking business, Salomon showed its willingness to increase the company's overall risk exposure, jeopardizing the strong and stable credit rating so important to its customers and reducing its ability to compete in the credit-sensitive, customer-based derivatives business.

When different businesses share the same corporate umbrella, then, the risk of each business is shared among all businesses. For Salomon, the combination of the two businesses destroyed value until financial engineering created an AAA-rated derivatives subsidiary that effectively decoupled the shared capital structure.

The Salomon example also underscores the reality that risk considerations permeate every major decision of the company. When a company changes its business strategy, it likely changes its risk profile, thereby either creating or destroying value. Risk management almost always requires making tradeoffs. These tradeoffs sometimes involve comparing the costs of reducing a particular risk with the benefits of that reduction; at other times, managers must trade off risks among businesses. Risk management decisions must be made on a company-wide level because the consequences of managing any particular risk affect the value of the entire company.

Integration of risk management can also add value to the firm by permitting the purchase of more efficient insurance contracts that provide a lower cost way to manage overall or "enterprise" risk. Consider a hypothetical company that faces non-operating risks of three types: losses from product liability, losses from fire, and losses from foreign exchange rate exposures. Suppose that the firm is willing to "self-insure" against these risks up to a maximum total loss of $3 million. If, as is typical, responsibility for each type of risk is delegated separately and a separate policy is purchased to protect for each, then to meet the overall firm maximum-loss constraint, the maximum deductible on each of the three policies is $1 million. However, this collection of separate policies provides more insurance than the firm really needs. For example, suppose that the firm experiences a product liability judgment of $2.5 million and no losses from either fire or foreign exchange. The firm is covered for all but $1 million even though it was prepared to take the entire $2.5 million loss within its maximum-loss limit. Of course, after the fact, the firm would have been happy to have the greater coverage. But beforehand, when it made its risk management decisions, the firm paid higher insurance premiums for that extra, unwanted coverage.

If instead the firm could purchase a comprehensive policy covering all three types of risks, it could have a deductible of $3 million and receive the coverage it actually wants. Because the three types of risks are not perfectly correlated with one another, the premium for the comprehensive policy with a $3 million deductible will be less than the sum of the three separate policies with $1 million deductible on each, even when all premiums are absolutely actuarially fair.[13] When the firm buys a comprehensive policy that insures against all three risks, it buys a different (and lower cost) product. Exposure of the firm's value, after all, does not depend on the source of the risk per se; instead, it depends on the total risk. So, the type of insurance needed by the firm is one that pays off when the effect of the aggregated risks exceeds a certain, pre-specified, amount. If what the firm really wants is to ensure that the risks do not lead to a drop of more than $3 million in value, then it should insure against the joint event that the combined risks do not lead to a drop of more than $3 million.

Multi-risk policies are just beginning to be used in practice. Some policies bundle together foreign exchange risks with coverage of more conventional insurance risks. And Reliance Insurance now offers an "omni-risk" policy that insures a company's earnings against all sorts of risks that are outside of management's control. However, a firm can only use these comprehensive policies effectively in the context of a firm-wide integrated risk management approach.

Moreover, the integration of different possible ways to manage risks can be just as important as the aggregation of the risks. As discussed earlier in the case of Microsoft, just as different categories of risks can affect firm value in a similar fashion, so different ways of managing risks can be combined to achieve a common objective. Thus, Microsoft can reduce its total risk through the operational policy of using temporary workers; it can also reduce that risk by carrying a low level of debt.[14] What is important to keep in mind, however, is

---

13. The point is very much analogous to buying an individual put option on each security in a portfolio versus buying a put option on the portfolio of securities itself. As is well known, the sum of premium charges for a portfolio of individual put options on each security is going to be larger than the premium for a put option on the overall portfolio. If all the investor cares about is protecting against losses on the overall portfolio value and not on each part separately, then the portfolio of put options provides too much coverage. Just so, the firm buys too much insurance when it buys a separate policy, or put option, for each risk.

14. Debt actually has a two-fold effect. First, lowering debt means lowering fixed costs, thereby reducing the firm's chances of getting into financial distress. Second, debt acts as a magnifier of other risks. So, while changing the debt level does not affect *whether* an operational risk occurs or not, if an operational risk *does* occur, a low debt level will cushion the impact of an operational risk, but a high debt level will exacerbate its effect.

that the goal of risk management is *not* to minimize the total risk faced by a firm per se, but to choose the *optimal* level of risk to maximize shareholder value. Effective risk management requires a thorough understanding of the firm's operations as well as its financial policies. Given the breadth of firm-specific knowledge required and the potential for impact on overall firm value, risk management is a direct responsibility of senior managers. It should be delegated neither entirely to outside risk experts nor to internal managers by type of risk (such as one policy for exchange rate risk, another for product obsolescence) or type of business.[15] Senior management must decide which risks are essential to the profitability of the firm, taking into account cross-risk and cross-business effects, and then develop an integrated strategy to manage those risks.[16]

Tools for Integrated Risk Management: Operations, Financial Instruments, and Capital Structure

At the foundation of risk management is the integration of the three mechanisms to alter the firm's risk profile. These three ways to manage risk—modifying the firm's operations, adjusting its capital structure, and employing targeted financial instruments—interact to form the firm's risk management strategy. Managers must weigh the advantages and disadvantages of any particular approach in order to find an optimal mix of the three. As in the preceding section, we explore each of these mechanisms in a series of examples.

Operational Risk Management

Managers typically have many different ways to address risk by adjusting operations. Microsoft's use of temporary workers discussed in the last section is an example, but there are many others. Consider the effect of weather on Disney's theme parks and their customers. Bad weather dramatically reduces the number of visitors, exposing the theme park's owners to considerable weather-related risk. This risk extends to customers as well. A vacation destination with unpredictably unpleasant weather compels potential visitors to bear some

---

15. Derivatives and other outside experts will be involved to the extent that they must provide information about whether it's feasible to manage a particular type of risk, and how costly it might be. Other consultants might be helpful in providing guidance on the type of information needed before embarking on a risk management program. But the one thing consultants do not typically have is an intimate understanding of the firm's business, the competitive landscape, and how the various risks feed back and affect firm value.

16. Of course, senior managers will rely upon the managers of a specific business unit or project to provide them with information to measure the firm's exposures. Likewise, the estimation of the costs of addressing those risks operationally necessitates business and project-specific information. The firm's senior management must then integrate the risks and their effects across businesses or projects.

weather risk. Disney's 1965 decision to build Disney World in a warm and sunny location (Orlando, Florida) reduced both its own exposure, and that of its customers, to inclement weather.[17]

But Disney's decision to locate in Florida, while reducing weather risk, also altered its risk exposure along other dimensions. At the time of Disney's 27,500-acre purchase, Orlando was not particularly near any population centers, and air travel was relatively expensive. So one cost of Disney's location choice was that most of its customers had to travel long distances to visit, increasing Disney's exposure to fuel prices, the cost of air travel, and fluctuations in the economy.

Another case where a company chose to eliminate a risk facing its customers was that of the producer of Fresh Samantha fruit juices. From their introduction, Fresh Samantha juices' hallmark was their freshly squeezed taste, attributable in large part to the fact that the juice was not pasteurized, a departure from standard industry practice. But without pasteurization, the risk of contamination increases. Furthermore, consumers are typically not the best bearers of this risk because they cannot easily detect contamination. In 1995, the magnitude of this risk became apparent. Odwalla, a California-based fresh (non-pasteurized) juice maker, sold juice contaminated with *Escherichia coli* bacteria, resulting in the death of one child and illness in 60 others. The incident raised consumer awareness of the potential heath risks associated with non-pasteurized juice, and had an immediate impact on sales of Fresh Samantha, even though Fresh Samantha was not involved in the episode. *Forbes* reported that "retailers demanded to know if Fresh Samantha was safe. Some threatened to cancel orders; several new accounts delayed payment."[18] Fresh Samantha's managers decided that the firm's product liability risk exposure (and that of its customers) was simply too great and responded by upgrading the firm's quality control department and pasteurizing its juice. As this case suggests, the impact of product failure or mismanagement on the reputation of a firm can be devastating, especially for those reputation-sensitive firms involved in financial services, food, medicine, or anything else that goes inside our bodies.

Jaguar cars faced a different product market risk; their limited product line was focused on a very narrow segment of the luxury car market, which left Jaguar more exposed to economic fluctuations than other luxury car manufacturers whose customers might shift down to one of their less expensive luxury cars in more difficult economic times. Jaguar recently expanded its product line by introducing a less-expensive model, the S-type model. Jaguar surely had multiple reasons for broadening its product line. But whether intended or

---

17. Customers are rarely the best bearers of risk. In this instance, customers are unlikely to be exceptionally skilled weather forecasters, suggesting they may not be the ideal bearers of risk.
18. *Forbes*, April 6, 1998.

not, this decision has risk management implications for the firm. Introduction of the S-type helps buffer Jaguar against a softening of the luxury car market and volatility in the overall state of the economy. But, of course, this decision was not without its own risks; one potential cost of Jaguar's product expansion was the possibility that the S-type would dilute Jaguar's high-end image.[19]

Disney's theme park locations, Fresh Samantha's pasteurization decision, and Jaguar's expanded product line all illustrate how changes in the firm's operations can alter its risk exposure. Risk management is not only a decision about how much risk the firm should bear, it is also a decision about how much risk the firm's customers or suppliers are prepared to bear. As a more general matter, suppliers, customers, community members, firm shareholders, and employees are all potential risk bearers for the firm. Managers must determine the optimal level of risk for all parties and consider not only how each individual risk affects the firm's total risk exposure, but also evaluate the optimal way of managing and distributing those risks.

Risk Management Using Targeted Financial Instruments

Some risks cannot be managed effectively through the operations of the firm, either because no feasible operational approach exists or because an operational solution is simply too expensive to implement or too disruptive of the firm's strategic goals. Targeted financial instruments such as derivatives (futures, swaps, or options) or insurance can be an alternative to using operations directly to reduce risk. Such instruments are available for many commodities, currencies, stock indices, and interest rates; and the menu is continually expanding to reflect a variety of other risks, including even the weather. Targeted financial instruments affect the firm's risk profile in the sense that if a risk does occur, targeted financial instruments can reduce or eliminate the effect on firm value. In Disney's case, purchasing insurance against bad weather might be a substitute for locating in a warm and sunny climate.[20] Whether buying weather insurance dominates physically locating in a temperate climate depends upon the relative cost of the insurance versus the cost of putting the theme park in the middle of Florida.

To illustrate how financial contracts can be used as an alternative to operational solutions, we return to the case of Jaguar, but this time when it was an independent British company (that is, prior to its acquisition by Ford). Although almost all of Jaguar's production was located in the United Kingdom, more than 50% of its revenue came from sales in the United States, subjecting

19. Jaguar is entirely owned by Ford, which surely affects its risk profile and thus its risk management strategy. The text that follows offers another example drawn from Jaguar when it was an independent company that illustrates the application of financial instruments as an alternative risk management tool to operational actions.
20. Such insurance was not available in 1965 when Disney made its decision.

the firm to sterling–dollar exchange rate risk. Moreover, Jaguar's main competitors in the luxury car market in the United States—Daimler-Benz, BMW, and Porsche—were German car manufacturers that produced their cars in Germany. The German car manufacturers' U.S.-based sales, both individually and collectively, swamped those of Jaguar. Jaguar therefore had little influence on market prices of luxury cars sold in the United States, which depended more on prices set by the German car manufacturers—prices that were sensitive to the mark–dollar exchange rate. The competitive environment in U.S. luxury cars, then, exposed Jaguar to substantial exchange rate risk from movements in the mark relative to the dollar, even though Jaguar had neither sales nor production in Germany. Such currency risk could have been hedged using derivatives, such as currency futures or forward contracts.[21]

In a similar vein, suppose that the demand for Jaguars is found to be sensitive to the stock market, both because many potential owners work in financial services and because employees often use bonuses and stock option gains to buy luxury cars. A partial hedge could be constructed using futures, swaps, or options on the stock market. Or if interest rates and the price of gasoline were found to be linked to consumer demand for luxury cars, then derivatives on interest rate and gasoline may buy Jaguar further protection. To be sure, integrated risk management requires more than an observation that Jaguar can manage its risk using targeted financial instruments; it calls for continuous assessment of the firm's total risks and of the costs of the various ways to manage those risks. After engaging in an integrated risk management evaluation, Jaguar's managers may decide that using contractual agreements to decrease Jaguar's product line exposure to overall economic fluctuations in this fashion is too costly, or too difficult to execute. They may instead conclude that, to achieve the optimal level of total firm risk, they can more profitably moderate some of Jaguar's other risks.

That risk exposures individually can be difficult to hedge directly using existing financial instruments is not of course limited to luxury car manufacturers. Microsoft's continued success will depend upon the future evolution of the Internet, on the technology sector more broadly, and perhaps on the outcome of the government's antitrust suit. Hedging each of these risks individually would be difficult using traditional derivative instruments. Instead, Microsoft might choose to buy put options on its own stock to reduce its aggregate risk of loss in stock value from all sources; or it might buy insurance to protect its operating earnings against adverse events that are

21. For a more detailed description of Jaguar and its risk exposures, see Timothy A. Luehrman, "The Exchange Rate Exposure of a Global compeititor," *Journal of Int'l Business Studies* Vol. 21, No. 2(1990): 225–42.

beyond management's control. Although companies do sometimes buy limited quantities of put options on their own stock, such strategies also have significant shortcomings in implementation. Market participants may view the firm's decision to buy puts as negative information, either about the firm's future prospects or its future volatility.[22] A similar issue arises with earnings-protection insurance. As noted previously, Reliance Group has announced that it will sell such an insurance product covering events outside management's control. But determining what is or is not under management's control is no easy task.[23]

Targeted financial instruments are especially suited for firms with large exposures to commodity prices, currencies, interest rates, or the overall stock market. These exposures derive not only from the firm's inputs, outputs, or production processes, but also from risks passed along from its suppliers, employees, customers, or competitors. A candy producer, for instance, may have a substantial risk exposure to sugar prices and can hedge this risk using sugar futures. Likewise, an oil producer can sell its production forward to reduce its exposure to oil price risk. A manufacturer of recreational vehicles typically has substantial exposure to oil and gasoline price risk; it can hedge these risks contractually through oil or gasoline futures or forwards. So the benefit of risk management via targeted financial instruments is that specific risks can be offset without disrupting the firm's operations. But this type of risk management is effective only against the risks that managers are able to foresee in type and magnitude.

It is also possible to manage risk by changing the payment form of the firm's debt. A case in point is the ability to issue debt denominated in a foreign currency or to issue debt denominated in an asset other than money, such as debt denominated in gold or oil. Foreign currency debt can lower the firm's exchange rate exposure, and gold- or oil-denominated debt can reduce the firm's exposure to oil or gold prices. Catastrophe (CAT) bonds are another example of debt tailored to address a specific type of risk, namely that of a catastrophic event, which can reduce the risk exposure of the issuing insurance company. CAT bonds pay off only if the pre-specified event risk does not occur. Such structured approaches to risk management might just as easily be classified as a capital structure tool as a financial instrument tool. The boundaries between the two are indeed both permeable and imprecise.

22. Because a firm can also issue or buy stock to convert its puts to calls and vice versa, inferring a directional signal from its actions may be difficult. Still, the firm's purchases of puts *does* convey information about its belief concerning expected future volatility.
23. Of course, earnings insurance could introduce a substantial moral hazard problem, as managers who have such insurance might have little incentive to work hard. Also, the insurance company will face significant asymmetric information problems when it tries to sort out the "bad" managers from the "good" ones.

Risk Adjustment via the Capital Structure

The third tool to manage risk does not require a precise forecast of the source or magnitude of a specific risk. By decreasing the amount of debt in the capital structure, managers reduce the shareholder's total risk exposure. Besides reducing the probability of financial distress, lower debt means that the firm has fewer fixed expenses and thus greater flexibility in responding to any type of volatility that affects firm value. Equity provides an all-purpose risk cushion against loss. There are some types of risks that a firm can anticipate and measure relatively precisely and these can be shed through targeted risk management. Equity provides protection against risks that cannot be readily anticipated or measured, or for which there are no specific targeted financial instruments. The greater the risk that cannot be accurately measured or shed, the larger the firm's equity cushion should be.

A well-known disadvantage of using equity as a risk management tool is the loss of the interest tax shield that debt provides. Another disadvantage of managing risk via the capital structure is that a reduction in debt can create or exacerbate certain agency problems, including a well-documented tendency of managers to waste "free cash flow" and excess capital.[24] In contrast, managers who use operational adjustments and targeted financial instruments as a substitute for more equity capital typically have greater flexibility to avoid the negative tax and incentive consequences of their risk management actions. And as this argument implies, managers can effectively increase their firm's debt capacity by reducing risks operationally or with targeted financial instruments.

Implementing Integrated Risk Management

Having explored the three basic tools for firm-wide risk management, I close by framing the broad managerial issues surrounding the development and implementation of a risk management system. Whether risk reduction actually increases firm value depends upon the cost of that reduction. Managers must estimate the effect of each risk on firm value, understand how each risk contributes to total firm risk, and determine the cost of reducing each risk.

In order to quantify the value of a given risk management strategy and so arrive at the value-maximizing strategy, this information must be incorporated into a model of firm value that encompasses management's knowledge of the economics of the business and the competitive environment, as well as its beliefs about the ways in which risk potentially affects firm value. By varying the inputs to the model, managers can observe how firm value changes when various risks are hedged or not. In this fashion, managers will be able to deter-

---

24. See Tufano, "Agency Costs," on agency costs of risk management.

FIGURE 4.1

Risk Review

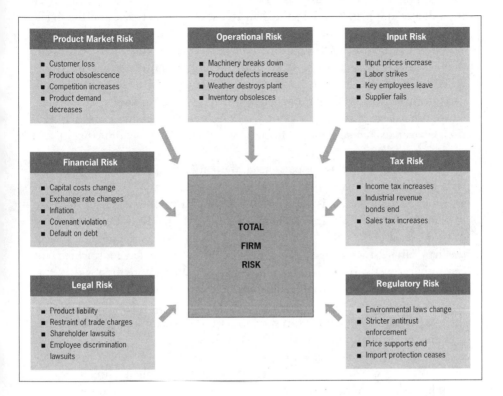

mine the optimal level of total risk, the configuration of risks constituting this level of risk (i.e., the risks to be divested, and the risks to be retained), and the best way to achieve the desired risk profile. Of course, creating such a valuation model requires extensive information about consumer demand and the nature of competition in the industry as well as continuous refinement.

The first key step in the development of a risk management strategy is to inventory all the risks faced by the firm. As shown in figure 4.1, corporate risks can be classified into seven categories. Operational risk, product market risk, input risk, tax risk, regulatory risk, legal risk, and financial risk constitute the broad classes of risks faced by most firms. After management has both inventoried the various risks and assessed the probability of their occurrence (both as separate events and concurrently), the next step is to estimate the effect of a particular risk on firm value.

To illustrate how one might begin mapping a risk management strategy, consider the risks faced by a rapidly growing company. The managers know that the firm's rapid growth introduces substantial risk. The goal of the risk inventory is to transform this general observation into a more detailed description of how the risks associated with a growth strategy are likely to affect the value of the firm. Suppose the firm is a toy manufacturer, and the firm's rapid growth is a result of the success of one particular toy. The managers expect the demand for this toy to drop as the fad wanes, so volatile consumer demand is one major source of risk for this firm. Suppose further that the firm is based in Japan and exports much of its product to the United States. In this case, the firm's U.S. sales may depend upon relative yen–dollar exchange rates, where the nature of the competition in the United States determines the relation between exchange rates and firm value. For simplicity, assume that the toy manufacturer has no other risks.

The managers of the company need to identify the precise ways that these risks are expected to affect firm value. If consumers tire of the toy, how much will sales decrease? What is the expected length of time before a sharp decrease in demand occurs? Can the toy company prolong the fad through advertising or by decreasing the price? Volatile demand also increases the possibility that the firm will be stuck with obsolete inventory after the toy fad ends, which will certainly be costly. If the firm has expanded by buying more toy-making machinery, does this machinery become obsolete as well, or can it be used in the production for other toys? If it can be used for other toys, how profitable are these other toys likely to be?[25] In sum, precision in specifying risks translates into greater ability to measure the effects of those risks.

To then evaluate the effect of exchange rates, managers must first determine how sales are related to exchange rates, and then explicitly link firm sales to exchange rates in their valuation model. A useful valuation model will specify how much the U.S. market price will change with a given percentage movement in the yen–dollar exchange rate, and then define how a shift in the market price will affect demand for the product in the U.S. The toy company's managers should also assess the probability of large and small exchange rate movements, and whether or how exchange rate risk is correlated to the expected life of the toy.[26]

Of course, none of this information is likely to be known with certainty. Managers can analyze past fads and complement this historical information with their insights about why their particular product might be either longer- or shorter-lived. The marketing area might be able to contribute information about the expected duration of high demand, as well as information about how

---

25. An operational approach to managing the risk of toy fads is that the machinery used to produce toys can be easily adapted to produce a variety of toys, rather than be specific to one toy.
26. That is, they must estimate the probability density function of exchange rate changes and the covariance between exchange rate changes and the expected life of the toy.

sales change in response to price decreases. Likewise, the operations area may be the best source for information on how practicable and costly it is to use the machinery for other purposes. Managers need to collect the necessary information about how both revenues and costs will shift with changing demands, which in turn will enable them to arrive at an estimated probability—or, better yet, a probability distribution—for the toy's life.

Challenges in Creating an Integrated Risk Management System

Corporate risk management is evolving rapidly, but the practice of risk aggregation is not yet widespread. Instead, the typical firm tends to isolate and manage risks by type. The treasurer's office manages exchange rate exposures and, in some cases, credit risk. Commodity traders, sometimes located within the purchasing area, focus on commodity price risk. Production and operations management consider risks associated with the production process. The insurance risk manager focuses on property and casualty risks. Human resources typically addresses employment risks. As a practical matter, integrated risk management requires the coordination (at least for the function of risk management) of all these previously independent organizational units. The firm, rather than the type of risk, provides a frame of reference.

And coordination of risk management across separate areas is only the first step. Managers must expand the often narrow focus of their current risk management practices, moving from a "tactical" to a "strategic" approach. Whereas tactical risk management typically confines itself to hedging specific contracts or other explicit future firm commitments, strategic risk management addresses the broader question of how risk affects the value of the firm and the firm's competitive environment—the pricing of its products, the quantity sold, the costs of its inputs, and the response of other firms in the same industry. Indeed, a firm can be completely hedged tactically, yet still have substantial strategic exposure. Integrated risk management demands that managers look beyond the usual definition of "hedging."

Because an integrated approach to risk management departs from the rigid compartmentalization of risks, and requires a thorough understanding of the firm's operations as well as its financial policies, risk management is the clear responsibility of senior managers. It cannot be delegated to derivatives experts, nor can management of each individual risk be delegated to separate business units. Although management will no doubt seek counsel from managers of business units or projects, it must ultimately decide which risks are essential to the profitability of the firm, taking into account cross-risk and cross-business effects, and develop a strategy to manage those risks. The rapidly expanding universe of tools available for risk measurement and management offers managers significant opportunities for value creation, but this growth also creates new responsibilities. Managers must understand how the tools work, and then make decisions about how and when their use is likely to add value.

LISA K. MEULBROEK is Professor of Business Administration at the Harvard Business School.

PART II

Corporate Uses of the Products

A S DISCUSSED EARLIER, Merton Miller described the social role of derivative markets as that of "a gigantic insurance company" whose aim is to
bring about "efficient risk-sharing" throughout the economy. In "Rethinking
Risk Management" (chapter 5), René Stulz presents a theory of corporate risk
management that uses Miller's idea of comparative advantage in risk-bearing
to go beyond the "variance-minimization" model that dominates most academic discussions. Stulz argues that the primary goal of risk management is
not to dampen swings in corporate cash flows or value but, rather, to provide
protection against the possibility of costly lower-tail outcomes—situations
that would cause financial distress or make a company unable to carry out its
investment strategy. By reducing the odds of financial trouble, risk management has the power to change not only the optimal capital structure of the
firm but its optimal ownership structure as well. Besides increasing corporate
debt capacity, the reduction of downside risk also facilitates larger equity stakes
for managers by shielding their investments from "uncontrollables."

The chapter's most significant departure from the standard theory, however, is in Stulz's suggestion that some companies may have a comparative advantage in bearing certain financial market risks—an advantage that could
derive from information acquired through normal business activities. Although such specialized market information may lead some companies to
take speculative positions in commodities or currencies, it is more likely to
encourage "selective" hedging, a practice in which the risk manager's "view"
of future price movements influences the percentage of the exposure that is
hedged. But if such view-taking becomes an accepted part of a company's risk
management program, managers' "bets" should be evaluated on a risk-adjusted
basis and relative to the market. As Stulz notes in closing, "If risk managers
want to behave like money managers, they should be evaluated like money
managers."

In "An Analysis of Trading Profits: How Trading Rooms Really Make Money" (chapter 6), Albèric Braas and Charles Bralver of Oliver, Wyman & Co. attempt to correct some popular misconceptions about the profitability of bank trading operations. Based on their consulting work with more than 40 large trading operations, Braas and Bralver conclude that, for most trading rooms, speculative "positioning" is not a reliable source of profits. The primary source of profit is dealings with customers. Stable profits can also be expected from inter-dealer, trade, but only from traders who work for large institutions with heavy order flows and who adopt a "jobber" style of trading. These findings could have major implications for financial institutions, natural resource firms, and, indeed, any corporation that aims to derive a significant portion of its value from trading activities.

In "Theory of Risk Capital in Financial Firms" (chapter 7), Nobel laureate Robert Merton and André Perold present a concept of risk capital that can be used to guide the capital structure, performance measurement, and strategic planning decisions of commercial and investment banks, insurance companies, and other firms engaged in principal financial activities. In the wake of the new Bank for International Settlements capital guidelines, not only banks, but also most financial institutions have been forced to revisit the issue of capital adequacy. The concept of risk capital presented in these pages differs significantly, however, from "both regulatory capital, which attempts to measure risk capital according to a particular accounting standard, and from cash capital, which represents the up-front cash required to execute a transaction." After illustrating their concept of risk capital with a series of examples, Merton and Perold demonstrate its application to a number of challenging problems faced by financial firms—specifically, allocating the costs of risk capital to individual businesses or projects in performance measurement and accounting for the benefits of internal diversification among business units in strategic planning.

In "Value at Risk: Uses and Abuses" (chapter 8), Christopher Culp, Merton Miller, and Andrea Neves use a number of derivatives disasters to illustrate some pitfalls in using the popular risk measurement technique called "value at risk" (VaR). VaR is a method of measuring the financial risk of an asset, portfolio, or exposure over some specified period of time. By facilitating the consistent measurement of risk across different assets and activities, VaR is said to enable companies to monitor, report, and control their risks in a manner that relates risk control to targeted and actual economic exposures.

Nevertheless, as Culp et al. argue, reliance on VaR can result in serious problems when used improperly, and would-be users are urged to heed the following three pieces of advice:

1. VaR is a tool for firms engaged in *total value* risk management. Companies concerned with the volatility of a *flow of funds,* rather than with the value

of a stock of assets and liabilities over a specific time horizon, often are better off eschewing VaR altogether in favor of a measure of cash flow volatility.

2. VaR should be applied very carefully to companies that practice "selective" risk management—those firms that choose to take certain risks as a part of their primary business. When VaR is reported in such situations without estimates of the corresponding expected profits, the information conveyed by the VaR estimate can be extremely misleading.

3. As a number of derivatives disasters of the 1990s are used to illustrate, no form of risk measurement—including VaR—is a substitute for good management. Risk management as a process encompasses much more than just risk measurement. Indeed, risk measurement (whether using VaR or some of the alternatives proposed in this chapter) is pointless without a well-developed organizational infrastructure and information technology system capable of supporting the complex and dynamic process of risk taking and risk control.

In "Allocating Shareholder Capital to Pension Plans" (chapter 9), Robert Merton discusses the corporate challenge of providing retirement income to employees while limiting the costs and risks of defined-benefit (DB) pension plans to the companies. Although the pension shortfalls have been the focus of attention, Merton argues that the more serious concern is the risk stemming from the mismatch between pension assets and pension liabilities—that is, the funding of debt-like liabilities with equity-heavy asset portfolios. Without offering specific solutions, Merton presents a framework for analyzing the problem from a strategic perspective that can be used in formulating a company's pension policy. In particular, he recommends that companies take an integrated perspective that views pension assets and liabilities as parts of the corporate balance sheet, and the pension asset allocation decision as a critical aspect of a corporate-wide enterprise risk management program. One possible solution is a partial or complete immunization accomplished by substituting bonds for stocks, in which case management must take pains to communicate its new policy to the rating agencies and investors. A different solution is to convert DB plans to defined-contribution (DC) plans. But for companies taking that step, Merton counsels that political realities make it likely that DC plans without *some* corporate oversight or responsibility for results will not be a viable long-term solution.

In "The Uses and Abuses of Finite Risk Reinsurance" (chapter 10) Christopher Culp and J. B. Heaton provide a general overview of finite risk solutions and products, describing their main features and their legitimate role in helping (mainly) industrial companies manage timing, funding, and insurance risks. Finite risk solutions generally take the form of structured insurance products that are designed to help companies manage risks often regarded as exotic or "tail" risks, such as environmental or asbestos liability. Although such products are underwritten by insurance or reinsurance companies, they typically involve limited risk transfer (hence the name "finite risk") while providing the insured companies with a means of pre-funding their expected losses, or what is often called "pre-loss" financing. Given the limited risk transfer, companies could choose to self-insure such risks by establishing a reserve for future losses. But, as Culp and Heaton argue, finite risk provides a more credible and transparent alternative—one that reassures investors both by capping the liability and eliminating the possibility for manipulation of reserves that often takes place under self-insurance.

The authors also warn companies against potential abuses of finite risk products and offers guidance on how to avoid the pitfalls. The abuses of finite risk products usually concern the degree to which transactions are accounted for, disclosed, and represented to investors as achieving "significant risk transfer" when there is little or no such transfer. In the authors' words, "Users of finite should regularly ask themselves. Does this transaction help my financial statements more clearly represent the true economic income and risks of the business? If not, then consider not doing the deal."

In the final chapter in Part II, entitled "Does Risk Management Add Value? A Survey of the Evidence" (chapter 11), Charles Smithson and Betty Simkins provide an overview of almost 30 years of broad-based, stock-market–oriented academic studies that address one or more of the following questions:

- Are corporate financial price risks—that is, interest rate, exchange rate, and commodity price risks—reflected in stock price movements?

- Is volatility in corporate earnings and cash flows related in a systematic way to corporate market values?

- Is the corporate use of derivatives associated with reduced risk and higher market values?

The answer to the first question, at least in the case of financial institutions and interest rate risk, is a definite "yes"; all studies with this focus find that the stock returns of financial firms are clearly sensitive to interest rate changes. The stock returns of industrial companies exhibit no pronounced interest rate exposure (at least as a group), but industrial firms with significant cross-border revenues and costs show considerable sensitivity to exchange rates (although such sensitivity actually appears to be reduced by the size and geographical diversity of the largest multinationals). What's more, the corporate use of derivatives to hedge interest rate and currency exposures appears to be associated with lower sensitivity of stock returns to interest rate and foreign exchange (FX) changes.

But does the resulting reduction in price sensitivity affect value—and, if so, how? Consistent with a widely cited theory that risk management increases value by limiting the corporate "underinvestment problem," a number of studies show a correlation between lower cash flow volatility and higher corporate investment and market values. Smithson and Simkins also cite a small but growing group of studies that show a strong positive association between derivatives use and stock price performance (typically measured using price-to-book ratios). But, as they concede, one cannot conclude from such studies that derivatives use is a significant *cause* of such higher values.

Perhaps the nearest the research comes to establishing causality are two case studies described in chapter 14 of this book. One case studies companies that hedge FX exposures, and another case studies airlines' hedging of fuel costs. They both show that, in industries where hedging with derivatives is common, companies that hedge outperform those that don't.

CHAPTER 5

Rethinking Risk Management

RENÉ M. STULZ

THIS CHAPTER EXPLORES an apparent conflict between the theory and current practice of corporate risk management. Academic theory suggests that some companies facing large exposures to interest rates, exchange rates, or commodity prices can increase their market values by using derivative securities to reduce their exposures. The primary emphasis of the theory is on the role of derivatives in reducing the variability of corporate cash flows and, in so doing, reducing various costs associated with financial distress.

The actual corporate use of derivatives, however, does not seem to correspond closely to the theory. For one thing, large companies make far greater use of derivatives than small firms, even though small firms have more volatile cash flows, more restricted access to capital, and thus presumably more reason to buy protection against financial trouble. Perhaps more puzzling, however, is that many companies appear to be using risk management to pursue goals other than reducing variance.

Does this mean that the prevailing academic theory of risk management is wrong, and that "variance-minimization" is not a useful goal for companies using derivatives? Or, is the current corporate practice of risk management misguided and in urgent need of reform? In this chapter, I answer "no" to both questions while at the same time suggesting there may be room for improvement in the theory as well as the practice of risk management.

The chapter begins by reviewing some evidence that has accumulated about the current practice of corporate risk management. Part of this evidence takes the form of recent "anecdotes," or cases, involving large derivatives losses.

This chapter was previously published as an article in the *Journal of Applied Corporate Finance* Vol. 9, No. 3 (Fall 1996): 8–25. I am grateful for comments by Steve Figlewski, Andrew Karolyi, Robert Whaley, and participants at a seminar at McKinsey, at the Annual Meeting of the International Association of Financial Engineers, and at the French Finance Association.

Most of the evidence, however, consists of corporate responses to surveys. What the stories suggest, and the surveys seem to confirm, is the popularity of a practice known as "selective" as opposed to "full-cover" hedging. That is, while few companies regularly use derivatives to take a "naked" speculative position on foreign exchange (FX) rates or commodity prices, most corporate derivatives users appear to allow their views of future interest rates, exchange rates, and commodity prices to influence their hedge ratios.

Such a practice seems inconsistent with modern risk management theory, or at least the theory that has been presented thus far. But there is a plausible defense of selective hedging—one that would justify the practice without violating the efficient markets tenet at the center of modern financial theory. In this chapter, I attempt to explain more of the corporate behavior observed by pushing the theory of risk management beyond the variance-minimization model that prevails in most academic circles. Some companies, I argue below, may have a comparative advantage in bearing certain financial risk (while other companies mistakenly think and act as if they do). I accordingly propose a somewhat different goal for corporate risk management—namely, the *elimination of costly lower-tail outcomes*—that is designed to reduce the expected costs of financial trouble while preserving a company's ability to exploit any comparative advantage in risk-bearing it may have. (In the jargon of finance specialists, the fundamental aim of corporate risk management can be viewed as the purchase of "well-out-of-the-money put options" that eliminate the downside while preserving as much of the upside as can be justified by the principle of comparative advantage.)

Such a modified theory of risk management implies that some companies should hedge all financial risks, other firms should worry about only certain kinds of risks, and still others should not worry about risks at all. But, as I also argue below, when making decisions whether or not to hedge, management should keep in mind that risk management can be used to change both a company's capital structure and its ownership structure. By reducing the probability of financial trouble, risk management has the potential both to increase debt capacity and to facilitate larger equity stakes for management.

This paper also argues that common measures of risk such as variance and value at risk (VaR) are not useful for most risk management applications by non-financial companies, nor are they consistent with the objective of risk management presented here. In place of both VaR and the variance of cash flows, I suggest a method for measuring corporate exposures that, besides having a foundation in modern finance theory, should be relatively easy to use.

I conclude with a discussion of the internal "management" of risk management. If corporate risk management is focused not on minimizing variance, but rather on eliminating downside risk while extending the corporate quest for comparative advantage into financial markets, then much more attention must be devoted to the evaluation and control of corporate risk management activities. The closing section of the chapter offers some suggestions for evaluating the performance of risk managers whose "view-taking" is an accepted part of the firm's risk management strategy.

Risk Management in Practice

In one of their series of papers on Metallgesellschaft, Chris Culp and Merton Miller make an observation that may seem startling to students of modern finance: "We need hardly remind readers that most value-maximizing firms do not hedge."[1] But is this true? And, if so, how would we know?

Culp and Miller refer to survey evidence—in particular, to a Wharton-Chase study that sent questionnaires to 1,999 companies inquiring about their risk management practices.[2] Of the 530 firms that responded to the survey, only about a third answered "yes" when asked if they ever used futures, forwards, options, or swaps. One clear finding that emerges from this survey is that large companies make greater use of derivatives than smaller firms. Whereas 65% of companies with a market value greater than $250 million reported using derivatives, only 13% of the firms with market values of $50 million or less claimed to use them.

What are the derivatives used to accomplish? The only uses reported by more than half of the corporate users are to hedge contractual commitments and to hedge anticipated transactions expected to take place within 12 months. About two-thirds of the companies responded that they never use derivatives to reduce funding costs (or earn "treasury profits") by arbitraging the markets or by taking a view. Roughly the same proportion of firms also said they never use derivatives to hedge their balance sheets, their foreign dividends, or their economic or competitive exposures.

The Wharton–Chase study was updated in 1995, and its results were published in 1996 as the Wharton–CIBC Wood Gundy study. The results of the 1995 survey confirm those of its predecessor, but with one striking new finding: Over a third of all derivative users said they sometimes "actively take positions" that reflect their market views of interest rate and exchange rates.

1. Christopher Culp and Merton Miller, "Hedging in the Theory of Corporate Finance: A Reply to Our Critics," *Journal of Applied Corporate Finance* Vol. 8 (Spring 1995): 122. For the central idea of this chapter, I am indebted to Culp and Miller's discussion of Holbrook Working's "carrying-charge" theory of commodity hedging. It is essentially Working's notion—and Culp and Miller's elaboration of it—that I attempt in this chapter to generalize into a broader theory of risk management based on comparative advantage in risk-bearing.
2. The Wharton School and the Chase Manhattan Bank, N.A., Survey of Derivative Usage Among U.S. Non-Financial Firms (February 1994).

This finding was anticipated in a survey of Fortune 500 companies conducted by Walter Dolde in 1992, and published the following year.[3] Of the 244 companies that responded to Dolde's survey, 85% reported having used swaps, forwards, futures, or options. As in the Wharton surveys, larger companies reported greater use of derivatives than smaller firms. And, as Dolde notes, such a finding confirms the experience of risk management practitioners that the corporate use of derivatives requires a considerable upfront investment in personnel, training, and computer hardware and software—an investment that could discourage small firms.

But, as observed earlier, there are also reasons why the demand for risk management products should actually be greater for small firms than for large—notably the greater probability of default caused by unhedged exposures and the greater concentration of equity ownership in smaller companies. And Dolde's survey provides an interesting piece of evidence in support of this argument. When companies were asked to estimate what percentages of their exposures they chose to hedge, many respondents said that it depended on whether they had a view of future market movements. *Almost 90% of the derivatives users in Dolde's survey said they sometimes took a view.* And, when the companies employed such views in their hedging decisions, the smaller companies reported hedging significantly greater percentages of their FX and interest rate exposures than the larger companies.

Put another way, the larger companies were more inclined to "self-insure" their FX or interest rate risks. For example, if they expected FX rates to move in a way that would increase firm value, they might hedge only 10% to 20% (or maybe none) of their currency exposure. But if they expected rates to move in a way that would reduce value, they might hedge 100% of the exposure.

Like the Wharton surveys, the Dolde survey also found that the focus of risk management was mostly on transaction exposures and near-term exposures. Nevertheless, Dolde also reported "a distinct evolutionary pattern" in which many firms "progress from targeting individual transactions to more systematic measures of ongoing competitive exposures."[4]

The bottom line from the surveys, then, is that corporations do not systematically hedge their exposures, the extent to which they hedge depends on their views of future price movements, the focus of hedging is primarily on near-term transactions, and the use of derivatives is greater for large firms than small firms. Many of the widely reported derivative problems of recent years are fully consistent with this survey evidence, and closer inspection of such cases provides additional insight into common risk management prac-

3. Walter Dolde, "The Trajectory of Corporate Financial Risk Management," *Journal of Applied Corporate Finance* Vol. 6, No. 3 (Fall 1993): 33–41.
4. Ibid., 39.

tices. I briefly recount two cases in which companies lost large amounts of money as a result of risk management programs.

Metallgesellschaft

Although the case of Metallgesellschaft continues to be surrounded by controversy, there is general agreement about the facts of the case. By the end of 1993, MG Refining & Marketing, Inc. (MGRM), the U.S. oil marketing subsidiary of Metallgesellschaft AG, contracted to sell 154 million barrels of oil through fixed-price contracts ranging over a period of 10 years. These fixed-price contracts created a huge exposure to oil price increases that MGRM decided to hedge. However, it did not do so in a straightforward way. Rather than hedging its future outflows with offsetting positions of matching maturities, MGRM chose to take "stacked" positions in short-term contracts, both futures and swaps, and then roll the entire "stack" forward as the contracts expired.

MGRM's choice of short-term contracts can be explained in part by the lack of longer-term hedging vehicles. For example, liquid markets for oil futures do not go out much beyond 12 months. But it also appears that MGRM took a far larger position in oil futures than would have been consistent with a variance-minimizing strategy. For example, one study estimated that the minimum-variance hedge position for MGRM would have required the forward purchase of only 86 million barrels of oil, or about 55% of the 154 million barrels in short-maturity contracts that MGRM actually entered into.[5]

Does this mean that MGRM really took a position that was long some 58 million barrels of oil? Not necessarily. As Culp and Miller demonstrate, had MGRM adhered to its professed strategy and been able to obtain funding for whatever futures losses it incurred over the entire 10-year period, its position would have been largely hedged.[6]

But even if MGRM's net exposure to oil prices was effectively hedged over the long haul, it is also clear that MGRM's traders had not designed their hedge with the aim of minimizing the variance of their net position in oil during the life of the contracts. The traders presumably took the position they did because they thought they could benefit from their specialized information about supply and demand—and, more specifically, from a persistent feature of oil futures known as "backwardation," or the long-run tendency of spot prices to be higher than futures prices. So, although MGRM was effectively hedged against

---

5. A. Mello, and J.E. Parsons, "Maturity Structure of a Hedge Matters: Lessons from the Metallgesellschaft Debacle," *Journal of Applied Corporate Finance* Vol. 8, No. 1 (Spring 1995): 106–20.

6. More precisely, Culp and Miller's analysis shows that, ignoring any complications arising from basis risk and the daily mark-to-market requirement for futures, over the 10-year period each rolled-over futures contract would have eventually corresponded to an equivalent quantity of oil delivered to customers.

changes in spot oil prices, it nevertheless had what amounted to a long position in "the basis." Most of this long position in the basis represented a bet that the convenience yields on crude oil—that is, the premiums of near-term futures over long-dated futures—would remain positive as they had over most of the past decade.

When spot prices fell dramatically in 1993, MGRM lost on its futures positions and gained on its cash positions—that is, on the present value of its delivery contracts. But because the futures positions were marked to market while the delivery contracts were not, MGRM's financial statements showed large losses. Compounding this problem of large "paper losses," the backwardation of oil prices also disappeared, thus adding real losses to the paper ones. And, in response to the reports of mounting losses, MGRM's management chose to liquidate the hedge. This action, as Culp and Miller point out, had the unfortunate consequence of "turning paper losses into realized losses" and "leaving MGRM exposed to rising prices on its remaining fixed-price contracts."[7]

Daimler-Benz

In 1995, Daimler-Benz reported first-half losses of DM1.56 billion, the largest in the company's 109-year history. In its public statements, management attributed the losses to exchange rate losses due to the weakening dollar. One subsidiary of Daimler-Benz, Daimler-Benz Aerospace, had an order book of DM20 billion, of which 80% was fixed in dollars. Because the dollar fell by 14% during this period, Daimler-Benz had to take a provision for losses of DM1.2 billion to cover future losses.

Why did Daimler-Benz fail to hedge its expected dollar receivables? The company said that it chose not to hedge because the forecasts it received were too disperse, ranging as they did from DM1.2 to DM1.7 per dollar. Analysts, however, attributed Daimler-Benz's decision to remain unhedged to its view that the dollar would stay above DM1.55.[8]

These two brief case studies reinforce the conclusion drawn from the survey evidence. In both these cases, management's view of future price movements was an important determinant of how (or whether) risk was managed. Risk management did not mean minimizing risk by putting on a minimum-variance hedge. Rather, it meant choosing to bear certain risks based on a number of different considerations, including the belief that a particular position would allow the firm to earn abnormal returns.

Is such a practice consistent with the modern theory of risk management? To answer that question, I first review the theory.

---

7. Christopher Culp and Merton Miller, "Metallgesellschaft and the Economics of Synthetic Storage," *Journal of Applied Corporate Finance* Vol. 7, No. 4 (Winter 1995): 63.
8. See *Risk Magazine*, October 1995, p. 11.

The Perspective of Modern Finance

The two pillars of modern finance theory are the concepts of efficient markets and diversification. Stated as briefly as possible, market efficiency means that markets don't leave money on the table. Information that is freely accessible is incorporated in prices with sufficient speed and accuracy that one cannot profit by trading on it.

Despite the spread of the doctrine of efficient markets, the world remains full of corporate executives who are convinced of their own ability to predict future interest rates, exchange rates, and commodity prices. As evidence of the strength and breadth of this conviction, many companies during the late 1980s and early 1990s set up their corporate treasuries as "profit centers" in their own right—a practice that, if the survey evidence can be trusted, has been largely abandoned in recent years by most industrial firms. And the practice has been abandoned with good reason: Behind most large derivative losses—in cases ranging from Orange County and Baring Brothers to Procter & Gamble and BancOne—there appear to have been more or less conscious decisions to bear significant exposures to market risks with the hope of earning abnormal returns.

The lesson of market efficiency for corporate risk managers is that the attempt to earn higher returns in most financial markets generally means bearing large (and unfamiliar) risks. In highly liquid markets such as those for interest rate and FX futures—and in the case of heavily traded commodities like oil and gold as well—industrial companies are unlikely to have a comparative advantage in bearing these risks. And so, for most industrial corporations, setting up the corporate treasury to trade derivatives for profit is a value-destroying proposition. (As I will also argue later, however, market efficiency does not rule out the possibility that management's information may be better than the market's in special cases.)

But if the concept of market efficiency should discourage corporations from *creating* corporate exposures to financial market risks, the companion concept of diversification should also discourage some companies from *hedging* financial exposures incurred through their normal business operations. To explain why, however, requires a brief digression on the corporate cost of capital.

Finance theory says that the stock market, in setting the values of companies, effectively assigns minimum required rates of return on capital that vary directly with the companies' levels of risk. In general, the greater a company's risk, the higher the rate of return it must earn to produce superior returns for its shareholders. But a company's required rate of return, also known as its cost of capital, is said to depend only on its non-diversifiable (or "systematic") risk, not on its total risk. In slightly different words, a company's cost of capital depends on the strength of the firm's tendency to move with the broad market (in statistical terms, its "covariance") rather than its overall volatility (or "variance").

In general, most of a company's interest rate, currency, and commodity price exposures will not increase the risk of a well-diversified portfolio. Thus, most corporate financial exposures represent "non-systematic" or "diversifiable" risks that shareholders can eliminate by holding diversified portfolios. And because shareholders have such an inexpensive risk management tool at their disposal, companies that reduce their earnings volatility by managing their financial risks will not be rewarded by investors with lower required rates of return (or, alternatively, with higher price/earnings [P/E] ratios for given levels of cash flow or earnings). As one example, investors with portfolios that include stocks of oil companies are not likely to place higher multiples on the earnings of petrochemical firms just because the latter smooth their earnings by hedging against oil price increases.

For this reason, having the corporation devote resources to reducing FX or commodity price risks makes sense only if the cash flow variability arising from such risks has the potential to impose "real" costs on the corporation. The academic finance literature has identified three major costs associated with higher variability: (1) higher expected bankruptcy costs (and, more generally, costs of financial distress); (2) higher expected payments to corporate "stakeholders" (including higher rates of return required by owners of closely held firms); and (3) higher expected tax payments. The potential gains from risk management come from its ability to reduce each of these three costs—and I review each in turn below.[9]

Risk Management Can Reduce Bankruptcy Costs

Although well-diversified shareholders may not be concerned about the cash flow variability caused by swings in FX rates or commodity prices, they will become concerned if such variability materially raises the probability of financial distress. In the extreme case, a company with significant amounts of debt could experience a sharp downturn in operating cash flow—caused in part by an unhedged exposure—and be forced to file for bankruptcy.

What are the costs of bankruptcy? Most obvious are the payments to lawyers and court costs. But, in addition to these "direct" costs of administration and reorganization, there are some potentially larger "indirect" costs. Companies that wind up in Chapter 11 face considerable interference from the bankruptcy court with their investment and operating decisions. And such interference has the potential to cause significant reductions in the ongoing operating value of the firm.

9. For a discussion of the benefits of corporate hedging, see Clifford Smith and René Stulz, "The Determinants of Firms' Hedging Policies," *Journal of Financial and Quantitative Analysis* Vol. 20 (1985): 391–405.

FIGURE 5.1

Debt, Equity, and Firm Value with Bankruptcy Costs

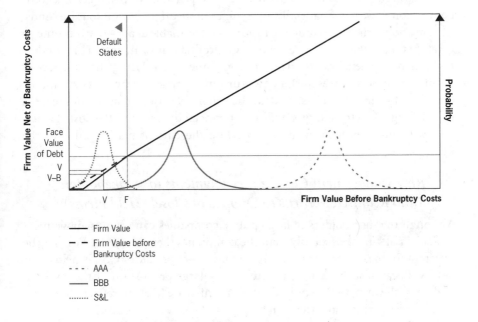

If a company's shareholders view bankruptcy as a real possibility—and to the extent the process of reorganization itself is expected to reduce the firm's operating value—the expected present value of these costs will be reflected in a company's *current* market value. A risk management program that costlessly eliminates the risk of bankruptcy effectively reduces these costs to zero and, in so doing, increases the value of the firm.

The effects of risk management on bankruptcy costs and firm value are illustrated in figure 5.1. In the case shown, hedging is assumed to reduce the variability of cash flow and firm value to the degree that default is no longer possible. By eliminating the possibility of bankruptcy, risk management increases the value of the firm's equity by an amount roughly equal to BC (bankruptcy costs) multiplied by the probability of bankruptcy if the firm remains unhedged (pBU). For example, assume the market value of the firm's equity is $100 million, bankruptcy costs are expected to run $25 million (or 25% of current firm value), and the probability of bankruptcy in the absence of hedging is 10%. In this case, risk management can be seen as increasing the current value of the firm's equity by $2.5 million (10% × $25 million), or 2.5%. (Keep in mind that this is the contribution of risk management to firm value *when the company is healthy*; in the event that cash flow and value should decline sharply from current levels, the value added by risk management increases in absolute dollars, and even more on a percentage-of-value basis.)

This argument extends to distress costs in general. For instance, as a company becomes weaker financially, it becomes more difficult for it to raise funds. At some point, the cost of outside funding—if available at all—may become so great that management chooses to pass up profitable investments. This "underinvestment problem" experienced by companies when facing the prospect of default (or, in some cases, just a downturn in earnings[10]) represents an important cost of financial distress. And, to the extent that risk management succeeds in reducing the perceived *probability* of financial distress and the costs associated with underinvestment, it will increase the current market value of the firm.

Risk Management Can Reduce Payments to "Stakeholders" (and Required Returns to Owners of Closely Held Firms)[11]

Although the shareholders of large public companies can often manage most financial risks more efficiently than the companies themselves, the case may be different for the owners—or owner-managers—of private or closely held companies. Because such owners tend to have a large proportion of their wealth tied up in the firm, their required rates of return are likely to reflect all important sources of risk, those that can be "diversified away" by outside investors as well as those that cannot. In such circumstances, hedging financial exposures can be thought of as adding value by reducing the owners' risks and hence their required rates of return on investment.

And it's not just the owners of closely held companies that value the protection from risk management. In public companies with dispersed ownership, non-investor groups such as managers, employees, customers, and suppliers with a large stake in the success of the firm typically cannot diversify away large financial exposures. If there is a chance that their "firm-specific" investments could be lost because of financial distress, they are likely to require added compensation for the greater risk. Employees will demand higher wages (or reduce their loyalty or perhaps their work effort) at a company where the probability of layoff is greater. Managers with alternative opportunities will demand higher salaries (or maybe an equity stake in the company) to run firms where the risks of insolvency and financial embarrassment are significant. Suppliers will be more reluctant to enter into long-term contracts, and

10. This argument is made by Kenneth Froot, David Scharfstein, and Jeremy Stein in "Risk Management: Coordinating Corporate Investment and Financing Policies," *Journal of Finance* Vol. 48 (1993): 1629–58.

11. The discussion in this section and the next draws heavily on Neil Doherty and Clifford Smith, "Corporate Insurance Strategy: The Case of British Petroleum," *Journal of Applied Corporate Finance* Vol. 6, No. 3 (Fall 1993).

trade creditors will charge more and be less flexible, with companies whose prospects are more uncertain. And customers concerned about the company's ability to fulfill warranty obligations or service their products in the future may be reluctant to buy those products.

To the extent risk management can protect the investments of each of these corporate stakeholders, the company can improve the terms on which it contracts with them and so increase firm value. And, as I discuss later in more detail, hedging can also facilitate larger equity stakes for managers of public companies by limiting "uncontrollables" and thus the "scope" of their bets.

Risk Management Can Reduce Taxes

The potential tax benefits of risk management derive from the interaction of risk management's ability to reduce the volatility of reported income and the progressivity (or, more precisely, the "convexity") of most of the world's tax codes. In the United States, as in most countries, a company's effective tax rate rises along with increases in pre-tax income. Increasing marginal tax rates, limits on the use of tax-loss carry forwards, and the alternative minimum tax all work together to impose higher effective rates of taxation on higher levels of reported income and to provide lower percentage tax rebates for ever larger losses.

Because of the convexity of the tax code, there are benefits to "managing" taxable income so that as much of it as possible falls within an optimal range—that is, neither too high nor too low. By reducing fluctuations in taxable income, risk management can lead to lower tax payments by ensuring that, over a complete business cycle, the largest possible proportion of corporate income falls within this optimal range of tax rates.

Risk Management and Comparative Advantage in Risk Taking

Up to this point, I have shown that companies should not expect to make money consistently by taking financial positions based on information that is publicly available. But what about information that is not publicly available? After all, many companies in the course of their normal operating activities acquire specialized information about certain financial markets. Could not such information give them a comparative advantage over their shareholders in taking some types of risks?

Let's look at a hypothetical example. Consider company X that produces consumer durables using large amounts of copper as a major input. In the process of ensuring that it has the appropriate amount of copper on hand, it gathers useful information about the copper market. It knows its own demand for copper, of course, but it also learns a lot about the supply. In such a case, the firm will almost certainly allow that specialized information to play some role in its risk management strategy.

For example, let's assume that company X's management has determined that, when it has no view about future copper prices, it will hedge 50% of the next year's expected copper purchases to protect itself against the possibility of financial distress. But, now let's say that the firm's purchasing agents persuade top management that the price of copper is far more likely to rise than fall in the coming year. In this case, the firm's risk manager might choose to take a long position in copper futures that would hedge as much as 100% of its anticipated purchases for the year instead of the customary 50%. Conversely, if management becomes convinced that copper prices are likely to drop sharply (with almost no possibility of a major increase), it might choose to hedge as little as 20% of its exposure.[12]

Should the management of company X refrain from exploiting its specialized knowledge in this fashion, and instead adhere to its 50% hedging target? Or should it, in certain circumstances, allow its market view to influence its hedge ratio?

Although there are clearly risks to selective hedging of this kind—in particular, the risk that the firm's information may not in fact be better than the market's—it seems quite plausible that companies could have such informational advantages. Companies that repurchase their own shares based on the belief that their current value fails to reflect the firm's prospects seem to be vindicated more often than not. And though it's true that management may be able to predict the firm's future earnings with more confidence than the price of one of its major inputs, the information companies acquire about certain financial markets may still prove a reasonably reliable source of gain in risk management decisions.

The Importance of Understanding Comparative Advantage

What this example fails to suggest, however, is that the same operating activity in one company may not necessarily provide a comparative advantage in risk bearing for another firm. As suggested above, the major risk associated with "selective" hedging is that the firm's information may not in fact be better than the market's. For this reason, it is important for management to understand the source of its comparative advantages.

To illustrate this point, take the case of a foreign currency trading operation in a large commercial bank. A foreign currency trading room can make a lot of money from taking positions provided, of course, exchange rates move in

---

12. For a good example of this kind of selective hedging policy, see the comments by John van Roden, chief financial officer of Lukens, Inc., in the "Bank of America Roundtable on Corporate Risk Management," *Journal of Applied Corporate Finance* Vol. 8, No. 3 (Fall 1995). As a stainless steel producer, one of the company's principal inputs is nickel; and Lukens' policy is to allow its view of nickel prices to influence how much of its nickel exposure it hedges. By contrast, although it may have views of interest rates or FX exposures, such views play no role in hedging those exposures.

the anticipated direction. But, in an efficient market, as seen, banks can reliably make money from position-taking of this sort only if they have access to information before most other firms. In the case of FX, this is likely to happen only if the bank's trading operation is very large—large enough so that its deal flow is likely to reflect general shifts in demand for foreign currencies.

Most FX dealers, however, have no comparative advantage in gathering information about changes in the value of foreign currencies. For such firms, management of currency risk means ensuring that their exposures are short-lived. The most reliable way to minimize exposures for most currency traders is to enlarge their customer base. With a sufficient number of large, highly active customers, a trading operation has the following advantage: If one of its traders agrees to buy yen from one customer, the firm can resell them quickly to another customer and pocket the bid-ask spread.

In "An Analysis of Trading Profits: How Trading Rooms Really Make Money," Alberic Braas and Charles Bralver present evidence suggesting that most FX trading profits come from market-making, not position-taking.[13] Moreover, as the authors of this article point out, a trading operation that does not understand its comparative advantage in trading currencies is likely not only to fail to generate consistent profit, but to endanger its existing comparative advantage. If the source of the profits of the trading room is really the customer base of the bank, and not the predictive power of its traders, then the bank must invest in maintaining and building its customer base. A trading room that mistakenly believes that the source of its profits is position-taking will take large positions that, on average, will neither make money nor lose money. More troubling, though, is that the resulting variability of its trading income is likely to unsettle its customers and weaken its customer base. Making matters worse, it may choose a compensation system for its traders that rewards profitable position-taking instead of valuable coordination of trading and sales activities. A top management that fails to understand its comparative advantage may waste its time looking for star traders while neglecting the development of marketing strategies and services.

How can management determine when it should take risks and when it should not? The best approach is to implement a *risk-taking audit*. This would involve a comprehensive review of the risks to which the company is exposed, both through its financial instruments and liability structure as well as its normal operations. Such an audit should attempt to answer questions like the following: Which of its major risks has the firm proved capable of "self-insuring" over a complete business cycle? If the firm chooses to hedge "selectively," or leaves exposures completely unhedged, what is the source of the firm's comparative

---

13. See Alberic Braas and Charles Bralver, "An Analysis of Trading Profits: How Trading Rooms Really Make Money," *Journal of Applied Corporate Finance* Vol. 2, No. 4 (Winter 1990).

advantage in taking these positions? Which risk management activities have consistently added value without introducing another source of volatility?

Once a firm has decided that it has a comparative advantage in taking certain financial risks, it must then determine the role of risk management in exploiting this advantage. As I argue below, risk management may paradoxically enable the firm to take *more* of these risks than it would in the absence of risk management. To illustrate this point, let's return to the example of company X and assume it has valuable information about the copper market that enables it to earn consistently superior profits trading copper. Even in this situation, such trading profits are by no means a sure thing; there is always the possibility that the firm will experience significant losses. Purchasing far-out-of-the-money calls on copper in such a case could actually serve to increase the firm's ability to take speculative positions in copper. But, as I argue in the next section, a company's ability to withstand large trading losses without endangering its operating activities depends not only on its risk management policy, but also on its capital structure and general financial health.

The Link Between Risk Management, Risk Taking, and Capital Structure

In discussing earlier the benefits of risk management, I suggested that companies should manage risk in a way that makes financial distress highly unlikely and, in so doing, preserves the financing flexibility necessary to carry out their investment strategies. Given this primary objective for risk management, one would not expect companies with little or no debt financing—and, hence, a low probability of financial trouble—to benefit from hedging.

In this sense, risk management can be viewed as a direct substitute for equity capital. That is, the more the firm hedges its financial exposures, the less equity it requires to support its business. Or, to put it another way, the use of risk management to reduce exposures effectively increases a company's debt capacity.

Moreover, to the extent one views risk management as a substitute for equity capital—or, alternatively, as a technique that allows management to substitute debt for equity—then it pays companies to practice risk management only to the extent that equity capital is more expensive than debt. As this formulation of the issue suggests, a company's decisions to hedge financial risks—or to bear part of such risks through selective hedging—should be made jointly with the corporate capital structure decision.

To illustrate this interdependence between risk management and capital structure, consider the three kinds of companies pictured in figure 5.2. At the right-hand side of the figure is company AAA, so named because it has little

FIGURE 5.2

Optimal Hedging for Firms AAA, BBB and S&L

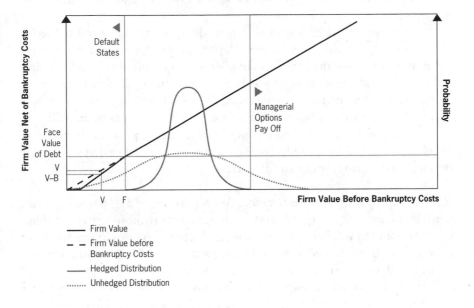

- —— Firm Value
- — — Firm Value before Bankruptcy Costs
- —— Hedged Distribution
- ······· Unhedged Distribution

debt and a very high debt rating. The probability of default is essentially zero; and thus the left or lower tail of AAA's distribution of potential outcomes never reaches the range where low value begins to impose financial distress costs on the firm. Based on the theory of risk management just presented, there is no reason for this company to hedge its financial exposures; the company's shareholders can do the same job more cost effectively. And, should investment opportunities arise, AAA will likely be able to raise funds on an economic basis, even if its cash flows should decline temporarily.

Should such a company take bets on financial markets? The answer could be yes, provided management has specialized information that would give it a comparative advantage in a certain market. In AAA's case, a bet that turns out badly will not affect the company's ability to carry out its strategic plan.

But now let's consider the company in the middle of the picture; let's call it BBB. Like the company shown in figure 5.1, this firm has a lower credit rating, and there is a significant probability that the firm could face distress. What should BBB do? As shown in figure 5.1, this firm should probably eliminate the probability of encountering financial distress through risk management. In this case, even if management feels that there are occasional opportunities to profit from market inefficiencies, hedging exposures is likely to be the best policy. In company BBB's case, the cost of having a bet turn sour can be substantial, since this would almost certainly imply default. Consequently, one would not expect the management of such a firm to let its views affect the hedge ratio.

Finally, let's consider a firm that is in distress—and let's call it "S&L." What should it do? Reducing risk once the firm is in distress is not in the interest of shareholders. If the firm stays in distress and eventually defaults, shareholders will end up with near-worthless shares. In these circumstances, a management intent on maximizing shareholder value will not only accept bets that present themselves, but will *seek out* new ones. Such managers will take bets even if they believe markets are efficient because introducing new sources of volatility raises the probability of the "upper-tail" outcomes that are capable of rescuing the firm from financial distress.

Back to the Capital Structure Decision. As seen in the case of company AAA, firms that have a lot of equity capital can make bets without worrying about whether doing so will bring about financial distress. One would therefore not expect these firms to hedge aggressively, particularly if risk management is costly and shareholders are better off without it.

The major issue that such companies must address, however, is whether they have too much capital—or, too much equity capital. In other words, although risk management may not be useful to them *given their current leverage ratios,* they might be better off using risk management and increasing leverage. Debt financing, of course, has a tax advantage over equity financing. But, in addition to its ability to reduce corporate taxes, increasing leverage also has the potential to strengthen management incentives to improve efficiency and add value. For one thing, the substitution of debt for equity leads managers to pay out excess capital—an action that could be a major source of value added in industries with overcapacity and few promising investment opportunities. Perhaps even more important, however, is that the substitution of debt for equity also allows for greater concentration of equity ownership, including a significant ownership stake for managers.

In sum, the question of what is the right corporate risk management decision for a company begs the question of not only its optimal capital structure, but optimal *ownership* structure as well. As suggested above, hedging could help some companies to increase shareholder value by enabling them to raise leverage—say, by buying back their shares—and increase management's percentage ownership. For other companies, however, leaving exposures unhedged or hedging "selectively" while maintaining more equity may turn out to be the value-maximizing strategy.

Corporate Risk Taking and Management Incentives

Management incentives may have a lot to do with why some firms take bets and others do not. As suggested, some companies that leave exposures unhedged or take bets on financial markets may have a comparative advantage in so doing; and, for those companies, such risk taking may be a value-increasing strategy. Other companies, however, may choose to take financial risks without having a comparative advantage, particularly if such risk taking somehow serves the interests of those managers who choose to expose their firms to the risks.

Little convincing empirical evidence exists on the extent of risk taking by companies, whether public or private. But there is one notable exception—a study by Peter Tufano of the hedging behavior of 48 publicly traded North American gold mining companies that was published in the September 1996 issue of the *Journal of Finance*.[14] The gold mining industry is ideal for studying hedging behavior in the sense that gold mining companies tend to be single-industry firms with one very large price exposure and a wide range of hedging vehicles, from forward sales, to exchange-traded gold futures and options, to gold swaps and bullion loans.

The purpose of Tufano's study was to examine the ability of various corporate risk management theories to explain any significant pattern of differences in the percentage of their gold price exposures that the companies choose to hedge. Somewhat surprisingly, there was considerable variation in the hedging behavior of these 48 firms. One company, Homestake Mining, chose not only to hedge none of its exposure, but to publicize its policy while condemning what it called "gold price management." At the other extreme were companies like American Barrick that hedged as much as 85% of their anticipated production over the next 3 years. And whereas about one in six of these firms chose to hedge none of its exposure and sold *all* of its output at spot prices, another one in six firms hedged 40% or more of its gold price exposure.

The bottom line of Tufano's study was that the only important systematic determinant of the 48 corporate hedging decisions was managerial ownership of shares and, more generally, the nature of the managerial compensation contract. In general, the greater management's direct percentage share of ownership, the larger the percentage of its gold price exposure a firm hedged. By contrast, little hedging took place in gold mining firms where management owns a small stake. Moreover, managerial compensation contracts that emphasize options or option-like features were also associated with significantly less hedging.

---

14. Peter Tufano, "Who Manages Risk? An Empirical Examination of the Risk Management Practices of the Gold Mining Industry," *Journal of Finance* (September 1996).

As Tufano acknowledged in his study, this pattern of findings could have been predicted from arguments that Clifford Smith and I presented in a theoretical paper in 1985.[15] Our argument was essentially as follows: As we saw in the case of closely held companies, managers with a significant fraction of their own wealth tied up in their own firms are likely to consider all sources of risk when setting their required rates of return. And this could help explain the tendency of firms with heavy managerial equity ownership to hedge more of their gold price exposures. In such cases, the volatility of gold prices translates fairly directly into volatility of managers' wealth, and manager-owners concerned about such volatility may rationally choose to manage their exposures. (How, or whether, such hedging serves the interests of the companies' outside shareholders is another issue, one that I return to shortly.)

The propensity of managers with lots of stock options but little equity ownership to leave their gold price exposures unhedged is also easy to understand. As shown in figure 5.3, the one-sided payoff from stock options effectively rewards management for taking bets and so increasing volatility. In this example, the reduction in volatility from hedging makes management's options worthless (that is, the example assumes these are well out-of-the-money options). But if the firm does not hedge, there is some probability that a large increase in gold prices will cause the options to pay off.

What if one makes the more realistic assumption that the options are *at the money* instead of far out of the money? In this case, options would still have the power to influence hedging behavior because management gains more from increases in firm value than it loses from reductions in firm value. As seen in the case of the S&L presented earlier, this "asymmetric" payoff structure of options increases management's willingness to take bets.[16]

But if these differences in hedging behavior reflect differences in managerial incentives, what do they tell us about the effect of risk management on shareholder value? Without directly addressing the issue, Tufano implies that neither of the two polar risk management strategies—hedging none of their gold exposure versus hedging 40% or more—seems designed to increase share-

15. Smith and Stulz, "Determinants of Firms' Hedging Policies."
16. Additional empirical support for the importance of the relation between the option component of managerial compensation contracts and corporate risk taking was provided in a recent study of savings and loan institutions (S&Ls) that changed their organizational form from mutual ownership to stock ownership. The study finds that those "converted" S&Ls where management has options choose to increase their 1-year gaps and, hence, their exposure to interest rates. The study also shows that the greater the percentage of their interest rate exposure an S&L hedges, the larger the credit risk it takes on. The authors of the study interpret this finding to argue, as I do here, that risk management allows firms to increase their exposures to some risks by reducing other risks and thus limiting total firm risk. See C.M. Schrandt and H. Unal, "Coordinated Risk Management: On and Off-balance Sheet Hedging and Thrift Conversion" (unpublished working paper, The Wharton School, University of Pennsylvania, Philadelphia, 1996).

FIGURE 5.3

Impact of Options in Managerial Compensation Contracts

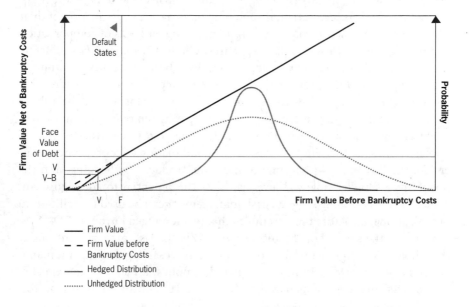

──── Firm Value

── ── Firm Value before
        Bankruptcy Costs

──── Hedged Distribution

········ Unhedged Distribution

holder value while both appear to serve managers' interests. But can we therefore conclude from this study that neither of these approaches benefits shareholders?

Let's start with the case of the companies that, like Homestake Mining, choose to hedge none of their gold price exposure. As seen earlier, companies for which financial distress is unlikely have no good reason to hedge (assuming they see no value in changing their current capital structure). At the same time, in a market as heavily traded as gold, management is also not likely to possess a comparative advantage in predicting gold prices. And, lacking either a motive for hedging or superior information about future gold prices, management has no reason to alter the company's natural exposure to gold prices. In further defense of such a policy, one could also argue that such a gold price exposure will have diversification benefits for investors seeking protection against inflation and political risks.

On the other hand, as Smith and I pointed out, because stock options have considerably more upside than downside risk, such incentive packages could result in a misalignment of managers' and shareholders' interests. That is, stock options could be giving managers a one-sided preference for risk taking that is not fully shared by the companies' stockholders; and, if so, a better policy would be to balance managers' upside potential by giving them a share of the downside risk.

But what about the opposite decision to hedge a significant portion of gold price exposures? Was that likely to have increased shareholder value? As Tufano's study suggests, the managers of the hedging firms tend to hold larger equity stakes. And, as seen earlier, if such managers have a large fraction of their wealth tied up in their firms, they will demand higher levels of compensation to work in firms with such price exposures. *Given that the firm has chosen to concentrate equity ownership*, hedging may well be a value-adding strategy. That is, if significant equity ownership for managers is expected to add value by strengthening incentives to improve operating performance, the role of hedging is to make these incentives even stronger by removing the "noise" introduced by a major performance variable—the gold price—that is beyond management's control. For this reason, the combination of concentrated ownership, the less "noisy" performance measure produced by hedging, and the possibility of higher financial leverage[17] has the potential to add significant value. As this reasoning suggests, risk management can be used to facilitate an organizational structure that resembles that of a leveraged buyout (LBO)![18]

To put the same thought another way, it is the risk management policy that allows companies with large financial exposures to have significant managerial stock ownership. Without the hedging policy, a major price exposure would cause the scope of management's bet to be too diffuse, and "uncontrollables" would dilute the desired incentive benefits of more concentrated ownership.

Although Tufano's study is finally incapable of answering the question, "Did risk management add value for shareholders?," the study nevertheless has an important message for corporate policy. It says that, to the extent that risk taking within the corporation is decentralized, it is important to understand the incentives of those who make the decisions to take or lay off risks.

Organizations have lots of people doing a good job, and so simply doing a good job may not be enough to get promoted. And, if one views corporate promotions as the outcome of "tournaments" (as does one strand of the academic literature), there are tremendous incentives to stand out. One way to stand out is by volunteering to take big risks. In most areas of a corporation, it is generally impossible to take risks where the payoffs are large enough to be noticeable if things go well. But the treasury area may still be an exception. When organized as a profit center, the corporate treasury was certainly a place where an enterprising executive could take such risks and succeed. To the extent such

17. Although Tufano's study does not find that firms that hedge have systematically higher leverage ratios, it does find that companies that hedge less have higher cash balances.
18. For a discussion of the role of hedging in creating an LBO-like structure, see René Stulz, "Managerial Discretion and Optimal Financing Policies," *Journal of Financial Economics* (1990): 3–26.

possibilities for risk taking still exist within some corporate treasuries, top management must be very careful in establishing the appropriate incentives for their risk managers. I return to this subject in the final section of the paper.

Measuring Risk (or, Improving on VaR)

As I mentioned at the outset, the academic literature has focused on volatility reduction as the primary objective of risk management, and on variance as the principal measure of risk. But such a focus on variance, as seen, is inconsistent with both most corporate practice and with the theory of risk management presented in this chapter. Rather than aiming to reduce variance, most corporate risk management programs appear designed just to avoid "lower-tail outcomes" while preserving upside potential. Indeed, as I suggested earlier, some companies will hedge certain downside risks precisely in order to be able to increase their leverage ratios or to enlarge other financial exposures in ways designed to exploit their comparative advantage in risk taking.

Many commercial banks and other financial institutions now attempt to quantify the probability of lower-tail outcomes by using a measure known as value at risk (VaR). To illustrate the general principle underlying VaR, let's assume you are an investor who holds a stock portfolio that is fully diversified across all the major world markets. To calculate your (VaR) you will need the kind of information that is presented graphically in figure 5.4, which is a histogram showing the distribution of monthly returns on the Morgan Stanley Capital International world market portfolio from September 1985 through December 1995.

How risky is that portfolio? One measure is the standard deviation of the portfolio's monthly returns. Over that roughly 10-year period, the average monthly return was 1.23%, with a standard deviation of 4.3%. This tells you that, about two thirds of the time, your actual return would have fallen within a range extending from a loss of 3.1% to a gain of 5.5%.

But what if one of your major concerns is the size of your monthly losses if things turn out badly, and you thus want to know more about the bottom third of the distribution of outcomes? Let's say, for example, that you want to know the maximum extent of your losses in 95 cases out of 100—that is, within a 95% "confidence interval." In that case, you would calculate the VaR evaluated at the 5% level, which turns out to be a loss of 5.9%. This VaR, represented by the vertical line in the middle of figure 5.4, is obtained by taking the monthly average return of 1.23% and subtracting from it 1.65 times the standard deviation of 4.3%. And, if you wanted to know the dollar value of your maximum expected losses, you would simply multiply 5.9% times the

FIGURE 5.4

World Market Portfolio Returns September 1985–December 1995

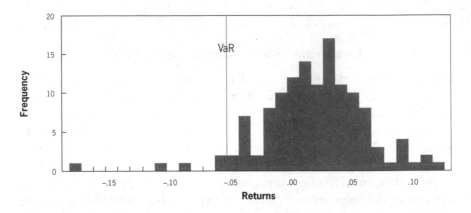

dollar value of your holdings. That number is your monthly VaR at the 95% confidence level.

Although the VaR is now used by some industrial firms to evaluate the risks of their derivatives portfolios, the measure was originally designed by J.P. Morgan to help financial institutions monitor the exposures created by their trading activities. In fact, for financial institutions that trade in liquid markets, a *daily* VaR is likely to be even more useful for monitoring trading operations than the monthly VaR illustrated above. Use of a daily VaR would tell an institution that it could expect, in 95 cases out of 100, to lose no more that X% of its value before unwinding its positions.

The special appeal of VaR is its ability to compress the expected distribution of bad outcomes into a single number. But how does one apply such a measure to the corporate risk management under discussion? Despite its advantages for certain uses, VaR cannot really be used to execute the risk management goal presented in this chapter—namely, the elimination of lower-tail outcomes to avoid financial distress. The fact that there is a 95% probability that a company's loss on a given day, or in a given month, will not exceed a certain amount called VaR is not useful information when management's concern is whether firm value will fall below some critical value *over an extended period of time*. The question management would like to be able to answer is this: If we define financial distress as a situation where we cannot raise funds with a rating of BBB, or where our cash flows or the value of equity fall below some target, what is the probability of distress over, say, the next 3 years? VaR by itself cannot answer this question—nor can traditional measures of volatility.

It is relatively simple to calculate VaR for a financial institution's portfolio over a horizon of a day or a week. It is much less clear how one would compute the VaR associated with, say, an airline's ongoing operating exposure to oil prices. In evaluating their major risks, most non-financial companies will want to know how much volatility in their cash flows or firm value an exposure can be expected to cause over periods of at least a year, and often considerably longer. Unfortunately, there are at least two major difficulties in extending the VaR over longer time horizons that may not be surmountable.

First, remember that a daily VaR at the 99th percentile is one that is expected to occur on one day out of 100. The relative precision of such a prediction makes it possible to conduct empirical checks of the validity of the model. With the large number of daily observations, one can readily observe the frequency with which the loss is equal to or greater than VaR *using reasonably current data*. But, if we attempt to move from a daily to, say, a 1-year VaR at the same 99th percentile, it becomes very difficult to calculate such a model, much less subject it to empirical testing. Since an annual VaR at the 99th percentile means that the loss can be expected to take place in only 1 year in every 100, one presumably requires numerous 100-year periods to establish the validity of such a model.

The second problem in extending the time horizon of VaR is its reliance on the normal distribution. When one is especially concerned about "tail" probabilities—the probabilities of the worst and best outcomes—the assumption made about the statistical distribution of the gains and losses is important. Research on stock prices and on default probabilities across different classes of debt suggests that the tail probabilities are generally larger than implied by the normal distribution. A simple way to understand this is as follows. If stock returns were really normally distributed, as many pricing models assume, market declines in excess of 10% in a day would be extremely rare—say, once in a million years. The fact that such declines happen more often than this is proof that the normal distribution does not describe the probability of lower-tail events correctly.

Although this is not an important failing for most applications in corporate finance, including the valuation of most securities, it can be critical in the context of risk management. For example, if changes in the value of derivatives portfolios or default probabilities have "fatter tails" than those implied by a normal distribution, management could end up significantly understating the probability of distress.

An Alternative to VaR: Using Cash Flow Simulations to Estimate Default Probabilities. Moreover, even if we could calculate a 1-year VaR for the value of the firm and be reasonably confident that the distribution was normal, the relevant risk measure for hedging purposes would not be the VaR computed at the 1-year horizon. A VaR computed at the 1-year horizon at the 99th percentile answers the question: What is the maximum loss in firm value that I can expect in 99 years out of 100? But when a company hedges an exposure, its primary concern is the likelihood of distress during the year, which depends on the value of the cumulative loss throughout the year. Thus, it must be concerned about the path of firm value during a period of time rather than the distribution of firm value at the end of the period.

Given this focus on cumulative changes in firm value during a period of time, perhaps the most practical approach to assessing a company's probability of financial distress is to conduct sensitivity analysis on the expected distribution of cash flows. Using Monte Carlo simulation techniques, for example, one could project the company's cash flows over a 10-year horizon in a way that is designed to reflect the combined effect of (and any interactions among) all the firm's major risk exposures on its default probability. The probability of distress over that period would be measured by the fraction of simulated distributions that falls below a certain threshold level of cumulative cash flow. Such a technique could also be used to estimate the expected effect of various hedging strategies on the probability of distress.[19]

One of the advantages of using simulation techniques in this context is their ability to incorporate any special properties (or "non-normalities") of the cash flows. As seen earlier, the VaR approach assumes that the gains and losses from risky positions are "serially independent," which means that if your firm experiences a loss today, the chance of experiencing another loss tomorrow is unaffected. But this assumption is likely to be wrong when applied to the operating cash flow of a non-financial firm: If cash flow is poor today, it is more likely to be poor tomorrow. Simulation has the ability to build this "serial dependence" of cash flows into an analysis of the probability of financial distress.

Managing Risk Taking

As seen, a hedging strategy that focuses on the probability of distress can be consistent with an increase in risk taking. With such a strategy, the primary goal of risk management is to eliminate lower-tail outcomes. Using risk management in this way, it is possible for a company to increase its volatility while also limiting the probability of a bad outcome that would create financial dis-

---

19. For an illustration of the use of Monte Carlo analysis in risk management, see René Stulz and Rohan Williamson, "Identifying and Quantifying Exposures," in *Treasury Risk Management*, ed. Robert Jameson (London, Risk Publications), forthcoming.

tress. One example of such a strategy would be to lever up the firm while at the same time buying way out-of-the-money put options that pay off if the firm does poorly. Focusing on lower-tail outcomes is also fully consistent with managing longer-term economic or competitive exposures, as opposed to the near-term transaction exposures that most corporate risk management seems designed to hedge.

But how would the firm decide whether the expected payoff from taking certain financial bets is adequate compensation for not only the risk of losses, but also the expected costs of financial distress? And, once management decides that it is a value-increasing proposition to undertake certain bets, how would the firm evaluate the success of its risk-taking efforts?

To evaluate if the bet is worth taking, let's start by supposing that we are willing to put an explicit cost on the increase in the probability of distress resulting from betting on certain markets. In that case, the tradeoff for evaluating a bet for the company becomes fairly simple: The expected profit from the bet must exceed the increase in the probability of distress multiplied by the expected cost of distress.[20] Thus, a bet that has a positive expected value and no effect on the probability of distress is one that the firm should take. But a bet with positive expected profit that significantly increases the probability of financial distress may not appear profitable if the costs of a bad outcome are too large. In such cases, it makes sense for the firm to think about using risk management to reduce the probability of distress. By hedging, management may be able to achieve a reduction in cash flow variability that is large enough that an adverse outcome of the bet will not create financial distress.

Given that management has decided the bet is worth taking, how does it evaluate the outcome of the strategy? Consider first the case of firm AAA discussed earlier. Recall that this firm is not concerned about lower-tail outcomes and thus has no reason to hedge. When evaluating the outcome of the bet in this case, the appropriate benchmark is the expected gain *adjusted for risk*. It is

20. One possible approach to quantifying the *expected* costs of financial distress involves the concept of American "binary options" and the associated option pricing models. An example of a binary option is one that would pay a fixed amount, say, $10, if the stock price of International Business Machines (IBM) falls below $40. Unlike standard American put options, which when exercised pay an amount equal to (the strike price of) $40 minus the actual price, the holder of a binary option receives either $10 or nothing, and exercises when the stock price crosses the $40 barrier. Such options can be priced using modified option pricing models.

The connection between binary options and risk management is this: The present value of a binary option is a function of two major variables: the probability that firm value will fall below a certain level (in this case, $40) and the payoff in the event of such a drop in value ($10). By substituting for the $10 payoff its own estimate of how much *additional value the firm is likely to lose once its value falls to a certain level and gets into financial trouble*, management can then estimate the expected present value of such costs using a binary option pricing model. This is the number that could be set against the expected profit from the firm's bet in order to evaluate whether to go ahead with the bet.

not enough that the bet ends up earning more than the risk-free rate or even more than the firm's cost of capital. To add value for the company's sharehold-ers, the bet must earn a return that is higher than investors' expected return on other investments of comparable risk.

For example, there is considerable evidence that holding currencies of high-interest rate countries earns returns that, on average, exceed the risk-free rate. This excess return most likely represents "normal" compensation for bearing some kind of risk—say, the higher inflation and interest rate volatility associated with high-interest-rate countries. And because such a strategy is thus *expected* to earn excess returns, it would not make sense to reward a cor-porate treasury for earning excess returns in this way. The treasury takes risks when it pursues that strategy, and the firm's shareholders expect to be compen-sated for these risks. Thus, it is only the amount by which the treasury exceeds the expected return—or the "abnormal return"—that represents *economic profit* for the corporation.

So, the abnormal or excess return should be the measure for evaluating bets by company AAA. But now let's turn to the case of company BBB, where the expected increase in volatility from the bet is also expected to raise the probability of costly lower-tail outcomes. In such a case, as seen earlier, man-agement should probably hedge to reduce the probability of financial trouble to acceptable levels. At the same time, however, top management should also consider subjecting its bets to an even higher standard of profitability to com-pensate shareholders for any associated increase in expected financial distress costs.

How much higher should it be? One method would be to assume that, in-stead of hedging, the firm raises additional equity capital to support the ex-pected increase in volatility associated with the bet. In that case, the bet would be expected to produce the same risk-adjusted return on capital as the bet taken by company AAA, but on a larger amount of imputed "risk" capital.[21]

In sum, when devising a compensation scheme for those managers en-trusted with making the firm's bets, it is critical to structure their incentive payments so that they are encouraged to take only those bets that are expected

21. The amount of implicit "risk capital" (as opposed to the actual cash capital) backing an activity can be calculated as a function of the expected volatility (as measured by the standard deviation) of the activity's cash flow returns. For the distinction between risk capital and cash capital, and a method for calculating risk capital, see Robert Merton and André Perold, "Theory of Risk Capital for Financial Firms," *Journal of Applied Corporate Finance* Vol. 6, No. 3 (Fall 1993). For one company's application of a similar method for calculating risk capital, see Edward Zaik et al., "RAROC at Bank of America: From Theory to Practice," *Journal of Applied Corporate Finance* Vol. 9, No. 2 (Summer 1996). For a theoretical model of capital budgeting that takes into account firm-specific risks, see Kenneth Froot and Jeremy Stein, "Risk Management, Capital Budgeting, and Capital Structure Policy for Financial Institutions: An Integrated Approach" (Working Paper 96–030, Harvard Business School Division of Research).

to increase shareholder wealth. Managers should not be compensated for earning average returns when taking larger-than-average risks. They should be compensated only for earning more than what their shareholders could earn on their own when bearing the same amount of risk.

This approach does not completely eliminate the problem discussed earlier caused by incentives for an individual to stand out in large organizations by taking risks. But traditional compensation schemes only reinforce this problem. If a risk taker simply receives a bonus for making gains, he [or she] has incentives to take random bets because he gets a fraction of his gains while the firm bears the losses. Evaluating managers' performance against a risk-adjusted benchmark can help discourage risk taking that is not justified by comparative advantage by making it more difficult for the risk taker to make money by taking random bets.

Conclusion

This chapter presents a theory of risk management that attempts to go beyond the "variance-minimization" model that dominates most academic discussions of corporate risk management. I argue that the primary goal of risk management is to eliminate the probability of costly lower-tail outcomes—those that would cause financial distress or make a company unable to carry out its investment strategy. (In this sense, risk management can be viewed as the purchase of well-out-of-the-money put options designed to limit downside risk.) Moreover, by eliminating downside risk and reducing the expected costs of financial trouble, risk management can also help move companies toward their optimal capital and ownership structure. Besides increasing corporate debt capacity, the reduction of downside risk could also encourage larger equity stakes for managers by shielding their investments from "uncontrollables."

This chapter also departs from standard finance theory in suggesting that some companies may have a comparative advantage in bearing certain financial market risks—an advantage that derives from information it acquires through its normal business activities. Although such specialized information may occasionally lead some companies to take speculative positions in commodities or currencies, it is more likely to encourage selective hedging, a practice in which the risk manager's view of future price movements influences the percentage of the exposure that is hedged. This kind of hedging, while certainly containing potential for abuse, may also represent a value-adding form of risk taking for many companies.

But, to the extent that such view-taking becomes an accepted part of a company's risk management program, it is important to evaluate managers' bets on a risk-adjusted basis and relative to the market. If managers want to behave like money managers, they should be evaluated like money managers.

■ RENÉ STULZ holds the Reese Chair in Banking and Monetary Economics at Ohio State University, and is also a Bower Fellow at the Harvard Business School and a Research Associate at the National Bureau of Economic Research. Professor Stulz is editor of the *Journal of Finance*, and is currently at work on a textbook entitled *Derivatives, Risk Management, and Financial Engineering*.

CHAPTER 6

An Analysis of Trading Profits

How Most Trading Rooms Really Make Money

ALBÉRIC BRAAS AND

CHARLES N. BRALVER

O UR OBSERVATION OF more than 40 large trading operations has led us to conclude that most trading rooms should be managed to generate stable profits by taking little positioning risk. This prescription is founded on three basic observations, each of which is developed in one of the three main sections of this chapter:

1. **The Myth of Speculative Positioning as the Best Source of Profit.** In this section we argue that, for most trading rooms, positioning is not a reliable source of revenues and profits.

2. **The Value of the Turn.** Here we take the view that more money is made trading interdealer volume than is customarily believed— but that it only happens if traders adopt a "jobber" style of trading.

3. **The Power of Customer Business.** Here we show the value of trading with customers and conclude that, for most trading rooms, it should be viewed as the primary source of revenue and profit.

The Myth of Speculative Positioning as Best Source of Profit

Traders are naturally inclined to believe that the primary source of earnings in trading fixed income securities, equities, or foreign exchange is positioning. The underlying premise is that quality traders are able to predict the movements of interest rates, foreign exchange rates, and stock prices with sufficient accuracy to "beat the market"—if not consistently, then at least more often than not.

This chapter was previously published as an article in *Journal of Applied Corporate Finance* Vol. 2, No. 4 (Winter 1990): 85–90.

FIGURE 6.1

Price Change versus Position Size

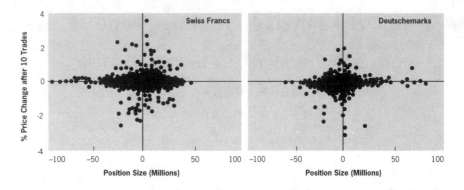

Having analyzed trading rooms around the world, for smaller operations in regional centers as well as major players, our experience suggests the above premise is ill-founded. For most trading rooms and traders, the financial markets are in fact very efficient, and betting on price movements is not a sound business proposition. Just as economists cannot consistently predict interest rates and mutual fund managers do not outperform the market year after year, traders cannot be expected to "outguess" movements in the value of trading instruments with any degree of reliability.

It is instructive to track the pattern of traders' positions relative to subsequent market movements. Figure 6.1, which reflects our analysis of a large foreign exchange trading desk in New York, shows the relationship (or the conspicuous absence thereof) between one group of successful traders' positions in Swiss francs and deutsche marks and subsequent changes in the spot market prices of those currencies. If these traders were consistently making money by taking positions, long positions would be strongly correlated with up movements and short positions with down movements; the dots would lie along an upward-sloping diagonal running from lower left to upper right. In this case, they do not—and it is our experience as advisers that they seldom do.

There are, however, a few significant exceptions. We know of three situations in which traders can make money by positioning. First, positioning tends to be profitable when the market experiences a lift or slide of significant duration. One example is the decline of the dollar in 1987, when most foreign exchange traders went short and made money. The slide may not have been forseeable; but once it was under way, it seemed easy to call. Unfortunately, such situations are rare, and hence cannot be relied upon to generate sustained profits over time. Second, traders can make money by positioning when they have some proprietary source of information. And, third, consistent profits from positioning can also be expected if the firm has sufficient market power to influence prices. Most markets have a handful of dealers large enough to be "trend-setters"—dealers whose quotations get everybody's attention. Besides being able to influence price by their actions, these influential players also benefit from a kind of proprietary information because they trade in larger volume with the largest institutional investors (some of which are large enough to move the markets themselves). They may be better able to anticipate market movements as they see the order flow from such dominant customers. Being a lead dealer to those customers and receiving those orders before the rest of the market constitutes a significant advantage.

Furthermore, in some cases, the use of increasingly sophisticated computer models to track and analyze data appears to have become another source of proprietary information and competitive advantage. For example, some investment banks seem to owe their success in the mortgage-backed securities market to their computer-driven fixed-income research and to the sheer volume of their trading—both of which allow them to structure, hedge, and price the instruments with more confidence and accuracy than their competitors.

In sum, position-taking is not for everybody. Only market leaders can leverage the competitive advantage acquired in the interdealer markets or in working with their customer base into their house positions; others are best advised to minimize speculative positions most of the time. This prescription also applies to institutions that hire successful traders from other trading houses; such traders often "lose their touch" when they find themselves in a disadvantaged environment. All too often, we find trading rooms that have no competitive advantage taking positions as if they did. Almost invariably, revenues and profits are disappointing and unreliable. Even in cases where there are initial or periodic bursts of profit and enthusiasm, such profits are typically dissipated in subsequent years or quarters. In these cases, the present value of the revenue stream is not likely to justify investment in state-of-the-art infrastructure and multi-desk trading floors. Our experience, in short, is that few trading rooms earn an acceptable return on the capital put at risk through positioning; and many even fail to cover expenses.

This is not to say, however, that trading must be a losing game for those institutions that do not have the competitive leverage to position effectively against market movements. There are other, more reliable, sources of profits from a trading room.

The Value of the Turn (or, Who Keeps the Bid-Offer Spread?)

Any trading market, at any point in time, consists of all the parties prepared to buy or sell at specified prices. Where the buying and selling pressure meets is within the "bid-ask" (or "bid-offer") spread—the spread in the interdealer market between the best posted bid and the best posted offer at a point in time. The bid-ask spread is relatively high on illiquid securities like municipal bonds and junk bonds but very thin on liquid assets like foreign exchange.

Some traders argue that there is no such thing as a bid-offer spread in a transaction, that each trade is a bargain struck, and that the range between the bid and the offered prices is simply a negotiating framework within (or outside of) which the bargain is concluded. Our view, however, is that the price at which an interdealer bargain is struck is a function of the relative power of the two parties in the instrument traded. One party's offered price often becomes the counterparty's bid price. In repeated transactions between these two parties, this counterparty will consistently find itself on the wrong side of the market bid-offer in the bargain.

The advantaged parties in such situations generally turn out to be those players with stronger market-making capacity, and the other dealers with whom they trade are essentially forced to trade at the prices quoted by those market-makers. The possession of such an advantage in turn seems to be a function of market share. This phenomenon is especially clear in our analysis of thousands of trades for a primary dealer in U.S. government securities. As illustrated in figure 6.2, the percentage of the spread retained interdealer in each of six different trading instruments appears to be a direct function of the dealer's share of the interdealer volume in a given instrument.

Our experience has convinced us, then, that a bid-ask spread materializes when dealers with larger market share transact with smaller dealers. And, as our analysis has consistently demonstrated, a given trader's average, long-run tendency to retain that spread is a function of the "market power" of his or her institution. Market power translates into control of "bargains," which in turn translate into revenues.

A head fixed-income trader for a New York powerhouse put it best when he told us, "Any trader I put in the 5- to 7-year note chair makes a lot of money for us. Each of them thinks he is making the money with his smart calls. But it's really the chair that makes the money." Although there is some exaggeration in this statement, the message here is that the predictability and sustainability of trading profits is the result of the market-maker's ability to retain a disproportionate share of the bid-offer spread in a large volume of trades. Like the "golden crumbs" in Tom Wolfe's *Bonfire of the Vanities*, 70% spread retention on billions of dollars of daily volume represents a sizable and consistent stream of revenue.

FIGURE 6.2

Market Share versus Interdealer Strength

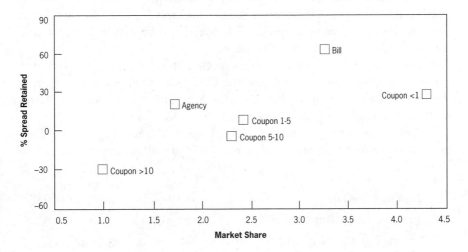

There are two keys to spread retention. First, the firm must have considerable financial muscle and trade flows. Second, traders must adopt a "jobbing" attitude, striving continuously to buy at or close to the bid side and to resell quickly at the offer side. This implies a lot of volume, but relatively small positions of short duration (and hence low risk).

The Power of Customer Business

A good predictor of long-term success in a trading room is the status of salespeople relative to traders. The most successful Wall Street firms have long recognized that distributing and selling securities (or other financial instruments) to smaller dealers and to institutional customers not only keeps them better-informed than their competitors, but also is a stable source of earnings. Too often salespeople are viewed as second-class citizens in trading rooms—because, once again, the myth of position-taking as the best source of profit overshadows the added value in the customer side of the business. One typical result of this misconception is an undervalued, undermotivated sales force that is required to sell an irregular flow of products based on traders' house positions and "views." The ultimate effect is a dissatisfied customer base and highly volatile earnings.

It is often argued that the interdealer business and the customer business are so closely interrelated that it is not possible to separate the revenue and the profits generated by each. We believe, however, that by marking large numbers of transactions to market (that is, determining where the actual price of each stood relative to the market prices at the time of sale), senior management can set transfer prices between trading and sales that provide a reasonably reliable split of revenues between the two.

Our examinations of over 40 trading desks around the world have shown that, contrary to popular belief, customer business represents a significant portion of trading revenues—generally between 60% and 150% (in which case positioning loses money) of total revenues.

One of our clients, for example, reported about $10 million of pre-tax profit for a given time period in trading U.S. government securities. During the period, the client had conducted almost $400 billion of customer business and over $500 billion of interdealer business.

Upon closer examination by marking individual trades to market, we decomposed the firm's "gross trading profit" of $30 million into the following categories:

Customer revenue	$26 million
Spread retention (interdealer)	8 million
Trading profit (positioning)	(4 million)
Gross trading profit	$30 million
Expenses	(20 million)
Net profit (pre-tax)	$10 million

In this case, which is far more representative than one might think, customer revenues were actually covering up positioning *losses*—losses that amounted to 40% of net profit.

Not all dealings with customers are profitable, however. As shown in figure 6.3, many (particularly small) trades are in fact priced below cost. This tends to happen either because too few trading rooms really understand their fully loaded costs or because their business has become too competitive.

In general, though, a large portion of customer business yields mark-ups relative to true interdealer prices; and the value of the mark-ups is often greater than the cost of a well-organized sales force. Dealing with customers allows you to price sales not only at the offer but often above it, while purchasing at or below the bid. Even when customers are powerful enough to avoid any mark-up relative to dealers' prices, they typically buy at or close to the major dealers' offer prices and sell at or close to the bid prices. For those dealers who can source most of their trades at the market bid prices and resell at the market offer, customer business generates a consistently profitable revenue stream.

As shown in table 6.1, one of our clients (also a primary government securities dealer) was able to retain a consistently large percentage of the bid-offer

FIGURE 6.3

Cost, Revenue Per Customer versus Deal Size

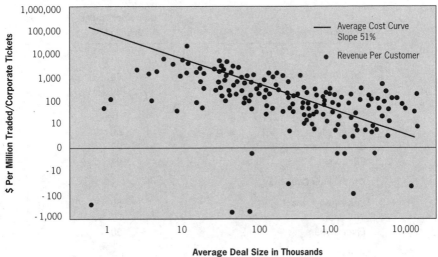

Average Deal Size in Thousands

spread in dealing with its larger customers. As in the case illustrated in figure 6.2, the percentage retained in each instrument was shown to vary directly with the institution's relative position in that instrument.

Of course, the largest institutional customers sometimes hold market power comparable to that of the major dealers. Those customers, while providing essential information flows, often "play the markets" themselves and know how to take advantage of the dealers' willingness to provide market liquidity. With such customers, dealers can rarely price to gain full compensation for that service.

The key to a profitable customer business, then, is to concentrate on those customer segments in which one holds (or can build) some type of comparative advantage. For this reason, the appropriate market focus will differ for every sales force. The largest dealers typically do well with the large institutional investors who use them selectively as first-tier suppliers of securities, and whose main concerns are product depth and a knowledgable sales force. Regional dealers or banks generally have a competitive advantage with smaller institutional investors in their region—and that business, we have observed, can be very profitable.

It is also often argued that by making markets (by standing ready to quote prices continuously to customers), dealers often end up with unwanted positions that must be unwound at a net loss over time. The resulting losses, it is

TABLE 6.1

Percentage of Bid-Offer Spread Retained

Products	Customer Trades Over $1 MM
Bills	
On-the-run	94
Off-the-run	100
Active Coupons	
2, 3, 4 years	56
5, 7, 10 years	92
20, 30 years	94
Off-the-Run Coupons	
Less than 1 year	59
1–5 years	73
Over 5 years	100
Agencies	
Less than 5 years	91
Over 5 years	88

further argued, tend to offset much if not all of the other revenue from customer business.

By tracking traders' positions, however, we have demonstrated over and over again that, except in rare periods of large price movements, this argument is fundamentally groundless. Inventories, to be sure, must often be maintained in illiquid markets to allow efficient sale of securities to customers. And although such inventories are subject to the ups and downs of the markets, the resulting exposure from taking such long positions should be viewed as simply one of the costs of functioning as a market-maker—a cost that when properly managed, as our own work repeatedly bears out, is far outweighed by the value of a strong customer franchise.

Even in liquid markets, moreover, it is clear that customer flows determine the ability to generate consistent trading profits. The more continuous the flow of customer orders, the less positioning risk any given trader is forced to bear, thus allowing him or her to function strictly as a broker. For example, in an analysis of a client that deals in the U.K. equity market, we found that its trading in stocks with high customer-volume ratios produced consistently higher profits than stocks with smaller customer order flows. Further supporting

FIGURE 6.4

Forex Trading Profits: Large U.S. and European Foreign Exchange Banks, 1988

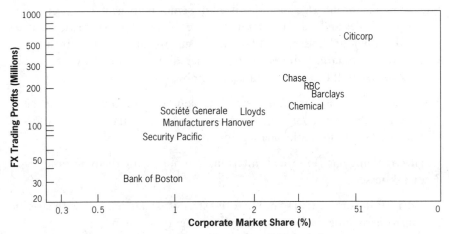

Sources: Annual Reports, Bernstein Research, Euromoney, OWC Analysis

evidence comes from our observation (illustrated in fig. 6.4) that the overall foreign exchange trading profits of some of the major banks around the world are strongly correlated with the degree of their penetration of the *customer* side of their markets.

For most trading rooms, then, sales are and will remain the principal source of consistent and stable revenue and profits. For many operations, "trading" and "trading and sales" are misnomers. The business should really be called "sales and trading," because much of what are called "trading" profits are really the result of a good customer base and the resulting flow of orders and information.

With advances in technology and increasing customer sophistication, margins in the business have narrowed; and today there are more salespeople than the industry can profitably employ. But, in our view, the current problem of oversupply (and hence excess costs) will not reduce the value of sales in the trading environment. Customer business will simply have to be executed in a cheaper and more efficient fashion in the future.

Conclusion

The above insights have major implications for managing the vast majority of trading desks, including those who erroneously believe they can trade head to head with the Salomons of this world.

First, sales (and not speculative trading) is the only reliable source of stable revenues for most trading rooms. The "trading" strategy should be subordinated to the "sales" strategy and speculative positioning should be kept to the strict minimum necessary to be credible and to operate. This, of course, implies a low-risk profile that should suit many senior managements.

Second, sales and trading are much more than an opportunistic business driven by individual traders' skills at outguessing the market. It is a business in which profits are largely driven by fundamental competitive advantage. The business lends itself to strategic management by:

- Understanding and monitoring the real sources of revenue—in essence opening the "black box" and creating a meaningful management information system for senior management;

- Recognizing one's existing limitations and not letting them become weaknesses;

- Identifying one's existing or potential strengths (particularly with specific customer segments) and focusing one's energy on them.

The third major implication is that positioning (and market arbitrage) should be pursued as a goal in itself only by the very few competitors that, through market power or sophisticated, proprietary computer systems, can price, evaluate risk, or set trends in a manner that most others cannot.

ALBÉRIC BRAAS AND CHARLES N. BRALVER are both senior as well as founding partners of Oliver, Wyman & Co., a strategic management consulting firm specializing in financial services. Mr. Braas is based in New York while Mr. Bralver is Managing Director of the firm's London office. Over the past several years, they have conducted numerous sales and trading analyses and assisted in the development of strategies for the trading floors of some of the largest financial institutions as well as regional dealers in North America, Europe, and the Far East.

CHAPTER 7

Theory of Risk Capital in Financial Firms

ROBERT C. MERTON AND ANDRÉ F. PEROLD

THIS CHAPTER DEVELOPS a concept of risk capital that can be applied to the financing, capital budgeting, and risk management decisions of financial firms. The development focuses particularly on firms that act as a *principal* in the ordinary course of business. Principal activities can be asset related, as in the case of lending and block positioning; liability related, as in deposit-taking and writing of guarantees (including insurance, letters of credit, and other contingent commitments); or both, as in the writing of swaps and other derivatives for customers.

For the purposes of this chapter, principal financial firms have three important distinguishing features. The first is that their customers can be major liabilityholders; for example, policyholders, depositors, and swap counterparties are all liabilityholders as well as customers. By definition, a financial firm's customers strictly prefer to have the payoffs on their contracts as unaffected as possible by the fortunes of the issuing firm. Hence, they strongly prefer firms of high credit quality. Investors, by contrast, expect their returns to be affected by the profits and losses of the firm. Hence, they are less credit sensitive provided, of course, they are compensated appropriately for risk. This means that A-rated firms, for example, can generally raise the funds they need to operate, but are at a disadvantage in competing with AAA-rated firms in businesses such as underwriting insurance or issuing swaps. The presence of credit-sensitive customers thus greatly increases the importance of risk control of the overall balance sheet.[1]

This chapter was previously published as an article in *Journal of Applied Corporate Finance* Vol. 6, No. 3 (Fall 1993): 16–32. An earlier version appeared as "Management of Risk Capital in Financial Firms," in Samuel L. Hayes III, ed., *Financial Services: Perspectives and Challenges* (Boston: Harvard Business School Press, 1993), 215–45.

1. For an elaboration on the difference between "customers" and "investors" of the financial-service firm as a core concept, see Robert C. Merton, *Continuous-Time Finance*, rev. ed. (Oxford: Basil

A second distinguishing feature of principal firms is their opaqueness to customers and investors.[2] That is, the detailed asset holdings and business activities of the firm are not publicly disclosed (or, if disclosed, only with a considerable lag in time). Furthermore, principal financial firms typically have relatively liquid balance sheets that, in the course of only weeks, can and often do undergo a substantial change in size and risk.[3] Unlike manufacturing firms, principal financial firms can enter, exit, expand, or contract individual businesses quickly at relatively low cost. These are changes that customers and investors cannot easily monitor. Moreover, financial businesses—even non-principal businesses like mutual fund management—are susceptible to potentially enormous "event risk" in areas not easily predictable or understood by outsiders.[4]

All of this implies that principal firms will generally experience high "agency" and "information" costs in raising equity capital and in executing various types of customer transactions.[5] (We later refer to these "dissipative" or "deadweight" costs collectively as *economic costs of risk capital*, in a manner to be made more precise.) Risk management by the firm is an important element in controlling these costs.

A third distinguishing feature of principal financial firms is that they operate in competitive financial markets. Their profitability is thus highly sensitive to their cost of capital, and especially their cost of risk capital. Allocating the costs of risk capital to individual businesses or projects is a problem for organizations that operate in a more or less decentralized fashion. As we shall discuss, there is no simple way to do so. Moreover, any allocation must necessarily be *imputed*, if only because highly risky principal transactions often require little or no up-front expenditure of cash.

Blackwell, 1992); R.C. Merton, "Operation and Regulation in Financial Intermediation: A Functional Perspective," in Peter England, ed., *Operation and Regulation of Financial Markets* (Stockholm: The Economic Council, 1993), 17–67; and R.C. Merton and Zvi Bodie, "On the Management of Financial Guarantees," *Financial Management* Vol. 21 (Winter 1992): 87–109.

2. The notion of "opaqueness" of financial institutions is developed by Stephen Ross in "Institutional Markets, Financial Marketing, and Financial Innovation," *Journal of Finance* Vol. 44 (July 1989): 541–56. For further discussion, see Merton, "Operation and Regulation."

3. As reported in *The Wall Street Journal*, October 24, 1991, the investment bank of Salomon Brothers reduced its total assets or "footings" by $50 billion in a period of approximately 40 days.

4. For example, consider the potentially large exposures from the "scandals" at E.F. Hutton (check writing), Merrill Lynch ("ticket in drawer"), Salomon Brothers (Treasury auction), Drexel Burnham Lambert (Financial Institutions Reform Recovery and Enforcement Act or FIRREA/collapse of high-yield debt market), and T. Rowe Price Associates (money-market-fund credit loss).

5. For detailed development and review of the literature on asymmetric information and agency theory in a financial market context, see Amir Barnea, Robert Haugen, and Lemma Senbet, *Agency Problems and Financial Contracting* (Englewood Cliffs, NJ: Prentice Hall, 1985); Michael Jensen, "Agency Costs of Free Cash Flow, Corporate Finance, and Takeovers," *American Economic Review* Vol. 76 (May 1986): 323–29; and especially N. Strong and M. Walker, *Information and Capital Markets* (Oxford: Basil Blackwell, 1987).

For example, an underwriting commitment can be executed with no immediate cash expenditure. However, the customer counterparty would not enter into the agreement if it did not believe that the underwriting commitment would be met. The commitment made by the underwriting business is backed by the entire firm. Therefore, the strength of this guarantee is measured by the overall credit standing of the firm. The problem of capital allocation within the firm is thus effectively the problem of correctly charging for the guarantees provided by the firm to its constituent businesses.

These three distinctive features of principal financial firms—credit sensitivity of customers, high costs of risk capital (resulting from their opaqueness), and high sensitivity of profitability to the cost of risk capital—should all be taken into account explicitly by such firms when deciding which activities to enter (or exit), how to finance those activities, and whether to hedge its various market or price exposures.

What Is Risk Capital?

We define *risk capital* as *the smallest amount that can be invested to insure the value of the firm's net assets against a loss in value relative to the risk-free investment of those net assets*. By *net assets*, we mean gross assets minus customer liabilities (valued as if these liabilities are default free). Customer liabilities can be simple fixed liabilities such as guaranteed insurance contracts (GICs), or complex contingent liabilities such as property and casualty insurance policies. With fixed customer liabilities, the riskiness of net assets (as measured, e.g., by the standard deviation of their change in value) is the same as the riskiness of gross assets. With contingent customer liabilities, however, the riskiness of net assets depends not only on the riskiness of gross assets, but also on the riskiness of customer liabilities and the covariance between changes in the value of gross assets and changes in the value of customer liabilities. The volatility of the change in the value of net assets is the most important determinant of the amount of risk capital.

As defined, risk capital differs from both *regulatory capital*, which attempts to measure risk capital according to a particular accounting standard, and from *cash capital*, which represents the up-front cash required to execute a transaction. Cash capital is a component of *working capital* that includes financing of operating expenses like salaries and rent. Cash capital can be large, as with the purchase of physical securities—or small, as with futures contracts and repurchase agreements—or even negative, as with the writing of insurance.

The organization of the chapter is as follows. In the next section, a series of examples is presented to show that the amount of risk capital depends only on the riskiness of net assets, and not at all on the form of financing of the net assets. These examples further establish how risk capital funds, provided mainly by the firm's shareholders (except in the case of extremely highly leveraged firms), are then either implicitly or explicitly used to purchase asset insurance from various sources. Besides third-party guarantors, other potential issuers of asset insurance to the firm are the firm's stakeholders, including customers, debtholders, and shareholders.

We next discuss how standard methods of accounting can fail to measure risk capital and its associated costs correctly in the calculation of firm profitability, and how this can lead to an overstatement of profitability. The economic costs of risk capital to the firm are shown to be the "spreads" on the price of asset insurance arising from information costs (adverse selection and moral hazard) and agency costs. We then use this framework to establish the implications for hedging and risk management decisions.

Finally, for multi-business firms, we discuss the problems that arise in trying to allocate the risk capital of the firm among its individual businesses. It is shown that, for a given configuration, the risk capital of a multibusiness firm is less than the aggregate risk capital of the businesses on a stand-alone basis. Therefore, full allocation of risk capital across the individual businesses of the firm is generally not feasible, and attempts at such a full allocation can significantly distort the true profitability of individual businesses.

Measuring Risk Capital

We now use a series of hypothetical but concrete examples to illustrate the concept of risk capital. In the first set of examples, there are no customer liabilities, so that gross assets equal net assets. After that, we consider two cases with customer liabilities, one with fixed liabilities and the other with contingent liabilities.

Consider the hypothetical newly formed firm of Merchant Bank, Inc., a wholly owned subsidiary of a large AAAA-rated[6] conglomerate. The firm currently has no assets. Merchant Bank's one and only deal this year will be a $100 million participation in a 1-year bridge loan promising 20% interest ($120 million total payment at maturity). It does not plan to issue any customer liabilities. Merchant Bank's net assets will thus consist of this single bridge loan.

The bridge loan is a risky asset. We assume in particular that there are only three possible scenarios: A likely "anticipated" scenario, in which the loan pays off in full the promised $120 million; an unlikely "disaster" scenario, in

---

6. By "AAAA-rated," we mean a firm with default-free liabilities that without question will stay that way.

which the borrower defaults but at maturity the lender recovers 50 cents on the dollar—that is, collects $60 million; and a rare "catastrophe" scenario, in which the lender recovers nothing.

To invest in the bridge loan requires $100 million of *cash* capital. Because this asset is risky, the firm also needs risk capital.

Merchant Bank wants to finance the cash capital by means of a 1-year note issued to an outside investor. The firm wants the note to be default free. If these terms can be arranged, then at the current riskless rate of 10%, $110 million would be owed the noteholder at maturity.

In general, a firm has essentially two ways to eliminate the default risk of its debt liabilities. Both involve the purchase of insurance: The first is to do so indirectly through the purchase of insurance on its *assets*; the second and more direct method is to purchase insurance on its (debt) liabilities. (Combinations of these would also work.) As we shall see, the two are economically equivalent. The risk capital of the firm is equal to the smallest investment that can be made to obtain complete default-free financing of its net assets.

Risk Capital and Asset Guarantees

Suppose that Merchant Bank buys insurance on the bridge loan from a AAAA-rated bond insurer. Suppose further that, for $5 million, Merchant Bank can obtain insurance just sufficient to guarantee a return of $110 million on the bridge loan.[7] With this asset insurance in place, the value of Merchant Bank's assets at the end of the year will equal or exceed $110 million. The noteholders of Merchant Bank are thus assured of receiving the full payment of their interest and principal, and the note will be default free.

It follows from the definition of risk capital that the price of the loan insurance ($5 million) is precisely the amount of risk capital Merchant Bank requires if it holds the bridge loan. Merchant Bank would need to fund it with a $5 million cash equity investment from its parent. Once these transactions have been completed, Merchant Bank's accounting balance sheet will be as shown in table 7.1.

If the bridge loan pays off as promised at the end of the year, Merchant Bank will be able to return a total of $10 million pre-tax to its parent ($20 million in interest income less $10 million in interest expense). If the bridge loan defaults, the asset insurance covers any shortfall up to $110 million, and Merchant Bank will just be able to meet its note obligations. There will be nothing to return to the parent. The risk capital used to purchase the insurance will have been just sufficient to protect the firm from any loss on the underlying

---

7. That is, *full insurance*. The insurance would take the form of paying Merchant Bank the difference between the promised debt payments and actually received cash flows on the bridge loan.

TABLE 7.1

Accounting Balance Sheet A

Bridge loan	$100	Note (default free)	$100
Loan insurance	5	Shareholder equity	5
(from insurance company)			

TABLE 7.2

Payoff Structure A

Bridge Loan	Loan Insurance	Bridge Loan + Insurance	Firm Stakeholders	
			Note	Shareholder
Anticipated scenario				
120	0	120	110	10
Disaster scenario				
60	50	110	110	0
Catastrophe scenario				
0	110	110	110	0

Note that, in this example, Merchant Bank's accounting balance sheet corresponds to what we shall call the firm's *risk-capital balance sheet*:

TABLE 7.3

Risk Capital Balance Sheet A

Bridge loan	$100	Note (default free)	$100
Loan insurance	5	Risk capital	5
(from insurance company)			

asset (including financing expense of the cash capital). And, of course, the risk capital itself will have been lost. In this arrangement, the insurance company bears the risk of the asset; Merchant Bank's parent as shareholder bears the risk of loss of the risk capital itself.

The payoffs (cash flows) at maturity to the various stakeholders in Merchant Bank is summarized in table 7.2.

TABLE 7.4

Accounting Balance Sheet B

Bridge loan	$100	Note (default free)	$100
		Shareholder equity	0

Note that, in this example, Merchant Bank's accounting balance sheet (table 7.3) corresponds to what we shall call the firm's *risk-capital balance sheet*.

By inspection of the two balance sheets, "shareholder equity" is equal to the firm's risk capital, and the non-equity liabilities are default free. We shall see, however, that the accounting and risk-capital balance sheets are in general quite different.

Risk Capital and Liability Guarantees

A parent guarantee of the note is an alternative, and perhaps the most common, form of credit enhancement for the debt of a subsidiary such as Merchant Bank.[8] This way, the parent makes no cash equity investment in Merchant Bank. At the outset, the firm's accounting balance sheet is shown in table 7.4.

Here Merchant Bank again obtains the necessary $100 million in cash capital through issuance of a default-free note; however, all asset risk is now borne by the parent. Thus the risk capital is merely taking the form of the parent guarantee of the note. This guarantee is an additional asset of the subsidiary—one that does not appear on its balance sheet. Suppose that the value of this guarantee is worth $G million. Then the parent's (off-balance-sheet) equity investment in Merchant Bank is worth $G million, and Merchant Bank's balance sheet can be restated in terms of its risk-capital balance sheet as shown in table 7.5.[9]

8. This insurance could take the form of the parent either paying the noteholder the $110 million promised payment in the event of default, and then seizing Merchant Bank's assets, or paying the noteholder the difference between the promised payment and actual payments Merchant Bank is able to make. The parent guarantee avoids outside lenders becoming involved in any bankruptcy of the subsidiary, and gives the parent some "choice." For our purposes here, we can abstract from such details of structure.

9. For a real-world application of this "extended" balance-sheet approach to capture the "hidden" asset and corresponding equity investment arising from parent guarantees of its subsidiary's debt, see R.C. Merton, "Prepared Direct Testimony of Robert C. Merton on Behalf of ARCO Pipe Line Company," Federal Energy Regulatory Commission, Washington, D.C., Docket No. OR78-1-011 (Phase II), Exhibits II N-C-34-0-34-4 (November 28, 1983). For a similar approach to analyze corporate pension assets and liabilities and the firm's guarantee of any shortfall on the pension plan, see Zvi Bodie, "The ABO, the PBO, and Pension Investment Policy," *Financial Analysts Journal* Vol. 46 (September–October 1990): 27–34.

TABLE 7.5

Risk-Capital Balance Sheet B

Bridge loan	$100	Note (default free)	$100
Note guarantee	G	Risk capital	G
(from parent)			

TABLE 7.6

Payoff Structure B

Bridge Loan	Note Sans Guarantee	Note Guarantee	Note + Guarantee	Shareholder
Anticipated scenario				
120	110	0	110	10
Disaster scenario				
60	60	50	110	0
Catastrophe scenario				
0	0	110	110	0

As in the previous example, if the bridge loan pays off as promised, Merchant Bank will be able to return a total of $10 million pre-tax to its parent ($20 million in interest income less $10 million in interest expense). If the bridge loan defaults, so too will Merchant Bank on its note, and the noteholder either collects any unpaid amounts from the parent, or the parent pays out the promised $110 million and receives back the value of the bridge-loan asset seized; either way the economic effect is the same. Merchant Bank of course will have nothing to return to its parent as equityholder. In this arrangement, the parent bears the risk of the asset as guarantor of its subsidiary's debt; the parent also bears the risk of loss of the risk capital as shareholder of Merchant Bank. Table 7.6 summarizes in terms of payoffs at maturity.

A comparison of table 7.2 and table 7.6 demonstrates the economic equivalence of liability insurance and asset insurance.[10] In both, the noteholder bears

10. This equivalence may not apply exactly if one takes account of the various bankruptcy costs and delays in payments which could occur, for example, if Merchant Bank sought Chapter 11 bankruptcy protection.

TABLE 7.7

Accounting Balance Sheet C

Bridge loan	$100	Note (risky)	$100 – D
		Shareholder equity	D

no risk and the parent, solely in its capacity as shareholder of Merchant Bank, obtains the same cash flows: $10 million in the "anticipated" scenario and zero otherwise. Moreover, the note guarantee has the same cash flows as the bridge-loan insurance. The note guarantee therefore is also worth G = $5 million. Thus, risk capital is once again $5 million.[11]

Liabilities with Default Risk

We now turn to the more typical case where our hypothetical firm, Merchant Bank, is willing to issue liabilities with some default risk. Suppose it issues the same 10% note (promising $110 million at maturity), but without any of the credit enhancements of the previous case. This now-risky note will sell at a discount $D to par (at a promised yield to maturity higher than 10%), leaving Merchant Bank $D short of its need for $100 million cash capital. The shortfall in initial funding must be supplied in the form of a cash equity investment. Merchant Bank's beginning balance sheet is shown in table 7.7.

Once again, if the bridge loan pays off as promised, Merchant Bank will be able to pay a total of $10 million pre-tax to its parent.[12] If the bridge loan defaults, so too will Merchant Bank default on its note, and the noteholder will be at risk for any shortfall on the bridge loan under $110 million. Merchant Bank will have nothing to return to its parent.

Merchant Bank's shareholder here receives the same payoffs as it did in the previous examples. This economic equivalence implies that the firm's equity must be worth D = $5 million initially. Correspondingly, the risky note will have an initial value of $95 million (with a *promised* yield to maturity of $15 on $95, or 15.8%).

To see where risk capital enters, consider the position of the debtholder. The debtholder can interpret its purchase of the risky note as equivalent to the following three-step transaction: First, the purchase of default-free debt

11. The assumption that economically equivalent cash flows have the same value is made only for expositional convenience in this part of the chapter. Later in the discussion of the management of risk capital, the assumption is relaxed to take account of differences in information and agency costs among alternative guarantors.
12. $20 million in interest income less $15 million in cash plus amortized interest expense plus $5 million return of capital.

TABLE 7.8

Risk-Capital Balance Sheet C

Bridge loan	$100	Note (default free)	$100
Asset insurance	5	Risk capital	5
(from note holder)			

TABLE 7.9

Payoff Structure C

Bridge Loan	Asset Insurance	Default-free Note	Risky Note= Default-free Note–Asset Insurance	Shareholder
Anticipated scenario				
120	110	0	110	10
Disaster scenario				
60	50	110	60	0
Catastrophe scenario				
0	110	110	0	0

from Merchant Bank for $100 million; second, the sale to Merchant Bank of debt insurance for $5 million; and third, the netting of payments owed the debtholder on the default-free debt against payments owed the firm if the insurance is triggered. It is perhaps easiest to see this by observing the economic identity:[13]

$$\text{Risky note} + \text{note insurance} = \text{Default-free note}$$

so that:

$$\text{Risky note} = \text{Default-free note} - \text{note insurance}.$$

As already shown (see tables 7.2 and 7.6), note insurance is economically equivalent to asset insurance. Thus, the debtholder can interpret its purchase of the risky note as equivalent to the purchase of default-free debt coupled with

13. For a full development and applications of this identity, see R.C. Merton, "The Financial System and Economic Performance," *Journal of Financial Services Research* Vol. 4 (December 1990): 263–300; and Merton and Bodie, "On the Management."

the *sale* to Merchant Bank of *asset* insurance (on the bridge loan) for $5 million. In other words:

Risky note = Default-free note – asset insurance.

This relation allows the restatement of the accounting balance sheet (see table 7.8) in its risk-capital form. The payoffs at maturity associated with this risk-capital balance sheet are shown in table 7.9.

Each of the examples (A, B, C) has a different accounting balance sheet. Yet all have very similar risk-capital balance sheets. They have the same amount of risk capital—because the underlying asset requiring the risk capital is the same in all cases. They differ only in which parties bear the risk of insuring the asset: the insurance company (example A), the parent (example B), or the noteholder (example C).

A More General Case

The concept of risk capital is now further expanded by analyzing a more general balance sheet. The goals here are to illustrate the case of fixed customer liabilities and the purchase of asset insurance from multiple sources.

Consider a firm with an investment portfolio of risky assets worth $2.5 billion. The firm has customer liabilities outstanding in the form of 1-year guaranteed investment contracts (GICs) promising 10% on their face value of $1 billion. Because the riskless rate is also 10%, the *default-free* value of these customer liabilities is $1 billion. The net assets—equal to assets minus the default-free value of customer liabilities—are thus worth $1.5 billion.

The riskiness of the portfolio is assumed to be such that the price of insurance to permit the portfolio to be financed risklessly for a year is $500 million. Since the customer liabilities are fixed, it follows that the price of insurance to permit the *net* assets to be financed risklessly for a year is also $500 million.[14] Therefore, $500 million is the required risk capital based on a 1-year horizon.

The firm's investor financings are in two forms: 1-year junior debt promising 10% on its face value of $1 billion and shareholder equity. Thus, the total promised payment on fixed liabilities at the end of the year is $2.2 billion, comprised of $1.1 billion of GICs and $1.1 billion of debt that is junior to the GICs.

---

14. By the end of the year, the gross assets will have experienced a loss relative to a risk-free investment if they fall below $2,750 million (110% of $2,500 million). The *net* assets will have experienced a loss relative to a risk-free investment if they fall below $1,650 million (110% of $1,500 million). Since year-end net assets always equals year-end gross assets minus $1,100 million, any shortfall in year-end *gross* assets is exactly equal to the shortfall in year-end *net* assets, and vice versa. Therefore, the loss to the insurer of gross assets is identical to the loss to the insurer of net assets, and the prices of the two policies are the same.

FIGURE 7.1

Payoffs to a Firm's Capital Providers

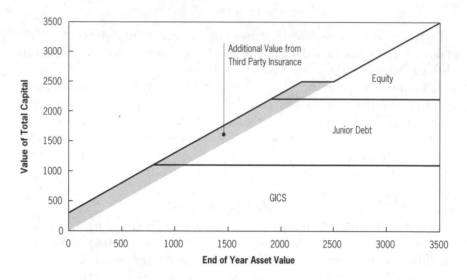

Suppose that the firm has formally obtained *partial* insurance on its investment portfolio, arbitrarily chosen to cover the *first* $300 million of decline of value of portfolio value below $2.5 billion. The insurance is thus structured to guarantee the portfolio value at $2.5 billion at year end, but is capped at a maximum payout of $300 million; therefore, the cap will be reached if the portfolio value falls below $2.2 billion. Assume, moreover, that the value of this "third-party" insurance is $200 million. The value of the policy appears as an additional asset on the firm's accounting balance sheet.

Figure 7.1 shows the payoffs on the various liabilities of the firm depending on the value of the investment portfolio at year end. Because the portfolio is only partially protected from loss by the firm-owned insurance policy, the junior debt and the customer liabilities are both potentially at risk to receive less than their promised payments.

As the senior liability, the GICs are most protected against a decline in the firm's asset values. As shown in figure 7.1, customers holding the GICs are at risk only if the value of the firm's portfolio has fallen below $800 million at year end, a decline in value of more than 68%. Accordingly, the GICs trade at only a small percentage discount to par. In our example, we assume that this discount is 1%, thus implying a price of $990 million and a promised yield to maturity of 11% ($110 on $990).

TABLE 7.10

Accounting Balance Sheet D

Investment portfolio	$2,500	GICs (par $1,000)	$990
"Third-party" insurance	200	Debt (par $1,000)	900
(insurance company)		Equity	810
Total assets	2,700	Total liabilities	2,700

The junior debt is considerably riskier: the holders are exposed to loss if the value of the firm's portfolio falls below $1.9 billion by year end, a decline of about 24%. This debt therefore will trade at a larger discount to par. In our example, we assume that the discount is 10% for a price of $900 million, with a promised yield to maturity of 22.2% ($200 on $900). The value of the firm's equity is equal to $810 million, the difference between the value of total assets ($2.7 billion) and the market value of customer- and investor-held liabilities ($990 million + 900 million). The accounting balance sheet (valuing assets and liabilities at market) is shown in table 7.10.

We now construct the risk-capital balance sheet for this firm. As in our earlier discussion of liabilities with default risk, the economic interpretation of the GIC holders is that, in effect, they have purchased default-free GICs and simultaneously *sold* some asset insurance to the firm, with the two transactions netted against each other. GIC holders are at risk only in the least likely of circumstances, and so they provide a kind of "catastrophe" insurance. As shown in figures 7.1 and 7.2, the catastrophe insurance pays off only if the portfolio value falls by more than 68%. The (implicit) price of this insurance is the discount from the default-free value of the GICs, or $10 million ($1 billion–$990 million). Similarly, the debtholders' position is as if they purchased default-free debt and simultaneously sold to the firm asset insurance with a value of $100 million ($1 billion–900 million). This insurance pays off if the firm's portfolio falls below $1.9 billion, but the maximum payoff is capped at $1.1 billion. The risk to the debtholders is greater than the risk to the GIC holders, but is still relatively small. As illustrated in figure 7.2, it is a kind of "disaster" insurance.

We have so far accounted for total premiums of $310 million for asset insurance: third-party ($200 million) + debtholders ($100 million) + GICs ($10 million). But we know that it takes $500 million in premiums to insure the portfolio fully. Hence, the balance of the insurance representing $190 million in premiums must effectively be provided by the equity-holders. Because this insurance covers all the risks not covered by the other kinds of insurance, we

FIGURE 7.2

Components of Asset Insurance

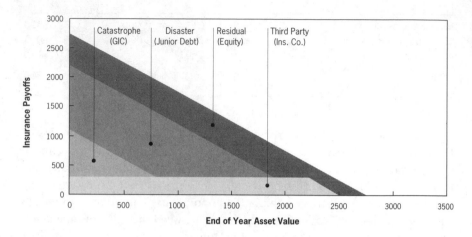

call it "residual" insurance. (figure 7.2 shows the combination of all sources of asset insurance.)

The total insurance has the same payoff structure as a *put option* on the portfolio with an exercise price equal to the current value of the portfolio ($2.5 billion) plus one year of interest at the riskless rate ($250 million), or $2.75 billion. The aggregate value of this asset insurance, or "put option," is equal to $500 million—as assumed at the outset. This is the risk capital of the firm.[15]

---

15. An alternative interpretation of the coverage provided by the four sources of insurance is as follows: The equityholders fully insure the gross assets at a level of $2.75 billion by year end, but purchase reinsurance from the insurance company that insures the assets to a level of $2.5 billion by year end. The insurance company in turn purchases reinsurance from the debtholders that insures the gross assets to a level of $1.9 billion by year end. The debtholders then purchase reinsurance from the firm's GIC customers that insures the gross assets to a level of $1.1 billion by year end. Equivalently, this can be expressed in terms of *put options*: The equityholders sell to the firm, for $500 million, a put option on the gross assets with exercise price $2.75 billion. They in turn spend $310 million of the $500 million proceeds to buy a put option from the insurance company with exercise price $2.5 billion. The insurance company then spends $110 million to buy a put option from the debtholders with exercise price $1.9 billion. Finally, the debtholders spend $10 million to purchase a put option from the GIC customers with exercise price $1.1 billion. The equityholders, insurance company, and debtholders have thus each sold a put option on the gross assets at one exercise price, and purchased reinsurance in the form of a second put option at a lower exercise price. For the formal development of the correspondence between loan guarantees and put options, see R.C. Merton, "An Analytical Derivation of the Cost of Deposit Insurance and Loan Guarantees: An Application of Modern Option Pricing Theory," *Journal of Banking and Finance* Vol. 1 (June 1977): 3–11; see also Merton, *Continuous-Time Finance*; and Merton, "Operation and Regulation."

TABLE 7.11

Risk-Capital Balance Sheet D

Asset portfolio	$2,500	Cash capital (default free)	
		Customers (GICs)	$1,000
Asset insurance		Debtholders	1,000
Equityholders ("residual")	190	Equityholders	500
Insurance Co ("third-party")	200	Total cash capital	2,500
Debtholders ("disaster")	100		
Customers ("catastrophe")	10	Risk capital	
Total insurance	500	(Equityholders)	500
Total assets	3,000	Total capital	3,000

The equityholders can think of their $810 million investment as serving three functions: providing $500 million of default-free cash-capital financing (bringing the total cash capital to $2.5 billion), providing $500 million of risk capital to pay for asset insurance, and selling to the firm a portion of that asset insurance worth $190 million. The equityholders' net cash contribution is $500 plus $500 minus $190 million, which equals $810 million.

The risk-capital balance sheet of the firm is shown in table 7.11.

This balance sheet encapsulates three basic functions of capital providers. First, *all provide cash capital*. Second, *all are sellers of asset insurance* to the firm, although in varying degrees. Customers and other senior providers of cash capital are typically sellers of catastrophe-type insurance—the kind that is called upon to pay in only the rarest of instances. This level of exposure is typical because customers prefer to have their contract payoffs insensitive to the fortunes of the issuing firm. Customers will buy contracts from the firm only if they perceive the risk of default on those contracts to be very low. "Mezzanine" debtholders and equityholders are investors who provide cash capital and sell to the firm almost all the insurance not purchased from third-party providers.

The third function is the provision of risk capital, which is the cash required for the purchase of asset insurance. It is almost always performed by equityholders, as in all our illustrations. (Non-equity liabilityholders and other stakeholders in the firm will also be providers of risk capital if the market value of the underlying assets is less than the value of promised liabilities, capitalized at the riskless rate.)

A comparison of the risk-capital balance sheet with the accounting balance sheet thus illustrates that the debt and equity values of the firm need not, and generally will not, sum to the firm's cash capital; nor does the value of the equity necessarily equal the firm's risk capital. Cash capital is determined by the assets of the firm. Risk capital is determined by the riskiness of the net assets of the firm. Debt and equity, defined in the *institutional* sense, represent the netting of asset insurance against the provision of riskless cash capital and risk capital.

Contingent Customer Liabilities

As mentioned earlier, with contingent customer liabilities, the riskiness of net assets will in general differ from the riskiness of gross assets. The following example illustrates this difference.[16]

Consider again a principal financial firm with no equity, but with liabilities fully guaranteed by an AAAA parent. Suppose the firm issues a contingent liability in the form of a 1-year Standard and Poor's (S&P) 500 index-linked note that promises to pay $100 million times the total return per dollar on the S&P index over the year. The purchaser of the note is a customer, say, a pension fund, that wants the return on its $100 million portfolio to match exactly that of the S&P 500 stock index. The customer has chosen this method of investing as an alternative to investing in an S&P 500 index fund. At the instant the transaction is consummated, the firm's accounting balance sheet is shown in table 7.12.

How the firm chooses to invest the $100 million will determine its risk capital. For instance, the firm might invest in 1-year U.S. Treasury bills paying 10%. If it does so, the *gross* assets are riskless, but the *net* assets are extremely risky. In fact, the net assets are equivalent to a short position in the S&P 500.[17] By year end, the parent as guarantor will have to make up a shortfall that is equal to the total return on $100 million worth of the S&P 500 minus $10 million, the return on U.S. Treasury bills, if this amount is positive. This shortfall payment is the same payoff as that promised by a European call option on $100 million worth of the S&P 500 with a strike price of $110 million.[18,19] The risk capital of the firm—the smallest amount that can be invested to insure the value of its net assets—is thus equal to the value of this call option.

As an alternative to U.S. Treasury bills, the firm might invest in the actual portfolio of stocks comprising the S&P 500. Assume it can do so costlessly. In this case, the *gross* assets are risky, but they exactly match the liabilities, so that

---

16. For an illustration of this point in the case of gross and net assets of a corporate pension plan, see Bodie, "ABO, the PBO, and Pension Investment Policy."
17. Assuming the firm receives full use of the proceeds of the short sale.
18. The option must be protected from dividend payouts.
19. We saw previously that the purchase of insurance was economically equivalent to the purchase of a put option on the net assets. That is also the case here since a European call option on the S&P 500 is equivalent to a European put option on a *short* position in the S&P 500, that is, a put option on the net assets.

TABLE 7.12

Accounting Balance Sheet E

Cash	$100	Index-linked note	$100
		Shareholder equity	0

the *net* assets are *riskless. When the assets are invested this way, the firm's risk capital is zero.*

As another alternative, the firm might invest in a customized portfolio of stocks that tracks fairly closely the S&P 500, but that omits the companies that the firm believes will underperform the S&P 500 index. In this case, the riskiness of the net assets is determined by the potential deviations in performance between the customized portfolio and the index. The risk capital of the firm will equal the value of a guarantee that pays the amount by which the customized portfolio underperforms the index, if it does so at all.[20]

These examples illustrate how the riskiness of the net assets can be significantly less than or greater than the riskiness of the gross assets. They also show that it is the riskiness of *net* assets that determines the type of insurance required to permit default-free financing for the firm, and hence it is the riskiness of net assets that determines the amount of the firm's risk capital.

Accounting for Risk Capital in the Calculation of Profits

As discussed above, risk capital is implicitly or explicitly used to purchase insurance on the net assets of the firm from a variety of potential providers. Insurance is a financial asset, and the gains or losses on this asset should be included along with the gains or losses on all other assets in the calculation of profitability. Standard methods of accounting often fail to do this, however. For example, as discussed earlier, when a parent guarantees the performance of a subsidiary, the guarantee is not usually accounted for as an asset on the balance sheet of the subsidiary.

To illustrate, consider a securities underwriting subsidiary of a principal financial firm. The subsidiary anticipates deriving $50 million in revenues from underwriting spreads over the next year. It anticipates customary expenses of

20. Thus, the value of *perfect* stock-selection skills equals the value of the risk capital of the portfolio since *with such skills*, the portfolio *never* underperforms the index and its risk capital is thus reduced to zero. For a theory that equates the value of market timing to the value of a portfolio guarantee, see R.C. Merton, "On Market Timing and Investment Performance Part I: An Equilibrium Theory of Value for Market Forecasts," *Journal of Business* Vol. 54 (July 1981): 363–406.

TABLE 7.13

Accounting Balance Sheet F

Net working capital	$10	Shareholder equity	10

TABLE 7.14

Accounting Income Statement F

Revenues (underwriting spreads)	$50
Customary expenses	(30)
Profit before tax	20
Pre-tax ROE	200%

$30 million, so that its profit before tax is anticipated to be $20 million. (This profit figure assumes no mishaps such as occurred, for example, in the underwriting of British Petroleum shares in 1986.[21]) The subsidiary has an ongoing net working capital requirement of $10 million. It has no other formal assets or liabilities and so its equity capital is $10 million.

Thus, the subsidiary's pre-tax return on equity (ROE) is anticipated to be 200% for the year, and its accounting balance sheet and income statement are shown in tables 7.13 and 7.14, respectively.

This accounting analysis, however, ignores risk capital, which in this case is the price of the insurance (implicitly provided by the parent) needed to ensure that the subsidiary can perform its underwriting commitments. Suppose such insurance would cost $15 million in premiums. Then the risk capital balance sheet of the subsidiary would include the insurance as an asset, and total shareholder equity would be $25 million, consisting of $10 million of cash capital and $15 million of risk capital (table 7.15).

After the fact, if the underwriting business performs as anticipated, the parent guarantee will not have been needed. Thus, the insurance that enabled the subsidiary to get the business in the first place will have expired worthless. As shown in table 7.16, including the cost of this insurance (which expired

21. In October 1987, prior to the stock market crash, the British government arranged to sell its $12.2 billion stake in British Petroleum to the public. The underwriting firms agreed to pay $65 per share, a full month before the offering would come to market. The shares fell to $53 post-crash. According to the *New York Times*, October 30, 1987, the four U.S. underwriters collectively stood to lose in excess of $500 million. A subsequent price guarantee from the Bank of England reduced these losses to an estimated $200 million after tax.

TABLE 7.15

Risk-Capital Balance Sheet F

Net working capital	$10	Cash capital	$10
Underwriting guarantee	15	Risk capital	15
(from parent)			
Total assets	25	Shareholder equity	25

TABLE 7.16

Anticipated Net Profit Including Risk Capital

Revenues (underwriting spreads)	$50
Customary expenses	(30)
Underwriting insurance	(15)
Profit before tax	5
Pre-tax ROE	20%

worthless) in the income statement results in an anticipated net profit of $5 million, or a pre-tax return of 20% on *economic* equity of $25 million.

The expensing of the $15 million cost of insurance shown in table 7.16 is standard accounting practice if the insurance is obtained from arms-length providers. The fact that the parent provides the insurance should not change the treatment. Thus, the proper internal accounting would book the $15 million insurance premium as an expense to the underwriting subsidiary, and as revenue to the parent in its role as guarantor. Correspondingly, any "claims" paid on the guarantee should be considered revenue to the sub and an expense to the parent.

Even though this treatment of revenue and expense does not affect consolidated accounting, it can materially affect the calculated profit rates of individual businesses within the firm. In particular, the omission of risk capital "expended" on insurance overstates profits when the underlying assets perform well (because the insurance expires worthless) and understates profits when the underlying assets perform poorly (because the insurance becomes valuable).

The Economic Cost of Risk Capital

Accounting for risk capital in the calculation of actual after-the-fact profits is important for reporting and other purposes, such as profit-related compensation. For the purposes of decision making *before the fact*, however, *expected* profits must be estimated. This requires estimation of the *expected* or *economic* cost of risk capital. Since risk capital is used to purchase insurance, and insurance is a financial asset, risk capital will not be costly in the economic sense if the insurance can be purchased at its "actuarially" fair market value. For example, the purchase of $100 worth of International Business Machines (IBM) stock is not costly in this sense if it can be purchased for $100.

Usually, however, transacting is not costless. Typically, a spread is paid over fair market value. These spread costs are "deadweight" losses to the firm. In terms of traditional use of "bid-ask" spread, the bid price from the firm's perspective is the fair value and the ask price is the amount the firm must actually pay for the insurance. The *economic cost* of risk capital to the firm is thus the spread it pays in the purchase of this insurance.

The reasons for such spreads in insurance contracts vary by type of risk coverage, but the largest component for the type discussed here generally relates to the insurer's need for protection against various forms of information risks and agency costs:

Adverse selection is the risk insurers face in not being able to distinguish "good" risks from "bad." Unable to discriminate perfectly, they limit amounts of coverage and set prices based on an intermediate quality of risk, and try to do so to profit enough from the good risks to offset losses incurred in the underpricing of bad risks.[22]

Moral hazard is the risk insurers face if they are not able to monitor the actions of the insured. Once covered, those insured have an incentive to increase their asset risk.

Agency costs are the dissipation of asset values through inefficiency or mismanagement. As residual claimants with few contractual controls over the actions of the firm, equityholders bear the brunt of these costs.

Because principal financial firms are typically opaque in their structure, insurers of such firms—capital providers included—are especially exposed to these information and agency risks. Spreads for providing asset insurance to these types of firms—and hence their economic cost of risk capital—will therefore be relatively higher than for more transparent institutions.

The cost of risk capital is likely to depend on the form in which the insurance is purchased. The spreads on each form of insurance are determined differently. For example, in an all-equity firm, the required asset insurance is "sold" to the firm by its shareholders. The cost of risk capital obtained in this way will tend to reflect high agency costs (given the extensive leeway afforded

---

22. For a general discussion of these risks and costs in the context of insurance contracts, see Karl H. Borch, *Economics of Insurance* (Amsterdam: North-Holland, 1990).

to management by this structure), but little in the way of moral-hazard costs since there is no benefit to management or the firm's shareholders from increasing risk for its own sake. Debt financing, on the other hand, can impose a discipline on management that reduces agency costs. But then moral-hazard spreads can be high, especially in highly leveraged firms in which debtholders perceive a strong incentive for management to "roll the dice." The task for management is to weigh the spread costs of the different sources of asset insurance to find the most *efficient* way of "spending" the firm's risk capital.

Managing the firm most efficiently does not necessarily imply obtaining the lowest cost of risk capital. Consider the case of signaling costs. Firms faced with high spread charges can try to obtain lower spreads by making themselves more transparent, signaling that they are "good" firms. For example, "good" firms can report on a mark-to-market basis knowing that the cost to "bad" firms of doing so would be prohibitive (they would be seized by creditors and/ or lose their customers). Transparency, however, can also impose costs of its own. For example, increasing transparency could lead to greater disclosure of proprietary strategies or self-imposed trading restraints that prevent it from taking advantage of short-lived windows of opportunity. Thus, the principal firm has to trade off between paying higher spread costs of risk capital for opaqueness and paying signaling costs and sacrificing potential competitive advantages to achieve transparency.

In calculating expected profitability for the overall firm, risk-capital costs should be expensed along with cash-capital costs. To illustrate, consider the example of balance sheet D (table 7.10) in which the firm required $2.5 billion of cash capital and $500 million of risk capital. Because the cash capital is riskless, its cost is the AAAA rate (a little less than the London interbank offered rate (LIBOR), assumed to be 10% per annum. Suppose that the spread or economic cost of one-year risk capital for this firm is $30 million.[23] That is, the fair value "bid price" of the insurance provided by risk capital is $470 million and the "ask price" is $500 million. The $30 million spread is thus 6% of the ask price. Then total economic capital costs for the firm will be as follows:

Cash capital costs:	$250	(10% of $2.5 billion)
Risk capital costs:	30	(6% of $500 million)

The rate paid for cash capital is the same for all firms, the riskless rate, here 10%. Risk capital costs could vary considerably among firms, and in a few special cases they could be negligible.[24]

23. For an explicit model of these spread costs, see Merton, "Operation and Regulation."
24. For example, an open-end mutual fund is highly transparent. Moreover, the liabilityholders are principally customers who can redeem shares daily. Enforced by the securities laws, the selection

This example differs importantly from the previous securities underwriting example (table 7.16). In table 7.16, we deducted the full "premium" expended on the purchase of insurance, while here we consider only that portion of the premium attributable to the spread or economic cost. The full insurance premium is deducted when the purpose of the analysis is to measure profits after the fact, or *ex post*. But when the purpose of the analysis is to measure the cost of capital *ex ante*, only the economic cost is deducted because, *ex ante*, insurance purchased free of spread costs at its actuarial fair value is just that—costless.

We next apply our concept of risk capital to two important areas of firm management.

Hedging and Risk Management

The implications of our framework for hedging and risk management decisions are straightforward. Exposures to broad market risk—such as stock market risk, interest rate risk, or foreign exchange risk—usually can be hedged with derivatives such as futures, forwards, swaps and options. By definition, hedging away these risk exposures reduces asset risk. Thus, hedging market exposure reduces the required amount of risk capital.

Firms that speculate on the direction of the market, and therefore maintain a market exposure, will require more risk capital. By purchasing put options to insure against these market risks, the firm can maintain its desired exposures with the least amount of risk capital.

If there were no spread costs for risk capital, larger amounts of risk capital would impose no additional costs on the firm. In this case, firms may well be indifferent to hedging or not.[25] But if there are spread costs, and if these costs depend on the amount of risk capital, then a reduction in risk capital from hedging will lead to lower costs of risk capital if the hedges can be acquired at relatively small spreads.[26] That will usually be the case with hedging instruments for broad market risks where significant informational advantages among market participants are unlikely.[27]

---

of assets matches the promised contingent payments on customer liabilities, as expressed in the fund's prospectus. Hence *net* assets are virtually riskless.

25. Except if it changes the transparency or opaqueness of the firm, as discussed previously.

26. Merton, "Operation and Regulation," provides a model of spread costs that produces this result.

27. For example, for an explanation of the very narrow observed spreads on stock-index futures relative to the spreads on individual stocks, see James F. Gammill and A.F. Perold, "The Changing Character of Stock Market Liquidity," *Journal of Portfolio Management* Vol. 15 (Spring 1989): 13–18.

Capital Allocation and Capital Budgeting

Financial firms frequently need to consider entering new businesses or getting out of existing businesses. The cost of risk capital can be a major influence on these decisions. As always, the marginal benefit must be traded off against the marginal cost. But to evaluate the net marginal benefit of a decision is difficult, because in principle it requires a comparison of total firm values under the alternatives being considered.

One simplifying assumption is that the incremental cost of risk capital is proportional to the incremental *amount* of risk capital. This might be reasonable, for example, if the decision does not lead to disclosures that materially change the degree of transparency or opaqueness of the firm. In this case, calculation of the economic cost of risk capital for a particular business is equivalent to the calculation of the risk capital applicable to that business.

Even if there are no economic costs of risk capital, calculation of the amount of risk capital of a particular business is still relevant. As discussed in example F (see tables 7.13 through 7.16 and discussion thereof), allocations of risk capital to individual businesses within the firm are necessary to calculate their after-the-fact profits. Such profit calculations can then serve, for example, as the basis for incentive compensation awards.

In general, the incremental risk capital of a particular business within the firm will differ from its risk capital determined on the basis of a stand-alone analysis. As we shall demonstrate, this results from a diversification effect that can dramatically reduce the firm's overall risk capital. The importance of this externality from risk sharing depends on the correlations among the profits of the firm's various businesses. Its presence means that a full allocation of all the risk capital of the firm to its constituent businesses is generally inappropriate.

We illustrate with an example of a firm with three distinct businesses. Table 7.17 shows the current gross assets, customer liabilities, net assets (investor capital), and 1-year risk-capital requirements of each business on a stand-alone basis.[28] The businesses all have the same amounts of gross assets, but different amounts of net assets because they have different amounts of customer liabilities. Business 1 requires substantial amounts of investor capital but relatively little stand-alone risk capital. Business 3 is the riskiest, requiring the most

---

28. Risk capital in this example is computed using the loan guarantee model in Merton, "Analytical Derivation," which is based on the Black-Scholes option-pricing model. Risk capital for this model will be roughly proportional to the standard deviation of profits. See the Technical Appendix for the precise calculations. For an extensive bibliography of more general models for valuing loan guarantees, see Merton, *Continuous-Time Finance*; and Merton and Bodie, "On the Management."

TABLE 7.17

($ Millions)

	Gross Assets	Customer Liabilities	Investor Capital	Stand-Alone Risk Capital
Business 1				
	$1,000	$500	$500	$150
Business 2				
	1,000	600	400	200
Business 3				
	1,000	700	300	250
Total				
	$3,000	$1,800	$1,200	$600

stand-alone risk capital; however, it has the least investor capital. Business 2 is fairly risky and requires a moderate amount of investor capital.

Table 7.18 shows how the profits of the three businesses are correlated. With a correlation coefficient of .5, the profit streams of business 1 and business 2 are fairly highly correlated. The profits of business 3, by contrast, are completely uncorrelated with those of businesses 1 and 2.

Because the businesses are not perfectly correlated with one another, there will be a diversification benefit: the risk of the portfolio of businesses will be less than the sum of the stand-alone risks of the businesses. Risk capital—the value of insurance on the portfolio of assets—will therefore mirror this effect, and the risk capital for the total firm will be less than the sum of the (stand-alone) risk capital necessary to support each of the three businesses. For example, based on the correlations in table 7.18, the risk capital of the firm can be shown to be $394 million, a 34% reduction relative to the aggregate risk capital on a stand-alone basis (see Technical Appendix).

TABLE 7.18

Correlation among Businesses

	Business 1	Business 2
Business 2	.5	
Business 3	0	0

TABLE 7.19

Combination of Businesses	Required Risk Capital for Combination	Marginal Business	Marginal Risk Capital
1+2+3	$394		
2+3	320	1	$74
1+3	292	2	102
1+2	304	3	90
	Summation of marginals:		$266

The reduction in risk capital derives from the interaction among the risks of the individual businesses. The less-than-perfect correlation among their year-to-year profits leaves room for one business to do well while another does poorly. In effect, the businesses in the portfolio coinsure one another, thus requiring less external asset insurance.

An important implication of this risk-reduction effect is that businesses that would be unprofitable on a stand-alone basis because of high risk-capital requirements might be profitable within a firm that has other businesses with offsetting risks. Thus, the true profitability of individual businesses within the multi-business firm will be distorted if calculated on the basis of stand-alone risk capital. A decision-making process based on this approach will forgo profitable opportunities.

The alternative approach of allocating the risk capital of the combined firm across individual businesses also suffers from this problem. To show why, we examine the *marginal* risk capital required by a business. This can be done by calculating the risk capital required for the firm without this business, and subtracting it from the risk capital required for the full portfolio of businesses. Doing so for the three businesses in our example produces the results in table 7.19.

The first line of table 7.19 shows the required risk capital for the combination of all three businesses, taking into account the less than perfect correlations among the businesses. As already noted, this amounts to $394 million. The next three lines of table 7.19 show the calculation of the marginal risk capital of each business. For example, in the second line, we calculate the required risk capital for a firm composed of just businesses 2 and 3, taking into account the zero correlation between these businesses. It amounts to $320 million. The difference between $320 million and the required risk capital for all three businesses is $74 million. This is the marginal risk capital for business 1. It is the reduction in risk capital that a firm in businesses 1, 2, and 3 would achieve by exiting business 1; or it is the additional risk capital required for a firm in businesses 2 and 3 to enter business 1.

For the purposes of making the marginal decision, the cost of marginal risk capital should be used. As shown in the last line of table 7.19, however, the summation of marginal risk capital, $266 million, is only two thirds of the full risk capital of $394 million required for the firm. Thus, if marginal risk capital is used for allocation among businesses, $128 million (32% of total risk capital) will not be allocated to any business.[29]

The discrepancy between the total risk capital of the firm and the sum of the marginal risk capital of its businesses will of course depend on the specifics of those businesses, but it can be very large. Using the aggregate of marginal risk capital, figure 7.3 illustrates how much of the firm's total risk capital goes unallocated as a function of the number of businesses in the firm, and the correlation among their profits. The analysis assumes that all businesses are the same size (in terms of stand-alone risk capital) and are symmetrically correlated. As shown in figure 7.3, the unallocated capital is larger at lower correlations. Only at the extreme of perfect correlation among the businesses is all of the capital allocated. In all other cases, at least some is not allocated. In the case of no correlation among the businesses, for example, the marginal risk capital of the individual businesses can account for as little as 50% of firm risk capital, so that as much as 50% can (and should) go unallocated.

These conclusions hold quite generally. Full allocation of the firm's risk capital overstates the marginal amount of risk capital. And the risk capital of a business evaluated on a stand-alone basis overstates the marginal risk capital by an even greater amount.[30]

Taking into account correlations among profits of individual businesses in capital-budgeting analysis may seem at odds with the traditional capital asset pricing model based notion that the only correlations that matter are those between individual business units and the broad market. Correlations among business units matter here because, by affecting the total amount of risk capital needed to support the businesses, they ultimately affect the total economic costs of risk capital. Per our earlier discussion, the economic cost of risk capital is the deadweight loss of spreads. The firm must expect to earn profits in excess of this cost as well as the cost of cash capital, which is the riskless rate of interest.

---

29. "Grossing up" the marginal allocations (by 32 percent in the example) to "fully allocate" the firm's risk capital does not solve the problem. Instead, it overstates the benefits of reductions in risk capital from dropping businesses or not starting new ones.
30. See the Technical Appendix for a formal proof of these propositions. Merton, "Operation and Regulation," provides another extensive example. The fact that risk capital cannot be allocated stems from the "externality" arising out of the less-than-perfect correlations among the profits of individual businesses and the asymmetric risk faced by providers of insurance: limited upside and potentially large downside.

FIGURE 7.3

Unallocated Risk Capital*

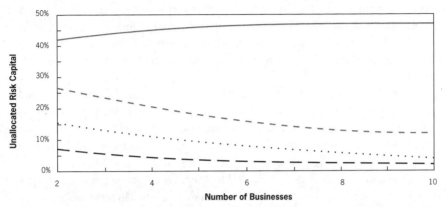

*Percentage of total firm risk capital not accounted for by the marginal risk capital of the individual businesses. Calculations assume businesses are symmetrically correlated and have the same stand-alone risk capital.

——— Correlation = 0
– – – Correlation = .25
· · · · · Correlation = .50
— — Correlation – .75

In traditional capital-budgeting procedures, estimates of cash flow correlations with the market portfolio are used to determine their stand-alone asset values. In our framework, these stand-alone asset values are assumed as given. Hence, correlations of business units with the broad market enter only indirectly—that is, in determining the amount of risk capital. As an insurance premium, risk capital is a function of the riskiness of the net assets as well as the value of the net assets. The *riskiness* of the net assets is affected by correlations among business units; the *value* of net assets is affected by their correlation with the broad market.

Summary and Conclusions

Financial firms that act as principal in the ordinary course of business do so in terms of asset-related as well as liability-related activities. Liability-related activities (such as deposit-taking and issuing guarantees like insurance and letters of credit) are mostly customer driven, which makes such businesses credit sensitive. Principal activities create a special set of financing, capital budgeting, and risk management decisions for the firm.

We have developed a framework for analyzing those decisions within the principal financial firm. The framework is built around a concept of risk capital, which we define as the smallest amount that can be invested to insure the *net* assets of the firm against loss in value relative to a risk-free investment. Using this definition of risk capital, the paper develops a number of important conclusions.

The amount of risk capital is uniquely determined, and depends only on the riskiness of the net assets. It is not affected by the form of financing of net assets.

Risk capital funds are provided by the firm's residual claimants, usually shareholders (except in the case of extremely highly leveraged firms). Implicitly or explicitly, this capital is used to purchase asset insurance. Potential issuers of asset insurance to the firm are third-party guarantors and the firm's stakeholders, including customers, debtholders, and shareholders.

The economic costs of risk capital to the firm are the spreads on the price of asset insurance that stem from information costs (adverse selection and moral hazard) and agency costs.

For a given configuration, the risk capital of a multi-business firm is less than the aggregate risk capital of the businesses on a stand-alone basis. Full allocation of risk capital across the individual businesses of the firm therefore is generally not feasible. Attempts at such a full allocation can significantly distort the true profitability of individual businesses.

TECHNICAL APPENDIX

Calculation of Risk Capital

For a given business, let the value of gross assets at time t be denoted by A_t, and the default-free value of customer liabilities be denoted by L_t, for $0 \leq t \leq T$. Gross assets and customer liabilities may both have uncertain, contingent payoffs. The value of the net assets at time t is $A_t - L_t$. If the net assets were invested risklessly, they would amount to $(A_0 - L_0) \exp(rT)$ at time T, where r is the continuously compounded riskless rate of interest. The shortfall in net assets relative to a riskless return is thus $(A_0 - L_0) \exp(rT) - (A_T - L_T)$, so that insurance to permit default-free financing of the net assets must pay max $\{(A_0 - L_0) \exp(rT) - (A_T - L_T), 0\}$ at time T. This is the same payoff structure as a European put option on the net assets with exercise price $(A_0 - L_0) \exp(rT)$. Under the assumption that the gross assets and customer liabilities both follow geometric Brownian motions, the value of this put option, and hence the amount of risk capital, is given by:

$$\text{Risk Capital} = A_0 F(1,1,0,T,\sigma)$$

where $F(S,E,r,T,\sigma)$ is the Black-Scholes (1973) formula[31] for a European call option on a stock with initial value S, exercise price E, riskless rate r, expiration date T, and volatility σ.[32] Here, σ is the volatility of profits as measured by the volatility of percentage changes in the ratio of gross assets to customer liabilities A_t/L_t (or simply the percent volatility of gross assets if customer liabilities are fixed or are non-existent.) As shown by Taylor's expansion for $\sigma\sqrt{t}$ not too large, the formula for risk capital is closely approximated by:

$$\text{Risk Capital} \approx .4A_0\sigma\sqrt{T}.$$

The formula used here for the variance rate of profits for a combination of N businesses is given by $\Sigma\Sigma w_i w_j \rho_{ij}\sigma_i\sigma_j$, where ρ_{ij} is the correlation between the profits of businesses i and j, and w_i is the fraction of gross assets in business i. The formula is an approximation that applies exactly only if investments in the businesses are continuously rebalanced so that the volatilities of the profits of the individual businesses maintain their relative proportions over the interval 0 to T. For the purposes here, this approximation has no material effect.

In table 7.17, the volatility of business profits was assumed to be 37.5%, 50%, and 62.5% per annum, respectively. Using the above variance formula, the volatility of the profits of the combination of three businesses evaluates to 32.75% per annum. This low percentage volatility of the three businesses combined stems directly from the diversification effect. The pairwise combinations show a similar effect.

Table 7.20 shows that for the range of parameter values used here the approximation $.4A_0\sigma\sqrt{T}$ is very close to the exact Black-Scholes option value.

The Relationship of Marginal Risk Capital to Combined and Stand-alone Risk Capital

This section establishes the general propositions that (a) the sum of the risk capital of stand-alone businesses exceeds the risk capital of the businesses combined in one firm; and (b) the risk capital of a combination of businesses exceeds the sum of the marginal risk capital of each of those businesses.

31. Set forth in F. Black and M. Scholes, "The Pricing of Options and Corporate Liabilities," *Journal of Political Economy* Vol. 81 (May–June 1973): 637–54.

32. $\sigma^2 = \sigma^2_A + \sigma^2_L - \sigma_A\sigma_L\sigma_{AL}$, where σ_A is the volatility of gross asset returns, σ_L is the volatility of customer liability "returns," and σ_{AL} is the correlation between gross asset returns and customer returns. See Stanley Fischer, "Call Option Pricing When the Exercise Price Is Uncertain, and the Valuation of Index Bonds," *Journal of Finance* Vol. 33 (March 1978): 169–76; William Margrabe, "The Value of an Option to Exchange One Asset for Another," *Journal of Finance* Vol. 33 (March 1978): 177–86; and, especially, René Stulz, "Options on the Minimum or the Maximum of Two Risky Assets: Analysis and Applications," *Journal of Financial Economics* Vol. 10 (July 1982): 161–85.

TABLE 7.20

($ Millions)

	Gross Assets	Standard Deviaton (σ)	Approximate Risk Capital ($.4A_0\sigma\sqrt{T}$)	"Exact" Risk Capital (Black-Scholes)
Business 1				
	$1,000	37.5%	$150	$148.7
Business 2				
	1,000	50.0%	200	197.4
Business 3				
	1,000	62.5%	250	245.3
Businesses 1+2				
	2,000	38.0%	304	301.4
Businesses 1+3				
	2,000	36.4%	292	288.8
Businesses 2+3				
	2,000	40.0%	320	317.0
Businesses 1+2+3				
	3,000	32.8%	394	390.8

As in the first part of this appendix, let $X=(A_0-L_0)\exp(rT)-(A_T-L_T)$ be the shortfall (or surplus if it is negative) in the net assets of a business at time T. Let there be N individual businesses, and let X_i be the shortfall for business i. From the above, insurance to permit default-free financing of the net assets of business i must pay $f(X_i)=\max\{X_i, 0\}$ at time T. Note that the function $f(.)$ is convex and satisfies $f(0)=0$.

The sum of the insurance payoffs to the stand-alone businesses is $\Sigma f(X_i)$, and the insurance payoff to the combined businesses is $f(\Sigma X_i)$. Since $f(.)$ is convex, we can apply Jensen's inequality to obtain:

$$\Sigma f(X_i) \geq f(\Sigma X_i)$$

which establishes the first proposition.[33]

To establish the second proposition, we note that $f(\Sigma_{j\neq i}X_j)$ is the insurance payoff to the firm consisting of all businesses except i. Thus the marginal insurance payoff for business i is

$$f(\Sigma X_i)-f(\Sigma_{j\neq i}X_j).$$

33. This is the well-known proposition that a portfolio of options always returns at least as much as the corresponding option on a portfolio of underlying securities.

We now observe the identity:

$$\Sigma X_i = \Sigma_i (\Sigma_{j \neq i} X_j)/(N-1).$$

Therefore, by Jensen's inequality,

$$f(\Sigma X_i) \leq \Sigma_i f((\Sigma_{j \neq i} X_j)/(N-1)).$$

Applying Jensen's inequality a second time and using the fact that $f(0)=0$, we obtain

$$(N-1)f(\Sigma X_i) \leq \Sigma_i f(\Sigma_{j \neq i} X_j)$$

from which it follows that

$$Nf(\Sigma X_i) - \Sigma_i f(\Sigma_{j \neq i} X_j) \leq f(\Sigma X_i)$$

or

$$\Sigma_k \{ f(\Sigma X_i) - f(\Sigma_{j \neq k} X_j) \} \leq f(\Sigma X_i).$$

This proves that the sum of the marginal insurance payoffs is at most the insurance payoff to the combined firm. Therefore, the risk capital of a combination of businesses exceeds the sum of the marginal risk capital of each of those businesses.

■ **ROBERT C. MERTON** is George Fisher Baker Professor of Business Administration at Harvard University's Graduate School of Business Administration.

■ **ANDRÉ F. PEROLD** is Sylvan C. Coleman Professor of Financial Management at Harvard University's Graduate School of Business Administration.

CHAPTER 8

Value at Risk

Uses and Abuses

CHRISTOPHER L. CULP, MERTON H. MILLER,

AND ANDREA M.P. NEVES

VALUE AT RISK (VaR) is now viewed by many as *indispensable* ammunition in any serious corporate risk manager's arsenal. VaR is a method of measuring the financial risk of an asset, portfolio, or exposure over some specified period of time. Its attraction stems from its ease of interpretation as a summary measure of risk and consistent treatment of risk across different financial instruments and business activities. VaR is often used as an approximation of the "maximum reasonable loss" a company can expect to realize from all its financial exposures.

VaR has received widespread accolades from industry and regulators alike.[1] Numerous organizations have found that the practical uses and benefits of VaR make it a valuable decision support tool in a comprehensive risk management process. Despite its many uses, however, VaR—like any statistical aggregate—is subject to the risk of misinterpretation and misapplication. Indeed, most problems with VaR seem to arise from what a firm *does* with a VaR measure rather than from the actual computation of the number.

Why a company manages risk affects *how* a company should manage—and, hence, should measure—its risk.[2] In that connection, we examine the

This chapter was previously published as an article in *Journal of Applied Corporate Finance* Vol. 10, No. 4 (Winter 1998): 26–38. The authors thank Kamaryn Tanner for her previous work with us on this subject.

1. See, for example, Global Derivatives Study Group, *Derivatives: Practices and Principles* (Washington, DC: July 1993); and Board of Governors of the Federal Reserve System, *SR Letter* 93–96 (1993). Most recently, the Securities and Exchange Commission (SEC) began to require risk disclosures by all public companies. One approved format for these mandatory financial risk disclosures is VaR. For a critical assessment of the SEC's risk disclosure rule, see Merton H. Miller and Christopher L. Culp, "The SEC's Costly Disclosure Rules," *Wall Street Journal*, June 22, 1996.

2. This presupposes, of course, that "risk management" is consistent with value-maximizing behavior by the firm. For the purpose of this chapter, we do not consider whether firms *should be*

four "great derivatives disasters" of 1993–95—Procter & Gamble, Barings, Orange County, and Metallgesellschaft—and evaluate how *ex ante* VaR measurements likely would have affected those situations. We conclude that VaR would have been of only limited value in averting those disasters and, indeed, actually might have been *misleading* in some of them.

What Is VaR?

Value at risk is a summary statistic that quantifies the exposure of an asset or portfolio to market risk, or the risk that a position declines in value with adverse market price changes.[3] Measuring risk using VaR allows managers to make statements like the following: "We do not expect losses to exceed $1 million on more than 1 out of the next 20 days."[4]

To arrive at a VAR measure for a given portfolio, a firm must generate a probability distribution of possible changes in the value of some portfolio over a specific time or "risk horizon"—for example, 1 day.[5] The value at risk of the portfolio is the dollar loss corresponding to some pre-defined probability level—usually 5% or less—as defined by the left-hand tail of the distribution. Alternatively, VaR is the dollar loss that is expected to occur no more than 5% of the time over the defined risk horizon. Figure 8.1, for example, depicts a 1-day VaR of $10X at the 5% probability level.

The Development of VaR

VaR emerged first in the trading community.[6] The original goal of VaR was to systematize the measurement of an active trading firm's risk exposures across its dealing portfolios. Before VaR, most commercial trading houses measured and controlled risk on a desk-by-desk basis with little attention to firm-wide exposures. VaR made it possible for dealers to use risk measures that could be compared and aggregated across trading areas as a means of monitoring and limiting their consolidated financial risks.

managing their risks. For a discussion of that issue, see Christopher L. Culp and Merton H. Miller, "Hedging in the Theory of Corporate Finance: A Reply to Our Critics," *Journal of Applied Corporate Finance* Vol. 8, No. 1 (Spring 1995): 121–27; and René M. Stulz, "Rethinking Risk Management," *Journal of Applied Corporate Finance* Vol. 9, No. 3 (Fall 1996): 8–24.

3. More recently, VaR has been suggested as a framework for measuring credit risk, as well. To keep our discussion focused, we examine only the applications of VaR to market risk measurement.

4. For a general description of VaR, see Philippe Jorion, *Value at Risk* (Chicago: Irwin Professional Publishing, 1997).

5. The risk horizon is chosen exogenously by the firm engaging in the VaR calculation.

6. An early precursor of VaR was standard portfolio analysis of risk (SPAN™) developed by the Chicago Mercantile Exchange for setting futures margins. Now widely used by virtually all futures exchanges, SPAN is a non-parametric, simulation-based "worst case" measure of risk. As will be seen, VaR, by contrast, rests on well-defined probability distributions.

VaR received its first public endorsement in July 1993, when a group representing the swap dealer community recommended the adoption of VaR by all
active dealers.[7] In that report, the Global Derivatives Study Group of the Group
of Thirty urged dealers to "use a *consistent measure* to calculate daily the market risk of their derivatives positions and compare it to market risk limits.
Market risk is best measured as 'value at risk' using *probability analysis* based
upon a common confidence interval (e.g., two standard deviations) and *time
horizon* (e.g., a one-day exposure)."[8]

The italicized phrases in the Group of Thirty recommendation draw attention to several specific features of VaR that account for its widespread popularity among trading firms. One feature of VaR is its *consistent* measurement of
financial risk. By expressing risk using a "possible dollar loss" metric, VaR
makes possible direct comparisons of risk across different business lines and
distinct financial products such as interest rate and currency swaps.

In addition to consistency, VaR also is *probability based*. With whatever
degree of confidence a firm wants to specify, VaR enables the firm to associate
a specific loss with that level of confidence. Consequently, VaR measures can
be interpreted as forward-looking approximations of potential market risk.

A third feature of VaR is its reliance on a *common time horizon* called the
risk horizon. A 1-day risk horizon at, say, the 5% probability level tells the firm,
strictly speaking, that it can expect to lose no more than, say, $10X on the next
day with 95% confidence. Firms often go on to assume that the 5% confidence
level means they stand to lose more than $10X on no more than 5 days out of
100, an inference that is true only if strong assumptions are made about the
stability of the underlying probability distribution.[9]

The choice of this risk horizon is based on various motivating factors.
These may include the timing of employee performance evaluations, key
decision-making events (e.g., asset purchases), major reporting events (e.g.,
board meetings and required disclosures), regulatory examinations, tax assessments, external quality assessments, and the like.

Implementing VaR

To estimate the value at risk of a portfolio, possible future values of that portfolio must be generated, yielding a distribution—called the "VaR distribution"—
like that seen in figure 8.1. Once the VaR distribution is created for the chosen
risk horizon, the VaR itself is just a number on the curve—namely, the change

7. This was followed quickly by a similar endorsement from the International Swaps and Derivatives
   Association. See Jorion, *Value at Risk*.
8. Global Derivatives Study Group, *Derivatives*; emphasis added.
9. This interpretation assumes that asset prices changes are what the technicians call independently
   and identically distributed (IID)—that is, that price changes are drawn from essentially the same
   distribution every day.

FIGURE 8.1

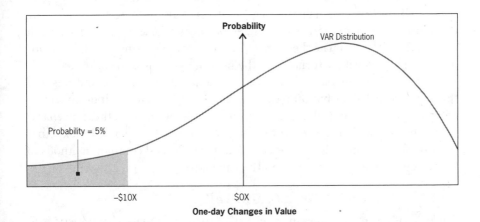

in the value of the portfolio leaving the specified amount of probability in the left-hand tail.

Creating a VaR distribution for a particular portfolio and a given risk horizon can be viewed as a two-step process.[10] In the first step, the price or return distributions for each individual security or asset in the portfolio are generated. These distributions represent possible value changes in all the component assets over the risk horizon.[11] Next, the individual distributions somehow must be aggregated into a portfolio distribution using appropriate measures of correlation.[12] The resulting portfolio distribution then serves as the basis for the VaR summary measure.

An important assumption in almost all VaR calculations is that the portfolio whose risk is being evaluated *does not change* over the risk horizon. This assumption of no turnover was not a major issue when VaR first arrived on the

10. In practice, VaR is not often implemented in a clean two-step manner, but discussing it in this way simplifies our discussion—without any loss of generality.
11. Especially with instruments whose payoffs are non-linear, a better approach is to generate distributions for the underlying "risk factors" that affect an asset rather than focus on the changes in the values of the assets themselves. To generate the value change distribution of an option on a stock, for example, one might first generate changes in the stock price and its volatility and *then* compute associated option price changes rather than generating option price changes "directly." For a discussion, see Michael S. Gamze and Ronald S. Rolighed, "VAR: What's Wrong with This Picture?" (Unpublished manuscript, Federal Reserve Bank of Chicago, 1997).
12. If a risk manager is interested in the risk of a particular financial instrument, the appropriate risk measure to analyze is *not* the VaR of that instrument. Portfolio effects still must be considered. The relevant measure of risk is the *marginal risk* of that instrument in the portfolio being evaluated. See Mark Garman, "Improving on VAR," *Risk* Vol. 9, No. 5 (1996): 61–63.

scene at derivatives dealers. They were focused on 1- or 2-day—sometimes *intra*-day—risk horizons and thus found VaR both easy to implement and relatively realistic. But when it comes to generalizing VaR to a longer time horizon, the assumption of no portfolio changes becomes problematic. What does it mean, after all, to evaluate the *1-year* VaR of a portfolio using only the portfolio's contents *today* if the turnover in the portfolio is 20% to 30% per day?

Methods for generating both the individual asset risk distributions and the portfolio risk distribution range from the simplistic to the indecipherably complex. Because our goal in this chapter is not to evaluate all these mechanical methods of VaR measurement, readers are referred elsewhere for explanations of the nuts and bolts of VaR computation.[13] Several common methods of VaR calculation are summarized in the Appendix.

Uses of VaR

The purpose of any risk measurement system and summary risk statistic is to facilitate risk reporting and control decisions. Accordingly, dealers quickly began to rely on VaR measures in their broader risk management activities. The simplicity of VaR measurement greatly facilitated dealers' reporting of risks to senior managers and directors. The popularity of VaR owes much to Dennis Weatherstone, former chairman of JP Morgan & Co., Inc., who demanded to know the total market risk exposure of JP Morgan at 4:15 pm every day. Weatherstone's request was met with a daily VaR report.

VaR also proved useful in dealers' risk *control* efforts.[14] Commercial banks, for example, used VaR measures to quantify current trading exposures and compare them to established counterparty risk limits. In addition, VaR provided traders with information useful in formulating hedging policies and evaluating the effects of particular transactions on net portfolio risk. For managers, VaR became popular as a means of analyzing the performance of traders for compensation purposes and for allocating reserves or capital across business lines on a risk-adjusted basis.

Uses of VaR by Non-dealers. Since its original development as a risk management tool for active trading firms, VaR has spread outside the dealer community.

13. See, for example, Jorion, *Value at Risk*; Rod A. Beckström and Alyce R. Campbell, "Value-at-Risk (VAR): Theoretical Foundations," in *An Introduction to VAR*, ed. Rod Beckström and Alyce Campbell (Palo Alto, CA: CAATS Software, Inc., 1995); and James V. Jordan and Robert J. Mackay, "Assessing Value at Risk for Equity Portfolios: Implementing Alternative Techniques," in *Derivatives Handbook*, ed. Robert J. Schwartz and Clifford W. Smith Jr. (New York: John Wiley & Sons, Inc., 1997).

14. See Rod A. Beckström and Alyce R. Campbell, "The Future of Firm-Wide Risk Management," in *An Introduction to VAR*, ed. Rod Beckström and Alyce Campbell (Palo Alto, CA: CAATS Software, Inc., 1995).

VaR now is used regularly by non-financial corporations, pension plans and mutual funds, clearing organizations, brokers and futures commission merchants, and insurers. These organizations find VaR just as useful as trading firms, albeit for different reasons.

Some benefits of VaR for non-dealers relate more to the exposure monitoring facilitated by VaR measurement than to the risk measurement task itself. For example, a pension plan with funds managed by external investment advisers may use VaR for policing its external managers. Similarly, brokers and account merchants can use VaR to assess collateral requirements for customers.

VaR and Corporate Risk Management Objectives

Firms managing risks may be either *value risk managers* or *cash flow risk managers*.[15] A value risk manager is concerned with the firm's total value at a particular point in time. This concern may arise from a desire to avoid bankruptcy, mitigate problems associated with informational asymmetries, or reduce expected tax liabilities.[16] A cash flow risk manager, by contrast, uses risk management to reduce cash flow volatility and thereby increase debt capacity.[17] Value risk managers thus typically manage the risks of a *stock of assets*, whereas cash flow risk managers manage the risks of a *flow of funds*. A risk measure that is appropriate for one type of firm may not be appropriate for others.

Value Risk Managers and VaR-Based Risk Controls

As the term value at risk implies, organizations for which VaR is best suited are those for which value risk management is the goal. VaR, after all, is intended to summarize the risk of a stock of assets over a particular risk horizon. Those likely to realize the most benefits from VaR thus include clearing houses, securities settlement agents,[18] and swap dealers. These organizations have in common a concern with the value of their exposures over a well-defined period of time and a wish to limit and control those exposures. In addition, the relatively

15. For a general discussion of the traditional corporate motivations for risk management, see David Fite and Paul Pfleider, "Should Firms Use Derivatives to Manage Risk?" in *Risk Management: Problems & Solutions*, ed. William H. Beaver and George Parker (New York: McGraw-Hill, Inc., 1995).

16. See, for example, Clifford Smith and René Stulz, "The Determinants of Firms' Hedging Policies," *Journal of Financial and Quantitative Analysis* Vol. 20 (1985): 391–405.

17. See, for example, Kenneth Froot, David Scharfstein, and Jeremy Stein, "Risk Management: Coordinating Corporate Investment and Financing Policies," *Journal of Finance* Vol. 48 (1993): 1629–58.

18. See Christopher L. Culp and Andrea M.P. Neves, "Risk Management by Securities Settlement Agents," *Journal of Applied Corporate Finance* Vol. 10, No. 3 (Fall 1997): 96–103.

short risk horizons of these enterprises imply that VaR measurement can be accomplished reliably and with minimal concern about changing portfolio composition over the risk horizon.

Many value risk managers have risks arising mainly from *agency* transactions. Organizations like financial clearing houses, for example, are exposed to risk arising from intermediation services rather than the risks of proprietary position taking. VaR can assist such firms in monitoring their customer credit exposures, in setting position and exposure limits, and in determining and enforcing margin and collateral requirements.

Total versus Selective Risk Management

Most financial distress-driven explanations of corporate risk management, whether value or cash flow risk, center on a firm's *total risk*.[19] If so, such firms should be indifferent to the *composition* of their total risks. *Any* risk thus is a candidate for risk reduction.

Selective risk managers, by contrast, deliberately choose to manage some risks and not others. Specifically, they seek to manage their exposures to risks in which they have no comparative informational advantage—for the usual financial ruin reasons—while actively exposing themselves, at least to a point, to risks in which they *do* have perceived superior information.[20]

For firms managing total risk, the principal benefit of VaR is facilitating explicit risk control decisions, such as setting and enforcing exposure limits. For firms that selectively manage risk, by contrast, VaR is useful largely for diagnostic monitoring *or* for controlling risk in areas where the firm perceives no comparative informational advantage. An airline, for example, might find VaR helpful in assessing its exposure to jet fuel prices; but for the airline to use VaR to analyze the risk that seats on its aircraft are not all sold makes little sense.

Consider also a hedge fund manager who invests in foreign equity because the risk/return profile of that asset class is desirable. To avoid exposure to the exchange rate risk, the fund could engage an "overlay manager" to hedge the currency risk of the position. Using VaR on the *whole position* lumps together two separate and distinct sources of risk—the currency risk and the foreign equity price risk. And *reporting* that total VaR without a corresponding expected return could have disastrous consequences. Using VaR to ensure that the currency hedge is accomplishing its intended aims, by contrast, might be perfectly legitimate.

---

19. See, for example, Smith and Stulz, "Determinants"; and Froot et al., "Risk Management."
20. See Culp and Miller, "Hedging"; and Stulz, "Rethinking."

VaR and the Great Derivatives Disasters

Despite its many benefits to certain firms, VaR is not a panacea. Even when VaR is calculated appropriately, VaR *in isolation* will do little to keep a firm's risk exposures in line with the firm's chosen risk tolerances. Without a well-developed risk management infrastructure—policies and procedures, systems, and well-defined senior management responsibilities—VaR will deliver little, if any, benefits. In addition, VaR may not always help a firm accomplish its particular risk management objectives, as we shall see.

To illustrate some of the pitfalls of using VaR, we examine the four "great derivatives disasters" of 1993–1995: Procter & Gamble, Orange County, Barings, and Metallgesellschaft.[21] Proponents of VaR often claim that many of these disasters would have been averted had VaR measurement systems been in place. We think otherwise.[22]

Procter & Gamble

During 1993, Procter & Gamble (P&G) undertook derivatives transactions with Bankers Trust that resulted in over $150 million in losses.[23] Those losses traced essentially to P&G's writing of a put option on interest rates to Bankers Trust. Writers of put options suffer losses, of course, whenever the underlying security declines in price, which in this instance meant whenever interest rates rose. And rise they did in the summer and autumn of 1993.

The put option actually was only one component of the whole deal. The deal, with a notional principal of $200 million, was a fixed-for-floating rate swap in which Bankers Trust offered P&G 10 years of floating-rate financing at 75 basis points below the commercial paper rate in exchange for the put and fixed interest payments of 5.3% annually. That huge financing advantage of 75 basis points apparently was too much for P&G's treasurer to resist, particularly because the put was well out-of-the-money when the deal was struck in May 1993. But the low financing rate, of course, was just premium collected for writing

---

21. In truth, Procter & Gamble was the only one of these disasters actually *caused* by derivatives. See Merton H. Miller, "The Great Derivatives Disasters: What Really Went Wrong and How to Keep It from Happening to You" (Speech presented to JP Morgan & Co., Frankfurt, June 24, 1997; and chapter two in Merton H. Miller, *Merton Miller on Derivatives* (New York: John Wiley & Sons, Inc., 1997).

22. The details of all these cases are complex. We thus refer readers elsewhere for discussions of the actual events that took place and limit our discussion here only to basic background. See, for example, Stephen Figlewski, "How to Lose Money in Derivatives," *Journal of Derivatives* Vol. 2, No. 2 (Winter 1994): 75–82.

23. See, for example, Figlewski, "How to Lose Money"; and Michael S. Gamze and Karen McCann, "A Simplified Approach to Valuing an Option on a Leveraged Spread: The Bankers Trust, Procter & Gamble Example," *Derivatives Quarterly* Vol. 1, No. 4 (Summer 1995): 44–53.

the put. When the put went in-the-money for Bankers Trust, what once seemed like a good deal to P&G ended up costing millions of dollars.

VaR would have helped P&G, if P&G also had in place an adequate risk management infrastructure—which apparently it did not. Most obviously, senior managers at P&G would have been unlikely to have approved the original swap deal if its exposure had been subject to a VaR calculation. But that presupposes a lot.

Although VaR would have helped P&G's senior management measure its exposure to the speculative punt by its treasurer, much more would have been needed to stop the treasurer from taking the interest rate bet. The first requirement would have been a system for measuring the risk of the swaps *on a transactional basis*. But VaR was never intended for use on single transactions.[24] On the contrary, the whole appeal of the concept initially was its capacity to aggregate risk *across* transactions and exposures. To examine the risk of an individual transaction, the *change* in portfolio VaR that would occur with the addition of that new transaction should be analyzed. But that still requires first calculating the total VaR.[25] So, for P&G to have looked at the risk of its swaps in a VaR context, its entire treasury area would have needed a VaR measurement capability.

Implementing VaR for P&G's entire treasury function might *seem* to have been a good idea *anyway*. Why not, after all, perform a comprehensive VaR analysis on the whole treasury area and get transactional VaR assessment capabilities as an added bonus? For some firms, that *is* a good idea. But for other firms, it is not. Many non-financial corporations like P&G, after all, typically undertake risk management in their corporate treasury functions for *cash flow* management reasons.[26] VaR is a *value* risk measure, not a cash flow risk measure. For P&G to examine value at risk for its *whole* treasury operation, therefore, presumes that P&G was a *value* risk manager, and that may not have been the case. Even had VaR been in place at P&G, moreover, the assumption that P&G's senior managers would have been *monitoring* and *controlling* the VaRs of individual swap transactions is not a foregone conclusion.

---

24. Recently, some have advocated that derivatives dealers should evaluate the VaR of specific transactions *from the perspective of their counterparties* in order to determine counterparty suitability. Without knowing the rest of the counterparty's risk exposures, however, the VaR estimate would be meaningless. Even with full knowledge of the counterparty's total portfolio, the VaR number still might be of no use in determining suitability for reasons to become clear later.

25. See Garman "Improving on VAR."

26. See, for example, Judy C. Lewent and A. John Kearney, "Identifying, Measuring, and Hedging Currency Risk at Merck," *Journal of Applied Corporate Finance* Vol. 2, No. 4 (Winter 1990): 19–28; and Deana R. Nance, Clifford W. Smith, and Charles W. Smithson, "On the Determinants of Corporate Hedging," *Journal of Finance* Vol. 48, No. 1 (1993): 267–84.

Barings

Barings PLC failed in February 1995 when rogue trader Nick Leeson's bets on the Japanese stock market went sour and turned into over $1 billion in trading losses.[27,28] To be sure, VaR would have led Barings senior management to shut down Leeson's trading operation in time to save the firm—*if they knew about it.* If P&G's sin was a lack of internal management and control over its treasurer, then Barings was guilty of an even more cardinal sin. The top officers of Barings lost control over the trading operation *not* because no VaR measurement system was in place, but because they let the same individual making the trades also serve as the recorder of those trades—violating one of the most elementary principles of good management.

The more interesting question emerging from Barings is why top management seems to have taken so long to recognize that a rogue trader was at work. For that purpose, a fully functioning VaR system would certainly have helped. Increasingly, companies in the financial risk-taking business use VaR as a monitoring tool for detecting unauthorized increases in positions.[29] Usually, this is intended for *customer* credit risk management by firms like futures commission merchants. In the case of Barings, however, such account monitoring would have enabled management to spot Leeson's run-up in positions in his so-called "arbitrage" and "error" accounts.

VaR measurements at Barings, on the other hand, would have been impossible to implement, given the deficiencies in the *overall* information technology (IT) systems in place at the firm. At any point in time, Barings' top managers knew only what Leeson was telling them. If Barings' systems were incapable of reconciling the position build-up in Leeson's accounts with the huge wire transfers being made by London to support Leeson's trading in Singapore, no VaR measure would have included a complete picture of Leeson's positions. And without that, no warning flag would have been raised.

Orange County

The Orange County Investment Pool (OCIP) filed bankruptcy in December 1994 after reporting a drop in its market value of $1.5 billion. For many years,

27. See, for example, Hans R. Stoll, "Lost Barings: A Tale in Three Parts Concluding with a Lesson," *Journal of Derivatives* Vol. 3, No. 1 (Fall 1995): 109–15; and Anatoli Kuprianov, "Derivatives Debacles: Case Studies of Large Losses in Derivatives Markets," in *Derivatives Handbook: Risk Management and Control*, ed. Robert J. Schwartz and Clifford W. Smith Jr. (New York: John Wiley & Sons, Inc., 1997).

28. Our reference to rogue traders is not intended to suggest, of course, that rogue traders are only found in connection with derivatives. Rogue traders have caused the banks of this world far more damage from failed real estate (and copper) deals than from derivatives.

29. See Christopher Culp, Kamaryn Tanner, and Ron Mensink, "Risks, Returns and Retirement," *Risk* Vol. 10, No. 10 (October 1997): 63–69.

Orange County maintained the OCIP as the equivalent of a money market fund for the benefit of school boards, road building authorities, and other local government bodies in its territory. These local agencies deposited their tax and other collections when they came in and paid for their own wage and other bills when the need arose. The OCIP paid them interest on their deposits—handsomely, in fact. Between 1989–94, the OCIP paid its depositors 400 basis points more than they would have earned on the corporate pool maintained by the state of California—roughly $750 million over the period.[30]

Most of the OCIP's investments involved leveraged purchases of intermediate-term securities and structured notes financed with "reverse repos" and other short-term borrowings. Contrary to conventional wisdom, the OCIP was making its profits *not* from "speculation on falling interest rates" but rather from an investment play on the *slope* of the yield curve.[31] When the Federal Reserve started to raise interest rates in 1994, the intermediate-term securities declined in value and OCIP's short-term borrowing costs rose.

Despite the widespread belief that the leverage policy led to the fund's insolvency and bankruptcy filing, Miller and Ross, after examining the OCIP's investment strategy, cash position, and net asset value at the time of the filing, have shown that the OCIP was *not* insolvent. Miller and Ross estimate that the $20 billion in total assets on deposit in the fund had a positive net worth of about $6 billion. Nor was the fund in an illiquid cash situation. OCIP had over $600 million of cash on hand and was generating further cash at a rate of more than $30 million a month.[32] Even the reported $1.5 billion "loss" would have been completely recovered within a year—a loss that was realized only because Orange County's bankruptcy lawyers forced the liquidation of the securities.[33]

Philippe Jorion has taken issue with Miller and Ross's analysis of OCIP, arguing that VaR would have called the OCIP investment program into question long before the $1.5 billion loss was incurred.[34] Using several different VaR

---

30. Miller.
31. When the term structure is upward sloping, borrowing in short-term markets to leverage longer-term government securities generates positive cash carry. A surge in inflation or interest rates, of course, could reverse the term structure and turn the carry negative. That is the real risk the treasurer was taking. But it was not much of a risk. Since the days of Jimmy Carter in the late 1970s, the U.S. term structure has never been downward sloping and nobody in December 1994 thought it was likely to be so in the foreseeable future.
32. Merton H. Miller and David J. Ross, "The Orange County Bankruptcy and Its Aftermath: Some New Evidence," *Journal of Derivatives* Vol. 4, No. 4 (Summer 1997): 51–60.
33. Readers may wonder why, then, Orange County did declare bankruptcy. That story is complicated, but a hint might be found in the payment of $50 million in special legal fees to the attorneys that sued Merrill Lynch for $1.5 billion for selling OCIP the securities that lost money. In short, *lots* of people gained from OCIP's bankruptcy, even though OCIP was not actually bankrupt. See Miller, and Miller and Ross, "Orange County Bankruptcy."
34. Philippe Jorion, "Lessons From the Orange County Bankruptcy," *Journal of Derivatives* Vol. 4, No. 4 (Summer 1997): 61–66.

calculation methods, Jorion concludes that OCIP's 1-year VaR at the end of 1994 was about $1 billion at the 5% confidence level. Under the usual VaR interpretation, this would have told OCIP to expect a loss in excess of $1 billion in 1 out of the next 20 years.

Even assuming Jorion's VaR number is accurate, however, his interpretation of the VaR measure was unlikely to have been the OCIP's interpretation—at least not *ex ante* when it could have mattered. The VaR measure in isolation, after all, takes no account of the *upside* returns OCIP was receiving as compensation for that downside risk. Remember that OCIP was pursuing a very deliberate yield curve, net cost-of-carry strategy, designed to generate high expected cash returns. That strategy had risks, to be sure, but those risks seem to have been clear to OCIP treasurer Robert Citron—and, for that matter, to the people of Orange County who re-elected Citron treasurer in preference to an opposing candidate who was criticizing the investment strategy.[35]

Had Orange County been using VaR, however, it almost certainly *would* have terminated its investment program upon seeing the $1 billion risk estimate. The reason probably would *not* have been the actual informativeness of the VaR number, but rather the fear of a public outcry at the number. Imagine the public reaction if the OCIP announced one day that it expected to lose more than $1 billion over the next year in one time out of 20. But that reaction would have far less to do with the actual risk information conveyed by the VaR number than with the lack of any corresponding expected profits reported *with* the risk number. Just consider, after all, what the public reaction would have been if the OCIP publicly announced that it would *gain* more than $1 billion over the next year in one time out of 20![36]

This example highlights a major abuse of VaR—an abuse that has nothing to do with the meaning of the value at risk number but instead traces to the presentation of the information that number conveys. Especially for institutional investors, a major pitfall of VaR is to highlight large potential losses over long time horizons *without conveying any information about the corresponding expected return*. The lesson from Orange County to would-be VaR users thus is an important one—for organizations whose mission is *to take some risks*, VaR measures of risks are meaningful *only* when interpreted alongside estimates of corresponding potential *gains*.

Metallgesellschaft

MG Refining & Marketing, Inc. (MGRM), a U.S. subsidiary of Metallgesellschaft AG, reported $1.3 billion in losses by year-end 1993 from its oil trading

---

35. Miller and Ross, "Orange County Bankruptcy."
36. Only for the purpose of this example, we obviously have assumed symmetry in the VaR distribution.

activities. MGRM's oil derivatives were part of a marketing program under which it offered long-term customers firm price guarantees for up to 10 years on gasoline, heating oil, and diesel fuel purchased from MGRM.[37] The firm hedged its resulting exposure to spot price increases with short-term futures contracts to a considerable extent. After several consecutive months of *falling* prices in the autumn of 1993, however, MGRM's German parent reacted to the substantial margin calls on the losing futures positions by liquidating the hedge, thereby turning a paper loss into a very real one.[38]

Most of the arguments over MGRM—in press accounts, in the many lawsuits the case engendered, and in the academic literature—have focused on whether MGRM was "speculating" or "hedging." The answer, of course, is that like all other merchant firms, they were doing both. They were definitely speculating on the oil "basis"—inter-regional, inter-temporal, and inter-product *differences* in prices of crude, heating oil, and gasoline. That was the *business they were in.*[39] The firm had expertise and informational advantages far beyond those of its customers or of casual observers playing the oil futures market. What MGRM did not have, of course, was any special expertise about the level and direction of oil prices generally. Here, rather than take a corporate "view" on the direction of oil prices, like the misguided one the treasurer of P&G took on interest rates, MGRM chose to hedge its exposure to oil price *levels.*

Subsequent academic controversy surrounding the case has mainly been not whether MGRM was hedging, but whether they were *over*-hedging— whether the firm could have achieved the same degree of insulation from price level changes with a lower commitment from MGRM's ultimate owner-creditor Deutsche Bank.[40] The answer is that the day-to-day cash-flow volatility of the program *could* have been reduced by any number of cash flow variance-reducing hedge ratios.[41] But the cost of chopping off some cash drains when prices fell was that of losing the corresponding cash inflows when prices spiked up.[42]

---

37. A detailed analysis of the program can be found in Christopher L. Culp and Merton H. Miller, "Metallgesellschaft and the Economics of Synthetic Storage," *Journal of Applied Corporate Finance* Vol. 7, No. 4 (Winter 1995): 62–76.

38. For an analysis of the losses incurred by MGRM—as well as why they were incurred—see Christopher L. Culp and Merton H. Miller, "Auditing the Auditors," *Risk* Vol. 8, No. 4 (1995): 36–39.

39. Culp and Miller, "Metallgesellschaft" and "Hedging," explain this in detail.

40. See Franklin R. Edwards and Michael S. Canter, "The Collapse of Metallgesellschaft: Unhedgeable Risks, Poor Hedging Strategy, or Just Bad Luck?" *Journal of Applied Corporate Finance* Vol. 8, No. 1 (Spring 1995): 86–105.

41. See, for example, Froot et al., "Risk Management."

42. A number of other reasons also explain MGRM's reluctance to adopt anything smaller than a "one-for-one stack-and-roll" hedge. See Culp and Miller, "Metallgesellschaft" and "Auditing."

Conceptually, of course, MGRM could have used VAR analysis to measure its possible financial risks. But why would it have wanted to do so? The combined marketing/hedging program, after all, was *hedged* against changes in the *level* of oil prices. The only significant risks to which MGRM's program was subject thus were basis and rollover risks—again, the risk that MGRM was *in the business of taking*.[43]

A much bigger problem at MGRM than the change in the *value* of its program was the large negative *cash flows* on the futures hedge that would have been offset by eventual gains in the future on the fixed-price customer contracts. Although MGRM's former management claims it had access to adequate funding from Deutsche Bank (the firm's leading creditor and stockholder), perhaps some benefit might have been achieved by more rigorous cash flow simulations. But even granting that, VaR would have told MGRM very little about its *cash flows* at risk. As we have already emphasized, VaR is a *value*-based risk measure.

For firms like MGRM engaged in *authorized* risk taking—like Orange County and unlike Leeson/Barings—the primary benefit of VaR really is just as an internal "diagnostic monitoring" tool. To that end, estimating the VaR of MGRM's basis trading activities *would* have told senior managers and directors at its parent what the basis risks were that MGRM actually was taking. But remember, MGRM's parent appears to have been fully aware of the risks MGRM's traders were taking *even without a VaR number*. In that sense, even the monitoring benefits of VAR for a proprietary trading operation would not have changed MGRM's fate.[44]

Alternatives to VaR

VaR certainly is not the *only* way a firm can systematically measure its financial risk. As noted, its appeal is mainly its conceptual simplicity and its consistency across financial products and activities. In cases where VaR may *not* be appropriate as a measure of risk, however, other alternatives *are* available.

---

43. The claim that MGRM was in the business of trading the basis has been disputed by managers of MGRM's parent and creditors. Nevertheless, the marketing materials of MGRM—on which the parent firm signed off—suggests otherwise. See Culp and Miller, "Hedging."

44. Like P&G and Barings, what happened at MGRM was, in the end, a *management* failure rather than a *risk management failure*. For details on how management failed in the MGRM case, see Culp and Miller, "Metallgesellschaft" and "Hedging." For a redacted version of the story, *see* Christopher L. Culp and Merton H. Miller, "Blame Mismanagement, Not Speculation, for Metall's Woes," *Wall Street Journal Europe*, April 25, 1995.

Cash Flow Risk

Firms concerned *not* with the value of a stock of assets and liabilities over a specific time horizon but with the volatility of a *flow of funds* often are better off eschewing VaR altogether in favor of a measure of cash flow volatility. Possible cash requirements over a *sequence* of future dates, for example, can be simulated. The resulting distributions of cash flows then enable the firm to control its exposure to cash flow risk more directly.[45] Firms worried about cash flow risk for preserving or increasing their debt capacities thus might engage in hedging, whereas firms concerned purely about liquidity shortfalls might use such cash flow stress tests to arrange appropriate standby funding.

Abnormal Returns and Risk-Based Capital Allocation

René Stulz suggests managing risk-taking activities using abnormal returns— that is, returns in excess of the risk free rate—as a measure of the expected profitability of certain activities. Selective risk management then can be accomplished by allocating capital on a risk-adjusted basis and limiting capital at risk accordingly. To measure the risk-adjusted capital allocation, he suggests using the cost of new equity issued to finance the particular activity.[46]

On the positive side, Stulz's suggestion does not penalize selective risk managers for exploiting perceived informational advantages, whereas VAR does. The problem with Stulz's idea, however, lies in any company's capacity actually to implement such a risk management process. More properly, the difficulty lies in the actual estimation of the firm's equity cost of capital. And in any event, under M&M proposition three, all sources of capital are equivalent on a risk-adjusted basis. The source of capital for financing a particular project thus should not affect the decision to undertake that project. Stulz's reliance on equity only is thus inappropriate.

Shortfall Risk

VaR need not be calculated by assuming variance is a complete measure of "risk," but in practice this often *is* how VaR is calculated. (See the Appendix.) This assumption can be problematic when measuring exposures in markets characterized by non-normal (i.e., non-Gaussian) distributions—for example, return distributions that are skewed or have fat tails. If so, as explained in the Appendix, a solution is to generate the VaR distribution in a manner that does *not* presuppose variance is an adequate measure of risk. Alternatively, other summary risk measures can be calculated.

45. See Stulz, "Rethinking."
46. Ibid.

For some organizations, asymmetric distributions pose a problem that VaR on its own *cannot* address, no matter how it is calculated. Consider again the OCIP example, in which the 1-year VaR implied a $1 billion loss in 1 year out of 20. With a symmetric portfolio distribution, that would also imply a $1 billion gain in 1 year out of 20. But suppose OCIP's investment program had a *positively skewed* return distribution. Then, the $1 billion loss in 1 year out of 20 might be comparable to, say, a $5 billion gain in 1 year of 20.

One of the problems with interpreting VaR thus is interpreting the confidence level—namely, 5% or 1 year in 20. Some organizations may consider it more useful *not* to examine the loss associated with a chosen probability level but rather to examine the risk associated with a *given loss*—the so-called "doomsday" return below which a portfolio must *never* fall. Pension plans, endowments, and some hedge funds, for example, are concerned primarily with the possibility of a "shortfall" of assets below liabilities that would necessitate a contribution from the plan sponsor.

Shortfall risk measures are alternatives to VaR that allow a risk manager to define a specific target value below which the organization's assets must *never* fall and they measure risk accordingly. Two popular measures of shortfall risk are below-target probability (BTP) and below-target risk (BTR).[47]

The advantage of BTR, in particular, over VaR is that it penalizes large shortfalls more than small ones.[48] BTR is still subject to the same misinterpretation as VAR when it is reported without a corresponding indication of possible *gains*. VaR, however, relies on a somewhat arbitrary choice of a "probability level" that can be changed to exaggerate or to de-emphasize risk measures. BTR, by contrast, is based on a real target—for example, a pension actuarial contribution threshold—and thus reveals information about risk that can be much more usefully weighed against expected returns than a VaR measure.[49]

Conclusion

By facilitating the consistent measurement of risk across distinct assets and activities, VaR allows firms to monitor, report, and control their risks in a manner that efficiently relates risk control to desired and actual economic exposures. At the same time, reliance on VaR can result in serious problems when improperly used. Would-be users of VaR are thus advised to consider the following three pieces of advice.

---

47. See Culp et al., "Risks." For a complete mathematic discussion of these concepts, see Kamaryn T. Tanner, "An Asymmetric Distribution Model for Portfolio Optimization" (Unpublished manuscript, Graduate School of Business, University of Chicago, 1997).
48. BTP accomplishes a similar objective but does *not* weight large deviations below the target more heavily than small ones.
49. See Culp et al., "Risks," for a more involved treatment of shortfall risk as compared to VaR.

VaR is useful only to certain firms and only in particular circumstances. Specifically, VAR is a tool for firms engaged in *total value* risk management, where the consolidated values of exposures across a variety of activities are at issue. Dangerous misinterpretations of the risk facing a firm can result when VaR is wrongly applied in situations where total value risk management is *not* the objective, such as at firms concerned with *cash flow* risk rather than value risk.

Second, VaR should be applied very carefully to firms selectively managing their risks. When an organization deliberately takes certain risks as a part of its primary business, VaR can serve at best as a diagnostic monitoring tool for those risks. When VaR is analyzed and reported in such situations with no estimates of corresponding expected profits, the information conveyed by the VaR estimate can be extremely misleading.

Finally, as all the great derivatives disasters illustrate, no form of risk measurement—including VaR—is a substitute for good management. Risk management as a process encompasses much more than just risk measurement. Although judicious risk measurement can prove very useful to certain firms, it is quite pointless without a well-developed organizational infrastructure and IT system capable of supporting the complex and dynamic process of risk taking and risk control.

APPENDIX
Calculating VaR

To calculate a VaR statistic is easy *once you have generated the probability distribution for future values of the portfolio*. Creating that VaR distribution, on the other hand, can be quite hard, and the methods available range from the banal to the utterly arcane. This appendix reviews a few of those methods.

Variance-Based Approaches

By far the easiest way to create the VaR distribution used in calculating the actual VaR statistic is just to *assume* that distribution is normal (i.e., Gaussian). Mean and variance are "sufficient statistics" to fully characterize a normal distribution. Consequently, knowing the variance of an asset whose return is normally distributed is all that is needed to summarize the risk of that asset.

Using return variances and covariances as inputs, VaR thus can be calculated in a fairly straightforward way.[50] First consider a single asset. If returns on

---

50. A useful example of this methodology is presented in Anthony Saunders, "Market Risk," *The Financier* Vol. 2, No. 5 (December 1995).

that asset are normally distributed, the 5th percentile VaR is always 1.65 standard deviations below the mean return. So, the variance is a sufficient measure of risk to compute the VaR on that asset—just subtract 1.65 times the standard deviation from the mean. The risk horizon for such a VaR estimate corresponds to the frequency used to compute the input variance.

Now consider two assets. In that case, the VaR of the portfolio of two assets can be computed in a similar manner using the variances of the two assets' returns. These variance-based risk measures then are combined using the correlation of the two assets' returns. The result is a VaR estimate for the portfolio.

The simplicity of the variance-based approach to VaR calculations lies in the assumption of normality. By *assuming* that returns on all financial instruments are normally distributed, the risk manager eliminates the need to come up with a VaR distribution using complicated modeling techniques. All that *really* must be done is to come up with the appropriate variances and correlations.

At the same time, however, by assuming normality, the risk manager has greatly limited the VaR estimate. Normal distributions, after all, are symmetric. Any potential for skewness or fat tails in asset returns thus is totally ignored in the variance-only approach.

In addition to sacrificing the possibility that asset returns may *not* be normally distributed, the variance-only approach to calculating VaR also relies on the critical assumption that asset returns are totally independent across increments of time. A multi-period VaR can be calculated only by calculating a single-period VaR from the available data and then extrapolating the multi-day risk estimate. For example, suppose variances and correlations are available for historical returns measured at the *daily* frequency. To get from a 1-day VaR to a T-day VaR—where T is the risk horizon of interest—the variance-only approach requires that the 1-day VaR is multiplied by the square root of T.

For return variances and correlations measured at the monthly frequency or lower, this assumption may not be terribly implausible. For daily variances and correlations, however, serial independence is a very strong and usually an unrealistic assumption in most markets. The problem is less severe for short risk horizons, of course. So, using a 1-day VaR as the basis for a 5-day VaR might be acceptable, whereas a 1-day VAR extrapolated into a 1-year VaR would be highly problematic in most markets.

Computing Volatility Inputs

Despite its unrealistic assumptions, simple variance-based VaR calculations are probably the dominant application of the VaR measure today. The approach is especially popular for corporate end users of derivatives, principally because the necessary software is cheap and easy to use.

All variance-based VaR measures, however, are not alike. The sources of inputs used to calculate VaR in this manner can differ widely. The next several subsections summarize several popular methods for determining these variances.[51] Note that these methods are *only* methods of computing *variances* on single assets. Correlations still must be determined to convert the VaRs of individual assets into portfolio VaRs.

Moving Average Volatility. One of the simplest approaches to calculating variance for use in a variance-based VaR calculation involves estimating a historical moving average of volatility. To get a moving average estimate of variance, the average is taken over a rolling window of historical volatility data. For example, given a 20-day rolling window,[52] the daily variance used for 1-day VAR calculations would be the average daily variance over the most recent 20 days. To calculate this, many assume a zero mean daily return and then just average the squared returns for the last 20 trading days. On the next day, a new return becomes available for the volatility calculation. To maintain a 20-day measurement window, the first observation is dropped off and the average is recomputed as the basis of the next day's VaR estimate.

More formally, denote the daily return from time t–1 to time t as r_t. Assuming a zero mean daily return, the moving average volatility over a window of the last D days is calculated as follows:

$$V_t^2 = \left[\frac{1}{D}\right] \sum_{i=0}^{D-1} r_{t-i}^2$$

where v_t is the daily volatility estimate used as the VaR input on day t.

Because moving-average volatility is calculated using equal weights for all observations in the historical time series, the calculations are very simple. The result, however, is a smoothing effect that causes sharp changes in volatility to appear as plateaus over longer periods of time, failing to capture dramatic changes in volatility.

Risk Metrics. To facilitate 1-day VaR calculations and extrapolated risk measures for longer risk horizons, JP Morgan—in association with Reuters—began making available their RiskMetrics™ data sets. This data includes historical variances and covariances on a variety of simple assets—sometimes called "primitive securities."[53] Most other assets have cash flows that can be "mapped" into these simpler RiskMetrics assets for VaR calculation purposes.[54]

---

51. For more methods, see Jorion.
52. The length of the window is chosen by the risk manager doing the VaR calculation.
53. See Jorion.
54. For a detailed explanation of this approach, see J.P. Morgan/Reuters, *RiskMetrics—Technical Document*, 4th ed. (1996).

In the RiskMetrics data set, daily variances and correlations are computed using an "exponentially weighted moving average." Unlike the simple moving-average volatility estimate, an exponentially weighted moving average allows the most recent observations to be more influential in the calculation than observations further in the past. This has the advantage of capturing shocks in the market better than the simple moving average and thus is often regarded as producing a better volatility for variance-based VaR than the equal-weighted moving average alternative.

Conditional Variance Models. Another approach for estimating the variance input to VaR calculations involves the use of "conditional variance" time series methods. The first conditional variance model was developed by Robert Engle in 1982 and is known as the autoregressive conditional heterskedasticity (ARCH) model.[55] ARCH combines an autoregressive process with a moving average estimation method so that variance still is calculated in the rolling window manner used for moving averages.

Since its introduction, ARCH has evolved into a variety of other conditional variance models, such as generalized ARCH (GARCH), integrated GARCH (IGARCH), and exponential GARCH (EGARCH). Numerous applications of these models have led practitioners to believe that these estimation techniques provide better estimates of (time-series) volatility than simpler methods.

For a GARCH (1,1) model, the variance of an asset's return at time t is presumed to have the following structure:

$$v^2_t = a_0 + a_1 r^2_{t-1} + a_2 v^2_{t-1}$$

The conditional variance model thus incorporates a *recursive* moving average term. In the special case where $a_0 = 0$ and $a_1 + a_2 = 1$, the GARCH (1,1) model reduces *exactly* to the exponentially weighted moving average formulation for volatility.[56]

Using volatilities from a GARCH model as inputs in a variance-based VaR calculation does not circumvent the statistical inference problem of presumed normality. By incorporating additional information into the volatility measure, however, more of the actual time-series properties of the underlying asset return can be incorporated into the VaR estimate than if a simple average volatility is used.

Implied Volatility. All of the above methods of computing volatilities for variance-based VaR calculations are based on historical data. For more of a

55. Robert Engle, "Autoregressive Conditional Heteroskedasticity with Estimates of the Variance of United Kingdom Inflation," *Econometrica* Vol. 50 (1982): 391–407.
56. See Jorion.

forward-looking measure of volatility, option-implied volatilities sometimes can be used to calculate VaR.

The implied volatility of an option is defined as the expected future volatility of the underlying asset over the remaining life of the option. Many studies have concluded that measures of option-implied volatility are, indeed, the *best* predictor of future volatility.[57] Unlike time-series measures of volatility that are entirely backward-looking, option-implied volatility is "backed-out" of actual option prices—which, in turn, are based on actual transactions and expectations of market participants—and thus is inherently forward-looking.

Any option-implied volatility estimate is dependent on the particular option pricing model used to derive the implied volatility. Given an observed market price for an option *and* a presumed pricing model, the implied volatility can be determined numerically. This variance may then be used in a VaR calculation for the asset underlying the option.

Non-variance VaR Calculation Methods

Despite the simplicity of most variance-based VaR measurement methods, many practitioners prefer to avoid the restrictive assumptions underlying that approach—namely, symmetric return distributions that are independent and stable over time. To avoid these assumptions, a risk manager must actually generate a full distribution of possible future portfolio values—a distribution that is neither necessarily normal nor symmetric.[58]

Historical simulation is perhaps the easiest alternative to variance-based VaR. This approach generates VaR distributions merely by "re-arranging" historical data—namely, re-sampling time-series data on the relevant asset prices or returns. This can be about as easy *computationally* as variance-based VaR, and it does *not* presuppose that everything in the world is normally distributed. Nevertheless, the approach is highly dependent on the availability of potentially massive amounts of historical data. In addition, the VaR resulting from a historical simulation is totally sample dependent.

More advanced approaches to VaR calculation usually involve some type of forward-looking simulation model, such as Monte Carlo. Implementing simulation methods typically is computationally intensive, expensive, and heavily dependent on personnel resources. For that reason, simulation has remained largely limited to active trading firms and institutional investors. Nevertheless, simulation does enable users to depart from the RiskMetrics normality assumptions about underlying asset returns without forcing them

---

57. See, for example, Philippe Jorion, "Predicting Volatility in the Foreign Exchange Market," *Journal of Finance* Vol. 50 (1995): 507–28.
58. Variance-based approaches avoid the problem of generating a new distribution by *assuming* that distribution.

to rely on a single historical data sample. Simulation also eliminates the need to assume independence in returns over time—namely, VaR calculations are no longer restricted to 1-day estimates that must be extrapolated over the total risk horizon.

■ CHRISTOPHER L. CULP is Director of Risk Management Services, CP Risk Management LLC.

■ MERTON H. MILLER is Robert R. McCormick Distinguished Service Professor of Finance Emeritus, Graduate School of Business, the University of Chicago.

■ ANDREA M. P. NEVES is Senior Risk Management Consultant, CP Risk Management LLC.

CHAPTER 9

Allocating Shareholder
Capital to Pension Plans

ROBERT C. MERTON

G OOD EVENING, it's a pleasure to be here and thank you all for coming. It will not come as news to any of you that adequate provision for retirement through a combination of state, employer, and personal savings is a worldwide concern. It's a major concern in Asia and South America, in the United States and continental Europe, and, of course, here in the United Kingdom. For corporations with defined benefit (DB) pension plans, the problem has manifested itself in a funding shortfall between pension assets and pension liabilities. The shortfall is a consequence of the large decline in equities in the first 3 years of this decade, in combination with drops in interest rates that have raised the value of the liabilities. The falling stock prices during that period also coincided with—and indeed reflected—reductions in the companies' earnings and hence in their ability to fund their shortfalls out of business operations.

The new accounting treatment of pensions in the United Kingdom—a version of which is now being considered by the Financial Accounting Standards Board (FASB) in the United States—will make these shortfalls more transparent to interested parties, particularly investors, rating agencies, and regulators. And as the new rules come into force, they are likely to have real effects, such as limiting dividends and other distributions to shareholders. Some companies are responding by capping or shutting down their DB plans, and then creating defined contribution (DC) plans.[1]

This chapter was previously published as an article in *Journal of Applied Corporate Finance* Vol. 18, No. 1 (Spring 2006): 15–24. The original article is an edited transcript of a speech delivered in London on October 21, 2004, at a conference on pensions sponsored by BNP Paribas. Some events that have occurred since that time are reflected in the footnotes that have been appended to the talk.

1. The recent announcement by International Business Machines (IBM) of its shift to a DC plan could turn out to be a watershed event that precipitates the unraveling of the DB system. If healthy and employee-centric companies are getting rid of DB plans even for existing employees, what kind of companies are going to pay ever larger premiums to remain part of the system insured by the Pension Benefit Guaranty Corporation?

There are of course multiple facets to this very important issue. My remarks this evening will focus primarily on the corporate challenge of providing retirement income to employees while limiting the costs and risks of retirement plans to the firms, and ensuring that investors and rating agencies understand both the risks and corporate efforts to deal with them. My main focus throughout will be on the real economic import and consequences of such issues and not how they are reflected on financial statements. This is not to suggest that accounting issues are unimportant, only that accounting is not my expertise—and because I value the time you are spending with me, I will concentrate on what I know a bit more about.

In the rest of this talk I will address five questions:

- What are the major issues and challenges surrounding pensions? We all know that the shortfall has been the focus of attention. However, I will make a case that while the gap between assets and liabilities is important, of far greater concern for the future is the risk mismatch between pension assets and pension liabilities. Most U.K. and U.S. companies have been funding debt-like liabilities with investments in equity-heavy asset portfolios.[2]

- To what extent do the equity market and equity prices reflect the shortfall in pension funding and the mismatch in risk? Do the markets see through the smoothing of pension earnings by accounting convention and consider pension shortfalls and mismatch risks in valuing the equity? What does the evidence tell us? Moreover, even if the market appears capable of reflecting pension risk, is it possible that analysts' price/earnings (P/E) multiples and management's assessments of cost of capital are distorted by failure to take full account of the risks associated with pension assets?

- How should management analyze and formulate strategic solutions? I will offer no specific solutions tonight because each firm faces somewhat different circumstances and no one prescription fits all. Nevertheless, I do want to lay out a framework for analyzing the problem from a strategic perspective that can be used in formulating a company's pension policy. In particular, I will recommend that companies take an integrated perspective that views pension assets and liabilities as parts of their economic value and risk balance sheets—and one that accordingly treats the pension asset allocation decision as a critical aspect of a corporate-wide

---

2. One notable difference between U.S. and U.K. companies is that the latter provide workers with inflation-indexed benefits, and such benefits can be immunized with inflation-linked "Gilts."

enterprise risk management program. Finally, I will offer the concept of a *risk budget*—basically, a list of all of a company's major exposures along with an estimate of the amount of equity capital necessary to support each one. One important use of such a risk budget is to enable management to address the question of how much equity capital must be allocated to the risk positions, or risk mismatches, that are created by asset allocation decisions in DB pension plans.

- The fourth question has to do with issues of implementation. If a company chooses to make a major change in its pension policy, such as a partial or complete immunization accomplished by substituting bonds for stocks, how would you communicate the risk implications of the new policy to the rating agencies and investors? How would your approach be affected by whether your plan is fully funded, underfunded, or overfunded? If underfunded, should one borrow to fully fund the plan?

- The fifth and final section discusses the challenges associated with moving from a DB plan to a DC plan. What are the major issues to be thinking about when contemplating such a change?

I will confess to you at the outset that most of the examples I will discuss come from the United States rather than the United Kingdom. The only defense I offer for such provincialism is to plead my own familiarity with U.S. companies and numbers. But let me suggest that most of the U.S. cases I will present have rough counterparts in the United Kingdom—and that if you make some effort to translate the numbers and the circumstances into a U.K. context, I think you will find that the main issues that I raise tonight apply, with roughly equal force, to U.K. companies.

The Apparent Issue—Funding Shortfall

The funding shortfall has been the focus of analysts, the rating agencies (which have treated the shortfall as a form of debt for at least a decade), and regulators. You heard the numbers in my introduction; these are big numbers and the problem needs to be addressed. But I have no magic solution if you are underfunded by $1 billion; I cannot tell you how to wave a wand or give you a strategy that makes the underfunding disappear in true economic terms. And just to be clear, when I say "underfunded," I mean that the current marked-to-market value of the pension assets is less than the current marked-to-market value of the pension liabilities.

Underfunding has long been a problem, though it was largely hidden in the 1990s. This was partly driven by a mistaken tendency to equate higher *expected* returns with higher *realized* returns. Like most economists, I agree that equity returns in general are expected to be higher than fixed-income returns. However, the concept of higher expected equity returns has been translated, thanks to a misapplication of actuarial science, into the statement, "For companies with a long enough time horizon, higher expected returns can be assumed to imply higher realized returns for certain." And from there it is a short step to the idea that $1 invested today in stocks is worth more than $1 invested in bonds. This mistaken way of thinking,[3] which is effectively embedded in pension accounting and actuarial smoothing of pension returns, has been a major driver of corporate pension allocations. What such thinking ignores, of course, are the very different levels of risk associated with the higher expected returns on equities, a reality that became very clear during the market experience of 2000–2002.

The Real Issue—Risk Mismatch

But, again, I believe that the biggest pension problem facing corporate America and its investors is not the shortfall, but the risk mismatch between pension assets and liabilities. Suppose you were looking at two companies. For Company A, the ratio of its pension assets and liabilities on a marked-to-market basis is 1.0. For Company B, the ratio of assets to liabilities is 1.05 to 1.0. Which company should we be more worried about? With no other information about the companies or their plans, common sense of course says that the firm that is 5% overfunded is in a better position.

But let me now give you the rest of the story. Company A's allocation of pension assets is to choose 100% bonds with the same duration as its pension liabilities. Company B has 85% of its pension asset portfolio in equities. Now, which of the two should you watch more closely? The point I'm making with this simple example is that balance sheet numbers, whether marked-to-market or not, are *static* and therefore of limited use. They are a picture of where the firm and its assets and liabilities are right now. They reveal nothing about the risk that those two numbers may change, either by how much or with what likelihood.

In the first case, as long as Company A maintains its policy, even though the plan is just fully funded, that funding will be completely adequate; you do not need to be overfunded if you always hold assets that precisely hedge the

---

3. The fallacy of treating expected stock returns as risk free has been demonstrated by Paul Samuelson in several of his writings: "Lifetime Portfolio Selection by Dynamic Stochastic Programming," *Review of Economics and Statistics* Vol. 51 (1969), and "The Long-Term Case of Equities and How it Can be Oversold," *Journal of Portfolio Management* (Fall 1994); and, more recently, by Zvi Bodie, in "On the Risk of Stocks in the Long Run," *Financial Analysts Journal* (May–June 1995). As discussed later, still another way of demonstrating this fallacy is to note that a 40-year return asset return swap in which one receives the cumulative total return on the Standard and Poor's (S&P) 500 over 40 years and pays the cumulative return on either U.S. treasury bills (rolled over) or U.S. treasury 10-year bonds can be purchased for $0.

risk of the liabilities. In the second case, however, even a funding ratio of 1.05 is probably not sufficient. While it is quite true that the company's funding ratio could jump from 1.05 to 1.20 in a year's time, it could just as quickly fall to 0.85. The balance sheet numbers that purport to measure a pension surplus or deficit give no indication of risk.

The risk mismatch is likely to be of greatest concern in cases where the ratio of pension assets to the market capitalization of equity is high. For publicly traded U.S. companies with DB pension plans near the end of 2001, the median ratio of pension assets to the market cap of equity for the top quintile of firms (ranked by that ratio) was 2 to 1.[4] That underscores the point that pension assets are not small relative to the total equity of the firm. Moreover, it is typical to have 60% to 70% of the pension assets in equities. This means that for at least 20% of the companies in this sample, the equities holdings in their pension portfolios are larger than the entire market cap of the firm's equity (60% of 2.0 is 1.2).

Take the case of General Motors (GM), which has the largest corporate pension fund in the United States, with total assets of approximately $90 billion. If we assume that 65% of those assets are devoted to equities—which, again, is standard U.S. corporate practice—that means the company has approximately $60 billion invested in equities. At the moment, GM has a market cap of approximately $22 billion, which means that it may well have almost three times its own market cap invested in the equities of other companies.[5] Even for large firms, if you are thinking in terms of the size of the pension investment versus such things as the amount of equity capital, this is quite considerable. We need to be aware of that in our thinking.

Now consider a corporate balance sheet that includes $60 billion of equity on the asset side and a $60-billion liability that is perfectly matched in terms of value but not risk. This mismatched combination of assets and liabilities would not show up any differently on accounting statements—even under the new international accounting standard (IAS) rule—than $60 billion of debt assets that were perfectly matched in risk to the pension liability. The first of these two combinations is equivalent to making a $60-billion bet on the stock market and financing it with $60 billion of fixed-rate, long-term debt. For those of you who are familiar with derivatives, this is equivalent to entering into a

4. For the pension quintile ratios of pension assets to market cap, I am indebted to a presentation by Michael Gilberto of J.P. Morgan Chase at a JPM Investment Management Conference on October 4, 2001.

5. Although GM recently reported that the 2005 gains in its pension fund have given it a pension surplus of some $6 billion, the economic reality—again based on the assumption that 60% of the fund is in equities—is that the value at risk (VaR) or equity capital necessary to support that risk exposure is several times the firm's current (January 24, 2006) equity market cap of $13 billion.

$60-billion asset return swap where you pay a fixed rate of interest in return for receiving the total realized market return on equities.

Recognizing the Risk

As you know, when a swap is first done on standard terms, it has essentially no value; in terms of the balance sheet, it thus has no entry. What about its risk? Would you say there is a fair amount of risk if you bought $60 billion of equity and financed it with $60 billion of fixed-rate debt? That is a huge risk position. I am not saying that risk-taking is wrong, but failing to recognize the size of that risk position is a mistake. Imagine a chief executive officer (CEO), accompanied by his or her chief financial officer (CFO) or finance director, announcing to an audience of shareholders, creditors, and other stakeholders, "Our current market capitalization is $15 billion. Our strategy for the coming year is to buy $60 billion of equities and finance the purchase with $60 billion of long-term fixed-rate debt." I think that recommendation would evoke a considerable amount of discussion.

And this brings me to the issues of transparency and framing. I am not suggesting that companies are consciously attempting to mislead investors about their pension policies. What I am trying to emphasize is the importance of acknowledging the economic reality that the pension assets *are* the shareholders' assets, and then framing the risks accordingly. Pension assets are "encumbered" assets in the sense that there is a lien against them by the pensioners in the plan, but the residual gains and losses from that pension asset portfolio basically flow to the shareholders.

Now, there is one important exception to this rule—namely, companies with pension deficits facing a significant probability of default and bankruptcy. Since the pension losses of such firms are likely to end up being borne by the Pension Benefit Guaranty Corporation in the United States—and by the Pension Protection Fund in the United Kingdom—the value-maximizing strategy may well be to maintain and even enlarge the risk mismatch of their pensions in the hope that large pension gains can help rescue the firm by covering the shortfall and limiting future contributions to the plan. But, for reasonably healthy companies, pension assets are effectively (though not institutionally) assets of the corporation; and pension liabilities are liabilities of the corporation, no matter what happens to the pension assets. It is an obligation of the corporation, much like payments of interest and principal on its debt.

In this sense, then, pension risks *are* corporate risks. And as I discuss in more detail later, how one frames the risks in corporate DB plans will affect corporate decisions to continue or modify such plans as well as the choice of assets to fund them. When you consider the magnitude of the total value changes stemming from the mismatch of risk, it becomes very clear that the mismatch is a bigger problem than the current shortfall in funding. For companies with large DB plans, the impact on corporate values of a recession-induced drop in equities combined with a drop in interest rates—a combination similar to what we saw during the first years of this decade—could end up dwarfing the effects of a downturn on the operating businesses. The risks associated with today's pension asset-liability mismatches are very big risks indeed.

Accounting for Value Mismatch and Risk

My second major point has to do with how the markets seem to take account of both the value mismatch—that is, the size of any pension surplus or shortfall—and the risk mismatch. In terms of value, research done over a decade ago at the National Bureau of Economic Research on U.S. companies—and I have no reason to think it would be materially different for U.K. companies—supports the idea that share prices do in fact reflect the value of pension surpluses or shortfalls. In particular, companies with large pension deficits appear to trade at lower P/E multiples and price-to-book ratios than firms with fully or overfunded DB plans.[6]

This finding did not come as a surprise. But I have to confess to some surprise at the findings of some recent work I did with colleagues Zvi Bodie and Li Jin on the value effects of pension risk mismatch.[7] And let me remind you once more of the proposition we were testing: You could have a pension plan in which pension assets and pension liabilities are roughly equal in value, meaning there is no shortfall or surplus. But if the pension assets were largely in equities and the liability is largely fixed-rate debt, the risk exposure would be huge. And the question we were attempting to answer in our study was: Does the market capture that risk? Given the arcane accounting and institutional separation between the pension plan and the rest of the business, I did not think the market would take it into account.

But our results suggest that, during the period of our study[8] (1993–98) the U.S. stock market did a pretty good job of picking up the differences in risk. More specifically, a company with a larger fraction of equity in its pension portfolio tended, all other things equal, to have a larger "beta"—a widely used measure of risk that reflects, among other things, the "systematic-risk" volatility of the stock price itself. In other words—and this is simplifying things a

6. See, for example, Martin Feldstein and Stephanie Seligman, "Pension Funding, Share Prices, and National Savings," *Journal of Finance* Vol. 4, No. 36 (1981).
7. See Li Jin, Robert C. Merton, and Zvi Bodie, "Do a Firm's Equity Returns Reflect the Risk of Its Pension Plan?" *Journal of Financial Economics*, forthcoming.
8. In 1993, companies were required for the first time to report Employment Retirement Income Security Act (ERISA) form 5500, which provides a list of the firm's pension holdings as of year end.

bit—the greater risk associated with equity-heavy pension plans seemed to show up in more volatile stock prices.

What's especially interesting to me about these findings is that they apply to a period that preceded the large market decline that started in 2000. It's relatively easy to see how investors could become sensitized to the possibility of pension losses during a market downturn. But the evidence of our study seems to show that share prices do take account of pension risk, even when most pensions are in surplus—and when the risk shows up nowhere on the accounting balance sheet. And to the extent the marketplace charges firms for bearing that added pension risk, our findings have some important implications for corporate policy and investment decisions that I will discuss later.

To repeat my point, then, our evidence comes not from surveying analysts, but from looking at what actually happens to share prices. And this, of course, is supportive of the idea of an efficient stock market. But we are not out of the woods yet. It is entirely possible that some equity analysts do not pay much attention to pension risk when assessing P/E multiples and comparing companies. It's also possible that some corporate managers may not be taking account of the contribution of pension risk to overall corporate risk when making major capital allocations among their different businesses. And, as discussed below, the result could be distortions of both analysts' valuations and strategic corporate business decisions.

Calculating the Weighted Average Cost of Capital

To illustrate this point, let's say you are a corporate executive considering a decision to expand into more or less the same business you are in now. In that case, the standard capital budgeting approach is to estimate the expected future cash flows and then discount those flows at the firm's weighted average cost of capital (WACC). How do you get estimates of your WACC? If you are a publicly traded company, you can typically observe the historical movement of your share prices, and then estimate the beta of the share returns. When you do this, you are really assuming that the historical volatility of the stock is a reliable proxy for its risk—and, in this sense, beta is a wholly *market-based* measure of risk. The market may be completely wrong about this, but this is how investors perceive the risk of your stock.

Now, in valuing a project, unless the firm is financed entirely with equity, you cannot simply take the firm's beta and come up with a cost of equity capital. You have to take account of the use of debt in the firm's capital structure. To do that, you "de-leverage" the equity to come up with the WACC, which is an average of your debt and equity rates; you get the equity rates from the riskiness measured historically. Your debt rates are your observed debt rates. That is standard procedure for estimating WACC.

But the use of WACC to evaluate this project is based on a couple of important premises. First, as mentioned, the project in question should have roughly the same operating risk and be able to support the same leverage ratio as the rest of the firm's assets. Second, the calculation of the firm's leverage ratio should reflect all senior corporate obligations, not just on balance-sheet debt.[9]

Incorporating Pension Risk into WACC

Given our focus on pension assets and liabilities, this suggests there may be a problem with this standard procedure for estimating WACC: its failure to take account of the risk of other important assets that are not reflected on generally accepted accounting principles (GAAP) balance sheets. As we have already seen, pension assets can be a significant fraction of total corporate assets. And for companies with large DB plans, an equity-heavy asset portfolio can be one of the main sources of total volatility on the left side of the balance sheet—in some cases as large as the operating business itself.

On the other side of the balance sheet, pension liabilities are missing from the standard procedure as well. Pension liabilities are debt. Though collateralized by the pension assets, they are an obligation of the firm and thus part of the leverage or gearing of the firm.

By failing to take account of their pension assets and pension liabilities when estimating their cost of capital, companies are probably distorting their measures of operating, or project, risk in two ways. First, they are effectively assigning the firm's total risk to its business operations, when a potentially significant part of that risk could in fact come from the pension fund assets. Second, because the standard analysis does not take account of the pension liabilities, it understates the firm's leverage ratio.

The typical effect of these two distortions is to overstate WACC for an operating project. If our analysis instead used a pension-adjusted leverage ratio and included the pension assets on the left-hand side of the balance sheet, the resulting estimates of "unleveraged" operating beta for most companies with large DB plans would fall.

To sum up, then, if management estimates WACC by the standard method, it can lead to a major distortion of the capital allocation decision. It means applying too high a hurdle rate to projects, which means the firm may not under-

9. For illustrative purposes, all the calculations of the effect of the pension plan on beta estimates for WACC are based on the assumption that corporations do not pay income taxes. In practice, companies need to incorporate into their WACC analysis an estimate of the company's marginal corporate tax rate. If the company is and expects to be fully taxable at all times, a portion of the value of the pension assets and the pension liabilities are "owned" by the government and so therefore are their risks. But that computation is very firm-specific and not required for the level of demonstration here.

TABLE 9.1

Errors in Estimates of Weighted Average Cost of Capital: Examples

	Pension Assets ($bn)	Pension Liabilities ($bn)	Pension Surplus/ Deficit ($bn)	Market Cap ($bn)	Book Value of Debt ($bn)	Standard WACC*	WACC Adjusted for Pension Risks*
Boeing	33.8	32.7	1.1	30.9	12.3	8.80%	6.09%
DuPont	17.9	18.8	(0.9)	42.6	6.8	9.44%	8.15%
Eastman Kodak	7.9	7.4	0.5	8.6	3.2	9.75%	7.47%
Textron	4.5	3.9	0.6	5.9	7.1	7.98%	6.81%

*WACC numbers are based on a risk-free rate of 5% and a market-risk premium of 7%.
Source: "The Real Problem with Pensions," *Harvard Business Review*, December 2004.

take all the projects that are expected to increase its value. Taken by itself, it does not imply anything about the optimal asset allocation in the pension fund plan; but it is one possible consequence of not taking account of it.

Illustrations

To give you an idea of how big that distortion could be for some real companies, let's look at four examples: Boeing, DuPont, Eastman Kodak, and Textron.[10] As shown in table 9.1, all but DuPont have pension surpluses. And DuPont's pension shortfall is tiny compared to both its total liabilities and assets, and to its market cap. These are financially healthy companies; they are surely not high on anyone's list of the type of pension issues that normally concern us.

Calculating a standard WACC, which fails to take account of the risk of the pension assets and the gearing of the pension liabilities, leads to an estimated cost of capital for Boeing of 8.8%. But when we make an adjustment for the company's pension risk that reflects the extent of its asset-liability mismatch—and take account of the size of the pension liabilities, which changes the firm's leverage ratio—Boeing's estimated WACC drops to about 6%, implying an overstatement of almost 300 basis points by the standard methods. That is the extreme case in the sample, but estimates of the overstatements for all four firms exceed 100 basis points.

This is not to say that the managements of these four companies are actually making this mistake; I have not worked with any of these companies and have no knowledge of their capital budgeting process. What I am saying is that if they follow the standard textbook procedure for estimating WACC, without

10. These examples appear in Lin et al., "Firm's Equity Returns."

adjusting for the risk and size of the pension fund, they could be materially overstating their cost of capital. And since we know that stock-price multiples are roughly inversely related to required returns or cost of capital, analysts who are overstating the estimates of cost of capital are also likely to be underestimating the multiples of the companies they cover.

In sum, pension decisions in terms of both asset size and allocation have the potential to affect the management of the entire firm at the most fundamental level. Strategic investment and risk management decisions can be affected by the allocation of pension assets. And for reasons I've just illustrated, the failure of corporate managements to view pension assets and liabilities as part of the firm may well be leading to underinvestment in the operating part of the business.

Strategic Analysis and Policy Development

My third major point is about strategic analysis and working toward developing a pension plan policy. I hope the preceding remarks have demonstrated the need for an integrated enterprise-wide approach, one that views pension assets and liabilities as parts of the firm's comprehensive economic and risk balance sheets. To evaluate their sources and impact at the strategic level, pension risks should be evaluated not only in terms of implementation of the pension plan, but within the context of the firm's other objectives, risks, and strategic plans, including effects on credit ratings.

Or to turn this thought upside down, all of a company's major business and financing decisions should be informed by a well-structured analysis that views capital allocation, capital structure, *and* pension plan decisions as parts of an integrated strategy. Much of my emphasis to this point has been on the potential effects of pension asset allocation on corporate capital allocation and capital structure choices. It is precisely because of these effects—of this linkage between the pension and the operating business—that pension asset allocation should be considered a strategic issue, one that is overseen at the highest level of corporate decision making.

But if we continue to view the pension fund as an off-balance sheet entity with no ties to the firm, our decision making will likely also continue to be distorted by the higher expected returns on equities, even if the new accounting rules force us to report actual rather than expected returns in our financial statements. After all, shifting pension assets from equities to bonds will lower the expected returns on our asset portfolio and raise the contributions needed, at least in the near-term, to meet plan obligations. And that sounds like a bad thing, a value-reducing proposition—until one begins to consider the effect on risk. When you look at the whole picture, lowering the expected returns on the assets also lowers the risk of the entire firm. And by lowering risk, you create the capacity for the firm to take other risks—core operating risks, if you will, that are likely to add more value than passive equity investments in other companies.

That brings me to the concept of a "risk budget" I mentioned earlier. I find it useful to think of companies as having risk budgets that are very much analogous to their capital budgets. Reducing risk in one place releases capacity to increase risk elsewhere without having to add more equity capital to the firm. And this means that the total opportunity created by reducing risks in the pension fund is to enable the firm to take more risk in its operating businesses, which is presumably where it is most likely to find positive net present value opportunities. The expected net effect of such changes is an increase in firm value. Although you reduce the expected return on your pension assets, you gain more from the new operating assets that you are now able to hold without additional equity capital—all of which is made possible by the reduction of risk in the pension fund.

Having said this, let me also hasten to add that 100% bonds will not be the optimal pension portfolio for all DB plans. But the possibility for such gains from reducing pension risk is a good reason to view your pension assets and liabilities as part of an enterprise-wide risk framework. As with any other decision that affects corporate balance sheets or income statements, changes in pension strategy and risk are bound to show up somewhere else. And, as I said a moment ago, it is because of their effects on the rest of the firm that pension decisions must be overseen by decision makers at high levels in the corporate organization, people entrusted with managing the risks and maximizing the value of the entire enterprise.

An Illustration

As a hypothetical illustration of how to evaluate the risk of a company's operating assets *and* its pension plan, let's take the case of a company called LT. Table 9.2 provides standard balance sheet estimates of operating asset risk and WACC, without considering the pension plan. All numbers are market values, not book values. We arrived at the value of the operating assets by taking the market value of equity and the market value of debt—$21 billion and $19 billion, respectively—and adding those up to arrive at $40 billion, which is equal to the value of total assets.

To do a conventional calculation of WACC for LT, we began by estimating its beta from historical market returns—and our estimate turned out to be 2.0. Then, taking account of the firm's debt and its level of risk, we determined that the weighted risk of debt and equity results in an "unleveraged" or "asset" beta of 1.05. If LT's management team were using this method to evaluate a project similar to the company's other operations, the project would be valued using a WACC based on a risk factor of 1.05. Using a risk-free rate of 5% and a market-risk premium of 7%, we would come up with a WACC of around 12%.

TABLE 9.2

Effect of Pension Asset Risk Mismatch on Equity Risk and Cost of Capital: LT Corporation (with Fully Funded Pension Plan)

	Standard Balance Sheet Estimates			Value ($bn)	Risk (Beta)
	Value ($bn)	Risk (Beta)			
Operating assets	$40	1.05	Debt	$19	0.00
			Equity	$21	2.00
Total assets	**$40**	**1.05**	**Total L&E**	**$40**	**1.05**

Estimated WACC operating assets = 12.35%

In table 9.3, we show what happens when you adjust the conventional analysis to incorporate a full economic balance sheet—one that takes account of risk as well as value and so includes the pension assets and pension liabilities. The pension plan is fully funded—$46 billion of assets and $46 billion of liabilities—and since there is no surplus or shortfall, there is no entry on the traditional balance sheet. Since 60% of the pension assets are invested in equities, LT does have a significant risk exposure to equities; but, again, that exposure is not recorded on its GAAP balance sheet. When we expand the balance sheet to include the pension assets and liabilities, we have a much larger company—$86 billion of total assets instead of $40 billion, and $65 billion of total debt instead of $19 billion. We can easily estimate the risk of the pension asset portfolio—a well-diversified portfolio of equities and debt—just by look-

TABLE 9.3

Effect of Pension Asset Risk Mismatch on Equity Risk and Cost of Capital: LT Corporation (with Fully Funded Pension Plan)

	Full Economic Balance Sheet Estimates			Value ($bn)	Risk (Beta)
	Value ($bn)	Risk (Beta)			
Operating assets	$40	0.36	Debt	$19	0.00
Pension assets	$46	0.60	Pension liabilities	$46	0.00
			Equity	$21	2.00
Total assets	**$86**	**0.49**	**Total L&E**	**$86**	**0.49**

Estimated WACC operating assets = 7.52%

ing at its composition: If we assume that the stocks have a beta of 1.0 and the bonds have a beta of 0, a portfolio with 60% equities can be assumed, pretty much by definition, to have a beta of 0.60.

The next step, then, using the firm's equity beta of 2.0, is to use LT's leverage ratio and its pension assets and liabilities to "back out" the firm's operating asset risk, which turns out to be 0.36. In this particular case, then—perhaps an extreme one, but useful in making my point—the operating assets actually have a materially lower systematic risk than the pension fund assets![11] Moreover, when we evaluate the total asset risk, which includes the risk of both the operating assets and the pension assets, we get 0.49, which is less than half the estimate we came up with—1.05—doing the analysis the conventional way.

But for purposes of project valuation and capital budgeting, the relevant comparison for LT's management in this case is not between 1.05 and 0.49, but between 1.05 and 0.36. If we were to do a capital budgeting analysis of contemplated projects for LT's core business, we would use 0.36 in calculating WACC; and if we did so, the cost of capital would fall from over 12% to 7.5% (5% + {0.36 × 7.0}). For projects with an expected life of ten years, the effect of overestimating the discount rate by some 450 basis points can be an underestimation of project values on the order of 30% to 40%. And as this example is meant to suggest, neglecting the risk of the pension plan can lead to major distortions of the capital budgeting process.

Besides improving capital allocation decisions, use of this expanded balance sheet approach provides a better picture of your firm in terms of its value and risk allocations between your operating businesses and other activities such as pension asset investments, which are largely passive investments. Your pension plan may make use of active fund managers; but unless you are a financial firm, managing financial assets is probably not part of your core business. Use of an expanded risk balance sheet can give top management a better picture of the composition and risk character of the firm.

Considering Alternative Pension Policies

Now I will try to show how the economic and risk balance sheets from table 9.3 can be used to explore alternative pension asset allocation policies and their implications for capital structure and firm risk. Before I go any further, let me warn you that I'm not offering a specific policy recommendation for LT or any other firm. What I'm presenting is a framework for thinking about the effects of different asset allocation on the risk of the enterprise.

The conventional analysis of a change in pension asset allocation—say, a major shift from stocks to bonds—focuses mainly on the effects of the

---

11. This is in fact not uncommon for the kind of companies that have DB plans—in many cases, basic industrial companies with relatively low betas.

TABLE 9.4

Effect of Pension Fund Asset Allocation on Asset and Equity Risk: LT Corporation

Fraction of Pension Assets in Equities	Pension Asset Beta	Total Asset Beta	Firm Equity Beta
0.00	0.00	0.17	0.70
0.25	0.25	0.30	1.23
0.60	**0.60**	**0.49**	**2.00**
0.75	0.75	0.57	2.34
1.00	1.00	0.70	2.88

change in expected return on corporate balance sheets and income statements. At least from the vantage point of GAAP—though less so with the new U.K. standard—the primary effect of such a change is to reduce reported earnings.[12] In addition to such accounting effects, conventional analysis also takes account of any effects on the stand-alone risk of the pension fund.

The main focus of economic analysis, however, begins with the changes in risk. When a company alters the mix of its pension assets between fixed-income and equities, it changes its equity risk and the risk of the overall firm. For example, as can be seen in table 9.4, if LT were to raise its pension allocation of equities from 60% to 100%, our analysis suggests that the firm's total asset risk factor would increase from 0.49 to 0.70—a significant increase in the risk of the total company. And the beta of the firm's equity is estimated to jump from 2.0 to 2.88—though, again, I ask you not to take the precision of these numbers seriously. In this case, you see nearly a 50% increase in the risk of the firm's equity. Investors require a higher expected return for this kind of increase in risk.

Now, let me also say that such an increase in risk is not inherently bad. What is important, however, is to understand the change and any possible firm-wide effects.

A decision to go to 100% equities, though not necessarily a bad idea for all companies, does mean a higher return requirement by your equity holders. When you think of the higher expected return on the equities in your pension fund, the good news is that you can indeed expect them to produce higher returns, at least over a sufficiently long time horizon. The bad news, however, is that because of the risk associated with your pension assets, your own share-

12. But if the firm also maintains its total risk posture by simultaneously issuing new debt and using the proceeds to buy back stock, the effect on earnings per share (EPS) is not clear; EPS could increase.

holders will demand a higher return than they did before and lower the P/E multiple on your stock. So, even if your future pension contributions turn out to be lower and your reported earnings higher as a consequence of an all-equity pension, the reduction in your multiple may leave your stock price unaffected or even lower than otherwise.

But, again, I am not offering a specific prediction or recommendation here. My purpose is simply to show how overall firm risk and its equity risk are influenced by pension asset allocation, and to note that such changes could end up increasing the firm's cost of capital and lowering its multiple. Neither of these effects is necessarily bad, but you should prepare yourself for the probable changes.

Effects of Pension Change on Optimal Capital Structure

As we change the pension asset allocation, what are the implications for the capital structure or the amount of equity capital required to keep the risk of our equity unchanged? Let's return to the case of LT, and assume that the company's management and shareholders are comfortable with their current equity risk factor of 2.0. Let's further assume that one of the firm's key risk management objectives is to maintain the beta risk of its equity at that level.

As we saw in table 9.4, an increase in the allocation of pension asset to equities increases the risk of the total assets. And if we increase the risk on the left-hand side of the balance sheet, in order to keep the risk of our equity unchanged we have to reduce leverage or gearing. If you increase asset risk and leave the capital structure unchanged, equity risk goes up. Another way of saying this is that, for your creditors and equityholders to be as comfortable as they were before the pension change, any increase in asset risk will have to be offset by taking less risk with your capital structure. There is no free lunch in that sense.

Table 9.5 provides an indication of how much equity capital the firm would need to maintain an equity risk of 2.0 for a range of pension asset allocation choices. We begin with the assumption that LT's management and shareholders are comfortable with the status quo, at least in the sense that the combination of a 60% pension equity allocation with $21 billion of shareholders' equity meets the firm's risk management criterion of maintaining an equity beta of 2.0. But, according to table 9.5, if management took the extreme step of increasing the pension allocation to 100% equities, the firm would have to issue $9 billion of new equity in order to maintain the same risk for LT's equityholders. In other words, to keep its equity risk the same, the firm would have to deleverage or reduce the gearing by $9 billion; and, as shown in table 9.5, its debt-to-equity ratio would drop from 0.9 to 0.33. At the other extreme, if the firm were to shift the entire pension into bonds that perfectly match the pension liabilities, the amount of equity capital needed to keep the equity risk at 2.0 would fall to $7 billion from $21 billion—and the debt-to-equity ratio would rise above 4.0.

TABLE 9.5

Tradeoff between Pension Asset Allocation and Firm Capital Structure

Fraction of Pension Assets in Equities	Total Asset Beta	Firm Equity Beta	Equity Capital ($bn)	Debt/Equity Ratio
0.00	0.17	2.00	7.3	4.48
0.25	0.30	2.00	12.9	2.10
0.60	**0.49**	**2.00**	**21.0**	**0.90**
0.75	0.57	2.00	24.5	0.63
1.00	0.70	2.00	30.1	0.33

Cushioning Your Risks with Capital

Tables 9.4 and 9.5 provide just two illustrations of how, once you have set the analysis up correctly, you can begin to discuss pension asset allocation in an integrated way, taking into account the impact you are having on the capital structure and risk of the business. You can use this tool to ask how much capital you are holding in the firm to cushion the risk mismatch of the pension fund versus the amount needed to support the risk of the operating businesses.

You are not going to trade on the precision of these numbers, but the magnitudes and implications here are essentially valid and will stand up to more sophisticated applications. In fact, my firm Integrated Finance Limited (IFL) has done this kind of analysis for clients who were surprised to discover how much of their total risk, and therefore the total amount of capital allocation, had to do with the risk mismatch in their pension fund.

Does this say that all companies should immunize their pension liabilities and thus avoid a risk mismatch in their pension fund? The answer is no.[13] Our

13. Immunization of the pension liabilities, although the value-maximizing approach in many cases, will not *always* be the optimal solution. The problem with current immunization practices, or those that now go under the name "LDI," or liability driven investment, is that they apply asset-liability management (ALM) only with respect to the pension assets and pension liabilities alone instead of considering ALM with respect to the assets and liabilities of the *entire* corporation.

When determining an optimal policy, one must define the objectives and condition under which you are assessing alternative pension fund policies. If you frame the problem as: What provides the maximum assurance to plan participants of the benefits that they have accrued in a plan that is currently fully funded (to the level of the ABO at true marked-to-market valuations) and that *will continue* to be fully funded as future benefits accrue *pari passu* with the existing benefits of the plan, the answer is indeed immunization. This particular framing takes as given the amount and terms of the promised benefits and *assumes* that the firm cannot in the future "dilute" the security of the current beneficiaries' claims by either promising additional

analysis says only that you should understand how much risk your shareholders are bearing as a result of the mismatch, how much capital you are using to
support it, and how your cost of capital is affected by it. An integrated approach requires you to look at all of these factors and consider all the choices
that can be made. And when you do that, you are in a position to make an informed strategic decision.

benefits in the future without immediately fully funding them or by changing the investment
policy of the fund. To my knowledge, neither of these future financing and investment
conditions is set either by employee contract or by ERISA law for typical U.S. DB plans.

From a general equilibrium perspective, pension asset optimization should consider the
perspective of the firm and its shareholders as well as the beneficiaries of the plan in terms of the
"bargain" between the two since the equilibrium level of promised pension benefits the firm
will agree to is determined in part by the cost of providing those benefits, which in turn depends
on the terms of the arrangement between the firm and its beneficiaries. I believe that over the
past two decades, firms did not recognize how costly the benefits they offered were at the time
they agreed to them, but they do now; and as we see everywhere, they are rapidly closing their
DB plans for new members and freezing them for existing members.

No insurance company offers full-faith and credit of the U.S. government for its retirement
annuity liabilities, even though very large AAA companies can be downgraded (AIG). In
principle, the market could provide full faith and credit annuities with individual segregated
accounts for each of its annuity participants. But it doesn't, and I suspect that few customers
would be so risk averse as to be willing to pay the high incremental cost to move from AA-rated
commingled funds of regulated insurers to segregated full-faith and credit asset accounts. That
is, for the bulk of retirees, the competitive market equilibrium is probably not at that "corner
solution" of extreme risk aversion.

To return to my original point, when one views the pension allocation decision in the
context of all the firm's assets and all its liabilities—that is, when one practices ALM for the
entire firm — one can surely imagine a solution in which the optimal asset risk position in
the pension fund is not complete immunization and thus zero correlation with the exposure
of the firm's net operating assets. In some cases, the optimal asset exposure could turn out to
be one that is negatively correlated with the operating assets of the firm, which in turn would
reduce the entire risk of the corporate asset base and improve the (implied) credit rating of
the pension liabilities more effectively than simply holding debt securities with match
duration to the pension liabilities.

The limitation of immunization, then, is not that matching pension assets and liabilities will
fail to add value, but that it may not be the value-maximizing strategy. Since returns on equities,
in the vast majority of cases, will be positively correlated with a firm's operating assets, holding
equities in the pension fund is not likely to be an outcome of the firm-wide analysis recommended
here. Immunization-like positions in bonds or long-dated fixed rate swaps will be an important
part of the portfolio composition. However, when optimal tax, liquidity considerations, and
hedge accounting rules are taken into account, it is entirely possible that the optimal pension
asset mix could include significant holdings of alternatives like true "zero-beta" hedge funds
(which are often highly taxed if held on the corporate balance sheet) and long-dated, illiquid
equity put warrants on selected industries as well as interest rate, currency, credit default swaps
to offset "passive" exposures of the operating businesses. See my article, "You Have More
Capital than You Think," Harvard Business Review Vol. 83, No. 11 (November 2005): 84–94.

In sum, I do not believe that in 2006 the optimal pension asset allocation decision should be
reduced to the "one size fits all" prescription of complete immunization.

Implementation

When you have done this analysis and decided on a pension policy, you then have to decide how to communicate that policy to the rating agencies, to your shareholders, to analysts, and to others. We believe that a good way to do that is to provide a full reasoned analysis in support of your new policy, one that includes a demonstration of how much risk-reduction credit you expect to get from changing a 60% equity allocation to, say, one of 25%. If you accept the number in the LT example, for example, you could eliminate almost $8 billion in equity.

But that estimate would simply provide a starting point for your discussion. You would then have to see how much the rating agencies would actually allow you to reduce equity without affecting the rating when you show them how much risk you are taking out on a permanent basis. This is an unsettled question, and the answer to it can be expected to change over time as the rating agencies and credit markets develop greater understanding of pension risk and its effect on overall firm risk. But to repeat my point: effective communication is an important element of the implementation.

Underfunding

The LT case is an example of a fully funded plan with no surplus or deficit. If the firm were underfunded, what might you want to consider? One possibility is to issue debt to fund the plan if you can. I'm not going to comment on whether that's the best strategy; the only answer I can give is that it depends on the firm and its circumstances. In making such a decision, some of the big issues will include taxes, whether you are a profitable firm, and how your communication with the rating agencies goes. Funding the plan may well be the optimal decision—or you may choose to fund the plan while making a change in the asset mix of the pension. And, of course, debt and equity are not the only possibilities for pension assets; there are other assets, including all variety of derivatives.

Overfunding

If you have a surplus, what do you do? Even if you want to match-fund the risk of what you owe, do you take risk with the surplus and, if so, what kinds of risk? Those are all part of the equation of what you need to analyze when thinking about and implementing a policy. There is no single answer for all cases.

Moving from a DB to a DC Plan

To those of you who decide that the answer is to end your DB plan and start a DC plan, I offer some observations. Suppose that an employee, upon retirement, would like to receive a stream of income comparable to the one earned in the latter part of his or her working life in order to maintain more or less the same standard of living. Although some plans are more generous than others, the basic idea of a DB plan is that it provides something near to one's final income, perhaps scaled down somewhat. When this arrangement works, it's wonderful because the employees do not need to know anything; they simply have to believe it will happen, and the benefits have to materialize at the appointed time.

With a DC plan, life becomes simpler for the corporation in some ways. The moment it pays its fraction of income into the plan, it has seemingly carried out all of its obligations. The problem, however, is that in making this change, you are now putting your employees in the position of having to make some quite complex investment decisions. Imagine if you were approached by a 42-year-old who told you he wanted to retire at 67, and to have an income during retirement that was roughly equal to 70% of his average earnings between the ages of 62 and 67. What would you tell him he had to invest in and how much he should be contributing in order to hit that target? We do not even know today what that person will be making in 20 years' time, so this is quite a complex problem.

We do not ask people to do their own medical surgery, or other kinds of important activities which require a great deal of specialization. Yet, when addressing one of the most important challenges in their lives, funding their retirements, employees in DC plans are essentially forced to obtain advice that is typically based in large part on the assumption that history will simply repeat itself. However, a reasonable question for any of us as consumers to ask is, "What happens if history does not repeat itself?"

What other major product do consumers buy where they allow someone to hand them the product, tell them this is an important part of their lives, and then warn them that "If it does not work, it is your problem"? I am not just pointing fingers, because I am also in this business. I do not know the optimal solution, but I know that we can do better than simply leaving individuals to make these complex decisions about risks.

That does not mean that DC plans are bad. What it does suggest, however, is that DC plans as they are commonly carried out today, particularly in the United States, are not the long-run answer. We have to design a product that works institutionally from a DC plan, but has an output that looks more like a DB plan. This kind of product is on the drawing board.

Conclusion

Corporations today face huge challenges in managing DB plans, and, if we go to the DC plans, there are huge challenges there as well. When I worked at a large investment bank, we had a focus group that aimed to design a great financial product for retired people. Focus groups were held all over the United States, and participants included non-profit institutions as well as private corporations. The most common response from participants when asked what they thought of our product proposals was that "the products are too good to be true; we do not believe it can happen." But once we suggested that such products might be made available through their employers, their response was quite different: "Anything offered through the employer plan has been scrubbed; it has been studied by financial experts and lawyers. We trust our employers."

I cannot imagine that the response would be much different here in the United Kingdom. Consumers everywhere are looking for solutions they can trust—and, by and large, they seem to trust their employers. It is important to recognize that, with a DC plan, the firm may eliminate—at least on paper—a lot of risks and future obligations, but keep in mind that once you change the plan to a DC, your employees will expect you to have done a great job for them. If lots of people do not receive in the future what they were promised, companies may find themselves making good, either voluntarily or otherwise, on what prove to be the implicit obligations associated with being a long-lived institution.

■ **ROBERT C. MERTON** is a cofounder and Chief Science Officer of Integrated Finance Limited (IFL), a strategic advisory and pension-solutions firm, as well as John and Natty McArthur University Professor at the Harvard Business School. He was awarded the 1997 Nobel Prize in Economics for his contributions to modern finance, particularly in the area of option pricing.

CHAPTER 10

The Uses and Abuses of Finite Risk Reinsurance

CHRISTOPHER L. CULP AND J. B. HEATON

F INITE RISK HAS BECOME what derivatives were 10 years ago—a hot button for controversy and the likely subject of investigations, litigation, and (heaven forbid) new regulations. American International Group (AIG) has borne the brunt of the assault to date as the target of New York State Attorney General Eliot Spitzer's scrutiny. AIG's troubles began with an investigation by the Securities and Exchange Commission (SEC) into a relatively small finite risk deal. Before long, the company's long-time chairman was gone and the company's accounts faced significant restatement. Brightpoint and the now-defunct HIH Insurance in Australia—as well as an increasing number of other firms—have also been associated with potential finite risk abuses. This article deliberately avoids discussion of any company-specific alleged abuses of finite risk. There is too little in the public domain to permit fair and complete analysis and this chapter should not be used out of context to address the facts of those particular examples.

Our objective instead is to provide a general introduction to finite risk (or just "finite," as it is known in the trade). Finite is a type of reinsurance contract. Finite risk solutions limit the reinsurance company's downside compared to traditional reinsurance, leaving more of that risk with the insured. The insured party also participates in its own positive claims experience, sharing some of the gains that insurance companies typically keep to themselves. In this sense, finite risk is a hybrid of risk finance and risk transfer. There is risk finance because the insured has access to capital to meet timing risk but bears the cost of its own risks. There is risk transfer because some risk is

This chapter was previously published as an article in *Journal of Applied Corporate Finance* Vol. 17, No. 3 (Summer 2005): 18–31. Much of the original article is based on chapter 24 (by Culp and Heaton) in C. Culp, *Structured Finance and Insurance: The ART of Managing Capital and Risk* (New York: Wiley, 2005).

transferred to the reinsurer even if less obviously than in traditional reinsurance programs.

Finite risk solutions have two main sets of applications: (1) as blended risk finance and risk transfer for corporate end users, and (2) as a form of reinsurance or retrocession for insurance companies. For consistency, we shall use the terms *finite* and *finite risk* to refer to corporate uses of this product type, which are the main focus of this article. The term *financial reinsurance* typically refers to applications within the reinsurance industry.[1] Importantly, most allegations of abuse of finite risk programs have involved financial reinsurance rather than deals done by corporations.

We begin with a brief overview of the structured insurance market. Finite risk solutions are a part of that market. We then describe the kind of risk management problems that lend themselves to finite risk solutions. Next, we provide a more precise definition of finite risk, first by distinguishing its main features from those of traditional insurance and then by discussing the kinds of risks that companies can manage with finite risk. We also describe a number of specific finite products and illustrate their applications with brief case studies. Finally we explore the potential for abuse of finite risk programs and suggest some guiding principles to help firms steer clear of such abuses.

The Risk Management Landscape

All companies face risks doing business. Corporate risk management involves identifying and classifying such risks into two categories: core and non-core. A firm's *core* risks are those in its primary business. *Non-core* risks are risks that the firm does not need to retain to engage in its primary business. Non-core risks include non-financial or "insurance" risks such as property damage, casualty, liability, and the like, but may also include financial risks, for example, airlines' exposure to jet fuel price risk.[2]

The firm's *retention decision* splits risks among three strategic alternatives: *retain, neutralize,* or *transfer* the risk in question. Figure 10.1 illustrates this decision.

The firm's *retained risk* or *retention* is the collection of risks that the firm decides to bear rather than neutralize or transfer. Retained risks may be either *funded* or *unfunded*. In the case of all retained risks, however, the firm's equity share capital must eventually absorb the loss. Whether or not a retention is

---

1. Not everyone adheres to this terminological distinction. A recent highly critical assessment of financial reinsurance by Fitch Ratings was titled *Finite Risk Reinsurance*, despite being focused entirely on reinsurance applications and not corporate uses of this product.

2. For an interesting exploration into the nuances of core versus non-core risk, see P. Tufano, "Who Manages Risk? An Empirical Examination of Risk Management Practices in the Gold Mining Industry," *Journal of Finance* Vol. 51 (1996).

FIGURE 10.1

Risk Management Alternatives

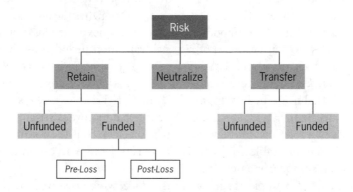

funded—and if so, how—does not change that fact. For that reason, we generally refer to any kind of contract or structure that firms use to address their
planned retentions as *risk finance.*[3]

A funded retention is a retained risk for which the firm sets aside specific
funds or sources of funds before the risk event translates into realized losses. If a
firm decides to retain a specific risk and pay for any losses as they occur without
setting aside particular funds, then that risk is unfunded. When losses occur, the
firm can either use its current free cash reserves, divert funds away from planned
investment spending, or issue new securities, provided the loss is not so large that
it deprives the firm of access to new capital. A company may choose instead to
fund some or all of its retention of certain risks—perhaps to protect against the
problem of having its cash unexpectedly depleted and, as a result, having to forgo
promising investment opportunities (a situation known as "the underinvestment
problem"). In this case, the risk is funded; the firm literally sets aside cash or a
source of cash to pay for all or part of a loss in the event the loss occurs.

As Figure 10.1 also shows, the firm can fund a retained risk on a *pre-loss* or
post-loss basis. This distinction relates to when the cash is actually raised to pay
for losses that materialize. Pre-loss financing is cash raised before the loss event,
and post-loss financing arrangements allow firms to pre-negotiate a means of
raising cash—including the terms on which it will be provided—in the event the
loss occurs. Setting aside cash in a dedicated reserve to cover a possible future

3. The practice of raising risk finance need not be motivated by accounting considerations. A firm's
motivation for pre-loss of post-loss funding of a retention may be completely driven by economics
(i.e., non-accounting) concerns. When a firm engages in *legitimate* risk financing, we're assuming
it has some reason to do so that is related to its liquidity or cash flows, even where the accounting
impacts of the transaction might be attractive.

loss is an example of pre-loss financing. Negotiating a line of credit on which the firm can draw following a loss is an example of post-loss finance.

If a firm does not wish to retain a source of risk to which its business naturally exposes it, one alternative is *risk neutralization*, which is the process by which a firm reduces either the likelihood or the size of an unexpected loss without engaging in risk transfer. Examples of risk neutralization include prevention and loss control, which are actions designed to eliminate or lessen the particular risk.

Finally, *risk transfer* is the explicit process by which the adverse impacts of a risk are shifted from the firm to others. Transferred risks can be systematic or idiosyncratic, financial or non-financial, core or non-core. Virtually the only limitation on the risk or bundle of risks to be transferred is the ability to define the risk in an enforceable contract. Risk transfer can be accomplished using derivatives, insurance, or asset divestitures.

Consider, for example, traditional insurance, which involves the payment of a premium by the insured (the "cedant" in insurance terms) to an insurance company. Traditional insurance gives the cedant the right to reimbursement for actual economic injury on the occurrence of a specific triggering event. Reinsurance is the purchase of insurance by an insurance company. Retrocession or retro is the purchase of reinsurance by a reinsurer.[4] Insurance, reinsurance, retro, and retro on retro are all forms of risk transfer because the contract shifts (some or all of) the financial impact to another entity, be it the insurance company or the reinsurance company.

Structured insurance, also known as *alternative risk transfer* (ART), refers to non-traditional risk management products and solutions in which the provider is still usually an insurance or reinsurance company. Structured insurance solutions or ART forms include both risk transfer and risk finance and often provide a mixture of the two. Examples of structured insurance solutions include the following:

- Captive insurance companies, mutuals, and protected cell companies
- Risk securitizations and insurance-linked notes
- Integrated multi-line, multi-year insurance coverage
- Dual-trigger insurance
- Contingent or committed capital
- Contingent insurance (also called "contingent cover").

Finite risk is a form of structured insurance.[5]

---

4. For a detailed review of traditional (re-)insurance and the emerging structured insurance markets, see C. Culp, *Structured Finance*.
5. Finite was originally developed and offered by Centre Re (later to become Centre Solutions, a division of Zürich Financial Services). For a review of the historical evolution of finite, see

A Simple Example of Finite

We begin by presenting an example of a finite risk structured insurance transaction that demonstrates the kinds of problems that finite risk addresses. Suppose we have a company whose primary business has given rise to an asbestos liability risk. The company is willing to take its lumps for this and sets aside $500 million to cover the present value of claims as they flow in over the next 5 years. This is a start, but the company faces three ongoing potential problems.

First, claims may not show up in the expected pattern over the 5-year period. If claimants want their cash now, so that all the claims arrive tomorrow, then the $500 million estimate of present value may be too low. Second, what happens if the actual loss comes in well above the $500 million? Many corporate users of finite face exotic risks, such as asbestos liability, that are awfully hard to quantify and thus require additional insurance coverage on top of the $500 million already set aside to finance the risk. The $500 million estimate itself, after all, presumably came from some probabilistic estimation. If the $500 million estimate reflected the expected loss, then there is a lot of room for the actual loss to be higher.

Finally, what does the firm *do* with the $500 million it wants to set aside? If it merely takes a charge against earnings to set up a reserve, investors are likely to be suspicious. Nothing really keeps a firm from using those funds for other purposes, or from arbitrarily deciding to add them back to earnings in the future when revised estimates of the loss might help the company meet an earnings target. Reaching into a $500 million cookie jar is awfully tempting, after all. And if the firm *does* reach into the cookie jar and reverse a reserve, it can send a very negative signal to the capital markets.

Finite could be a good solution—perhaps the *only* good solution—for a company in this situation. A typical finite structure would require the company to pay a $500 million premium to a highly rated reinsurance company for, say, $600 million in asbestos liability insurance over a 3-year term.[6] The $500 million would be expensed against earnings as the premium is paid—probably on a quarterly basis over the life of the program. This would reduce earnings in a way that accurately represents the loss for which the functional equivalent of a reserve is being taken.

B. Dyson, "Striking the Vital Balance," *Reactions* (January 2001); and R. Monte and A. Barile, *A Practical Guide to Finite Risk Insurance and Reinsurance* (New York: John Wiley, 1995).

6. We would say in that case that the firm has retained and pre-funded the first $500 million in losses and has bought insurance for the "$100 million XS $500 million layer"—that is, the firm has bought $100 million in insurance to cover losses in excess of its $500 million retention up to a policy limit of $600 million.

If the claims materialize, the company is covered for up to $600 million in losses, even if they occur more rapidly than anticipated. If claims are lower than expected, the company gets a low-claims bonus (a partial refund of its premium).

By means of such a finite transaction, then, the company has converted a potentially huge risk into a currently known expense, and has done so in a way that is *transparent* and *credible* to investors. As the case also shows, finite risk products can help finance liabilities whose outcomes are unknown while simultaneously transferring the risk that the firm has underestimated the true retention associated with those risks. In this sense, finite risk offers companies an attractive combination of a credible pre-loss financing structure with a classical risk transfer component.

But what if the firm doesn't actually have $500 million in cash sitting around to pay the insurer up front (or to fully fund the reserve)? In that case, the insurer may enter into a different kind of finite structure that essentially allows the company to obtain $100 million in insurance and to borrow the $500 million retention when and if the asbestos claims arrive. The company then repays the $500 million at a more convenient time. This is a classic form of risk finance and, if properly disclosed, can be useful when there simply is no capacity for insurance below the $500 million "attachment point."

Non-insurance corporations typically find finite risk products useful for managing exotic tail risks that are not core to their primary business activities. More specifically, such products can be used for "ring-fencing" (that is, isolating) assets or business risks in mergers and acquisitions (M&A) transactions or in conjunction with project financing, for managing runoff solutions (for example, when exiting a business line), and for funding retentions when standard insurance is not available in the loss layers the firm would prefer to insure outright but cannot.

The bottom line, then, is that finite risk transactions, when properly motivated, implemented, and disclosed, can provide companies with protection against hard-to-predict catastrophic risks, enhance the quality of their earnings, and achieve a reputation with investors for having effective risk management *and* credible disclosure.

Typical Finite Risk Structures

Now that we have introduced and motivated the concept of finite by way of an example, let's turn to the more practical and specific aspects of finite risk coverage. As noted, finite risk is more of a structuring methodology than a financial or reinsurance product. It is the process by which risk finance and risk transfer are integrated into a single hybrid risk management program that enables a customer to pre-fund a retention, manage the timing risks of that retention, and obtain excess-of-loss risk transfer for losses above the retention. There are many products and solutions that potentially fall under this umbrella.

To provide more detail to our characterization of finite risk solutions, we now consider the following:

- Features that typically distinguish finite risk structures from traditional (re-)insurance;

- The nature of the liabilities typically covered by finite risk programs; and

- The degree to which the program is fully, partially, or not funded.

Characteristics of Finite Risk Structures

The features that distinguish finite risk solutions from traditional insurance are subtle but critically important in helping firms determine which risk solution is the right one. Not every finite contract will have all of these features, and the characteristics discussed cannot be considered a definitive list of necessary and sufficient conditions for a structure to be considered a finite risk deal. For the most part, however, this set of characteristics seems adequate for describing a typical finite transaction.

Material Risk Transfer. Insurance and reinsurance contracts generally involve at least four types of risk:

- *Underwriting risk:* the risk that premiums collected (generally set to cover *expected* claims payments plus transaction costs) are insufficient to cover *actual* claims payments;

- *Credit risk:* the risk that a (re-)insurer will not fully honor all of its contingent obligations to its cedants;

- *Investment risk:* the risk that the income generated by an insurer when premium is collected and invested in assets will be below the expected income reflected in the (re-)insurer's premium pricing; and

- *Timing risk:* the risk that actual loss claims occur faster than expected and that invested reserves (including investment income) are too low to fund those claims when they occur.

A true finite risk contract must involve material risk transfer of all four of the above risks. To be sure, some predecessors of today's finite risk products (and perhaps a few of the recent, more controversial ones as well) focused purely on the transfer of timing risk to the exclusion of underwriting risk. For example, an early Lloyd's of London structure known as a *time and distance* policy involved the payment of a large premium by the cedant to a reinsurer and then specified a fixed schedule by which premiums were returned to the cedant. This schedule, however, did not have anything to do with the actual timing of claims made by the ceding insurer and essentially represented more of a cash deposit than a risk transfer device. Accordingly, the only material risk transferred in a time and distance policy was timing risk, and the main purpose of these transactions seems to have been pure income stabilization—that is, cash flow or earnings smoothing. Such a policy would not be considered a legitimate finite risk transaction today.

Determining what constitutes material risk transfer depends, of course, on why the determination is being made. As suggested earlier, the optimal amount of risk transfer in a finite structure should in theory be a function primarily of the company's optimal capital structure. In practice, however, decisions to transfer risk will also be affected by tax, disclosure, accounting, and other regulations. Regulations, of course, must be respected, but even regulatory definitions of "adequate risk transfer" have been ambiguous to date. Clearly, a traditional insurance contract represents "full risk transfer" in the sense that the cedant has paid a premium equal to its *expected* loss to avoid bearing *actual* losses, and the reinsurer in turn bears most if not all of the risk that actual losses exceed the expected loss reflected in the premium. At the other extreme, the time and distance policy described above involves no risk transfer since the only payment obligation of the reinsurer is to honor a fixed schedule of payments unrelated to actual loss development experience. Partial risk transfer is everything in between.

Until very recently, the rule of thumb practiced by most accountants was to deem a transaction as involving material risk transfer if there was at least a 10% probability that the reinsurer would incur an underwriting loss on an amount equal to at least 10% of the policy limit. A program with a $1.05 million policy limit and a $1 million premium would fail that so-called 10/10 test or 10/10 rule. The maximum loss to the insurer would be only $50,000 under such a policy; and even if that loss were 95% likely to occur, $50,000 is only 5% of the policy limit. Similarly, a $1.1 million policy limit and a $1 million premium (called a $100,000 XS $1,000,000 program) would also fail the test if the risk of a loss in excess of $1 million were under 10%.

Unfortunately for companies seeking regulatory certainty, this rule of thumb was only ever just that—a rule of thumb, not a statutory or regulatory requirement. It was also subject to modeling interpretation when it came to assessing the probability of exceedance.

Following some of the recent widely publicized controversies about finite, many accountants now prefer a 15/15 rule or, in some cases, as much as 25/25—that is, at least a 25% chance of reaching the policy limit with losses above $1 million in a $250,000 XS $1,000,000 program.

Cedant Participates in Positive Claims Experience. A long-standing marketing problem faced by (re-)insurers has always been the perception that (re-)insurance does not add value if claims are rarely made. The reality, of course, is that there can be substantial risk even in cases where losses are rare events. A loss is just an adverse outcome of a risk, but risk does not always lead to losses. The right time to determine whether or not (re-)insurance increases the value of the firm is ex ante, before the losses materialize.

Nevertheless, reinsurers also recognize that their rates reflect certain assumptions about adverse selection and moral hazard—assumptions that tend to raise prices when reinsurers have less information than purchasers of the reinsurance. Over time, if the claims experience of a customer helps the reinsurer realize that it has not insured a "lemon,"[7] then it makes sense to allow the customer to participate in its positive claims and loss development experience through a partial rebate of the premium. A partial premium rebate can also make sense purely for marketing purposes, depending, of course, on the level of the initial premium.

Finite risk premiums often are quite high, but looking only at premiums on these ART contracts can be misleading for the aforementioned reason. Regardless of the quoted premium, the total cost to the cedant of a finite risk program is usually a function of the actual claims or loss experience. Investment income also may be included in the overall assessment of a cedant's experience with the policy.

The mechanics by which profit and loss sharing is accomplished in a finite risk transaction depend on the nature of the transaction and the particular counterparties involved. In general, this sharing is accomplished through the use of an *experience account* that tracks the paper profits and losses on the actual underlying deal. The premium paid by the cedant to the (re-)insurer is credited to the account, as is interest on invested premium reserves, while losses and various charges incurred by the (re-)insurer are debited to the account. At the end of the term of the finite risk structure, the (re-)insurer and cedant essentially split the balance in the experience account, whether a net gain or loss.

Limited Liability for the Reinsurer. Notwithstanding the requirement that a finite transaction involve material transfer of all risk types, a distinguishing feature of a finite risk contract is generally that it exposes the (re-)insurer to a limited or finite amount of underwriting risk. Limitation-of-liability provisions are by no means unique to finite risk. Indeed, virtually all traditional insurance and reinsurance contracts involve some kind of policy limit. What is special about finite risk contracts is usually the mechanisms by which the underwriting risk of the (re-)insurer is limited.

---

7. G.A. Akerlof, "The Market for 'Lemons': Quality Uncertainty and the Market Mechanism," *Quarterly Journal of Economics* Vol. 84 (August 1973).

The policy limit, of course, is important, but perhaps more important in a typical finite structure is the level of the premium relative to the policy limit. The premium on traditional reinsurance is generally equal to the expected claims payment plus a mark-up to reflect the costs to the reinsurer of underwriting the policy (including retrocession costs). If a customer chooses voluntarily to cede more than that amount to the carrier as premium, the amount in excess of the actuarial premium plus load is essentially a form of pre-loss risk finance. As noted earlier, firms may wish to do this to avoid the cash flow risk of an unfunded retention leading to underinvestment or other liquidity problems.[8] We will return later to a discussion of the benefits of finite risk contracts, but the high premium relative to the policy limit is often a significant part of that benefit.

Multi-Year. For reasons of historical convention (owing in part to the role of brokers), almost all traditional insurance and reinsurance contracts have a life of 1 year. This puts the cedant at risk of price increases and capacity or coverage contractions every year. Like most ART and structured insurance products and unlike most traditional (re-)insurance, finite risk contracts generally have a tenor of more than a year—usually 3 to 5 years.

Risk in the Risk Transfer Component

Finite risk structures can be either *prospective* or *retrospective* with regard to the risks the structures are intended to cover. Figure 10.2 depicts the distinction between retrospective and prospective cover (as well as a third possibility, retroactive risk, that is *not* a legitimate basis for insurance). In this figure, we can distinguish between prospective, retrospective, and retroactive risks by comparing four different dates in the life of a would-be insurance policy:

- *Policy Underwritten*: a policy is bound that allows the insurance purchaser to pay a premium in exchange for the right to make a claim of loss and to receive all or partial reimbursement of that loss upon the occurrence of a specific triggering event during a specified risk cover period;

- *Liability incurred*: the event that exposes the insurance purchaser to a risk of loss occurs;

- *Policy triggered*: the risk of loss actually becomes a known loss, thereby triggering the insurance contract; and

- *Claim made*: the insurance purchaser files a claim for reimbursement of actual damage sustained.

8. K.A. Froot, D.S. Scharfstein, and J.C. Stein, "Risk Management: Coordinating Investment and Financing Policies," *Journal of Finance* Vol. 48 (1993).

FIGURE 10.2

Retrospective versus Prospective versus Retroactive Cover

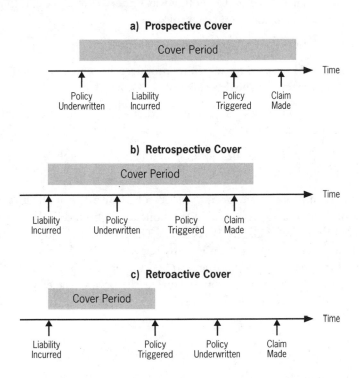

A lot of confusion arises about the distinction between the date on which a liability is incurred and the date a policy is triggered. The distinction is the same as that which distinguishes a risk from a loss. A liability is effectively incurred at the time the firm assumes a risk, whereas the policy trigger date is the date on which that risk no longer represents a *potential* loss but in fact has become an *actual* loss.

If the policy has not been triggered before the policy underwriting date and the risk coverage period have passed, the outcome of the policy is not known. The insurance purchaser is *at risk*, which means that the risk might still translate into a loss. But once the policy trigger has been pulled or the risk coverage period has ended without the trigger being pulled, the outcome is known with certainty. This situation is what we call a *retroactive* cover—a cover that is intended to pay off based on an event whose outcome is known at the time the policy is signed. This is *not* insurance, and does *not* represent risk transfer.

If the possibility for a loss exists when the policy is signed, however, the policy can in principle involve material risk transfer even if the liability or risk exposure was incurred before the policy was underwritten. We call that a retrospective policy. Consider some examples:

- A crime occurred but has not yet been detected;

- A product was released for which its producer faces product liability as a result of a defect, but the defect is not yet known;

- A chemical thought to be safe is dumped in a residential stream but is later found to cause cancer;

- A typhoon destabilizes the foundation underlying shoreline property, but the instability is undetected initially.

These examples of retrospective risk can be legitimate applications of insurance or finite risk deals provided the policies are bound before the uncertainty about the loss exposure is revealed. That the event leading to the loss exposure occurred in the past is not really relevant.

The third possibility is that the policy is underwritten before the liability is even incurred, which means by definition the policy trigger has not been pulled. On such prospective programs, there is little doubt that there is risk transfer.

Pre-Loss versus Post-Loss Funded Finite

Yet another important distinction between different finite risk solutions is the degree to which the structure is pre-loss or post-loss funded. Let's again use a simple example to differentiate between the two.

Consider a corporation facing potential environmental clean-up cost liabilities of $400 million over the next, say, 3 years. The first $350 million has about a 50% chance of being realized, and the next $50 million has about a 15% probability. Figure 10.3 compares pre-loss funded and post-loss funded finite risk solutions to help manage this risk. For simplicity, we ignore transaction costs, including arrangement fees.

In panel A of figure 10.3, we first consider a pre-loss funded program. The corporation essentially sets aside the first $350 million in cash but is concerned that a balance sheet reserve will not be as credible to investors as a finite program. So, the company enters into a finite program for 3 years in which it cedes the initial $350 million to a reinsurer at the inception of the program. If the liability turns into a realized loss over the life of the program, the reinsurer uses the premium to cover the first $350 million in losses and provides an additional $50 million XS $350 million in cover. Losses above $400 million are

FIGURE 10.3

Pre-Loss versus Post-Loss Funded Finite Structures

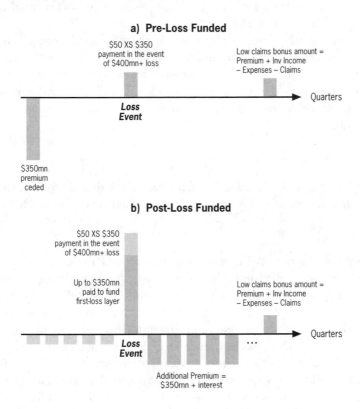

a) Pre-Loss Funded

$50 XS $350
payment in the event
of $400mn+ loss

Low claims bonus amount =
Premium + Inv Income
– Expenses – Claims

Quarters

*Loss
Event*

$350mn
premium
ceded

b) Post-Loss Funded

$50 XS $350
payment in the event
of $400mn+ loss

Up to $350mn
paid to fund
first-loss layer

Low claims bonus amount =
Premium + Inv Income
– Expenses – Claims

Quarters

*Loss
Event*

Additional Premium =
$350mn + interest

retained by the company. If losses are below what is expected, at the end of the program the company is eligible for a low-claims bonus, paid out of any program surplus, where the program surplus is equal to the premium collected plus investment income earned on that premium minus claims payments and expenses.

Now consider in panel B of figure 10.3 a program that is substantially the same but post-loss funded. The corporation pays only a commitment fee or small premium to the reinsurer in advance of any loss. If no loss occurs, a low-claims bonus is again possible based on the surplus after 3 years. But now suppose a loss occurs. In this case and unlike the previous one, the firm has not pre-funded the first $350 million layer, but has retained that layer. In effect, the reinsurer makes a $350 million payment to the company to cover the first layer of losses. The reinsurer also provides excess cover of $50 million XS $350 million. But in this case, the company's subsequent premiums on the program now rise so that the present value of those future premiums is equal to $350 million as of the date of the loss.

The additional premium required on the unfunded program is often called *retrospectively rated premium,* or *contingent premium.* In effect, the additional premium in the program is economically equivalent (at least in this example) to the principal and interest on a $350 million loan made by the reinsurer to the corporation on the loss event date through the end of the life of the program.

The Products

Although finite risk is more a structuring technique than a product, the market has identified a handful of specific products that are considered to be finite risk.

Loss Portfolio Transfers. A loss portfolio transfer (LPT) occurs when a firm cedes all remaining unclaimed losses associated with a previously incurred liability. In addition to paying an arrangement fee, the cedant also typically pays a premium equal to the net present value of reserves it has set aside for the transferred liability *plus* a premium to compensate the (re-)insurer for the underwriting and other risks assumed. An LPT thus enables a firm to exchange an uncertain liability in the form of a stream of unrealized losses over time for a certain liability whose present value is equal to the expected net present value (NPV) of the unrealized losses plus a risk premium and a fee. An LPT is generally a pre-loss funded finite risk structure intended to deal with retrospective liability.

The principal risk that the cedant transfers to the (re-)insurer through the LPT is the risk that losses or claims arrive at a much faster rate than expected. In that case, the investment income on the reserves—and perhaps the reserves themselves—may be inadequate to fund the losses. A time series of losses that occurs more slowly than expected, by contrast, will represent an opportunity for a net gain that the (re-)insurer would typically share with the cedant. LPTs thus are risk-financing mechanisms through which firms can address the timing risk of a liability. But they also include a sufficient amount of pure risk transfer—in the form of excess-of-loss reinsurance on top of the premium and reserve—to qualify as insurance.

LPTs can be attractive for various reasons. For insurers, they provide a low-cost means of synthetically exiting or ring-fencing a business very quickly. LPTs can help corporations that have captives, for example, wind up certain self-insurance lines if the firm alters its retention decision for certain risks. LPTs are also useful to non-financial corporations in securing financing for runoff solutions, especially in the area of environmental claims and clean-up cost allocation.

The principal benefit of an LPT is that it enhances a firm's quality of earnings by enabling it to take a credible reserve. If the firm cannot cede its reserves to a reinsurer through a mechanism like an LPT, the firm is left with an escrow account. Even if the firm can account for the reserves in earnings, all the problems of reserves apply—they can appear to be cookie jars, they can cause underinvestment problems, and they can send negative signals to investors when they are reversed. An LPT suffers from none of these problems.

Adverse Development Covers. An adverse development cover (ADC)— sometimes called a *retrospective excess of loss cover* (RXL)—is a finite risk ART form in which a (re-)insurer agrees to provide excess-of-loss (XOL) coverage for losses incurred on a retrospective liability that exceed the cedant's current reserves or planned retention. ADCs are commonly used by firms to manage liabilities that have been incurred but not reported (IBNR).

ADCs do not involve the cession either of a liability/loss portfolio or of reserves by the cedant to the (re-)insurer. As a result, ADCs do not really provide firms with the opportunity to combine any pre-loss financing with their excess-of-loss protection. Instead, the (re-)insurer simply agrees to compensate the cedant for any losses above an attachment point equal to a defined retention level. The retention may be funded by the purchaser of the ADC; but if so, the funds are left with the protection purchaser and *not* ceded to the reinsurer as they would be in an LPT. ADCs may also involve a policy limit, but a cedant is free to layer ADCs in the same way that traditional XOL reinsurance can be layered to address concerns over catastrophic loss development layers.

ADCs can be useful for firms in a variety of situations. They are commonly used to cap old liabilities that are of concern in a merger or acquisition. In addition, they are widely regarded as important devices for combating adverse selection problems associated with "black hole" risks that investors consider impossible to estimate reliably and reserve against. A firm that records a charge to earnings for a liability that has not been fully realized, for example, may be suspected of possessing superior information about the liability that leads to under-reporting. Or a firm that first announces a tail-end risk event, such as environmental liability, will almost certainly be suspected of underestimating the total liability its first time around. A firm wishing to assuage investor suspicion can take out an ADC to lock in its liability at the

Using an LPT to Ring-Fence an Environmental Liability

The Case of Stauffer Management*

The Iron Mountain Copper Mine is a Superfund site in Redding, California, that is owned by the Stauffer Management Co. of Wilmington, Delaware. Stauffer Management is the sole potentially responsible party (PRP) under Superfund, which generally holds any PRP to a Superfund site jointly and severally liable for the entire clean-up costs of that site. Stauffer Management became the PRP to Iron Mountain because it manages the assets and liabilities of the former Stauffer Chemical Co., which acquired Mountain Copper Ltd. in the 1960s. It was Mountain Copper's mining operations above and below ground that fractured Iron Mountain, creating the Superfund liability by exposing the mountain's mineral deposits to oxygen, water, and bacteria, which in turn generated substantial acidic runoff.

Mining operations ceased at Iron Mountain in 1963, at which time the federal government developed the Spring Creek Debris Dam to control the release of acidic water runoff from the mine. The Environmental Protection Agency (EPA) listed Iron Mountain as a Superfund site in 1983 with Stauffer as the sole PRP responsible for its clean-up. Eleven years later, the state of California and the EPA concluded the dam was not enough and ordered Stauffer to begin removing all the contaminants from the water.

Stauffer Management settled its Superfund claim in 2000 with the EPA and several other federal and California agencies for approximately $160 million. Of that amount, $7.1 million was a settlement with the EPA, $10 million represented a mandatory contribution to other federal and California agencies for future regional environmental improvement projects, and $139.4 million was the premium Stauffer paid for a finite risk LPT obtained from American International Specialty Lines Insurance Co., a subsidiary of AIG.

Under the LPT agreement, the parties have agreed to contract with IT Corp. for the actual clean-up of the Iron Mountain site. The parties estimated the cost of clean-up to be about $4.1 million per annum over the next three decades, for an inflation-adjusted total of about $201 million. Under the finite risk policy, Stauffer cedes all of its past, current, and future liabilities on the Iron Mountain site to AIG along with the finite risk premium. The premium payment of $139.4 million was funded by Stauffer out of its current clean-up reserves for the site, plus some insurance coverage under prior policies.

* Background for this example was obtained from D. Lenckus, "Finite Risk Superfund Deal Set," *Business Insurance* (November 6, 2000).

continued

The LPT agreement also obliges AIG to reimburse IT Corp. for 90% of the actual clean-up costs incurred each year on the Iron Mountain site, up to a maximum of $4.1 million per year. IT Corp. bears the risk of higher annual clean-up costs subject to two other protections. First, if inflation causes an increase in costs by up to $900,000 in a single year, IT Corp. can carry forward that additional cost into a subsequent year in which costs are below $4.1 million. Second, AIG also provides IT Corp. with $100 million in aggregate excess-of-loss coverage for cost overruns triggered specifically by catastrophic perils such as excessive rainfall or earthquakes, subject to a $5 million limit per peril.

IT Corp. must finance the remaining 10% of its actual annual clean-up costs as a co-payment on the finite risk policy, although Stauffer agreed to pre-pay in a lump sum approximately $2.5 million to IT Corp. that it can use toward its 10% residual co-pay requirement. IT Corp. bears all of the timing risk on how that additional 10% in costs is accrued, as well as the timing risks on the clean-up costs themselves. In return, the finite risk policy includes a type of experience account in which IT Corp. retains some of the surplus if aggregate clean-up costs fall below $201 million over the next 30 years. The EPA receives another portion of whatever surplus exists.

charge-off amount and thus signal its confidence that the charge-off was indeed correct.[9]

Finally, ADCs can improve the ability of cedants to find favorable pricing for catastrophic XOL layers with lower attachment points above the policy limit on the ADC itself. Especially if there is limited or no capacity for insurance in primary or excess layers, an ADC may be the only way a firm can obtain coverage.

Retrospective Aggregate Loss Covers. A retrospective aggregate loss cover (RAL), involves a cession of reserves to a reinsurer that represents only a *partial* prefunding of expected losses. In a typical RAL, the cedant can finance existing and IBNR losses by paying a premium to a (re-)insurer equal to the current value of those reserves but less than the present value of *all* expected liabilities. In our earlier example of the firm that expected $350 million in environmental claims, $150 million of those claims might be IBNR or existing claims and might correspond to a funded reserve. Just as in an LPT, the RAL purchaser

9. See P. Shimpi, *Integrating Corporate Risk Management* (New York: Texere, 2001); and Swiss Re, *Sigma 5* (1997).

Three Cases Illustrating the Uses of ADCs*

Covering the Excess Layer for Asbestos Liability

Turner & Newall, a U.K. manufacturer of motor components, used an ADC to reassure its investors and analysts that it had adequately reserved against a series of asbestos claims associated with some of its discontinued operations. The company self-insured its asbestos claims by establishing a captive and then reinsured some of that underwriting risk with an ADC for $815,000 XS $1,125,000. The ADC had a 15-year tenor and, like other finite risk products, contained an agreement for a partial premium rebate if actual loss developments were favorable relative to its reserve holdings after the 15 years.

Ring-Fencing the Liabilities of a Discontinued Business

In a more general case, the multinational firm Hanson PLC was concerned when it acquired building materials company Beazer PLC that Beazer's discontinued U.S. operations would create an impediment to growth for the new conglomerate. Hanson self-insured the liabilities of Beazer's U.S. operations through a captive, and the captive in turn acquired $80 million XS $100 million through a perpetual ADC—that is, the insurance coverage lasts forever. In so doing, Hanson effectively shifted all remaining liability for Beazer's discontinued U.S. operations to a reinsurer.

Exiting a Business Line (Runoff Solution)

Frontier Insurance Company was a specialized property/casualty insurer that ran into financial problems in 2000. It had $70 million in debt and had suffered significant losses on its physicians' malpractice insurance line. Frontier's losses were due both to inadequate reserves to cover total losses and to the unexpectedly rapid development of losses on the portfolio. The company had to replenish reserves several times to cover the time path of claims.

In the second quarter of 2000, Frontier entered into an option on a bundled finite risk agreement with Berkshire Hathaway's National Indemnity. If

* Background for these examples was obtained from Gerling Global Financial Products, *Modern ART Practice* (London: Euromoney Institutional Investor, 2000); and "Frontier Gets a New Lifeline," *Reactions* (November 2000).

continued

exercised, the option delivered $800 million in cover to Frontier, of which $514 million was an ADC that created excess-of-loss reinsurance for any aggregate losses in excess of Frontier's then-current reserves. The remaining $286 million in cover involved a cession of its current reserves to National Indemnity through an LPT that protected Frontier from further unexpected accelerations in the timing of its claims submissions. In providing such an option, National Indemnity effectively enabled Frontier to transfer the underwriting risks and finance the timing risks associated with its existing physicians' malpractice line. As things turned out, Frontier exercised its option to obtain the $800 million in cover in late 2000. After ring-fencing its liabilities in this way, the company was able to cleanly exit this line of business and withdraw from the market in 2001.

cedes both the $150 million *and* the associated liability to the (re-)insurer. But unlike an LPT, an RAL also usually includes a provision that requires the cedant to pay (in the form of retrospectively rated premiums) for any losses over the ceded amount or above a defined loss ratio when those losses are actually incurred by the cedant.

In the LPT, the risk of a very large claim arriving unexpectedly early in the loss development cycle is borne solely by the (re-)insurer, perhaps subject to an aggregate or per-risk policy limit. But the RAL specifically forces the cedant to retain some of this timing risk. At the same time, however, the RAL is less cash-intensive and tends to allow the firm to pre-finance losses in its working capital layer. Thus, for companies less concerned about pre-loss finance *outside* the working capital layer, an RAL can make sense.

Nevertheless, firms that use RALs must be particularly attentive to disclosure issues. At face value, an RAL can be used to increase the balance sheet equity of the cedant by replacing the technical reserves allocated to an unknown liability with a fixed premium payment whose value is less than the current technical reserves. But precisely because the value of the premium is below the expected loss, the retrospectively rated premiums in the program give rise to a contingent liability that can be significant.

Others. As we have emphasized, the universe of finite risk solutions is far more expansive than a short list of named products. The principles of finite risk can be applied to a range of risk management problems that is limited only by the willingness of counterparties to do the deals.

Partially Funding a High Retention

A large energy firm found that its mandated retentions had escalated to $5 million for property, boiler and machinery, mechanical breakdown, and transmission and distribution coverage, but the firm was comfortable pre-funding only $2.5 million of that retention. Its reinsurer—Zürich Corporate Solutions—helped the client convert the $2.5 million XS $2.5 million layer of its retention into a more fungible layer of debt capital through an unfunded finite program that blended a $2.5 million XS $2.5 million post-loss risk finance layer with a $5 million XS $5 million layer of pure risk transfer (using an integrated multi-line program).

This example illustrates that post-loss funded programs need not be problematic just because they are funded after the loss occurs. As in the case of many users of post-loss funded programs, the post-loss funded risk finance layer is not pre-funded mainly because the firm cannot obtain risk transfer coverage at that layer. And rather than leave the risk unaddressed, the firm essentially enters into a contingent debt facility to fund the part of its retention between the lower attachment point that it can fund and the lower attachment point of the true risk transfer layer.

Opportunities for Abuse

As we have shown, finite risk programs can provide companies with real economic benefits without raising questions of impropriety. Let's turn now to some of the features of finite programs that create opportunities for abuse. The common denominator of abuse usually concerns the degree to which the transaction is accounted for, disclosed, and represented to investors as achieving "significant risk transfer" when there is in fact little or no such transfer. The fact that a finite program contains a risk financing component is not in and of itself a problem. The desire of a company to manage the timing, and hence the cash flow, risk of an as-yet-unknown liability is a legitimate economic motive. But a program that transfers only timing risk will not qualify as insurance. Such a transaction is a deposit or a loan, not an insurance contract, and must be accounted for as such. On the other hand, a program with a component intended to address timing risk is not automatically suspect.

So where, then, are the problems? Let's explore some specific areas of potential abuse.

Replacing a Non-Renewed Multi-Line, Multi-Year Integrated Program*

A professional services firm had been relying on a multi-line, multi-year integrated program for its financial lines insurance coverage. When that program did not renew, the services firm also found that replacing certain of the coverage lines in the traditional single-year, single-line market was prohibitively expensive and that coverage was only available at extremely high attachment points. Not only was the company unable to secure the coverage it wanted on fiduciary liability and on a blanket bond, but the services firm had contracts with customers that required errors and omissions (E&O) coverage at specified limits the firm could no longer obtain. Apart from facing extraordinarily high rates at undesirably high attachment points, the firm literally found its core business at risk from its seeming inability to insure non-core E&O risks.

AIG Risk Finance proposed a blended E&O, fiduciary liability, and blanket bond finite program. The program involved a combination of retentions, coinsurance, high aggregate limits, premium installment payments, retrospectively rated premiums, and more, but ultimately delivered a solution that secured the desired coverage.

This program again illustrates that post-loss funded finite solutions are not always problematic. This program also illustrates, however, the need to be careful in representing a program accurately. If the customers of this firm simply require E&O exposure indemnification, a post-loss funded finite program like the one described will work fine. But the company would want to be clear in its representations that some portion of this exposure has been financed. In the end, AIG has indeed covered the risk, but it has done so by financing a part of the risk. The customer in this or a similar case probably would not want to claim that the insurance program was 100% risk transfer or equivalent to classical indemnity insurance. But provided it is disclosed properly and conforms to the requirements set forth by the firm's customers, the program is quite sensible on its face.

* This case is based on information presented in P. Raybin, "When One Door Closes . . . ," *AIG Risk Finance Review* Vol. 2, No. 2 (2003).

Retroactive Cover

Finite risk structures, as we have seen, can be used to manage both prospective and retrospective liabilities. When dealing with retro*active* liabilities, however, the contract is no longer insurance. If there is no risk, after all, there is no risk transfer.

To put it bluntly, trying to execute retroactive insurance is equivalent to insuring against a known outcome. As long as there is still risk and uncertainty about the outcome of a liability—will the risk damage the firm or not, and if so, by how much?—then finite or any other insurance contract can be underwritten. But the moment the damage is known with certainty, any contract predicated on that particular backward-looking trigger is no longer managing risk; it is just shifting funds—or financing the loss.

Firms can still *do* this, of course. They just cannot account for and disclose what they are doing as insurance. Under U.S. generally accepted accounting principles (GAAP), a firm is allowed to net the benefit of an insurance program against the associated loss as long as the recovery is considered "probable." At the same time, the premium paid can be expensed over the life of the policy. But if the recovery is "possible" but not "probable," the insurance cannot be used to reduce the size of the loss. And if the recovery is "known with certainty," then the recovery can be netted against the loss, but in that case the *entire premium* must be expensed in the same quarter in which the loss and recovery are recognized and netted.

For example, suppose a firm buys $1.1 million of insurance at a cost of $1 million to cover the risk of the failure of a machine over the next five years. If the machine is teetering on the brink so that a recovery is probable, the firm can charge off the loss on the machine *and* net the $1.1 million recovery now against that expected loss. The $1 million in premium is expensed gradually over 5 years. The $1 million premium expense represents the retained portion of the loss that the firm wishes to pay but cannot credibly reserve against. So far, so good.

Suppose instead that the machine failed 2 months ago and a policy is now written to cover any failure of the machine from last year through the end of 5 years from now. What the firm *should* do is take the $1.1 million charge-off now for the loss of the machine, net the $1.1 million recoverable on the contract against it now, *and* expense the entire $1 million in premium *now*. There is no risk, so there is no risk transfer and hence no justification for amortizing the premium over the life of a redundant policy.

But let's suppose the firm has already told investors it had a great quarter and then discovers that the machine has gone kaput. If it wants to play accounting games, the firm could try and inappropriately treat this finite deal as insurance, using the $1.1 million expected recovery to offset the $1.1 million charge-off and avoiding any hit to current earnings. Instead, the firm would gradually take the hit to earnings over the next 5 years. This is *not* okay—it is earnings smoothing, plain and simple.

The problem here, however, is not with the contract structure itself. The problem is entirely a failure by the firm to account for a retroactive contract as a depository instrument. If there is no risk transfer, there can be no accounting for and disclosure of the structure as risk transfer.

Undisclosed Debt in Post-Loss Funded Programs

Post-loss funded finite programs can be very useful. When insurance markets are "hard" and coverage is not available for firms in the primary or excess layers, post-loss funded finite may be literally the only way to obtain some kind of cover. And most would agree that risk finance for the forced retention is better than wandering into the risk event completely unprotected. In other words, risk transfer can help protect the firm's equity holders. But when risk *transfer* is not available, risk *financing* can be a way to secure new debt to be issued post-loss but on pre-loss terms, thus protecting debtholders from the costs of distress debt financing or the deepening insolvency problem,[10] while also protecting equity holders from strategy interruption and underinvestment. For a cash-strapped firm in particular, risk finance is better than nothing at all.

At the same time, insurance is insurance—and debt is debt. Many unfunded finite programs are essentially a blend of contingent debt and excess-of-loss insurance coverage. There is nothing inherently "wrong" with contingent debt.[11] The question that many have asked about post-loss funded programs is whether or not they have been properly accounted for and disclosed. If a firm has a $50 million XS $350 million post-loss funded finite program, a loss event of $400 million will involve a pure insurance payment of $50 million by the reinsurer and a loan to the cedant of $350 million to cover the retained first layer. That $350 million is then paid back through contingent or retrospectively rated premiums—premiums that are really principal and interest on the debt, but that investors might not perceive as such.

Debt and insurance are accounted for differently, and the difference can be significant. As Enron has taught us, the amount of term debt carried by a company can be a very important variable, affecting debt covenants, credit lines, credit enhancements, collateral requirements, and the like. Concealing term debt inside an insurance program can thus be considered both misleading and fraudulent accounting.

10. For a detailed discussion of "deepening insolvency," see J.B. Heaton, "Deepening Insolvency," *Journal of Corporation Law* Vol. 30, No. 3 (2005): 465–500.
11. See C. Culp, "Contingent Capital," *Journal of Applied Corporate Finance* Vol. 15, No. 1 (Spring 2002).

The bigger problem is arguably with *disclosure*. If you have disclosed that you have $400 million in "insurance" on the above program, investors and other firms are likely to believe that you have $400 million in risk transfer. That's quite a different story from telling investors you have borrowed $350 million contingent on the loss event and then have $50 million of insurance.

There is an easy solution to this problem. If a firm wants to do an un-funded program, the better way might be to combine a true contingent debt structure[12] with a $50 million XS $350 million insurance cover. If the excess insurance is multi-year and multi-line, a firm can probably still get the benefits of a low-claims bonus. The firm only really sacrifices the appearance that the first layer is insurance—which it isn't. So, the answer is to go ahead and do the structure in which you borrow the $350 million retention and insure the excess, but by using contingent debt and insurance rather than finite. This will result in the appropriate accounting and tax treatment, and, equally important, the proper disclosure.

We're not saying that *all* post-loss funded finite programs are irresponsible, disclosed improperly, or debt in disguise. That's plainly not true. And we're not trying to indict the whole class of post-loss funded finite products. Our goal is simply to highlight opportunities for abuse—and easy ways to assure concerned investors that management is not availing itself of those opportunities.

Other Potentially Troublesome Features

Finite structures may contain various other provisions designed to affect the degree of true risk transfer and the timing of cash flows under the program. These additional features can help users of the products achieve a significant degree of customization in their risk management programs. But they can also present opportunities for concealing the true nature of the finite program, especially with respect to the true amount of risk finance versus risk transfer in the structure. Consider some examples below of additional features often found in finite deals that can cause trouble when firms are anything other than transparent in their disclosure of these terms.

Loss Corridors and "Blending." The term "blended" has several different meanings in a finite risk context. To some, it merely reinforces the fact that finite itself blends risk finance and risk transfer. To others, blended finite programs refer to finite programs combined or integrated with other ART

---

12. Such as Swiss Re's Committed Long-Term Capital Solutions (CLOCS™). For a discussion of CLOCS and its uses, see Culp, "Contingent Capital."

forms. It is not uncommon, for example, to see a captive insurance company or a mutual seek protection that includes a finite program integrated with a multi-line cover. Such a program might well be called "blended finite."

Blending can also refer to the manner in which the risk transfer component of the structure is integrated into the deal at various attachment points. In the environmental clean-up example we used earlier, we had a $400 million program that consisted of a $350 million pre-loss financing layer and a $50 million pure insurance component. The latter encompassed the $50 million XS $350 million layer. But suppose instead that the program was structured so that a $1 million insurance layer attached after every $7 million in retention up to $400 million. In other words, insurance would cover $1 XS $7, $1 XS $15, $1 XS $23, and so on, up through $1 XS $391 and $1 XS $399. The total coverage would still be $400 million, with a total retention of $350 million and total insurance of $50 million. The only difference is the layering.

It's possible that the above kind of layering is intended to match a corporate retention need, but not likely. More likely is that the blending scheme is intended to distribute the insurance part of the program into lower loss layers so as to increase the probability that the risk transfer component will be used. This can make sense, as it may lead to greater risk transfer than if all $50 million is in the layer that exceeds $350 million. At the same time, this sort of program is awfully confusing and hard to describe, much less to rationalize. Beware.

Mandatory Reinstatement Provisions. A *reinstatement* in a (re-)insurance program occurs if a policy limit can be refreshed after a loss has reached its limit. Optional reinstatement provisions are common features of ART forms like multi-line programs. With an optional reinstatement provision, the insurer has the right to pay additional premium to reinstate a policy limit after it is exhausted. This is a type of *contingent cover* or *contingent insurance*.

Mandatory reinstatement means that the protection purchaser in a finite program is automatically assessed an additional premium to reinstate a limit following a loss. On the one hand, this would seem to increase the risk transfer component of the structure. On the other hand, the mandatory reinstatement creates a source of additional known premium payments for the insurer. On a probability-adjusted basis, the net impact can be *reduced* risk transfer. If the aggregate limit of cover is reached in the last 6 months of a 3-year structure, for example, the probability that the entire aggregate limit would be exhausted *again* over the next 6 months is remote at best. A mandatory reinstatement of the full limit in that case would be largely redundant from a capacity perspective, but it could increase the total premium outlay by enough to significantly reduce the risk borne by the reinsurer.

Abuse of the Low-Claims Bonus Feature. One of the essential features of most finite deals is the low-claims bonus. If premium plus investment income less expenses and claims result in a surplus, at least some of that surplus is likely to revert to the insurance purchaser. This represents a contingent asset that may cause the insurance purchaser some tax and accounting headaches. Provided the policy runs its natural course, this feature of a program does not in any way reduce the ex ante risk transfer. It merely takes any favorable result ex post and divides the gain between the reinsurer and the cedant.

The real problem lies in programs that combine a low-claims bonus with *retroactive cover*. Recall that retroactive cover applies when there is no real risk or uncertainty about the outcome of the insurable event—it either happened or it didn't. Suppose that Company Scully enters into a finite structure with Reinsurer Mulder. The premium is $50 million, the policy limit is $75 million, and the cover is retroactive. If the event *did* occur and caused $50 million in damage, Scully has essentially used the finite transaction to make a $50 million *deposit* with Mulder. If the event did *not* occur, Scully is still assured of getting $50 million back (plus interest and less expenses). Again, Scully has made a deposit.

Early Termination and Tear-up Agreements. Some finite risk deals include early termination provisions. In and of itself, this does not necessarily reduce the risk transfer component of a structure. It depends entirely on how the program is structured. If a program allows for early termination in such a way that the premium reverts back to the cedant, a tear-up clause can function much like an abused low-claims bonus—as a means by which a premium deposit is returned to a cedant without any real risk transfer occurring in the process.

Sound Principles for Finite

In today's environment, like it or not, some users of finite should be losing sleep—and will lose more as regulatory scrutiny increases and litigation builds. Properly used and disclosed, however, finite is a valuable risk management tool. Indeed, some firms *not* using finite may be avoiding it at the expense of their shareholders.

Like junk bonds in the 1980s and derivatives in the 1990s, finite risk invites scrutiny mainly because it is not well understood and has been associated with a few high-profile abuses. There is one thing we know about financial innovation: accounting, disclosure, and regulation have a hard time keeping up. What's a responsible firm to do?

With the recent attacks on finite, the best approach for current and potential users is to hunker down and determine whether finite is appropriate for them and, most important, whether it is being accounted for and disclosed properly.

After the derivatives losses that the mid-1990s, many firms undertook derivatives risk audits. This is sound advice to firms thinking of what finite means to them is to implement a similar insurance risk and disclosure audit.

Those seeking a simple checklist of things to do to make finite acceptable won't find it. As with all structured finance and structured insurance, there are too many variations on deal terms and themes to draw sweeping generalizations— a fact that regulators may also have forgotten. There simply is no list of magic conditions that are both necessary and sufficient to make finite or any other structured program "okay." We can, however, get halfway there and identify a few conditions that are *necessary* for responsible transacting, even if not always sufficient.[13]

Economic Purpose

A structured transaction should be undertaken because it is consistent with firm value maximization and because it fits into the integrated risk and capital management strategy of the firm. If an economically motivated deal can also be structured to achieve desirable accounting, tax, and regulatory treatment, great! But the underlying motivation for the deal should not be to "reverse engineer" a specifically desired tax or accounting target.

Transparency

Here's an easy litmus test: If the only way that a structured insurance deal makes sense is if no one ever finds out you did it, then don't do it. As obvious as this seems, a lot of the structuring business involves proprietary modeling and product design. There is a natural tension between the desire to disclose details of a deal to assuage any concerns or misunderstandings about their economic purpose and the desire to protect costly proprietary information. But in this environment, the scale is tipped toward the former. Without adequate transparency and disclosure, it is likely that the deal will be misunderstood or questioned. The real decision is whether or not to do the deal—and if it is worth doing, it is worth disclosing in detail. At a minimum, disclosure about the economic purpose and basic design of structured programs should be included in the management discussion and analysis (MD&A) section of 10-Ks. Better still is to provide descriptive information about the deal publicly—on the firm's Web site, through interviews with key financial reporters, and the like.

Worth noting is that limited disclosure is hardly unique to finite risk products. In fact, most corporations today engage routinely in very limited

---

13. These principles were initially developed by the head of an ART practice at a major reinsurer and are adapted here with permission.

voluntary disclosures about their insurance activities, whether structured or traditional. This strikes us as a missed opportunity. Especially in today's environment, clear explanations of how a firm is using insurance for the benefit of its security holders is not only advisable but arguably essential if the firm expects to extract the full value of insurance. How can a firm realize the full benefits of risk transfer, after all, if its investors do not really know what risks have been transferred and how?

Adverse Selection and Credibility

Beware of cookie jars. Structured insurance and finite can often be remedies to cookie jar problems, but of course they can also *create* cookie jars. For example, trying to classify a retroactive cover (which is essentially a deposit) as insurance is just shifting earnings around in time and is a classic cookie jar problem. Attention should be paid to making structures credible, and part of this means making them intelligible. Over-engineered deals in a post-Enron world immediately raise a red flag that there is a cookie jar lurking somewhere inside those hundreds of special-purpose entities and finite deals.

One way to avoid the cookie jar syndrome in the finite area is to use finite mainly for managing non-core business risks. When finite is used on a core risk that is directly under management's control, moral hazard comes into play and there is too much temptation to use the program specifically to achieve a desired earnings result. When finite is applied to non-core risks, however, management cannot affect the outcome of the risk—nor do the firm's earnings depend so critically on the result. There is thus less temptation to manipulate the resolution.

Quality of Earnings

Earnings are not always a reliable guide to a company's underlying profitability and value, and far too much attention tends to be paid to the reported numbers. Given that companies will likely continue to have an earnings fixation, however, one of the best ways to evaluate the effect of structured finance and insurance products on the investment community may be to assess how they affect the quality of information an earnings release conveys.

When a firm cannot take an accounting reserve for a loss that is hard to estimate (i.e., the recovery is possible but not probable), traditional insurance is a good alternative. But when risk transfer is either not desired at lower retentions or not available, finite is a credible alternative to a loss reserve and makes the firm's earnings more informative than just setting aside cash that investors cannot see and that does not affect the firm's earnings.

This sword cuts both ways, however. Most finite programs increase shareholder equity or, for insurance companies, the surplus by replacing an unknown stream of liabilities with a known premium outlay. That can be an accurate representation of the economics of the deal if the finite structure contains adequate risk transfer. But if not, finite can be used to conceal leverage and overstate the value of equity, thus reducing the informativeness of financial statements and earnings.

Users of finite should regularly ask themselves the following question: Does this transaction help my financial statements more closely represent the true economic income and risks of the business? If not, then consider not doing the deal—or disclose the purpose and impact of the deal in excruciating detail. Alternatively, consider asking: Does this deal make my firm look financially stronger than it really is? If so, then don't do it.

Financial Flexibility

Structured insurance is generally intended to help companies optimize their risk and capital and their debt-equity mix. Programs that lock firms into inflexible solutions are often at odds with the corporate finance drivers that led firms to consider those solutions in the first place.

As we have noted, too much flexibility in a finite deal can limit the true risk transfer that occurs, and users must be alert to this possibility. At the same time, a certain degree of flexibility is what makes these structures more desirable than more rigid alternatives like captives or traditional insurance.

A Cautionary Policy Note

At the policy level, we urge reflection, restraint, and, where culpability is not clearly established, some degree of forbearance. Ambiguous accounting and disclosure rules—added to a post-Enron siege mentality—have led to a guilty-before-proven-innocent attitude toward finite risk tools and their users. Each finite application should be carefully evaluated on its own merits, with the awareness that finite can be used properly as well as abused. Rushing to judgment about finite is tempting, but dangerous. Consider how much insurance industry capital has already been burned up by the regulatory bulls in the china shop to date.

We agree that true abusers of finite must be held accountable for their actions. At the same time, a firm is innocent until proven guilty, even in highly complex insurance matters. Let's allow these firms to have their day in court before pronouncing sentence.

▪ CHRISTOPHER L. CULP is Director of Risk Management Consulting Services, Inc. in Chicago and Bern (Switzerland); Senior Fellow in Financial Regulation at the Competitive Enterprise Institute in

Washington, DC; adjunct professor of finance at the University of Chicago's Graduate School of Business; and Honorarprofessor at Universität Bern, Switzerland, in the Institut für Finanzmanagement.

■ J. B. HEATON is a trial lawyer and partner at Bartlit Beck Herman Palenchar & Scott LLP in Chicago, and adjunct professor of finance at the University of Chicago's Graduate School of Business. Dr. Heaton's opinions here are his own and do not reflect the position of Bartlit Beck Herman Palenchar & Scott LLP, its attorneys, or clients.

CHAPTER 11

Does Risk Management Add Value?

A Survey of the Evidence

CHARLES SMITHSON AND BETTY J. SIMKINS

IN HIS MARCH 8, 2003, letter to Berkshire Hathaway's shareholders, Warren Buffett described derivatives as "financial weapons of mass destruction, carrying dangers that, while now latent, are potentially lethal." Buffett argued that derivatives "can exacerbate trouble that a corporation has run into for completely unrelated reasons. This pile-on effect occurs because many derivatives contracts require that a company suffering a credit downgrade immediately supply collateral to counterparties. . . ."

Despite Buffett's warning, corporate managers appear to believe that derivatives are capable of adding value since they continue to make extensive use of them. When the International Swaps and Derivatives Association (ISDA) examined the annual reports and regulatory filings of the world's 500 largest companies in 2003, they found that 92% of the firms reported making some use of derivatives.[1] Of the users of derivatives, 92% reported using derivatives to manage interest rate risk, 85% reported using derivatives to manage currency risk, and 25% reported using derivatives to manage commodity price risk. Even Buffett himself, in that same March 2003 letter to shareholders, admitted to "engage[ing] in large-scale derivatives transactions in order to facilitate certain investment strategies."

Academics also seem to believe that the corporate use of derivatives generally works to increase shareholder wealth. In March 2004, ISDA surveyed finance professors at the top 50 business schools worldwide.[2] A total of 84 professors at 42 institutions provided responses. ISDA asked the professors whether they agreed with the statement, "Managing financial risk more effectively is a way for companies to build shareholder value." The results were as

This chapter was previously published as an article in *Journal of Applied Corporate Finance* Vol. 17, No. 3 (Summer 2005): 8–17.

1. International Swaps and Derivatives Association, "2003 Derivatives Usage Survey" (2003).
2. As ranked in *The Financial Times*, January 26, 2004.

follows: 44% strongly agreed, 47% agreed, 7% somewhat agreed, and only 2% somewhat disagreed.[3]

So it appears that both corporate executives and academics believe that risk management can increase the value of the firm. But is there any *evidence* that it does?

In this article, we will investigate this question by examining four more-specific questions:

1. Is financial price risk reflected in share price behavior?

2. Is the use of risk management tools (derivatives) associated with reduced risk?

3. Is cash flow volatility related to firm value?

4. Is there a relationship between the use of derivatives and the value of the firm?

For each of these four questions, we searched for all of the academic empirical evidence (whether published in an academic journal or in working paper form).[4] Although the research discussed below is not uniformly supportive of the corporate use of derivatives, the bulk of the evidence reinforces the idea that corporate risk management is a value-adding activity.

Question 1: Is Financial Price Risk Reflected in Stock Price Movements?

To answer this question, researchers need a model that tells them the rate of return an individual stock is expected to produce, *given the rate of return on the market as a whole*. The so-called "market" model does this by specifying a linear relationship between the rate of return on a particular equity, R_i, and that for the market portfolio, R_m:

$$R_{i,t} = \alpha_i + \beta_i R_{m,t} + \gamma_b R_{b,t} + \varepsilon_{i,t} \tag{11.1}$$

The market model can be viewed as a way of dividing the firm's risk into two different sources.[5] The parameter β_i measures the share of the total varia-

---

3. International Swaps and Derivatives Association, "A Survey of Finance Professors' Views on Derivatives" (2004).

4. We restricted our search to studies that included U.S. companies or foreign firms with American Depositary receipts (ADRs) traded on U.S. exchanges as part of the sample. One reason for so doing was to focus on an equity market that most would regard as efficient. The other reason is to keep the tables of manageable size.

5. The market model has been closely associated with the capital asset pricing model (CAPM). Note, however, that the market model is concerned only with the statistical relationship between returns to an individual stock and the market portfolio, while the CAPM makes additional assumptions about equilibrium pricing.

tion (or risk) in the share return that is attributable to changes in the broad market. The rest of the variation, which is reflected in the "error term," $\varepsilon_{i,t}$, is so-called "idiosyncratic" or firm-specific risk—risk that can be managed by investors simply by holding diversified portfolios.

Most researchers who have investigated Question 1 have done so by taking the market model and adding elements to it. For example, to detect the interest rate exposure of a company's market value—an exposure that is presumably reflected in the sensitivity of its stock price to changes in interest rates—researchers have added the rate of return from holding a constant-maturity, default-free bond, $R_{b,t}$, as in the following equation:

$$R_{i,t} = \alpha_i + \beta_i R_{m,t} + \gamma_b R_{b,t} + \varepsilon_{i,t} \qquad (11.2)$$

Or they have added the rate of change in interest rates, $\Delta r_t / r_t$:

$$R_{i,t} = \alpha_i + \beta_i R_{m,t} + \gamma_r \frac{\Delta r_t}{r_t} + \varepsilon_{i,t} \qquad (11.3)$$

In Equations (11.2) and (11.3), interest rate exposure is measured by γ_b (bond price exposure) or γ_r.

To examine the exchange rate exposure reflected in equity returns, researchers add the rate of change in a foreign exchange rate, $\Delta P_{FX,t} / P_{FX,t}$:

$$R_{i,t} = \alpha_i + \beta_i R_{m,t} + \gamma_{FX} \frac{\Delta P_{FX,t}}{P_{FX,t}} + \varepsilon_{i,t} \qquad (11.4)$$

where the firm's exposure to foreign exchange rates is measured by γ_{FX}.

Having made such additions to the market model, Question 1 is then rephrased as follows: Are γ_b, γ_r, and γ_{FX} different from zero?

We found 21 published studies and working papers that attempted to answer Question 1. Nine of the studies looked at the interest rate sensitivity of financial institutions and 12 studies examined either the foreign exchange exposure or the interest rate exposures of industrial corporations.[6] The findings of these studies are summarized in table. 11.1.

In the case of financial institutions, the answer to Question 1 is: "*Yes.*" All of the studies that examined stock returns following the increase in interest rate volatility at the end of the 1970s[7] (as well as some of the studies of earlier periods) found that the stock returns of financial institutions were sensitive to interest rate changes. Several of the studies also showed that the degree of the interest rate sensitivity of equity returns was related to the interest rate "riskiness"

---

6. Note that only one of the nine studies of financial institutions also investigated foreign exchange risk and only one of the 12 studies of industrial corporations investigated interest rate exposure. Clearly, as supported by the empirical evidence, academic research considers interest rate exposure a greater risk for financial institutions and exchange rate exposure a greater risk for industrial corporations.

7. This increase in interest rate volatility is contemporaneous with the Federal Reserve's change in monetary policy (from targeting interest rates to targeting money supply) in 1979.

TABLE 11.1

Is Financial Price Risk Reflected in Share Price Behavior?

Authors	What Was Examined? (Time Period)	Findings
Part 1—Empirical Examination of Financial Institutions		
Lloyd & Shick (1977)	Sensitivity of equity returns of 60 large banks to Salomon Brothers High-Grade Long-Term Corporate Bond Index (1969–72)	Only 8.3% of bank stocks exhibited significant sensitivity to the long-term corporate bond index. [Authors noted that (1) bank stocks should be sensitive to short-term interest rates, rather than the long-term bond index they used; and (2) during the 1969–72 period, returns on bonds were higher than those for equity—the average monthly return on a bond portfolio was 0.5% and the average return on an equity portfolio was 0.2%.]
Lynge & Zumwalt (1980)	Sensitivity of equity returns of 57 banks and all DJIA companies to short- and long-term interest rates (1969–75)	Approximately 80% of banks and half of industrial companies are sensitive to interest rates. Magnitude of bank exposures are larger than for industrial companies.
Chance & Lane (1980)	Sensitivity of bank equity returns to short-, intermediate-, and long-term interest rates (1972–76)	For the period 1972–76, the interest rate factor was not significant in a two-factor model.
Flannery & James (1984)	Interest rate sensitivity of 67 actively traded commercial banks and S&Ls (1976–81)	Direct relation between estimated interest rate risk parameter and the degree of maturity mismatch in assets and liabilities.
Booth & Officer (1985)	Interest rate sensitivity of 66 banks and a control group of 66 nonfinancials (1966–80)	Bank stocks are sensitive to actual, anticipated, and unanticipated changes in short-term interest rates, a result not found for the control group of nonfinancials.

Authors	What Was Examined? (Time Period)	Findings
Scott & Peterson (1986)	Interest rate risk of portfolios of 78 bank stocks, 8 S&L stocks, and 25 insurance company stocks (1977–84)	All portfolios exhibited significant sensitivity to interest rates. Interest rate sensitivity of S&L portfolio twice as great as for commercial banks or insurance companies portfolios.
Kane & Unal (1998)	Interest rate sensitivity of 31 banks and 8 S&Ls using a two-factor model that estimated time-varying coefficients (1975–85)	Interest-sensitivity varied significantly over time period. Bank equity returns were sensitive to interest rates only for 1979–82, while S&L returns were sensitive to interest rates over most of sample period.
Kwan (1991)	Interest rate sensitivity of 51 bank stock returns, using a two-factor model that controls for time-varying interest rate sensitivity (1976–82)	Bank stock returns are related to unanticipated interest rate changes, and the magnitude of the effect can be explained by the maturity composition of assets and liabilities.
Chol, Elyasiani, & Kopecky (1992)	Interest rate and exchange rate risks of 48 largest U.S. banks (1975–87)	Bank equity returns were significantly negatively related to interest rates only for the post–Oct. 1979 period. Money center bank returns were sensitive to FX rates—negative relation prior to Oct. 1979 and positive relation thereafter.

Part 2—Empirical Examination of Industrial Corporations

Authors	What Was Examined? (Time Period)	Findings
Sweeney & Warga (1986)	Interest rate sensitivity of industry portfolios focusing primarily on utilities (1960–79)	Utilities exhibited significant negative sensitivity to interest rates. No other industry portfolios exhibited significant interest rate sensitivity.
Jorion (1990)	FX sensitivity of 287 U.S. multinationals (1971–87)	Only 5% of firms exhibited significant FX exposure—estimated FX sensitivity increased as the firm's foreign involvement (as measured by foreign sales) increased.

continued

TABLE 11.1 (*Continued*)

Authors	What Was Examined? (Time Period)	Findings
Part 2—Empirical Examination of Industrial Corporations		
Amihud (1994)	Foreign exchange rate risk of 32 largest U.S. exporters (1979–88)	Strongest significance of FX risk parameter is detected with a lag of up to two quarters.
Bartov, Bodnar, & Kaul (1996)	Relation between volatility in share price returns and volatility in foreign exchange rates before and after the switch from fixed to floating exchange rates (1973)	Increased FX rate volatility associated with increased volatility in share price returns.
Choi & Mehra Prasad (1995)	FX sensitivity of 409 multinational firms and 20 industry portfolios (1978–89)	More firms exhibit significant FX sensitivity during weak-dollar periods than during strong-dollar periods. Cross-sectional differences in FX sensitivity are related to foreign operating profits, sales, and assets.
Chow, Lee, & Solt (1997)	FX sensitivity of 213 multinational firms and 4 diversified stock portfolios (1977–91)	FX exposure increases with return horizon and is significantly related to firm size but not to foreign sales.
Martin, Madura, & Akhigbe (1999)	FX sensitivity of 168 U.S. multinational firms with foreign operations primarily in Europe (1979–95)	16% of firms exhibit FX sensitivity (reinforces Jorion's [1990] finding that FX sensitivity increases as the firm's foreign involvement increases). FX sensitivity is determined by the degree of imbalance in foreign cash inflows and outflows and the proportion of export sales.
Allayannis & Ihrig (2001)	FX sensitivity of returns of 18 U.S. manufacturing industry groups (1979–95)	Four of 18 industry groups exhibited significant FX sensitivity. Significant relation between FX sensitivity and industry markups—as industry markups fall (rise), exposure increases (decreases).

Authors	What Was Examined? (Time Period)	Findings
Pantzalis, Simkins, & Laux (2001)	FX sensitivity of returns of the 220 multinational firms in the Fortune 500 (1989–93)	Operational hedges can reduce FX sensitivity—firms with foreign subsidiaries spread across several foreign countries exhibited smaller FX sensitivity than those with more highly concentrated networks.
Williamson (2001)	FX sensitivity of automotive firms in the United States and Japan (1973–95)	Automotive firms face exposure to FX shocks. FX sensitivity determined by foreign sales and by operational hedging in the form of foreign production.
Bodnar & Wong (2000)	FX sensitivity of large U.S. firms (1977–96)	FX exposures are more significant at longer horizons. There is an inverse relation between firm size and exposure.
Pritamani, Shome, & Singal (2004)	FX sensitivity of subgroups of S&P 500: 28 "importer" firms and 67 "exporter" firms (1975–97)	Significant positive (negative) FX exposures for importers (exporters).

of the institutions, as reflected in operating as opposed to stock market measures. For example, a 1984 study by Flannery and James found that interest rate sensitivity was directly related to the extent of the maturity mismatch between assets and liabilities (a finding reinforced by Kwan [1991]). And a 1986 study by Scott and Peterson found that savings and loans (S&Ls), whose business model was based on the extreme mismatch between the durations of assets and liabilities, were more sensitive to interest rates than commercial banks or insurance companies (a finding confirmed by Kane and Unal [1988]).

In the case of industrial corporations, the answer to Question 1 is: "*It depends.*" All but one of the 12 studies of industrial companies' stock returns focused on foreign exchange rate risk. The one study that investigated interest rate risk—Sweeney and Warga (1986)—reported that the interest rate sensitivity of industrial companies was concentrated mainly in the utility industry, though industries like banking, finance, and real estate also showed some sensitivity during certain periods.[8] The studies of foreign exchange (FX) risk in industrial

---

8. A number of other industries—notably banking, finance, real estate, and "stone, clay, and glass"—showed significant negative exposures over certain time periods. Sweeney and Warga

companies reported that only a small percentage of individual firms exhibited (statistically) significant exposure. Moreover, a number of the studies found that significant FX exposures were associated with certain firm characteristics. For example, as one would expect, most of the studies reported that the FX sensitivity of a company's stock increases with the extent of the firm's foreign involvement.[9] As we would also expect, the sensitivity of equity returns to FX movements was shown to be negatively related to the degree of "operational hedging" done by the firm. Pantzalis, Simkins, and Laux (2001) found that companies with highly concentrated foreign networks (operating with a small number of foreign subs) had greater FX sensitivities than firms with more network "breadth." And Williamson (2001) reported that the FX sensitivity of U.S. and Japanese automotive companies was affected by the degree of foreign production—and, more specifically, that foreign sales were associated with increased FX exposure and foreign operations with reduced exposure. Finally, Chow, Lee, and Solt (1997) and Bodnar and Wong (2003) both reported an inverse relationship between FX exposure and the size of the firm. The intuition here is that although larger companies tend to be more multinational, the greater size and diversity of their overseas operations tend to function as natural hedges.[10]

Question 2: Is the Use of Risk Management Tools (Derivatives) Associated with Reduced Risk?

If companies are exposed to financial price risk (i.e., if the firm's equity returns are sensitive to changes in interest rates, foreign exchange rates, or commodity prices) and if they use derivatives to manage one or more of those exposures, a change in the sensitivity of their stock returns to those risks would be evidence that the market reacts to risk management activities. In the

---

(1986) also investigated whether the interest factor is priced within the framework of arbitrage pricing theory (APT) and found strong evidence for this effect in the utility industry (i.e., interest rate risk is priced in that it is recognized by market participants who expect a premium for bearing this risk).

9. This finding was first reported by Jorion (1990), who looked at U.S. multinationals over the period 1971–87. The finding was then reinforced by Choi and Prasad (1995), who looked at foreign operating profits, sales, and assets; and by Martin, Madura, and Akhigbe (1999), who looked at foreign cash inflows and outflows and export sales as a percentage of the firm's total sales. At the same time, Chow, Lee, and Solt (1997) found no relationship between FX sensitivity and foreign sales.

10. The overall evidence of FX exposure for non-financial firms is mixed. Possible explanations are as follows: the difficulty in obtaining stable measures of FX exposure; the long-term nature of FX risk (i.e., economic exposure), which is difficult to ascertain and not captured using the short-term return measures of most studies; the use of broad exchange rate indexes when firms have unique FX exposures; and the use of stock returns instead of cash flows to measure FX exposures. Also important is the fact that such studies don't take account of corporate risk management practices that work to reduce exposures.

context of Equations (11.2) through (11.4), Question 2 can be rephrased as: Does the use of derivatives affect the size of γ_b, γ_r, and/or γ_{FX}?

We found 15 studies that examined this question, six that focused on financial institutions and nine on industrial companies. The findings reported in these studies are summarized in table 11.2. In the case of financial institutions, the answer to Question 2 is: "*Yes.*" All six of the studies reported that the use of derivatives reduced the sensitivity of the equity returns to interest rates. And three other studies provided indirect supporting evidence: Ahmed, Beatty, and Takeda (1997) concluded that the use of derivatives reduced the volatility of net income for banks; Venkatachalam (1996) reported that derivatives disclosures affect share returns;[11] and Brewer, Jackson, and Moser (1996) found that, in addition to reducing the volatility of their stock returns, the use of derivatives by S&Ls was also associated with greater growth in their mortgage portfolios. Moreover, this last finding was reinforced by a later study of commercial banks (Brewer, Jackson, and Moser [2001]) that demonstrated a positive relationship between their derivatives use and the growth of their commercial and industrial (C&I) loan portfolios.[12]

In the case of industrial companies, while the studies are not unanimous, the weight of the evidence suggests that the answer to Question 2 is "*Yes.*" Eight of the nine studies reported that the use of (mainly FX) derivatives by non-financial firms reduced the sensitivity of their equity returns to financial (mainly currency) risks.[13]

Question 3: Is Cash Flow Volatility Related to Firm Value?

Finance theory suggests that risk management can increase the value of the firm by addressing the so-called corporate "underinvestment problem." The basic idea is that, by hedging financial risks with derivatives, companies reduce the variability of their cash flow, thereby ensuring they will have sufficient funds to undertake all promising projects.[14]

11. The findings suggest that the fair values of off-balance-sheet derivatives are correlated with equity values beyond the notional values for such derivatives. Across firms, the fair value gains and losses for on-balance-sheet derivatives were negatively correlated with fair value gains and losses on derivatives. However, for over 50% of the banks, changes in the fair values of derivatives were positively correlated with the fair values of net on-balance-sheet items—suggesting that some banks may be using derivatives to increase, rather than to reduce, risk.
12. They interpreted this to mean that derivatives usage reduces systematic risk, thereby increasing lending ability.
13. In addition, one study (Guay [1999]) found that the use of risk management was associated with a reduction in beta or market risk.
14. This idea is supported by a leading theoretical paper by Froot, Scharfstein, and Stein (1993), which demonstrated that when the costs of external capital include deadweight costs, companies that require outside financing will underinvest when internal operating cash flows are low. They also show that hedging can be designed to generate additional cash in these situations, thus providing a solution to the underinvestment problem.

TABLE 11.2

Is the Use of Risk Management Tools Associated with Lower Levels of Risk?

Authors	What Was Examined? (Time Period)	Findings
Part 1—Empirical Examination of Financial Institutions		
Choi & Elyasiani (1997)	Impact of interest rate and FX risk management activities of 59 large U.S. banks (1975–92)	Relation exists between the scale of interest rate and FX derivatives contracts and the corresponding sensitivity measures.
Chamberlain, Howe, & Popper (1997)	FX risk management activities of 30 largest U.S. bank holding companies (1986–92)	Negative relation between use of FX derivatives and FX sensitivity of share price.
Carter & Sinkey (1997)	Impact of use of interest rate derivatives on a sample of large U.S. banks (1991–94)	Use of interest rate derivatives associated with a reduction in interest rate sensitivity of bank stock returns.
Schrand (1997)	Interest rate sensitivity of 57 S&Ls (1984–88)	Derivatives usage associated with lower stock price sensitivity.
Hirtle (1997)	Relation between equity returns and use of interest rate swaps for 139 bank holding companies (1986–94)	Increased use of interest rate swaps associated with higher interest rate sensitivity for 1991–94 (no significant relation for earlier years).
Brewer, Jackson, & Moser (2001)	Effects of interest rate derivatives use on commercial and industrial lending activity by 154 bank holding companies (1986–94)	Derivatives users tend to have less exposure to interest rate risk than nonusers.
Part 2—Empirical Examination of Industrial Corporations		
Tufano (1998)	Impact of hedging on sensitivity of equity value to price of gold for North American gold producers (1990–97)	Negative relation between degree of hedging and sensitivity of equity value to price of gold.

Authors	What Was Examined? (Time Period)	Findings
Guay (1999)	Impact of interest rate and FX derivatives on equity returns of new users of derivatives—i.e., firms who previously had not reported using derivatives (1990–94)	Both interest rate and FX sensitivities of equity returns declined.
Petersen & Thiagarajan (2000)	Impact of gold hedging on risk exposures of two firms at opposite ends of derivatives-use spectrum (1976–94)	American Barrick's (hedger) gold exposure was only slightly smaller than Homestake Mining (non-hedger). Operational hedging and leverage are also important to exposure.
Allayannis & Ofek (2001)	Impact of use of FX derivatives on sensitivity of equity returns to FX for 378 nonfinancial firms (1992–94)	Strong negative relation between use of FX derivatives and FX sensitivity of equity returns.
Hentschel & Kothari (2001)	Impact of interest rate and FX derivatives use on equity returns of 325 U.S. nonfinancials (1990–93)	Sensitivities of equity returns to interest rates and FX not related to derivatives positions.
Allayannis, Ihrig, & Weston (2001)	Impact of financial (and operational) risk management on FX sensitivity of U.S. multinational firms (1996–98)	Financial risk management is related to lower FX sensitivity.
Carter, Pantzalis, & Simkins (2004)	Impact of financial (and operational) risk management on FX sensitivity of 208 U.S. multinational firms (1994–98)	Financial risk management is related to lower FX sensitivity.
Kim, Mathur, & Nam (2004)	Impact of financial (and operational) risk management on FX exposure of 424 firms (1996–2000)	Financial risk management is related to lower FX sensitivity.
Jin & Jorion (2004)	Risk management activities of 119 U.S. oil and gas producers (1998–2001)	Use of risk management reduces sensitivity of equity returns to oil and gas prices.

TABLE 11.3

Is Cash Flow Volatility Related to Firm Value?

Authors	What Was Examined? (Time Period)	Findings
Minton & Schrand (1999)	Financial statements of approximately 1,000 nonfinancial firms (1988–95)	(1) Negative relation between cash flow volatility and investment: firms with higher levels of cash flow volatility had lower capital expenditures, R&D expenditures, and advertising expenditures; and (2) positive relation between volatility and cost of debt and equity financing.
Shin & Stulz (2000)	Firms available on COMPUSTAT database and CRSP for the period 1962–99	Negative relation between cash flow volatility and shareholder wealth. Result stronger for firms that are financially weak and have poorer growth opportunities.
Allayannis & Weston (2001)	Earnings and cash flow volatility impact on firm value for COMPUSTAT/ CRSP firms with few missing observations (1986–2000); 3,390 firm-year observations	Negative relation between earnings and cash flow volatility on shareholder wealth. Value effect of earnings volatility greater than that of cash flow volatility.

We found only three studies (summarized in table 11. 3) that bear on this issue. In their study of about 1,000 non-financial companies over the period 1988–95, Minton and Schrand (1999) found that companies with higher cash flow volatility had lower capital expenditures, research and development (R&D), and advertising expenditures, thereby establishing the tie between volatility and lower investment. The link between volatility and lower value is furnished in two working papers. Looking at over 2,000 companies during the period 1986–2000, Allayannis and Weston (2003) found a negative relationship between earnings and cash flow volatility and shareholder value (as measured by price-to-book ratios). And Shin and Stulz (2000) reported much the same result in their study of companies from 1962 to 1999.

Question 4: Is There a Relationship between the Use of Derivatives and Firm Value?

Now to the question we started with: Does the use of risk management add value? Empirical research on this question is relatively recent. In all, we found ten studies, the first of which was published in 2001. To proxy for a firm's value, nine of the studies used Tobin's Q, which is the ratio of a company's market value to the replacement value of its assets. In table 11.4, we have arranged these studies into four groups:

1. One study of interest rate and FX risk management by financial institutions

2. Five studies of interest rate and FX risk management by industrial corporations

3. One study of commodity price risk management by commodity users

4. Three studies of commodity risk management by commodity producers

In the case of interest rate and FX risk management (parts 1 and 2 of table 11.4), the evidence shows a positive relationship between risk management and the value of the firm. The study of banks' use of interest rate and FX derivatives concludes that such activities are associated with higher firm value (as measured by Tobin's Q). Furthermore, all five studies of industrial companies' use of FX derivatives (including one study that also included interest rate derivatives) found evidence that risk management adds value.

The most-cited study (and one of the few published papers) in this line of research is Allayannis and Weston (2001) on the use of foreign currency derivatives by large non-financial firms between 1990 and 1995. Again using Tobin's Q as an approximation of firm value, they found that FX hedging is associated with a 4.8% premium for companies with FX exposure (as measured by foreign sales). But this finding presents the problem of distinguishing between correlation and causality: Could the corporate use of derivatives alone account for this almost 5% premium, or does a sophisticated risk management program presuppose some degree of corporate success? Another published study (Guay and Kothari [2003]) concluded that corporate derivatives positions in general are far too small to account for the valuation premium reported by Allayannis and Weston (2001),[15] and that the positive

---

15. Guay and Kothari (2003) reported that, for the median firm in their sample of 234 firms, a simultaneous three-standard-deviation change in interest rates, FX rates, and commodity prices would result in a cash inflow of only $15 million and would increase the value of the firm's derivatives portfolio by only $31 million.

association between derivatives and value is more a reflection of the tendency of successful companies to use derivatives.

Nevertheless, there are a number of other studies of FX and interest rate risk management that shed a more direct light on this question of causality. An important published study by Graham and Rogers (2002) examined a broad cross section of 442 companies and concluded that hedging FX and/or interest rates increases firm value by 1.1% through increased debt capacity and tax benefits.[16] Perhaps even more suggestive, Nain (2004) reported that companies that choose not to hedge FX risk in industries where the use of FX derivatives is common had 5% lower Tobin's Q than their hedged competitors.[17] The novel approach of this study may be the most effective way of addressing the question: What difference does hedging really make?

Now, let's turn to the case of commodity price risk management. As summarized in parts 3 and 4 of table 11.4, the evidence suggests that whether or not risk management adds value depends on whether the company is a user or producer of the commodity. Taking an approach similar to that of the Nain (2004) study, the single study of commodity risk management by commodity users (Carter, Rogers, and Simkins [2004]) found that fuel price hedging by airlines was associated with significantly higher firm values. More specifically, the study examined 29 U.S. airlines over the period 1992–2003 and found that (1) the stock prices of all the airlines were highly sensitive to fuel prices and (2) the prices of the airlines that hedged traded at a 12% to 16% premium over those that did not.[18] Such results do not seem unreasonable, especially when one considers that the annualized volatility of jet fuel prices is around 30% (as compared to, say, 11% for major currencies). Consider the recent hedging results for two major airlines, American Airlines and Southwest Airlines. At the end of 2004, AMR (parent company of American Airlines) had hedged roughly 5% of its 2005 fuel requirements and, as a result, expected to pay $1.3 billion *more* for

---

16. They found that hedging increases the mean (median) firm's debt ratio by 2.03% (2.46%), consistent with increased debt capacity resulting from lower income volatility. The higher debt ratios lead to tax deductions equal to about 1.1% of firm value.

17. While not included in the exhibit, additional support for this conclusion was provided by another study: Lin, Pantzalis, and Park (2005) found that the use of risk management by non-financial firms was associated with lower levels of equity undervaluation (measured as the deviation of a firm's equity value from its intrinsic or fundamental value using six different proxies of value including abnormal returns and analysts' forecasts). Other studies worth noting in this context are Lin and Smith (2003) and Dadalt, Gay, and Nam (2002). In their study of companies over the period 1992–96, Lin and Smith (2003) found that companies that hedge have a lower cost of equity than non-hedgers (in the range of 0.4–2.9%) using both ex post (average realized) and ex ante (expected) cost of equity measures. Dadalt et al. (2002) revealed that both the use of derivatives and the extent of derivatives usage were associated with lower asymmetric information in that analysts' earnings forecasts were more accurate and less dispersed.

18. They also note that analysts' forecasts for hedging airlines tended to be more accurate, an indirect benefit of hedging also mentioned by Guay and Kothari (2003).

TABLE 11.4

Is There a Relationship between Risk Management and the Value of the Firm?

Authors	What Was Examined? (Time Period)	Findings
Part 1—Empirical Examination of Impact of Interest Rate and/or FX Risk Management by Financial Institutions		
Cyree & Huang (2004)	Impact of interest rate and FX derivatives use by publicly traded banks or holding companies (1993–96)	Banks using derivatives have higher value (Tobin's Q) than non-users.
Part 2—Empirical Examination of Impact of Interest Rate and/or FX Risk Management by Industrial Corporations		
Allayannis & Weston (2001)	Impact of FX derivatives use on 720 large nonfinancial firms (1990–95)	Positive relation between use of FX derivatives and firm value (Tobin's Q).
Bartram, Brown, & Fehle (2004)	Impact of interest rate and FX derivatives use for 7,292 companies in U.S. and 47 other countries (2000–2001)	Use of derivatives associated with higher firm value (more significant for interest rates than FX).
Nain (2004)	U.S. firms (548 derivatives users and 2,711 non-derivative users) with ex ante FX exposure (1997–99)	FX risk management increases (does not affect) firm value as measured by Tobin's Q if many (few or zero) competitors hedge.
Kim, Mathur, & Nam (2004)	Impact of financial (and operational) risk management on FX exposure of 424 firms (1996–2000)	Financial risk management is associated with higher firm value.
Allayannis, Lei, & Miller (2004)	Impact of use of FX derivatives on firm value (Tobin's Q) for 379 firms (1990–99)	Significant positive premium for users of derivatives with FX exposures (positive but insignificant for firms with no exposure).
Part 3—Empirical Examination of Impact of Commodity Price Risk Management by Users of Commodities		
Carter, Rogers, & Simkins (2004)	Impact of fuel hedging on 26 U.S. airlines (1994–2000)	Positive relation between use of fuel price risk derivatives and firm value (Tobin's Q).

continued

TABLE 11.4 *(Continued)*

Authors	What Was Examined? (Time Period)	Findings
Part 4—Empirical Examination of Impact of Commodity Price Risk Management by Producers of Commodities		
Callahan (2002)	Impact of gold hedging on 20 North American gold mining firms (1996–2000)	Negative correlation between extent of gold hedging and performance of firm stock price.
Lookman (2004)	Exploration and production (E&P) firms that hedge commodity price risk; unbalanced panel set of 125 firms (364 firm-year observations) (1992–94 and 1999–2000)	For undiversified E&P firms where commodity price risk is a primary risk, hedging is associated with lower firm value. For diversified firms with an E&P segment, hedging is associated with higher firm value. In aggregate, no association with hedging and firm value is detected.
Jin & Jorion (2005)	Risk management activities of 119 U.S. oil and gas producers (1998–2001)	Risk management not related to firm value (Tobin's Q).

jet fuel in 2005 than in 2004 (a considerable amount, considering that 2004 revenues were $18.6 billion and the net loss for that year was $761 million). By contrast, Southwest Airlines' aggressive hedging program (which involved hedging over 80% of its 2005 fuel requirements, with some contracts extending up to 6 years) has saved the firm over $1 billion on fuel since 2000, allowing it to make important capital investments when strategic opportunities arise.[19]

But what about the three studies of commodity producers? Two studies of oil and gas firms and a study of gold mining companies all found that commodity risk management had either no effect or a negative effect on equity values. The most important paper of the three, Jin and Jorion (2005), studied the hedging activities of 119 U.S. oil and gas producers from 1998 to 2001 and concluded that, while hedging reduced the firm's stock price sensitivity to oil and gas prices, it did not appear to increase value. As the authors conclude, ". . . one might even argue that investors take positions in oil producers precisely to gain

19. For example, its hedging program has helped give Southwest Airlines the financial capability to make capital expenditures to increase its market position in weaker competitors' markets, aggressively expand new routes, and make energy-saving improvements, including the addition of blended winglets to 177 of their Boeing 737–700 aircraft (as of December 31, 2004).

exposure to oil prices. If so, an oil firm should not necessarily benefit from hedging oil price risk."[20]

Conclusions

Contrary to the implications of the capital asset pricing model (CAPM), the findings of academic studies suggest that financial price risks can affect the expected returns on stocks and hence stock prices themselves. For example, there is clear evidence that the equity returns of financial institutions are sensitive to interest rate changes. And industrial companies with foreign sales and cash flows (though not large-scale foreign operations) exhibit greater sensitivity to foreign exchange rate changes than most wholly domestic firms. What's more, the evidence also suggests that the corporate uses of derivatives to manage certain "diversifiable" risks reduces the sensitivity of their stock returns to those risks.

But how does reduced sensitivity to price risks translate into added value—and if so, how? The main argument offered by finance academics is that the resulting reduction in cash flow volatility reduces the likelihood that the company will become financially distressed or be forced to pass up valuable investment opportunities. And what little evidence we now have on this issue—which shows positive associations between higher cash flow volatility and both lower corporate investment and lower share values—is consistent with this argument.

Is there any direct evidence that risk management increases firm value? The answer is yes, but the evidence is fairly limited as yet. A number of more recent studies show a clearly positive correlation between higher share values and the use of derivatives to manage foreign exchange rate risk and interest rate risk. And one study provides fairly compelling evidence that the use of commodity price derivatives by commodity *users* increases share values. But studies of hedging by commodity producers provide no clear support for the argument that risk management adds value. At a minimum, whether hedging adds value appears to depend on the types of risk to which a firm is exposed.

For those of us who have spent much of our careers promoting the use of derivatives to manage financial price risk, the results of the research to date are reassuring. But it also raises questions that deserve more attention:

---

20. One published paper, while indirectly related to our question, provides evidence for a positive effect. Adam and Fernando (2005) found that firms in the gold mining industry have consistently realized positive cash flows from their derivatives transactions for gold. The authors documented that a key source of this cash flow is realized from gold producers trading on a persistent positive risk premium in the forward markets.

- The available evidence indicates that although the management of interest rate and foreign exchange rate risks does indeed add value, the effect is larger than would be expected. Is the observed effect the market's reaction to the risk management activity itself; or are we observing some kind of "self-selection" process in which successful firms are more likely to have the capital and other resources needed to run a derivatives program? How do shareholders react to a change in the scale of risk management activities; is more derivatives trading preferred to less? And are there other ways in which the use of derivatives might be adding value?

- Some of the studies suggest that the use of risk management reduces the sensitivity of the share price not only to the financial price being managed but to general market risk (b). How "robust" is this result? Can determinants of the size of this effect be identified?

- How is information on risk management being acquired by shareholders? Do security analysts provide more favorable ratings to companies that actively manage risk? If so, why?

CHARLES W. SMITHSON is the founder and principal owner of Rutter Associates, a risk management consulting firm that specializes in measuring and managing credit and market risks for financial institutions.

BETTY J. SIMKINS is an Associate Professor of Finance at Oklahoma State University.

References

Adam, T., and C. Fernando. "Hedging, Speculation, and Shareholder Value." *Journal of Financial Economics* (2005).

Ahmed, A., A. Beatty, and C. Takeda. "Evidence on Interest Rate Risk Management and Derivatives Usage by Commercial Banks." Unpublished working paper, 1997.

Allayannis, G., and J. Ihrig. "Exposure and Markups." *Review of Financial Studies* Vol. 14 (2001): 805–35.

Allayannis, G., J. Ihrig, and J. Weston. "Exchange-Rate Hedging: Financial vs. Operating Strategies." *American Economic Review Papers and Proceedings* Vol. 91 (2001): 391–95.

Allayannis, G., U. Lei, and D. Miller. Corporate working paper, Darden School of Business (University of Virginia) and Kelley School of Business (Indiana University), 2004.

Allayannis, G., and E. Ofek. "Exchange Rate Exposure, Hedging, and the Use of Foreign Currency Derivatives," *Journal of International Money and Finance* Vol. 20 (2001): 273–96.

Allayannis, G., and J. Weston. "The Use of Foreign Currency Derivatives and Firm Market Value." *Review of Financial Studies* Vol. 14 (2001): 243–76.

Amihud, Y. "Evidence on Exchange Rates and Valuation of Equity Shares," in Y. Amihud and R. Levich, eds., *Exchange Rates and Corporate Performance* Homewood, IL: Business One Irwin, 1994.

Bartov, E., G. Bodnar, and A. Kaul. "Exchange Rate Volatility and the Riskiness of U.S. Multinational Firms." *Journal of Financial Economics* Vol. 42 (1996): 105–32.

Bartram, S., G. Brown, and F. Fehle. "International Evidence on Financial Derivatives Usage." Unpublished working paper, Kenan-Flagler Business School (University of North Carolina), 2004.

Booth, J., and D. Officer. "Expectations, Interest Rates, and Commercial Bank Stocks." *Journal of Financial Research* Vol. 8 (1985): 51–58.

Bodnar, G., and M. H. Wong. "Estimating Exchange Rate Exposures: Issues in Model Structure." *Financial Management* (Spring 2000): 35–67.

Brewer III, E., W. Jackson III, and J. Moser. "Alligators in the Swamp: The Impact of Derivatives on the Financial Performance of Depository Institutions." *Journal of Money, Credit and Banking* Vol. 28 (1996): 482–97.

Brewer III, E., W. Jackson III, and J. Moser. "The Value of Using Interest Rate Derivatives to Manage Risk of U.S. Banking Organizations." *Economic Perspectives*, Federal Reserve Bank of Chicago, 49–66.

Callahan, M. "To Hedge or Not To Hedge . . . That Is the Question: Empirical Evidence from the North American Gold Mining Industry 1996–2000." *Financial Markets, Institutions & Instruments* Vol. 11 (2002): 271–88.

Carter, D., C. Pantzalis, and B. Simkins. "Asymmetric Exposure to Foreign-Exchange Risk: Financial and Real Option Hedges Implemented by U.S. Multinational Corporations." *Proceedings of the Assurant/Georgia Tech Tenth International Finance Conference*, 2004.

Carter, D., D. Rogers, and B. Simkins. "Does Fuel Hedging Make Economics Sense? The Case of the U.S. Airline Industry." Unpublished working paper, Oklahoma State University and Portland State University, 2004.

Carter, D., and J. Sinkey, Jr. "The Use of Derivatives and the Interest-Rate Sensitivity of Bank Stock Returns." Unpublished working paper, University of Georgia, 1997.

Chamberlain, S., J. Howe, and H. Popper. "The Exchange Rate Exposure of U.S. and Japanese Banking Institutions." *Journal of Banking and Finance* Vol. 21 (1997): 871–92.

Chance, D., and W. Lane. "A Re-Examination of Interest Rate Sensitivity in the Common Stocks of Financial Institutions." *Journal of Financial Research* Vol. 3 (1980): 49–55.

Choi, J., and E. Elyasiani. "Derivative Exposure and the Interest Rate and Exchange Rate Risks of U.S. Banks." *Journal of Financial Services Research* Vol. 12 (1997): 267–86.

Choi, J., E. Elyasiani, and K. Kopecky. "The Sensitivity of Bank Stock Returns to Market, Interest and Exchange Rate Risks." *Journal of Banking and Finance* Vol. 16 (1992): 983–1004.

Choi, J., and A. Mehra Prasad. "Exchange Rate Sensitivity and Its Determinants: A Firm and Industry Analysis of U.S. Multinationals." *Financial Management* Vol. 24 (1995): 77–88.

Chow, E., W. Lee, and M. Solt. "The Economic Exposure of U.S. Multinational Firms." *Journal of Financial Research* Vol. 20 (1997): 191–210.

Cyree, K., and P. Huang. "Bank Hedging and Derivatives Use: The Impact on and Sources of Shareholder Value and Risk." Unpublished working paper, University of Mississippi and Massey University, 2004.

Dadalt, P., G. Gay, and J. Nam. "Asymmetric Information and Corporate Derivatives Use." *Journal of Futures Markets* Vol. 22 (2002): 241–67.

Flannery, M., and C. James. "The Effect of Interest Rate Changes on the Common Stock Returns of Financial Institutions." *The Journal of Finance* Vol. 39 (1984): 1141–53.

Froot, K., D. Scharfstein, and J. Stein. "Risk Management: Coordinating Investment and Financing Policies." *Journal of Finance* Vol. 48 (1993): 1629–58.

Graham, J., and D. Rogers. "Do Firms Hedge in Response to Tax Incentives?" *Journal of Finance* Vol. 57 (2002): 815–39.

Guay, W. "The Impact of Derivatives on Firm Risk: An Empirical Examination of New Derivative Users." *Journal of Accounting and Economics* Vol. 26 (1999): 319–51.

Guay, W., and S. P. Kothari. "How Much Do Firms Hedge with Derivatives?" *Journal of Financial Economics* Vol. 70 (2003): 423–61.

Hentschel, L., and S. P. Kothari. "Are Corporations Reducing or Taking Risks with Derivatives?" *Journal of Financial and Quantitative Analysis* Vol. 36 (2001): 93–118.

Hirtle, B. "Derivatives, Portfolio Composition, and Bank Holding Company Interest Rate Risk Exposure." *Journal of Financial Services Research* Vol. 12 (1997): 243–66.

Jin, Y., and P. Jorion. "Firm Value and Hedging: Evidence from U.S. Oil and Gas Producers." Unpublished working paper, California State University at Northridge and University of California at Irvine, 2004.

Jorion, P. "The Exchange-Rate Exposure of U.S. Multinationals." *Journal of Business* Vol. 63 (1990): 331–45.

Kane, E., and H. Unal. "Change in Market Assessments of Deposit-Institution Riskiness." *Journal of Financial Services Research* Vol. 1 (1988): 207–29.

Kim, Y., I. Mathur, and J. Nam. "Is Operational Hedging a Substitute for or a Complement to Financial Hedging?" Unpublished working paper, Northern Kentucky University, 2004.

Koutmos, G., and A. Martin. "Asymmetric Exchange Rate Exposure: Theory and Evidence." *Journal of International Money and Finance* Vol. 22 (2003): 365–83.

Kwan, S. "Re-examination of Interest Rate Sensitivity of Commercial Bank Stock Returns Using a Random Coefficient Model." *Journal of Financial Services Research* Vol. 5 (1991): 61–76.

Lin, B., C. Pantzalis, and J. Park. "Corporate Hedging Policy and Equity Mispricing." Unpublished working paper, University of South Florida, 2005.

Lin, C., and S. Smith. "Risk Management and the Cost of Equity." Unpublished working paper, Georgia State University, 2003.

Lloyd, W., and R. Shick. "A Test of Stone's Two-Index Model of Returns." *Journal of Financial and Quantitative Analysis* Vol. 12 (1977): 363–76.

Lookman, A. "Does Hedging Increase Firm Value? Evidence from Oil and Gas Producing Firms." Unpublished working paper, Carnegie Mellon University, 2004.

Lynge, M., and J. Zumwalt. *Journal of Financial and Quantitative Analysis* Vol. 15 (1980): 731–42.

Martin, A., J. Madura, and A. Akhigbe. "Economic Exchange Rate Exposure of U.S.-Based MNCs Operating in Europe." *Financial Review* Vol. 34 (1999): 21–36.

Minton, B., and C. Schrand. "The Impact of Cash Flow Volatility on Discretionary Investment and the Costs of Debt and Equity Financing." *Journal of Financial Economics* Vol. 54 (1999): 423–60.

Nain, A. "The Strategic Motives for Corporate Risk Management." Unpublished working paper, University of Michigan, 2004.

Pantzalis, C., B. Simkins, and P. Laux. "Operational Hedges and the Foreign Exchange Exposure of U.S. Multinational Corporations." *Journal of International Business Studies* Vol. 32 (2001): 793–812.

Petersen, M., and S. Thiagarajan. "Risk Management and Hedging: With and Without Derivatives." *Financial Management* Vol. 29 (2000): 5–30.

Pritamani, M., D. Shome, and V. Singal. "Foreign Exchange Exposure of Exporting and Importing Firms." *Journal of Banking and Finance* Vol. 28 (2004): 1697–1710.

Schrand, C. "The Association between Stock-Price Interest Rate Sensitivity and Disclosures about Derivative Instruments." *Accounting Review* Vol. 72 (1997): 87–109.

Scott, W., and R. Peterson. "Interest Rate Risk and Equity Values of Hedged and Unhedged Financial Intermediaries." *Journal of Financial Research* Vol. 9 (1986): 325–29.

Shin, H., and R. Stulz. "Shareholder Wealth and Firm Risk," School of Management, State University of New York at Buffalo, Ohio State University Dice Center

Working Paper No. 2000–19 and National Bureau of Economic Research
Working Paper, December 2000.

Sinkey, Jr., J., and D. Carter. "Evidence on the Financial Characteristics of Banks That Do and Do Not Use Derivatives." *Quarterly Review of Economics and Finance* Vol. 40 (2000): 431–49.

Sweeney, R., and A. Warga. "The Pricing of Interest-Rate Risk: Evidence from the Stock Market." *Journal of Finance* Vol. 41 (1986): 393–409.

Tufano, P. "The Determinants of Stock Price Exposure: Financial Engineering and the Gold Mining Industry." *Journal of Finance* Vol. 53 (1998): 1015–52.

Venkatachalam, M. "Value-Relevance of Banks' Derivatives Disclosures." *Journal of Accounting and Economics* Vol. 22 (1996): 327–55.

Williamson, R. "Exchange Rate Exposure and Competition: Evidence from the Automotive Industry." *Journal of Financial Economics* Vol. 59 (2001): 441–75.

PART III

Practitioner Perspectives

IN "IDENTIFYING, MEASURING, AND HEDGING CURRENCY RISK AT MERCK" (chapter 12), Judy Lewent and John Kearney describe the company's effort to understand and manage the effect of exchange rate volatility on worldwide revenues and earnings. In a thought process that parallels the one laid out in preceding chapters (by Smith, Stulz, and others), Merck's treasury arrived at the following conclusions: (1) the home currency value of cash flows regularly repatriated by its many overseas subsidiaries was vulnerable to a strengthening of the U.S. dollar; (2) although stock market analysts and investors do not appear much concerned about the exchange-related volatility of reported earnings, volatility in repatriated cash flows could interfere with the company's ability to make long-term investments in research and development and marketing (the principal sources of the company's future earnings); and (3) consistent with Stulz's argument that risk management should be designed to eliminate the lower tail of the distribution (and not to minimize variance), hedging (only part of) its currency options was the most cost-effective means of ensuring the company's ability to carry out its long-range strategic plan.

In "Corporate Insurance Strategy: The Case of British Petroleum" (chapter 13), Neil Doherty and Clifford Smith describe a radical shift in British Petroleum's approach to insuring property and casualty losses, product liability suits, and other insurable events. Conventional corporate practice—and until recently the long-standing risk management policy of British Petroleum (BP)—was to insure against large losses while "self-insuring" smaller ones. In this chapter, Doherty and Smith explain why BP chose to flout the conventional wisdom and now insures against most smaller losses while self-insuring larger ones.

The BP decision came down to factors affecting the market supply of insurance as well as the corporate demand for it. On the demand side, the authors demonstrate that the primary source of demand for insurance by large public companies is not, as standard insurance textbooks assume, to transfer risk away from the corporation's owners (corporate stockholders and bondholders, it turns out, have their own means of neutralizing the effect of such risks). The demand stems, rather, at least in BP's case, from insurance companies' comparative advantage in assessing and monitoring risk and in processing claims. On the supply side, Doherty and Smith explain why the capacity of insurance markets to underwrite very large or highly specialized exposures is quite limited—and can be expected to remain so.

Comparative advantage also plays a major role in "Hedging and Value in the U.S. Airline Industry" (chapter 14), in which David Carter, Daniel Rogers, and Betty Simkins summarize the findings of their study of fuel cost hedging by 28 U.S. airlines during the period 1992–2003. The results show that hedging is positively related to firm value, that the largest and most profitable airlines are the most consistent and active hedgers, and, perhaps most interesting, that the value premium associated with hedging increases with the level of the airline's capital spending.

Consistent with what finance theorists were suggesting almost 25 years ago, these findings could well be interpreted as saying that the main source of value added by hedging in the airline industry is its role in preserving the firm's ability to take advantage of investment opportunities—in this case, opportunities that arise when fuel prices are high, and airline operating cash flows and values are down. In other words, because only the largest, most profitable airlines are able to buy distressed assets during periods of industry weakness, such firms may well have the most to gain from hedging.

In "Enterprise Risk Management: Theory and Practice" (chapter 15), Brian Nocco, the Chief Risk Officer of Nationwide Insurance, and Rene Stulz attach considerable weight to the views of the rating agencies while discussing the design and implementation of an enterprise risk management (ERM) program. Nocco and Stulz begin by arguing that a well-designed ERM program—one that enables senior management to identify, measure, and limit to acceptable levels all material risks using a single, company-wide framework—can be a source of long-run competitive advantage. By managing the firm's net exposures mainly with the idea of cushioning downside outcomes and protecting the firm's credit rating, ERM helps maintain the firm's access to capital and other resources necessary to implement its strategy and business plan. Maintaining a high investment grade credit rating is especially critical for Nationwide since it affects the firm's ability to attract customers for its insurance and investment products.

But if much of the benefits of Nationwide's ERM program are expected to come from greater coordination and control from the top, there is also a major role for decentralized decision-making and accountability. To help ensure that risk-return trade-offs are carefully evaluated at the business unit and project levels, the company's business managers are required to provide information about the major risks associated with all new capital projects—information that senior management can then use to evaluate the marginal impact of the projects on the firm's total risk. And to encourage the operating managers to take account of the risk-return trade-offs in their own businesses, Nationwide's regular performance evaluations of its business units attempt to reflect the units' contributions to total risk by assigning them risk-adjusted levels of "imputed" capital. By requiring the operating heads to earn adequate returns on such capital, the performance evaluation system effectively forces managers to become important participants—the first line of defense, if you will—in the ERM program.

Among other matters of implementation, this chapter also raises the question of which risks a company should retain and which it should transfer to others. Guided by the principle of comparative advantage, Nationwide attempts to limit "non-core" exposures such as interest rate and equity risk, which has the effect of enlarging the firm's capacity to bear the "information-intensive, insurance-specific" risks that are at the core of its business and competencies.

In "The Rise and Evolution of the Chief Risk Officer: Enterprise Risk Management at Hydro One" (chapter 16) Tom Aabo, John Fraser, and Betty Simkins describe the 5-year implementation of enterprise risk management at Hydro One, a Canadian electric utility company that recently went public. Starting with the creation of the position of Chief Risk Officer (CRO) and the implementation of a pilot risk study involving one of the firm's subsidiaries, the ERM process has made use of a variety of tools and techniques, including the "Delphi Method," risk trends, risk tolerances, and risk rankings.

Among the most tangible benefits of ERM at Hydro One are said to be (1) a better-coordinated and more effective process for allocating capital and (2) a favorable reaction to the program by Moody's and Standard and Poor's, which has arguably improved the company's credit rating and lowered its cost of capital. But perhaps equally important is the company's progress in realizing the first principle of its ERM policy—namely, that "risk management is everyone's responsibility, from the Board of Directors to individual employees." The implementation process itself has reportedly helped make risk awareness an important part of the corporate culture; and as a result, Hydro One's management feels that the company is much better positioned today to respond to new business developments than it was 5 years ago.

Part III, and thus the book, closes with two roundtable discussions (chapter 17, "University of Georgia Roundtable on Enterprise-Wide Risk Management," and chapter 18, "Morgan Stanley Roundtable on Enterprise Risk Management and Corporate Strategy"), which brought together academics and practitioners of corporate risk management to discuss questions such as the following:

What are the primary goals of corporate risk management programs? Should such programs be designed mainly to reduce volatility in reported earnings, or are there other aims that translate more directly into adding value for shareholders?

What risks are companies paid to bear? To what extent can the economist's principle be used to guide corporate risk management decisions? For example, should oil companies hedge much of their oil price risk, or banks hedge their interest rate risk—or should such risks be borne mainly by the firms' shareholders? Can energy and financial firms use the information provided by their operations to make their trading operations a reliable source of profit?

What should companies tell investors about their risk management programs? To get recognition from the equity markets—say, in the form of a higher price/earnings ratio (P/E) multiple—for having an ERM program, companies may need to find a way to communicate at least their general risk management *policy* to their shareholders. But given the difficulty of qualifying for hedge accounting under FAS 133, how do companies communicate the effectiveness of their hedging programs to investors when even well-conceived and well-executed programs can produce large derivatives losses that flow through the profit and loss statement?

The second of the two roundtables—using the case of The Williams Companies, a risk management success story—offers a solution in the form of a commitment to regular and extensive disclosure. The Williams Companies is a highly regarded producer and distributor of natural gas that narrowly averted bankruptcy about 5 years ago. According to the company's CRO, Andrew Sunderman:

> In the case of Williams, which was [then] a BBB-rated energy company with a trading and marketing unit operating in the wake of the collapse of the largest U.S. merchant energy trading company—and I'm talking of course about Enron—derivatives and risk management were, and continue to be, an important part of our overall strategy.

Operating under difficult circumstances, the company initiated an extensive hedging program that helped restore its access to capital and jumpstart a recovery that has transformed Williams into one of the best performers on Wall Street in recent years.

One common response to the Williams case is to suggest that the firm was overleveraged from the start. But this misses a critical point of the story—that a mid-cap company like Williams is likely to face a considerably higher cost of equity than a firm like, say, BP, which does not hedge oil prices. And for companies with a relatively high cost of equity and a significant exposure to commodity prices, the combination of hedging and higher leverage (made possible by hedging) can serve as a substitute for expensive equity capital. To the extent this is so, the real lesson of the Williams story, as summed up by Morgan Stanley's John McCormack, is that:

> Williams's business model is fundamentally different from BP's, and the company's combination of hedging and higher leverage is likely to attract a different kind of investor than BP's. But, as long as Williams earns high rates of return on capital—and provided management makes it clear to the market how they are producing those returns and the risks they are taking in the process—the company will find investors willing to buy its shares.

The lesson from the Williams story is straightforward: If companies take the pains to communicate the aims and methods of their risk management programs, the market is likely to understand and reward their efforts.

CHAPTER 12

Identifying, Measuring, and Hedging Currency Risk at Merck

JUDY C. LEWENT AND A. JOHN KEARNEY

T HE IMPACT OF EXCHANGE RATE volatility on a company depends mainly on the company's business structure, both legal and operational, its industry profile, and the nature of its competitive environment. This article recounts how Merck assessed its currency exposures and reached a decision to hedge those exposures. After a brief introduction to the company and the industry, we discuss our methods of identifying and measuring our exchange exposures, the factors considered in deciding whether to hedge such risks, and the financial hedging program we put in place.

An Introduction to the Company

Merck & Co., Inc. primarily discovers, develops, produces, and distributes human and animal health pharmaceuticals. It is part of a global industry that makes its products available for the prevention, relief, and cure of disease throughout the world. Merck itself is a multinational company, doing business in over 100 countries.

Total worldwide sales in 1989 for all domestic and foreign research-intensive pharmaceutical companies are projected to be $103.7 billion. Worldwide sales for those companies based in the United States are projected at $36.4 billion—an estimated 35% of the world pharmaceutical market; and worldwide sales for Merck in 1989 were $6.6 billion. The industry is highly competitive, with no company holding over 5% of the worldwide market. Merck ranks first in pharmaceutical sales in the United States and the world, yet has only a 4.7% market

This chapter was previously published as an article in *Journal of Applied Corporate Finance* Vol. 2, No. 2 (1990): 19–28. The authors would like to thank Francis H. Spiegel, Jr., Senior Vice President and CFO of Merck & Co., Inc., and Professors Donald Lessard of M.I.T. and Darrell Duffie of Stanford for their guidance throughout.

share worldwide. The major foreign competitors for the domestic industry are European firms and emerging Japanese companies.

Driven by the need to fund high-risk and growing research expenditures, the U.S. pharmaceutical industry has expanded significantly more into foreign markets than has U.S. industry as a whole. In 1987, the leading U.S. pharmaceutical companies generated 38% of their sales revenues overseas; and 37% of their total assets were located outside the United States. In contrast, most U.S. industry groups report foreign sales revenues in the range of 20% to 30%. Merck, with overseas assets equal to 40% of its total and with roughly half of its sales overseas, is among the most internationally oriented of U.S. pharmaceutical companies.

The U.S. pharmaceutical industry also differs in its method of doing business overseas. In contrast to U.S. exporters, who often bill their customers in U.S. dollars, the pharmaceutical industry typically bills its customers in their local currencies. Thus, the effect of foreign currency fluctuations on the pharmaceutical industry tends to be more immediate and direct.

The typical structure is the establishment of subsidiaries in many overseas markets. These subsidiaries, of which Merck has approximately 70, are typically importers of product at some stage of manufacture, and are responsible for finishing, marketing, and distribution within the country of incorporation. Sales are denominated in local currency, and costs in a combination of local currency for finishing, marketing, distribution, administration, and taxes, and in the currency of basic manufacture and research—typically, the U.S. dollar for U.S.-based companies.

Identification and Measurement of Exposure

It is generally agreed that foreign exchange fluctuations can affect a U.S. company's economic and financial results in three ways:

1. By changing the dollar value of net assets held overseas in foreign currencies (known as "translation" exposures) or by changing the expected results of transactions in non-local currencies ("transaction" exposures).

2. By changing the dollar value of future revenues expected to be earned overseas in foreign currencies ("future revenue" exposures).

3. By changing a company's competitive position—for example, a competitor whose costs are denominated in a depreciating currency will have greater pricing flexibility and thus a potential competitive advantage ("competitive" exposures).

Competitive exposures have been the subject of much of the recent academic work done on exchange risk management. Such exposures are best exemplified by the adverse effect of the strong dollar on the competitive position of much of U.S. industry in the early 1980s. This was true not only in export markets but also in the U.S. domestic market, where the strengthening U.S. dollar gave Japanese- and European-based manufacturers a large competitive advantage in dollar terms over domestic U.S. producers.

For the pharmaceutical industry, however, the pricing environment is such that competitive exposure to exchange fluctuations is generally not significant. The existence of price controls throughout most of the world generally reduces flexibility to react to economic changes.

Hence, Merck's exposure to exchange tends to be limited primarily to net asset and revenue exposures. The potential loss in dollar value of net revenues earned overseas represents the company's most significant economic and financial exposure. Such revenues are continuously converted into dollars through interaffiliate merchandise payments, dividends, and royalties, and are an important source of cash flow for the company. To the extent the dollar value of these earnings is diminished, the company suffers a loss of cash flow—at least over the short term. And, as discussed in more detail later, the resulting volatility in earnings and cash flow could impair the company's ability to execute its strategic plan for growth.

With its significant presence worldwide, Merck has exposures in approximately 40 currencies. As a first step in assessing the effect of exchange rate movements on revenues and net income, we constructed a sales index that measures the relative strength of the dollar against a basket of currencies weighted by the size of sales in those countries.[1] When the index is above 100%, foreign currencies have strengthened versus the dollar, indicating a positive exchange effect on dollar revenues. When the index is below 100%, as was the case through most of the 1980s, the dollar has strengthened versus the foreign currencies, resulting in income statement losses due to exchange.

As figure 12.1 illustrates, the index was relatively stable from 1972 to 1980. But, as the dollar strengthened in the early 1980s, the index declined to the 60% level, resulting in a cumulative exchange reduction in sales of approximately $900 million. But, then, as the dollar weakened in the later 1980s, the index increased to roughly 97%, returning to its 1972–1980 range.

But, as figure 12.2 also shows, although the overall index returned as of 1988 to the earlier range, not all currencies have moved together against the dollar. The strengthening in the yen and the deutsche mark has offset the

---

1. The index uses 1978 as its base year. The currency basket excludes hyperinflationary markets where exchange devaluation is measured net of price increases.

FIGURE 12.1

Merck Sales Index

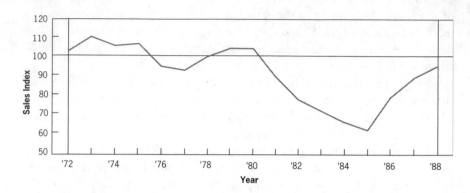

FIGURE 12.2

Merck Sales Index 1978—100%

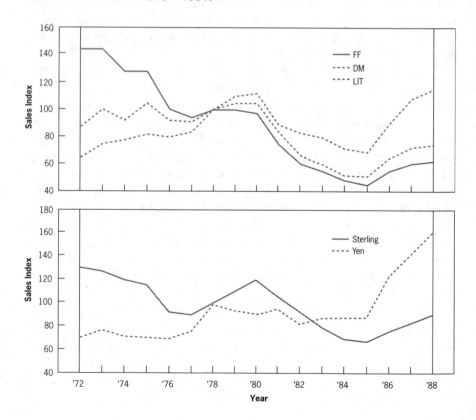

decline of historically weaker currencies such as the Italian lira and French franc, while the British pound is very near 1978 levels.

Resource Allocation

Given the significant exchange exposure of our net overseas revenues as reflected by our experience in the early 1980s, we next decided to review the company's global allocation of resources across currencies and, in the process, to determine the extent to which revenues and costs were matched in individual currencies. Our analysis (the main findings of which are illustrated in figure 12.3) revealed that the distribution of Merck's assets differs somewhat from the sales mix, primarily because of the concentration of research, manufacturing, and headquarters operations in the United States.

On the basis of this analysis, it was clear that Merck has an exchange rate mismatch. To reduce this mismatch, we first considered the possibility of redeploying resources in order to shift dollar costs to a different currency. This process would have involved relocating manufacturing sites, research sites, and employees such as headquarters and support staff. We soon reached the conclusion, however, that because so few support functions seemed appropriate candidates for relocation a move would have had only a negligible effect on our global income exposure. In short, we decided that shifting people and resources overseas was not a cost-effective way of dealing with our exchange exposure.

Hedging Merck's Exposures with Financial Instruments

Having concluded that resource deployment was not an appropriate way for Merck to address exchange risk, we considered the alternative of financial

FIGURE 12.3

Merck's Geographic Mix of Sales and Assets

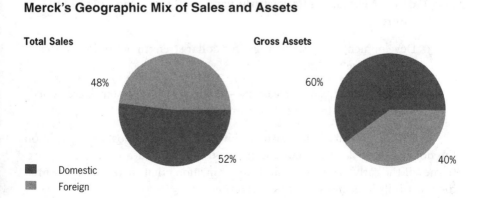

Total Sales

48%

52%

Gross Assets

60%

40%

■ Domestic
▨ Foreign

hedging. Thinking through this alternative involved the following five steps:

1. **Exchange Forecasts.** Review of the likelihood of adverse exchange movements.

2. **Strategic Plan Impact.** Quantification of the potential impact of adverse exchange movements over the period of the plan.

3. **Hedging Rationale.** Critical examination of the reasons for hedging (perhaps the most important part of the process).

4. **Financial Instruments.** Selection of which instruments to use and how to execute the hedge.

5. **Hedging Program.** Simulation of alternative strategies to choose the most cost-effective hedging strategy to accommodate our risk-tolerance profile (an ongoing process supported by a mathematical model we have recently developed to supplement our earlier analysis).

Step 1: Projecting Exchange Rate Volatility

Our review of the probability of future exchange rate movements was guided by four main considerations:

1. The major factors expected to affect exchange rates over the strategic plan period—for example, the U.S. trade deficit, capital flows, the U.S. budget deficit—all viewed in the context of the concept of an "equilibrium" exchange rate.

2. Target zones or government policies designed to manage exchange rates. To what extent will government policies be implemented to dampen exchange rate volatility, particularly "overshooting," in the future?

3. Development of possible ranges for dollar strength or weakness over the planning period.

4. Summary of outside forecasters—a number of forecasters were polled on the outlook for the dollar over the plan period.

Our review of outside forecasters showed they were almost evenly split on the dollar's outlook. Although almost no one predicted a return to the extremes of the early 1980s, we nonetheless concluded that there was a potential for a relatively large move in either direction.

We developed a simple method for quantifying the potential ranges that reflects the following thought process:

- Except for 1986, the upper limit of the year-to-year move in average exchange rates for the deutsche mark and the yen has been about 20%. We used this as the measure of potential volatility in developing the probabilistic ranges in the forecast. (The deutsche mark, incidentally, was used as a proxy for all European currencies.)

- The widest ranges would likely result from one-directional movements— that is, 5 years of continued strengthening or weakening.

- However, as the effect of each year's movement is felt in the economy and financial markets, the probability of exchange rates continuing in the same direction is lessened. For example, if the dollar were to weaken, the favorable effects on the trade balance and on relative asset values would likely induce increased capital flows and cause a turnaround.

Based in part on this concept of exchange rate movements as a "mean-reverting" process, we developed ranges of expected rate movements (as shown in figure 12.4) by assigning probabilities to the dollar continuing to move along a line of consecutive years' strengthening or weakening. For example, the dollar was considered to have a 40% probability of strengthening by 20% versus the deutsche mark in 1989. If the dollar does appreciate by 20% in 1989, then we also assume that the probability of its strengthening by a further 20% in 1990 is also 40%, but that the chance of this pattern continuing in 1991 is only 30% and falls to 20% in 1992.

Such ranges represent our best guess about the likely boundaries of dollar strength or weakness. The actual probability of exchange rate movements reaching or exceeding these boundaries is small, but the use of such extreme rates allows us to estimate the extent of our exposure. These exchange boundaries were also used in quantifying the potential impact of unfavorable exchange rate movements on our Strategic Plan.

Step 2: Assessing the Impact on the 5-Year Strategic Plan

To assess the potential effect of unfavorable exchange rates, we converted our strategic plan into U.S. dollars on an exchange neutral basis (that is, at the current exchange rate) and compared these cash flow and earnings projections to those we expected to materialize under both our strong dollar and weak dollar scenarios. (See figure 12.5.)

Further, we measured the potential impact of exchange rate movements on a cumulative basis as well as according to the year-to-year convention that

FIGURE 12.4

Probabilities of 20% Movement Per Year

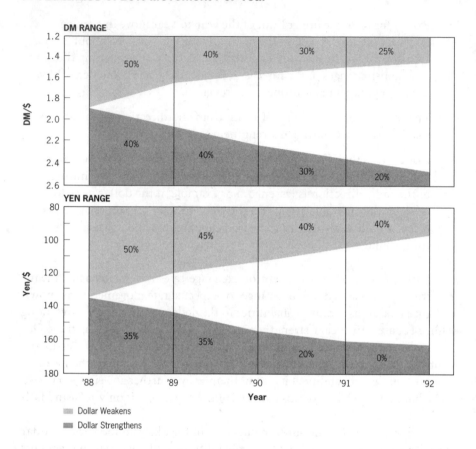

is standard in external reporting. Figure 12.6 shows the effect of translating the year-to-year data from figure 12.5 on a cumulative basis. (The total bar represents the cumulative variance, while the shaded portion represents the variance as determined by the change in rates from one period to the next.) Because it looks beyond a one-year period, the cumulative exchange variance provides a more useful estimate of the size of the exchange risk associated with Merck's long-range plan. Use of a cumulative measure also provides the basis for the kind of multi-year financial hedging program that, as we eventually determined, is appropriate for hedging multi-year income flows.

Step 3: Deciding Whether to Hedge the Exposure

Over the long term, foreign exchange rate movements have been—and are likely to continue to be—a problem of volatility in year-to-year earnings rather

FIGURE 12.5

Unhedged Net Income 1989–1992

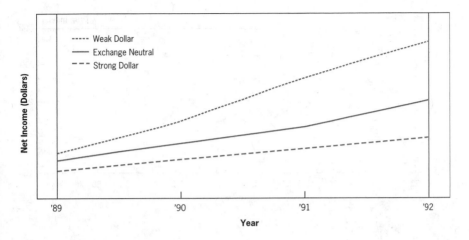

than one of irreversible losses. For example, most of the income statement losses of the early 1980s were recouped in the following three years. The question of whether or not to hedge exchange risk thus becomes a question of the company's own risk profile with respect to interim volatility in earnings and cash flows.

The desirability of reducing earnings volatility due to exchange can be examined from both external and internal perspectives.

FIGURE 12.6

Exchange Impact Strong Dollar Scenario

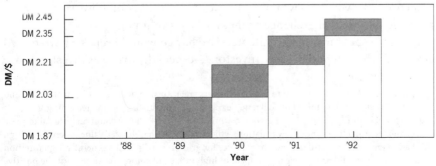

Total bar represents cumulative exchange impact. Shaded area represents year-on-year impact.

FIGURE 12.7

Trade Weighted Dollar Versus Drug Index

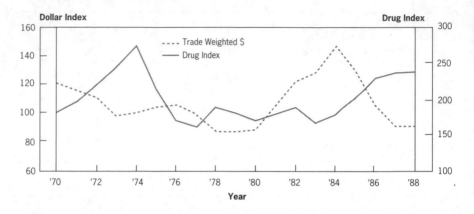

External Concerns. These center on the perspective of capital markets, and accordingly involve matters such as share price, investor clientele effects, and maintenance of dividend policy. Although exchange fluctuations clearly can have material effects on reported accounting earnings, it is not clear that exchange-related fluctuations in earnings have significant effects on stock price. Our own analysis (as illustrated in figure 12.7) suggests only a modest correlation in recent years between exchange gains and losses and share price movements, and a slight relationship in the strong dollar period—the scenario of greatest concern to us.

Industry analysts' reports, moreover, tend to support our analysis by arguing that exchange gains and losses are at most a second-order factor in determining the share prices of pharmaceutical companies. While invariably stressing the importance of new products as perhaps the most critical share price variable, analysts also often comment on the regulated price environment overseas (which, as we pointed out earlier, limits competitive exposure by reducing the effect of exchange changes on sales volume).[2]

With respect to investor clientele, exchange would seem to have mixed effects. To the extent that some investors—especially overseas investors—see

---

2. Some analysts have also claimed to detect an inverse relationship between drug stock prices and inflation that also acts to reduce currency exposure. Drug stocks, as this reasoning goes, are growth stocks and generally benefit from low inflation because the discount factor used to price growth stocks declines under low inflation, which increases shareholder value. Likewise, a high inflation environment will depress share prices for growth stocks. Since generally high inflation leads to a weaker dollar, the negative impact of high inflation would over time limit the positive effect of a weaker dollar, and the reverse would also be true.

Merck's stock as an opportunity for speculating on a weak dollar, hedging would be contrary to investors' interests. But, for investors seeking a "pure play" on the stocks of ethical drug companies, significant exchange risk could be undesirable. Thus, given this potential conflict of motives among investors, and recognizing our inability to ascertain the preferences of all of Merck's investor clienteles (potential as well as current), we concluded that it would be inappropriate to give too much weight to any specific type of investor.

On the issue of dividend policy, we came to a somewhat different conclusion. Maintaining Merck's dividend, while probably not the most important determinant of our share price, is nevertheless viewed by management as an important means of expressing our confidence in the company's prospective earnings growth. It is our way of reassuring investors that we expect our large investment in future research (funded primarily by retained earnings) to provide requisite returns. And, although both Merck and the industry in general were able to maintain dividend rates during the strong dollar period, we were concerned about the company's ability to maintain a policy of dividend *growth* during a future dollar strengthening. Because Merck's (and other pharmaceutical companies') dividend growth rates did indeed decline during the strong dollar 1981–1985 period, the effect of future dollar strengthening on company cash flows could well constrain future dividend growth. So, in considering whether to hedge our income against future exchange movements, we chose to give some weight to the desirability of maintaining growth in the dividend.

In general, then, we concluded that although our exchange hedging policy should consider capital market perspectives (especially dividend policy), it should not be dictated by them. The direct effect of exchange fluctuations on shareholder value, if any, is unclear; and it thus seemed a better course to concentrate on the objective of maximizing long-term cash flows and to focus on the potential effect of exchange rate movements on our ability to meet our internal objectives. Such actions, needless to say, are ultimately intended to maximize returns for our stockholders.

Internal Concerns. From the perspective of management, the key factors that would support hedging against exchange volatility are the following two: (1) the large proportion of the company's overseas earnings and cash flows; and (2) the potential effect of cash flow volatility on our ability to execute our strategic plan—particularly, to make the investments in R & D that furnish the basis for future growth. The pharmaceutical industry has a very long planning horizon, one that reflects the complexity of the research involved as well as the lengthy process of product registration. It often takes more than 10 years between the discovery of a product and its market launch. In the current competitive environment, success in the industry requires a continuous, long-term commitment to a steadily increasing level of research funding.

Given the cost of research and the subsequent challenges of achieving positive returns, companies such as Merck require foreign sales in addition to U.S. sales to generate a level of income that supports continued research and business operations. The U.S. market alone is not large enough to support the level of our research effort. Because foreign sales are subject to exchange volatility, the dollar equivalent of worldwide sales can be very unstable. Uncertainty can make it very difficult to justify high levels of U.S.-based research when the firm cannot effectively estimate the payoffs from its research. Our experience, and that of the industry in general, has been that the cash flow and earnings uncertainty caused by exchange rate volatility leads to a reduction of growth in research spending.

Such volatility can also result in periodic reductions of corporate spending necessary to expand markets and maintain supportive capital expenditures. In the early 1980s, for example, capital expenditures by Merck and other leading U.S. pharmaceutical companies experienced a reduction in rate of growth similar to that in R & D.

Our conclusion, then, was that we should take action to reduce the potential impact of exchange volatility on future cash flows. Reduction of such volatility removes an important element of uncertainty confronting the strategic management of the company.

Step 4: Selecting the Appropriate Financial Instruments

While we will not discuss the various hedging techniques in detail, we do wish to share the thought processes that led us to choose currency options as our risk management tool. Our objective was to select the most cost-effective hedging instrument that accommodated the company's risk preferences.

Forward foreign exchange contracts, foreign currency debt, and currency swaps all effectively fix the value of the amount hedged regardless of currency movements. With the use of options, by contrast, the hedging firm retains the opportunity to benefit from natural positions—albeit at a cost equal to the premium paid for the option. As illustrated in figure 12.8, under a strong dollar scenario (based on 1988 spot rates and forward points), Merck would prefer a forward sale because the contract would produce the same gains as the option but without incurring the cost of the option premium. But, under the weak dollar scenario, both the unhedged and the option positions would be preferred to hedging with the forward contract.

Given the possibility of exchange rate movements in either direction, we were unwilling to forgo the potential gains if the dollar weakened; so options were strictly preferred. We also concluded, moreover, that a certain level of

FIGURE 12.8

Alternative Hedging Instruments

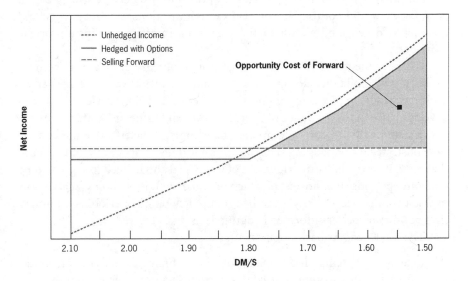

option premiums could be justified as the cost of an insurance policy designed to preserve our ability to carry through with our strategic plan.[3]

Step 5: Constructing a Hedging Program

Having selected currency options as our hedging vehicle and designated the 5-year period of our strategic plan as our hedging horizon, we then considered several implementation strategies, including:

Varying the term of the hedge. That is, using year-by-year rather than multi-year hedging.

Varying the strike price of the foreign exchange options. For example, out-of-the-money options were considered as a means of reducing costs.

Varying the amount. That is, different percentages of income could be covered, again, to control costs.

---

3. It was also recognized that to the extent hedge accounting could be applied to purchased options, this represents an advantage over other foreign currency instruments. The accounting ramifications of mark-to-market versus hedge accounting were, and remain, an important issue and we have continued to monitor developments with respect to the ongoing controversy over accounting for currency options.

After simulating the outcome of alternative strategies under various exchange rate scenarios we came to the following decisions: (1) we would hedge for a multi-year period, using long-term options to protect our strategic cash flow; (2) we would not use far-out-of-the-money options to reduce costs; and (3) we would hedge only on a partial basis and, in effect, self-insure for the remainder.

We continue to refine this decision through our use of increasingly more sophisticated modeling. Recognizing this as a quantitative process whereby decisions can be improved by application of better techniques, Merck has been developing (with the guidance of Professor Darrell Duffie of Stanford University) a state-of-the-art computer model that simulates the effectiveness of a variety of strategies for hedging. The model is a Monte Carlo simulation package that presents probability distributions of unhedged and hedged foreign income for future periods (the shortest of which are quarters). By so doing, it allows us to visualize the effect of any given hedging policy on our periodic cash flows, thus permitting better-informed hedging decisions.

The model has six basic components:

1. **Security Pricing Models:** State-of-the-art financial analytics are used to calculate theoretical prices for various securities such as bonds, futures, forwards, and options.[4]

2. **Hedging Policy:** We can specify a variety of hedging policies, with each representing a portfolio of securities to buy or sell in each quarter. The number of hedging policies is essentially unlimited, reflecting a variety of hedge ratios, proxy currencies, accounting constraints, security combinations, etc. For example, the model permits us to compare a hedging program of purchasing options that cover the exposures of the 5-year planning period and holding them until maturity with the alternative of a dynamic portfolio revision strategy. A dynamic hedge would involve not only the initial purchase of options, but a continuous process of buying and selling additional options based on interim changes in exchange rates.

4. In pricing options, we have the choice of using the Black-Scholes model or an alternative highly advanced valuation model. These models provide reasonably reliable estimates of the expected true cost, including transaction fees, of the option program. Although Black-Scholes is the predominant pricing model in pricing many kinds of options, alternative models appear to have an advantage in the pricing of long-dated currency options. Black-Scholes implicitly assumes that the volatility of exchange rates grows exponentially with time to maturity. Generally speaking, the further out the expiry date, the higher the price. The alternative model has a sophisticated approach in its assumption of a dampened exponential relationship between time to maturity, expected volatility, and price. For this reason, in the case of long-dated options, the Black-Scholes model generally overstates option prices relative to the alternative model.

3. **Foreign Income Generator:** Before simulating changes in hedging policy, however, we start by building our strategic plan forecast of local currency earnings into the model. The model then generates random earnings by quarter according to a specified model of forecast projections and random forecast errors. This process provides us with an estimate of the variability of local currency earnings and thereby allows us to reflect possible variations versus plan forecasts with greater accuracy.

4. **Exchange Rate Dynamics:** The model uses a Monte Carlo simulator to generate random exchange rates by quarter. The simulator allows us to adjust currency volatilities, rates of reversion, long-term exchange rates, and coefficients of correlation among currencies. We can test the sensitivity of the simulator to stronger or weaker dollar exchange rates by modifying the inputs. We can also use the Monte Carlo simulation package to re-examine the development of exchange scenarios and ranges described earlier.[5]

5. **Cash Flow Generator:** The model collects information from each of the above four components so as to calculate total cash flow in U.S. dollars by quarter for each random scenario.

6. **Statistical and Graphical Output:** The quarterly cash flow information for each of a large number of scenarios is collected and displayed graphically in frequency plots, and in terms of statistics such as means, standard deviations, and confidence levels. Figure 12.9 provides an example of the graphical output from our simulator, comparing distributions of unhedged and hedged cash flows. In this case, the hedged curve assumes 100% of Merck's exposure has been covered through the purchase of foreign currency options. Given the pattern of exchange rate movements simulated, the hedging strategy has shifted the hedged cash flow distribution to the right, cutting off a portion of unfavorable outcomes. In addition, the hedged cash flow distribution has a higher mean value as well as a lower standard deviation. Therefore, in this scenario hedging would be preferable to not hedging, resulting in higher returns as well as lower risk. (Again, of course, the trade-off is the initial cost of the option premiums that would have to be balanced against the improved risk/return pattern.)

5. The model will also have the ability to simulate historic exchange trends. The model will have access to a large database of historic exchange rates. We will be able to analyze the impact of hedging on a selected time period, for example, the strong dollar period of the 1980s. Or, we can have the model randomly select exchange rate movements from a historical period, resulting in a Monte Carlo simulation of that period.

FIGURE 12.9

Merck Foreign Cash Flow, Unhedged Versus Hedged*

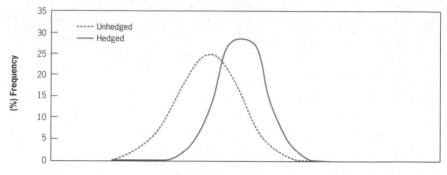

* Hedge of 100% of Cash Flow.

Other scenarios may indicate that a lower hedge ratio or not hedging is the preferred strategy.

In sum, the model provides Merck with a powerful tool to determine the optimal strategy for reducing our exposure to foreign currency risk. The simulator allows us to analyze a wide range (in fact, an infinite number) of exchange scenarios, hedging policies, and security combinations. This in turn gives us the ability to select the hedging policy that is both cost-effective and consistent with our desired risk profile.

Conclusion

Identifying a company's exchange risk and reaching a decision with respect to what action, if any, should be taken requires extensive analysis. We believe that, as a result of this kind of analysis of Merck's currency exposures, we have developed an appropriate financial hedging plan—one that provides management with what amounts to an insurance policy against the potentially damaging effect of currency volatility on the company's ability to carry out its strategic plan. We continue to refine the actual implementation process as we move forward.

▦ **JUDY C. LEWENT AND A. JOHN KEARNEY** are Vice President and Treasurer, and Assistant Treasurer, respectively, of Merck & Co., Inc. Ms. Lewent has spent nine years at Merck, and Mr. Kearney has been with the company for 20 years.

CHAPTER 13

Corporate Insurance Strategy

The Case of British Petroleum

NEIL A. DOHERTY AND CLIFFORD W. SMITH, JR.

INSURABLE EVENTS such as product liability suits, toxic torts, and physical damage to corporate assets represent major production costs for industrial corporations. For large public companies, conventional practice is to buy insurance to hedge against large potential losses while self-insuring against smaller ones. The underlying logic of this strategy, which is reflected in insurance textbooks,[1] is essentially this: For large- and medium-sized corporations, small losses—the kind that stem from localized fires, employee injuries, vehicle crashes, and so forth—occur with such regularity that their total cost is predictable. To the extent such losses are predictable in the aggregate, buying insurance amounts simply to exchanging known dollars of premium for roughly equivalent and relatively known dollars of loss settlements (a practice called "trading dollars" in the profession). Larger losses, by contrast, are rare and much less predictable. Because such losses are borne by the company's owners (mainly by its stockholders but also, if the losses are large enough, by its bondholders), they should be hedged with insurance.

Recently, however, British Petroleum (BP), one of the largest industrial companies in the world, decided on a major change in its insurance strategy that turns the conventional wisdom on its head. In this article, we analyze why BP now insures against most smaller losses while self-insuring against the larger ones. Our analysis focuses on factors affecting the market *supply* of insurance as well as the corporate demand for it. On the demand side, we demonstrate that the primary source of demand for insurance by widely held public companies is not, as standard insurance textbooks assume, to transfer

This chapter was previously published as an article in *Journal of Applied Corporate Finance* Vol. 6, No. 3 (1993): 4–15. The authors wish to thank Judith Hanratty and Rodney Insall of British Petroleum for many discussions and insightful comments.

1. See, for example, G.E. Rejda, *Principles of Insurance* (Glenview, IL: Scott Foresman, 1989), 52–53; and C.A. Williams, *Risk Management and Insurance* (New York: McGraw Hill, 1989), Chapter 13.

risk from the corporation's owners, but rather to take advantage of insurance companies' efficiencies in providing risk-assessment, monitoring, and loss-settlement services. On the supply side, we explain why the capacity of insurance markets to underwrite very large (or highly specialized) exposures is quite limited. Given BP's size, when losses become large enough to be of concern, they exceed the capacity of the industry. In essence, BP has a comparative advantage relative to the insurance industry in bearing large losses.

A Framework for Evaluating Corporate Insurance

Before discussing the case of BP, we first provide a general framework for analyzing the corporate insurance decision—one that identifies the benefits and costs of insurance from the perspective of a corporate management intent on maximizing shareholder value.

The Important Difference Between Individual and Corporate Insurance[2]

Let's begin with the simplest case: the purchase of insurance by individuals. Insurance allows individuals to transfer risks to insurance companies, thus reducing uncertainty about their net worth and standard of living. In return for accepting the risk of losses, the insurance company charges a premium. The *expected cost* of the insurance, known as the "premium loading," is the difference between the premium and the present value of expected losses.

The decision to purchase insurance can be justified if the insurance company has a comparative advantage over the policyholder in bearing the risks in question. Such an advantage can derive from two sources: the reduction of risk accomplished by pooling a large portfolio of similar risks and better access to capital markets.

It is not hard to see that, relative to the risk-bearing capacity of insurance companies, the ability of most individuals to self-insure against large risks is quite limited. Private assets are not protected by the "limited liability" provision that shelters other assets of corporate stockholders. Thus, decisions by individuals to pay premiums to insure their hard assets and human capital are economically rational choices based primarily on insurance companies' advantages in pooling such risks.

Private or closely held corporations are likely to purchase insurance for the same reason—namely, their limited ability to bear certain risks relative to

2. This discussion draws heavily on three articles by David Mayers and Clifford Smith, "On the Corporate Demand for Insurance," *Journal of Business* (1982): 281–96; "The Corporate Insurance Decision," *Chase Financial Quarterly* (Spring 1982): 47–65; "Corporate Insurance and the Underinvestment Problem," *Journal of Risk and Insurance*, LIV (1987): 45–54.

the risk-bearing capacity of insurance companies. The owners of such companies often have a large proportion of their wealth tied up in the firm; and, whether out of a desire to maintain control or some other motive, they choose not to diversify their own holdings fully. For most closely held and private companies, then, logic and experience tell us that the companies' owners will self-insure only against those risks where they have specialized expertise and, hence, their own kind of comparative advantage.

The case of large, widely held public corporations, however, presents some important differences that standard insurance textbooks fail to acknowledge. The conventional wisdom says, in effect, that because the owners of corporations (their stockholders and bondholders) are individually risk-averse,[3] financial managers should attempt to minimize their exposure to large risks. What this explanation fails to recognize, however, is that the company's stockholders and bondholders generally diversify their own portfolios of corporate securities. In so doing, they effectively diversify away the kinds of risks insurable through insurance companies.

Now, it's true that the stock market effectively assesses corporations a risk premium when setting their minimum required rates of return on capital. In general, the greater a company's risk, the higher the rate of return it must earn, on average, to produce superior returns for its shareholders. But a company's required rate of return (also known as its cost of capital) depends only on its non-diversifiable risk.[4] And because most insurable risks can be readily managed by investors through diversification, capital markets will not reward companies for eliminating them.

In short, insurance purchases reduce the expected variance of a company's cash flows, but not its cost of capital. Thus, corporate purchases of insurance

---

3. In the financial economics literature, risk aversion refers to an individual who prefers the average outcome, or the "expected value" of a gamble, to taking a chance on the distribution of possible outcomes. Thus, a risk-averse individual would pay to get out of a risky situation or, alternatively, would demand a higher rate of return for holding a riskier security.

4. One of the cardinal principles of modern finance is that, on average and over long periods of time, investors both expect and receive rewards commensurate with the risks they bear. As the bulk of the academic evidence also shows, however, average returns on investment correlate most strongly with systematic or non-diversifiable risk. The measure of this risk, known as "beta," is a measure of the sensitivity of individual stock prices to market-wide and general economic developments; such risk cannot be eliminated by investors' diversification of their holdings. Nor is a company's systematic risk likely to be reduced by purchasing insurance—because insurable risks, to the extent they have no discernible correlation with broad economic cycles, are completely diversifiable for investors.

To the extent insurable losses do represent systematic risk, insurance will reduce the firm's cost of capital. But then insurance premiums paid must include an appropriate risk premium, which will offset any possible gain in terms of the firm's discount rate associated with competitively priced insurance. See N.A. Doherty and S.M. Tinics, "A Note on Reinsurance under Conditions of Capital Market Equilibrium," *Journal of Finance* 36 (1982): 949–53.

intended solely to reduce *investors'* exposures to such risks are negative net present value projects; the loading built into insurance premiums represents a pure transfer from the company to the insurer.

The Real Benefits of Insurance

Why, then, do large corporations buy insurance? In this section, we describe a number of services and functions performed by insurance companies that provide the basis for a rational corporate demand for insurance—functions having nothing to do with stockholders' risk aversion. As described in sequence below, insurance purchases can increase shareholder value by:

- avoiding underinvestment and other problems faced by companies whose financial solvency (or even just liquidity) could be threatened by uninsured losses;

- transferring risk from non-owner corporate stakeholders—managers, employees, suppliers—at a disadvantage in risk-bearing;

- providing efficiencies in loss assessment, prevention, and claims processing;

- reducing taxes; and

- satisfying regulatory requirements.

Avoiding the Underinvestment (and Associated Illiquidity) Problem. Although well-diversified shareholders and bondholders may not be concerned about the prospect of uninsured losses *per se*, they will become concerned if such losses materially raise the probability of financial insolvency. Shareholders are concerned about insolvency mainly because of its potential to cause significant reductions in companies' *operating* values—that is, reductions in the present value of expected operating cash flows.

There are two important things to keep in mind about a firm's operating cash flows in this context. First, large uninsured losses do not in and of themselves reduce ongoing operating values, but should be thought of instead as one-time reductions of a company's equity, or stock of capital (a point we return to below). Second, because operating cash flows are before interest expense, a company's operating value can also be viewed as the sum of the bondholders' and the stockholders' claims on the company. This sharing of value between the two groups can create problems that end up reducing the operating value of the firm.

How does financial trouble, or just the prospect of trouble, reduce a company's operating value? To begin with the extreme case, companies that wind up in Chapter 11 face considerable interference from the bankruptcy court with their investment and operating decisions, not to mention substantial direct costs of administration and reorganization. But, even short of bankruptcy, financial difficulty can impose large indirect costs. One important source of such costs is a potential "underinvestment problem." This problem arises from conflicts of interest between stockholders and bondholders in companies with significant amounts of debt. As the example below illustrates, insurance can help manage this problem.

Consider a company with a large amount of debt outstanding that chooses not to purchase fire insurance for its plants. Suppose also that a large and highly profitable plant is destroyed at a time when a downturn in operating cash flow has depleted the company's cash reserves and driven down its stock price.

The company is then faced with a potentially difficult reinvestment decision—that is, whether and, if so, when to rebuild the plant. In these circumstances, the large casualty loss has the effect of cutting further into the firm's already deflated equity cushion, and so further raising its effective leverage ratio. This, needless to say, would be a difficult time for management to approach capital markets for funding.

In this situation, if the company's debt burden is heavy enough, a management acting on behalf of its shareholders would have an incentive to pass up such a positive-NPV investment. As Stewart Myers demonstrated years ago,[5] this would be a rational decision (not just the result of managerial shortsightedness) if enough of the value of the new investment went to shoring up the bondholders' position. The new equity issue would amount to a major wealth transfer from stockholders to bondholders—and a shareholder-wealth-maximizing management would thus choose either not to rebuild the plant, or to defer it, thereby reducing overall firm value.[6]

Even if stockholders would end up sharing some of the benefits from reinvestment, such a severe liquidity problem could still tempt management to defer raising capital until the company's stock price increased. But, in this case, there would be a significant loss in operating value as a consequence of deferring the investment.

5. More technically, insurance controls an aspect of Stewart Myers' underinvestment problem involving the joint effect of risk, limited liability, and leverage on project selection (see S. C. Myers, "Determinants of Corporate Borrowing," *Journal of Financial Economics* 5 [1997]: 147–76). With debt in the capital structure, the firm's stockholders can face incentive to turn down positive-NPV projects. An uninsured casualty loss reduces firm value, increasing the firm's leverage and thereby exacerbating this incentive. Such behavior is anticipated by rational bondholders and will be reflected *ex ante* in the bond price. Thus the loss of value from distortions in project selection falls *ex ante* on shareholders. For a discussion of how insurance can control such incentives, see Mayers and Smith (1982), cited in note 2.
6. Such stories can be told about corporate decisions to invest in routine maintenance and safety projects; in highly leveraged or financially distressed firms, insurance purchases effectively force managements to make necessary maintenance investments by reducing their cash premiums for so doing.

Now let's go back to the beginning of this story and assume that management instead purchases fire insurance. (In fact, debt covenants typically *require* companies to buy such insurance—in part to control this underinvestment incentive.) In that case, insurance effectively serves as a funding source. If the loss is large and the facilities must be replaced quickly, it provides a "leverage-neutral" source of financing that permits the company to avoid the costs of a hurried new issue. In so doing, insurance reduces the likelihood that management is confronted with this kind of decision.

A Note on Insurance and Capital Structure. An alternative solution to this underinvestment problem, of course, would be to reduce the amount of corporate debt. Indeed, one could argue that, as a general rule, corporate decisions to retain large exposures effectively reduce the optimal amount of debt—and, conversely, insurance purchases increase corporate debt capacity. But this conclusion, though correct as far as it goes, obscures an important feature of large casualty losses—their infrequency. Large uninsured losses, as suggested above, do not reduce ongoing operating values, but represent instead one-time reductions of a company's equity cushion. A company that chooses to self-insure such large exposures is thus making a decision that affects the adequacy of its *stock* of capital—including its ability to raise additional funds on short notice—rather than its ability to service a predictable *flow* of interest and principal payments out of regular operating cash flows.

Because large exposures are by definition infrequent events, an alternative way to manage them would be to arrange lines of credit available specifically in the event of a large uninsured loss. Such lines of credit, at least for larger, more creditworthy companies that can obtain them at reasonable cost, potentially provide a more economical, custom-tailored solution to the problem of insuring against extreme illiquidity—while allowing the firm to use its remaining debt capacity more effectively.

For smaller companies, however, insurance is likely to be more valuable. To the extent such companies have lower liquidity and face higher transactions costs for new issues, they will find insurance to be both a lower-cost funding source and an indispensable means of increasing their corporate debt capacity.

Risk Shifting within the Firm. Up to this point, we have viewed the corporation from the perspective of its investors and owners. Of course, the corporation is a vast network of contracts among various parties with conflicting as well as common interests. In addition to bondholders and stockholders, other corporate constituencies such as employees, managers, suppliers, and customers all have vested interests in the company's success.

Like the owners of private or closely held companies, the corporation's managers, employees, suppliers, and customers may not be able to diversify insurable risks; and such risks, if not insured, can affect their future payoffs under their respective contracts. (In many cases, of course, these contracts are implied rather than explicit.) Because they are also risk-averse, these groups are likely to require extra compensation to bear any risk not assumed by the owners or transferred to an insurance company. Employees will demand higher wages (or reduce their loyalty or perhaps their work effort) at a company where the probability of layoff is greater. Managers with alternative opportunities will demand higher salaries (or maybe an equity stake in the company) to run firms where the risks of insolvency and financial embarrassment are significant. Suppliers will be more reluctant to enter into long-term contracts, and trade creditors will charge more and be less flexible, with companies whose prospects are more uncertain. And customers concerned about the company's ability to fulfill warranty obligations or service their products in the future may be reluctant to buy those products.

Because of limited liability, the amount of risk that can be allocated to the stockholders is limited by the capital stock of the company. Companies in service industries, for instance, are often thinly capitalized. And, for such companies, where the claims—and thus the risks—of managers and employees are likely to be very large relative to the claims of investors, there may be substantial benefits from transferring those risks to an insurance company.

Even if companies self-insure, the above argument can also be extended to the design of *management compensation* contracts. Effective compensation plans achieve an appropriate balance between two partly conflicting aims: strengthening managers' performance incentives and insulating them from risks beyond their control. Incentive considerations require that compensations be linked to performance measures such as share price and earnings. A potential problem with such performance proxies is that they contain significant variation (or "noise") that is unrelated to management's performance. Because uninsured losses are a potential source of such noise, companies may achieve economies in risk-bearing by excluding uninsured losses from performance measures that serve as the basis for managerial evaluations and bonuses. In so doing, though, companies should be mindful of avoidable losses and ensure that managers still have strong incentives to take sensible measures to control such risks.

Service Efficiencies. Besides transferring risk, insurance companies often provide a set of related services—and at a significantly lower cost than offered elsewhere. One obvious example, as mentioned earlier, is insurers' comparative advantage in processing and settling claims, an advantage that derives from specialization and economies of scale. Thus, we would expect part of the corporate demand for insurance to be explained by insurers' expertise and efficiency in providing low-cost claims administration.[7]

Other services for which insurance companies are likely to have a comparative advantage are the assessment of loss exposures (more precisely, estimation of the parameters of the loss distribution) and the design, administration, and auditing of safety and other loss-control programs. Although these services are occasionally priced and sold separately, they are typically bundled with insurance. When insurers accumulate large numbers of exposures, they not only reduce risks through pooling, but also achieve economies of scale and other benefits from specialization that economists typically refer to as "organizational capital."

The most tangible aspect of this organizational capital is the large data base built up by an insurance company over years of underwriting. The data base allows for extensive and precise actuarial analysis, which in turn enables the insurer to estimate and classify individual exposures more accurately and price their products appropriately.[8] Indeed, this data base constitutes one of an insurer's principal comparative advantages over its policyholders in insuring many corporate risks—namely, its greater confidence in forecasting its policyholder's loss distribution for events such as fires, vehicle collisions, and workers' injuries.

In general, then, it is the frequency of events that makes them amenable to statistical analysis. But, for exposures in which new or specialized technology is employed—especially if losses are infrequent—more subjective and hence less precise estimation techniques such as engineering risk assessment must take the place of statistical analysis. In these cases, the industrial companies that have developed the new technology can generally use their own organizational capital to assess the risks posed by the technology. (Also, if the company is better able to assess the risk than the insurer, adverse selection becomes a serious problem—a point we discuss below.) Hence, insurance companies are likely to operate at a competitive disadvantage in indemnifying those companies for such risks. In this sense, insurance companies' inability to apply actuarial analysis to the pricing of their products helps to define the limits of the insurance industry's products.

7. A striking confirmation of this general argument is the existence of "claims-only" insurance contracts—those in which the insurance company provides only claims-management services while the insured firm pays all the claims. Claims-only policies, moreover, represent only an extreme of a spectrum of insurance policies that allow the insured company to maintain a degree of self-insurance. More often employed are policies that use retrospective ratings that continually adjust the premium to reflect actual claims experience over the life of the policy. This means the insured is effectively bearing most of the risk of claims losses.

8. From the insurer's perspective, this is necessary to quote competitive insurance premiums. Failure of an insurer to categorize individuals accurately by loss expectation leads to adverse selection by policyholders.

Similar issues of comparative advantage arise in connection with safety, loss control, and loss prevention. Insurers' data bases permit them to identify common types of accidents, often enabling them to advise clients as to potential sources of risk and cost-effective means of reducing expected losses. Some specialist insurers—factory mutual insurance firms, for example—focus as much on safety audits as on the provision of insurance services. As suggested above, however, the more specialized and complex the technology, the more likely is the producer, not the insurer, to have a comparative advantage in designing and implementing a loss-prevention program. In such cases, producers are likely to perform these functions themselves.

One specific area, however, in which insurers are almost certain to have superior expertise is the defense of lawsuits. Access to the insurer's lawyers and other defense resources can reduce the expected costs of third-party liability claims. Insurers regularly defend such cases, whereas individual policyholders see them infrequently. Moreover, the adverse reputation effects that could come from vigorous defense of a lawsuit are partly shifted to the insurer that effectively conducts the case. This is particularly useful in cases where third-party claimants have a continuing relationship with the firm, as in the case of workers-compensation or product-liability claims.

Tax Benefits. The tax benefits of corporate insurance derive from the interaction of two factors: (1) the ability of corporate insurance to reduce the volatility of reported income and (2) the effective progressivity of most of the world's tax codes.

In the United States, and most other jurisdictions throughout the world, tax codes permit the deduction of both insurance premiums and of uninsured losses. Given (1) a constant marginal tax rate and (2) actuarially fair premiums, such provisions would have a neutral effect on the decision to purchase insurance. That is, the expected present value of tax deductions would be the same with insurance as without.

In practice, however, the marginal tax rate in the United States (and in most other jurisdictions) is not constant, but rather "convex"; that is, a company's effective tax rate rises along with increases in pre-tax income. Increasing marginal tax rates, tax shields such as depreciation allowances and interest expense, the inability to earn interest on tax-loss carryforwards, and the alternative minimum tax all work together to impose higher effective rates of taxation on higher levels of reported income and to provide lower percentage rebates for ever larger losses. Given U.S. tax treatment of insurance premiums and uninsured losses, the reductions in the volatility of taxable income resulting from insurance effectively reduce corporate taxes.

In the case of multinational corporations, tax liabilities are imposed by a number of different jurisdictions (the various countries in which they operate).

Reductions in the expected tax liabilities in different jurisdictions can reduce expected taxes incurred in each, thereby reducing a multinational's overall worldwide taxes. For this reason, local purchases of insurance can add value by reducing expected local tax obligations, although they have little or no effect on the risk of aggregate corporate income.

Regulatory Requirements. Financial-responsibility laws sometimes require insurance coverage. For example, many jurisdictions require that an operator of motor vehicles have insurance or other evidence of financial capability to discharge third-party liability claims. Similar requirements are often found in workers' compensation insurance. A further example in the United States is the financial-responsibility requirement associated with handling hazardous materials under the Resource Control and Recovery Act of 1976.

These requirements are generally modest relative to the resources of medium- to large-sized companies. For example, in the United States the requirement for automobile liability insurance is typically in the range of $30,000 to $50,000. Such regulatory requirements tend to increase the demand for insurance covering relatively small losses.

The Supply Side of Corporate Insurance

As stated earlier, the gross profit to an insurer from underwriting a given policy, known as the premium loading, is defined as the difference between the expected loss and the premium. The insurance premium can be further decomposed into the expected indemnity payment, administrative costs (including the costs of providing services), a normal profit, and any rent, or "abnormal profit," that might be captured by the insurer.

Thus, some elements of the loading are not a cost to the policyholder—for example, the expected cost of various services bundled with the coverage. But other parts of the loading represent a transfer to the insurer and thus deter the purchase of insurance. This is true not only of insurer rents, but also of the component of expected indemnity payments attributable to moral hazard and adverse selection—two well-known problems confronting insurance underwriters that we discuss below. These factors affect the comparative advantage of insurance versus other risk-management strategies.

Effective Competition. Expected rents depend on the degree of competition. Some sectors of the insurance market are highly competitive; barriers to entry are low, insurers sell large numbers of homogenous policies with low correlation among payoffs, and expected losses are easily estimated. Since aggregate losses are fairly predictable, relatively little capital is required to ensure the solvency and maintain the creditworthiness of the insurer. Moreover, the routine nature of the business and the presence of established independent selling networks—that is, independent agents and brokers—serve to reduce the required investment in underwriters, actuaries, engineers, and individuals with other technical skills. Such markets include those for routine small property and liability losses incurred by large companies[9] as well as various kinds of insurance for small businesses and individuals.

In contrast, the markets for large losses and for certain specialized risks are characterized by significantly less competition. For example, writing pollution insurance requires a large investment in the ability to provide environmental audits and risk assessment; there are few U.S. insurers active in this market (AIG and Reliance are the two best-known). There are also few insurers that offer coverage of very large exposures. Such business requires a large surplus—that is, equity—and substantial investment in establishing reinsurance facilities. Such an investment can be viewed as necessary reputational capital. Success in selling policies for such large exposures depends critically on the insurer's ability to assure the insured that the contract will be honored if losses occur. A large stock of equity capital may be the only credible means of backing that promise.

A significant portion of worldwide capacity for insuring very large and unusual exposures is provided by Lloyd's of London. In part, this is due to its distinctive organizational form. With unlimited liability, Lloyd's syndicates have additional implicit reserves in the form of a call on the wealth of their members. But since the value of this call depends on the net worth of the members, the ultimate capacity of Lloyd's is limited.[10] Thus, the markets for pollution and other unusual lines of insurance, for high-risk lines, and for very high levels of all lines of insurance are characterized by less competition and higher expected insurer rents.

The effective supply of insurance coverage is not limited by the financial capability of *individual* insurers. Insurance is commonly syndicated among several insurers. Alternatively, policyholders can "layer" insurance protection by purchasing separate policies from several insurers (known as "surplus-lines" insurers). In yet another alternative, the capacity of individual insurers can be extended by selling secondary claims on some of its policies—or on its entire portfolio—in the reinsurance market. In most cases, some combination

---

9. For example, the fire insurer insuring 5,000 independently owned retail grocery stores will significantly improve its diversification by insuring one additional policyholder which is a chain owning 4,000 stores. It might further improve its diversification by insuring the smaller losses on much bigger risks, for example small fire losses (e.g., not exceeding $500,000) on department stores, electronics manufacturers, etc.

10. There are also some questions concerning the enforceability of claims against members' wealth. Following recent catastrophic loss experience in a number of syndicates, Lloyds is facing a number of lawsuits from members who are alleging negligent underwriting and challenging the call on their wealth.

of these mechanisms is used to spread coverage over the market through a complex network.

Yet, in spite of these possibilities for combining insurer capacity, there are still limits to the amount of insurance protection available in the marketplace for certain kinds of exposures. For example, it is difficult to place insurance for exposures in excess of $500 million, and virtually impossible to find protection for exposures in excess of $1 billion, even on restricted terms.

Even for policies well under $500 million, the "quality" of insurance is not constant. In insurance markets, the expected value of coverage falls with the size of the claim for a number of reasons. First, a large claim can cause an insurer to become insolvent, and insurance contracts are not fully enforceable against an insolvent insurer. Even if large claims do not trigger insolvency, they often cause significant financial difficulty for insurers, especially in the surplus-lines market where the variance of claims is usually high relative to the insurer's surplus (equity). Enforcing contracts against such insurers can be very costly since they can dispute their obligations under the contract and otherwise delay settlements. The costs of enforcing contracts include legal costs of the actions as well as increases in the costs of writing future contracts because reputational capital has depreciated. These problems can be particularly acute since the expected adverse reputation consequences of disputing claims are less of a restraint on an insurer facing a higher probability of insolvency.

Moral Hazard and Adverse Selection. Moral hazard and adverse selection arise naturally in insurance markets. Moral hazard—loosely speaking, the tendency for insured parties to exercise less care and thus to experience greater losses than the uninsured—is one factor that works against insurance purchase by all potential policyholders. The expected costs of the average policyholder's actions will be built into the insurance premium. Adverse selection—the likelihood that insurers will get a riskier-than-average sample, given the tendency of less risky parties to self-insure—discourages the purchase of insurance by those policyholders that are of low risk relative to their class. The industry practice of "experience rating"—in which the premiums for future insurance contracts are based on prior claim experience—is widely used to control moral hazard and adverse selection problems. In the case of insurable risks involving frequent losses, experience rating is an especially effective control device: it motivates the policyholder to reduce the risk of losses, thereby reducing moral hazard; and it quickly reveals loss characteristics, thus reducing the costs of adverse selection.

When losses are infrequent, however, experience rating is less useful. Simply because large losses occur much less often than small ones, the costs of adverse selection and moral hazard built into the premiums of very large insurance policies tend to be much larger than the same costs confronting purchasers of small policies.

The Case of British Petroleum

BP comprises four operating companies. BP Exploration is the upstream company, which is responsible for exploration and development of new oil and gas resources. BP Oil is the downstream business, whose activities include refining, distribution, and retailing of petroleum products. The remaining two companies are BP Chemicals, which concentrates in petrochemicals, acetyl, and nitrates, and BP Nutrition, a relatively small company in the animal-feed business.

Perhaps the most striking feature of BP is its size. It is the largest company in the U.K., and the second largest in Europe. BP's equity capital is approximately $35 billion, and its debt is approximately $15 billion. After-tax profit has averaged $1.9 billion over the previous 5 years with a standard deviation of $1.1 billion.[11]

BP's major assets include exploration and extraction licenses, and scientific and technical capital specific to the oil industry in the form of rigs, pipelines, refineries, ships, road tankers, and filling stations. While the company has operations worldwide (for example, it has some 13,000 service stations in some 50 countries), it has two major concentrations of value: its production licenses and its facilities in the North Sea and on the Alaska North Slope. This concentration of value, together with the limited range of the company's activities, imply that significant aspects of its business risk are relatively undiversified.

BP's Loss Exposures

BP's loss exposure ranges from routine small losses to potential losses in the multi-billion-dollar range. At the low end of this scale, there are vehicle accidents, minor shipping accidents, industrial injuries, small fires, and equipment failures. On a larger scale, potential losses include refinery fires or explosions, minor environmental damage from oil spills, and loss of (nautical) oil tankers. Very large losses could result from clean-up costs arising from major oil spills, tort claims for widespread injuries caused by release of toxic chemicals, liability for defective fuel causing a major airline disaster, and loss of an offshore rig with major loss of life (as in the Piper Alpha case). Perhaps one of the largest foreseeable losses to an oil firm would be the withdrawal of operating licenses as a consequence of political backlash in response to environmental damage.

BP employed independent actuarial consultants to estimate its loss distribution. The actuaries had access to extensive industry and BP loss data. Table 13.1 provides a summary of BP's estimated loss exposure—one that is based not

---

11. These numbers reflect BP's balance sheet and income statement as of year-end 1991, the last full year for which data were available when the authors were assisting in the analysis of the company's insurance strategy.

TABLE 13.1

Actuary's Estimate of BP's Loss Distribution at 1990 (Millions of Dollars)

Loss Range	Number per year	Average Loss	Expected Annual Loss	Standard Deviation
$0–$10	1845.00	$0.03	$52	$12
$10–$500	1.70	40.00	70	98
$500 plus	0.03	1000.00	35	233
Whole distribution	1846.73	$0.66	$157	

Note: This table covers all insurable losses whether or not they were previously insured.

only on BP's experience but also on that of other firms in the oil and chemical industries.[12]

A comparison of these figures with other BP financial statistics provides some useful insights. For example, assuming a corporate tax rate of 35%, an uninsured pre-tax loss of $500 million represents less than a 1% reduction of the market value of BP equity; it also amounts to only 17% of average annual after-tax earnings over the last five years, and about 30% of the standard deviation of average earnings.

Historically, BP has insured its property and liability exposures. It has also insured, to a very limited extent, business-interruption exposures where insurance coverage has been available. Liability insurance and business-interruption insurance has been placed largely with external insurers, though some insurance has been purchased from an oil-industry mutual called OIL (of which BP was a joint owner). OIL in turn reinsures the upper tail of its exposures. Some property has been insured directly by independent insurers, other property through a captive insurer, which also reinsures.

Thus, in the past, BP has purchased considerable external insurance protection. Virtually all of this insurance covers the first two loss ranges—those under $10 million and those between $10 and $500 million—and most has been in the $10–$500 million category. With only one or two exceptions, insurance has been unavailable above $500 million, and BP has historically self-insured in this range.

---

12. Curve fitting permits estimation of the tail of the loss distribution despite the absence (or virtual absence) of very large losses in the loss record. Distributions such as the compound poisson are found to fit reasonably well. In addition, loss scenarios are constructed for possible large and unusual events that are not in the loss record but which nevertheless are considered to be feasible. (Note also that it would be rare for an insurer to undertake a study of this intensity to estimate the loss distribution for an individual client.)

Using the cost-benefit framework presented earlier in this article, BP recently undertook a comprehensive re-examination of its insurance strategy. In the pages that follow, we describe BP's new approach to each of the three loss categories.

Coverage for Losses Below $10 Million

Under the new approach, losses below $10 million are now the responsibility of the managers of the local operating unit. (Such decisions were previously made by BP's insurance subsidiary.) Where there is a demonstrable need for insurance, local managers may buy it from BP's captive insurer or seek competitive quotations in local markets.

Expected changes in firm value (and leverage ratios) resulting from uninsured losses at this level are small. The standard deviation of after-tax earnings for BP exceeds $1 billion. In comparison, self-insuring losses under $10 million increases the standard deviation of earnings by only $12 million. Thus, the expected benefits of insurance in controlling financial-distress costs are trivial at this level.

The decision to allow local managers to insure small losses reflects other considerations:

• Because markets for losses at this level are very competitive, market forces effectively eliminate expected insurer rents.

• Insurers have a comparative advantage in service-provision activities such as claims administration. Because losses within this range are frequent and routine, insurers have an informational advantage in loss assessment and control, and contract enforcement is reliable.

• Insurance coverage satisfies local financial-responsibility requirements.

• Insurance reduces noise in the performance measures employed for local managers, producing stronger incentives for good performance.

• Because of the localized nature of some of BP's tax liabilities, there are potential tax-related benefits of insurance.

Coverage for Losses Between $10 Million and $500 Million

Losses above $10 million are not to be insured using external insurance markets except in specific circumstances (for example, in cases where insurance is required under existing bond indentures or joint-venture provisions). This represents a major change in policy, since most of the company's losses in the $10–$500 million range were previously insured. This strategy change reflects the following considerations:

- At this level, effective competition in insurance markets is limited.

- The costs of enforcing contracts are high.

- Over this range of losses, insurers do not have a comparative advantage in supplying safety and other services that are bundled with financial indemnification.

- The impact of such losses on total corporate value is quite limited (as shown in table 13.1, self-insuring losses between $10 million and $500 million increases the standard deviation of annual earnings [and cash flow] by only $98 million).

Over the ten-year period ending in 1989, BP paid $1.15 billion in premiums and recovered $250 million in claims (both in present values). In effect, this amounts to a 360% loading on realized losses. This loading can be broken down into several components: (1) a reserve against catastrophe losses, (2) a payment for bundled insurance services, (3) a payment for transaction costs, and (4) rents for the insurer. Transaction costs and bundled services typically account for 10% to 30% of premiums. We doubt that the size of this loading can be explained as a catastrophe reserve. The difference of $900 million between premiums and losses is simply too large to be accounted for by the prospect of large losses that, owing to chance, failed to materialize over the 10-year span.[13] Thus, we can only conclude that insurers received extraordinary rents in insuring these losses.

The explanation for this rent is found partly in the limited competition in this market. Few insurers are willing to make a market in risks the size and nature of BP's. Much of the market capacity, as mentioned earlier, is provided by Lloyd's syndicates. A large loss, however, would have a material impact on Lloyd's financial position. For example, a $500 million loss would amount to about 8% of Lloyd's total annual premium, 90% of profits, and 4% of surplus. Moreover, these statistics reflect the combined numbers of all Lloyd's syndi-

13. Suppose the total premiums paid, $1.15 billion (present values), were competitively priced in the sense that they represent the expected value of losses of $880 million plus a typical expense loading of about 20%. We can approximate this as a sequence of ten annual expected losses each having a present value of $88 million. (We cannot compare this $88 million directly with the table 13.1 estimate of $70 million for second-tier losses since not all losses in this tier were insured.) If we use the coefficient of variation from the second tier in the table (13.1), this yields an estimate for the standard deviation of annual aggregate losses actually insured of $108.4 million. If losses are time independent, the standard deviation of the aggregate losses for the ten-year period is $[(10)(108.4)^2]^{1/2} = \$342$ million. The realized losses for the period are $250 million, which is 1.84 standard deviations below the assumed total expected losses of $880 million. Using standard normal tables, there is only a .033 chance that revealed losses could be that low. This estimate is conservative since the loss distribution is skewed to the right. For such cases, use of the standard normal table will normally overestimate the probability mass in the left-hand tail and underestimate the mass in the right-hand tail.

cates, even though only a subset made a market for BP. In short, the potential for a large loss to impose financial stress on BP's insurers is great.

This problem arising from limited competition is aggravated by several contractual and institutional features of insurance markets.

Enforcement Costs. In the case of large losses, enforcement problems are higher due to the low frequency of such losses, which in turn reduces the effectiveness of reputational restraints on opportunistic behavior by insurers. To illustrate potential enforcement costs, consider that in the only large liability loss BP has filed with its insurers, settlement with the insurers was not reached until several years after settlement with the plaintiff. The insurance settlement, moreover, was only 70% of the liability claim; and, to secure this 70%, BP estimated that its expenses, legal costs, and management time in resolving this dispute amounted to approximately $1 million.

There are good reasons to view this as a representative rather than an unusual experience. Small losses occur routinely but large losses are rare. Indeed, the data in table 13.1 contain the implication that losses greater than $500 million occur only about once every 30 years. Although insurers are unlikely to sacrifice their reputational investments with clients for modest savings in disputing small claims, concerns about reputation are a much less effective restraint on insurers' opportunism when faced with large, infrequent losses.

Small losses also tend to come from repetitions of similar events such as damage to cars at autowashers, customer accidents, or crashes of road tankers. Given the large body of accumulated experience in negotiating past claim settlements and the experience of courts in interpreting contracts, there is little room for disagreement on coverage. Larger losses, by contrast, often present unusual facts and challenges for which there is little experience. The scope for different legal interpretations and, hence, the expected enforcement costs are correspondingly larger.

For large losses, the unlimited liability structure of the Lloyd's syndicates can make contract enforcement difficult. Lloyd's closes its accounts after three years and distributes surplus. Thus, much of a syndicate's reserves for long-gestation losses, such as liability claims, takes the form of a call on the personal wealth of the underwriting members. In recent years, attempts to recover deficits from members have met legal challenges (such as malpractice suits against the underwriter). Costly access to reserves and surplus raises expected enforcement costs.

The potential for dispute under large claims can be further increased by insurers' practice of laying off risks through the purchase of reinsurance. If a primary insurer disputes a claim and loses the ensuing litigation, the primary insurer must settle the claim to its policyholder and the reinsurer is then bound to the primary firm. However, if the primary settles a claim without a challenge, but the reinsurer considers that the loss was not covered by the primary contract language, the reinsurer might dispute its settlement to the primary. Consequently, when deciding whether to settle or fight claims, primary firms have to anticipate both the chances of being successful in litigation with their policyholder and whether they can bind their reinsurer in any settlement. (Similarly, the threat of legal challenges to syndicates at Lloyd's from their members may act as an important factor in resisting settlements.) Since large losses generally involve reinsurance contracts, this further raises enforcement costs for large losses.

Comparative Advantage in Risk Assessment. In operating its production, refining, and distribution activities, BP has considerable engineering and related skills. These are put to further use in safety programs that relate to design of facilities, inspection, *post mortem* on actual losses, and analysis of loss records. Given the scale and specialized nature of its operations, BP has a comparative advantage over its insurers in providing these services.

Management Incentives and Self-Insurance. The decision to self-insure against losses within this range has, however, created one problem that management has chosen to address. Uninsured losses, while posing little risk to aggregate firm value, can introduce significant "noise" into local and regional performance measures. Because such losses are infrequent and discrete events, the corporation has adopted a policy of eliminating this noise from performance measures on an *ad hoc* basis. That is, losses will not be charged against profit centers—and thereby reduce management bonuses—except insofar as the loss reflects poor management (say, a failure to enforce adequate safety standards).

Coverage for Losses Above $500 Million

BP has chosen to continue self-insuring very large losses—primarily for supply considerations: As the size of the loss becomes material for BP, it exceeds the capacity of the insurance market.

Such expected losses, moreover, are not necessarily as large as they look because of what amount to generous coinsurance provisions in many countries' tax codes, especially the United Kingdom's. Uninsured casualty losses generate tax shields, thus allowing BP to share these losses with the tax authorities. The tax code thus provides an implicit insurance policy with a coinsurance rate equal to the effective tax rate.

Losses greater than $500 million are most likely to occur in BP's two major geographical concentrations, the North Sea and the North Slope of Alaska. BP's effective tax rate for income from its North Sea production is 87%. Thus a

$2 billion North Sea loss would result in only a $260 million reduction in firm value (and the expected cost of negotiation with the Inland Revenue Service over the tax treatment for losses in this range appears modest).

Another consideration reinforcing BP's decision to self-insure very large losses is that such losses could actually lead to increases in oil prices. For example, an oil rig fire of the magnitude of the Piper Alpha disaster in the North Sea could result in new safety regulations; or a large tanker spill like the one experienced by the Exxon Valdez in Alaska could lead to the withdrawal of operating licenses. Because BP has what amounts to a very large long-position in oil, the expected price increases from such supply reductions reduce BP's net exposure.

Work in Progress

To manage its remaining exposure more effectively, BP is considering some additional adjustments. As one example, the three-tiered insurance strategy described above makes use of the tendency for both the costs and the benefits of insurance to increase with loss size. The tax effects just noted, however, suggest the need for some refinement of this strategy. Given the wide variation in marginal tax rates for different jurisdictions (ranging from zero to the 87% rate for North Sea production), losses of the same pre-tax value can result in widely different after-tax costs to BP. The initial allocation of exposures to the various tiers was based on pre-tax losses. This strategy is being fine-tuned to reflect after-tax costs.

A second issue to be examined more carefully is the effect of self-insurance on BP's optimal capital structure. As we observed earlier, the expected costs of financial distress can be reduced by combining a policy of self-insurance with lower financial leverage. However, the use of dedicated standby lines of credit, especially in the case of a large, creditworthy firm like BP, can be used to provide additional liquidity while limiting the required reduction in financial leverage.

In addition to lines of credit, financial instruments that include financial "shock absorbers" could also be used to lower the cost of an uninsured casualty loss. Consider, for example, the effect of substituting a convertible for a straight bond issue. A convertible bond gives bondholders, in effect, both a non-convertible bond and a call option on the stock. In return for this option, bondholders reduce the rate of interest on the bonds, thereby reducing the probability of financial difficulty.

Conclusion

British Petroleum, one of the largest industrial companies in the world, recently revised its corporate insurance strategy in a way that stands the conventional wisdom on its head. This change reflects recent developments in the theory of corporate finance and applications of the theory to the practice of corporate risk management.

In the past decade, financial economists have begun to re-examine the benefits and costs of corporate risk management from a shareholder-value perspective. To date, academic attention has been focused almost entirely on factors affecting the corporate *demand* for risk management products. But, in our analysis of British Petroleum's recent and marked shift in insurance strategy, we demonstrate that this new approach also depends critically on supply considerations across different sizes of potential claims.

Based on this supply-side analysis of the insurance industry as well as distinctive aspects of the *corporate* demand for insurance, this very large public company reached the conclusion that it has a substantial comparative advantage over the insurance industry in bearing the risk of its largest exposures. For this reason, BP purchases coverage only for its smallest tier of losses (under $10 million). Even in these cases, the primary motive for buying insurance is not to transfer risk, but rather to exploit the insurance industry's comparative efficiency in providing risk-assessment and claims-administration services.

Having completed and acted upon this rethinking of its insurance strategy, BP is now in the process of reviewing the way it manages its other significant exposures. In addition to property and casualty risks, oil price changes, currency fluctuations, and interest rate changes all affect the value of BP in fairly systematic ways, thus imposing risk. Over the past decade, hedging instruments such as exchange-traded futures and options and over-the-counter swaps have become available to manage these kinds of exposures. In an effort to formulate a comprehensive risk management strategy, BP is extending the analytical framework described here to weigh the benefits of managing such financial risks against the costs associated with these other forms of insurance.

■ **NEIL A. DOHERTY** is a professor in the Department of Insurance and Risk Management at the University of Pennsylvania's Wharton School of Business.

■ **CLIFFORD W. SMITH, Jr.** is the Clarey Professor of Finance at the University of Rochester's Simon School of Business.

CHAPTER 14

Hedging and Value in the U.S. Airline Industry

DAVID A. CARTER, DANIEL A. ROGERS, AND BETTY J. SIMKINS

If we don't do anything, we are speculating. It is our fiduciary duty to hedge fuel price risk.
—Scott Topping, Vice President and Treasurer, Southwest Airlines[1]

IN THE PAST FEW YEARS, a growing number of companies have devoted major resources to implementing risk management programs designed to hedge financial risks, such as interest rate, currency, and commodity price risk. Because of the increasing reliance on such programs, it is important to ask the question: "Does hedging add value to corporations?"[2] And if it does, the obvious follow-up question is: "How does it add value?"

Finance theorists have proposed a number of ways that hedging and, more generally, risk management can increase corporate market values. Stated briefly, risk management has the potential to add value by (1) reducing corporate income taxes; (2) reducing the probability and expected costs of financial distress; and (3) preserving management's ability and incentives to carry out all positive-NPV projects (incentives that can otherwise be distorted by the pressure for near-term cash flow faced by financially troubled firms).[3]

This chapter was previously published as an article in *Journal of Applied Corporate Finance* Vol. 18, No. 4 (2006): 21–36.

1. Quote made by Scott Topping on April 29, 2003 in a presentation at Oklahoma State University.
2. Although the answer is far from definitive, the initial evidence would appear to support a guarded "yes." George Allayannis and James Weston presented the first empirical work regarding the value effect of hedging by looking at the relationship between the use of foreign currency derivatives and value for a sample of large U.S. nonfinancial firms. (See George Allayannis and James Weston, "The Use of Foreign Currency Derivatives and Firm Market Value," *Review of Financial Studies* 14 (2001): 243–76.) Additionally, a recent survey by Charles Smithson and Betty Simkins of the empirical literature on the relation between hedging and firm value finds that most evidence is consistent with the notion that hedging adds value. Charles Smithson and Betty Simkins, "Does Risk Management Add Value? A Survey of the Evidence," *Journal of Applied Corporate Finance* 17 (2005): 8–17.
3. Other possible motives for hedging discussed in the literature include reducing the cost of capital, asymmetric information, and managerial incentives.

Competition, Fuel Costs, and Consumer Prices

Fuel prices are an external factor that airlines cannot control. What can they do to react and minimize the damage? A comparison with other modes of transportation is revealing. Fuel represents a roughly comparable proportion of expenses for railroads and many trucking companies (in the mid-teens percent range), but they have not been hurt by higher fuel prices to nearly the same degree.

Part of the difference is due to more active hedging programs by these freight transportation companies, but most is due to the fact that many of their contracts with corporate customers allow them to pass through higher fuel costs in the form of surcharges. Airlines have tried repeatedly to raise fares in response to high fuel costs, but with little success. [T]he problem comes back to a lack of pricing power in a very competitive market.

Philip Baggaley, Managing Director, Standard & Poor's (June 3, 2004), testimony before the U.S. House of Representatives Committee on Transportation and Infrastructure.

To answer the questions of whether hedging adds value and, if so, how, we conducted a study of the fuel price hedging of 28 airlines over the period of 1992–2003 that was published in *Financial Management* in 2006.[4] The aim of this article is to summarize and evaluate the practical import of the findings of that study.

We chose to investigate the relation between hedging and value in the airline industry for a number of reasons. First, the industry is by and large competitive and remarkably homogeneous. Second, by studying airlines, we were able to focus on the hedging of a single, volatile input commodity—jet fuel—that represents a major economic expense for the industry. Although fuel costs have historically been a distant second to labor costs, the two have almost converged in recent years.[5] Third, jet fuel prices are not only highly volatile (our estimate of annualized jet fuel price volatility during 1992–2003 was about 27%, as compared to about 10% for major currencies),[6] but the *levels of volatil-*

---

4. See David Carter, Daniel Rogers, and Betty Simkins, "Does Hedging Affect Firm Value? Evidence from the U.S. Airline Industry," *Financial Management* 35 (2006): 53–86.

5. In 2005, labor costs and fuel costs at the 10 major U.S. airlines averaged 27.5% and 25% of revenues, respectively. And for some airlines, fuel costs exceeded labor costs for the first time.

6. Guay and Kothari report that the annualized volatility of major currencies is only 11% (measured over 1988–1997). See Wayne Guay and S.P. Kothari, "How Much Do Firms Hedge with Derivatives?" *Journal of Financial Economics* 70 (2003): 423–61.

ity are themselves highly variable. The notable variation in both price and volatility levels during the period we studied allowed us to examine more closely the source of potential value from hedging, and how that value is reflected under different price conditions. Fourth, fuel price increases cannot be easily passed through to customers (see box 14.1) because of competitive pressures in the airline industry. Fifth, and finally, airlines face significant "costs" associated with financial trouble. Perhaps most important, airlines facing a sharp downturn in operating cash flow are likely, especially when faced with a material probability of default, to "underinvest" in their future, making cutbacks in discretionary expenditures on everything from advertising to maintenance.[7] Hedging fuel costs, as the results of our study suggest, can help the airlines manage this potential underinvestment problem while also limiting other costs of financial trouble.

Some Background on the Companies

We analyzed all publicly held U.S. passenger airline companies (SIC codes 4512 and 4513) for which information was available for at least two years during the period 1992–2003. That fuel price risk is a major risk factor for the airlines is clear from the disclosures about their hedging programs that appear in many of their annual financial statements. At the same time, a number of other airlines that say nothing about hedging *future* jet fuel purchases draw attention to their use of other risk-management tactics, such as fuel pass-through agreements with major carriers or charter arrangements that allow for fuel costs to be passed along to the organization chartering the flight.[8]

Table 14.1 provides descriptive data on our sample of 28 airlines. The second and third columns list the airline classification (major carrier, national carrier, or regional/commuter) and the years for which information about the airline was available.[9] As shown in the fourth column of table 14.1, fuel costs averaged about 13.75% of operating expenses for all years, with a range of 8.5%

7. Kenneth Froot, David Scharfstein, and Jeremy Stein, "Risk Management: Coordinating Corporate Investment and Financing Policies," *Journal of Finance* 48 (1993): 1629–58.
8. It should be noted that fuel pass-through and charter agreements do not lock in a price for future jet fuel, as is the case when airlines hedge future fuel purchases. Rather, users of these operational-type hedging mechanisms experience higher fuel costs as fuel prices increase, but have some flexibility to pass some or all of the higher jet fuel cost to another party, such as the partner airline or the chartering client.
9. Airline carrier classifications are based on the Air Transport Association of America definitions. Major carriers are defined as an airline with annual revenue of more than $1 billion, and national carriers are airlines with annual revenues between $100 million and $1 billion. Regional carriers are airlines with annual revenues of less than $100 million whose service generally is limited to a particular geographic region.

TABLE 14.1

Fuel Usage and Derivatives Hedging by Sample Airlines (1992–2003)

Airline	Airline Classification	Sample Years	Jet Fuel as a Percentage of Operating Expenses (Average Over Sample Period)	Years Jet Fuel Hedged	Maximum Maturity of Hedge (Years)	Average Percentage of Next Year Hedged
Airtran Holdings	National	1993–2003	18.84%	1999–2003	1.0	14%
Alaska Air Group	Major	1992–2003	13.92%	1992–96, 2000–03	3.0	22%
America West Holdings	Major	1992–2003	13.30%	1997–2003	<1.0	11%
AMR Corp	Major	1992–2003	11.97%	1992–2003	3.0	28%
Amtran	National	1992–2003	18.44%	1998–2001	0.75	3%
Atlantic Coast Airlines	National	1994–2003	12.73%	1997–2000	1.0	5%
CCAir	Regional	1994–1998	8.69%	None		
Comair Holdings	National	1994–1999	10.19%	None		
Continental Airlines	Major	1992–2003	15.14%	1992–93, 1996–2002	1.0	18%
Delta Air Lines	Major	1992–2003	12.20%	1996–2003	3.0	34%
Express Jet Holdings	National	2002–2003	11.62%	None		
Frontier Airlines	National	1994–2003	15.58%	2002–2003	2.0	2%
Great Lakes Aviation	National	1994–2003	15.28%	None		

Airline	Type					
Hawaiian Airlines	National	1994–2002	17.11%	1997–2002	2.0	8%
Jetblue Airways	National	2002–2003	16.07%	2002–2003	1.25	43%
Mesa Air Group	National	1994–2003	15.09%	None		
Mesaba Holdings	National	1993–2003	8.45%	None		
Midway Airlines	National	1995–2000	12.52%	None		
Midwest Express Holdings	National	1994–2003	16.53%	1997–2002	0.75	4%
Northwest Airlines	Major	1992–2003	13.57%	1997–2002	1.0	11%
SkyWest	National	1994–2003	12.20%	None		
Southwest Airlines	Major	1992–2003	14.51%	1992–2003	6.0	43%
Tower Air	National	1994–1998	18.36%	1998	N/A	0%
TransWorld Airlines (TWA)	Major	1994–1999	13.00%	1998–1999	2.0	1%
UAL Corp	Major	1992–2003	12.30%	1995–2003	1.0	19%
US Airways Group	Major	1992–2003	9.69%	1994–97, 2000–03	2.0	12%
Vanguard Airlines	Regional	1995–2001	17.61%	None		
World Airways	National	1994–2003	9.97%	None		
Average			**13.75%**			**15%**

(for Mesaba Holdings) to 18.8% (Airtran Holdings). The last three columns in the table report three pieces of information about the companies' fuel hedging programs: (1) the calendar years in which fuel hedges were in place at the fiscal year-end; (2) the maximum maturity of the hedge (expressed in years); and (3) the percentage of next year's fuel requirements hedged.

The major airlines, as can be seen in the table, are much more likely to hedge future jet fuel purchases than the smaller firms. Only AMR and Southwest Airlines had hedges in place at the end of every year for which we have data. But other fairly regular and extensive hedgers included Continental, Delta, Alaska Air, and JetBlue. Of the 28 airlines, 18 (or 64%) reported hedging jet fuel in at least one year.

But among those airlines that hedged, there was considerable variation in the amount of fuel hedged. While the average percentage of next year's fuel consumption hedged was only about 15%, some airlines—notably Southwest—have often hedged up to 80% of the next year's fuel requirements. And in an interesting development, a few major airlines such as Southwest and AMR have been increasing the maximum length of hedging horizons in recent years.

But, as the case of Delta Air Lines makes clear, fuel hedging is not a panacea. For much of our sample period, Delta maintained fairly high levels of fuel hedging. At the end of 2002, the company had hedged 65% of its fuel requirements for 2003, and this level was fairly representative of its hedging policy from 1998 through 2003. But Delta drastically increased its leverage in the post–9/11 environment, perhaps in the belief the industry downturn would be short-lived. By the end of 2003, Delta's long-term debt as a percentage of total assets had grown to 48% (up from 27% at the end of 2000), with about $1 billion coming due in 2004. Meanwhile, during the years of 2001–2003, Delta reported operating losses of almost $3 billion while servicing $1.9 billion of interest expense. Delta's Standard and Poor's (S&P) credit rating declined steadily from BBB- before September 11, 2001 to BB- by the end of 2003. By March of 2004, its credit rating had been cut further to B-. In February of 2004, Delta liquidated its existing fuel hedge contracts to raise $83 million of cash, leaving the company completely exposed to further price shocks.

Hedging and Value in the Airline Industry

To investigate whether and how the jet fuel hedging activities of airlines affect their values, we estimated the empirical relationships between a number of measures of the extent of a firm's jet fuel hedging activities and a widely used measure of value added called "Tobin's Q" ratio. Tobin's Q, in brief, is the ratio of the firm's market value to its replacement cost—and we used the following simplified version:

> market value of equity + liquidation value of preferred stock
> + the book values of long-term debt and current liabilities – current assets
> + book value of inventory]/divided by total assets.[10]

We used a number of different measures of fuel hedging activity, including the percentage of next year's fuel requirements hedged and a fuel hedging "indicator" variable (that received a value of 1 if the airline hedges its jet fuel exposure and 0 if it does not). In addition to variables measuring hedging behavior, we also included several other control variables in our analysis, including: firm size (measured by the natural logarithm of total assets), a dividend indicator, long-term debt-to-asset ratio, cash-flow-to-sales ratio, capital-expenditures-to-sales ratio, advertising-to-sales ratio, S&P credit rating score, and Altman's Z-score.[11] We also included indicator variables to proxy for the possible effects on firm value of other risk management techniques, such as fuel pass-through agreements, charter operations, and interest-rate or foreign-exchange hedging.[12] Finally, we included the ratio of cash to sales as a measure of liquidity, since excess cash can serve as a partial substitute for hedging and risk management.[13]

Table 14.2 summarizes the results of our analysis of the relation between Tobin's Q and fuel hedging, as measured by the percentage of next year's fuel requirements hedged. We tested this relationship using three different models.[14] Our results when using Models 1 and 2 provide evidence of a link between

---

10. Because of data limitation, we used a simple approximation of Tobin's Q rather than a more rigorous construction. See Kee Chung and Stephen Pruitt, "A Simple Approximation of Tobin's Q," *Financial Management* 23 (1994): 70–74. Prior research has documented that a simple Q calculation is preferable in most empirical applications because of the ease of computation, data availability, and because the simple approximation is highly correlated with more rigorous calculations. Peter DaDalt, Jeffrey Donaldson, and Jacqueline Garner, "Will Any Q Do? Firm Characteristics and Divergences in Estimates of Tobin's Q," *Journal of Financial Research* 26 (2003).

11. Altman's Z-score is a measure of the likelihood of bankruptcy. A score above 3.0 indicates that bankruptcy is unlikely, while a score below 1.8 indicates bankruptcy is likely.

12. Wayne Guay and S. P. Kothari report in a 2003 *Journal of Financial Economics* article that the annualized volatility of major currencies is only 11% (measured over 1988–1997). See Wayne Guay and S.P. Kothari, "How Much Do Firms Hedge with Derivatives!" *Journal of Financial Economics* 70 (2003): 423–61.

13. Prior research notes that airlines with greater liquidity demonstrated less stock price sensitivity in response to the September 11, 2001 attacks. See David Carter and Betty Simkins, "The Market's Reaction to Unexpected Catastrophic Events: The Case of Airline Stock Returns and the September 11th Attacks," *Quarterly Review of Economics and Finance* 44 (2004): 539–58.

14. We used pooled ordinary least squares regression (OLS) with robust standard errors to estimate Models 1 and 3 and a feasible generalized least squares regression (FGLS) with heteroskedastically consistent standard errors to estimate Model 2. Model 3 differs from Model 1 in that we used changes in our variables to explore the effect of changes in jet fuel–hedging behavior on the change in firm value. We also included year-dummy variables in all regressions. Because all airlines did not operate in all years of our sample, we had a total of 251 firm-year observations.

Southwest Airlines: An Example of a Successful Hedging Program

Southwest Airlines is both the most active hedger of fuel costs and the most profitable among U.S. airlines. At the end of 2005, Southwest posted a profit for its 33rd consecutive year. This success is unprecedented in an industry that has collectively failed to turn a profit for the past five years. Southwest attributes much of that success to its fuel-hedging program. As they point out in their 2005 10K report: "This performance was driven primarily by strong revenue growth, as the Company grew capacity, and effective cost control measures, including a successful fuel-hedge program." And, in the words of Scott Topping, Southwest's Vice President and Treasurer, "Fuel hedging will continue to play a strategic role in the industry and be a potential source of competitive advantage."

In 2005, Southwest's fuel costs totaled $1.342 billion and represented 19.8% of operating expenses. Their fuel-hedging program resulted in an estimated reduction of "fuel and oil expense" during 2005 of $892 million. The airline paid an average of $1.03 per gallon after hedging gains and used 1.3 billion gallons of fuel for the year. The following insert summarizes Southwest's hedging program objectives, commodities used and instruments considered, and other considerations.

Hedging Program Objectives

- Strategically manage the second largest expense category on P&L statement

- Integral to unit cost management & competitive advantage

- Manage upside risk and participate on the downside (requires an investment)

- Be opportunistic

Commodities Used in Hedging

- Crude oil, heating oil, unleaded gasoline, and jet fuel

- Considerations in choice of commodities include expected performance of the hedge, basis risk, liquidity, and accounting issues (i.e., FAS 133)

continued

Hedging Instruments Considered

- Swaps—no initial cost but highest risk

- Differential swaps—restructure hedge to manage basis risk

- Collars—can be structured at no cost or premium collars; carries a moderate risk. Premium collars are often used.

- Call options—highest cost, lowest risk, and can create synthetically (swap plus put option)

Considerations in Hedging and Operations

- Point in commodity price cycle—swaps look more favorable at low prices, collars in the mid-range, and options at high prices.

- Uncertainty beyond fundamentals

- Cost/budget

- Other portfolio management objectives or market opportunities (example: volatility)

- Counterparties—prefer OTC trading and counterparties must be investment grade

- FAS 133—goal is to maintain hedge accounting without sacrificing opportunity

Example of Protection at $1.20 per Gallon using Swap, Call Option, and Collar

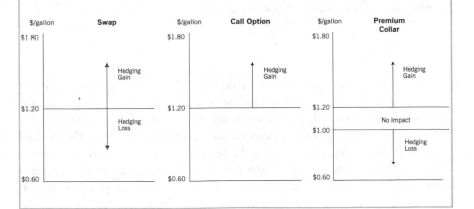

TABLE 14.2

Regression Analysis of the Relation Between Firm Value and Jet Fuel–Hedging Behavior for Airlines (1992–2003)[a]

	Constant	Firm Size	Percentage of Next Year's Fuel Req'ts Hedged	LTD-to-Asset Ratio	R^2	Wald X
Panel A Relation Between Value and Jet Fuel Hedging						
Model 1 Pooled OLS						
Dep. Var. = ln(Q)	−0.085	−0.174***	0.348*	0.710*		
(n = 228)	(0.908)	(0.003)	(0.069)	(0.074)	0.463	—
Model 2 FGLS						
Dep. Var. = ln(Q)	−0.557	−0.115***	0.332***	0.819***		
(n = 228)	(0.179)	(0.000)	(0.005)	(0.000)	—	340.97***
Panel B Relation Between the Change in Value and the Change in Jet Fuel Hedging						
Model 3 Pooled OLS						
Dep. Var. = Δln(Q)	−0.164	−0.298**	0.188*	0.897***		
(n = 200)	(0.341)	(0.049)	(0.068)	(0.006)	0.439	—

[a.] Models 1 and 3 were estimated with OLS using robust standard errors that account for the clustered sample. Model 2 was estimated using time-series feasible generalized least squares with heteroskedastically consistent standard errors. Control variables listed in the text and year-dummy variables were included in all regressions, but not reported. p-values are reported in parentheses below the coefficients.

   * indicates significance at the 10 percent level.
   ** indicates significance at the 5 percent level.
   *** indicates significance at the 1 percent level.

hedging and value for airlines. The estimated coefficients for the percentage of next year's fuel requirements hedged were 0.348 for Model 1 and 0.332 for Model 2 (both statistically significant at the 10% level). In the case of Model 1, the coefficient of 0.348 can be interpreted as saying that an airline that hedges 100% of its jet fuel requirements would be expected to command a value premium of almost 35% over an airline that hedges none of its jet fuel requirements. For those airlines in our sample that hedged, the average percentage of next year's fuel requirements hedged was 29.4%. Thus, our findings suggest

Lufthansa Airlines: An Example of a Successful Hedging Program by an International Airline

A successful fuel-hedging program is simply one that accomplishes its hedge objectives, like systematic reduction of risk, catastrophe insurance or budget protection
—*Helmut Fredrich, General Manager of Corporate Fuel Management, Lufthansa**

German airline Lufthansa is not new to risk management. The company began hedging jet fuel–price risk in 1990 and was one of the first airlines to do so. In 1997, Lufthansa became fully privatized and listed its shares on the stock market when the German government sold off its remaining stake in the company. In 2003, Energy Risk named Lufthansa as the "Energy Risk Manager of the Year—End User."

In 2005, fuel consumption accounted for approximately 14% of operating expenses. Like Southwest, Lufthansa has also hedged its fuel-cost risk with option structures, including collars, as well as swaps.

Commodities Used in Hedging

- Crude oil, gasoil, kerosene

Hedging Instruments Considered

- Swaps including differential swaps

- Crack spreads

- Collars

- Options

Lufthansa hedges up to 90% of its planned fuel requirements on a revolving basis over a period of 24 months ahead. As the figure above illustrates, beginning 24 months into the future (see M+24 in figure), they start hedging 5% of their requirements using Brent Crude Oil Collars each month, incre-

---

* Source: "Energy Risk Manager of the Year–End User," *Energy Risk*, Vol. 7, No. 12 (March 2003).

continued

Example of Lufthansa's Current Hedging Policy: Medium-Term Crude Oil Hedging Combined with Short-Term Crack Hedging†

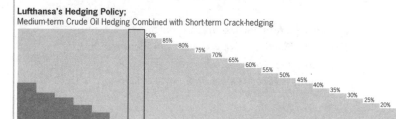

Lufthansa's Hedging Policy;
Medium-term Crude Oil Hedging Combined with Short-term Crack-hedging

● Brent Collar ● Crack Collar ○ Crude Oil (Brent) Average Price of 18 Individual Prices

mentally increasing the level to 90% at seven months into the future (see M+7 in figure). To minimize basis risk (i.e., the price difference between crude oil and kerosene), Lufthansa also hedges using crack collars. Since hedging crack is expensive, Lufthansa has modified its hedging approach to combine its hedging of crude oil with its short-term hedging of crack. Lufthansa starts implementing the crack-hedging strategy six months ahead (see M+6 in figure) at a monthly rate of 7.5%. As a result, 45% of basis risk is hedged using crack collars by the time the fuel is used (see M+1).

Accounting rules are also an important concern. As Helmut Fredrich states: "We have to follow the IASB (International Accounting Standards Board) rules, to make sure our instruments are seen as just hedges and not trading. But as we go more towards the U.S. GAAP regulations, it is more difficult to stay within the rules, especially if you want to do more intelligent hedges."‡

† *Source:* Lufthansa Investor Relations public documents on hedging and other public sources.
‡ See "Energy Risk Manager of the Year-End User."

that an average hedging airline exhibits a value premium of around 10% $(0.35 \times 29.4\%)$.[15]

Models 1 and 2 are concerned with the relation between levels of hedging activity and levels of value. Another way of estimating the value consequences of hedging is to measure the change in values when companies change their

15. We also estimated the same models using Tobin's Q, total assets, leverage, and capital expenditures adjusted for operating leases. While not shown in this article, the results continue to suggest a statistically significant hedging premium.

hedging policies. Our results using Model 3 show that changes in jet fuel hedging are positively related to changes in the value of the firm. The estimated coefficient for a change in the percentage of next year's fuel requirements hedged was 0.188 (which was also statistically significant at the 10% level). This result implies that a change from a policy of no hedging to the average level of hedging (for hedging firms) of 29.4% is associated with an increase in value of approximately 5.5% (0.188×29.4%).[16]

Finally, we performed a very simple analysis of stock returns (which was not part of our published study) with no controls for size or other potential factors, and we found that hedgers outperformed non-hedgers in 7 of the 10 years we studied. Furthermore, in 2 of the 3 years that the hedgers failed to outperform the non-hedgers (2001–2002), the weaker performance of the hedging airlines was most likely due to factors other than hedging. In particular, the stock market heavily punished large airlines (almost all of which hedge) in the post–9/11 period since they were more likely targets of terrorist attacks.

How Does Hedging Add Value for Airlines?

Having found evidence that hedging adds value for airlines, we now ask, "How?" In his recent book on *Risk Management and Derivatives* (2003),[17] René Stulz offered a variation on the M&M irrelevance proposition that he called the "risk management irrelevance proposition." Like the famous M&M theorems, Stulz's proposition says that, under a set of artificial conditions known as "perfect financial markets" (i.e., no asymmetric information, no taxes, and no transactions [including bankruptcy] costs), hedging should not affect the value of the firm.

But in the real world, where most, if not all, the assumptions of perfect financial markets are violated, the question becomes: "Under what conditions might hedging add value?" As mentioned earlier, the ways in which hedging can add value can be reduced to three main categories: (1) reducing taxes; (2) reducing the costs associated with reorganizing financially troubled companies; and (3) preserving (or strengthening) managers' incentives to invest in the company's future. In what follows, we briefly describe how airline hedging of jet fuel–price risk might affect firm value in the context of risk management theory.

16. In a simple analysis of stock returns (i.e., not controlling for size or other factors), hedgers outperformed non-hedgers in 7 of the 10 years we studied. Furthermore, for 2 of the years that the hedgers did not outperform non-hedgers (2001–2002), the weaker performance of hedging airlines was most likely due to factors other than hedging. The stock market heavily punished large airlines (almost all of which hedge) in the post–9/11 period since they were more likely targets of terrorist attacks.

17. See René M. Stulz, *Risk Management and Derivatives* (South-Western/Thomson Publishing, 2003.)

Hedging and Investment Behavior: The Case of Southwest and ATA

A recent example that illustrates the investment behavior discussed above occurred after ATA's (formerly known as Amtran) Chapter 11 bankruptcy filing on October 27, 2004. Rising jet fuel prices contributed to ATA's deteriorating financial condition as spot prices for Gulf Coast jet fuel rose from below $1.00 per gallon at the start of 2004 to an average of more than $1.50 per gallon during October 2004—a ten-month period during which ATA was not hedged against fuel price increases. At the time of its bankruptcy filing, ATA announced that Airtran had agreed to purchase its Chicago Midway operation along with some additional gates and landing slots at other airports for $87.5 million in cash. In contrast to ATA, Airtran had hedged about 29% of its 2004 fuel commitments hedged by the end of 2003, and it increased its hedged position to 35% during the first quarter of 2004. However, the Midway operation was to be put up for auction, and even at the time of the bankruptcy filing, it was speculated that other bidders would emerge.

Southwest Airlines ultimately won the bidding for ATA's Chicago Midway property with a $117 million bid on December 17, 2004. Southwest had over 80% of its 2004 fuel commitments hedged at the end of 2003; and in its 2005 10-K filing, the airline reported that its gains from fuel hedging amounted to $455 million during 2004. Thus, one interpretation of these events is that Southwest's fuel hedging provided the cash flow (and market valuation) that gave management the confidence to bid aggressively for the distressed ATA assets.

Preserving Managers' Normal Investment Incentives

In a paper published in the *Journal of Financial and Quantitative Analysis* in 1984, Cliff Smith, and Stulz himself, argued that one of the most important benefits of corporate risk management was its role in limiting the probability and costs of financial distress. Such costs can take the form of direct, out-of-pocket costs, such as the costs of reorganizing a company that defaults. Or they can be indirect, such as the tougher terms exacted by the suppliers and employees—not to mention the reluctance of consumers—when dealing with financially troubled companies. But potentially the greatest of these indirect costs, at least for companies with significant growth opportunities, is the tendency of managers to underinvest when facing pressure to meet interest payments (and analysts' forecasts). Risk management, by helping to ensure a minimal level of cash flow or capital, can preserve management's incentives and ability to invest in all positive-NPV projects.[18]

In a 1993 article in the *Journal of Finance*, Ken Froot, David Scharfstein, and Jeremy Stein proposed an interesting variation on this argument that maintained that the value of hedging is likely to depend heavily on the *correlation* between a company's investment opportunities and the cash-flow effects associated with hedgeable risks.[19] For example, if an airline's investment opportunities tend to dry up when jet fuel prices are high and operating cash flow (in the absence of hedging) is down, then the case for hedging is relatively weak; the firm doesn't really need much excess capital under those circumstances. On the other hand, if investment opportunities are greatest when industry cash flows are depressed by high fuel costs, the case for hedging becomes much clearer. In this event, hedging ensures that the firm will have sufficient capital for investment at a time when raising outside capital would likely be very expensive.

In support of this version of the underinvestment hypothesis, our study provides evidence that investment by the airline industry was *not negatively* correlated with jet fuel costs, as one might expect—and, indeed, was positive during parts of the period we studied.[20] That is to say, investment opportunities and, as discussed later, actual airline capital spending was greater in periods when fuel prices were high or rising. Consistent with our findings, other studies have shown that periods of economic downturn result in failure and/or asset sales by financially weak airlines. In such cases, the more profitable airlines may be in a position to buy the assets at "fire sale" prices.[21]

Managing Other Costs of Financial Distress

In addition to its role in managing the corporate underinvestment problem, hedging can also be used to manage other costs associated with financial distress, everything from the fees incurred in reorganizing debt claims to the higher costs of attracting and keeping concerned suppliers, customers, and employees. But this raises an interesting question about the real underlying objectives of airline hedging. If the fundamental purpose of hedging is really to preserve value by avoiding a costly reorganization and reassuring creditors, then we might expect the smaller, and more highly leveraged, airlines to be the most active hedgers. To the extent there are major costs associated with

18. Clifford Smith, Jr., and René Stulz, "The Determinants of Firms' Hedging Policies," *Journal of Financial and Quantitative Analysis* 20 (1984): 391–405.
19. See Kenneth Froot, David Scharfstein, and Jeremy Stein, "Risk Management: Coordinating Corporate Investment and Financing Policies," *Journal of Finance* 48 (1993): 1629–1658.
20. See Carter et al., "Does Hedging Affect Firm Value?" pp. 61–62.
21. See Todd C. Pulvino, "Do Asset Fire Sales Exist? An Empirical Investigation of Commercial Aircraft Transactions," *Journal of Finance* 53 (1998): 939–78, and Todd C. Pulvino, "Effects of Bankruptcy Court Protection on Asset Sales," *Journal of Financial Economics* 52 (1999): 151–86.

TABLE 14.3

S&P Credit Ratings for Senior Debt of Sample Airlines

Airline	Median Rating (1988–2004)	May 2004 Rating
Airtran Holdings	B-	B-
Alaska Air Group	BB+	BB-
America West	B+	B-
AMR	BBB-	B-
Amtran	B	CCC
Atlantic Coast Airlines	B	B-
Continental Airlines	B+	B
Delta Air Lines	BBB-	B-
Midway Airlines	B-	Bankrupt
Northwest Airlines	BB	B+
Southwest Airlines	A-	A
Tower Air	CCC	Bankrupt
Trans World Airlines	CCC	Purchased by AMR
UAL	BB+	Bankrupt
US Airways Group	B+	CCC+

financial distress, such costs would likely represent a higher percentage of firm value for the smaller airlines. On the other hand, if the main purpose of hedging is to enable the strongest airlines to buttress their already strong strategic positions by acquiring assets at fire-sale prices, then it may make sense that the most consistent hedgers are also the largest, most successful operators. (And, as discussed below, to the extent that hedging and strategic risk management require an up-front investment in "learning," the largest most successful firms are also likely to be the first, if not the main, users.)

In order to investigate the extent of financial distress costs in the industry, we began by examining the airlines' credit ratings and how they have changed over time. For the period 1988–2004, table 14.3 reports the median S&P ratings of the senior debt of the 15 sample airlines with ratings reported in the Compustat database. As shown in the table, in 1988 six airlines had investment grade ratings. During the next 17 years, three airlines filed Chapter 11 and one was purchased after filing bankruptcy. As of this writing, only one airline had an investment grade credit rating—Southwest. And as these credit ratings suggest, the airline industry's access to external capital markets has been diminishing over time.

One major reason for this decline in ratings can be seen in Figure 14.2, which shows the heightened volatility of airline profit margins. Moreover, there is a clear negative correlation between operating profits (not including hedging gains or losses) and jet fuel prices.[22] The combination of volatile cash flow and limited access to capital (especially during weak industry conditions) might provide an incentive for airlines to protect cash flow against a spike in fuel prices.

More Evidence on How Fuel Hedging Adds Value

In an additional effort to determine the motives for airline hedging, we conducted a series of multivariate regressions designed to test the relation of the percentage of jet fuel requirements hedged with a number of other potentially important variables, the results of which are summarized in table 14.4.[23] One of the variables was the credit ratings themselves. As reported in table 14.4, the airlines with the higher credit ratings (i.e., the lower S&P credit rating numbers), and those with the least debt (when counting operating leases as debt) as a percentage of book value of total assets hedged the largest proportions of their future fuel requirements. And as we also noted earlier—and as shown in table 14.4—it is also the larger airlines that tend to hedge a larger percentage of their fuel requirements.

Both of these results are somewhat surprising, at least to the extent that one expects smaller, riskier airlines to have the highest expected costs of financial distress (as a percentage of firm value). But there are at least two possible explanations. One is that the smaller airlines have lacked either the resources to invest in acquiring a hedging capability or the strategic foresight to make that kind of investment. A second, and more intriguing possibility, is that the larger, stronger airlines actually have larger costs of financial distress (even as a percentage of firm value) in the form of more growth opportunities that could be lost as a result of high leverage and financial risk. Recall the positive relation between Tobin's Q and hedging activity that we noted earlier (and reported in table 14.2). To the extent that an airline's Tobin's Q serves as a proxy for the market's assessment of its value from growth opportunities (which is standard interpretation of Tobin's Q in the finance literature), this result is consistent with the underinvestment hypothesis. That is, if it is mainly just the largest airlines that are able to buy distressed assets during periods of weak industry cash flows, then such firms may also have the most to gain from hedging and the most to lose from high leverage.

For the smaller airlines, it's true that the probability of getting into financial trouble may be quite high. But it also may well be true that the financial distress costs for such organizations are relatively low. For example, to the extent that the airlines are able to operate efficiently in Chapter 11 (and the "stay"

---

22. The Pearson Correlation Coefficient over the period 1992–2003 is -42 percent.

23. Table 14.4 reports a subset of the results from the complete random effects Tobit regressions reported in our *Financial Management* article. For the complete set of results and discussion, see Carter et al., "Does Hedging Affect Firm Value?" pp. 66–71.

TABLE 14.4

Random Effects Tobit Regression Analysis of the Relation Between Amount of Jet Fuel Hedged and Underinvestment Hypothesis Variable for Airlines (1992–2003)[a]

	Tobin's Q	Long-term Debt-to-Assets	Ln(Assets)	Credit Rating
Model 1 No adjustments for operating leases Dep.Var.=Amt. of fuel hedged (n=215)	0.1367** (0.0.017)	−0.0848 (0.579)	0.0532* (0.056)	−0.0226*** (0.000)
Model 2 Adjustments for operating leases Dep. Var.=Amt. of fuel hedged (n=206)	0.2249*** (0.007)	−0.2729** (0.043)	0.0492** (0.032)	−0.0214*** (0.000)

[a] The dependent variable in each regression is the percentage of next year's jet fuel requirements hedged as of the end of the fiscal year. The results shown above are a subset of the full regressions and are taken from Table V on page 69 of our *Financial Management* article entitled, "Does Hedging Affect Firm Value? Evidence from the US Airline Industry."
* indicates significance at the 10 percent level.
** indicates significance at the 5 percent level.
*** indicates significance at the 1 percent level.

on creditors' claims provided by the bankruptcy court may have a stabilizing effect), there may be relatively little disruption of normal operating routines. What is likely to be lost in Chapter 11, however, is the ability to invest in major growth opportunities.

Hedging and Investment Opportunities

Consistent with the possibility that the primary aim of airlines in hedging fuel costs is to protect their ability to invest, our study also found a strong correlation between hedging activity and the level of capital expenditures for individual airlines. More specifically, we re-estimated the models of the relation between hedging and value reported in table 14.2 while adding a term measuring the interaction between airline hedging and capital expenditures (capex). While the results of this test (reported in table 14.5) show no significant relation between firm value and fuel hedging, the coefficient on the interaction

TABLE 14.5

Regression Analysis of the Relation Between Firm Value and the Interaction Between Capital Expenditures and Jet Fuel–Hedging Behavior for Airlines (1992–2003)[a]

	Constant	Firm Size	Percentage of Next Year's Fuel Req'ts Hedged	Percentage of Next Year's Fuel Req'ts Hedged X Capital Exp.	R^2	Wald^2
Model 1						
Pooled OLS						
Dep. Var. = ln(Q)	−0.048	−0.174 ***	0.036	1.825 *	0. 469	
(n = 228)	(0.947)	(0.003)	(0.889)	(0.063)		
Model 2						
FGLS						
Dep. Var. = ln(Q)	−0.438	−0.125 ***	0.060	1.772 ***		572.25 ***
(n = 228)	(0.269)	(0.000)	(0.707)	(0.003)		

[a]Model 1 was estimated with OLS using robust standard errors that account for the clustered sample. Model 2 was estimated using time-series feasible generalized least squares with heteroskedastically consistent standard errors. Control variables listed in the text and year dummy variables were included in all regressions, but not reported. p-values are reported in parentheses below the coefficients.

* indicates significance at the 10 percent level.

** indicates significance at the 5 percent level.

*** indicates significance at the 1 percent level.

of capital expenditures and hedging was positive (e.g., 1.825 in Model 1) and statistically significant in both models. Moreover, it seems plausible to interpret this result as saying that, for those airlines that hedge future fuel purchases, the higher capital spending made possible in part by hedging is an important contributor to the higher firm value.

To interpret the value premium associated with hedging for the average hedging airline, we used the estimated coefficients for the percentage of next year's fuel requirements hedged (0.036) and the interaction between hedging and capital expenditures (1.825) along with the average level of capital expenditures-to-sales (11.7%) and average hedge ratio for hedgers (29.4%). Using these values, the average hedging airline is expected to be valued around 7% higher than a non-hedging airline [(1.825 × 0.117 × 0.294) + (0.036 × 0.294)]. This hedging premium consists of two components. The first term in parentheses corresponds to the portion of the hedging premium associated with capital expenditures, and accounts for approximately 86% of the total. The second term is the hedging premium associated only with hedging, which suggests that most of the value premium (86% in this case) is due to investment opportunities.

While not a direct test that jet fuel hedging reduces underinvestment for airlines, this finding does suggest that investors place a higher value on capital spending by hedgers than non-hedgers. In other words, investors may believe that hedgers are able to invest more and such investment tends to be value adding. One explanation for such investor behavior is that hedging makes future capital spending less vulnerable to future increases in jet fuel prices. In such cases, investors view today's capital expenditures as a more reliable proxy for tomorrow's.

The Hedging Premium Over Time

Prior research has shown the hedging value premium for companies with foreign currency exposure is highest during years in which the U.S. dollar appreciates.[24] This suggests, as might be expected, that the market places higher values on companies that hedge during periods that the hedging instruments produce positive payoffs.

As part of our study, we investigated whether the jet fuel–hedging premium changes over time by re-estimating Models 1 and 2 from table 14.2 and including a term that interacts the percentage of next year's fuel requirements hedged with year-indicator variables. As reported in Panel A of table 14.6, our results show an increase in the hedging premiums over the time period studied. The largest hedging premiums occurred in 2002 in both models, a year in

24. See Allayannis and Weston, "Use of Foreign Currency Derivatives."

TABLE 14.6

Jet Fuel Hedging Premium Over Time (1992–2003)[a]

	Estimated Coefficients on the Percentage of Next Year's Fuel Req'ts Hedged X Year (or Regime) Indicator Variable	
	Model 1 Pooled OLS Dep. Var.=ln(Q)	Model 2 FGLS Dep. Var.=ln(Q)
Panel A Hedging Premiums by Year		
1994	−0.027	−0.294
1995	−0.768	−0.834
1996	0.509	0.299
1997	0.087	0.185
1998	0.111	0.307*
1999	0.249	0.252
2000	0.632	0.606**
2001	0.337	0.428*
2002	1.191**	0.936***
2003	0.575*	0.467**
Panel B Hedging Premiums by Fuel Price Regime		
1992–1996 (low prices & volatility)	−0.290	−0.129
1997–1998 (declining prices)	0.049	0.135
1999–2000 (increasing prices)	0.257	0.134
2002–2003 (high prices & volatility)	0.772**	0.713***

[a] Model 1 was estimated with OLS using robust standard errors that account for the clustered sample. Model 2 was estimated using time-series feasible generalized least squares with heteroskedastically consistent standard errors. Control variables listed in the text and year dummy variables were included in all regressions, but not reported.
* indicates significance at the 10 percent level.
** indicates significance at the 5 percent level.
*** indicates significance at the 1 percent level.

which fuel prices were both high and volatile. (In addition, the premiums are statistically significant in both models for 2002 and 2003.)

Moreover, as shown in Figure 14.1, we classified jet fuel prices into four different "regimes"—(1) low prices and volatility (1992–1996), (2) declining prices (1997–1998), (3) increasing prices (1999–2000), and (4) high prices and volatility (2002–2003)—and then estimated hedging value premiums during each of these periods. As reported in Panel B of table 14.6, we found that the premium value for hedging generally increased over these four time periods, with the highest premiums occurring in 2002–2003, the period covered by our study that experienced the highest prices and volatility. And if we were to create a

FIGURE 14.1

Jet Fuel Prices over 1992–2003

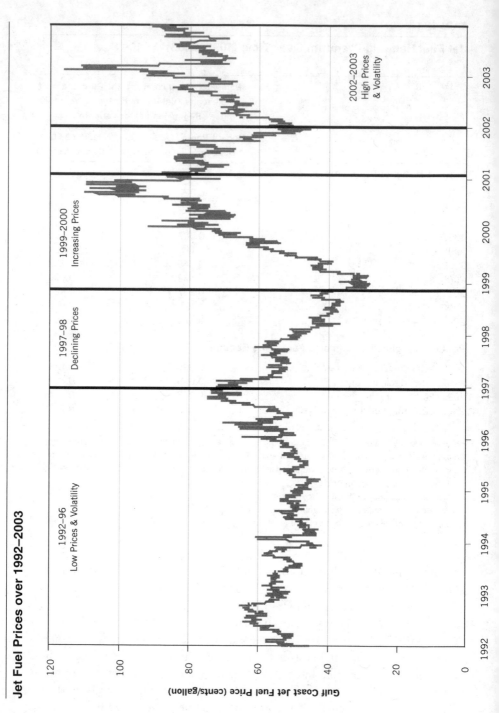

FIGURE 14.2

Net Profit Margin (%) of the U.S. Airline Industry over 1992–2003

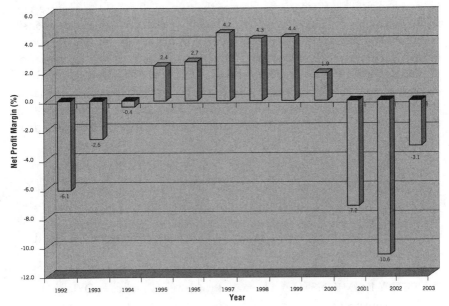

Source: Air Transport Association Economic Reports

fifth period running from 2004 to the time of this writing (October 2006)—a period in which the level and volatility of fuel costs have continued to rise—our best guess is that the hedging value premium would have continued to grow along with them.

Conclusions

In response to the question posed at the beginning of the article: "Does hedging add value to corporations?" our response is a definite "yes" for the 28 airlines in our sample. Those airlines that hedge their fuel costs have Tobin's Q ratios that are 5–10% higher than those of airlines that choose not to hedge. Our results also suggest that the main source of value added by hedging is its role in preserving the firm's ability to take advantage of investment opportunities that arise when fuel prices are high and airline operating cash flows and values are down. Specifically, we find that the value premium associated with hedging increases with the level of the firm's capital investment.

We also find that the more active hedgers of fuel costs among the airlines are the larger firms with the least debt and highest credit ratings. This result is somewhat surprising, at least to the extent the smaller airlines might be expected to have larger financial distress costs (as a percentage of firm value), and hence greater motive to hedge. One explanation is that the smaller airlines have lacked either sufficient resources or the strategic foresight to acquire a derivatives hedging capability. A second possibility, however—one that is consistent with our main findings—is that the largest airlines also have highest costs of financial distress (even as a percentage of firm value) in the form of more growth opportunities that could be lost as a result of high leverage and financial risk. Conventional wisdom says it is mainly just the largest airlines that are able to buy distressed assets during periods of weak industry cash flows—and to the extent this is so, such firms may also have the most to gain from hedging.

DAVID A. CARTER is an Associate Professor of Finance at Oklahoma State University.

DANIEL A. ROGERS is an Associate Professor of Finance at Portland State University.

BETTY J. SIMKINS is an Associate Professor of Finance at Oklahoma State University.

CHAPTER 15

Enterprise Risk Management

Theory and Practice

BRIAN W. NOCCO AND RENÉ M. STULZ

THE PAST TWO DECADES have seen a dramatic change in the role of risk management in corporations. Twenty years ago, the job of the corporate risk manager—typically, a low-level position in the corporate treasury—involved mainly the purchase of insurance. At the same time, treasurers were responsible for the hedging of interest rate and foreign exchange exposures. Over the last ten years, however, corporate risk management has expanded well beyond insurance and the hedging of financial exposures to include a variety of other kinds of risk—notably operational risk, reputational risk, and, most recently, strategic risk. What's more, at a large and growing number of companies, the risk management function is directed by a senior executive with the title of chief risk officer (CRO) and overseen by a board of directors charged with monitoring risk measures and setting limits for these measures.

A corporation can manage risks in one of two fundamentally different ways: (1) one risk at a time, on a largely compartmentalized and decentralized basis; or (2) all risks viewed together within a coordinated and strategic framework. The latter approach is often called "enterprise risk management," or "ERM" for short. In this article, we suggest that companies that succeed in creating an effective ERM have a long-run competitive advantage over those that manage and monitor risks individually. Our argument in brief is that, by measuring and managing its risks consistently and systematically, and by giving its business managers the information and incentives to optimize the trade-off between risk and return, a company strengthens its ability to carry out its strategic plan.

This chapter was previously published as an article in *Journal of Applied Corporate Finance* Vol. 18, No. 4 (2006): 8–20. We are grateful for comments from Don Chew, Michael Hofmann, Joanne Lamm-Tennant, Tom O'Brien, Jérôme Taillard, and William Wilt.

In the pages that follow, we start by explaining how ERM can give companies a competitive advantage and add value for shareholders. Next we describe the process and challenges involved in implementing ERM. We begin by discussing how a company should assess its risk "appetite," an assessment that should guide management's decision about how much and which risks to retain and which to lay off. Then we show how companies should measure their risks. Third, we discuss various means of laying off "non-core" risks, which, as we argue below, increases the firm's capacity for bearing those "core" risks the firm chooses to retain. Though ERM is conceptually straightforward, its implementation is not. And in the last—and longest—section of the chapter, we provide an extensive guide to the major difficulties that arise in practice when implementing ERM.

How Does ERM Create Shareholder Value?

ERM creates value through its effects on companies at both a "macro" or company-wide level and a "micro" or business-unit level. At the macro level, ERM creates value by enabling senior management to quantify and manage the risk-return tradeoff that faces the entire firm. By adopting this perspective, ERM helps the firm maintain access to the capital markets and other resources necessary to implement its strategy and business plan.

At the micro level, ERM becomes a way of life for managers and employees at all levels of the company. Though the academic literature has concentrated mainly on the macro-level benefits of ERM, the micro-level benefits are extremely important in practice. As we argue below, a well-designed ERM system ensures that all material risks are "owned," and risk-return trade-offs carefully evaluated, by operating managers and employees throughout the firm.

The Macro Benefits of Risk Management

Students in the first finance course of a master's of business administration program often come away with the "perfect markets" view that since shareholders can diversify their own portfolios, the value of a firm does not depend on its "total" risk. In this view, a company's cost of capital, which is a critical determinant of its price/earnings ratio, depends mainly on the "systematic" or "non-diversifiable component of that risk (as typically measured by a company's "beta"). And this in turn implies that efforts to manage total risk are a waste of corporate resources.

But in the real world, where investors' information is far from complete and financial troubles can disrupt a company's operations, a bad outcome resulting from a "diversifiable" risk—say, an unexpected spike in a currency or commodity price—can have costs that go well beyond the immediate hit to cash flow and earnings. In the language of economists, such risks can have large "deadweight" costs.[1]

To illustrate, if a company expects operating cash flow of $200 million for the year and instead reports a loss of $50 million, a cash shortfall of this size can be far more costly to the firm than just the missing $250 million. First of all, to the extent it affects the market's expectation of future cash flows and earnings, such a shortfall will generally be associated with a reduction in firm value of much more than $250 million—a reduction that reflects the market's expectation of lower growth. And even if operating cash flow rebounds quickly, there could be other, longer-lasting effects. For example, assume the company has a number of strategic investment opportunities that require *immediate* funding. Unless the firm has considerable excess cash or unused debt capacity, it may be faced with the tough choice of cutting back on planned investments or raising equity in difficult circumstances and on expensive terms. If the cost of issuing equity is high enough, management may have little choice but to cut investment. And unlike the adjustment of market expectations in response to what proves to be a temporary cash shortfall, the loss in value from the firm having to pass up positive net present value (NPV) projects represents a *permanent* reduction in value.

For most companies, guarding against this corporate "underinvestment problem" is likely to be the most important reason to manage risk. By hedging or otherwise managing risk, a firm can limit (to an agreed-upon level) the probability that a large cash shortfall will lead to value-destroying cutbacks in investment. And it is in this sense that the main function of corporate risk management can be seen as protecting a company's ability to carry out its business plan.

But which risks should a company lay off and which should it retain? Corporate exposures to changes in currencies, interest rates, and commodity prices can often be hedged fairly inexpensively using derivatives such as forwards, futures, swaps, and options. For instance, a foreign exchange hedging program using forward contracts typically has very low transaction costs; and when the transfer of risk is inexpensive, there is a strong case for laying off economic risks that could otherwise undermine a company's ability to execute its strategic plan.

On the other hand, companies in the course of their normal activities take many strategic or business risks that they cannot profitably lay off in capital markets or other developed risk transfer markets. For instance, a company with a promising plan to expand its business typically cannot find an economic

---

1. There is a large academic literature that investigates how firm value depends on total risk. For a review of that literature, see René Stulz, *Risk Management and Derivatives* (South-Western Publishing, 2002).

hedge—if indeed there is any hedge at all—for the business risks associated with pursuing such growth. The company's management presumably understands the risks of such expansion better than any insurance or derivatives provider—if they don't, the company probably shouldn't be undertaking the project. If the company were to seek a counterparty to bear such business risks, the costs of transferring such risks would likely be prohibitively high, since they would have to be high enough to compensate the counterparty for transacting with a better informed party and for constructing models to evaluate the risks they're being asked to hedge. For this reason, we should not be surprised that insurance companies do not offer insurance contracts that provide complete coverage for earnings shortfalls or that there is no market for derivatives for which the underlying is a company's earnings. The insured companies would be in a position not only to know more than the insurers about the distribution of their future earnings, but to manipulate that distribution to increase the payoffs from such insurance policies. A firm that entered into a derivatives contract with its earnings as the underlying would have a similar advantage over a derivatives dealer.

More generally, in making decisions whether to retain or transfer risks, companies should be guided by the principle of *comparative advantage in risk-bearing*.[2] A company that has no special ability to forecast market variables has no comparative advantage in bearing the risk associated with those variables. In contrast, the same company should have a comparative advantage in bearing information-intensive, firm-specific business risks because it knows more about these risks than anybody else. For example, at Nationwide Insurance, exposures to changes in interest rates and equity markets are managed in strict ranges, with excess exposures reduced through asset repositioning or hedging. At the same time, Nationwide retains the vast majority of its insurance risks, a decision that reflects the firm's advantage relative to any potential risk transfer counterparty in terms of experience with and knowledge of such risks.

One important benefit of thinking in terms of comparative advantage is to reinforce the message that companies are in business to *take strategic and business risks*. The recognition that there are no economical ways of transferring risks that are unique to a company's business operations can serve to underscore the potential value of reducing the firm's exposure to other, "non-core" risks.[3] Once management has decided that the firm has a comparative advantage in taking certain business risks, it should use risk management to help the firm make the most of this advantage. Which brings us to a paradox of risk

---

2. For an extended treatment of this concept, see René Stulz, "Rethinking Risk Management," *Journal of Applied Corporate Finance* Vol. 9, No. 3 (Fall 1996).
3. For a discussion of core and non-core risks, see Robert Merton, "You Have More Capital Than You Think," *Harvard Business Review*, November, 2005.

management: By reducing non-core exposures, ERM effectively enables companies to take more strategic business risk—and greater advantage of the opportunities in their core business.

The Micro Benefits of ERM

As discussed above, an increase in total risk can end up reducing value by causing companies to pass up valuable projects or otherwise disrupting the normal operations of the firm. These costs associated with total risk should be accounted for when assessing the risk-return trade-off in all major new investments. If the company takes on a project that increases the firm's total risk, the project should be sufficiently profitable to provide an adequate return on capital *after* compensating for the costs associated with the increase in risk. This risk-return trade-off must be evaluated for all corporate decisions that are expected to have a material impact on total risk.

Thus, a major challenge for a company implementing ERM is to ensure that decision-making not just by senior management, but by business managers *throughout the firm*, takes proper account of the risk-return trade-off. To make this happen, the risk evaluations of new projects must be performed, at least initially, on a decentralized basis by the project planners in the business units. A completely centralized evaluation of the risk-return trade-off of individual projects would lead to corporate gridlock. Take the extreme case of a trader. Centralized evaluation would require the CRO's approval of each of the trader's decisions with a potentially material impact on the firm's risk. But in a decentralized evaluation of the risk-return trade-off, each unit in the corporation evaluates this trade-off in its decision making. An important part of senior management's and the CRO's job is to provide the information and incentives for each unit to make these trade-offs in ways that serve the interests of the shareholders.

There are two main components of decentralizing the risk-return trade-off in a company:

a) First, managers proposing new projects should be required to evaluate all major risks in the context of the marginal impact of the projects on the firm's total risk. The company's decision-making framework should require the business managers to evaluate project returns in relation to the marginal increase in firm-wide risk to achieve the optimal amount of risk at the corporate level.

b) Second, to help ensure that managers do a good job of assessing the risk-return trade-off, the periodic performance evaluations of the business units must take account of the contributions of each of the units to the total risk of the firm. As we will see later, this can be done by assigning a level of additional "imputed" capital to the project to reflect such incremental risk—capital on which the project manager will be expected to earn an adequate

return. By so doing, the corporation not only measures its true economic performance, but also creates incentives for managers to manage the risk-return
trade-off effectively by refusing to accept risks that are not economically
attractive.

With the help of these two mechanisms that are essential to the management of firm-wide risk, a company that implements ERM can transform its
culture. Without these means, risk will be accounted for in an *ad hoc*, subjective way, or ignored. In the former case, promising projects could be rejected
when risks are overstated. In the latter case, systems that ignore risk will end
up encouraging high-risk projects, in many cases without the returns to justify
them. Perhaps even more troubling, one division could take a project that another would reject based on a different assessment of the project's risk and associated costs. With the above capital allocation and performance evaluation
system mechanisms put in place when ERM is implemented, business managers are forced to consider the impact of all material risks in their investment
and operating decisions. In short, every risk is "owned" since it affects someone's performance evaluation.

Spreading risk ownership throughout the company has become more important as the scope of risk management has expanded to include operating
and reputational risks. Ten or 20 years ago, when risk management focused
mainly on financial risks, companies could centrally measure and manage
their exposures to market rates. But operational risks typically cannot be
hedged. Some of these risks can be insured, but companies often choose to reduce their exposure to such risks by changing procedures and technologies.
The individuals who are closest to these risks are generally in the best position
to assess what steps should be taken to reduce the firm's exposure to them. So,
for example, decisions to manage operating risks are often entrusted to line
managers whose decisions are based on their knowledge of the business, and
supplemented by technical experts where appropriate.

Nationwide has developed a "factor-based" capital allocation approach for
its management accounting and performance evaluation system. Capital factors are assigned to products based on the perceived risk of such products. For
example, the risk associated with, and capital allocated to, insuring a home in
a hurricane- or earthquake-prone area.is greater than that for a home in a non-
catastrophe-exposed region.

One of the most important purposes of such a risk-based capital allocation
system is to provide business managers with more information about how
their own investment and operating decisions are likely to affect both
corporate-wide performance and the measures by which their performance
will be evaluated. When combined with a performance evaluation system in
this way, a risk-based capital allocation approach effectively forces the business
managers to consider risk in their decision-making. Nationwide's risk factors

are updated annually as part of the strategic and operational planning process, reflecting changes in risk and diversification. Decision-making authority is delegated by means of a risk limit structure that is consistent with Nationwide's risk appetite framework.

Determining the Right Amount of Risk

How should a company determine the optimal amount of total risk to bear? To answer this question, it's important to start by recognizing that the costs associated with the cash shortfalls we discussed earlier would not exist if the firm had a larger buffer stock of equity capital invested in liquid assets. But carrying excess equity also, of course, has costs. For example, a recent study concludes that, for some companies (typically larger, mature companies), the last dollar of "excess" cash is valued by the market at as little as 60 cents.[4]

By reducing risk, a company can reduce the amount of expensive equity capital needed to support its operating risks. In this sense, risk management can be viewed as a substitute for equity capital, and an important part of the job of the CRO and top management is to evaluate the trade-off between more active risk management and holding a larger buffer stock of cash and equity.

As we saw earlier, for companies without a larger buffer of excess equity, a sharp drop in cash flow and value can lead to financial distress and a further (permanent) loss of value from underinvestment. Let's define "financial distress" to be any situation where a company is likely to feel compelled to pass up positive NPV activities.

Many companies identify a level of earnings or cash flow that they want to maintain under almost all circumstances (i.e., with an agreed-upon level of statistical confidence, say 95%, over a one-year period) and then design their risk management programs to ensure the firm achieves that minimum. For example, in the case described earlier of the firm with a $250 million shortfall, management may want to explore steps that would ensure that the firm almost never loses more than, say, $100 million in a year, since that may be the point where management begins to feel pressure to cut projects. But, as the mention of statistical confidence intervals suggests, a company cannot—nor should it attempt to—*guarantee* that its cash and earnings will never fall below the level it's aiming to protect. As long as a company operates in a business that promises more than the risk-free rate, there will be some risk of falling into financial distress.

---

4. By contrast, for riskier companies with lots of growth opportunities, the same dollar can be worth as much as $1.50. See Lee Pinkowitz and Rohan Williamson, "What is the Market Value of a Dollar of Cash Holdings?" working paper, Georgetown University.

What management can accomplish through an ERM program, then, is not to minimize or eliminate, but rather to *limit*, the probability of distress to a level that management and the board agrees is likely to maximize firm value. *Minimizing* the probability of distress, which could be achieved by investing most of the firm's capital in Treasury bills, is clearly not in the interests of shareholders. Management's job is rather to *optimize* the firm's risk portfolio by trading off the probability of large shortfalls and the associated costs with the expected gains from taking or retaining risks.

Let's refer to this targeted minimal level of resources (which can be formulated in terms of cash flow, capital, or market value) as the company's financial distress "threshold." Many companies use bond ratings to define this threshold. For example, management may conclude that the firm would have to start giving up valuable projects if its rating falls to Baa. In that case, it would adopt a financial and risk management policy that aims to limit to an acceptably low level the probability that the firm's rating will fall to Baa or lower. Given a firm's current rating—and let's assume it is Aa—it is straightforward to use data supplied by the rating agencies to estimate the average probability that the firm's rating will fall to Baa or lower. A study by Moody's using data from 1920 to 2005 shows that the probability of a company with an Aa rating having its rating drop to Baa or lower within a year's time is 1.05%, on average.[5]

Whether such a probability is acceptable is for top management and the board to decide. For a company with many valuable growth opportunities, even just a 1% chance of having to forgo such investments may be too risky. By contrast, a basic manufacturing firm with few growth opportunities is likely to be better off making aggressive use of leverage, maximizing the tax benefits of debt, and returning excess funds to shareholders. For such a firm, the costs associated with financial trouble would be relatively low, at least as a percentage of total value.

For financial companies like Nationwide, however, there is another important consideration when evaluating the costs of financial distress that is specific to financial institutions: financial trouble has an adverse impact on liabilities like bank deposits and insurance contracts that constitute an important source of the value of banks and insurance companies.[6] Because such liabilities are *very* credit-sensitive, these financial institutions generally aim to maximize their value by targeting a much lower probability of distress than the typical industrial firm.

5. Moody's Default and Recovery Rates of Corporate Bond Issuers, 1920–2005, March 2006. We compute probabilities that assume that the rating is not withdrawn.
6. See Robert C. Merton, "Operation and Regulation in Financial Intermediation: A Functional Perspective," in *Operation and Regulation of Financial Markets*, ed. P. Englund (Stockholm: The Economic Council: 1993).

TABLE 15.1

Transition Matrix from Moody's

Rating From:	Rating To: Aaa	Aa	A	Baa	Ba	B	Caa-C	Default
Aaa	91.75%	7.26%	0.79%	0.17%	0.02%	0.00%	0.00%	0.00%
Aa	1.32%	90.71%	6.92%	0.75%	0.19%	0.04%	0.01%	0.06%
A	0.08%	3.02%	90.24%	5.67%	0.76%	0.12%	0.03%	0.08%
Baa	0.05%	0.33%	5.05%	87.50%	5.72%	0.86%	0.18%	0.31%
Ba	0.01%	0.09%	0.59%	6.70%	82.58%	7.83%	0.72%	1.48%
B	0.00%	0.07%	0.20%	0.80%	7.29%	80.62%	6.23%	4.78%
Caa-C	0.00%	0.03%	0.06%	0.23%	1.07%	7.69%	75.24%	15.69%

Average one-year rating transition matrix, 1920–2005, conditional upon no rating withdrawal.
Source: Moody's Default and Recovery Rates of Corporate Bond Issuers, 1920–2005, March 2006.

Let's suppose for the moment that a rating is a completely reliable and suffi-cient measure of the probability that a company will default—an assumption we will reexamine later. And let's consider a company that would have to start giving up valuable projects if its rating fell to Baa or below (i.e., Baa would serve as its financial distress threshold). Assume also that management and the board have determined that, for this kind of business, the optimal level of risk is one where the probability of encountering financial distress is 7% over a one-year period. Such an optimal level of risk would be determined by comparing the costs associated with financial distress and the benefits of having a more levered capital structure and taking on riskier projects.

To the extent that ratings are reliable proxies for financial health, compa-nies can use a rating agency "transition matrix" to estimate the amount of cap-ital necessary to support a given level of risk. The transition matrix shown in table 15.1 can be used to identify the frequency with which companies moved from one rating to another over a certain period (in this case, 1920 to 2005).[7] For any rating at the beginning of the year (listed in the left-hand column of the table), the column of numbers running down from the heading "Baa" tells us the probability that a company will end up with a Baa rating at the end of the year.

Again, let's assume management wants the probability of its rating falling to Baa or lower over the next year to average around 7%. To determine the

7. See Stulz, "Rethinking Risk Management."

probability of a downgrade to or lower than Baa for a given initial rating, we add up the probabilities of ending with a rating equal to or lower than Baa along the row that corresponds to the initial rating. The row where the probabilities of ending at Baa or lower is closest to 7% is the one corresponding to an A rating. Consequently, by targeting an A rating, management would achieve the probability of financial distress that is optimal for the firm.

In practice, however, the process of determining a target rating can involve more considerations, which makes it more complicated. For example, Nationwide analyzes and manages both its probability of default and its probability of downgrade, and it does so in separate but related frameworks. The company's optimal probability of default is anchored to its target Aa ratings and reflects the default history of Aa-rated bonds. By contrast, the probability of downgrade to Baa or below is assumed to be affected by, and is accordingly managed by limiting, risk concentrations such as those arising from natural catastrophes and equity markets.

In the example above, the company is assumed to maximize value by targeting a rating of A. As we noted earlier, equity capital provides a buffer or shock absorber that helps the firm to avoid default. For a given firm, a different probability of default corresponds to each level of equity, so that by choosing a given level of equity, management is also effectively choosing a probability of default that it believes to be optimal.

As can be seen in table 15.1, an A rating is associated with a probability of default of 0.08% over a one-year period. Thus, to achieve an A rating, the company in our example must have the level of (equity) capital that makes its probability of default equal to 0.08%. If we make the assumption that the value of a company's equity falls to a level not materially different from zero in the event of default, we can use the probability of default to "back out" the amount of equity the firm needs to support its current level of risk.

Although the probability of default is in fact a complicated function of a number of firm characteristics, not just the amount of equity, the analytical process that leads from the probability of default to the required amount of capital is straightforward. To see this, suppose that the company becomes bankrupt if the firm's value at the end of the fiscal year falls below a default threshold level, which is a function of the composition and amount of the firm's debt.[8] Given this assumption, the firm needs the amount of equity capital that will make the probability of its value falling below the default threshold level equal to 0.08% (or alternatively, the amount that will ensure that its

---

8. If all debt were due at the end of the year, the default threshold level would be the principal amount of debt outstanding plus interest due. However, if debt matures later, firm value could fall below the principal amount of debt outstanding without triggering a default. So, the default threshold level is lower than the principal amount of debt outstanding when the firm has long-term debt.

value will not fall below the default threshold level with a probability of 99.92%).

A company can also assess its costs of financial distress by using criteria other than ratings and ratings thresholds. For instance, in addition to a rating downgrade, Nationwide Insurance identifies a number of other scenarios that it views as imposing large costs on the company. Chief among them are high levels of volatility in earnings and capital that, while not alone sufficient to cause a rating downgrade, could contribute to an increase in overall risk and hence the required level of capital. For each of these critical variables and scenarios, Nationwide sets target probability levels and acceptable tolerances that enable the firm to limit its volatility risk within those targeted levels.

When thinking about acceptable levels of volatility, and the equity capital needed to support them, many financial companies use a risk measure called Value-at-risk, or VaR for short. VaR is the amount of the loss that is expected, with some pre-specified probability level, to be reached or exceeded during a defined time period. For instance, if a portfolio of securities has a 1-year VaR at the 5% probability level of $20 million, there is a 5% chance the portfolio will have a loss that exceeds $20 million in the next year. VaR can also be computed for an entire company by assessing the distribution of firm value. When the determination of the buffer stock of equity proceeds along the lines described so far, the company in our example must have an amount of equity equal to its firm-wide 1-year VaR determined at a probability level of 0.08%.

For some companies, VaR conveys the same information as the volatility of its stock price or market value, which would allow the firm using VaR to focus on these more direct measures of volatility of its value.[9] But for those companies for which the distribution of firm value changes is not "normal" or symmetric, the analysis of risk provided by VaR can be quite different from the information provided by volatility—and in such cases, VaR must be estimated directly.

But whether management uses VaR or volatility, given a targeted probability of default or financial distress, the company faces a trade-off, as illustrated in figure 15.1, between its level of VaR or volatility and the size of its buffer stock of equity capital. As VaR or volatility increase, the firm requires more capital to achieve the same probability of default. And as can also be seen in the upward shift from line x to line y in figure 15.1, this trade-off becomes steeper if management chooses to reduce the targeted probability of default.

Now suppose that based on its estimate of volatility, management concludes that the firm needs $5 billion of equity capital to achieve its target probability

9. In particular, VaR is a multiple of volatility when the variable for which VaR is estimated has a normal distribution.

FIGURE 15.1

Required Equity Capital to Achieve a Target Probability of Default as Function of Firm Volatility or VaR

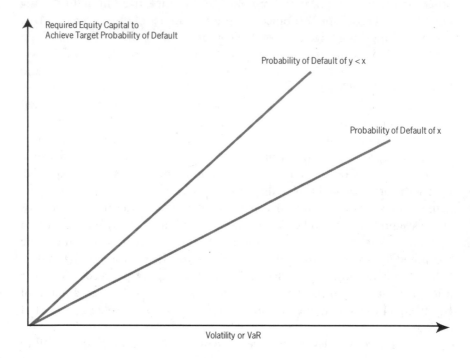

of default. As noted earlier, the company can reduce its required level of equity by using risk management to reduce the probability of default, which would make sense if that option were deemed less costly than holding the $5 billion of equity. In making this trade-off between managing risk and holding more equity, the company should aim to position itself "at the margin" where it is indifferent between decreasing risk and increasing capital. Management can satisfy itself that it has achieved this position if, after having decided on a certain combination of risk management and capital, it can show that, for example, spending another $10 million to decrease risk by 1% will save the firm roughly $10 million in equity capital costs. In this event, it has achieved the optimal amount of risk.

Using this approach, the company can evaluate the marginal impact of a project on both its risk of default and its risk of financial distress. As total risk increases, the firm requires more capital to support that risk. Moreover, the cost of the additional capital provides a useful measure of the cost of the project's contribution to the firm's total risk. The project is worth undertaking only if its NPV is large enough to cover that additional cost. Similarly, when evaluating the performance of a unit within the firm, the unit contributes to shareholder wealth only insofar as its economic value-added exceeds the cost of its contribution to the risk of the firm. In this way, then, the capital required to support the contribution of an activity to the total risk of the firm becomes itself a measure of risk—a measure that, because of its simplicity, can easily be added up across different activities or risks.

The conceptual framework of ERM can thus be summarized as follows:

1. Management begins by determining the firm's risk appetite, a key part of which is choosing the probability of financial distress that is expected to maximize firm value. When credit ratings are used as the primary indicator of financial risk, the firm determines an optimal or target rating based on its risk appetite and the cost of reducing its probability of financial distress.

2. Given the firm's target rating, management estimates the amount of capital it requires to support the risk of its operations. In so doing, management should consider the probability of default.

3. Management determines the optimal combination of capital and risk that is expected to yield its target rating. For a given amount of capital, management can alter its risk through hedging and project selection. Alternatively, for a given amount of total risk, the company can increase its capital to achieve its target rating. At the margin, the firm should be indifferent between changing its capital and changing its risk.

4. Top management decentralizes the risk-capital trade-off with the help of a capital allocation and performance evaluation system that motivates managers throughout the organization to make investment and operating decisions that optimize this trade-off.

Implementing ERM

But if ERM is conceptually straightforward, its implementation is challenging. For a company to succeed in implementing ERM, it is critical that people throughout the organization understand how it can create value. Managers must understand that it is not an academic exercise but a critical tool for executing the firm's strategy. Thus ERM must be "sold to" and "bought into" by all levels of the organization. For the whole organization to get behind it, considerable thought must be devoted to the design of managerial performance evaluation and incentives. We now consider the main challenges involved in making ERM work.

Inventory of Risks

The first step in operationalizing ERM is to identify the risks to which the company is exposed. A common approach is to identify the types of risks that will be measured. In the early days of corporate risk management, financial institutions focused mainly on market and credit risks. Eventually operational risk was added. As a result, a common practice for banks is to classify all risks into one of three categories: market, credit, and operational. But for such an approach to capture all the risks the firm is exposed to, operational risk has to be a catch-all category that includes all risks that are not market and credit risks.[10]

Many companies have gone beyond measuring market, credit, and operational risks. In recent years, some firms have also attempted to measure liquidity, reputational, and strategic risks. Further, the three-party typology used in banking often does not correspond well to the risks faced in other industries. For example, because insurance companies have risks on their asset side—that is, the risks associated with their investment portfolio—as well as their liability side, such companies generally use a different typology. Nationwide Insurance regularly measures and monitors its asset, liability, operating, liquidity, and strategic risks—and it considers reputational risks in the context of each of these risks and of its overall business. (Market and credit risks are both treated as parts of asset risks.)

Having identified all of the company's major risks, management must then find a consistent way to measure the firm's exposure to these risks—a common approach that can be used to identify and quantify all of the firm's significant exposures. Without such a method, exposure to the same risk could have different effects on the performance evaluation and decision-making of different business units and activities. The resulting possibility that identically risky activities would be allocated different amounts of capital would almost certainly create tension within the firm. Furthermore, risk would gradually migrate within the organization to those parts of the firm where it received the lowest risk rating and smallest capital allocation.

For an inventory of risks to be useful, the information possessed by people within the organization must be collected, made comparable, and continuously updated. Organizations that have grown through acquisitions or without centralized information technology departments typically face the problem of

---

10. For banks, the definition of operational risk that prevails in the Basle II accord is much narrower; for instance, it ignores the reputational risks that are today a major concern of many financial institutions. As a result, for banks, there will be a tension between the measurement of operational risk for regulatory purposes and from the perspective of ERM.

incompatible computer systems. Companies must be able to aggregate common risks across all of their businesses to analyze and manage those risks effectively.

Nationwide employs both a top-down and a bottom-up process of risk identification. From a top-down perspective, the company's ERM leadership and corporate level risk committee have identified all risks that are large enough in aggregate to threaten the firm with financial distress in an adverse environment. The bottom-up process involves individual business units and functional areas conducting risk-control self-assessments designed to identify all material local-level risks. The goal is to identify all important risks, quantify them using a consistent approach, and then aggregate individual risk exposures across the entire organization to produce a firm-wide risk profile that takes account of correlations among risk. For example, Nationwide analyzes and establishes aggregate limits for the equity risk stemming from three main sources: (1) the stock holdings in its property and casualty insurance investment portfolio; (2) the fee levels that are tied to equity values in the variable annuity and insurance contracts of its life insurance business; and (3) the asset management fees that are tied to equity values in its investment management business.

Corporate failures to conduct thorough "inventories" of their risks on a regular basis have been responsible for a striking number of major corporate disasters over the last 20 years. Business units often resist such monitoring efforts because they are time-consuming and distract from other activities. A well-known example of such resistance that ultimately created massive problems for the old UBS took place when the firm attempted to include its equity derivatives desk into its risk measurement system. Because the equity derivatives desk used a different computer system, such an undertaking would have required major changes in the way the desk did its business. But since the desk was highly profitable, it was allowed to stay outside the system. Eventually, the operation incurred massive losses that fundamentally weakened the bank and led it to seek a merger.[11]

Economic Value versus Accounting Performance

Although credit ratings are a useful device for helping a company think about its risk appetite, management should also recognize the limitations of ratings as a guide to a value-maximizing risk management and capital structure policy. Because of the extent of their reliance on "accounting" ratios as well as analysts' subjective judgment, credit ratings are often not the most reliable estimates of a firm's probability of default. For example, a company might feel confident that the underlying economics of its risk management and capital

11. See Dirk Schütz, La Chute de l'UBS, Bilan, 1998.

structure give it a probability of default that warrants an A rating, but find itself assigned a Baa rating—perhaps because of a mechanical application of misleading accounting-based criteria—by the agencies. In such cases, management should rely on its own economics-based analysis, while making every effort to share its thinking with the agencies.

But having said this, if maintaining a certain rating is deemed to be critical to the success of the organization, then setting capital at a level that achieves the probability of default of the targeted rating may not be enough. Management may also have to target some accounting-based ratios that are important determinants of ratings as well.

This question of economic- or value-based management versus accounting-based decision-making raises a fundamental question of risk management: What is the shortfall that management should be concerned about? Is it a shortfall in cash flow or in earnings? Is it a drop in a company's GAAP net worth or a market-based measure of firm value?

If the company is managing its probability of default, it should obviously focus on the measure that is most directly linked to that outcome. For example, an unexpected drop in this year's cash flow may not be a problem for a company if its future cash flows are clearly unaffected. If the firm finds it easy to borrow against its future cash flows or tangible assets, a shortfall in this year's cash flow is unlikely to lead the firm to default. But those companies that cannot borrow against future cash flows, perhaps because they are too speculative and have few tangible assets, may be affected much more adversely. In such cases, the shortfall in cash flow, by triggering financing constraints, could push the firm into financial distress. It is these kinds of companies that are likely to focus their risk management efforts on measures of cash-flow volatility.

But if a company is more likely to experience financial distress because the *present value* of future cash flows is low than because of a drop in cash flow, management must model the risk of changes in firm value, which reflects the present value of expected future cash flows, rather than the risk of changes in cash flows. There are a number of top-down approaches that provide estimates of total risk based on industry benchmarks that are cheap and easy to implement. Unfortunately, such approaches are not useful for managing risk within a company because they do not make it possible to relate corporate actions to firm-wide risk. For instance, management could obtain an estimate of the volatility of firm value or cash flows by looking at the distribution of the value or cash flows of comparable companies. But such an approach would provide management with little understanding of how specific risk management policies, including changes in capital structure, would affect this estimate.

Thus, a management intent on implementing ERM must estimate the expected distribution of changes in firm value from the bottom up. When, as is typical, a company's value is best estimated as the present value of its expected future cash flows, management should "build" its estimates of firm value by modeling the distribution of future cash flows. As a fundamental part of its ERM program, Nationwide has developed stochastic models that generate multi-year cash flow distributions for its main businesses.

The Accounting Problem. By focusing on cash flows, then, a company focuses on its economic value. But while helping the firm achieve its target probability of default, such an approach could also result in more volatile accounting earnings. For example, under the current accounting treatment of derivatives, if a company uses derivatives to hedge an economic exposure but fails to qualify for hedge accounting, the derivatives hedge can reduce the volatility of firm value while at the same time increasing the volatility of accounting earnings. And thus a company that implements ERM could end up with higher earnings volatility than a comparable firm that does not.

While companies should pursue economic outcomes whenever possible, there will clearly be situations where they need to limit the volatility of reported accounting earnings. Companies with debt covenants that specify minimal levels of earnings and net worth are one example. Another is provided by companies that face regulatory requirements to maintain minimal levels of "statutory" capital, which is typically defined in standard accounting terms. Yet another are companies whose ability to attract customers depends in part on credit ratings, which in turn can be affected by earnings volatility. Nationwide Insurance, for example, operates in many businesses that are highly sensitive to credit ratings. And to the extent its ratings could be affected by high (or unexplained) levels of accounting volatility, management's decision-making must clearly take such volatility into account. In such cases, the challenge of an ERM system is to meet the lenders' and regulators' accounting requirements while still attempting to manage risk from the perspective of economic value. Nationwide's approach is to make economically based decisions to maximize value while treating its targeted "Aa" ratings vulnerability as a "constraint." A significant amount of effort is devoted to minimizing the effect of this constraint through disclosure and communication with the rating agencies.

Aggregating Risks

A firm that uses the three-part typology of market, credit, and operational risk mentioned earlier generally begins by measuring each of these risks individually. If the firm uses VaR, it will have three separate VaR measures, one each for

FIGURE 15.2

Typical Market, Credit and Operational Risk Distributions

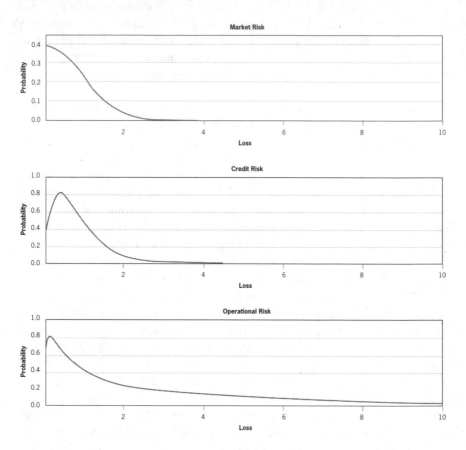

market risk, for credit risk, and for operational risk. These three VaRs are then used to produce a firm-wide VaR.

As shown in figure 15.2, these three types of risks have dramatically different distributions.[12] Market risk behaves very much like the returns on a portfolio of securities, which have a "normal" or symmetric distribution. In contrast, both credit and operational risk have asymmetric distributions. With credit risk, either a creditor pays in full what is owed or it does not. In general, most creditors pay in full, but some do not—and when a creditor defaults, the loss can be large. With operational risk, there tends to be large

---

12. This is also the case when risks are divided into asset risks, operational risks, and liability risks.

numbers of small losses, so that small operational losses are almost predictable. There is also, however, some chance of large losses, so that the distribution of operational losses has a "long tail." Statisticians describe distributions as having "fat tails" when the probability of extreme losses is higher than can be described by the normal distribution. While many use the normal distribution to estimate the VaR of market risk, such an approach is not appropriate for credit and operational risks because these risks have fat tails.

When aggregating the risks, one must also estimate their correlations. The probability of experiencing simultaneously highly adverse market, credit, and operational outcomes is typically very low. This means that there is diversification across risk categories, and that the firm-wide VaR is thus less than the sum of the market risk, credit risk, and operational risk VaRs. How much less depends on the correlation between these risks. The estimation of the correlations between certain types of risks is at present more art than science. For this reason, many companies choose to use averages of correlations used by other firms in their industry rather than relying on their own estimates.[13] But regardless of whether they use their own or other firms' correlation measures, companies should keep in mind the tendency for correlations to increase in highly stressed environments.

One important issue in estimating correlations across types of risks is the importance of recognizing that such correlations depend to some extent on the actions of the company. For example, the total risk of an insurance company depends on the correlation between its asset risk and its liability risk. By changing its asset allocations, the company can modify the correlation between its asset risk and its liability risk. As a consequence, an insurance company's asset portfolio allocations can be an essential part of its risk management effort. For example, Nationwide Insurance uses a sophisticated asset/liability model to create an efficient frontier of investment portfolios. The actual target portfolio selected takes into consideration the firm's tolerance for interest rate, equity market, and other risks as well as the opportunity for expected economic value creation.

Measuring Risks

Some companies focus mostly on tail risk—the low-probability, large-loss outcomes. As a result, when they measure the risk of changes in the present value of cash flows, they use a measure like VaR at a probability level that corresponds to a default threshold. Some of these companies also complement their

---

13. For data on correlations used in practice for financial institutions, see Andrew Kuritzkes, Til Schuermann, and Scott M. Weiner, "Risk Measurement, Risk Management and Capital Adequacy in Financial Conglomerates," *Brookings-Wharton Papers on Financial Services,* (2003): 141–93.

VaR estimates with stress tests in which they investigate the impact on firm value of rare events (such as the crisis period of August and September 1998 that followed Russia's default on some of its debt).

Though VaR is widely used, it is important to understand its limitations and to complement its use with other risk measures. Perhaps the main problem is that while VaR measures the loss that is expected to be exceeded with a specified probability, it says nothing about the expected size of the loss in the event that VaR is exceeded. Some have argued that companies should instead focus on the expected loss if VaR is exceeded. But focusing on this risk measure, which is often called *conditional VaR*, instead of focusing on VaR has little economic justification in the context of firm-wide risk management. Setting the company's capital at a level equal to the conditional VaR would provide the firm with a lower probability of default than the targeted level, leading to an excessively conservative capital structure.

But a more important reason for companies to look beyond a VaR measure estimated at the probability level corresponding to a default threshold is that ERM adds value by optimizing the probability and expected costs of *financial distress*. It is therefore critical for companies to make sure that the equity capital set based on a VaR estimate leads to the targeted optimal probability of financial distress. Such an effort requires a broader understanding of the distribution of firm value than is provided by a VaR estimate for a given probability of default. Further, since different levels of financial distress have different costs, a company can take these different costs into account and focus on the probability distribution of different levels of financial distress.

To compound the problem, when a company has a high rating target, the estimation of VaR becomes more of an art as the estimated VaR corresponds to an extremely low probability level. To see this, consider a company that has determined that an A rating is optimal. Since the probability of default for an A-rated company is only 0.08% over a 1-year period, to estimate its optimal amount of capital the firm must therefore estimate the loss in value that is exceeded with a probability of 0.08%. The problem, however, is that few A-rated companies have any experience of losses that come anywhere near that level. And without any historical experience of such losses, it is difficult for management to estimate the VaR at that probability level and then evaluate the result.

For most investment grade companies, then, it is much easier to evaluate the distribution of changes in firm value over the range of changes that encompasses not default, but just a ratings downgrade. For example, using the Moody's transition matrix data (table 15.1), one can say with some confidence that an A-rated firm has a 5.67% chance on average of being downgraded to a Baa rating over a 1-year period; in other words, such an event is expected to happen in more than 1 year out of 20. (In contrast, default is expected to happen in approximately 1 year out of 1,000.) Because of the abundance of data on downgrades as opposed to defaults for A-rated companies, the distribution of changes in firm value that corresponds to a downgrade to Baa can be estimated more precisely. Over that much narrower range of possible outcomes, the problems created by "asymmetries" in the distribution of firm value changes and the so-called "fat-tail" problems (where extreme negative outcomes are more likely than predicted by common statistical distributions) are not likely to be as severe. In such cases, management may have greater confidence in its estimates of the distribution of value changes corresponding to a downgrade rather than a default and will be justified in focusing on managing the probability of a downgrade.

As discussed previously, it is also important to understand and take account of risk correlations when analyzing and managing default and distress probabilities. Nationwide Insurance incorporates in its economic capital model a correlation matrix that reflects sensitivity-tested stress correlations. It is also now in the process of exploring event-driven correlation analysis for scenarios that include terrorist attacks, mega hurricanes, and pandemics.

Regulatory versus Economic Capital

The amount of equity capital required for the company to achieve its optimal rating may bear little relation to the amount of capital regulators would require it to hold. A firm that practices ERM may therefore have an amount of capital that substantially exceeds its regulatory requirements because it maximizes shareholder wealth by doing so. In this case, the regulatory requirements are not binding and would not affect the firm's decisions.

The company would be in a more difficult situation if its required regulatory capital exceeded the amount of capital it should hold to maximize shareholder wealth. Nationwide Insurance refers to this excess as "stranded capital." To the extent that economic and regulatory capital are subject to different drivers, the difference between the two can be arbitraged to some degree to minimize the level of stranded capital. Nationwide allocates any residual stranded capital to its businesses and products. If all the potential competitors of the firm face the same onerous regulatory capital requirements, the capital the firm has to hold that is not justified on economic grounds is simply a regulatory tax. If some potential competitors could provide the firm's products without being subjected to the same regulatory capital, these less regulated competitors could offer the products at a lower price and the firm would risk losing business to them. In this case, the firm would have to factor in the cost of regulatory capital of its various activities and would want to grow its portfolio of activities in a way that requires less regulatory capital.

Regulatory capital is generally defined in terms of regulatory accounting. For purposes of an ERM system, companies focus on generally accepted accounting principles (GAAP) and economic capital. An exclusive focus on accounting capital is mistaken when accounting capital does not accurately reflect the buffer stock of equity available to the firm. The firm may have valuable assets that, although not marked to market on its books, could be sold or borrowed against. In such cases, the firm's book equity capital understates the buffer stock available to it that could be used to avoid default.

Thus, in assessing the level of a company's buffer of capital, this suggests that the amount of its GAAP equity capital is only part of the story. The composition and liquidity of the assets matters as well. If the firm incurs a large loss and has no liquid assets it can use to "finance" it, the fact that it has a large buffer stock of book equity will not be very helpful. For this reason, many companies now do separate evaluations of their liquidity and the amount of equity capital they require. As the practice of ERM evolves, we would expect such companies to pay more attention to the relation between the optimal amount of equity and the liquidity of their assets.

Using Economic Capital to Make Decisions

As we saw earlier, if companies could simply stockpile equity capital at no cost, there would be no deadweight costs associated with adverse outcomes. Management could use its liquid assets to finance the losses, and the bad outcome would have no effect on the firm's investment policy. But in the real world, there are significant costs associated with carrying too much equity. If the market perceives that a company has more equity than it needs to support the risk of the business, it will reduce the firm's value to reflect management's failure to earn the cost of capital on that excess capital.

When a company undertakes a new risky activity, the probability that it will experience financial distress increases, thus raising the expected costs of financial distress. One way to avoid these additional costs is by raising enough additional capital so that taking on the new risky activity has no effect on the probability of financial distress. Consequently, the most straightforward way to estimate the cost of the impact of a new risky activity on the firm's total risk is to evaluate how much incremental capital would be necessary to ensure that the new risky activity has no impact on the firm's probability of financial distress.

To illustrate, suppose that before the company takes on the new activity, the VaR estimate used to set the firm's capital is $5 billion. Now, with the new activity, this VaR estimate increases to $5.1 billion. Thus, for the firm to have the same probability of financial distress as it had before it undertook the new risky activity, it would need to raise capital of $100 million. Moreover, this capital would have to be invested in such a way that the investment does not increase the risk of the firm, since otherwise the VaR of the firm would further increase. If the risky new activity is expected to last one year, and the cost to the firm of having this additional $100 million available for 1 year is estimated to be $8 million, then the economic value added of the new activity should be reduced by $8 million. If the firm ignores this cost, it effectively subsidizes the new risky activity. To the extent that riskier activities have higher expected payoffs before taking into account their contribution to the firm's probability of financial distress, a firm that ignores the impact of project risk on firm-wide risk ends up favoring riskier projects over less risky ones.

Though the example just discussed is straightforward, the implementation of this idea in practice faces several difficulties. A company is a collection of risky projects. At any time, a project's contribution to the firm's total risk depends on the risk of the other project and their correlations. When business units are asked to make decisions that take into account the contribution of a project to firm-wide risk, they must have enough information when making the decision to know how to evaluate that contribution. They cannot be told that the contribution will depend on everything else that is going to happen within the firm over the next year, and then have a risk charge assigned to their unit *after the fact*.

Many companies sidestep this issue and ignore correlations altogether when they set capital. In that case, the capital required to support a project would be set so that the project receives no benefit from diversification, and the contribution of the project to firm-wide risk would then be the VaR of the project itself. To account for diversification benefits under this system, the firm would reduce the cost of equity. But when evaluating the performance of a business unit, the VaR of the business unit would be used to assess the contribution of the unit to the firm's risk and the units would effectively get no credit for diversification benefits.

When decentralizing the risk-return trade-off, the company has to enable the managers of its business units to determine the capital that has to be allocated to a project to keep the risk of the firm constant with the relatively simple information that is readily available to them. Nationwide's factor-based capital allocation and performance evaluation system is an example of such an approach. The company allocates diversification benefits within major business units, but not across them. This means that a project whose returns have a low correlation with the other activities within its unit will receive "credit" for such diversification benefits in the form of a lower capital allocation for the unit. But investments of a business unit that have low correlations with activities of other major business units are not credited with firm-wide diversification benefits. The rationale for this policy is that it enables Nationwide's top management to take account of the effects of new investments on risk at the corporate level while at the same time holding the business managers who make those decisions accountable for earning returns consistent with their competitive operating environment.

The Governance of ERM

How does a company know that its ERM is succeeding? While one outcome of effective ERM should be a better estimate of expected value and better understanding of unexpected losses, ERM does not eliminate risk. Thus, extreme negative outcomes are still a possibility, and the effectiveness of ERM cannot be judged on whether such outcomes materialize. The role of ERM is to limit the probability of such outcomes to an agreed-upon, value-maximizing, level. But what if the probability of default is set at one in 1,000 years? Quite apart from whether this is indeed the value-maximizing choice, such a low probability means that there will be no obvious way to judge whether the CRO succeeded in managing risk so as to give the firm its target probability of default.

To evaluate the job of a CRO, the board and the CEO must attempt to determine how well the company's risk is understood and managed. A company where risk is well understood and well managed is one that can command the resources required to invest in the valuable projects available to it because it is trusted by investors. In such cases, investors will be able to distinguish bad outcomes that are the result of bad luck rather than bad management, and that should give them confidence to keep investing in the firm.

Conclusion

In this article, we have discussed how enterprise risk management creates value for shareholders and examined the practical issues that arise in the implementation of enterprise risk management. Although the key principles that underlie the theory of ERM are well-established, it should be clear from this article that additional research is needed to help with the implementation of ERM. In particular, while much attention has been paid to measures of tail risk like VaR, it has become clear from attempts to implement ERM that a more complete understanding of the distribution of firm value is required. Though correlations between different types of risks are essential in measuring firm-wide risk, existing research provides little help in how to estimate these correlations. Companies also find that some of their most troubling risks—notably, reputational and strategic risks—are the most difficult to quantify. At this point, there is little research that helps practitioners in assessing these risks, but much to gain from having a better understanding of these risks even if they cannot be quantified reliably.

In sum, there has been considerable progress in the implementation of ERM, with the promise of major benefits for corporate shareholders. And, as this implementation improves with the help of academic research, these benefits can only be expected to grow.

BRIAN W. NOCCO is the Chief Risk Officer of Nationwide Insurance.

RENÉ M. STULZ is the Reese Chair of Banking and Monetary Economics at Ohio State University's Fisher School of Business and a research fellow at the NBER and at the European Corporate Governance Institute. He is also a member of the executive committee of the Global Association of Risk Professionals (GARP).

CHAPTER 16

The Rise and Evolution of the Chief Risk Officer

Enterprise Risk Management at Hydro One

TOM AABO, JOHN R. S. FRASER, AND BETTY J. SIMKINS

危機 THE CHINESE SYMBOLS for risk shown at left capture a key aspect of enterprise risk management. The first symbol represents "danger" and the second "opportunity." Taken together, they suggest that risk is a strategic combination of vulnerability and opportunity. Viewed in this light, enterprise risk management represents a tool for managing risk in a way that enables the corporation to take advantage of value-enhancing opportunities. A missed strategic opportunity can result in a greater loss of (potential) value than an unfortunate incident or adverse change in prices or markets.

As in the past, many organizations continue to address risk in "silos," with the management of insurance, foreign exchange risk, operational risk, credit risk, and commodity risk each conducted as narrowly focused and fragmented activities. Under the new enterprise risk management (ERM) approach, all would function as parts of an integrated, strategic, and enterprise-wide system.[1] And while risk management is coordinated with senior-level oversight, employees at all levels of the organization are encouraged to view risk management as an integral and ongoing part of their jobs.

While there are theoretical arguments for corporate risk management,[2] the main drivers for the implementation of ERM systems have been studies such as

This chapter was previously published as an article in *Journal of Applied Corporate Finance* Vol. 17, No. 3 (2005): 62–75.

1. We view the terms "integrated," "strategic," and "enterprise-wide" as interchangeable in what we call enterprise risk management.
2. In the hypothetical Modigliani and Miller world of corporate finance, risk management does not add value. However, in the non-fictionless environment of the real world, risk management by the firm can create value in one or more of the following ways that investors cannot duplicate for themselves: (1) facilitate the risk management efforts of the firm's equity holders; (2) decrease financial distress costs; (3) lower the risk faced by important non-diversified investors (such as managers and employees); (4) reduce taxes; (5) reduce the firm's capital costs through better performance evaluation and reduced monitoring costs; and (6) provide internal funding for

the Joint Australian/New Zealand Standard for Risk Management, Committee of Sponsoring Organizations of the Treadway Commission (COSO) in the United States (in response to the control problems in the S&L industry), the Group of Thirty Report in the United States (following derivatives disasters in the early 1990s), CoCo (the Criteria of Control model developed by the Canadian Institute of Chartered Accountants), the Toronto Stock Exchange Dey Report in Canada following major bankruptcies, and the Cadbury report in the United Kingdom.[3] In addition, large pension funds have become more vocal about the need for improved corporate governance, including risk management, and have stated their willingness to pay premiums for stocks of firms with strong independent board governance.[4] These studies point out that boards of directors need to have a thorough understanding of the key risks in the organization and what is being done to manage such risks.

What's more, security rating agencies such as Moody's and Standard and Poor's have recently begun to take account of ERM systems in their ratings methodology. As reported in a recent study by Moody's:

> Increasing numbers of companies are undertaking enterprise-level approaches to risk—a more encompassing and systematic review of potential risks and their mitigation than most companies have undertaken in the past. Business units are tasked with identifying risks and, where possible, quantifying and determining how to mitigate them. These assessments typically are rolled up to a corporate level, sometimes

investment projects and facilitate capital planning. Refer to Lisa Meulbroek, "A Senior Manager's Guide to Integrated Risk Management," *Journal of Applied Corporate Finance* Vol. 14, No. 4 (Winter 2002) for more information on these benefits. Another view of how risk management can maximize firm value is that risk management should eliminate costly "lower-tail outcomes," while preserving as much of the upside as possible; see R. Stulz, "Rethinking Risk Management," *Journal of Applied Corporate Finance* Vol. 9, No. 3 (Fall 1996). Corporate risk management should include choosing the optimal mixture of securities and risk management products and solutions to give the company access to capital at the lowest possible cost; see Christopher Culp, "The Revolution in Corporate Risk Management: A Decade of Innovations in Process and Products," *Journal of Applied Corporate Finance* Vol. 14, No. 4 (Winter 2002).

3. The Joint Australian/New Zealand Standard for Risk Management (AS/NZS 4360:1999), first edition published in 1995, provides the first articulation of practical enterprise risk management. This guide covers the establishment and implementation of the risk management process involving the identification, analysis, evaluation, treatment, and ongoing monitoring of risks.

   Committee of Sponsoring Organizations of the Treadway Commission (COSO) (September 1992); Group of Thirty, *Derivatives: Practices and Principles* (Washington, DC: 1993); "Where Were the Directors?" *Guidelines for Improved Corporate Governance in Canada*, Report of the Toronto Stock Exchange Committee on Corporate Governance in Canada (December 1994); Criteria of Control Board of the Canadian Institute of Chartered Accountants (CoCo); and Committee on the Financial Aspects of Corporate Governance (Cadbury Committee, Final Report and Code of Best Practices, issued December 1, 2002).

4. In McKinsey & Company, "Corporate Boards: New Strategies for Adding Value at the Top" (a study of 50 money managers) *Institutional Investor* (1996).

with direct input from the board or audit committee. These assessments have often been relatively broad, focusing on reputation, litigation, product development, and health and safety risks, rather than focusing solely on financial risks. Where we have seen these assessments implemented we have commented favorably, particularly when the board or the audit committee is actively involved.[5]

Given the overwhelming incentives and pressures to employ an enterprise-wide approach to risk management, we are surprised that more firms are not doing so. One deterrent is the scarcity of case studies describing successful implementations of ERM. A recent study by the Association of Financial Professionals noted that while most senior financial professionals see their activities evolving into a more strategic role, most also feel that more education and training are needed to meet these future challenges.[6] The Joint Australian/New Zealand Standard for Risk Management mentioned above provides the first practical prescription for implementation of ERM using generic examples. While some articles and reports provide examples and insights into the potential benefits of ERM, most lack a useful framework and sufficient practical detail to guide other firms.[7] One case study published in this journal in 2002 by Scott Harrington, Greg Niehaus, and Kenneth Risko describes how United Grain Growers combined protection against financial (such as currency and interest rate) risk and conventional insurance risk using an integrated risk management policy provided by Swiss Re.[8] However, there is a crucial need for case studies that help firms to better understand the totality of risks faced—that is, a more holistic view of ERM—and not just those that are easier to quantify.[9]

5. Refer to *Moody's Findings on Corporate Governance in the United States and Canada: August 2003–September 2004* (New York: Moody's Investors Service, October 2004).
6. See the Association for Financial Professionals, "The Evolving Role of Treasury: Report of Survey Results" (November 2003).
7. See, for example, "University of Georgia Roundtable on Enterprise-Wide Risk Management," *Journal of Applied Corporate Finance* Vol. 15, No. 4 (Fall 2003); "Strategic Risk Management: New Disciplines, New Opportunities," CFO Publishing Corporation (2002); Marie Hollein, "Measuring Risk: A Strategic Review and Step-by-Step Approach," *AFP Exchange* Vol. 23, No. 6 (Nov/Dec 2003); and James C. Lam and Brian M. Kawamoto, "Emergence of the Chief Risk Officer," *Risk Management* (September 1997); and similar articles in *CFO Magazine* (http://www.cfo.com).
8. See S. Harrington, G. Niehaus, and K. Risko, "Enterprise Risk Management: The Case of United Grain Growers," *Journal of Applied Corporate Finance* Vol. 14, No. 4 (Winter 2002); and Chapter 6 of T.L. Barton, W.G. Shenkir, and P.L. Walker, *Making Enterprise Risk Management Pay Off* (Financial Executives Research Foundation, Inc., 2002).
9. As reported in a recent survey, companies indicated that quantifiable risks are still absorbing too much of their attention and that they need to better understand the totality of the risks their firm faces. See "Uncertainty Tamed? The Evolution of Risk Management in the Financial Services Industry," a joint project by PricewaterhouseCoopers and the Economist Intelligence Unit (2004).

While there is no "one-size-fits-all" approach to ERM, companies can benefit by following the best practices of successful firms. The purpose of this case study is to fill this gap in the literature by providing the process by which one firm, Hydro One., Inc. has successfully implemented ERM. This firm is considered by many to be at the forefront of ERM, especially in the comprehensive management of risks faced. Risk managers from the World Bank, the Auditor General of Canada, Fluor Corporation, Toronto General Hospital/Universal Health Network, and other firms from various economic sectors have visited Hydro One in order to learn from its experiences.

This case study examines the implementation of ERM at Hydro One by describing the process the firm followed, beginning with the creation of the Chief Risk Officer position (the rise of the CRO). We describe the steps of implementation, which started with a pilot study involving workshops conducted with one of the subsidiaries. The purpose of the pilot study was to determine if ERM should be deployed throughout the firm. We next analyze the ERM process and describe various tools and techniques such as the "Delphi Method," risk trends, risk maps, risk tolerances, risk profiles, and risk ranking as it relates to the capital expenditure process. Finally, we note that ERM has become such an integral part of the workplace that the corporate Chief Risk Officer is now becoming a low-maintenance position (the evolution of the CRO) within the company.

Hydro One

Hydro One, Inc. is the largest electricity delivery company in Ontario, Canada, and one of the ten largest such companies in North America. Its predecessor, Ontario Hydro, was founded nearly a century ago, principally to build transmission lines to supply municipal utilities with power generated at Niagara Falls. Hydro One came into being in 1999 after legislation divided Ontario Hydro's delivery and generation functions into two separate companies. Hydro One today consists of three businesses—transmission, distribution, and telecom. Its main business (contributing 99% of revenue) is the transportation of electricity through the high-voltage provincial grid and low-voltage distribution system to municipal utilities, large industrial customers, and 1.2 million end-use customers.

Hydro One has total revenues of Canadian dollars (CAD) 4.1 billion, total assets of CAD 11.3 billion, and approximately 4,000 employees. Total equity is CAD 4.3 billion, or 38% of total assets, and all the shares are owned by the Ontario government. In 2001, the Ontario government announced its intention to proceed with an initial public offering (IPO). However, special interest groups successfully challenged the IPO in the Supreme Court of Ontario, and the prospectus was withdrawn. Long-term financing for Hydro One is provided by access to the debt markets, including a medium-term note program. Short-term liquidity is provided through a commercial paper program. The company's long-term debt is rated A2 by Moody's and A by Standard and Poor's, and its commercial paper is rated Prime-1 and A-2.

Getting Started with ERM

Enterprise risk management was established at Hydro One in 1999. As part of the firm's spin-off from the previous Ontario Hydro, the management and board of Hydro One set high goals for being a best-practices organization with superior corporate governance and business conduct. Hydro One wanted to look at risks and opportunities in an integrated way that would lead to a better overall allocation of corporate resources. At the same time, the scheduled de-regulation of the electricity markets posed a new external challenge that had to be addressed. Finally, the increased scrutiny on corporate governance called for a comprehensive risk management program.

Corporate Risk Management Group

At first, the attempts to implement ERM were led by external consultants, but no lasting benefits or transfer of knowledge appeared to result from those initiatives. Then, in late 1999, the Head of Internal Audit, John Fraser (one of the authors of this article), was asked to take on the additional role of Chief Risk Officer (CRO). A Corporate Risk Management Group was established consisting of the CRO (part-time) and two full-time professionals, one with a degree in industrial engineering and one with a master's of business administration in process re-engineering and organizational effectiveness. The group was given six months to prove its worth. If it failed to demonstrate its value during this period, the idea of implementing ERM would be abandoned and the Corporate Risk Management Group dissolved.

In early 2000, the Corporate Risk Management Group prepared two documents with the help of experienced consultants: an ERM Policy (figure 16.1) and an ERM Framework (figure 16.2). The ERM Policy set forth the governing principles and who was responsible for specific aspects of risk management activities, and the ERM Framework set out the procedures for ERM in greater detail. The Corporate Risk Management Group took the ERM Policy and ERM Framework to the Executive Risk Committee for discussion and approval. The Committee, which consisted of the CEO and the most senior executives, suggested that a pilot study be undertaken with one of the small subsidiaries before formal approval of the Policy and Framework was sought from the Audit and Finance Committee of the Board.

FIGURE 16.1

ERM Policy

Hydro One Inc.: Enterprise Risk Management Policy

Hydro One Inc. and its subsidiaries use an enterprise-wide portfolio approach for the management of key business risks. Enterprise risk management provides uniform processes to identify, measure, treat and report on key risks.[1] It supports the Board's corporate governance needs and the due diligence responsibilities of senior management. It also helps to strengthen our management practices in a manner demonstrable to external stakeholders.

MANAGEMENT PRINCIPLES

To fulfill this commitment, we abide by the following seven principles:

1. Risk management is everyone's responsibility, from the board of directors to individual employees. Each is expected to understand the risks that fall within the limits of their accountabilities and is expected to manage these risks within approved risk tolerances.

2. Hydro One will manage its significant risks through a portfolio approach that optimizes the trade-offs between risk and return across all business functions. Optimization ensures that the corporation accepts the appropriate level of risk to meet its business objectives.

3. Each subsidiary or line of business is expected to undertake risk assessments on no less than an annual basis for the business as a whole, and as determined locally for elements below the subsidiary level.

4. Enterprise risk management will be integrated with major business processes such as strategic planning, business planning, operational management, and investment decisions to ensure consistent consideration of risks in all decision-making.

5. Enterprise risk management is a comprehensive, disciplined, and continuous process in which risks are identified, analyzed and consciously accepted or mitigated within approved risk tolerances.

6. Enterprise risk management will continue to evolve to reflect industry best practices and Hydro One Inc.'s needs. This policy will be reviewed

continued

annually by the Senior Management Team and the Audit & Finance Committee of the board.

7. Local risk management policies and processes will be consistent with this corporate policy and its companion Framework. Additionally, all local policies and processes will facilitate the upward consolidation and review of all significant business risks.

RESPONSIBILITIES AND ACCOUNTABILITIES (GOVERNANCE STRUCTURE)

- The *Audit & Finance Committee* of the board reviews annually with the officers of the corporation: the corporation's risk profile; the risk retention philosophy/risk tolerances of the corporation; and the risk management policies, processes and accountabilities within the corporation.

- The *President and Chief Executive Officer* has ultimate accountability for managing the corporation's risks. The Chief Financial Officer has specific accountability for ensuring that enterprise risk management processes are established, properly documented and maintained by the corporation.

- The Senior Management Team provides management oversight of the Hydro One risk portfolio and the corporation's risk management processes. It provides direction on the evolution of these processes and identifies priority areas of focus for risk assessment and mitigation planning.

- Each of the *President's direct reports* has specific accountabilities for managing risks in their subsidiary or function. Each will establish specific risk tolerances for their lines of business that do not exceed the limits of corporate risk tolerances. On an annual basis, each is also expected to formally attest that the unit's risk management process is in place, operating effectively and is consistent with this policy.

- *Line and functional managers* are responsible for managing risks within the scope of their authority and accountability. Risk acceptance or mitigation decisions will be made explicitly and within the risk tolerances specified by the head of the subsidiary or function.

- The *Chief Risk Officer* provides support to the President and Chief Executive Officer, CFO, Senior Management Team and key managers within the

continued

corporation. This support includes developing risk management policies, frameworks and processes, introducing and promoting new techniques, preparing annual corporate risk profiles, maintaining a registry of key business risks, and facilitating risk assessments across the corporation.

DEFINITIONS

Risk: The potential that an event, action or inaction will threaten Hydro One's ability to achieve its business objectives. Risk is described in terms of its likelihood of occurrence and potential impact or magnitude. Broad categories of risk in Hydro One include strategic, regulatory, financial and operational risks.

Risk Assessment: The systematic identification and measurement of business risks, on a project, line of business or corporate basis. It also includes the review or establishment of risk tolerances, the evaluation of existing mitigation/controls and conscious acceptance or treatment of residual risk.

Risk Mitigation/Treatment: Actions or decisions by management that will change the status of a risk. Options include retaining the risk (either completely or partially), increasing the risk (where mitigation is not cost-effective), avoiding the risk (by withdrawing from or ceasing the activity), reducing the likelihood (by increasing preventive controls), reducing the consequences (by emergency or crisis response), and/or transferring the risk (by outsourcing, insurance, etc.).

Risk Profile: The results of any risk assessment, assembled into a consolidated view of the significant strategic, regulatory, financial and operational risks at play in a project, line of business or across the corporation.

Risk Tolerances: Guidelines that establish levels of acceptable and unacceptable exposure from any risk. Tolerances define the range of possible impacts (from minor to worst case) that risks might have on business objectives. Risk tolerances are established for the corporation and reviewed annually. Each project, function or line of business assessing its risks is expected to use or develop a set of risk tolerances that does not exceed established corporate limits.

[1] Details on these processes are available in the companion Enterprise Risk Management Framework.

FIGURE 16.2

Risk Management Process

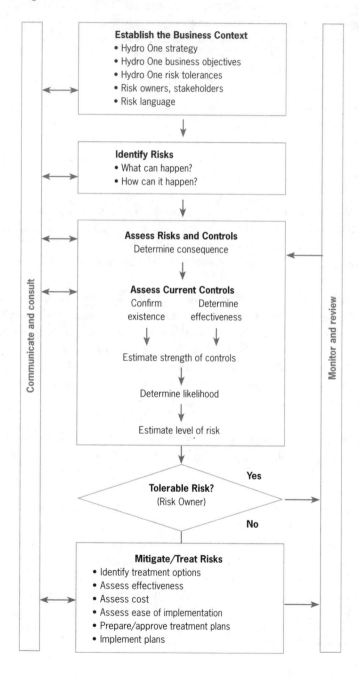

Pilot Study

With some consulting assistance, the Corporate Risk Management Group planned the first ERM workshop in the subsidiary. Using its own staff, the Group executed the first ERM workshop in Spring 2000.

The workshop followed a conventional format. Prior to the workshop, a list of some 80 potential risks or threats to the business was developed and e-mailed to the management team of the subsidiary. Each member of the team was asked to choose the ten most critical risks facing the company—and based on these choices, a list of the top eight was prepared. Then, at the workshop, these eight risks were discussed one at a time and their relative importance voted on by the management team. Voting was accomplished using the Delphi Method,[10] which involves a combination of facilitated discussions and iterative anonymous voting technology designed to quickly identify and prioritize risks based on magnitude and probability and to evaluate the quality of controls.

The first vote on the perceived magnitude of a particular risk—with risk defined on a five-point scale: Minor, Moderate, Major, Severe, and Worst Case—often showed wide dispersion. In each case, the initial vote was followed by discussion of the definition of the particular risk, and of its causes and consequences. Depending on the dispersion of votes in the first voting session, the discussion could be long or short. A second vote was then taken; and until a clear alignment or a clearly defined cause of disagreement was established, this sequence of discussion and voting might be repeated (usually no more than three votes were needed in practice). Then, with the voting and prioritization of risks completed, preliminary action plans were discussed and managers identified as "Champions" with the responsibility of developing more concrete action plans.

---

10. The Delphi Method, originally developed by the RAND Corporation in 1964 for technological forecasting, is a way of estimating future measures by asking a group of experts to make estimates, re-circulating the estimates back to the group, and repeating the process until the numbers converge. It is a formal method used to generate expert collective decisions. The Delphi Method recognizes human judgment as legitimate and useful inputs in generating forecasts. Single experts sometimes suffer biases and group meetings may suffer from "follow-the-leader" syndromes and/or reluctance to abandon previously stated opinions. The Delphi Method is characterized by anonymity, controlled feedback, and statistical response. The Rand report is still interesting to read and contains many innovations that are used in the analysis and describes Delphi results. For instance, the report presents arguments for using median values rather than the mean values of the group's responses and also illustrates how ranges of opinions can be presented graphically; see T.J. Gordon and Olaf Helmer, *Report on a Long Range Forecasting Study*, R-2982 (Rand Corporation, 1964). For a broad review of the literature on Delphi and references to the method and past studies, refer to Fred Woudenberg, "An Evaluation of Delphi," *Technological Forecasting and Social Change* (September 1991). For further information on practical applications, see Michael Adler and Erio Ziglio (eds.), *Gazing into the Oracle: The Delphi Method and its Application to Social Policy and Public Health* (Philadelphia: Jessica Kingsley Publishers, 1996).

The discussions proved to be very valuable. Issues that managers had thought about but never openly discussed were addressed. Concerns about some risks were allayed and new risks were identified; but in any case there was the beginning of a common understanding of risks and of a corporate plan for prioritizing action and resources to manage such risks. Since this was a pilot study for the Corporate Risk Management Group, the participants were asked to evaluate the quality and benefits of each workshop. The programs received high ratings and the managers of the subsidiary requested a follow-up session to discuss and rank the next eight risks that had been identified.

Final Approval

Following the pilot study in the subsidiary, the Corporate Risk Management Group returned to the Executive Risk Committee for debriefing. The pilot study was considered a success, and the Chief Risk Officer presented the ERM Policy and the ERM Framework to the Audit and Finance Committee of the Board for approval. In the summer of 2000, the Audit and Finance Committee approved the documents, and a roadmap for implementing ERM at Hydro One was established.

Processes and Tools

The overall aim of Hydro One's ERM Framework (figure 16.2) is not risk elimination or risk reduction *per se*, but rather attainment of an optimal balance between business risks and business returns.

The Business Context

The ERM Policy of Hydro One in figure 16.1 defines risk as follows:

> The potential that an event, action, or inaction will threaten Hydro One's ability to achieve its business objectives. Risk is described in terms of its likelihood of occurrence and potential impact or magnitude. Broad categories of risk in Hydro One include strategic, regulatory, financial, and operational risks.

Since risk is defined by its potential to threaten the achievement of business objectives, it is imperative to clearly state these objectives and how they contribute to Hydro One's overall strategy. The Corporate Risk Management Group found that objectives were not always clearly articulated, and that the workshop process from the pilot study helped in achieving clarity of business objectives needed to achieve the corporate mission.

The same was true of risk tolerances. Risk tolerances are guidelines that establish levels of acceptable and unacceptable exposures to any given risk

TABLE 16.1

Risk Tolerances

Business Objectives	Event Impact Description	5 Worst Case	4 Severe	3 Major	2 Moderate	1 Minor
Financial	Net income shortfall (after tax, in one year)	$>150M shortfall	$75–150M shortfall	$25–75M shortfall	$5–25M shortfall	<$5M shortfall
Reputation	Negative media attention; opinion leader and public criticism	International media attention; opinion leaders/ customers nearly unanimous in public criticism	National media attention; most opinion leaders/ customers publicly critical	Provincial profile; several opinion leaders/ customers publicly critical	Local profile	Letter to government or senior management
System reliability	Outages on the Hydro One system	One of: >100,000 customers distribution or >1000MW Tx for more than seven days or failure to meet NERC minimum standards	One of: 40k–100k customers Dx or 400– 1000MW Tx for 4–7 days or failure to meet minimum standards	One of: 10k–40k customers Dx or 100– 400MW Tx for 2–4 days or concern expressed by NERC	One of: 1k–10k customers Dx or 10– 100MW Tx for 4–24 hours or near threshold of many NERC standards	One of: <1000 customers Dx or <10MW Tx for <4 hours or near threshold for one NERC standard

Definition of Risk Tolerances: (1) Minor: Noticeable disruption to results; manageable; (2) Moderate: Material deterioration in results; a concern; may not be acceptable; management response would be considered; (3) Major: Significant deterioration in results; not acceptable; management response required; (4) Severe: Fundamental threat to operating results; immediate senior management attention; (5) Worst Case: Results threaten survival of company in current form, potentially full-time senior management response until resolved.

(table 16.1 shows risk tolerances for three categories of risk out of 16). Tolerances define the range of possible impacts (on a five-point scale from Minor to Worst Case) of specific risks on business objectives. Through the workshops, a common understanding was developed as to how to categorize impacts from a particular risk on the firm's ability to accomplish key business objectives.[11]

As an example, Hydro One has a financial objective related to earnings stability—namely, to limit the risk of a major shortfall in net income and the associated possibility of financial distress costs. One source of the risk to net income is loss of competitiveness; another is the volatility of financial markets.

A second important corporate objective of Hydro One is maintaining its reputation and public profile. One potential source of reputational risk is pollution damage; another is inappropriate employment contracts. In this case, the magnitude of the risk is not measured in dollar terms, but in terms of the extent of public criticism both on a local as well as an international basis.

Although the ERM Policy of Hydro One states that "risk management is everyone's responsibility, from the Board of Directors to individual employees," the risk facing a specific project or line of business will typically fall under the accountability of a primary risk "owner," typically the project manager or the business's CEO.

Identification and Assessment of Risks and Controls

The approach to risk identification depends on the depth and breadth of the activities under review and the extent to which these activities are "new" to Hydro One. As described above, however, the process typically involves the identification of 50–70 business risks which are then narrowed down to the ten most significant risks through interviews and focus groups. In assessing risks, the aim is to understand both the size of the potential losses as well as the associated probability of occurrence. In theory, the correct way to portray the estimated effect of a risk is to use a probability curve that reflects the potential outcomes and associated probabilities. But given the practical difficulties of "building" such a curve, Hydro One has instead chosen to focus on the "worst credible" outcome within a given time frame and its associated probability of occurrence. This has proven to be a practical and efficient way to focus on major risks while avoiding excessive detail and complex calculations.

For all risks deemed to be "major," Hydro One defines the "worst credible" outcome as the greatest loss that can result in the event that certain key con-

11. The two scales (risk tolerance and probability rating) form the backbone of the quantification of risks at Hydro One and make comparisons possible between impacts that are easily quantifiable in monetary terms (e.g., shortfall in net income) with impacts that are more qualitative in nature (e.g., extent of criticism). For example, a risk that has an impact of 3 in relation to objective A and an impact of 2 in relation to objective B is a more serious threat to Hydro One in relation to objective A than it is in relation to objective B.

TABLE 16.2

Probability Rating Scale

Score	Rating	Description
5	Virtually certain	95% probability that the event will occur in the next 5 years
4	Very likely	75% probability that the event will occur in the next 5 years
3	Even odds	50% probability that the event will occur in the next 5 years
2	Unlikely	25% probability that the event will occur in the next 5 years
1	Remote	5% probability that the event will occur in the next 5 years

trols fail. (As so defined, worst credible outcomes differ both from "inherent magnitudes," which assume that all controls fail or are absent, and "residual magnitudes," which assume that all key controls are in place and functioning.) The probability of such outcomes is evaluated for a specific time frame, generally two to five years, though for special projects the period is as short as six or nine months. As shown in table 16.2, Hydro One uses a probability rating scale from "Remote" (a 5% probability that the event will occur in the stipulated time frame) to "Virtually Certain" (95% probability).

After the Corporate Risk Management Group has helped management estimate the "worst credible" outcome, the impact on various objectives, and the associated probabilities for each risk (by workshops and the Delphi Method), the next step is to produce a "risk map" like the one presented in figure 16.3. The bubbles in the figure represent the expected effect of the risk on a certain objective in terms of its estimated impact (reflected on the horizontal axis) and the estimated probability that the impact materializes (on the vertical axis). In the case of each risk, the estimated probabilities represent the relevant experts' best guess that the "worst credible" outcome will materialize. Management also uses the risk map to track the historical development of particular risks and to project expected future developments.[12]

---

12. For another example of how a firm uses risk maps in enterprise risk management, refer to Chapter 5 on Microsoft Corporation in T.L. Barton et al., *Making Enterprise Risk Management Pay Off.*

FIGURE 16.3

Risk Map

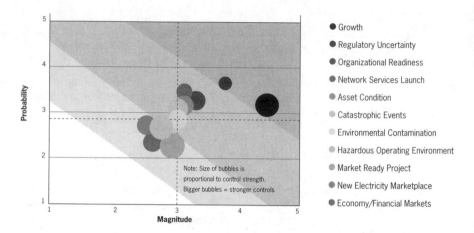

The size of the bubbles in the figure indicates the extent of management's confidence in the effectiveness of the company's controls and efforts to limit individual exposures. Control assessment involves the strength of existing organizations, processes, systems, and feedback loops that are in place to manage the risk. The company has developed a "control strength" model that is designed to complement its risk tolerances. For any given magnitude of risk (from Minor to Worst Case), there is a corresponding strength of control, with "1" representing few controls and "5" representing full prescriptive controls with executive oversight.

Tolerability of Risk—and Risk Mitigation

Once risks and controls are assessed, a rank-ordered list of "residual risks" is assembled. The risk owner (for example, the subsidiary CEO or the project manager) then determines the firm's tolerance for each risk. Within the limits of the risk owner's accountability, the risk owner decides either to accept the risk as is or to take (further) steps to mitigate it. If the risk owner accepts the risk as is, the risk is monitored and reviewed in the normal future course of risk management processes. If the risk owner decides to mitigate the risk, the process of risk mitigation is defined.

Risk owners thus have seven possible ways of dealing with significant risks:

- **Retain:** Risk exposure is accepted as is without further mitigation, since the potential return is viewed as desirable and the downside exposure is not significant.

- **Retain, but change mitigation:** A partially mitigated exposure is maintained, but a change in mitigation reduces the cost of control.

- **Increase:** Risk exposure is increased, either because the potential return is viewed as desirable or the controls in place are not cost-effective.

- **Avoid:** Risk exposure will be eliminated entirely (perhaps by withdrawal from a business area or ceasing the activity), since the potential return does not offset the downside exposure.

- **Reduce the likelihood:** Risk exposure will be reduced cost-effectively through new or enhanced preventive controls.

- **Reduce the consequences:** The impact of any risk that materializes will be reduced through emergency preparedness or crisis response.

- **Transfer:** Risk exposure will be transferred to others (perhaps through an insurance policy or an outsourcing arrangement).

As can be seen from the list, risk mitigation is not necessarily the same as risk elimination or risk reduction. As previously mentioned, the purpose of strategic risk management at Hydro One is to balance business risks and business returns by taking into account the potential upside as well as the downside associated with a particular risk. Thus, a balancing act may involve an *increase* in risk. In practical terms, however, an increase in risk at Hydro One is most likely to be decided at the strategic level. Once the strategic plan is set, the primary focus is on limiting the downside risk of failure to achieve stated business objectives.

Monitor and Review

Risks do not remain static. The magnitude and probability of a certain risk is affected by internal controls (mitigation) as well as external changes in the environment. Monitoring and reporting are fundamental to effective management of business risks. Furthermore, risks may not always be categorized correctly in the first place. Risks are notoriously hard to predict, and assessing risks is to a large extent a matter of qualitative guesswork. As physicist Niels Bohr observed, "Prediction is very difficult, especially about the future."

A nice example of changing risk tolerances is Hydro One's decision to issue shares on the New York Stock Exchange. During the period leading up to the scheduled offering, one of management's greatest fears was the possibility of an unfavorable news story in the international press. As things turned out, however, the IPO was shelved. Then, in October 2003, the company had an oil spill that overflowed into a small stream and received a lot of press in Ontario.[13] When this got the attention of both the Ontario Government (Hydro One's shareholder) and the company's Board of Directors, the Corporate Risk Management Group quickly realized that their greatest reputational exposure was not to the international press, but to the local press and its power to inflame the sensitivities of Hydro One's primary stakeholders. As a consequence, negative provincial press stories are now identified as a worst-case scenario—considerably worse than their international counterparts—and strong measures are taken to avoid them.

Corporate Risk Profile

The risk management process described in the previous section serves as the basic framework for managing risks at Hydro One. The framework can be used in the normal conduct of business or for new projects.

To aggregate the information from these processes in a form suitable for the senior management and board of directors, the Risk Management Group prepares a Corporate Risk Profile twice a year. Table 16.3 provides an illustration of the risk profile using the same risk sources contained in the risk map in figure 16.3.

The purpose of the Corporate Risk Profile is to ensure that the senior management team shares a common understanding of the principal risks facing the organization and to provide a basis for allocating resources to address risks based on their priority. The Corporate Risk Profile is based on structured interviews with the top 40 to 50 executives together with databases from other sources (such as annual business plans and workshops). The profile reflects the executives' assessments of both previously identified risks and risks that may have been identified since the last profile in workshops, media scans, or other sources.

Description of Risk Sources

The June 2000 Corporate Risk Profile in table 16.3 shows the list of the top risks ranked as "Very High," "High," and "Medium." As of June 2000, eleven key risks had been identified. The figure also shows how these risks were rated in the previous profile and the estimated trend. And as the changes and trends

13. Refer to Hydro One news releases on October 1 and 2, 2003, about the oil spill in Pickering. Initially, the city of Pickering was very upset about the oil spill from a station, the largest single transformer station in North America, in a residential community (see "Hydro Plant Oil Spill Riles Mayor of Pickering," *Bell Globemedia*, October 2, 2003). Later, the mayor praised Hydro One's quick response to the clean up (see "Hydro One Picks Up Tab for Oil Spill," *Electricity Forum News*, October 2003).

TABLE 16.3

Corporate Risk Profile

Risk Source	Risk Rating Dec. 1999	Risk Rating June 2000	Risk Trend
Growth	Very High	Very High	↑
Regulatory uncertainty	Very High	Very High	↑
Organizational readiness	High	High	↑
Network services launch	N/A	High	New
Asset condition	High	High	→
Catastrophic events	High	High	↓
Environmental contamination	High	High	→
Hazardous operating environment	Medium	Medium	↑
Market ready project	Medium	Medium	→
New electricity marketplace	Medium	Medium	→
Economy/financial markets	Medium	Medium	↓

suggest, the Corporate Risk Profile is by no means a static document. New risks arise with legislation or new initiatives. The severity of some risks can be reduced by mitigation efforts or changes in external factors. And the estimated severity of some risks can also change because the risks (and the consequences of mitigation) are better understood.

In addition to the major sources of risk and their trends, the Corporate Risk Profile also describes the corporate objectives that are likely to be most affected by such risks and the corporate controls being used to mitigate such risks. Below we describe each of the eleven major risks as evaluated in June 2000 and the corporate measures to manage such risks.

1. **Growth:** Hydro One has plans for significant growth through acquisitions of both existing and related businesses within and

beyond Ontario. This is a major risk source because there are many substantial barriers to the achievement of the planned growth. Business development and financial results are the objectives most likely to be affected. The actions of the Government (as owner) create the largest part of this risk because the degree of owner support for the acquisition strategy is not always clear and firm. Hydro One has limited experience in identifying, negotiating, and integrating significant acquisitions. The exposure to Government actions is mitigated by senior management participation in Government review processes and a proactive Government Relations function. Acquisition risks are mitigated by various means, including careful planning and analysis, staff skill development, and external advisors.

2. **Regulatory Uncertainty:** The objectives of Hydro One are greatly influenced by the actions of regulators. The rules under which regulators operate will likely change as experience in the restructured industry is gained. Also, other stakeholder groups will influence regulatory decisions. The objectives most likely affected are financial results, legal/regulatory status, and reputation. Methods for mitigating this risk include increased and more effective interactions with the Government and the Ontario Energy Board, increased priority and profile for regulatory matters within the company, and restoration of the company's regulatory staff capability through the addition of senior regulatory staff.

3. **Organizational Readiness:** Organizational readiness reflects the ability of the company to provide effective services to customers and to improve operating efficiency in the new business environment. Many systems and processes are recognized to be less than optimally efficient and some inefficiencies are amenable to information technology solutions. Readiness has been both helped and made more complex by the departure of 1,400 of the most seasoned employees through the recent voluntary retirement program. This risk source impacts competitiveness and customer service. Methods being used to mitigate this risk source include performance contracting, compensation programs, labor relations strategies, and improved technology prioritization processes.

4. **Network Services Launch:** The risks associated with the creation of a separate subsidiary to provide wire network services in the open market are many and varied, including uncertainty about the form of the future competitive market, the ability of the business to achieve a

competitive cost structure, and the regulatory treatment of the business's reorganization costs. Possible consequences of such risks are reductions in competitiveness, reliability of customer service, and financial results. Mitigating this risk source involves a carefully crafted strategy and transition plan.

5. **Asset Conditions:** The aging of asset wires and the possibility of underfunded maintenance and incomplete information about the condition of assets represent risks to customer service and reputation. Ways to mitigate this risk include redundancy on the transmission system, emergency response capability, and increased attention to this issue through higher planning priority.

6. **Catastrophic Events:** Hydro One has assets covering a very large geographical area, and the firm thus faces some exposure to destructive natural events such as tornadoes, which damage facilities every year, and ice storms, which are less frequent but can cause widespread damage and disruption of service. These events affect customer service, reputation, and financial results. Methods used to mitigate this risk include those listed under Asset Conditions (see above), as well as emergency preparedness plans and rehearsals, weather forecasting, and insurance.

7. **Environmental Contamination:** This risk is largely driven by lands owned by the company that are contaminated with arsenic trioxide. Other contaminants are penta poles, transformer oils, and PCBs. To mitigate such risks to the firm's reputation and financial results, as well as to the environment itself, the firm uses a combination of limited insurance coverage with initiatives designed to prevent such contamination.

8. **Hazardous Operating Environment:** Essentially all Hydro One facilities are electrically energized and so represent a threat to employees, contractors, and the public. In order to protect the firm's reputation as well as ensure employee and public safety, risk mitigation is accomplished through facilities design, asset maintenance, safe work practices, and employee training and supervision.

9. **Market Ready Project:** The Market Ready Project is a major complex undertaking with uncertain requirements and has the potential to cause Hydro One to delay the province's market opening, to cause significant customer or regulator dissatisfaction, or to well exceed its projected budget. Mitigation is provided by giving the project a high

priority and profile. The recently announced delay in market opening reduces this risk, although it does not eliminate it, as even the delayed schedule is seen as tight.

10. **New Electricity Market:** The evolving electricity market exposes Hydro One to a wide range of unpredictable actions by competitors, customers, generators, and regulators. Any one of these parties may be able to erode the company's market position or increase its costs, thereby harming financial results. To limit this risk, the company's management is active on the IMO Board (the Independent Electricity Market Operator) and is negotiating a comprehensive operating agreement with the IMO.

11. **Economy/Financial Markets:** Changes in commodity prices, exchange rates, or interest rates can have adverse effects on net income and cash flows. Hydro One has no commodity risk and does not trade in energy derivatives. The direct effect of fluctuations in exchange rates is considered insignificant, although this may change in the future if the company issues foreign currency debt. (All debt is currently denominated in local currency.) The company is, however, exposed to fluctuations in interest rates through its floating-rate debt (though corporate policy specifies that at most 15% of total debt can have floating rates) and through the refinancing of its maturing longer-term debt. Besides limiting its use of floating rate debt, the company also periodically uses interest rate swap agreements to manage interest rate risk. Management estimates that a 100-basis-point increase in interest rates would reduce net income by roughly CAD 25 million—a risk deemed to be "Minor" or "Moderate" on the risk tolerance scale. All prudent expenses, including interest, are part of the rate base and recoverable through billing rates, so that any interest rate increase would eventually be recovered, but it would not be regarded as good management by the board and would show up as a reduction of profits in the current year.

Hydro One has some exposure to credit risk, both from its customers and from the possibility of counterparty default on its interest rate swaps. The credit risk associated with customers is effectively managed through a broadly diversified customer base. The counterparty default risk is limited by the company's policy of transacting only with highly rated counterparties, limiting total exposure levels with individual counterparties, and entering into master agreements that allow "net settlement."

Quantifying the Unquantifiable

The final step of the ERM process at Hydro One is to prioritize the use of resources for investment planning based on the risks identified. Hydro One is inherently an asset management company in the sense that most of its assets have a life expectancy of from 30 to 70 years. The Investment Planning Department of Hydro One collaborated with the Corporate Risk Management Group to develop a risk-based approach for allocating resources. Using this approach, the company has managed to find an innovative way of "quantifying the unquantifiable."

The approach rests on three pillars:

1. the five-point risk tolerance scale (from Minor to Worst Case) for assessing the estimated impact of a given risk on a given corporate objective (illustrated earlier in table 16.1 and Figure 16.3);

2. the five-point probability rating scale (from Remote to Virtually Certain) for evaluating the probability that a given impact will materialize (shown in table 16.2 and figure 16.3); and

3. the quality of controls (or other risk management mechanisms) designed to reduce the residual risks.

Table 16.4 illustrates this risk-based approach for determining capital expenditures. Each class of asset or type of expenditure is categorized into different levels as follows:[14]

- Highest Risk Exposure: an unacceptable level of risk that must be funded as a priority (and shown in table 16.4).

- Minimum Funding Level: the level of service at which the risk to the company's business objectives is considered barely tolerable.

- Level 1: at this level of funding, the risk to business objectives is materially lower than at the Minimum Funding Level.

- Levels 2 and 3 (not illustrated in the table): At these levels of funding, the risk to business objectives is materially lower than at Level 1. A description of the expenditures and associated risks is provided for each level.

---

14. A useful analogy for this methodology is to consider in a typical household that each asset (e.g., house, car, kids' education) has certain expenditure requirements that are broken down into levels of expenditure; for example, the car has levels defined as Red Zone = fixing brakes (impacts safety objectives), Minimum Funding Level = changing oil to lengthen life (long-term financial objective; could also be viewed as Level 1), Level 3 = paint job (improve the family's social image).

TABLE 16.4

A Risk-Based Structural Approach to Investment Planning at Hydro One

Program	Level	Cost	Cumulative Cost	Risk if Not Done	Bang for the Buck	
Tree trim	Highest risk	$ 2	$ 2	4.6 ˙	—	⎤
Lines	Highest risk	$ 6	$ 8	4.5	—	Intolerable
Poles	Highest risk	$ 1	$ 9	3.9	—	⎦ risk
Tree trim	Minimum level	$ 1	$10	2.8	2.80	⎤
Lines	Level 1	$ 3	$13	3.0	1.00	
Tree trim	Level 1	$ 2	$15	1.9	0.95	"Bang for
Lines	Minimum level	$ 5	$20	3.2	0.64	the buck"
Poles	Minimum level	$12	$32	2.3	0.19	⎦

This table illustrates Hydro One's risk-based structural approach for determining capital expenditures. The first three projects have the highest risk exposure measure and will have the top priority for resource allocation. This type of ranking of projects across work programs is very useful for resource allocation prioritization in the capital expenditures process. "Bang for the Buck" equals "risk if not done" divided by dollar cost.

The investment levels are associated with specific accomplishments—for example, numbers of kilometers of line cleared, or numbers of calls answered within 30 seconds.

As also shown in table 16.4, all investment levels for each asset class are risk-rated based on magnitude and probability for the major corporate objectives using a grid. This grid defines intolerable combined levels of magnitude and probability (shown as Highest Risk in table 16.4), and assigns a risk rating based on a scale for the combined rating. Each class of asset is stratified into different levels of risk (Highest Risk, Minimum Funding Level, Level 1, and so on). As an example, "Tree Trim" is broken down into several categories, each with its own risk rating. Highest Risk might be minimum clearance near urban centers, while Level 2 might correspond to a deeper clearance on small lines with lower risk.

Hydro One has applied a method named "Bang for the Buck" to be used in prioritizing expenditures for non–Highest Risk risks. The Bang-for-the-Buck index prioritizes by calculating the risk reduction per dollar spent. For example, at the top of the Bang-for-the-Buck index in table 16.4 is "Tree Trim" (Minimum Level), which shows 2.8 risk units ("Risk if not done") eliminated by spending one dollar ("Cost"). This gives a Bang-for-the-Buck value of 2.8. At the other end of the scale, the elimination of 2.3 risk units in relation to Poles (Minimum Level) by spending $12 gives a more modest Bang-for-the-Buck value of 0.18.

At the point where the cumulative expenditures reach the level of the available resources, the planned work for the year is determined. The documented prioritization of planned investments in assets is then the subject of a formal two-day meeting between the senior asset managers and the executives that is designed to probe and validate assumptions before the investment plan is presented to the Board of Directors as part of the annual business planning process.

Using this approach to enterprise risk management, the company then attempts to combine the qualitative, imaginative strengths of scenario planning with the quantitative rigor associated with real options analysis.[15] Scenario planning is a well-established approach (the origins of which are generally traced to practices at Royal Dutch/Shell[16]) for thinking about major sources of corporate uncertainty. Real options, on the other hand, is a more scientific, finance-oriented approach that, at least in well-defined cases, can be used to quantify possible outcomes and the value of different strategies for dealing with such outcomes. In the case of an oil exploration company, for example, scenario planning might be used to help management anticipate the set of political and economic events that could lead to $100-per-barrel oil prices. Real options could be used to estimate how much the firm would be worth while also providing management with a value-maximizing schedule for developing its reserves.

Benefits of ERM and Outcomes at Hydro One

Hydro One's 2003 Annual Report summarizes the benefits of ERM as follows: "An enterprise-wide approach enables regulatory, strategic, operational, and financial risks to be managed and aligned with our strategic business objectives." Table 16.5 reflects our attempt to list and elaborate on some of the key benefits. While most are qualitative and difficult to quantify, all are perceived as valuable.

---

15. See, for example, Kent D. Miller and H. Gregory Waller, "Scenarios, Real Options and Integrated Risk Management," *Long Range Planning* Vol. 36 (2003): 93–107, for a good general discussion.

16. See, for example, Paul J. H. Schoemaker and Cornelius A.J.M. van der Heijden, "Integrating Scenarios into Strategic Planning at Royal Dutch/Shell," *Planning Review* Vol. 20, No. 3 (May–June 1992): 41–46.

TABLE 16.5

Benefits of ERM and Outcomes at Hydro One

Examples of ERM Benefits	Hydro One Experiences
Achieve lower cost of debt	Realized higher debt rating and lower interest costs than expected on $1 billion debt issue, which was the first issue as a new company. Issue was heavily oversubscribed. Ratings analysts stated ERM was a significant factor in the ratings process for Hydro One.
Focus capital expenditures process on managing/allocating capital based on greatest mitigation of risk per $ spent	Capital expenditures are allocated and prioritized based on a risk-based structural approach. An "optimal portfolio" of capital investments is achieved providing the greatest risk reduction per $ spent. Also, ERM has been used in the management of major projects such as the 88 corporate utility acquisitions during 2000 and the potential building of an underground cable to the USA.
Avoid "land mines" and other surprises	Since starting ERM, there have been many unusual occurrences at the company. Two significant ones were spelled out in the Corporate Risk Tolerances ahead of time: the dismissal of the Board of Directors and the reaction to a large oil spill.
Reassure stakeholders that the business is well-managed—with stakeholders defined to include investors, analysts, rating agencies, regulators, and the press	During the IPO road shows, the Corporate Risk Management Group was told that the ERM workshops had greatly assisted the executive team in articulating the risks they faced and what was being done about them. There are many other examples.
Improve corporate governance via best practices guidelines	Hydro One has moved from the Board Committees asking why these risk summaries were being brought to them to a point at which they now routinely expect this information. Directors recognize that Hydro One is ahead of other companies on whose boards they sit.

TABLE 16.5

Benefits of ERM and Outcomes at Hydro One

Examples of ERM Benefits	Hydro One Experiences
Implement a formalized system of risk management that includes an ERM system (a required component of the 1995/1999/2004 Australian Standard for Risk Management)	Hydro One has a formalized system that drives periodic assessment, documentation, and reporting of all risks.
Identify which risks the company can pursue better than its peers	Although not neccessarily attributable solely to ERM: • A subsidiary involved in marketing electricity was sold due to high commodity risks. • Several processing and administrative functions were outsourced to transfer labor union and labor cost risks.

From a finance perspective, the most direct evidence of a benefit from ERM is the positive reaction of the credit rating agencies and the resulting reduction in the company's cost of debt.[17] In 2000, Hydro One issued $1 billion of debt, its first issue as a new company after the split-up of Ontario Hydro. According to recent conversations with senior ratings analysts at Moody's, ERM was then (and continues to be) a significant factor in the ratings process for the company.[18] The firm reportedly received a higher rating on this initial issue (AA− from Standard & Poor's and A+ from Moody's) than initially anticipated, and the issue was oversubscribed by approximately 50%. To quantify the potential yield savings, consider that since 2000, the long-term mean yield spread between AA and A has averaged approximately 20 basis points. And if we conservatively credit ERM with reducing the company's debt costs by, say, ten basis points, this translates into annual savings in interest costs of $1 million on the $1 billion in new debt.

17. For additional discussion and examples of ERM and its effect on the cost of capital, see "University of Georgia Roundtable on Enterprise-Wide Risk Management," *Journal of Applied Corporate Finance* Vol. 15, No. 4 (Fall 2003): 18–20.
18. On September 13, 2004, telephone interviews were conducted with senior ratings analysts at Moody's to verify the importance of Hydro One's ERM program in the credit rating process on their long-term debt. Moreover, as part of Moody's Enhanced Analysis Initiative, ratings methodologies measuring the quality of corporate governance and risk management include specific questions related to enterprise risk management. See, for example, Questions 16, 17, and 18 of Moody's Corporate Governance Assessment and Moody's research methodology.

Another clearly important benefit is the improvement of Hydro One's capital expenditure process using the risk mitigation prioritization index. As described in the previous section, this process takes into account the benefit of risk reduction in all major risk categories (that is, regulatory, financial, reliability, safety, reputation, and so on) by allocating capital expenditures according to the greatest overall risk reduction per dollar spent. While the system is complex and involves extensive computer modeling, the result is a capital allocation process that is much more likely to lead the firm toward the optimal (viewed on a risk-adjusted basis) portfolio of capital projects.

In addition to a lower cost of capital and improved capital allocation, our discussions with Hydro One's management also suggest a number of less tangible benefits, some of which are described in table 16.5. Perhaps most important, top management seems convinced that employees at all levels of the organization now have a much better understanding of the firm's risks and what they can do to manage them. And, as described in the next section, this process appears to have led to an impressive change in the company's corporate culture.

Current Status

Instead of the title "Current Status," we could have substituted "The Evolution of the CRO." At the outset of the ERM initiative, the Corporate Risk Management Group consisted of the CRO (part-time) and two full-time professionals. To date, the group has conducted more than 180 workshops and authored numerous internal reports on strategic risk management. Some of these reports were prepared in the normal conduct of business and were issued regularly. Other reports were requested *ad hoc*, such as the strategic risk management analysis of a voluntary retirement program at Hydro One that is summarized in the box insert.

From the end of 2003 until the present, there have been no full-time members of the Corporate Risk Management Group. The CRO devotes 20% of his time to this role, and his previous staff have been reassigned to other jobs, although they are occasionally "borrowed back" for certain specific high-risk ERM projects. This reduction in personnel is not a sign of failure, but rather of two notable accomplishments:

- The transfer and generation of knowledge on strategic risk management throughout the organization has been so effective that strategic risk management is considered to be embedded in the various subsidiaries and divisions to such an extent that the need for extensive central planning, implementation, and monitoring is significantly reduced. As evidence of Hydro One's success in making "risk management everyone's responsibility," in 2002 the Corporate Risk Management Group received the firm's "Sir Graham Day Award for Excellence in Culture Change."[19] In the words of then CEO and President of the company,

> Thanks to this team, Hydro One is becoming a leader in enterprise risk management—a key best-practice in the energy industry, and a critical element of good corporate governance. . . . This group's progress to date has also garnered attention from other organizations. In fact, the risk managers from the World Bank and Toronto General Hospital have visited Hydro One to learn about our methods.

- Hydro One has become a well-established company both internally and externally. In 1999 it was a "new" company operating in a market that was to be deregulated and it was scheduled for privatization through an IPO. Today Hydro One has over five years of experience as an independent company. It has demonstrated its ability to compete in a market that *had been* deregulated (but is now moving toward more regulation), and its ownership structure is now considered stable. Thus, the extent to which Hydro One faces internal and external changes has been markedly reduced.

The CRO continues to provide support for senior managers and develop risk management policies, frameworks, processes, and other analyses as needed. But thanks to the success of the program, the demand for hosting numerous workshops and establishing a risk management culture is greatly diminished. In short, risk management and awareness has become a mature operation at Hydro One.[20]

Conclusion

This article describes the implementation over a 5-year period of enterprise risk management at Hydro One, a Canadian electric utility company that has experienced significant changes in its industry and business. Starting with the creation of the position of Chief Risk Officer and the deployment of a pilot

19. See Hydro One Inc.'s 2002 President's Awards.
20. Interestingly, the outcome of ERM at Hydro One is consistent with the predictions of a survey by The Conference Board of Canada in which respondents felt that the need for a specific risk officer may decline as it is more widely implemented in organizations and the CRO's responsibilities would then be distributed to the operating units or assimilated into the CFO's duties; see The Conference Board of Canada, "A Composite Sketch of a Chief Risk Officer" (2001).

Strategic Risk Management Analysis of Voluntary Retirement Package

In the early summer of 2000, the Risk Management Group was asked to perform an enterprise risk management analysis of the risks related to a Voluntary Retirement Package (VRP) that was offered to employees at Hydro One. The purpose of the Voluntary Retirement Package was to reduce staff and related costs in preparation for an IPO. However, the Voluntary Retirement Package turned out to be almost too much of a success. Hydro One lost 1,300 employees out of a total of over 6,000 employees—far more than the 800 that were expected to take the package. And the 1,300 employees were in most cases senior and experienced personnel. The senior management of Hydro One feared that without a rigorous analysis, some unjustified requests for personnel to replace those who had left would eradicate the economic benefits of the program. In risk map terms, the purpose of the enterprise risk analysis was to address the bubbles in the far right-hand corner and move these bubbles toward the lower left-hand corner as cost effectively as possible. (See figure 16.3 for an illustration of this concept.)

The Corporate Risk Management Group discussed business objectives and related risk tolerances with about 40 managers whose groups had experienced material VRP losses. The group asked the managers what actions they had taken or planned to compensate for VRP losses (such as efficiency improvements or dropping activities) and where they felt they still had a resource gap that could impact corporate objectives. The interviews allowed the Corporate Risk Management Group to identify units where the VRP losses resulted in material risk and what the impacts of those risks might be. The group vetted this feedback through a series of interviews with senior management responsible for each major functional area (Finance, Regulatory, and so on) to validate middle management's assessment of both the gap and the impacts. For areas of material risk ("Major" or higher), the group asked managers what could be done in order to reduce risk to a "Moderate" level or lower.

The managers indicated that they had taken actions or had plans underway to compensate for the loss of some of the employees. The most important mitigating technique was from planned efficiency gains, but the possibility of hiring contract / temporary workers was also planned. Overall, managers estimated that they could compensate for 1,100 employees out of the 1,300 employees lost, thus leaving a gap of some 200 employees to mitigate excessive levels of risks.

continued

The Corporate Risk Management Group developed a draft list of VRP risk sources, which the senior management team assessed and ranked at a two-hour facilitated workshop, using electronic voting technology and the Delphi Method. The result was a list of 11 risk sources ranked according to their significance. "Customer Relations" and "Network Services" topped the list with a risk score of 3.9 and 3.8 on a five-point scale integrating both magnitude and probability. For example, "Customer Relations" was voted as having a magnitude of 3.8 and a probability of 4.1, which gave an ultimate risk score of 3.9. Some of the risk sources pertained to specific organization units while other risk sources were generic (organization-wide). For the unit-specific risks, the Corporate Risk Management Group calculated on the basis of input from managers that a mitigation process that reduced all risks to a "Moderate" level or lower (1 or 2 on a five-point scale—see table 16.1) would require 126 full-time employees and CAD 4.4 million. For the generic risks, a combination of monitoring, planning, and risk assessment programs was proposed. The mitigation as to unit-specific risks as well as generic risks was not intended to eliminate the VRP as a source of risk but to reduce the risks to acceptable levels in a cost-effective way.

study involving one of the firm's subsidiaries, the ERM implementation process has made use of a variety of tools and techniques, including the "Delphi Method," risk trends, risk maps, risk tolerances, risk profiles, and risk rankings.

Among the most tangible benefits of ERM at Hydro One are a more rational and better-coordinated process for allocating capital and the favorable reaction of Moody's and Standard & Poor's, which has arguably led to an increase in its credit rating and a reduction of its cost of capital. But perhaps just as important is the company's progress in realizing the first principle of its ERM policy—namely, that "risk management is everyone's responsibility, from the board of directors to individual employees. Each is expected to understand the risks that fall within the limits of their accountabilities and is expected to manage these risks within approved risk tolerances." The implementation process itself has helped make risk awareness an important part of the corporate culture.

As a result, the management of Hydro One feels that the company is much better positioned today than 5 years ago to respond to new developments in the business environment, favorable as well as unfavorable. Indeed, ERM can be viewed as an integral part of the company's current business model. As Charles

Darwin noted over 150 years ago, in a world where mutability is the only permanent feature of the landscape, "It's not the strongest of the species that survive, nor the most intelligent, but those that are the most responsive to change."

■ TOM AABO is an Associate Professor at Aarhus School of Business (Denmark).

■ JOHN R. S. FRASER is Chief Risk Officer at Hydro One, Inc.

■ BETTY J. SIMKINS is an Associate Professor of Finance at Oklahoma State University.

CHAPTER 17

University of Georgia Roundtable on Enterprise-Wide Risk Management

ATLANTA, GEORGIA, NOVEMBER 18, 2002

James Verbrugge: Good morning, and on behalf of the University of Georgia's Terry College of Business and the Spencer Educational Foundation, let me welcome you to this discussion of corporate risk management. I'm Jim Verbrugge, Professor of Finance at the Terry College of Business and Director of its Center for Strategic Risk Management. I will be serving as one of the moderators of this discussion. My co-moderator is Don Chew, one of the founding partners of Stern Stewart & Co. and Editor-in-Chief of the *Journal of Applied Corporate Finance (JACF)*. As you may have heard, the *JACF* is now being co-published by Accenture, the well-known management consulting and technical services firm.

Our discussion will proceed in two main parts. In the first, we're going to focus on the goals of enterprise-wide risk management, or ERM for short. What is it that ERM programs are really supposed to accomplish? And before I go any farther, let me just explain that I'm going to be using the terms "ERM" and "strategic risk management" more or less interchangeably. Defined as briefly as possible, ERM and strategic risk management are corporate-wide, as opposed to departmentalized, efforts to manage *all* the firm's risks—in fact, its *total* liability structure—in a way that helps management to carry out its goal of maximizing the value of the firm's assets. It amounts to a highly coordinated attempt to use the right-hand side of the balance sheet to support the left-hand side—which, as finance theory tells us, is where most of the value is created.

For academics like me, who have been trained to believe that *all* corporate value comes from the asset side of the balance sheet, there's a bit of a paradox in the very idea of *corporate* risk management. The overall objective of most ERM or strategic risk management programs is often expressed in terms of

This chapter was previously published as an article in *Journal of Applied Corporate Finance* Vol. 15, No. 4 (2003): 8–26. Photographs by Tim Wilkerson/Atlanta.

reducing, or limiting, the variability of corporate earnings or cash flows. But according to the so-called "modern" theory of corporate finance, reductions in the volatility of earnings and cash flows per se should not be expected to increase a company's market value. As we teach our students, in the case of public companies owned by lots of well-diversified investors, higher volatility that is unrelated to broad swings in the economy or markets should not increase a company's "beta," and thus should not cause the company to have a higher required rate of return—or, what amounts to pretty much the same thing, to trade at a lower P/E ratio. So, the essential question we want to address in the first part of the discussion is whether corporate risk management programs are capable in theory of adding value for a company's investors; and, if the answer is yes, how do they do it? Are the risk management programs that we see in practice today really designed to add value?

The second part of the discussion will focus on the issues and obstacles companies face when they attempt to implement an ERM program. Who in the corporate organization should be held accountable for managing what risks, and how should corporate performance measurement be designed to enforce such accountability? What are some notable examples of corporate risk management failures, and what went wrong in those cases? And how do you know if your risk management program has accomplished its objectives?

To discuss these issues, we have assembled a distinguished group of academics and practitioners—a group that we expect will generate a lively exchange of views on the theory and practice of corporate risk management. I will start by introducing our two academic panelists:

Clifford Smith, in addition to being a friend of mine for over 20 years, is the Louise and Henry Epstein Professor of Business Administration at the University of Rochester's Simon School of Business. Cliff is one of the world's leading scholars in the areas of risk management, capital structure, and corporate finance. He has published several books and a very large number of articles in the best academic finance journals, and he continues to pile up awards for his teaching of Rochester MBAs.

Greg Niehaus is Professor of Risk Management and Insurance at the University of South Carolina's Moore School of Business. Greg has written a number of papers describing applications of risk management in various industries, including a case study of United Grain Grower's unique approach to managing weather risk that appeared in the *JACF* about a year ago.

Now I'll introduce our representatives from the business community:

Christie Briscoe works in the Chief Risk Officer's organization at AGL Resources, which is a distributor and seller of natural gas and which has recently started an enterprise risk program. Prior to joining AGL, Christie worked in Risk Management at Xcel Energy and Research and at the New York Mercantile Exchange.

Walter Coleman is a Senior Vice President in charge of audit at First Data Corporation, a company that has spent considerable time and effort implementing an enterprise risk management program. And I'm sure Walter will have some very interesting comments about that process and the issues they have faced along the way.

Keith Lawder is a Senior Vice President and Group Executive at Wachovia Bank. Banks, of course, have always faced risk management issues, particularly credit and interest rate risk, and they have been among the first organizations to develop ERM systems. As Wachovia's State Risk Officer for Georgia, Keith has been involved in the bank's efforts to manage the risks in its commercial credit portfolios as well as its approval process for taking on additional risk.

Sailesh Ramamurtie is Assistant Global Risk Control Officer at Mirant, the power generation and energy risk management company that was spun out of the Southern Company almost two years ago. Mirant is facing a unique set of challenges at the present time, and I'm hoping Sailesh will shed some light on how risk management is being used to respond to these challenges. Before joining Mirant, Sailesh was a member of the finance faculty at Georgia State University and a visiting scholar at the Atlanta Fed.

With these introductions behind us, I'll now turn over the floor to my co-moderator, Don Chew.

Does Risk Management Matter?

Chew: Thanks, Jim, for starting us off. And before we plunge into the subject, I want to thank you and the University of Georgia's Terry College of Business for all your efforts and support in putting this program together.

To provide a bit more perspective on Jim's opening comments, I'd like to begin with a little story. My colleague Joel Stern is fond of saying that when he started his MBA at the University of Chicago in the late 1960s, the phrase "nothing matters" was used with such frequency and fervor that he thought he was in the wrong place—he thought he had come to Berkeley. At that time, and for many years after, the teaching of corporate finance began and ended with the celebrated Modigliani and Miller irrelevance propositions. The M&M propositions, as you might recall from your school days, say that neither a company's capital structure nor its dividend policy should affect its value. Their basic insight was that corporate capital structure and dividend choices are nothing more than different ways of dividing up the firm's operating cash flows and repackaging them for investors. And because investors who would prefer a higher corporate leverage or dividend payout ratio can accomplish the same effect simply by buying stock on margin or periodically selling shares, two equally risky companies with the same (pre-interest) operating cash flows ought to have the same total "enterprise" value—that is, the value of debt plus equity—regardless of differences in their leverage or dividend policies.

And the same was said to be true of corporate risk management. Much as the company's investors can create homemade leverage and dividends, they can also neutralize any effects of interest rate and currency risk on corporate values just by holding well-diversified portfolios of stocks and bonds. Thus there was no good reason for a company that hedged a large currency exposure to trade at a higher P/E multiple than an otherwise identical firm that chose not to hedge.

But after having spent most of the 1960s showing why corporate finance should not matter, finance theorists in the 1970s shifted their focus to explaining how and why it *could* add value. And one of the finance scholars who played a very central role in taking finance theory beyond the M&M propositions is seated at this table—Cliff Smith. Besides being an old friend of Jim Verbrugge's, Cliff also happens to have been my first finance professor at the Simon School in the late 1970s. And I'm going to ask Cliff to start us off by telling us why financial economists think that corporate risk management *doesn't* matter—and then why they think it *does*.

Cliff Smith: Thanks, Don, for the kind words—and it's good to be back here in my home state and to get away from the Rochester tundra for a few days. When Don called and we started talking about this roundtable, I was reminded of some of the encounters I've had with the students in our Executive MBA programs at Rochester over the years. These people generally come to my finance course with considerable business experience, and their initial reaction to the idea of corporate risk management is to say, "Well, reducing risk is obviously a good idea. Who wants to take on risks that you can get rid of?"

But after spending some time talking about the Modigliani and Miller propositions and the way our capital markets operate, the students begin to rethink their original positions. The heart of the analysis here is that the corporate form of organizing business activities is a tremendously powerful risk management tool in and of itself. By selling claims on their future cash flow into the marketplace, companies allow their securities to be priced by individuals who hold well-diversified portfolios of securities. Thanks to this kind of diversification, investors manage a whole variety of corporate risks in ways that are compa-

Risk management can create value by strengthening managers' incentives to undertake all available positive-NPV investments (especially those with a long payoff horizon). By reducing the expected costs of bankruptcy or financial distress, hedging can also be viewed as increasing a firm's debt capacity and, in so doing reducing its cost of capital. Reducing the probability of financial trouble helps reassure not only creditors, but also other corporate "stakeholders"—groups such as employees, suppliers, and regulators, who are generally willing to provide the firm with better terms (or more slack) when the possibility of Chapter 11 seems remote.

—Cliff Smith

rable to what an insurance company does with a bunch of policies that are individually quite risky but whose total losses are fairly predictable using actuarial techniques. And just as the insurance company's ability to pool its risks allows it to charge lower premiums, stockholders' ability to diversify their portfolios ends up reducing the "price," or required rate of return, that they charge companies for holding their stock—a price that people in finance call the "cost of capital." For that reason, investors' ability to hold a company's stock in a diversified portfolio has the effect of raising the firm's stock price and its P/E ratio—that is, it raises the price the market is willing to pay for a given expected cash flow or earnings stream. And that's what I mean when I say that the corporate form of organization has a highly beneficial effect on the value of individual firms and on the allocation of risk across our economy. It's a very efficient way of spreading the risks associated with funding corporate growth.

So, the beginning of my finance course is aimed at persuading experienced financial executives that their original intuition about risk is wrong, and that the responsible approach for a corporate manager is to avoid wasting corporate resources on risk management activities that are effectively accomplished *at far lower cost* by investors. But having spent some time showing why corporate risk management doesn't matter, we then devote much of the rest of the course to showing why risk management—and corporate finance in general—*does* matter. That is, we try to demonstrate how CFOs and chief risk officers are capable of increasing corporate values.

The way we do this is to take the M&M propositions and give them something of a half twist. If it's been a while since you were sitting in a corporate finance classroom, let me remind you that the M&M propositions rest on three major assumptions. First, there are no taxes or transactions costs incurred by either companies or their investors, including the costs associated with reorganizing firms that get into financial trouble. Second, there are no "information" costs, which implies, among other things, that investors have as good a view of the company's prospects as the managers themselves. And third, corporate investment policy is assumed to be "fixed," which means that corporate investment and operating decisions are not affected by how the company finances itself or whether it manages risks. Using those assumptions and a handful of others that don't matter for our purposes, M&M showed that financing policy in general and risk management policy in particular should not affect a company's total market value, or the value of its debt plus equity.

Now, when we turn the M&M proposition on its head, we get the following: If financing policy or risk management activities *do* affect the value of the firm, then one of the factors that M&M assumed away must be important. So we are left with the argument that risk management can create value in one or more of the following ways: by reducing the overall tax liabilities of the corporation or its investors; by reducing the costs associated with investors' uncertainty about the firm's current profitability and prospects; by strengthening managers' incentives to undertake all available positive-NPV investments (especially those with a long payoff horizon) and walk away from the rest; and by reducing the probability of a costly reorganization or bankruptcy. I should also mention that hedging, by reducing the expected costs of bankruptcy or financial distress, can also be viewed as increasing a firm's debt capacity and, in so doing, reducing its cost of capital. And, by the way, it's not only the firm's bondholders and creditors who appreciate risk management; reducing the probability of financial trouble also helps reassure the firm's other corporate "stakeholders"—groups such as employees, suppliers, and regulators—who are generally willing to provide the firm with better terms (or more slack) when the possibility of Chapter 11 seems more remote.

So, to make a long story a little longer, the aim of my finance course is to get students to see that even though investors hold well-diversified portfolios of securities and the corporate form is a tremendously powerful risk management tool, there are important things that CFOs and CROs can do to add significant value.

Chew: Cliff, consistent with your argument about how our capital markets manage risk, Warren Buffett has said that he prefers a "lumpy" 15% rate of return to a smooth 12% return. Yet I often get the sense that most corporate managers, if given the same choice, would take the smooth 12%. To the extent our capital markets share Buffett's willingness to accept more volatility for higher overall returns, my concern is that managers who view risk management as primarily a tool for smoothing reported earnings are losing sight of the "real" economic functions of risk management that you cited, particularly its role in reducing the cost of capital and ensuring a company's ability to carry out its long-term investment policy and strategic plan.

Smith: This is one of those areas where I'd agree fairly readily with Mr. Buffett.

As I said a moment ago, there's an awful lot that individual investors can do about risk management simply through diversification. If you give me the opportunity to undertake a project with lumpy cash flows but an expected rate of return that is higher than the cost of capital, investors are generally in a good position to manage that kind of lumpiness themselves through their portfolio holdings; that's a big part of their job. And, as Jim suggested earlier, reductions in volatility per se, in the absence of any expected effects on real factors like taxes or bankruptcy costs or corporate investment decisions, are not a good reason to manage risk.

Why Earnings Might Matter

Sailesh Ramamurtie: Although Warren Buffett may prefer lumpy returns, my sense is that the majority of investors would choose the smooth 12% return over the lumpy 15%. So, to me, the decision by most corporations and managers to smooth earnings is a reasonable response to the behavior of investors. Most investments by individuals are made through portfolios of mutual funds. The performance of mutual fund managers is judged on a quarter-by-quarter basis. And to achieve their goal of steady price appreciation, the mutual fund managers in turn encourage the managements of the companies they invest in to report smooth earnings growth.

So, I don't believe that investors' portfolio diversification is an unmixed blessing for public companies. As I see it, the pressure for short-term performance and smooth earnings is coming *from* our capital markets, not in spite of them.

Greg Niehaus: I agree that there are outside influences that cause managers to care about volatility in earnings, but I also tend to think that these pressures are coming mainly from sell-side analysts, and not from the buy side. The fact that mutual fund managers have diversified portfolios means that fluctuations in the value of one stock can't really cause much of a change in their net asset values in a given period.

Ramamurtie: But mutual fund managers pay a great deal of attention to the analysts' reports. Analysts classify a stock as having lower or higher risk based in large part on the predictability of the company's income on a quarter-by-quarter basis; and those risk classifications are used by portfolio managers when justifying their decisions to buy or sell a stock. So I think the buy side is also contributing to the short-termism and earnings management of U.S. corporate managers.

Walter Coleman: It's really a question of investor time horizons that we're debating here. Warren Buffett is willing to live with short-term earnings volatility because his time horizon is much longer than that of the portfolio managers who are constantly rebalancing their portfolios. And I tend to agree with Sailesh's position that most investors are not like Buffett; most have a very short-term frame of reference in terms of dealing with predictability of earnings that makes them uncomfortable with volatility.

I would also argue that recent changes in laws and regulations governing the marketplace have made this problem worse. Take the recently passed fair disclosure requirements, or "Reg. FD" for short. By limiting the ability of analysts to obtain additional information from the companies they follow, Reg. FD has actually *increased* the level of uncertainty in the market. In this situation, investors will rationally attach *more* weight, not less, to quarterly earnings.

Let me give you an example. There is an analyst who follows First Data who has been determined to get the inside track on what's happening at the company. We own Western Union Financial Services, which is the largest money transfer corporation—the largest "nonbank" bank, if you will—in the world. We have 130,000 agents around the world who move money in about 15,000 different corridors for the "unbanked." The business is growing at a 20–30% rate a year because of the movement of people from Third-World nations to developed countries who transfer money back and forth for family purposes.

This analyst went out and interviewed some 15 or 20 of our 130,000 agents to get an indication of where the marketplace for money transfers was going. Based on his interviews, he concluded that the marketplace was slowing down. And he based his report on this slim evidence because he was no longer permitted to go to the company itself and ask the executives any questions other than those relating to the information that would be publicly disclosed.

When we released earnings this last quarter, we ended up exceeding expectations by a significant margin; and our stock price, which had been depressed by the analyst's report, jumped on the earnings release. When some of the other analysts came back and asked about that particular analyst's report, our CEO commented that the technique used to gather information was unreliable and the conclusions were incorrect.

So, Reg. FD places a lot of risk on analysts' efforts to try to get beyond public information. And this makes it even harder for management to communicate with the markets, which in turn increases the pressure to meet near-term earnings targets.

Chew: Walter, I agree with you that the main effect of Reg. FD has been to increase "information costs"—to make it even more difficult for companies to provide credible, forward-looking information to their investors. And this is likely to end up reducing all corporate values and cause investors to pay even more attention to quarterly earnings. But even so, I can't help feeling that corporate managements have brought a big part of this problem on themselves. It seems to me that managements are overly sensitive to volatility in earnings, much more sensitive than the investors themselves.

Coleman: Well, I think that what drives management's sensitivity is the reaction of the stock price to earnings misses. Our CEO likes to say that he has to manage for the future, but pay attention to the quarter—because the quarterly results are what the marketplace is looking at.

Chew: But there is another way to interpret this earnings-miss phenomenon you mention. The market knows that GAAP earnings are not a very reliable measure of either cash flow or value added, in part because corporate managements have so many ways to manipulate the numbers. And given the pressure managers are facing to meet earnings targets, an earnings miss thus suggests that actual corporate cash flows have fallen way short of the target. That seems like a fairly plausible account of how a one-penny earnings miss can lead to a 20% drop in the stock.

ERM and strategic risk management are corporate-wide, as opposed to departmentalized, efforts to manage all the firm's risks—in fact, its total liability structure—in a way that helps management to carry out its goal of maximizing the value of the firm's assets. It amounts to a highly coordinated attempt to use the right-hand side of the balance sheet to support the left-hand side—which, as finance theory tells us, is where most of the value is created.

—Jim Verbrugge

Ramamurtie: Back on the point about investor diversification, one thing we tend to overlook in discussions of required corporate returns and cost of capital is that a large portion of most investors' income and wealth comes from their employment, their jobs. When we talk about M&M and portfolio theory, we are talking about exchange economies where a typical investor's entire income is coming from his or her portfolio of securities. But the extent and kind of investors' diversification has to reflect *both* sources of income—their investment income and the income associated with their own employment.

So while portfolio diversification sounds fine in theory, I'm skeptical of the idea that everybody is going to hold the so-called market portfolio. What portfolio theory fails to take account of is that people hold portfolios that are diversified when viewed in the context of *all* their sources of income.

Smith: I agree that there are lots of people who don't hold well-diversified portfolios. In fact, corporate managers are a perfect example of a group of people who typically hold unbalanced, or highly concentrated, portfolios. *But that's the way it should be*. In the handful of cases where I have served on corporate boards, I have urged the compensation committee to structure the total compensation of top management so that future changes in their wealth are tied directly to changes in the long-run value of the firm. Specifically, we try to load up the managers with restricted stock—securities that are not tradable—because we want the managers to bear the consequences of their business decisions not just on a quarter-by-quarter basis, but over a period of as much as five or ten years. To see why that's important, consider top corporate managers with large equity positions that can be unloaded at will. In such cases, managers are much more likely to manage for the short term, use aggressive accounting practices, and even engage in the unethical behavior that we have read so much about in the popular press.

At any rate, my bottom line here is that if U.S. managers pay too much attention to the next quarter's earnings, or to the smoothness of earnings—which I find a doubtful proposition at best—most of the blame should be placed not on our capital markets, but on the managers themselves and on the boards that are supposed to oversee them. If we could find some way to see through all the "noise" in stock price reactions to earnings announcements, I think we would find that the investors who play the greatest role in setting long-run stock values behave a lot more like Warren Buffett than the momentum investors and day traders we hear so much about. And while I understand there are pressures for smooth earnings coming from some securities analysts, boards need to do a better job of encouraging managers to resist those pressures when that's clearly the right thing to do.

But having said that, I can also think of a number of *good* reasons for risk management programs to pay at least some attention to the volatility of earnings. For example, companies with bank or bond covenants that have minimum coverage ratios and net worth provisions want to ensure that they are able to report at least some minimal level of earnings.

Ramamurtie: In our risk management program at Mirant, we pay a lot of attention to the level and volatility of earnings as well as cash flow. We fund our operations with significant amounts of debt; and, as Cliff just suggested, a major part of our rationale for focusing on earnings is our need to meet the provisions of our covenants.

Smith: That's a good illustration, by the way, of how risk management can increase the firm's debt capacity. I would guess that Mirant couldn't support the kind of debt it does without at least some hedging of its earnings and cash flow.

Ramamurtie: That's right.

Smith: Another possible reason for managing earnings volatility has to do with some potentially beneficial effects on managers' decision-making. About ten years ago, Judy Lewent, who was then CFO (and is now a board member) of Merck, wrote a *Harvard Business Review* article that addressed the problem of maintaining Merck's R&D spending over time. Merck had a long-standing policy of setting R&D budgets as a percentage of earnings. But as Merck's international business grew and its earnings were increasingly subject to currency swings, Judy became concerned that Merck was walking away from promising R&D projects when the dollar strengthened and earnings fell. One possible solution to this problem was to go to the board and change the rule of thumb about determining the R&D budget. But another approach was risk management—to hedge the foreign currency exposure, reduce earnings volatility, and stabilize the R&D budget. And that's the course that Merck chose. At bottom, it was a decision to use risk management to ensure that managers' concern about earnings would not cause them to turn down positive-NPV projects.

Strategic Risk Management and the Search for Comparative Advantage

Verbrugge: Recently some academics have argued that corporate risk management policy should be guided by a concept called "comparative advantage in risk-bearing." The basic idea is that companies should retain only the business risks in which they have a comparative advantage and attempt to transfer all non-core risks to others who are in a better position to bear them. To what extent has this concept of comparative advantage become part of current risk management practice?

Ramamurtie: I think that's clearly what strategic risk management is about—determining which risks are best managed inside the corporation and which are best managed by outside investors or firms. Of course, any company that decides to be in a particular line of business has already made that decision to some extent. For example, my company, Mirant, is in both the power generation business and the energy trading business. And by virtue of our decision to be in the power business, we face what is known in the industry as "operations" risk. The question here is how best to manage production technologies and to limit technology failure rates and business interruption to acceptable levels. Do you buy insurance or do you self-insure? Many utilities manage their operations risk by building more capacity than they need so that if one unit goes out they can still provide power. In effect, they've made a decision to manage that risk internally by maintaining excess capacity. But in recent years, utilities have been forced to become increasingly sensitive to the possibility that carrying excess capacity is not always the value-maximizing strategy—hence the growing popularity of business interruption insurance and contingent supply contracts. Another risk that we have to worry about—and it's one that is currently attracting a lot of attention among financial and trading firms—is "operational" risk, the possibility that a rogue trader could do serious damage or even bring down the firm by circumventing trading limits. And the question, again, is how best to manage such risk. Some companies choose to improve their internal controls; but sometimes it's better to basically subcontract your mid- and back-office controls to a third party and concentrate on your core business activities.

Chew: Energy price risk is clearly another major risk for a power and energy trading company. Does Mirant feel that it has a comparative advantage in bearing energy price risk? Or do you generally try to transfer as much of that risk as you can through derivatives or long-term purchase contracts?

Ramamurtie: Well, if you're an energy company, then you have to decide whether to manage energy price risk at all. Following the logic of portfolio diversification and the Capital Asset Pricing Model, the managements of a lot of energy and mining companies are convinced that their shareholders want to bear the energy price exposure, and so they do little if any hedging of energy prices. But a growing number of companies are finding reasons to hedge a significant portion of their price risks, even though such risks may not affect the systematic risk that is supposed to determine investors' required rates of return.

The question is, what is the appropriate level of hedging activity for a given company? The way we answer that question at Mirant is by simulating possible earnings and cash flow outcomes based on different hedging strategies and our projected probability distribution for future energy prices. We try to put certain hedges in place and then see what happens to our projected earnings and cash flows while also trying to forecast the reaction of the marketplace to that outcome. And by pursuing this process, we try to determine the optimal level of hedging, the one that we expect to maximize our stock price and P/E multiple.

At the current moment, we at Mirant—along with most of the power producers I'm aware of—think that power prices are too low to do much hedging. If we lock in prices at current levels, we will never get enough revenue to earn the rate of return that our investors are demanding from us. So we'd rather take the risk of daily price fluctuations to preserve the possibility of benefiting from a sharp increase in prices and revenues.

Chew: That doesn't sound like hedging to me. By making a decision not to hedge when you think prices are low, aren't you effectively betting against a further drop in prices and, in so doing, taking a major price risk? How is that different from speculating on prices?

Ramamurtie: What we do at Mirant is not the so-called variance-minimizing hedging that you read about in finance textbooks; we don't hedge against the downside by giving away the upside. Instead we practice what is sometimes called *selective* hedging, or hedging "with a view." And it works like this: When we think prices are near their lows, we will hedge as little of our production as possible, just enough to make sure we have sufficient earnings and cash flow to maintain our credit rating if prices continue to fall. Hedging when prices are low is counterproductive because it eliminates the expected upside in the revenue stream from a price increase. But when prices are near historically high levels, we are likely to hedge a significant fraction of our expected revenues.

Chew: Cliff, how do you feel about the idea of selective hedging?

Smith: The first thing I like to do when talking about hedging strategy is to sort out whether in a particular market setting you are going to be active or passive. One way to take an active position is to decide *not* to hedge a given exposure under certain conditions. Like you, Don, I'm inclined to call that speculating rather than hedging.

My general advice to corporate treasurers is that when you're dealing in well-functioning liquid secondary markets—and in that category I would include global markets in interest rates, foreign exchange rates, and energy prices—there's an awful lot of information reflected in current prices, far more than any individual organization can possibly possess. And unless you have some kind of informational advantage over most other market participants, then your best bet is to interpret the current price—or, if there is one, the current *futures* price—as an "unbiased" predictor of the future price. If you operate under that assumption, your expected profit from holding an open long position in any commodity has got to be zero; it's just not a value-adding proposition.

But having said that, I'm willing to entertain the idea that having a natural position in an asset like oil or power conceivably gives you some advantage in trading that commodity. For example, it's possible that the old Chase Manhattan Bank, because of its continuous operations in money markets, had a comparative advantage in making markets in interest rate swaps. But I would be very reluctant to build a business strategy around that argument. In fact, if memory serves, Don's journal published an article about ten years ago showing that the profits from Chase's market-making activities haven't come from taking positions, but from acting as a go-between, collecting the bid-ask spreads, and *avoiding* large positions.

Managing interest rate and other financial risks is generally a two-part process. Each line manager or business manager is responsible for managing risk, at least to some extent. But the institution as a whole—the corporate risk management office, if you will—must then decide what to do with the *residual* risk, what's left over after all the line managers and traders have taken their positions. An ERM program helps management decide which risks are best managed at what levels in the organization and then to establish the optimal risk limits and permissible risk management strategies.

—Sailesh Ramamurtie

Ramamurtie: I tend to agree with both parts of your argument—and I feel that the second part describes our situation at Mirant. Given that we're in the power generation business, we've accumulated lots of experience with energy price markets that we can use in our market-making operations. Moreover, as an energy trader and market maker, we're not in a position to put on a static hedge and then just relax. Power generation can be thought of as giving us an option on the difference between the price at which we sell our output and the price we pay for it, and both of those prices move randomly and somewhat independently of each other. So if you want to hedge, you have to continuously adjust your positions. You might call this activity speculative, but we're always actively monitoring our hedging and trading to limit our exposures to acceptable levels.

And to repeat my earlier argument, we believe that our selective hedging policy reflects the risk preferences of our shareholders. That is, we protect them from a disastrous outcome by always hedging enough to ensure a minimal level of cash flow that's designed to preserve our credit rating. But at the same time, by limiting our hedging when prices are considered low, we preserve our shareholders' ability to participate in the upside that would result from a spike in energy demand. Given the current low level of prices, it simply wouldn't help our expected earnings or our share price to go out and hedge.

Niehaus: I'm not surprised that a company in the energy business would have information that would make selective hedging of energy price risk a value-increasing strategy, on average. By the same token, a gold-mining company might have information that makes selective hedging of gold price risk a value-adding activity. Of course, in both these cases the extent to which traders are allowed to engage in such activity must be limited and carefully monitored. But for those commodities or financial markets where companies do *not* have a natural position on a daily basis, I would clearly question the wisdom of selective hedging.

More on Comparative Advantage in Risk-Bearing: The Case of Interest Rate Risk

Smith: I would like to come back to this concept of strategic risk management—of keeping your core business risks and getting rid of other risks—that Jim mentioned earlier. My first job was working in a bank in Georgia (where my dad happened to be the president). This was long enough ago that if a bank originated a loan, the bank also owned the loan, serviced the loan, and bore the interest rate and credit risk. But if you look today at real estate mortgage loans, for example, securitization has led to a situation where all of those functions are performed by different entities; and each is priced very competitively, with the lowest-cost vendor getting most of the business.

 Different organizations can manage the same risk with different levels of effectiveness. And one goal of enterprise risk management should be to encourage corporate focus by getting rid of all the functions that can be performed more effectively outside the organization. In this sense, the thinking underlying strategic risk management is much the same as the rationale for corporate outsourcing. It's about determining where the corporation adds value, and focusing corporate efforts and resources on those areas while eliminating all distractions and risks that dilute that focus.

—Don Chew

And the same logic applies to risk management in general. If there is some outside firm or investor willing to bear a particular risk at a lower price than what it costs the firm to bear that risk internally, then it makes sense to lay off those risks. That's true if you're in the energy market, and you're talking about oil or gas or electricity prices; it's true if you're in the import-export business and you're talking about foreign exchange rates; and it's true if you're in the financial services industry and you're talking about interest rates. And I don't find the idea of "core" risks to be a very useful one because there may turn out to be *no core*; all the functions may end up being transferred outside the firm.

Niehaus: I don't see core risks as necessarily a set of risks that are fundamental to a business or an industry. I think that when people discuss core risks, what they're really talking about are the risks that they have a comparative advantage in bearing. A core risk is one that a particular firm can manage at lower cost than any outside entity. It's almost tautological—a core risk is a risk that is optimal for the firm to bear.

Chew: It might be more than a tautology in the sense that companies have to be very honest in assessing what they do well and what they don't. Different organizations can manage the same risk with different levels of effectiveness. And one goal of enterprise risk management should be to encourage corporate focus by getting rid of all the functions that can be performed more effectively outside the organization. In this sense, the thinking underlying strategic risk management is much the same as the rationale for corporate outsourcing. It's about determining where the corporation adds value, and focusing corporate efforts and resources on those areas while eliminating all distractions and risks that dilute that focus.

And that brings me to a question that has puzzled me for a long time: Is interest rate risk a core risk for a bank or not? And, Keith, since you're our representative banker, can I ask you to respond to this one?

Keith Lawder: All banks, as financial intermediaries that raise and hold deposits and make loans, are forced to bear some level of interest rate risk. It's impossible to get rid of 100% of it, but I think most banks try to limit their exposures. It goes back to what Cliff was saying earlier. When I got into banking back in the 1970s, it was a pretty simple proposition. If you wanted a mortgage loan, a car loan, or a business loan, you went to your banker—and the sources of funds on the other side of that transaction were pretty predictable, too, because whether you were a corporation or an individual, there were only certain types of deposits.

Deregulation on the deposit side of banks' balance sheets has brought a whole host of changes. Today, a commercial banker will probably be selling upwards of 250 different products. There is no way that any individual or group of individuals within a bank can be expected to manage all the interest rate risk associated with all the products they're selling.

So the bank has to manage the risks of their various businesses in a comprehensive fashion—and that, of course, is where enterprise-wide risk management comes in. Part of that process is to develop a vocabulary so that people can understand risk in the same way across different lines of business. In commercial banking, it's really a multilayered process of risk management, with each manager down the chain partly responsible for his or her portfolio of assets or risks, and senior management overseeing the process from the top. We are trying to get the people selling the products to understand the nature of at least some of the risks that are being created by the products they are selling. Without a common vocabulary and some common measurement systems, people operate at cross-purposes. And, as I see it, senior management has two main roles in this process: to coordinate the ERM process in a way that limits risk while eliminating duplication of hedging, controls, and costs; and to design an incentive system that encourages line managers to carry out the corporation's risk management goals.

Ramamurtie: That's right. Managing interest rate and other financial risks is generally a two-part process. Each line manager or business manager is responsible for managing risk, at least to some extent. But the institution as a whole—the corporate risk management office, if you will—must then decide what to do with the *residual* risk, what's left over after all the line managers and traders have taken their positions.

For example, our energy business in Canada exposes Mirant to both commodity price and exchange rate risks. We want the trader in Canada to be responsible for managing the commodity price risk, but the currency risk is managed at a higher and more centralized level. In both cases, the responsibility of ERM is to decide which risks are best managed at what levels in the organization and then to establish the optimal risk limits and permissible risk management strategies.

In this sense, we at Mirant think of ourselves as being in risk management both at an institutional level and at a desk level. We make clear to a particular trader what risks he or she will be responsible for managing, and we provide guidelines for doing so. And each trader's performance is evaluated on the basis of his or her return on capital.

Lawder: It's pretty much the same at Wachovia. For each line of business, we have objectives that are based on economic capital and risk-adjusted returns on net capital. And the managers are held accountable for meeting those objectives.

Chew: Keith, as a general proposition, do you think that the amount of interest rate risk that banks are taking has fallen over time? Years ago, I can remember Sandy Rose of *American Banker* saying that J.P. Morgan made most of its profits simply by riding the yield curve—funding short and investing heavily in long-term government bonds—and it was widely understood that many banks were doing this throughout the mid-to-late 1980s. But I can't imagine that this is still standard practice. I would think that the more businesses banks get into, and the riskier those businesses are, the more they would need to use their capital to support the new operations rather than speculate on the yield curve.

Lawder: Well, much as Sailesh was saying about energy trading companies, the larger commercial banks with a lot of trading activities will generally hedge selectively. That is, they will ride the yield curve and take some amount of interest rate risk in selected areas when they feel pretty confident about where rates are going. By contrast, smaller banks that are not sufficiently "in the flow" are likely to hedge much larger portions of their interest rate risk and avoid taking large positions.

 Banks have to manage the risks of their various businesses in a comprehensive fashion—and that, of course, is where ERM comes in. In commercial banking, it's really a multilayered process of risk management, with each manager down the chain partly responsible for his or her portfolio of assets or risks, and senior management overseeing the process from the top. Part of that process is to develop a vocabulary so that people can understand risk in the same way across different lines of business. We are trying to get the people selling the products to understand the nature of some of the risks that are being created by the products they are selling. Senior management has two main roles in this: to coordinate the ERM process in a way that limits risk while eliminating duplication of hedging, controls, and costs; and to design an incentive system that encourages line managers to carry out the corporation's risk management goals.

—**Keith Lawder**

What has changed significantly is the banks' approach to managing open positions. For example, in the old days, if a bank was trying to match LIBOR loans against LIBOR deposits and had a 90-day transaction on one side and a 180-day transaction on the other, there would be a 90-day gap on the back end. Over the years, and thanks to innovations in IT systems, these open positions have been managed down very significantly as banks have gotten better at evaluating their risks and finding more ways to manage those risks effectively.

Coleman: Another major change for banks, which also results from their adoption of an ERM perspective, is a fairly recent tendency to think in terms of portfolio theory about how the risks of their different business lines can be used to offset each other. For example, First Data is now getting heavily into the insurance business, which has a very different set of risks from our credit portfolio risk. The new risks are layered over our existing risks, creating new open positions that need to be managed.

Verbrugge: Keith, what is Wachovia's *overriding* risk management policy—and I don't mean in managing just interest rate risk, but in managing *all* the risks confronting the firm? Is it formulated in terms of limiting earnings or cash flow volatility to what top management feels is an acceptable level?

Lawder: Yes, that's essentially what we're doing. And our rationale is as follows: Although the P/E ratios of banks are fairly stable and predictable, they tend to vary sharply during different stages in the credit cycle. And it seems very clear that banks with more volatile earnings trade at lower multiples than banks with more consistent earnings.

What drives the consistency of earnings is for the most part a bank's ability to manage credit risk. Time and time again, bank stocks have been penalized for exceptional events—say, a major default—even though event risk is at normal levels and expected losses over a long period of time are not out of line. So the market really does hurt bank market values for unexpected losses, and we use risk management to limit such losses to what we deem to be acceptable levels.

ERM and the Costs of Capital, Creditors, and Other Stakeholders

Verbrugge: Cliff talked earlier about how risk management can be used to support corporate investment policy and carry out the company's strategic plan. He also said that a well-executed corporate risk management policy can increase corporate debt capacity and, in so doing, reduce the corporate cost of capital. But, for this to happen, a company's hedging policy will have to be coordinated in some fashion with its financing policy.

Sailesh, you told us earlier that your ERM policy at Mirant involves ensuring a certain minimal level of cash flow, in part to preserve your credit rating. So when you sit down and negotiate covenants with your debtholders, do you expose them to your ERM process? Do you show them your models?

Ramamurtie: We try to explain just about everything. We tell them exactly what we think are our core competencies, we explain our business model, and we tell them what the funds will be used for. We also explain to them the workings of our ERM program, including the operational controls that we have put in place to ensure that our program gets carried out as planned. So it's a fairly involved process.

I should also point out that we operate with fairly significant amounts of leverage, and that most of our funding is nonrecourse. That means we create a project company, and the bondholders have claims to only the revenues of the project company.

Niehaus: So, to the extent you can convince your debtholders that you are managing risk well, it lowers your interest costs and otherwise improves the terms on which you contract with them?

Ramamurtie: That's right. And we go through essentially the same process with both the bond rating and the credit rating agencies. The agencies are becoming more familiar with the idea of applying ERM to nonfinancial companies.

And in case I haven't already made this sufficiently clear, energy companies—and especially energy merchants like Mirant—are natural candidates for enterprise risk management. We have trading positions in highly volatile commodities that in many cases are equal in size to the positions held and traded by the largest U.S. investment banks. In addition to our financial assets, we also have real assets such as power plant generators that put tremendous demands on cash flow. But because we don't have the balance sheet and liquidity of a bank, we have to manage not just our market risks, but significant credit and liquidity risks as well.

Given the current problems in energy trading, we are going to see even more attention paid to—and innovations in—enterprise risk management by the energy sector in the next couple of years. A good example is the move towards centralized clearing arrangements for over-the-counter transactions. By allowing for overall reductions in the collateral posted by counterparties, centralized clearing will reduce the amount of capital that is now required to manage two-way credit risks.

Coleman: At First Data we are seeing another, though clearly related, kind of benefit from risk management. We are going through the renewal of our

D&O insurance, and the insurers are taking a look at our entire ERM process. This is the first time we've experienced what I would call a top-level evaluation of our risk management process—one that involves providing significantly more information to the underwriters than ever before. What's interesting to me is that the outcome of that examination will clearly affect the premium we pay for the insurance. This is yet another instance where having a good risk management system has the effect of reducing costs and adding value.

Lawder: Having an effective risk management system, as Cliff suggested earlier, can also help companies in their dealings with regulators. If a bank, for example, consistently operates within certain limits on a particular operation, then it isn't necessary to scrutinize it as closely.

Verbrugge: Christie, as a risk manager of a natural gas producer and distributor, you must have a lot of dealings with regulators, which probably creates its own risks.

Christie Briscoe: That's right. In fact, I would say that regulatory risk is the biggest risk that we face at AGL. To cite one example, we tried to implement a so-called weather hedge in Virginia that would have protected our earnings against the effects of deviations from expected seasonal weather patterns. The problem we faced, however, was that if we took losses on that hedge, we would be unable to treat the loss as a cost that we could recoup through adjustments to our rate base. And if we gained on the hedge, we would have to give back the gains to the rate payers.

As things worked out, we ended up having to go to the Virginia Commission for permission to implement weather "normalization," a strategy that allows revenues to be adjusted to levels that correspond to the ten-year average. Although this strategy was not necessarily in the best interest of the shareholders or the rate payers, it did succeed in reducing our earnings volatility.

So, we tend to have an unusual view of risk in that even if something is fundamentally sound on a financial or operational basis, we always have regulatory concerns. We even have to weigh the pros and cons of taking certain write-offs based on what they would do to the return authorized by the state public utility regulatory bodies.

At present, we're in a very preliminary stage of enterprise risk management. Our enterprise risk group has only been in existence for about a year. And as I said, our largest risk by far is regulatory risk since over 90% of our revenues are subject to the regulators in Virginia or Georgia. We are looking at how we can reframe regulatory risk and view it as a risk that overlays our other operating risks, as opposed to a source of uncertainty that in the past has been managed with each new change in political leadership. Our measurements are very crude right now, and they are still generally on a situation-by-situation basis, whether it's our asset management operations down in Houston or in our regulated distribution operations in Georgia, Tennessee, and Virginia. Our next task, as I said, is to find a way to figure out how regulatory risk interacts with the other risks in our business—to find out if there are any predictable relationships that we can use to develop a more systematic risk management approach.

Risk Management, Performance Evaluation, and Incentive Compensation

Verbrugge: To summarize what we've just been saying, then, risk management can be used to reduce uncertainty and risk for a number of important corporate stakeholders—and we've just mentioned creditors, suppliers (in the form of insurance providers), and regulators. And as finance theory suggests, this reduction in uncertainty should reduce the firm's costs in contracting with these stakeholders.

But there's another important stakeholder group that is likely to benefit significantly from ERM—and that's management and employees. In theory, a more predictable corporate earnings and cash flow stream should make managers and employees more confident about their own future employment income; and with the reduction of uncertainty, they should be willing to work for less. As Cliff suggested earlier, risk management can also play a positive role when managers' bonuses are tied to reported earnings. Can you tell us how you see that happening, Cliff?

Smith: In most contracting situations, there's a good deal of uncertainty about how things are going to turn out in the future. Some of that uncertainty is controllable by the person or organization entering into the contract, but much of it is outside their control. In the good old days before derivatives, whenever things turned out badly, the people in the hot seat could blame poor performance on things that weren't their fault. They could say that a jump in interest rates reduced the profitability of their book of loans, or that a plunge in oil prices was responsible for their drop in revenue.

But thanks to the development of derivatives, we now have a set of markets that allow us to isolate those things that are outside the executive's control and take them off the table. As a result, we're left with a clearer picture of the true operating performance of a particular enterprise. So, in one sense, it makes the manager more comfortable by not being held responsible for events that he or she can't control. But from the corporate board's perspective, if things turn out badly, there are fewer places for managers to hide.

 There are lots of metrics for evaluating success. At First Data, we expect to find the value of enterprise-wide risk management not so much in financial variables but in the quality of the dialogue that we have with managers around those variables. In essence, our risk management system forces the organization to take a look at various measures, talk about their determinants and the relationships among them, and then decide what to do from a resources standpoint.

—Walter Coleman

Niehaus: But it isn't really necessary for the company to actually hedge those risks in order to insulate managers from those risks. In cases where the company chooses not to hedge, you can simply adjust a manager's performance by backing out the effects of unexpected changes in those factors that are clearly beyond the manager's control.

Ramamurtie: That's true—and very much consistent with how we try to evaluate the performance of our traders at Mirant. As I said earlier, when we are transacting in Canada, we don't want our traders taking positions in Canadian dollars. All the currency risk associated with those trades is transferred to and managed centrally by our treasury group. Our traders' performance is then evaluated in U.S. dollars, but using an exchange rate assigned by our treasury group that is meant to ensure that traders neither benefit from nor are penalized by unexpected currency movements. And our performance evaluation systems handle interest rate risk essentially the same way.

But that's not how we handle energy commodity price risk. We believe that our traders and, to a lesser extent, the managers of our power generation assets should function as part of our "front line" in responding to fluctuations in power and commodity prices. Thus, managing energy price risk continues to be a primary responsibility of our traders, with performance targets and commodity trading limits clearly specified. In the case of our power asset managers, there are effectively two tiers of price responsibility. Our performance evaluation system ensures that our asset managers bear the price risk associated with "forced outages." At the same time, it gives them the opportunity to shift most of the "normal" energy price risk to a more centralized portfolio management function.

So, as Cliff suggested, eliminating the fluctuation in results caused by interest rate and exchange rate movements makes the implementation of performance targets and incentives far more rational and straightforward. And by removing the volatility in performance that results from unexpected changes in financial markets, we greatly increase the odds that what we're seeing is "true" performance. But, at the same time, we're effectively operating under the assumption that our traders have some comparative advantage in anticipating energy price movements—and so we hold them responsible for managing energy price risk.

In talking to the managers at United Grain Growers, I got the sense that just going through this process gave the managers greater comfort and a better understanding of everything they are doing and helped to direct them strategically. As an academic, I was much more focused on the analytical approach—quantifying the risks, measuring the costs and benefits of various solutions, and so on. But the message we got from everybody was that the value was in the dialogue. And it's hard to measure the value of a better understanding of all the firm's risks that comes out of this dialogue.

—Greg Niehaus

Chew: Keith, are product managers at Wachovia held accountable for interest rate risk, or is that typically excluded from their evaluations?

Lawder: As I said earlier, there is a group of people at Wachovia responsible for managing our overall portfolio of assets and liabilities, and they are held accountable for the effects of changes in interest rates—that is part of their job description. But for our line people, the story is more complicated. To a certain extent all line managers share accountability for interest rate risk by virtue of the mix of maturities of the assets they add to our portfolio simply by selling one product rather than another. At the same time, however, our salespeople receive "guidance"—in the form of forecasts and incentives for selling certain products—from the portfolio managers. So the salespeople both are expected, and have strong incentives, to respond to that guidance. But, again, the main responsibility for managing interest rate risk really rests at the corporate level, where the view of the book is clearest.

ERM, the Internal Dialogue, and Changes
in Corporate Structure

Verbrugge: We've talked about a number of benefits of risk management, such as reductions in the cost of capital and more favorable terms from the company's non-investor stakeholders. Are there other reliable indicators of a successful ERM program?

Coleman: There are lots of metrics for evaluating success. At First Data, we expect to find the value of enterprise-wide risk management not so much in financial variables but in the quality of the dialogue that we have with managers around those variables. In essence, our risk management system forces the organization to take a look at various measures, talk about their determinants and the relationships among them, and then decide what to do from a resources standpoint.

Niehaus: It's interesting you should say that, because I got the same sense from talking to the managers at United Grain Growers, a Canadian company that provides grain storage and shipping services to farmers in western Canada. Going through this process gave the managers greater comfort and a better understanding of everything they are doing and helped to direct them strategically. As an academic, I was much more focused on the analytical approach—quantifying the risks, measuring the costs and benefits of various solutions, and so on. But the message we got from everybody was that the value was in the dialogue. And it's hard to measure the value of a better understanding of all the firm's risks that comes out of this dialogue.

Smith: One thing an ERM program can accomplish is to get people within the organization to take a step back and look at where and how the interactions among business units occur. Most managers get to be the organization's acknowledged expert in their particular area. And while they implicitly understand that they interact with other people and business units in the organization, the actual step of exploring an enterprise risk management program sometimes allows that interaction to take place in a somewhat less threatening way.

What's more, going back and taking a fresh look at the organization as a whole can highlight potential issues in a control system that, like most systems, may have evolved over time in piecemeal fashion. Rather than putting one more Band-Aid on what's already there, it may make sense to start with a clean slate and ask whether there's a more efficient way to achieve our corporate goals, a more comprehensive package that we can put in place. That kind of organizational re-engineering can be a useful exercise, and one of its by-products, as Walter said, is a dialogue among various parts of the organization.

In the course of my consulting work, I have found that as a more common vocabulary becomes established within the organization, people across business units with similar problems wind up developing a rapport and a language that allows them to swap insights and solutions. And this means that the next time they develop a problem, they are less likely to have to bring in consultants from the outside to deal with them.

Coleman: We have spent a lot of time talking about managing financial risks. But companies are also paying a lot of attention and devoting a lot of effort to managing operating risks. And since most corporations are now being asked to do more with less, one of the major issues that arises is how to balance the demand for more effective controls while at the same time reducing the overall cost of control.

In most corporations, controls end up being layered on top of other controls because a lot of people feel that they need more controls to avoid a catastrophe. But my feeling is that most companies are spending too much money on needless controls, and that ERM can result in both more effective and less costly risk management. To reach that point requires an extensive dialogue with all of the company's important managers. And that's the process we've been going through at First Data.

Verbrugge: Keith, you earlier mentioned Wachovia's success in creating a common vocabulary for discussing risk. And Wachovia has long had a reputation as a bank with a very strong credit culture across all its operations, and one that has achieved very good credit risk performance. Could you comment on the role of risk measurement in affecting managers' behavior? It's also well known that Wachovia has a return on economic capital objective for each line of business. Do you measure the success of ERM by its effect on return on economic capital?

Lawder: Well, Jim, we set corporate risk and return objectives at the top of the company. These objectives provide line managers with guidance as to what is acceptable. While the mechanics for implementing risk-adjusted return measures continue to evolve, we do incorporate economic value, risk-adjusted returns, and, most especially, expected loss in our performance metrics. We believe that constructive use of these tools as part of our overall ERM system will lead to less volatile earnings and cash flows. Likewise, better information about economic profit and incentives built around economic profit are expected to lead to value-adding behavior.

Briscoe: We have had very similar experiences at AGL. The cross-functional internal dialogue about risk has proven to be extremely helpful. The ERM initiative has provided an education about risk and a vocabulary that has enabled managers to identify and measure all kinds of risks—operational, financial, price, market, environmental, and regulatory. We have worked hard to incorporate risk metrics into discussions of each of these risk categories with the aim of coming up with a list of material corporate-wide risks.

What we have found is that, even if the initial metric is not the most effective measure of a specific risk, it really focuses the attention of those involved with the direct management of the risk, enables them to understand and limit the risk, and, based on that experience, to further refine the metric. But in those areas of risk management where we have not implemented some kind of risk metric, the understanding of the risk has not come nearly as quickly or received the same level of support.

Communicating with Investors

Chew: We've talked a bit about creating a common language inside the firm and about the role of risk management in reassuring non-investor stakeholders about the future stability of the firm. What about disclosing your risk management policy to the outside investment community? It would seem to me that your stock value would be higher if your investors knew that this dialogue was going on inside the organization.

Coleman: That's an interesting idea. We can certainly say we have an enterprise-wide risk management process, but effectively describing it to the investor community is a different matter. We would probably have the lawyers all over us in terms of what we could or couldn't say.

There was a recent article in the *Atlanta Journal Constitution* about companies' willingness to disclose their thinking about future earnings, and the article suggested that companies are going to be less specific going forward and the earnings parameters will be broader. That's because pressure has been put on management to perform at a certain level—they've been held responsible down to the penny; and given the increased risk in the overall regulatory environment, they're balking.

In the days before Reg. FD, as I said earlier, analysts used to have private meetings with management. But now that those meetings are prohibited, we're finding that the SEC's disclosure requirements are much more demanding. For example, our next quarterly report is not going to look at all like a 10Q, but more like a 10K. It's gone from 30 pages to 80 pages; the segment information goes on forever. Now that we have "fair" disclosure instead of disclosure via the analysts, we have to prepare much more information.

And thanks to Sarbanes-Oxley, we have several additional committees on our board of directors, including a corporate governance committee, a certification committee, and a disclosure committee. I now have ten audit committee meetings a year where I used to have five. Everyone is trying to figure out exactly what they need to do to make sure there's full disclosure and that the playing field is kept level. In my view, the pendulum has swung way beyond what's necessary.

Chew: Michael Jensen wrote an article in this journal about a year ago entitled "Just Say No to Wall Street" in which he urged companies to stop making earnings forecasts and instead provide a more in-depth discussion of their various corporate policies. So, rather than offering precise forecasts of earnings, wouldn't it be more effective to try and educate your investor community about your strategic plan and the policies that will guide the execution of that plan? As part of these disclosures, you could also cite what you think are the key economic drivers of profitability at your firm, and then discuss the major risks associated with those drivers and the firm's policies in managing those risks.

Coleman: Well, one problem with that approach is that you might be releasing proprietary information that ends up weakening the company's competitive position.

Ramamurtie: Another problem is that it would be impossible to achieve uniformity in such disclosures. You might have one company disclosing certain things and other companies disclosing entirely different things. I'm skeptical that the answer lies in disclosing as much as possible. I think that it might be better to try and change our existing accounting framework so that it provides more useful information.

Chew: But even if we could change the existing framework to make GAAP income look more like economic profit, a single set of rules is never going to end up fitting all companies. And, as I think we're now finding out with Sarbanes-Oxley, an accounting framework that is too rigid can actually end up reducing information content and value. There's a strong case—and accounting scholars and financial economists have been making it for years—for allowing companies to report other measures alongside EPS, to customize their disclosure in a way that enables them to communicate more effectively with investors. My guess is that the more distinctive your disclosures—that is, the more they depart from standard GAAP reporting (while still complying with the law, of course)—the more likely you are to receive attention from the most sophisticated investors. Buy-side investors will start listening to what you have to say and begin to understand the volatility inherent in the business—the normal ups and downs—and how the company plans to deal with it. As a consequence, there will be less of a market reaction to each little bump in reported EPS.

 At AGL our CFO has a goal of communicating EPS projections to investors using a corporate Earnings at Risk (EaR) framework. We are still in the preliminary stages of developing this framework. But when completed, our EaR model will allow AGL to communicate ranges of expected outcomes with specific probabilities. And by helping investors understand the financial events that can be expected to lead to each of these outcomes, it should allow the market to become more comfortable with the volatility that's associated with our business.

—Christie Briscoe

Coleman: But my question is: Will the new policy end up increasing corporate values or reducing them? Think about what has happened recently at GE. When Jack Welch released quarterly earnings, he disclosed almost nothing. But when Jeffrey Immelt came on board, GE's stock was going down, and the first thing he did was to go out and disclose everything—and the stock went down further.

Chew: But that's not surprising. Investors were finally catching on to the earnings games that had been going on at GE all those years. Eventually, I think Immelt's decision is going to lead to a higher value for GE, and perhaps to a less diversified mix of businesses. To the extent GE's management reduces the priority of earnings stability as a corporate goal, it is likely to place less value on having a diversified "portfolio" of businesses.

Briscoe: Don, in response to your proposal, let me just say that our CFO at AGL has a goal of communicating EPS projections to investors using a corporate Earnings at Risk (EaR) framework. We are still in the preliminary stages of developing this framework. But when completed, our EaR model will allow AGL to communicate *ranges* of expected outcomes with specific probabilities. And by helping investors understand the financial events that can be expected to lead to each of these outcomes, it should allow the market to become more comfortable with the volatility that's associated with our business.

Why Risk Management Fails

Verbrugge: Let me put one more question on the table before we close. When failures in risk management have occurred, have they resulted from failures to understand and follow the basic premise of ERM—the idea that risk management must be designed to reduce the volatility of *real* variables like cash flow, as opposed to accounting earnings, in order to add or preserve corporate value? Or have the failures been due to bad risk measures or models or faulty techniques and processes for managing risk?

Ramamurtie: All of the above.

Smith: That's right. The list of things you cited aren't mutually exclusive. There are firms that have incurred spectacular losses in the name of risk management. But if you go back and look at what they have done, they've just gone out and speculated. Procter & Gamble, Gibson Greetings, and Orange County are all cases where people went into the derivatives securities markets and, while claiming to be engaged in risk management activities, were in fact turning the treasury into a profit center and *introducing* risk where there was no underlying core exposure.

Ramamurtie: From a theoretical or technical point of view, a risk management failure is one where the outcome doesn't accord with the volatility you are seeking. But from a practical standpoint, it's hard to find an example of a risk management failure that didn't involve some degree of moral hazard—cases where managers were actually amplifying rather than managing risks. In the case of Enron, for example, there was moral hazard everywhere. And while the risks of Enron's trading business were being managed quite effectively, top management was subjecting the firm to extraordinary levels of financial risk that ended up destroying the firm.

Still, even risk managers with the best intentions sometimes make mistakes. After all, they are often working with some very complex transactions. They try to model how the transaction will behave, but they may miss certain variables, and then there is a "surprise." The question is whether that surprise should have been anticipated and somehow accounted for in the model or risk management process. Clearly, there will be situations in which actual performance deviates from the expectation. But if the outcome turns out to fall short of or exceed expectations in virtually every case, then you have to go back and improve the model. A careful analysis of variance will show whether the performance deviation is due to risks that you are not addressing.

Smith: It's also important to realize that the instruments, policies, and markets for risk management have evolved over time; they weren't all carefully constructed by some incredibly bright oversight committee.

Initially, somebody tried something because they thought they could make a buck at it. If you go back to the early 1980s, bid-ask spreads in the swap market were big enough to drive a truck through. But as the participants became more experienced, they put better control systems in place, competition grew, and spreads started coming down.

There are all kinds of stories about failures to appreciate an esoteric operational risk. You may be familiar with what some people refer to as "Herstatt" risk, which is named after the now-defunct Herstatt Bank in Germany. The bank had, for all intents and purposes, a balanced swap book; and yet it became insolvent when a bunch of swaps defaulted because the settlement was on the same day but not in the same *hour* of the same day. All of a sudden there was a source of operational risk *within* an eight-hour workday. As a consequence, there's now lots of detail in the documentation to ensure that such mishaps won't happen again.

So things that were risks a year ago or a decade ago are much smaller problems today because the industry as a whole has had an opportunity to go to school on somebody else's tuition payment. It has also led to all kinds of operational policies to make sure that you understand your customer, understand the contract, understand the business, and have a proper appreciation of the array of risks that you're assuming.

Chew: As an example of that evolution, how is the Enron trading debacle changing the energy trading business and the way risks are hedged in the energy business?

Ramamurtie: The lesson that can be drawn from Enron is that no matter how good your risk management technology—and I include people, algorithms, systems, and reports—things can still go very wrong if you don't have a good alignment between management's interests and the shareholders' interests. Enron did not fail *because* of its trading systems, but *in spite* of them. But the trading certainly had an impact in terms of how quickly the firm failed once it got into trouble. Once the word of trouble spread, most of its trading counterparties simply refused to transact with them.

Briscoe: A number of energy trading companies failed simply because they believed that most of their risks were measured by VaR and other trading risk measurement methodologies. But the inability to anticipate actual risks, such as the effects of a credit downgrade in Enron's case, or the concentration of credit risk, proved much more important than having the right correlations for highly quantitative risk measurements.

The Future of Energy Trading

Chew: With Enron out of the game, which firm, or combination of firms, is going to fill the vacuum in energy trading?

Ramamurtie: That's a good question. Many people believe that the financial institutions are going to come in, and we certainly have seen increased enthusiasm from the energy commodity trading groups of banks to act as both market makers in commodities as well as clearers of OTC energy transactions. But I also believe that the merchant sector will come back, that the institutional arrangements in the industry, as Cliff was suggesting, will come back.

As I suggested earlier, we're likely to see the evolution of clearinghouses that take the credit risk out of energy trading. A big part of Enron's problems, as I just finished saying, stemmed from the fact that most transactions in the energy market are two-way deals that require counterparties—and when Enron got into trouble, its counterparties stopped dealing with it. In fact, the best transactional arrangement for the energy industry would be an exchange that bears *all* the residual counterparty credit risk. Enron tried in effect to become the exchange, a one-stop shop for all energy commodity trading. It became the counterparty of record for every transaction in the natural gas business. And while there were certainly some shenanigans in the trading to build up the volumes, most of Enron's problems were the result of its financial leverage and structure and investments outside its core energy business. It spent a lot of money in areas like water and broadband that had no revenue streams. To raise capital for those ventures, it entered into a lot of agreements with fairly restrictive covenants. In a sense, it was pledging its own equity as collateral for other funding—and because Enron was taking all the credit risk off all the counterparties, it had to post a lot of collateral. When the bubble burst, the collateral calls started coming. At the same time, liquidity started drying up and that led to a downward spiral.

If we do succeed in developing energy price clearinghouses, then I think we'll again see companies with real energy production assets making markets in energy commodities. Another major source of Enron's problems was its decision to make markets in commodities where it had no real assets. If you're making a market in something, real assets give you access to good information as well as capital.

Smith: I agree that having the assets themselves can be an important source of comparative advantage. One of the reasons that banks were instrumental in the original creation of the over-the-counter financial services market was their own asset-liability management activities. They had natural positions already, and the process of managing their core business exposures created an opportunity to engage in a market-making function.

Ramamurtie: Bankers Trust did exactly that. It had a matched book swap business where they did only offsetting legs on trades and they were exploiting their own balance sheet to hedge some of the trades they were doing for clients. Then, rather than insisting on a matched book, they started running a "risk" book where they were actually taking interest rate and FX exposure.

Smith: That kind of strategy makes me a little nervous. If you talk to a bookie over 50, they'll tell you that the number one rule to becoming a successful older bookie is never to fall in love with a horse—if you do, it's just a question of how soon it's going to be before you're insolvent. If you want a long, venerated career as a market maker, I would strongly recommend that perspective.

Now, I'm willing to believe that things might be a little different in energy markets, where having a natural position might end up giving you a comparative advantage as a trader. One of the big differences between Enron and the banking industry in general is that the major money center banks are all competing as market makers, whereas Enron had a dramatically larger share of the market, especially with regard to contracts with maturities over 5 years. The ability to manage a book of interest rate derivatives that consists mainly of three- and five-year contracts is helpful, but the problems become dramatically more difficult if you try to leverage that experience by making a book on 10-, 15-, or 20-year contracts.

What's more, if whoever is managing that book of business is compensated on the basis of what happens to its value—and that book of business won't turn to cash for decades and must be marked to market in a subjective way—then even with incredibly conscientious internal auditors who call up other people in the marketplace for independent quotes on the value of the contracts in your book, it ultimately comes back to the lead market maker to determine the value. This is the kind of thing that happened, for example, in some markets that were dominated by AIG. And that's why I say you have to be very, very careful about getting too far out in front.

Ramamurtie: That's right—and that gets back to my earlier observation about moral hazard. But there were also other risk factors at work that ended up turning what may have been minor difficulties into disastrous outcomes. In the case of energy trading, the industry as a whole wasn't sufficiently sensitive to the amount of credit exposure that some of these trading operations generated, and they certainly did not have the balance sheets to support it.

Verbrugge: This is the kind of discussion that could go on for hours, but I'm afraid we have to end it here. On behalf of the University of Georgia, Don and I want to thank the panel for participating.

CHAPTER 18

Morgan Stanley Roundtable on Enterprise Risk Management and Corporate Strategy

NEW YORK CITY, JUNE 21, 2005

John McCormack: Good morning and, on behalf of the joint sponsors of this event—Morgan Stanley and the Committee of Chief Risk Officers, or "CCRO" for short—let me welcome you all to this discussion of corporate risk management. I'm John McCormack, I work in equity research here at Morgan Stanley, and I will be serving as moderator.

Our topic is the potential role of derivatives and risk management in increasing the long-run profitability and value of companies. Our main focus will be on the energy and financial service sectors, where the uses of derivatives and risk management are probably easiest to see. And to the extent we can come up with a persuasive explanation for how risk management adds value in these companies, we can try to extend the framework to other industries. Here are some of the questions that we will address:

What are the primary goals of corporate risk management programs? Should such programs be designed mainly to reduce volatility in reported earnings, or are there other aims that translate more directly into adding value for shareholders? For example, academics like René Stulz have argued that risk management should ignore modest swings in earnings and cash flow while functioning mainly as a kind of catastrophic insurance policy that eliminates disastrous, "lower-tail" outcomes. In a somewhat related argument, Bob Anderson, who is Executive Director of the Committee of Chief Risk Officers and here with us today, has said that one good indication of an effective risk management program is its ability to help persuade Moody's or S&P to reaffirm or even raise a company's credit rating. Both of these arguments suggest that risk management may improve a company's access to capital and reduce its cost of capital.

This chapter was previously published as an article in *Journal of Applied Corporate Finance* Vol. 17, No. 3 (2005): 32–61. Photographs by Yvonne Gunner, New York.

What risks are companies paid to bear? A number of academics have used a concept called "comparative advantage in risk-bearing" to justify corporate decisions to transfer certain risks while retaining others. To what extent can this principle be used to guide corporate risk management decisions? For example, should oil companies hedge much of their oil price risk, or banks hedge their interest rate risk—or should such risks be borne mainly by the firms' shareholders? Can energy and financial firms use the information provided by their operations to make their trading operations a reliable source of profit? This is something the majors now appear to be doing and that many financial institutions seem to do with their "carry trade."

What should companies tell investors about their risk management programs? To get recognition from the equity markets—say, in the form of a higher P/E multiple—for having an effective risk management program, companies may need to find a way to communicate at least their general risk management *policy* to their shareholders. But this has all been complicated by FAS 133, which many claim has made it impossible to hedge real economic exposures without causing significant earnings volatility. Is this a problem—and, if so, how do companies deal with it? One recommendation is to make economically sensible hedging decisions and then report two earnings numbers, one that complies with GAAP and another that reflects the economic reality of the hedge. Will this approach work, and can it be done without running afoul of Sarbanes Oxley?

To discuss these issues, we have assembled a distinguished group that includes three former academics—all of whom are now working in the private sector—as well as a number of corporate practitioners. And let me start by telling you a little about each of our panelists.

Charles Smithson is the founder and principal owner of Rutter Associates, a risk management consulting firm that specializes in measuring and managing credit and market risks for financial institutions. Prior to starting his firm in 1999, Charles spent 15 years doing internal and external risk management consulting at Chase Manhattan Bank, Continental Bank, and CIBC. Charles earned his Ph.D. at Tulane and, before coming to New York in 1985, served on the economics faculty of Texas A&M University.

Tom Copeland has far too long a resume for me to even summarize here, so I will just tell you that he has been Head of the Finance Department at UCLA, Partner and Head of the Finance practice at McKinsey, and Managing Director of Corporate Finance at Monitor Group, the well-known strategy consulting firm. At present, he is a consulting director at Charles River Associates and senior lecturer at MIT's Sloan School of Management.

Harry Koppel is head of Corporate Risk Management at BP Finance and also carries the title BP Distinguished Advisor on Risk. He is responsible for monitoring BP's global exposure to financial risks and, where appropriate, for designing and implementing hedge strategies. He also looks after the Group's portfolio of marketable holdings. Harry has been with BP since 1987, when he completed a research fellowship at Imperial College in London. He also has an extensive operational background, having earned degrees in Systems Engineering and Operations Research at universities in his native Colombia and later in the Netherlands.

Joe Sullivan, besides being a former derivatives professional like me, is Vice President and Treasurer of Airgas, a distributor of industrial, specialty, and medical gases and related products. Prior to joining Airgas in 1998, Joe was Assistant Treasurer at Thomas & Betts Corporation, a manufacturer of electrical and electronic equipment. At other points in his career, Joe has been Director of Corporate Finance at Scott Paper Company and a Cash and Securities Manager at BT Futures Corp, a division of Bankers Trust, where he first gained experience with derivatives.

Andrew Sunderman is Chief Risk Officer of The Williams Companies, a company he joined in 1999. Both before and since joining Williams, Andrew has had extensive experience in trading energy derivatives. And as he will tell us, risk management and the use of derivatives recently played a critical role in moving Williams out of the financially distressed condition it faced as little as three years ago. Thanks in part to a carefully designed and well-executed risk management program, the company today has achieved considerable respect on Wall Street.

Bob Anderson, as I mentioned earlier, is Executive Director of the Committee of Chief Risk Officers, a group of corporate executives whose purpose is to bring companies together to share best practices in corporate risk management. Prior to taking on that job, Bob was Chief Risk Officer at El Paso Energy, where he helped the company work its way out of financial distress.

John Kapitan, until quite recently, was a Managing Director at ERisk, a consulting firm that focuses on risk management and the measurement and management of economic capital at financial institutions. Prior to joining ERisk,

John was a colleague of mine at the consulting firm Stern Stewart, where he was co-head of its financial institutions practice.

Trevor Harris is a Managing Director at Morgan Stanley and, until recently, served as head of the equity research group that I work in—namely, the global valuation and accounting group. Before coming to Morgan Stanley in 1999, Trevor was a tenured professor of accounting at Columbia University's Graduate Business School.

And, finally, my co-moderator in this discussion is Don Chew, editor of the *Journal of Applied Corporate Finance*. Before coming to Morgan Stanley last year, Don was a partner of Stern Stewart for 22 years—in fact, one of the founding partners.

How Does Risk Management Add Value?

McCormack: Today's topic—the relationship between risk management, corporate strategy, and shareholder value—is something I started thinking about when working as a derivatives trader at UBS in the 1980s. And it was something I was forced to think a lot harder about when running Stern Stewart's energy consulting practice in the '90s.

The relationship between risk management and value has been a controversial subject in the finance literature ever since Modigliani and Miller published their pioneering paper on capital structure back in 1958. The general assumption among most finance theorists in the wake of M&M has been that risk management transactions entered into at competitive market prices are at best "value neutral." And to the extent companies incur transactions costs in attempting to hedge corporate risks, the whole process was even suspected to be value-reducing. Today there are clearly lots of successful enterprises with risk management programs that make at least some use of derivatives and other risk management tools. In this sense, risk management has passed the "market test" with flying colors. But the question that finance theorists have struggled with is this: In a world where shareholders can readily diversify away many of the risks faced by companies, such as commodity and interest rate and FX risks, how does risk management *by the corporation* add value?

And with that, let's turn to Charles Smithson. Charles, what is the latest academic thinking on how risk management adds value?

Charles Smithson: Thanks for your generous introduction, John. What you didn't mention, though, is that my Ph.D. is in economics, not in finance. It was only after I joined the Chase Manhattan Bank in the mid-1980s that I began thinking about financial economics—and about derivatives and risk management in particular.

If derivatives and risk management are going to create value, they will do it in one of three ways. Either they reduce taxes for the firm and its shareholders—or they reduce reorganization or bankruptcy costs—or they help a company carry out its investment policy. Of these three reasons to manage risk, the one I seem to encounter most often is the role of risk management in helping the company carry out its investment policy, its strategic plan.

—Charles Smithson

When I was teaching economics at Texas A&M, my world view was the "deterministic" one that was the norm for microeconomists at the time. By that, I mean that my focus was on *expected* outcomes, and I didn't pay much attention to the distributions of outcomes. So when I discovered that these new financial instruments could be used to reduce the variance of corporate earnings and cash flows, my immediate reaction was, "The job of our salespeople should be easy—all companies are going to want these things."

When I started exploring financial economics, I was fortunate to have as my guide Professor Cliff Smith, who was at the time a consultant to Chase. Cliff responded to my enthusiasm about derivatives by giving me a reading list that included articles on Modern Portfolio Theory (MPT) and the Capital Asset Pricing Model (CAPM). The basic message of MPT and CAPM is that the stock market itself is an incredibly powerful and effective risk management device. The ability of investors to hold diversified portfolios has the effect of reducing the corporate cost of capital to the point where, at least according to the CAPM, the only risk that investors need to be paid to bear is so-called "market" risk. That is, a stock's market risk, or its beta, is all the investors care about when setting the stock's required rate of return. And so, armed with this information, my new position on derivatives was the reverse of my previous one: "Given the ability of shareholders to hold well-diversified portfolios, no publicly traded company will want to use these derivatives."

At that point Cliff gave me another reading list—this one dealing with the M&M irrelevance propositions that John mentioned earlier. The basic message of M&M is that, if three conditions hold—(1) no taxes, (2) no transactions costs, and (3) fixed corporate investment policy—a company's capital structure and dividend policies should not affect the *total* value of the firm, or the value of its debt plus its equity. And the same is true of risk management *at the corporate level*. Like capital structure and dividend choices, risk management decisions are just different ways of dividing up the firm's operating cash flows and repackaging them for investors. And in well-functioning markets, this repackaging function should not add significant value because investors can do most of this repackaging on their own.

So, how then does risk management add value? As Cliff likes to put it, the way to answer this question is to turn the M&M proposition upside down. That is, if risk management is capable of adding material value, it will do so in one of only three ways: (1) by reducing the total taxes paid by the company or its investors; (2) by reducing "transactions costs," including the costs of reorganizing troubled companies and the "information" costs faced by investors in learning about companies; and (3) by helping to ensure that management follows the classic NPV rule and invests in all projects that are expected to earn at least the cost of capital.

And this leads to my bottom line: If these derivatives—which have zero or even slightly negative net present values at origination—are going to create value, they are going to do so in one of these three ways. Either they reduce taxes for the firm and its shareholders—or they reduce reorganization or bankruptcy costs—or they help a company carry out its investment policy. Of these three reasons to manage risk, the one I seem to encounter most often is the role of risk management in helping the company carry out its investment policy, its strategic plan. In fact, this role is something that Harry Koppel and I have talked about at length in the context of BP—but I'll stop here and leave that to Harry.

McCormack: Before we turn to Harry and the other practitioners here, let's hear briefly from the other two former academics in our midst, Tom Copeland and Trevor Harris. Tom, do you want to add anything to what Charles has just told us?

Tom Copeland: I agree with Charles that probably the most important function of risk management is to help ensure a company's ability to carry out its business plan. And I can even think of an example where hedging with derivatives enabled a company to make a critical *change* in its business model.

Years ago I was working with a large, privately owned oil refinery in the Mediterranean. The company was essentially a tolling operation, taking other people's oil, charging a fee for processing it, and then giving it back to them for sale to the end customer. Our analysis showed that about a third of the firm's customers were not profitable because they didn't deliver the oil on time and they tended to be late in paying as well. So we recommended that the firm experiment with a new business model: drop the bad customers and, to maintain the current scale of the refining process, replace those customers by purchasing oil directly in the spot market, putting it through the refinery, and then selling the refined oil products.

The problem with this approach, however, is that refining takes about two or three weeks, which means that there's some oil price risk in this model. On first hearing our proposal, the company decided it was unwilling to take that risk and would prefer to keep the bad customers. To address this problem, we formed a hedge portfolio of futures contracts one or two months out in crude oil and heating oil and gasoline. And by reducing the price variability by about 80%, our hedging program allowed the company to shed its bad customers and process the oil themselves.

So, here's a case where, as Charles was suggesting, risk management was used to support a company's key investment and operating decisions. It allowed management to pursue the value-maximizing strategy.

Why Earnings Might Matter

McCormack: Although academics typically dismiss the idea, people often tell me that a primary goal of corporate risk management programs is to smooth reported earnings. The basic idea is that the market is willing to assign a higher P/E multiple to a more stable earnings stream.

Trevor, as a former academic and as the representative of the accounting profession at this table, would you comment on the interaction between risk management and earnings volatility?

Trevor Harris: In discussions with many of my colleagues at Morgan Stanley and its clients, I typically emphasize the limitations of reported earnings and other accounting numbers. And in the past few years, I've spent a good deal of my time trying to come up with adjustments to financial statements that are designed to produce something closer to what I like to call "sustainable earnings." But, in this discussion, where everybody is aware of the problems with accounting, I think my most constructive role is to start by making the positive case for earnings, by stressing the importance of the information that accounting provides.

Some proponents of efficient markets have argued that accounting or measurement systems should just "let the volatility happen, and the market will figure it out." But I think there are a couple of flaws in that argument, or at least a couple of good reasons to care about earnings volatility.

For years now, academics in finance and accounting have been devoting more attention to what they call "information asymmetries"—to the differences between what management and outside investors know about the firm's prospects for growth and profitability. And the longer I've worked on Wall Street, the clearer it has become to me that investors face major obstacles and significant costs in finding out how businesses are currently performing and how they are expected to perform in the future.

In order to make decisions to retain or lay off risks, companies need an in-depth understanding of all their major risks and how those risks correlate with each other. And if the company does choose to manage its exposures with derivatives or some other means, it needs to find a way to show the market that its program is working the way it's supposed to. At present, outside investors cannot find that kind of information in GAAP financial statements—nor do I believe that most companies have a complete and comprehensive enough understanding of their exposures to always make the best decisions.

But, with today's computing power, we expect in the next 5 years to see some significant advances in the analysis of corporate risk exposures and in companies' ability to provide information about their exposures. Part of the impetus for such changes is coming from a relatively new development in the investment community: the proliferation of hedge funds that manage the risk of their portfolios very differently.

—Trevor Harris

For better or worse, the information provided in financial statements is the primary *initial* source of information that investors look at when pricing stocks. I'm not saying it's the *only* source, but I would argue that a firm's financial statements are an important and even an essential source of information.

First of all, if you go way back to the basics, the reason accrual accounting exists is to smooth out the part of volatility in cash flow that does not reflect what is expected to happen going forward. In this sense, accrual accounting allows investors to apply price-earnings multiples to some measure of a company's earnings power. So the whole notion of an accrual accounting system, which has actually stood the market test over a long period of time, suggests that pure cash flow measures of performance can be highly misleading—in fact, far more misleading than earnings.

A second reason there may be some value to what many people call "earnings smoothing" has to do with the information asymmetries I mentioned earlier and the costs associated with providing investors with credible information. In a world where information is costly, I would argue that managing some risks at the corporate level can serve to increase the value of the firm simply by reassuring investors who don't have sufficient information to manage those risks themselves.

In his opening comments, John raised the question of whether companies should retain or lay off their commodity price risk or their foreign exchange risk. But in order to make those decisions, companies need an in-depth understanding of all their major risks and how those risks correlate with each other. Having reached that understanding, they then have to decide whether the remaining exposures should be managed, or are better left to the shareholders. And if the company does choose to manage its exposures with derivatives or some other means, it needs to find a way to show the market that the program is working the way it's supposed to. And this is where I think that managing earnings volatility can play at least some role. As John suggested earlier, eliminating all volatility in earnings is clearly not the most important role of corporate risk management. But corporate risk officers should at least consider the effects of their decisions on earnings.

This is by no means a simple task—and, as I'm sure we'll hear today, recent trends in accounting have not made it any easier. As accountants and regulators in the U.S. and Europe have moved closer to a mark-to-market or fair value approach, a major difficulty now facing the investment community—and I work a lot with our analysts and institutional clients on this issue—is how to interpret the earnings volatility that results from marking derivatives positions to market when trying to project future earnings streams. Thanks to FAS 133 and IAS 39, analysts and investors now have information about the market values of those derivatives positions. But the challenge is to use this information to estimate some kind of forward-looking "normalized" earnings that can serve as a basis for valuing the company.

And that brings me to my next point: the difficulty, and perhaps the futility, of trying to distinguish between hedging and speculative transactions. There's very little companies do that doesn't have at least some speculative component. For example, even in the case of Tom's tolling operation, the company's decision to purchase oil at any given point in time involves a kind of speculation as to what the market for the refined product is going to be a few weeks or months later. And in fact this is true of any business: Companies that buy inventory in advance of doing something with it could be viewed as hedging, as "locking in" the cost of a key input. But by choosing to lock in that cost today, as opposed to two days ago or two days later, they are also making a modest speculative bet about what they expect prices and sales to do over some interval of time.

So my view is that the whole notion of trying to define what's speculative and what's a hedge is almost beside the point. You will never be able to define "hedging" in a way that is transparent and meaningful. For this reason, corporate risk management to my mind is really more about thinking through these information asymmetries and determining who has the greatest comparative advantage in managing a given risk.

The last point I would make is that, as we look forward, we expect to see some significant developments in the analysis of corporate risk exposures. At the moment, as I suggested, outside investors don't have the ability to process all the information. But, with today's computing power, we expect to see a completely different environment five years from now. My expectation is that we are going to see rapid evolution of risk management practices with increases in companies' ability to provide information about their exposures. And part of the impetus for such changes is coming from a relatively new development in the investment community: the proliferation of hedge funds that can manage the risk of their portfolios very differently.

The Case of BP

McCormack: Thanks, Trevor. Let's now turn to Harry Koppel of BP. BP has clearly thought a lot about corporate risk management and the idea of comparative advantage in risk-bearing. In fact, one of my favorite articles on the subject was a 1993 piece in the *JACF* called "Corporate Insurance Strategy: The Case of British Petroleum." That article described the company's unconventional decision to self-insure its large property and casualty losses and product liability suits—a decision based on the insurance market's limited ability to underwrite large, specialized risks—while purchasing "claims only" insurance for smaller claims.

Harry, what is the current thinking at BP about the purpose of its corporate risk management program?

 A company's business strategy and its operations are the engine that drives its value. And that value comes from taking risks and choosing risks wisely—from taking risks where there is a comparative advantage. Once you understand the potential risks associated with major investment decisions, there are a number of choices. You can simply retain the risk and leave it as is, or you can manage the risk by taking certain operating measures, or you can transfer the risk to another party—say, by using insurance or derivatives contracts. This transfer of risk, or "hedging," is a relatively small part of the overall risk management process. The first thing to keep in mind when making these decisions is that where there is no risk-taking, there is no possibility for above-normal returns and therefore no value added.

—Harry Koppel

Harry Koppel: Let me start by returning to your original question, "How does risk management add value?" At BP we begin with the assumption that a company's value comes from its operations, from its business model and its success in implementing the model. And that means that the role of risk management is a derived or supporting one. But in order for risk management to play this supporting role, a corporate risk manager has to understand the big picture.

To answer your question, it is also important to make the distinction between "hedging" and "risk management," two terms that are often used to mean the same thing, but shouldn't be. And I will start by giving you a very succinct definition of risk management: it means "no surprises." That's something that we hold very close to our hearts at BP, from the CEO all the way down through the ranks. What does that entail? It means, first of all, measuring and understanding all your major risks. A large part of the risk manager's task is to understand the risks the company is facing, and to provide a picture of the downside possibilities as well as the upside opportunities.

Once you understand the potential risks associated with your major investment decisions, you have a number of possible choices. You can simply retain the risk and leave it as is. You can manage the risk by taking certain operating measures. Or you can transfer the risk to another party—say, by using insurance or derivatives contracts. This transfer of risk, or what is called "hedging," is a relatively small part of the overall risk management process. The first thing to keep in mind when making these decisions is that where there is no risk-taking, there is no possibility for above-normal returns and therefore no value added. As I suggested earlier, a company's business strategy and its operations are the engine that drives its value. And that value comes from taking risks and choosing risks wisely.

It's also important to understand, to the extent you can, the risk preferences of your shareholders. If your shareholders have made it clear that they want the company to retain its exposure to oil prices, then you're not likely to hedge oil prices. Another example of risk-taking, as John just mentioned, is our decision to retain our largest property and casualty exposures. Why did we do that? As Trevor was saying, it's a matter of comparative advantage. The size and diversity of our operations, combined with years of operating experience, put us in a better position than any insurance company to evaluate, price, and bear those risks.

McCormack: On the other hand, you also took out policies that insured you against small losses.

Koppel: That's right. There are legal and contractual requirements to take some of those policies. We also have to process a number of claims, and we use the claims-handling capability of our insurers to do this. That's something they can clearly do better than we can.

But now let's talk about BP's currency exposure, which can be a more complex issue. Since most of the commodities we sell are priced in U.S. dollars, we tend to view BP as a U.S.-dollar company. And to better match the currency of our liabilities and our assets, of our outflows and inflows, we generally aim to have our debt denominated in dollars. But because the lowest-cost debt is not always denominated in dollars, we often find ourselves issuing debt in other currencies and then swapping that debt into dollars. So, for example, we might borrow in Swiss francs and then swap into U.S. dollars. At the same time, we also have a preference for floating-rate rather than fixed-rate debt, mainly to avoid the illiquidity premium that is built into fixed rates. For instance, if we issue fixed-rate, non-U.S. debt, we may use currency and interest rate swaps to give us our targeted U.S.-dollar floating-rate profile. And as a result of our decision to hedge our currency exposure, you will see in our annual report that we have several billions of dollars of currency derivatives—many of which have the effect of swapping non-U.S. debt into U.S. dollars.

Harris: Harry, would your use of swaps to change the risk profile of your debt from one currency to another be clear to the outside shareholder or investor from your financial statements?

Koppel: You would find footnotes showing our debt issues in terms of the currencies they were issued in.

Harris: But if I look at your debt structure, would I just see the original issue debt or would I have a way of seeing what's actually been swapped and into what currencies? I ask because when we look at companies that have gone through the kind of transactions you've described, it has not been clear to us what has taken place. On the basis of your financials alone, we might conclude that your debt is still fixed-rate, non-U.S.-dollar debt.

Koppel: You may not be able to calculate the net FX exposure of our debt from our financials. But our Annual Report does include a clear statement saying in effect that we have swapped non-dollar currencies into U.S. dollars with the aim of giving us mostly floating-rate, U.S.-dollar debt.

Joe Sullivan: But does the accounting generally follow the way you manage the portfolio of risk? At my company, Airgas, we bundle all our interest rate risk for management purposes. But the accounting rules require that we match specific derivatives with specific debt instruments and then declare them as either "fair-market-value hedges" or "cash-flow hedges." In cases where we have designated something a fair market value hedge, we are required to mark to market both the derivative and the portion of debt that it hedges. These mark-to-market effects show up on our balance sheet—and the portion that is deemed "ineffective" runs through the P&L. And so even if our bundle of derivatives provides an effective hedge for the bundle of debt instruments—which is how we manage our interest rate exposure—it would be difficult for an investor to confirm that just from our GAAP statements. There really isn't enough information in the footnotes to allow investors to do that, which is why Airgas relies on a combination of GAAP and supplemental disclosure.

McCormack: What role do the supplemental disclosures play here? How are they likely to be used by investors?

Harris: Well, to the extent investors are trying to forecast the future cash flows of a business, they would need a good sense of its exposure to changes in interest rates, and how the firm is managing that exposure. But if you can't rely on financial statements for something as simple as the actual terms of the debt after taking account of the effects of the derivatives, then you're really operating in the dark. This is the information asymmetry problem I was talking about.

So, even if Joe's company is actually using derivatives to achieve what we would all agree is a sensible interest rate exposure, it's not clear that outside investors have the information to appreciate what you've effectively done. And in the effort to get what they take to be an optimal portfolio construction, they could end up holding your shares for the wrong reason; they may end up under- or overexposed to a certain risk because they misjudged your company's actual exposure.

Copeland: Let me reinforce that point with a simple example. When I was teaching at Harvard Business School, one of the students turned in a paper on the risk management of international equities funds. He called up the managers of ten funds and found out that they all were concerned about international currency risk. Eight out of the ten funds actually hedged the currency risk of their portfolio companies. How did they do it? They treated the domicile of the firm's headquarters as the currency in which the investment takes place. So, for example, a company like Johnson & Johnson, which has global operations and hence all kinds of natural hedges, was treated as a U.S.-dollar firm. And because the funds had very little idea of the actual currency exposures of their portfolio companies, they were probably creating exposures where none existed before.

Sullivan: In our case, I don't think it's that difficult to follow the trail of transactions because we change the composition of the fixed/floating mix only after consideration of the entire liability portfolio—as I said before, we manage our interest rate risk as a portfolio. But even with all the complexity introduced by fair value accounting, I think the analysts who take the time to read our accounts and our supplemental disclosures will understand that the fundamental purpose of our derivatives use is to transform our debt so that it has the mix of floating and fixed we think is optimal for Airgas.

Harris: Let me make one more observation about accounting and disclosure, because I think this issue bears directly on the relationship between risk management and value. Risk management can influence value by affecting the way investors make their forecasts of future earnings. Regardless of whether you use FAS 133 or IAS 39, or whether you use derivatives to hedge individual transactions or on a portfolio basis, the fact remains that most companies report their debt in the form it was originally issued, and not as it has been transformed with derivatives. And unless the companies also provide very explicit information about what has been swapped out, the analysts' forecasts will be based on what are at best guesses about the liability structure of the debt.

If investors have this much trouble figuring out a company's expected interest payments, imagine how difficult it is to understand all its other major risks and how they interact with each other. Because of this information gap between how managers perceive and manage their exposures and how investors perceive them and integrate that into their analysis, most companies will find it helpful to take some steps to reduce the volatility of their earnings—and if they don't do that, they will have to spend much more time and effort explaining their hedging and risk management policies than they have in the past.

Although we manage our interest rate exposure so that our bundle of derivatives provides an effective hedge for our bundle of debt instruments, it would be difficult for an investor to confirm that just from our GAAP statements. But we provide a significant amount of additional information in our press releases, on our conference calls, and in the MD&A section of our SEC filings. So, even with all the complexity introduced by fair value accounting, the analysts who take the time to read our accounts and our supplemental disclosures will understand that the fundamental purpose of our derivatives use is to transform our debt so that it has the optimal mix of floating and fixed.

—Joe Sullivan

The Case of Airgas

McCormack: Joe, let me follow up on your last point and ask you to elaborate a little on your interest rate risk management policy at Airgas and how much you disclose about your hedge book to the investment community. You mentioned that you have a portfolio hedging strategy, and it also sounds as if the representation of that strategy in your financial statements is not completely satisfactory from your point of view.

Sullivan: I am not a fan of FAS 133 . . . but I hasten to add that our accounting and disclosures are as prescribed by GAAP. Of course, GAAP is not forward-looking—that is one of its shortcomings.

McCormack: Are you prevented from providing other information that might allow your shareholder base to have a better understanding of your hedging policy?

Sullivan: No. In fact, we provide a significant amount of additional information in our press releases, on our conference calls, and in the MD&A ("Management Discussion and Analysis") section of our SEC filings. In our press releases and teleconference materials we report what we refer to as "adjusted debt." This removes the mark-to-market impact of the derivatives portfolio, removes non-recourse debt, and adds in our off-balance sheet accounts receivable securitization. The press release and teleconference slides provide a reconciliation of adjusted debt to GAAP debt.

We also make very comprehensive quarterly disclosures about risk management in the MD&A in general and in the Quantitative and Qualitative Disclosures section in particular. This includes the proportion of fixed-rate liabilities, how we measure those fixed-rate liabilities, and the approximate expected impact on interest expense of a 25-basis-point change in short-term rates, given current levels of liabilities and credit ratings. We need this level of disclosure—and we need it in print—to enable us to respond to the questions that come from our analysts about our risk management practices.

And by the way, I agree completely with Trevor's point that there's not enough required public information on derivatives positions for analysts to forecast future cash flows under different economic scenarios. But I also don't think this is a material problem when analysts forecast the impact of interest rate changes on our outstanding debt. Analysts tend to ask us to reveal our percentage of floating-rate debt, which we are happy to do. They make some assumption about the effect of our swaps based on what is reported in our disclosures. Some analysts go into more depth than others; but at the end of the day they're going to come up with something that's reasonably close to the firm's schedule of swap-adjusted interest rate exposure.

It's really on the commodities side where I think companies and their investors are facing the biggest risks. Fortunately for Airgas, we don't have a lot of exposure there. But for a lot of companies, it's possible for analysts to completely misunderstand a firm's actual economic exposure to commodity prices because of the lack of transparency surrounding derivatives positions and the difficulty of representing those positions in financial statements.

In terms of interest rate exposure, our policy at Airgas is to keep the proportion of our fixed rate liabilities between 40% and 60%. Currently we are nearer 60% fixed. Some people consider that to be a lot of floating rate debt for a sub-investment-grade company. But we are comfortable with that position because of the very strong cash flow characteristics of our business.

Airgas is a $2.4 billion company with a 20% market share of the U.S.-packaged industrial gas distribution and hardgoods market. The packaged gas business is very stable but the hard-goods business is more subject to economic cycles. That side of the business tends to give us a natural hedge against rising interest rates. When short-term interest rates go up, as they have been lately, our hard-goods revenue tends to go up as well—in fact, our same-store sales have been increasing at double-digit rates. And because of this strong positive correlation between our sales and interest rates, the high proportion of floating-rate debt provides what we feel is the right match between our assets and liabilities.

McCormack: How confident are you that this correlation would hold up in the event of a very large spike in interest rates?

Sullivan: Though past performance is not a guarantee of future results, the relationship has been pretty consistent over time.

Don Chew: Joe, do you discuss this kind of correlation analysis during presentations to analysts?

Sullivan: It's not part of our regular dialogue, but it has come up during investor calls. As I said earlier, analysts generally want to know our guidelines for fixed versus floating and why we have those guidelines. And as I also mentioned, we tell them that we aim for somewhere between 40% and 60% fixed rate debt—. and because they also know our debt balance, they are in a position to understand our interest rate exposure. I don't believe that the analyst community feels that we face a significant interest rate exposure as a result of that policy.

Chew: So, you're pretty confident about your ability to service your debt and avoid tripping debt covenants under virtually any interest rate scenario?

Sullivan: We are very confident about our approach. We have plenty of room under our existing debt covenants to accommodate a jump in interest rates. If we had a covenant package like those that are required for companies a couple of notches down the credit scale, then I would be a lot more concerned about rising interest rates. So, yes, rising interest rates could become a material concern for single-B credits with significant floating-rate debt. But given our current debt rating, and where our coverage ratio stands in relation to our covenants, we feel our current interest exposure is well under control.

Chew: Let's go back to the case of BP, then. Harry, is BP's preference for short-term funding based in part on an assessment that its revenues have a positive correlation with inflation and interest rates? Or did I hear you say it was mainly to take advantage of the liquidity savings in short rates or, what amounts to the same thing, to avoid the illiquidity premium built into long rates?

Koppel: We tend to fund short mainly because we know that, under normal circumstances and over long periods of time, short rates will turn out to be lower than long. There's really no attempt here to match the interest rate sensitivity of our liabilities with those of our assets.

I think what is important in carrying out such a policy is to maintain the discipline of the method, to implement it in a consistent way. We are not unwilling to shift risks when the costs of doing so are very low. When you have liquid markets, as is the case with the U.S./Euro market, we start by finding the funding source with the lowest all-in-cost interest rate. For instance, if the cheapest outcome involves the use of a Euro rate, we would fund in Euros and swap into U.S. debt. The transactions costs of so doing are minimal and it's fairly easy for management to explain the company's policy to shareholders.

The Case of The Williams Companies

McCormack: BP's reliance on floating-rate debt makes perfect sense to me. It is a very large company, with operations that are geographically as well as operationally diverse. And part of its overall risk management strategy is to fund those operations primarily with equity rather than debt.

But an investment-grade rating and heavy reliance on equity is not necessarily the value-maximizing strategy for all companies. In some cases, the use of derivatives and risk management can function to some extent as a substitute for equity capital. And the recent experience of The Williams Companies provides a good illustration of my point.

So let's now turn to Andrew Sunderman, who, as Chief Risk Officer of The Williams Companies, has played an important role in the company's recent recovery from a difficult set of circumstances. Andrew, can you tell us about the challenge the company faced a couple of years ago in servicing its debt load, and about the role of risk management in helping bring the company back from the brink of disaster?

Andrew Sunderman: The first statement I would make is that much of risk management and related kinds of financial decision-making is more academic when you have an AA balance sheet. In the case of Williams, which was a BBB-rated energy company with a trading and marketing unit operating in the wake of the collapse of the largest U.S. merchant energy trading company—and I'm talking of course about Enron—derivatives and risk management were, and continue to be, an important part of our overall strategy.

As John just told you, derivatives and risk management played an important role in our restoration to financial stability from our distressed situation three years ago—a time when our bonds were downgraded well below investment grade and our stock was trading below $1. As you drift downward, the financial distress discount on your debt and equity grows pretty quickly. The role of derivatives in this case has been mainly to eliminate the downside tail on our risk, the possibility that a sharp drop in oil or gas prices could make us unable to service our debt.

Williams operates in several distinct commodity businesses, including exploration and production of natural gas, power generation (involving the conversion of gas into electricity), the interstate transportation of natural gas, and the gathering and processing of natural gas and related natural gas liquids. When you view our portfolio of businesses, you can see that a large portion of our business is highly dependent on commodity prices—and it's important to keep in mind that these are the most volatile commodities in the world.

So, once again, for a company trying to continuously improve shareholder value and strengthen its credit standing, a continuing focus on managing our commodity price risk is critical for us to achieve these goals. In this sense, as both John and Charles suggested, an effective risk management program can help a distressed company lower its cost of capital.

McCormack: Andrew, can you tell us a bit about your disclosure policy, and can you comment on this issue of transparency that Trevor raised earlier? ˇ

Sunderman: We have disclosed increasingly more about how we use derivatives, how we trade our portfolio, and what exactly is in it. Besides providing more information in our filings, we make trips to New York twice a year in which we present to our investors the entire 20-year spectrum of our power trading book. This enables them to see when we are using derivatives, why we are using them, and exactly what the cash flows from them are going to be. This way they know when we use derivatives to hedge our production, our output.

As a result of our efforts, a number of publications have recently recognized our disclosure and investor relations program as the best in the energy sector. I personally have a lot of passion for this activity. As Harry said earlier, risk management is supposed to support a company's business and investment strategy—and that's the function it performs at Williams. By helping to understand, quantify, and in some cases eliminate the possibility of bad outcomes, it has reassured our investors and given us the confidence to invest in our business while paying down $8 billion in debt over the last three years.

 Corporate risk management involves much more than just the use of derivatives. For example, the design of the firm's supply contracts can be used to manage risk. Risk management can also influence the kinds of assets the firm purchases, some of which can provide a natural hedge for the firm's main businesses. And I imagine that these kinds of strategic risk management mechanisms are equally important for companies like BP. For companies with lots of hard assets, decisions to invest in assets can play a critical role in managing risk.

—Andrew Sunderman

Real Options as a Risk Management Strategy

Sunderman: But, as Harry said, it's important to keep in mind that corporate risk management involves much more than just the use of derivatives. For example, the design of the firm's supply contracts can be used to manage risk. Risk management considerations can also influence the kinds of assets the firm purchases, some of which can provide a natural hedge for the firm's main businesses. And I imagine that these kinds of strategic risk management mechanisms are equally important for companies like BP. For companies with lots of hard assets, decisions to invest in assets can play a critical role in managing risk.

Copeland: There are also ways to build flexibility into organizations that have the effect of reducing risk. You can accomplish this by making more flexible investments, you can do it by having an AA capital structure like BP, or you can do it by having a very active risk manager. How do you decide which is the preferred method at the margin?

Sunderman: At Williams we try to analyze the economic value—that is, the value over and above the cost—of each of these alternatives. So, let's say I want to own a commodity like natural gas. I have two basic ways of doing it: I can buy a futures contract or I can buy a company. In making that decision, we will consider factors such as our own operating expertise that could make asset ownership more valuable to us than to, say, financial buyers. And we also consider the opportunities that ownership of that asset would give us to build on and enlarge our own expertise. That to me is a critical part of risk management; it's keeping in mind the big picture that Harry was talking about.

Copeland: So, what we're really talking about here in part is the convergence of risk management with what academics have been calling "real options"; it's the idea that companies can manage some of their major business risks by consciously building flexibility into their operations. Just to give you one example, at Monitor we advised a client who was building a multi-billion-dollar, high-tech clean room. The facility was reengineered to be more modular, thus enabling management to respond to changes in technology and changes in demand.

Companies can manage some of their major business risks by consciously building flexibility into their operations, or creating what academics call "real options." A good example is J&J's venture capital program, which takes minority equity interests and deep-out-of-the-money warrants in small firms likely to produce breakthrough technologies. Although the investments are relatively small, they have the potential to create significant value for J&J by providing new sources of profit and protecting its core business from "disruptive" technologies. In this case, the company has literally created a portfolio of options, both financial and real.

—Tom Copeland

An even better example is provided by Johnson & Johnson's venture capital program. It takes minority equity interests and deep-out-of-the-money warrants in small firms that are considered likely to produce breakthrough technologies. Because the warrants are well out of the money, the investments are relatively small. But if one of the technologies materializes, the stock price jumps, the warrants move into the money, and J&J ends up with a significant equity ownership stake. This creates value for J&J by providing new sources of revenue and profits, and by protecting its core business from "disruptive" technologies. And it helps the target firms by providing what amounts to "just-in-time" equity financing—by which I mean that the equity needed for commercialization of the technology becomes necessary only if and when the technology and commercial opportunities have materialized. J&J's strategy is thus literally to create a portfolio of options—both financial options and real options.

Let me also mention that at MIT today, engineering courses are teaching real options as part of engineering design. So I think we're in a new age where the biggest risks today are not technical or environmental like Exxon's Valdez, but rather strategic risks—the possibility that you're in the wrong business at the wrong time. And if I'm right, designing operating flexibility will become an increasingly important part of long-term or strategic risk management.

Koppel: This "real options" way of thinking is also part of BP's project assessment framework. As I suggested earlier, we start with a value proposition and then analyze the risks that surround that value proposition. We consider not only the downside risks but also the upside potential—and much of our practice is designed to preserve our access to that upside. And that's where the real options analysis that Tom Copeland just mentioned comes into the picture.

There are, of course, some challenges in using real options theory to quantify the value of investments—and there's an article in the latest issue of the *JACF* by Simon Woolley, one of my colleagues at BP, that does a nice job of describing the issues. But let me repeat that real options thinking has long been pervasive at BP. We devote plenty of time and analysis to exploring both the potential value and the risks of our strategic investments; and whenever possible, we design those investments to limit the downside while preserving our options.

Managing Credit Risk

Smithson: Andrew, are you responsible for managing credit risk as well as commodity hedging at Williams?

Sunderman: That's right. I have the title of Chief Risk Officer of Williams, which means I'm responsible for analyzing, reporting, and developing strategies to help our Risk Management Committee manage the commodity risk and credit risk of the non-regulated units of the corporation. And I'm also the Chief Financial Officer of Williams Power, which was formerly our marketing and trading entity. Credit risk management today is different than it was five years ago, when we had a very liquid credit default swap market. In those days, if you entered into a contract and you had a customer that was always paying late, you could decide you didn't want to bear that credit exposure and transfer it to a third party either with a new position or through the purchase of credit protection—say, in the form of a credit default swap.

Today, however, that market is either very expensive or very illiquid, which has forced companies to manage much of their credit risk through netting agreements. When you deal with commodities today as a non-investment-grade company, most businesses now require basically 100% collateral posting for the set fair value of that derivative in or out of that money. Alternatively, you do it through the contract. The number one tool we use now is called master netting agreements. Under these arrangements, we would go to a BP and say that we want all entities within Williams and all entities within BP to net their positions every day, and so each day we would send money back and forth to avoid any future exposure from a default by a counter-party—though this is clearly something you wouldn't have to worry about if you were transacting with a firm like BP.

Smithson: How did Williams manage to find counterparties two years ago when it was facing all the problems and constraints and your credit was out of favor?

Sunderman: Part of the answer is going to sound very old-fashioned. Williams has been in business for almost 100 years and had built up a lot of good relationships. Because of these long-standing relationships, some of our suppliers were willing to give us good terms. In other cases, however, we were forced to pay cash up front.

Toward Enterprise-Wide Risk Management

McCormack: We haven't heard yet from Bob Anderson, who is Executive Director of the Committee of Chief Risk Officers. Bob, how does your recent experience with CCRO, and before that as Chief Risk Officer at El Paso, compare with what Harry and Andrew have been telling us about risk management in the energy business?

Bob Anderson: My experience as a CRO at El Paso was similar in many ways to what Andrew has just been through with Williams. We went through a period of financial difficulty and, as with Williams, the use of derivatives in hedging commodity price risk played a big role in getting our lenders to work with us and restoring our access to capital markets.

And now I'm running an organization, the Committee of Chief Risk Officers, whose purpose is to bring companies together to share best practices in corporate risk management. In my current role, I get to hear a lot from various companies about their problems as well as their solutions. As a result, I'm in a pretty good position to assess both the current state of risk management and what appear to be emerging practices.

One trend that I'm seeing very clearly is a major expansion of the focus of corporate risk officers beyond the use of derivatives to hedge specific financial risks into something that people are now calling "enterprise-wide" risk management. Ten years ago, risk management was mainly about the use of swaps and options to hedge interest rates and commodity prices, the kind of thing I did while working for BP in the early 1990s. Back then, risk management was thought of as a pretty much decentralized, or compartmentalized, activity that could help the firm mainly by making modest contributions to the P&L. But, as Harry has been telling us, the purview of today's risk manager is much broader; it encompasses all aspects of the corporation, including investment and operating decisions as well as financing. It's about ensuring the company's access to capital and its ability to carry out its strategic plan—and, in this sense, it is a critical part of the business model.

John earlier raised the question of whether oil and gas companies should be hedging their exposures to oil and gas prices. To answer that question, and to make the right decision, management needs to take a complete view of the firm's operations, from the perspective of outsiders as well as insiders. If a sharp drop in oil prices could make the firm default on its debt—the condition that Williams was facing—then it will be worthwhile to hedge at least enough of that exposure not only to avoid Chapter 11, but to carry out the investment plan. For equity-financed firms like BP, the question becomes one of comparative advantage: Who is in a better position, or more willing, to bear the firm's oil price risk? Is it the firm's shareholders, many of whom say they buy oil company shares for the oil price exposure, or is it investors who transact in the derivatives markets? So, in this sense, today's risk managers must understand not only how risk affects all the operations of the firm, but what role such risk plays in the expectations of the firm's investors—shareholders as well as creditors.

This may sound self-serving, but I believe that we have reached the point where all publicly traded companies should have a well-thought-out risk management policy. And as John said in his opening remarks, companies should make an effort to understand their comparative advantage or core competencies—and they should at least be aware of their options for transferring risks to third-party investors. Although good management will always be more art than science, it's probably fair to say that the days of the cowboy CEO who shoots from the hip are numbered. This is not to say that all companies are going to load up on "quants" and attempt to model all their exposures. What it does mean, however, is that risk management will increasingly be the responsibility of somebody near the top of the company—and that an important part of that responsibility will be to communicate the firm's policy to the investment community and other outside constituencies, possibly including regulators. That policy should attempt to strike a good balance between the firm's appetite and capacity for bearing risk, and between the expected upside and the ability to weather some adverse outcomes. It was essentially an imbalance between risk appetite and capacity that got the energy trading business into such trouble during the last 5 years. In a number of cases, top management had no idea of the risks that were being taken.

So, to repeat my basic point, risk management is in the process of becoming a truly corporate-wide undertaking. It's not just a series of isolated transactions, it's a strategic activity. As Andrew said, it encompasses everything from operating changes to financial hedging to the buying and selling of plants or new businesses—anything that affects the level and variability of cash flows going forward. When viewed in that light, risk management is clearly a senior management responsibility, one that requires input from and coordination of different parts of the company at all operating levels. And such internal coordination and understanding should in turn allow management to give a confident reporting of the risk management program to outsiders, one that gives Wall Street a clear picture of the program's objectives and how the program is being carried out.

Risk Management and Investor Clientele

McCormack: Bob, you mentioned a divergence between companies' appetite for certain risks and the risk preferences of their shareholders. Are you saying that managers didn't understand what their shareholders were looking for, or that they failed to understand the risks that underlay their own business?

Anderson: I think it was very clear to management 5 years ago that analysts and shareholders were looking for large and pretty much continuous increases in EPS. With hindsight it seems to be an extraordinarily silly idea that companies could grow their earnings at 15% a year in perpetuity. But the valuations that investors were giving some companies, especially in the tech sector, appeared to reflect that expectation. Such valuations in turn had the effect of putting management on a treadmill where they felt pressure to produce this kind of clearly unsustainable earnings growth. And the result was some aggressive accounting, and a lot of bad acquisitions that were driven in large part by cosmetic accounting effects.

One trend I'm seeing very clearly is a major expansion of the focus of corporate risk officers beyond the use of derivatives to hedge specific financial risks into something people are calling "enterprise-wide" risk management. Ten years ago, risk management was mainly about the use of swaps and options to hedge interest rates and commodity prices. It was pretty much a decentralized, and compartmentalized, activity whose main purpose was to smooth earnings or make modest contributions to the P&L. But the purview of today's risk manager is much broader; it encompasses all aspects of the corporation, including investment and operating decisions as well as financing. It's about ensuring the company's access to capital and its ability to carry out its strategic plan—and, in this sense, it is a critical part of the business model.

—Bob Anderson

Today things are much more complicated. Investors are paying less attention to earnings and putting greater emphasis on cash flow and returns on capital than in the past. And risk management is playing a greater role in the valuation process. Andrew has already provided some evidence that creditors value risk management; and to the extent that a risk management program reassures creditors and reduces the firm's cost of debt, it's also likely to reassure equity investors as well, particularly in cases where companies make aggressive use of their debt capacity. In other cases like BP, a good risk management program just reinforces a company's reputation for having an effective corporate governance and financial management system, which in turn should give the market the confidence to put a higher multiple on the firm's earnings and cash flow. And I think the Williams story provides even clearer evidence that risk management can increase overall value. As Andrew has told us, Williams now makes a point of publicizing its hedging program and, without taking correlation for causality, the company's market value has clearly risen along with the extent of its disclosure program. The ability of a company to communicate its exposure profile to outsiders, both shareholders and rating agencies, is to me the hallmark of a good risk management program.

Sunderman: In 1999 and 2000, investors seemed to be rewarding companies mainly just for revenue growth. During the Internet bubble, companies that had yet to realize a single dollar of economic value were being valued at billions of dollars. In cases where investors' expectations are clearly unrealistic, should it be management's responsibility to bring those expectations into line with its ability to deliver?

Let's come back to the case of Williams. In choosing to hedge much of our commodity price risk, we may have discouraged some kinds of investors from buying our shares—those investors who are looking mainly for a play on oil or gas prices. But if investors really want to bet on a company that takes commodity risk, there are much more direct ways to get that exposure—commodity futures and swaps will give you much more exposure for your dollar. I think it is management's responsibility to earn the highest return it can on the *total capital* at its disposal, on the total assets under management. In a company like Williams, which generates large and fairly stable cash flows, my belief is that we will end up earning higher rates of return by hedging and continuing to make fairly aggressive use of debt at lower costs of capital.

McCormack: So what you're saying, Andrew, is that risk management can function as a cheap substitute for equity capital?

Sunderman: I would say it provides a cheap alternative that must be considered. By eliminating the left-hand tail of our risk distribution, we give our lenders comfort and increase our debt capacity—and this in turn can reduce our cost of capital.

McCormack: So, as I was suggesting earlier, Williams's business model is quite different from BP's. It's one that's closer to that of an LBO, something we are starting to see in the energy industry. And I would guess that your combination of hedging and higher leverage is likely to attract a somewhat different kind of investor than BP does. But, as I think has become clear from your recent experience, if you find a way to add value, you will find investors who want to hold your shares.

Harris: I agree. The idea that all investors are the same is obviously wrong. So if you decide to make a major change in policy, such as hedging your price risk and levering up, you're likely to be able to find a group of investors who are attracted to the policy and want to buy your shares. Now, it's true that when you make that policy change, you will probably experience a change in your investor base; those investors who bought your shares mainly for the oil price exposure are likely to sell. But as long as you do a good job of explaining your new policy and the way you run your business, you should be able to find a set of investors willing to pay full value for your shares. Your shares will no longer attract people looking to add oil price exposure to their portfolios, but they will find a place in the portfolios of other investors who want exposure to a different kind of risk.

Another way of putting this is that companies should not feel bound to their existing investor base, or what people sometimes refer to as an investor "clientele." Companies are generally reluctant to change clienteles, mainly because the selling that takes place during a change in clientele creates a lot of price volatility, at least in the near term while the shift is taking place. But, as I said earlier, this price volatility reflects the large information costs faced by investors, and the generally poor job that companies have done in communicating major policy shifts. In most cases I'm aware of, companies have failed to provide investors with the information necessary to evaluate, say, a decision to cut the dividend to help fund a promising investment.

And this leads me to ask the following question: As we move toward enterprise risk management, do we really have the analytical tools that would allow us to measure and monitor and manage the exposures internally? And if so, do we also have the means of making this analysis transparent to outsiders? As we discussed earlier, financial statements provide very little guidance as to how companies are using derivatives—and a lot of hedging activity still takes place off the balance sheet. It's one thing to be able to get a clear picture of the firm's asset/liability mix looking out 1 year. But many derivatives contracts go out several years, and I'm skeptical that even corporate management, much less the investment community looking on from the outside, has the analytical capability to provide a good understanding of their exposures going out 5 years.

Anderson: Well, it depends on the company. They range in size and sophistication from multinationals like BP to small operations like Black Hills in Colorado. But with that qualification, my outlook is quite optimistic. Almost all the energy companies that are part of my organization know how to measure credit risk the way a bank would do it. A few years ago, most pipeline companies viewed all credit exposures as 60-day receivables even though the pipeline contracts with their customers were as long as 15 or 20 years. That doesn't happen anymore. Today, those companies think long and hard about potential credit risk, about what affects both their own credit ratings and those of their counterparties. So, in this sense, we are taking elements of the enterprise-wide approach that has grown up in the banking and finance industry and transporting them into the energy industry.

Now, the degree of progress varies depending on the type of risk we're talking about. I tend to think in terms of four major categories of risk: market, credit, operations, and business. I think that most energy companies today have pretty well mastered market risk. They have VaR measures and Monte Carlo price simulators to help them model the distribution of their operating cash flows over a range of different price scenarios—and they understand energy derivatives and how they can be used to hedge their market exposures. This has all been rich territory for consultants in the past few years. And as I was just saying, energy merchants have made major strides in understanding credit risk in the last year or so—though among utilities, there is still considerable room for improvement in this area.

But the case of operations risk is different. Here there's a pretty big hole and a lot of work to be done. When I think of operating risk at a bank, I think in terms of the telephones going down. But, in the case of energy companies and utilities, we're talking about entire plants and major disruptions in service provision. There is now talk of making operations risk part of companies' regular reporting profile, and of including that risk in the MD&A section of their annual reports; but there's still a lot of work to be done in this area.

That brings me to the case of business risk. Evaluating business risk is really about building scenarios, and a lot of companies today incorporate some form of scenario planning into their cash flow analysis. So things are improving here as well. Two or three years ago, we were only at the stage of reaching agreement on the four types of risk themselves, and we've come a long way during that time.

But what's next? In my view, the big improvements this year will come in the form of better disclosure. A lot of companies are going to showcase their emerging risk management practices in the MD&A section of their annual reports. You'll see a number of companies talk about the concept of "economic capital." Economic capital is a measure of the capital necessary to support an operation— a measure that is based mainly on the *volatility* of that operation. Although it's long been used by banks in their risk adjusted return on capital (RAROC) systems, energy companies are now beginning to use it for the first time.

In addition to the growing use of economic capital, we're also seeing attempts to treat market and credit risks in a consistent and coordinated way. More generally, companies would like to understand the extent to which all their major risks—market, credit, and operations—are correlated. Most companies realize that, in assessing their *overall* or *net* exposure, they can't simply add up the volatilities associated with each of their major risks. If you do that, you will overestimate your risk, which in turn could lead you to do too much hedging or keep too much capital on your balance sheet.

Now, this kind of correlation analysis is in a fairly early stage, and we're nowhere near the point that the banks have reached on this. But we're a lot farther along than we were just three or four years ago when I was CRO at El Paso. And that's one of the main reasons I'm excited about working with the companies in my organization. We're building consistency and standards. We're working together to develop a unified set of metrics that an outsider can use to compare the exposures of Williams and El Paso and BP and others. We will never get 100% comparability, but we're making progress.

Smithson: The answer to Trevor's question about whether we now have the tools for a truly enterprise-wide risk management system depends on the kind of company we're talking about. As Bob just said, new developments in risk management techniques tend to originate in the securities and banking firms, where most of the assets and liabilities can be readily marked to market—and then they spread to the industrial firms. And as Bob also mentioned, it was market risks—interest rate risk, foreign exchange rate risk, equity price risk, and commodity price risk—that were the first major focus of risk management programs. But about six years ago, the focus of risk management began to shift at most financial institutions. Lots of the people who had spent a great deal of time and energy thinking about VaR and how to apply it were suddenly asked to turn their attention to credit risk. And that effort has—or at least is about to—come of age.

So what is the next "new thing" in risk management? I think it is the application of the economic capital concept to industrial companies that Bob just cited. I am very excited about this idea because economic capital is really just a measure of risk—it's a way of putting market risks and credit risks and operational risks into a single dimension. Once all risks can be quantified and aggregated, the management of the firm can answer the payoff question: How much equity capital do we need to bear the collection of risks facing our firm?

If you look at recent annual reports and other disclosures by financial institutions, you will see that, instead of ROAs or ROEs, firms are increasingly talking about returns on economic capital—returns to risk or, if you prefer, risk-adjusted return. So if I had to choose a single major advance in corporate risk management for the rest of this decade, my guess would be the widespread adoption of some kind of risk-based capital measure. Most financial institutions are already doing it, and my prediction is that it will spread to industrial companies.

Risk Management, Performance Evaluation, and Management Incentives

McCormack: On that note, let me bring John Kapitan into this discussion. As a consultant to financial institutions, John has been personally involved in the proliferation of many of the new tools and measures, including economic capital, that Bob just described. John, would you give us your impression of the current state of the art of risk management at financial companies, and tell us about the role that economic capital is playing today and is likely to play in the near future?

John Kapitan: I'd be happy to. But let me start by commenting briefly on this question of investor clienteles that Trevor brought up a minute ago. I agree with his statement that there are all kinds of investors out there, and I also agree with his suggestion that corporate policies can and do influence who buys their shares. As Warren Buffett likes to say, companies get the shareholders they deserve. The way you communicate to your investors and what you choose to disclose—whether you provide only what's required or volunteer much more—has a lot to do with the kinds of investors you end up with. If you spend a lot of time forecasting quarterly earnings, then you will find a lot of momentum traders holding your shares. But if you downplay earnings and talk instead about goals and policies, then you're likely to attract longer-term holders—and not just pension funds, but some pretty sophisticated value investors.

So, for those managers who like to complain about the shortsightedness of their investors—the intensity of investors' focus on quarterly earnings—my suggestion is that they have no one to blame but themselves. And, more important, if they're not happy with their current investor group, there's probably something they can do about it.

Chew: They can either improve their disclosure—or they can go private.

Kapitan: Yes, going private is an option—and apparently a pretty popular one these days.

But let me now turn to this idea of economic capital that Charles Smithson was telling us about. Much of our discussion up to this point seems premised on the idea that companies, if not the analysts and investors who follow them, have accurate measures of risk. But we need to qualify this assumption a little. There are a lot of companies, including financial institutions, that have a long way to go before they have reached that point.

My own experience with a lot of financial institutions suggests that if they choose to make a major investment in a risk measurement system—and by "major" I mean anything from $500,000 for a fairly small bank to $10 million for a large one—they can attain a reasonable degree of accuracy. As both Bob and Charles mentioned, financial institutions today are fairly well down the path in terms of their ability to measure most market and credit risks. At the same time, most financials continue to struggle when measuring and managing their operational risk. But that's not an insurmountable problem; there are shortcuts capable of providing reasonable "guesstimates" of operational risk.

Now, once you make that investment and get a risk management system in place, you have the ability, as Charles was saying, of linking risk to capital—and then all kinds of wonderful things can happen to your organization. With the measures of economic or risk capital provided by your system, you can now calculate returns on economic capital—that is, risk-adjusted returns that allow top management to compare the performance of *all* the firm's businesses and investments. And with the help of such risk-adjusted returns, you can also make informed decisions about your comparative advantage in risk-bearing—that is, about which businesses to be in, and which businesses and risks to sell or transfer to others.

 Once you get a risk management system in place, you have the ability of linking risk to capital—and then all kinds of wonderful things can happen to your organization. With the measures of economic or risk capital provided by your system, you can now calculate returns on economic capital—that is, risk-adjusted returns that allow top management to compare the performance of all the firm's businesses and investments. To the extent your managers' rewards are tied to such measures, you end up with a more reasonable, and probably more effective, incentive comp program. And with the help of such risk-adjusted returns, you can also make informed decisions about your comparative advantage in risk-bearing—about which businesses to be in, and which businesses and risks to sell or transfer to others.

—John Kapitan

And this brings me to one other major benefit of accurate risk measurement. In his opening comments, Charles said that perhaps the most important function of risk management is to protect the firm's ability to carry out its long-term strategy. I agree with that, but would also add that a company's ability to carry out its strategy depends in large part on keeping its stakeholders happy, particularly its managers and employees. And one thing I really like about the idea of hedging away non-core risks is the clarity it can bring to your performance measurement system. If you're an exceptionally good manager in an E&P company, do you really want your results to depend in large part on the behavior of oil prices? If you have a lot of noise in your performance measurement system, how do you know if your strategy is working? How do you know whether your managers are good operators, or just lucky and riding favorable commodity price movements? By hedging and thus removing the effect of oil price volatility on its cash flow or earnings, an E&P company effectively ends up with a much less "noisy" performance measure.

And this is likely to be valuable for two reasons. First, to the extent a manager's rewards are tied to such measures, you end up with a more reasonable, and probably more effective, incentive compensation program. At the very least, you avoid the tendency of many companies to pay very large bonuses when commodity prices move favorably, but also to pay bonuses in the down years since managers can always come up with reasons why they are not "accountable" for unfavorable price movements. The other major benefit of less noisy performance measures has to do with the shareholders of E&P companies: because such investors always have the option of making bets on commodity price movements, they must be expecting management to bring some operating expertise to the table, to do something they can't do for themselves simply by taking positions in oil futures.

The Corporate Risk Management Center: Structure and Processes

Sunderman: At Williams, we also think our hedging policy has greatly improved our information systems and incentives. Much of what we're doing today has its roots in the investment banking world and our own marketing and trading company. We have taken those concepts that were really designed for and built around financial institutions and applied them to our businesses.

But, as Bob mentioned, the area that now needs the most attention is operational risk. In thinking a bit about this issue, I find it very interesting that BP chooses to self-insure its large product liability and environmental risk. And although what works for the super majors will not always work for a company like Williams, we too have learned that there are insurance markets where it just doesn't make sense to buy the insurance because of our own diversification.

McCormack: And besides diversification, you also have built up an asset knowledge that is comparable to, if not better than, any insurance company's.

Sunderman: That's right.

Koppel: And your record as a safe operator also plays a big role.

But let me repeat this point about diversification. Diversification has plenty to do with our decision to self-insure many of our risks, and it also turns out to be a critical factor in our overall risk management approach. Diversification has always been a key part of our business strategy. And business strategy, as I said earlier, is really the engine that drives our value. That value comes from taking risks—and from choosing to bear risks where we have a clear comparative advantage.

McCormack: Harry, let me ask you a question about your procedures for assessing and managing those risks. My understanding is that when you make these decisions to self-insure at BP, you use traditional, actuarial types of approaches in evaluating property and casualty risk. And I believe you have an insurance subsidiary.

Koppel: That's right, we have an in-house, or captive, insurance company based in Guernsey.

We are required to insure some risks for legal and contractual purposes, and we aim to use our own insurance company to handle these cases. We also have joint ventures, and our partners in such ventures often have a different risk profile and want insurance. But, as you mentioned earlier, John, we continue to involve insurance companies in processing claims to take advantage of their operational efficiencies. In such cases, we've determined that outsourcing claims administration is a value-adding proposition.

McCormack: Let me ask you a little more about this entity within BP that collects the risks of BP's operating units. I assume that the units pay premiums to the captive; and then, when something bad happens, the losses all show up in the Channel Islands company?

Koppel: In some cases where we take out insurance, the casualty losses are assumed by the captive insurance company.

McCormack: How does the fact that the losses from any accident or surprise show up in the Channel Islands company and not on the P&L of the individual units affect managers' investment decisions in those units? Does it encourage them to overlook risks when getting into new businesses or taking on new customers?

Koppel: In the cases where the operating companies pay premiums to the captive, it's really no different than insuring the risk externally. In assessing managerial performance, we try to identify the sources of gains or losses. And if

managers were systematically overlooking risks in their operating or investment decisions, this would show up in their results.

Our insurance team and the captive play a coordinating function within
BP—one that allows us to see the effects of our risks in the context of the whole
group, with losses in some areas being offset by gains in others. A similar approach is used in managing the credit risk associated with our receivables; we
evaluate and manage this on a corporate-wide rather than a business-unit
basis.

McCormack: It sounds as if this captive is evolving into a corporate risk
management center, one that's managing not just property and casualty risk
but perhaps some others as well. To illustrate what I mean by a risk management center, suppose one of your managers makes an E&P investment today
with a 15-year payback period. To protect that investment against the risk of
oil price declines, that manager may want to hedge future production by
locking in today's high oil prices—and I don't mean that the firm will literally go out and hedge that production, only that the manager's performance
will be evaluated *as if* the firm had put on that hedge. This way, as long as the
manager does a good job of discovering and producing hydrocarbons, his or
her project will be viewed as a success, even if a plunge in prices ends up
causing the value of the project to drop below expectations.

Is there any movement in BP or any other company here toward a system
where those kinds of potentially hedgeable risks get concentrated within a single, centralized entity?

Williams's business model is quite different from BP's, and the company's combination of hedging and higher leverage is
likely to attract a different kind of investor than BP's. But, as long as Williams
earns high rates of return on capital—
and provided management makes it clear
to the market how they are producing those returns and the
risks they are taking in the process—the company will find
investors willing to buy its shares.

—John McCormack

Koppel: Our insurance captive is definitely not involved in hedging oil price
risk, and there is no CRO or corporate risk management center at the Group
level. But we do have some highly centralized policies. In addition to insurance, our funding policy is also administered centrally—and there are also

very clear policies across the Group in terms of interest rates, foreign exchange, and bank relations. In fact, there are a number of policies at BP that, viewed as a whole, form a very cohesive set of processes for managing risks at the project level, at the business unit level, and at the Group level. We've also recently launched an initiative at BP called "enterprise risk management" where, as Bob was describing earlier, we attempt to view all of our major risks together to get an idea of our overall net exposure.

Sunderman: We too are moving toward a more centralized and enterprise-wide system. We now have a single place to analyze all commodity risk taken on by the corporation through our contracts—and the same is true of our credit risks, with the exception of our regulated pipeline.

We have also spent a lot of time thinking about how to motivate our people. A couple of years ago we put in place an EVA performance measurement and incentive plan with some help from Stern Stewart—and John McCormack can confirm this, since he was with Stern Stewart and in fact working with us at the time. The incentive plan we developed for our line managers does try to distinguish good performance from good luck by using performance measures that are adjusted for changes in commodity prices. For example, it removes the effect of commodity price changes on a business unit's return on capital, thus providing us with a measure of pure operating performance.

Kapitan: Some people argue that this is the wrong way to go—that to the extent the firm's shareholders are bearing commodity risk, managers should do the same. And they will say, "It's okay to pay big bonuses to managers whose results were mainly a result of good luck because shareholders got that value, too."

But while that logic may be appropriate for top management—for the people who decide the firm's risk profile—I don't think it's right to subject people at lower levels in the organization to all those risks. Incentive plans in large organizations need to be much more careful in how much and what kinds of risk they impose on operating managers and employees. Holding mid-level people accountable for things they have no control over, or say in, is not at all consistent with the idea of pay for performance; and when the uncontrollables go the wrong way, the effect is demoralizing. In this sense, risk management can play a role in convincing people that the firm they work for is a true meritocracy, one where the connection between operating performance and rewards is pretty straightforward and not distorted by financial "noise."

Risk Management and Credit Ratings

McCormack: How do credit agencies regard all this? Are they capable of understanding the consequences of enterprise risk management, and the difference between good and bad risk management programs? And how, if at all, does this affect the yield on your debt? Andrew, your debt is trading at a price consistent with a BBB or a BBB+ rating. But the debt is rated only B+. So, the rating agencies seem to be lagging the market in this respect. Does this lag suggest that the agencies have failed to appreciate your risk management program?

Sunderman: I think our rating reflects mainly our past troubles, and so in this sense I would say that the agencies are behind the curve. But, as long as our management team continues to deliver on its promises, I think you'll see the ratings agencies catch up with what the bond markets are saying—namely, that the company is now clearly solvent, it's no longer anywhere near bankruptcy, and it's trading like an investment-grade company.

Now, when it comes to risk management, one concern of the rating agencies is Williams's general policy of not owning the power-generating assets that help us generate our revenue. We provide the fuel, the asset owner provides the operational expertise to generate the power, and then we take the output and sell it. And that business model has a large debt component associated with it—because we've bought those options and we pay a fixed option premium every year for the right to do what we do. So, what the rating agencies see is a highly leveraged stand-alone business unit with long-term debt commitments without matching long-term guaranteed cash flows.

McCormack: But the bond market seems to have a different opinion than the rating agencies in this case.

Sunderman: I think the bond market sees a lot of the same things the rating agency sees, but it also appears to have recognized the future potential of the suite of Williams's businesses as well as expected improvements in power commodity markets. And it's also important to keep in mind where the agencies are coming from in the energy merchant space. They're still conscious of what happened with Enron.

I like much of what the rating agencies are doing today. They're very deliberate; they're trying to think things through in a systematic, methodical way. And they do respond well to companies that perform the way management says it will—and credibility is very important in securing and maintaining a rating. But I don't think the agencies completely understand everything that we present to them. They're moving in the right direction, but they're not quite there.

McCormack: Bob, is there anything else that corporate officers can do to persuade the rating agencies of the benefits and effectiveness of their risk management programs?

Anderson: My experience has been very similar to Andrew's. The agencies are clearly interested in risk management, and it has become a factor in their decision-making, but there's a lot more educating to be done.

At our invitation, a representative from S&P recently attended one of our CCRO discussion programs outlining the aims and accomplishments of corporate risk management to date. And I think we made some headway. Their energy analysts clearly understand much more about the merchant energy business, and the role of derivatives in that business, than they did a few years ago. Back in the late 1990s and early 2000s, I was struck by their almost total lack of comprehension of what was going on inside energy companies—while, at the same time, the analysts who covered the banking sector were pretty much on top of things. But the collapse of Enron and the troubles throughout the industry have clearly forced the agencies to upgrade their analytical skills and come to grips with emerging practices in risk management. In fact, S&P has expressed interest in working with us on another project.

What can a CRO do to make the case to the agencies? Mainly two things. The CRO should begin by explaining that his or her main job is to put in place an analytical framework for measuring all of a company's major risks and a set of controls and procedures for monitoring and managing them—and the fact that the company has seen fit to hire someone with the title of CRO should be interpreted as at least some indication of the company's commitment to the undertaking.

But that's only a first step. What the agencies really want is the opportunity to get your CEO and CFO in a room and ask them, "What is your chief risk measure or indicator?" And if your CEO says, "Well, we have a great VaR engine," then they're going to be disappointed, because that has nothing to do with what they really care about—and that's liquidity. And if your CEO and CFO don't understand that, the rating agencies are getting smart enough to know that something's wrong. They now understand that even though your company may have a great measurement system and a great CRO, if senior management hasn't bought into it and isn't going to take action based on it, it's all kind of pointless. It's liquidity—a system for measuring it, monitoring it, and ensuring it's there when needed—that is the rating agencies' number one concern right now.

Sunderman: To add to that, S&P recently put out a statement that was based on the CCRO's liquidity survey and the information the CCRO helped work through with them. In that statement they said they were surprised by the number of highly rated energy companies that didn't appear to have instantaneous access to risk measures that the agencies considered critical, such as how much liquidity you would need in the event of, say, a certain kind of price shock. The fact that most companies said they don't calculate such measures surprised and concerned them. So, for that reason alone, I think the agencies are getting smarter, and they are becoming more demanding in what they ask for.

Kapitan: Another thing that's important to understand about the rating agencies is the extent of their reliance on industry-wide ratios and rules of thumb. In my work with financial services companies, I've seen a lot of my clients work through their analysis and come to the conclusion that their current size, capital structure, and profitability would justify a certain rating—and let's say it's a single A—while their rating seems stuck at BBB. And they wonder why they are only BBB.

I think there are a number of different reasons for this disparity. Probably most important is that, in their desire to achieve comparability across companies in a given industry, the rating agencies have their particular sets of ratios and models that are not easy to challenge. Such models have been built up over the years using published information on all the different companies they rate. And because of this reliance on models and the need for comparability, the agencies have a hard time taking in specific information about a particular company—say, a highly sophisticated and effective risk analysis system that would enable the firm to operate with a significantly higher leverage. So, even if you have developed the most effective, foolproof risk management system imaginable, don't expect the agencies to raise your rating a couple of notches. You will get some credit for it—and more credit as the agencies become more familiar with sophisticated risk management approaches—but you probably won't get as much credit as you think you deserve.

I also agree with Bob's point on the agencies' skepticism about how risk management systems are being used. As Bob was saying, it's all well and good to calculate VaR, but the agencies want to hear about more than that. They want to know how a company's metrics and monitoring processes affect day-to-day business decision-making. How does a given change in interest rates or a key commodity price affect the firm's ability to service its debt or invest in maintenance or R&D or product support? What I think the agencies would *really like to hear*, what would really impress them, is that your risk management system is being used not just to avoid a meltdown, but as a key component of the firm's strategic decision-making and its performance management and reward system. What I have in mind here are the RAROC systems developed by some banks—systems that assign economic capital to different operations based on their degree of risk and that, in so doing, require the firm to earn higher rates of return on riskier businesses. If applied to industrial companies—and, like Charles, I think it's only a matter of time before this happens—this use of economic capital could be the single most important way of getting companies to manage their risk effectively.

According to a recent study, a dollar of "excess" cash translates into as much as $1.50 of market value for risky companies with lots of growth opportunities. But for larger, mature companies, the last dollar of cash can be worth as little as 60 cents. So, the value of cash and excess capital seems to depend on the company's investment opportunities and the risk of the business. And for companies without clear growth prospects, large cash holdings appear to be penalized by the market, presumably because investors don't see a profitable use for the cash.

—Don Chew

That's an important message to take to the rating agencies: We're measuring our risks and we're making sure our managers price the risks they're taking by holding them accountable for the capital necessary to support those businesses. And to the extent this kind of system creates sustainable increases in profits—or a less risky business—it should add to the firm's standing with creditors as well as shareholders.

McCormack: But to come back to my question, can a really good hedging program change your credit rating?

Sunderman: It certainly can't hurt, especially when you're faced with distress. But even then, it's clearly not sufficient by itself. I think what drives the credit rating is how you perform versus what you said you were going to do. I can't overemphasize that. The company has to solve its own problems, and I think Williams has proven it can do that.

But, again, I think your credit rating depends on your entire risk profile and not just your hedging program. Our cost of capital is a direct result of the amount of risk we have within the entire portfolio, operationally as well as from commodity exposure—and it also depends on the market's perception of how we manage that risk. And, in that regard, a good hedging program can help reduce your cost of capital.

More on Managing Counterparty Credit Risk

Smithson: Andrew, in addition to looking at S&P's and Moody's ratings, do you also look at another kind of information—the implied ratings that are generated by KMV?

Sunderman: When you buy Moody's ratings, the KMV implied rating comes with it. We also just purchased a new internal credit system with tools very similar to KMV's, and we plan on using that system to evaluate our counterparties.

Smithson: The KMV system essentially uses market data, especially the volatility of the stock price, to come up with an implied rating. So, using KMV, you can track what the market is saying about both your risk and perhaps your capital structure.

Do you also track your Credit Default Swap (CDS) price in the market? I ask because the CDS price for Williams will tell you the "instantaneous spread," which gives you a good idea about how the market is thinking about your credit.

Sunderman: We don't keep track of those spreads. But they should be fairly close to our bond spreads, which we do look at regularly. And we may have found a creative way to use these credit swaps. We sometimes have counterparties that won't do business with us unless we post collateral. One thing we have proposed is to fund a credit default swap and make the counterparty the beneficiary instead of prepaying the collateral. As of yet we haven't actually done a transaction like that, but it could provide an interesting alternative to cash or LCs.

Smithson: The use of credit derivatives by industrial corporations is still limited. But I can think of one interesting use of credit derivatives by a middle-market industrial company. Since middle-market companies don't have direct access to capital markets, the firm had been financing itself mainly through loans from their house bank. When the bank balked at accepting more credit exposure, the industrial company bought "default protection" in the form of a credit default swap that named the house bank as the beneficiary. With this extra layer of protection, the industrial company got the additional loan it needed.

But let me follow up on John's question about whether risk management activities can affect a firm's debt rating from S&P or Moody's. Your answer, Andrew, was that it may help a little, but that other things were much more important. But my guess is that your risk management practices are likely to have a greater, or maybe a more immediate, effect on your implied KMV rating and your CDS spreads than on your debt ratings. In my experience, they are more sensitive instruments for detecting changes in creditworthiness.

How Do Trading Operations Add Value?

Chew: The idea of comparative advantage in risk-bearing has come up a number of times today. And to me this idea raises the question about the rationale for trading operations. For example, the trading operations of large oil companies are routinely said to account for a certain portion of profits. And commercial and investment banks regularly attribute large portions of their earnings to fixed income and FX trading. My question is this: Do these trading profits come from taking what are essentially speculative positions, and turning out to be right more often than not? Or do the profits really come from "market making," from minimizing positions and just collecting the bid/ask spread on customer trades? I put the question this way because a study I published years ago by a couple of Oliver Wyman analysts reported that the recurring FX trading profits of the old Chase Manhattan Bank came almost entirely from market making, while the speculative positions essentially netted to zero over time.

Koppel: In the case of BP, our profits come both from taking positions *and* from market making. The rationale is pretty straightforward: Because of the scale and geographic diversity of our operations, we have a very good understanding of the oil and gas markets, and our traders use that expertise to take their positions.

Chew: Do your trading operations deliver a fairly stable earnings stream? And how do you communicate the value of your trading operation when you talk to Wall Street?

Koppel: Our IR people can probably respond to that question better than I can. But, as I said before, it seems clear to me that our position as a global owner and operator of hard assets is bound to give us some good insights into the market. And I think the market understands this advantage and is willing to give us credit for that earnings stream in much the same way it values the earnings from the rest of our businesses.

Chew: John, as an advisor to financial institutions, what can you tell us about banks' ability to generate trading profits from the carry trade and their interest rate forecasts?

Kapitan: It's really a matter of the bank's core competencies, of what it's in business to do and how it expects to add value. To the extent you are involved in the carry trade, you are choosing to take interest rate risk; you are in essence borrowing short, whether through actual borrowings or deposit taking, and then investing those funds in mortgage-backed securities or long-term Treasuries. Unless you're hedging, you have a mismatch between your assets and liabilities. And if that mismatch is a primary source of a bank's profit, management and the board needs to ask the question: what is our comparative advantage in taking that risk? Do we have some insight that the bond traders and the rest of the market don't?

Now, I'm willing to consider the possibility that a large, money-center bank can have some proprietary information because of its flow of business and trade with customers. But even in this case, the real underlying source of profit is likely to be the money they make on their bid/ask spread as a market maker. For smaller, regional, and middle-market banks, I think the best strategy is to avoid the carry trade and attempt to keep interest rate risk to very modest levels. In the case of middle-market banks, the market seems to be trying hard to determine how much of their profits come from the carry trade. And my sense is that, in cases where investors suspect that a large portion of a bank's earnings are not being generated by core bank operations, the bank's shares will carry a lower multiple.

But having said that, I also think there is one reason the carry trade may make sense for some banks—and that has to do with both the level and the design of capital requirements. In many cases, banks are required to hold more capital than they would probably choose to hold if left unregulated. And because the bank regulators don't have specific capital requirements for bearing interest rate risk, banks can do a kind of regulatory arbitrage by borrowing short and putting the capital in longer-term liquid securities that don't require much capital backing. In the process, you would be taking on a little bit of rate risk, at least temporarily, because you think that in the long term you're going to be able to put that capital to use in core operations like lending. And this kind of temporary use of the carry trade can make sense—you can unwind the positions relatively easily because it's such a liquid market and then either buy back shares or increase dividends or put it into core bank operations.

So, I can see the carry trade as a useful near-term strategy for reducing a bank's regulatory burden, but other than that I would caution banks against trying to out-trade the bond market.

Is Equity Expensive?

Koppel: John, your comment suggests that equity capital is expensive and that there's a significant penalty for having too much of it. Do we have any evidence that the market penalizes companies for carrying more equity than they need?

Kapitan: My feeling is that if a company carries a relatively small amount of excess capital, that's not going to be a problem. But it can become a major issue in cases where shareholders see a big cushion building up. First of all, idle cash earns a low rate of return, especially after taxes are taken out. But more important is the tendency of public companies to hoard capital and, in many cases, to waste it on bad ideas. When capital is abundant, the folks in corporate strategy can be counted on to find ways to spend it. And even if there aren't any acquisitions or major capital projects on the horizon, managers' natural instinct is to let the capital cushion keep building and building. We've seen this in the case of companies like Chrysler, whose cash build-up got the attention of Kirk Kerkorian. And I've seen it on a smaller scale in a number of financial institutions as well. Some banks with far more capital than profitable uses for it have devoted themselves almost entirely to the carry trade, in some cases with disastrous results. And that's why, as a general rule, the market wants you to return your excess capital in the form of dividends or stock repurchases.

Chew: To reinforce John's argument, a finance professor at Georgetown named Lee Pinkowitz has produced a study called "What is the Market Value of a Dollar of Cash Holdings?" The main finding of the study is that, for risky companies with lots of growth opportunities, a dollar of cash translates into as much as $1.50 of market value. But for larger, mature companies, the last dollar of cash can be worth as little as 60 cents. So, the value of cash and excess capital seems to depend on the company's investment opportunities and the risk of the business. And for companies without clear growth prospects, large cash holdings appear to be penalized by the market—again, because investors don't see a profitable use for the cash.

By the same token, when companies raise equity, there's a lot of variation in how the market responds to those offerings. We know that the market responds to announcements of new equity offerings by marking down the shares by about 3%, on average. But there's also a broad distribution around this average: in some cases, companies announcing their intention to raise equity will see their stock price drop by as much as 10%; and in other cases, typically companies in high-growth sectors, the market response is often very close to zero.

So, in this sense, what might be thought of as the incremental cost of equity capital can vary widely among different companies and circumstances. And the critical factor seems to be the intended use of the funds: are there profitable uses—or is management simply raising funds for a rainy day or, even worse, cashing out at what they think is the top?

FAS 133 and Corporate Disclosure

Chew: Let me ask one more question before we go. Corporate executives have been highly critical of FAS 133, arguing that it introduces artificial volatility into income statements that acts as a deterrent to a sound hedging policy. In an article that will be published along with this roundtable, Alex Pollock, the former president of the Federal Home Loan Bank for almost 15 years, argues that companies should make the right hedging decisions and then present their investors with what amount to two sets of earnings numbers: one that complies with FAS 133 and GAAP, and a "pro forma" number in which the firm's hedge is effectively treated as a hedge—that is, gains and losses are kept off the P&L and run through a capital account instead. Is this a workable disclosure policy?

Koppel: There are really two questions to answer here. Do the new accounting rules force you to do something different from what you would otherwise do—for example, would they prevent you from hedging an exposure? And are there ways to set up your hedges so that you can get hedge accounting treatment?

We have found it possible to obtain hedge accounting under IAS 39 for our economic hedges, but we have run into some obstacles. For example, although we hedge local subsidiaries' currency cash flows at the central level with respect to the Group functional currency, both IFRS and FAS 133 effectively view the functional currency only at the subsidiary level. This disparity between the accounting and the economic view forces us to document some hedges in a way that does not necessarily represent the economic rationale, but it does achieve the correct accounting treatment. So there are ways of dealing with the new accounting while carrying out our basic risk management policy, but they may involve structuring transactions a bit differently to comply with the accounting standards while achieving essentially the same economic results.

Chew: Let's say that your policy is to hedge a certain exposure, but FAS 133 prohibits hedge accounting treatment. Is it worth including a statement in the MD&A part of your annual report saying in effect that you've taken out a hedge that doesn't qualify as a hedge according to the FASB but you think it does a reasonably good job of hedging your exposure—and so you would like your investors to view your numbers as if you qualified for hedge accounting? Will this kind of "pro forma" approach work with investors?

Sunderman: That is essentially what we have been doing in our presentations to analysts in the last two or three quarters. We start by presenting GAAP financial statements and then we adjust those numbers to arrive at a measure that we call "segment profit after marking to market." This is a more cash-focused, accrual type of measure. We have told our analysts that this measure does a better job of reflecting the economic reality of our business. And, as I mentioned earlier, our company's disclosure practices were rated number one in the energy sector by *Institutional Investor Research Group* last year.

So I'm in favor of changing the rules on hedge accounting. Most of us understand that financial statements are not economic reality. But by making it so difficult to qualify for hedge accounting—it has been called a "privilege" rather than a "right"—FAS 133 has moved accounting numbers even farther from economic reality than they were before.

Sullivan: That's right. It's as if the regulators' primary aim is to make the rules for hedge accounting so tight that there's no ambiguity on how to do it. But, in the process, they have *created* a lot of ambiguity. I like the idea of mark-to-market accounting, but it needs to be applied consistently and comprehensively. What FAS 133 gives us is mark to market, or economic reality, for one side of the balance sheet—and in fact, it's only one part of one side of the balance sheet. And this one-sided treatment makes corporate financial statements a less reliable indicator of a company's ongoing or future earnings power, which is what I think we really want these statements to measure.

McCormack: Well, let's leave it at that. And let me thank you all for participating in this discussion.

Index